HOW TO PREPARE FOR THE

SCHOLASTIC APTITUDE TEST ®

HOW TO PREPARE FOR THE

SCHOLASTIC APTITUDE TEST ®

by Morton Selub and Doris Selub

Books for Professionals
Harcourt Brace Jovanovich, Publishers
San Diego   New York   London

Requests for permission to make copies of any part of the work should be
mailed to: Permissions, Harcourt Brace Jovanovich, Publishers, Orlando,
FL 32887

"Scholastic Aptitude Test" and "SAT" are registered trademarks of College En-
trance Examination Board. This publication was prepared by Harcourt Brace
Jovanovich, Inc., which is solely responsible for its contents. It is not endorsed by
any other organization.

The author wishes to thank the following: American Museum of Natural History, New
York, NY, for "Terns in Traffic" by M. Gochfeld, June/July 1978; "A Naturalist at Large:
Notes from a Rice Paddy" by Edwin Kessler, August/September 1978; and "The Enduring
Great Lakes: You'll Always Get Home" by R. McKee, August/September 1978. Reprinted
with permission from *Natural History Magazine.* Copyright © 1978 by the American
Museum of Natural History; *Esquire Magazine,* New York, NY, for "Pressure from
Below," copyright © 1978 by John Simon. First published in *Esquire Magazine; Harper's
Magazine,* New York, NY, for "Infant Thought" by Jerome Kagan and "Eagles, Doves,
and Hawks" by Tom Gervasi, copyright © 1978 by *Harper's Magazine.* All rights reserved.
Reprinted from the April 1978/May 1978 issues by special permission; The Hearst
Corporation, New York, NY, for "How They're Watching Us" and "51,000,000 Mistakes
Later," July 1976. Reprinted from *Popular Mechanics* copyright © 1976 by The Hearst
Corporation, All Rights Reserved; McGraw-Hill Book Company, New York, NY, for
Understanding Media by Marshall McLuhan. Copyright © 1964 by Marshall McLuhan.
Used with permission of McGraw-Hill Book Company; The New York Times Company,
New York, NY, for "Home of the Unicorn" by Bruce Chatwin reviewed by Ted Morgan
copyright © by The New York Times Company. Reprinted by permission; Michael
Steinberg, Boston, MA, for *Franz Schubert,* copyright © 1978 by Michael Steinberg.

Printed in the United States of America

Library of Congress Cataloging in Publication Data

Selub, Morton.
    How to prepare for the Scholastic aptitude test.

    (Books for professionals)
    1. Scholastic aptitude test—Study guides.   I. Selub,
Doris.   II. Title.   III. Series.
LB2353.57.S44   378'.1662   81-6410
ISBN 0-15-600085-7   AACR2

    K L M N

Contents

Contents

PART I

General Description of the Scholastic Aptitude Test

Time Schedule and Format of the SAT

The order of questions and the number of questions in each subsection of the actual test may vary somewhat from that shown in the chart below. Several different forms of the SAT are used at each scheduled date.

The chart indicates the basic makeup of the SAT and the time allotments. Note that there are two verbal sections consisting of a total of 85 questions and two mathematical sections consisting of a total of 60 questions. There is also an experimental section which may be mathematical or verbal; the score on this section is not included in the SAT score, and you will not know which of the five sections mentioned above is the experimental section. Finally, there is a Test of Standard Written English (TSWE) which consists of 50 questions on grammar and usage.

Each of the six sections discussed here has a separate time allotment of 30 minutes. All questions on the SAT and TSWE are of the multiple-choice type.

Your score on the TSWE is reported separately and is used mainly for suitable placement in an English course at college. The TSWE score is not used in determination of college admission, but only for placement.

Section of Test	Number of Questions	Time Allowed
Section 1: Verbal	15 Antonyms 10 Analogies 10 Sentence Completion 10 Reading Comprehension	30 minutes
Section 2: Verbal	10 Antonyms 10 Analogies 5 Sentence Completion 15 Reading Comprehension	30 minutes
Section 3: Mathematical or Verbal	25 or 40	30 minutes
Section 4: Mathematical	35	30 minutes
Section 5: Mathematical	25	30 minutes
Section 6: Test of Standard Written English	50 Grammar and Usage	30 minutes

Total Time = 180 minutes, or 3 hours

Scoring of the SAT

The system of scoring used for the SAT provides for a penalty for an incorrect answer. For each correct answer you receive one point and for omitted questions no points. However, one-quarter of a point is deducted for each incorrect answer to a question with five answer choices. Thus, if you take a test with 85 five-choice questions, answer 50 correctly, omit 6 and answer 29 incorrectly, your "raw score" will be computed as follows:

$$50 \text{ correct} - \frac{29 \text{ incorrect}}{4} = 50 - 7\frac{1}{4} = 42\frac{3}{4}.$$

This raw score is then converted to a score on the College Board scale of 200 to 800. In the mathematical portion of the test, the quantitative comparison questions are four-choice questions; here one-third of a point is deducted for each incorrect answer.

You will receive separate scores for the verbal ability and the mathematical ability. The verbal score also has subscores for vocabulary and reading comprehension, but these are reported on a 20 to 80 scale.

Is Guessing Advisable?

Since the system of scoring described above penalizes you for an incorrect answer, you should be cautious about guessing. If you are able to eliminate one or more answer choices, it is advisable to make an "educated" guess.

Types of Verbal Questions

The SAT attempts by means of its verbal questions to determine the degree to which you can read with understanding and the extent of your vocabulary.

The reading questions are of two types: sentence completion and reading comprehension. The vocabulary questions are also of two types: antonyms and analogies. These will be explained in detail in Part II.

The TSWE questions are also of two types: usage and sentence correction. The score on this section is recorded on a 20 to 60+ scale. These questions will be discussed further in Part II.

As explained, the experimental section may be verbal or mathematical. These verbal questions may include any of the types mentioned above as well as those on the TSWE.

Types of Mathematical Questions

The mathematical questions on the SAT are essentially of two types: the standard five-choice questions which make up about two-thirds of the mathematical portion and the four-choice quantitative questions which make up about one-third of the mathematical portion. The latter are described in detail in Part III.

The mathematical sections of the SAT deal essentially with arithmetic, elementary algebra, and informal geometry. The arithmetic requires an understanding of integers, fractions, percents, and averages. The algebra includes a knowledge of the formula, linear equation, and simple quadratic equation. The geometry requires an understanding of angle relationships, right triangle relationships, and the mensurational aspects of area, perimeter, and volume.

A review of all of these topics is presented in detail in Part III of this book, followed in Part IV by sets of practice exercises on each mathematical topic reviewed; these exercises are followed by explanatory answers.

PART II

The Verbal Section
of the Scholastic
Aptitude Test

What the Questions Are Like; What the Questions Test

The four parts of the verbal section of the Scholastic Aptitude Test are:

1. Vocabulary Questions, or Antonyms
2. Word Relationship Questions, or Analogies
3. Sentence Completion Questions
4. Reading Comprehension Questions, or Reading Passages

VOCABULARY QUESTIONS, OR ANTONYMS

The vocabulary part of the verbal section of the SAT, like each of the other parts, is made up of multiple-choice short-answer questions. You are given a word in capital letters, five words or phrases that are lettered from (A) through (E), and your task is to determine which of the lettered words or phrases is *most nearly opposite* in meaning to the capitalized word.

STRONG : (A) stout   (B) intense   (C) short   (D) weak   (E) poor

Answer: (D)

Of course the vocabulary questions on the actual test will probably not test you on words as familiar as the one in the example given above; however, the vocabulary that will be used will include words that you, a high school student, would be expected to come across in your general reading. Some words, undoubtedly, will not be as familiar to you as others, and some may be completely unfamiliar.

The antonym questions are intended to test the extent of your knowledge of vocabulary. This book, in a subsequent section, will tell you how you can improve your performance on the vocabulary questions and will provide you with comprehensive vocabulary lists for study.

WORD RELATIONSHIP QUESTIONS, OR ANALOGIES

In the word relationship, or analogies, question, you are given a pair of capitalized words, five other pairs of words that are lettered from (A) through (E), and you are asked to (a) see a relationship between the two words of the capitalized pair, and (b) select a lettered pair of words which are *related to one another in a way that is most similar to* that of the capitalized pair.

Note carefully how the word relationship question is written: The two words of each pair are separated by a colon or ratio symbol, as follows: *chef* : *recipe*, *doctor* : *diagnosis*, or *senator* : *legislation*. This colon or ratio symbol simply says in a kind of shorthand that *chef* is related to *recipe*, *doctor* is related to *diagnosis*, or *senator* is related to *legislation*. You must determine the nature of the relationship. Another symbol, a double pair of colons, separates the given, capitalized pair of words from the five pairs of lettered words. This symbol says that the given pair has a relationship that is similar to that of one of the lettered pairs.

HOT : COLD :: (A) fire : water (B) skilled : deft
(C) tall : short (D) now : later (E) hard : rock

Answer: (C)

Hot and *Cold* are adjectives that describe opposite qualities. Similarly, *tall* and *short* are adjectives which describe opposite qualities. *Fire* and *water* are opposed to one another, but they do not describe opposite qualities like the given pair or the pair in choice (C). Choices (B) and (E) are not opposites in any sense; they are not, therefore, possible answers. Choice (D) is out, too. The opposite of *later* is "earlier," not *now*.

The aim of the analogy question is to test your ability to see relationships between words, distinguish between types of relationships, and recognize which relationships are similar. This question tests the extent of your knowledge in various fields and your ability to engage in logical thinking.

The sample question presents the antonymous type of word relationship. The relationship in this question is not too difficult to perceive. Actual test questions will cover a fairly wide range of types of relationships and will vary in their levels of difficulty. Further on in this chapter you will find a section that will offer instruction on how to solve the word relationship, or analogy, question. That section will give examples of all the types of word relationships you are likely to need to be able to recognize in order to score high on the SAT. The instructional material will also teach you strategies for solving word relationship questions, so that by the time you finish working with this book, you will feel confident and secure about your ability to deal with this type of question.

SENTENCE COMPLETION QUESTIONS

For the sentence completion question you are given a sentence with one or two blanks in it where key words have been removed. From among five choices, lettered from (A) through (E), you are asked to select the word or words which, when substituted for the blanks, complete the meaning of the sentence. The words you select must be suitable from the point of view of meaning, correct usage, and grammatical aptness. The sentence, with the blanks filled, must be coherent and logical. Each sentence contains sufficient information through context and structure to permit you to ascertain the correct answer without any need for additional material or information.

The trustees of the Orchestral Society had hoped to reap substantial benefits through the sale of the paintings that Mr. Cooper had _____, but the proceeds from the auction, which was poorly attended as a result of the blizzard, were _____.

(A) retained . . unworthy
(B) lent . . confiscated
(C) bequeathed . . disappointing
(D) assembled . . enormous
(E) appraised . . taxable

Answer: (C)

The sentence states that the trustees had hoped to reap substantial benefits from the sale of the paintings. The word *but*, a reversal indicator, tells us that their expectations were not realized: The trustees either made less than they had hoped for or much more than they had hoped for. We can assume, since the attendance was poor because of the blizzard, that the proceeds were lower than expected, and that the trustees found the outcome of the sale *disappointing*, choice (C). The proceeds could have been *unworthy*, choice (A), but the first word in choice (A) does not make sense within the sentence. The trustees could not sell paintings that Mr. Cooper *retained* (kept). They can sell only paintings that were *bequeathed* (given) to them, choice (C).

The instructional section will instruct you in approaches to the various aspects of the problem and discuss appropriate questions to ask yourself when working on sentence completion questions. Among other things, the instructional section will deal with indicator words, sentence logic, linguistic elements, contextual clues, and the importance of correct usage in determining the proper choice of answer.

READING COMPREHENSION QUESTIONS, OR READING PASSAGES

In this part of the verbal section of the Scholastic Aptitude Test, you are given a passage to read, and you are asked to answer several questions about the material in that passage. Each question is followed by answer choices lettered from (A) through (E), and you are to select the one, based solely on the contents of the passage, that best answers the question.

The questions asked are of several types. Some are questions that ask for specific detail or information; some ask for the main idea of the passage; some ask for identification of supporting questions or ideas; some ask for the author's purpose in writing this passage, or for a characterization of the author's style or point of view. In each instance, however, the passage contains all the information needed to answer the question.

The example below is markedly shorter than a typical reading passage used in an actual SAT, but it is representative of the reading material used. The questions may be somewhat easier than the average SAT reading comprehension question, but they are very much like actual test questions. The instructional section of this book will cover the reading comprehension question very thoroughly. It will explore a number of approaches to the entire question of the best way to handle timed reading comprehension tests and make very specific suggestions as to how you should select the method that is best for you.

In the Great Lakes, the life cycles of individual organisms provide a number of fascinating, although brief, scenarios. But together, all the agents of change among the plants, birds, and fish become a full-length play on the massive stage of the Great Lakes basin.

Several important props must be described before we get to the play's narrative. One is the relative shallowness of the lakes, scraped out some 10,000 to 15,000 years ago by receding ice sheets. Another is the size of these inland seas, so enormous that the earth's rotation plays, through the Coriolis force, a major role in the dynamics of the Great Lakes, as it does in the oceans. And because the lakes all outflow either into each other or into the Saint Lawrence River and differ in surface size and in volume, they all have different water residence times.

1. Which of the following are directly stated in the passage?
     I. The Great Lakes all flow into the Saint Lawrence River or into each other.
    II. The Great Lakes basin is massive, but it is not very deep.
   III. The props needed for a full-length play about the Great Lakes would require a massive stage.

   (A) I only
   (B) II only
   (C) III only
   (D) I and II only
   (E) I, II, and III

2. From information given in the passage, we can infer that
   (A) the birds and fishes of the Great Lakes are unique organisms
   (B) the Coriolis force pushed the ice sheets back
   (C) the Great Lakes are as large as any of the oceans
   (D) water residence time is the length of time that a particular particle of water spends in one of the lakes before it flows out of that lake
   (E) water residence time varies from 10,000 to 15,000 years according to particular lake conditions

3. This passage probably is part of
   (A) a newspaper article on the decline in fish production in the Great Lakes
   (B) an article on the natural history of the Great Lakes
   (C) a prospectus offering waterfront land for real estate development
   (D) a treatise on the Coriolis force
   (E) a water pollution study, with emphasis on the Great Lakes
                              Answers: 1. (D) 2. (D) 3. (B)

In question 1, item I is directly stated in the last sentence; item II is stated in the last sentence of paragraph 1 and sentence 2 of paragraph 2. Item III is a mishmash of mistaken notions.

In question 2, the statement in choice (D) can be inferred from the last sentence in which the author concludes, ". . . they all have different water residence times," directly after stating ". . . because the lakes all . . . differ in size and volume. . . ," and tying size and volume together with the idea of outflow. We can conclude that any particular particle of water remains (resides) in a lake a longer or shorter length of time depending upon the size of that lake and the rate of its outflow, and that "water residence time" is what we call that length of time.

In the last question, we can deduce from the continuous thread dealing with "organisms," "plants," "birds," and "fish," and the geological beginning of the Great Lakes, that the passage is probably part of an article that will deal with phenomena that we recognize as part of the area of concern of natural history.

When you read the instructional section on the reading comprehension question, you will find information on the types of reading passages you are likely to find on the SAT, and you will be introduced to a wide variety of question types.

Vocabulary and the SAT Antonym Question

WHY YOU SHOULD STUDY VOCABULARY ... STARTING NOW

Some people say there is little use in studying vocabulary for the Scholastic Aptitude Test. They contend that you should have done something about your vocabulary all along. They say it's too late to do anything about improving your word power now.

Don't listen to them! It is better to do something about vocabulary than to do nothing about vocabulary! Do it now!

Despite anything you may hear to the contrary, you can learn a large number of new words in a comparatively short period of time. If you have six months until you take the SAT, you can learn literally thousands of words. If you have only six weeks, you can still learn a large and worthwhile number of new words. Of course, if you have left yourself with less time than that, you will learn fewer words, but every word that you do learn represents a possible point added to your raw score.

Enter the examination room as well prepared as possible!

Star athletes do not win important events unless they have trained rigorously. Great virtuosos practice continually to prepare for important concerts. Train for the SAT as you would for any other tough competitive event.

Immediately after this next part, which will thoroughly explain how to approach and deal with the antonym vocabulary question, you will find a complete outline of suggestions for learning more vocabulary to help you succeed with the vocabulary questions, and lists of words of the type you might expect to find on the SAT.

ANSWERING THE VOCABULARY OR ANTONYM QUESTION

An important step toward successfully answering any test question is understanding what the question is asking. It is a good idea to familiarize yourself beforehand with the general nature of the directions for each type of question on the SAT. However, no matter how familiar you are with the directions, be sure to read them carefully at the time that you take the test in order to be sure that no changes have been made. Below is a close paraphrase of the actual SAT directions for the antonym question:

> Directions: In each of the questions below, a capitalized word is followed by five words or phrases lettered from (A) through (E). Select the word or phrase most nearly *opposite* in meaning to the capitalized word. Since the questions may require that you make judgments that involve distinguishing among words that are close in meaning, consider all choices carefully before you make your final selection.

The wording of the directions may vary slightly, but the general sense will remain the same. You are required to find the word that is *most nearly opposite* in meaning to the given word.

You cannot find an opposite for a word unless you know what the word means, to start with. Use the following formula statement in order to focus attention on the task: Word *X* means: (State a synonym for word *X*), and the opposite is: (State your selection from among the choices).

> HARMONY : (A) adherence   (B) stimulation   (C) joy   (D) intonation   (E) conflict
>
> Answer: (E)

Applying the formula statement suggested above, you would say: *Harmony* means "accord" or "agreement," and the opposite is *conflict*.

Here are several thoughts to keep in mind:

Definitions. Words may have a number of meanings according to dictionary definitions. Sometimes your first reaction to a given word may trigger an alternate meaning that is not intended:

> FAIR : (A) angry   (B) glum   (C) homely   (D) hopeless   (E) judicious
>
> Answer: (C)

Fair means "attractive," as in "fair young maiden." The opposite is *homely*.

Your first reaction might have been that *fair* means "impartial" or "sunny" or "light-colored," referring to complexion, but you did not see any choices like "biased" or "stormy" or "brunet," which would have been opposites. In such cases it is necessary to consider other meanings that you know for the given word.

If you feel you know the given word, but you cannot find an opposite among the choices offered, ask yourself whether the word has another or several other meanings.

Pronunciation. Words sometimes have different meanings for different pronunciations. Also, a word that seems unfamiliar may sometimes be a word that you have heard spoken, but never seen in writing.

> CONSUMMATE : (A) compact   (B) imperfect   (C) crass   (D) bold   (E) active
>
> Answer: (B)

Consummate which rhymes with "date," is a verb which means "bring to completion." *Consummate*, which rhymes with "bit," is an adjective which means "perfect" or "superb." We speak of "consummate artistry," and "consummating a business deal."

> INDICT : (A) exonerate (B) cross-examine (C) prevail (D) respond (E) deny
>
> Answer: (A)

Indict means "to accuse of wrongdoing," and the opposite is *exonerate,* which means "to clear of blame." *Indict* is pronounced as if it were spelled "indite." If you had only heard it spoken, you might have known the meaning, but not recognized the word in print.

If you think you don't know a word, try pronouncing it several different ways. It may turn out to be a word you do know.

Antonyms. The SAT antonym questions ask you to find an opposite for the given word. There will not be, among the choices offered, any words with the same meaning as the given word.

Please note: Among the antonym questions on the simulated examinations in this book, the author *has* placed synonyms among the choices as a study aid, to help you build your vocabulary recognition skills.

Remember to use the formula statement: *Consummate* means "perfect" or "superb," and the opposite is *imperfect* (see example on the preceding page).

Synonyms. Very few words in the English language have exact synonyms, words that are the same in all their meanings, that can be used interchangeably in every instance. "I am sick," and "I am ill," are interchangeable expressions. However, the expression "an ill wind" cannot be rephrased "a sick wind." Similarly, very few words have exact opposites, words that are opposed in all their meanings. It is important to remember that you are directed to find a word that is *most nearly opposite* in meaning to the given word.

> CONCEAL : (A) harvest (B) depose (C) revere (D) espouse (E) unveil
>
> Answer: (E)

Conceal means "cover" or "remove from sight," and the opposite is *unveil,* which means "reveal" or "disclose." But *unveil* is usually used to mean "remove a veil or covering from, especially for the first time." Words like "expose" or "reveal" are probably more opposite in meaning to *conceal* than is *unveil,* but *unveil* is the only word among the choices that is opposite to the given word. It is, therefore, the one most nearly opposite in meaning to the given word.

> FRESH : (A) able (B) worn (C) nutritious (D) unsuitable (E) untried
>
> Answer: (B)

Fresh means "not worn," and the opposite is *worn.* Other opposites that might have been presented are: "canned," "trite," "adulterated," "salt" (as opposed to "not salt" water), and half a dozen others. You may not consider "canned" to be as much an opposite of *fresh* as the word "stale" is, but if it were substituted for choice (B) in the example above, it would be the choice most nearly opposite in meaning to the given word, *fresh.*

Your answer may be less than a perfect antonym, but if it is the one that is *most nearly the opposite of the given word,* it is the correct answer.

HOW TO FIGURE OUT THE MEANING OF A WORD WHEN YOU AREN'T SURE YOU KNOW IT

If you have a strong vocabulary and have practiced the approaches to the antonym question discussed in the previous section, you will undoubtedly do well on the vocabulary portion of the SAT. However, if you have some vocabulary deficiencies—or even if you haven't—there will be times when you will come across words whose meaning you either don't know or are uncertain of. What do you do then?

The one thing you don't do is concede any points until you are forced to do so. What you do is try alternative methods for unlocking the meanings of words you think you should know but don't.

Word Origins. If you are a student of a foreign language, your knowledge of that language may stand you in good stead. Languages are interrelated: Some words appear, in one form or other, in a number of different languages. English is especially rich with borrowings from other tongues. If you have a little Latin at your command, you will know that "precursor" is almost a direct translation of "forerunner," that "somnambulist" is a synonym for "sleepwalker," and that "remunerate" means "repay." You will find literally hundreds of other opportunities to "translate" from Latin into English, and vice versa. *Caveat emptor!* will not be Greek to you—it's Latin, of course—but rather another bridge to the meaning of what was previously unknown.

If French is your language, you will not have difficulty with a word such as "savant," which means "a man of extensive learning," since you will know that the French connection is the participle of the verb *savoir.* Knowing that *verte* means "green," you will conclude that *verdure* means greenery; familiar with *vendre,* the French word for "sell," you will feel sure that vendor means seller. So, too, with *gauche*—"clumsy," *naitre*—"nascent," and *pouvoir*—"puissant."

Whatever the other language you know, German, Spanish, Italian, Swedish, or Greek, you will find quite a number of words in English whose meaning will become clear by reference to words from the language of their origin. Keep in mind, however, that the foreign language connection will work only if you develop an awareness of the relationship between English and other languages.

Parts of Speech. Very often you find yourself puzzling over the meaning of a particular word, certain that you know it, yet unable to "see" the meaning. Then, suddenly, you realize that the word is similar to one you know, except that it is in a somewhat different form because it is a different part of speech: "predacious" is an adjective form of "predator"; "prevalent" is another form of "prevailing." You may be able to define "decant" if you think of "decanter," and decipher "heterogeneity" through "heterogeneous."

Words in Context. The brain is like a miraculous computer. Everything you have ever read or heard is in your brain's memory banks. The problem, sometimes, lies in not knowing the correct "button" to activate for item retrieval. That is, you can't recall what you have heard or read at the moment that you need the information. Sometimes, in fact, you are hardly aware of having the information stored away. Here's how to bring those "hidden" words to the fore: If the word seems the least bit familiar, try to remember when you heard it, where you heard it, where you saw it, who said it, and even a fragment of the context in which the word was said or written. Recall, if you can, the sentence that included the word in question, or failing that, a phrase of which the word was a part. Take the word "decant." Almost every high school student has heard that word, even if he or she is unaware of it. Sometime, in a science class somewhere, a teacher held up a flask with a fluid in it and said, "Now I'm going to decant the liquid from this flask into the beaker with the acid in it," and proceeded to pour off the liquid. This remembered context now clarifies the meaning of the word "decant."

If the word "covert" sticks in your brain, perhaps you can visualize your favorite anchorperson saying something about the "covert activities of the CIA," or else conjure up headlines about the "covert operations of the FBI." If you fall back on language likeness, the French "couvert" means "covered," and the word's meaning will open up for you, especially if one of the choices of an opposite is "open."

You have heard the word "incontrovertible" innumerable times as part of Castro Convertible's commercial jingle on radio. If you can just retrieve the line ". . . it's incontrovertible that the first to conquer living space is. . .," you may be able to define the word as meaning "not controvertible." Remember that "controvertible" stems from "controversy," which means "argument or dispute." Decide that *incontrovertible* means "can't be disputed" or "indisputable," and then note that "questionable" is one of the choices. And there's your answer!

Word-building Elements. The use of roots, stems, prefixes, and suffixes for vocabulary detective work is considered valuable by some and highly overrated by others. If you know how to use these word-building elements, by all means use them as another weapon in your word-attack arsenal.

It is useful to know that "tele-" is a combining form that means "distant" or "transmission over a distance," but be aware that another combining form that looks exactly the same, "tele-," is derived from a different Greek word and means "complete" or "end (purpose)." It is confusing to realize that the "ped-" in "pedagog" is different from that in "pedant," and different again from that in "pedology." However, the "ped-" in "pedal" has the same meaning as "pod-" in "podiatry" except that one comes from Latin, while the other comes from Greek. If you feel comfortable using roots, stems, and other word-building elements, combine their use with the other approaches.

All the methods outlined above can help you with words that are at least slightly familiar to you, but they can't help you much with words you really don't know. The ancillary, or auxiliary, methods for unraveling the meanings of words are useful, but your best bet, your basic approach, should be *knowing the words!* To do well on the antonym question of the SAT you would be well advised to strengthen your vocabulary. Which leads us directly to the next topic.

HOW TO IMPROVE YOUR VOCABULARY IN A LIMITED TIME—F.E.P (FOR EXAM PURPOSES)

No matter how strong your vocabulary is, you can improve it markedly between now and exam time. How much you improve will depend upon the amount of time you are willing to invest in this study project, but you can learn scores, even hundreds, of new words in a matter of weeks. Please understand, however, that this new knowledge will be primarily F.E.P.—for exam purposes. Learning vocabulary F.E.P. means you can memorize lists of words for the useful purpose of preparing for short-answer multiple-choice vocabulary questions such as the antonym questions and, to a lesser extent, the sentence completion and the analogy questions of the SAT, but you will not retain that vocabulary for very long if you stop reviewing the material. If, however, you want to make those words a permanent part of your background, you can do so by making a special effort to use those words frequently in your everyday conversation and in your writing.

Here is a program for improving your vocabulary. If you work at it, you will get good results.

1. You will need two paperback books: a good dictionary (get one even if you have a large hardbound desk or unabridged dictionary at home—carrying one of those around would be quite a task) and a thesaurus (a thesaurus is a book of synonyms and antonyms).

2. You will also need some packs of three- by five-inch index cards and a small memo book.

3. Keep lists of unfamiliar words that you come across in the course of each day. You will find unfamiliar words on the word lists in this book, in your various school textbooks, in your recreational reading, and in newspapers and magazines. You will hear unfamiliar words in class, on radio and TV programs, at the movies and the theater, as well as in conversations all about you. Whenever you hear an unfamiliar word, see an unfamiliar word, jot it down in your memo book.

4. At the end of the day or if you have a chance sometime during the school day (study hall, perhaps) transpose the words from your memo book to the index cards, one word to a card. Print the word in the center of the card in large clear letters. Look the word up in the dictionary and read the definition, then look the word up in the thesaurus.

5. On the other side of the index card, across the top of the card, copy several synonyms of the new word. Across the bottom of the card, copy several antonyms of the new word. Print or write the synonyms in the same color pen or pencil for each new word. Use that same color consistently for synonyms. Use another color consistently for the antonyms of the new word.

6. Use the index cards as flashcards. Carry them around with you. Whenever you have some spare time—at the dentist's office; on the school bus; while waiting for dinner; on a boring date; in the study hall—go over your index cards.

   Go over the index cards by looking at the word. Try to recall as many synonyms and antonyms as you can. Go on to the next word. When you find yourself getting a particular word right, put it into the "inactive" file. Go over the inactive file less frequently. If you see that words in the inactive file are fading from your memory, return them to the "active" file.

7. Bundle the cards in little packs of ten or fifteen. Don't go over your entire list each time. Go over a small pack four or five times in repeat drills.

8. Shuffle your cards so that you don't develop a dependency upon the sequential arrangement of the words as an aid to memory.

9. If you wish to fix the word in your mind even more firmly, write directly under the printed word on the front of the card the sentence in which the word appeared when you heard or read it.

10. Ask friends and relatives to help you use the cards. A variety of approaches eliminates some of the monotony of this kind of drill-work.

11. Use the new words in conversation and in writing as frequently as possible. If you are concerned about the possibility that you may embarrass yourself by using a word incorrectly, limit yourself to trying this only with family and really good friends.

The SAT test guide suggests that you engage in word games, read some moderately complex books or some good magazine articles on topics with which you are not familiar. Those are excellent suggestions, but those suggestions are not specific for helping you prepare for this exam. They are good in terms of what educational and intellectual growth is all about, but you should take direct steps, in addition, to increase your vocabulary F.E.P.—For Exam Purposes—and then, if you can, hold on to it F.L.—For Life.

You will find several lists of words in this book. The lists have not been compiled in terms of graded difficulty. There are no such things as difficult words; there are only familiar and unfamiliar words. If you know a word, no matter how polysyllabic, that word is easy for you. If you don't know a word, it is difficult for you even if it has only three or four letters.

No list of words can be considered comprehensive for SAT preparation. Use the materials in this book, your own list of words, lists from school, and any other vocabulary materials you can obtain. Your only limit should be the time you have to spare for this portion of your test preparation.

The SAT Analogies Question

THE SAT ANALOGY/WORD RELATIONSHIP QUESTION

The first thing to do to prepare yourself for the analogy/word relationship question of the SAT is to familiarize yourself with the format of the question and the instructions you must follow. While, to be sure, you must read the actual test directions carefully to make certain that no changes have been made, you should be completely familiar with the directions in advance to save yourself time under actual examination conditions. Immediately following is a set of directions that is worded almost exactly like those on past SAT examinations:

Directions: In each of the questions below, a related pair of words or phrases, in capital letters, is followed by five pairs of words or phrases lettered from (A) through (E). Select that lettered pair which expresses a relationship that is most similar to that of the capitalized pair.

The wording of the directions on the actual test may vary slightly from those above, but the general sense will remain the same. Your task is to find, among the lettered choices, that pair of words which forms a relationship similar to that of the given, capitalized pair.

As the directions indicate, the analogy/word relationship question looks like this:

HOT : COLD ::
    (A) sweet : soft
    (B) brittle : bright
    (C) dark : light
    (D) brilliant : radiant
    (E) constant : instant

Answer: (C)

The given pair of words, *hot* and *cold* are capitalized and set off by the colon, or ratio, sign. As you were told earlier, the colon is merely a kind of code or shorthand symbol that says that *word A* is related to *word B*. The double colon separates the given pair from the five choices, and it is a symbol that says "in the same way that." As you can now see, the question in the example reads as follows:

"*Hot* is related to *cold* in the same way that the words in one of the lettered choices are related to each other."

Although the analogy/word relationship question looks something like a ratio problem and is written in a similar fashion, *do not* express the problem as if it were a ratio problem. *Do not* say: *Hot* is to *cold* as dark is to light. Instead, say: *Hot* is the opposite of *cold* in the same way that dark is the opposite of light.

To sum up, then, in this part of the SAT verbal section, you are required to determine the significant relationship between the two words of a given pair of words, and find—among the choices offered—an analogous or similar relationship between another pair of words.

ANSWERING THE ANALOGY/WORD RELATIONSHIP QUESTION

You have been told *not* to express the analogy/word relationship problem in terms of a mathematical ratio problem. How, then, are you to express the problem?

The analogy/word relationship problem should always be expressed as a complete sentence that clearly indicates the relationship between the two given words, and links that relationship to a similar statement about one of the pairs among the choices. Thus, in the example given above, the statement showing the relationship between *hot* and *cold* is clearly expressed and then linked, by using the words "in the same way that," to the relationship between *dark* and *light*. Use this formula approach in all analogy/word relationship questions.

In the example, you were given the words *hot* and *cold*. If you were asked to indicate in what ways those words are related, you could observe that:

1. both words are adjectives,
2. both words describe the same kind of characteristic or physical state: temperature,
3. both words are terms that express comparative extremes of the same physical state—temperature.

But you could not have said which of the three observations was the most significant expression of the relationship between the two words until after you had examined the five answer choices. You would have noted that observation No. 1 applied to all five choices. However, observation No. 2 did not apply to choice (A) or choice (B): *sweet* and *soft* describe two entirely different kinds of physical characteristics, as do *brittle* and *bright*. The words in choice (E) do not fit observation No. 2, either; although they both describe aspects of time, they do not describe the same aspect. Only choices (C) and (D) fit observation No. 2: They both describe the same physical state—light intensity—but the words in choice (D) do not express opposite or extreme aspects of light intensity, while those in choice (C) do. The answer is choice (C).

Let's analyze another analogy/word relationship question:

> SURGEON : SCALPEL ::
>   (A) carpenter : cabinet
>   (B) architect : plans
>   (C) musician : instrument
>   (D) baker : oven
>   (E) sculptor : chisel
>
> Answer: (E)

You can state the relationship between the given words as follows: A *surgeon* uses a *scalpel* as a tool or instrument. Examining the five choices, you find that the only pairs of words for which similar statements can be made are those in choices (C) and (E):

> "A *musician* uses an *instrument* as a tool or instrument."
> "A *sculptor* uses a *chisel* as a tool or instrument."

Since the directions stress that the answer must be the lettered pair which expresses a relationship that is *most similar* to the given pair, you must decide which of the two relationships expressed above is closer to the given relationship.

Look at the choices again. While *surgeon* and *scalpel* are very specific terms, *musician* and *instrument* are not. "String instrumentalist" and "violin" would be better. *Sculptor* and *chisel* are as specific as the words in the given pair, and the relationship is similar. You can state your answer, then, as follows: "A surgeon uses a scalpel as a tool or instrument in the same way that a sculptor uses a chisel as a tool or instrument."

Here are some points to remember:

· The statement about the pairs of words always uses the words in the same order that those words appear in the question. Do not reverse the order to say, "A *scalpel* is used by a *surgeon*," or "A *chisel* is used by a *sculptor*." Sometimes incorrect choices with reversed word orders are used to distract you. Routinize your formula statement; that is, always use the words in the statement in the same order in which they appear in the question.

· Be sure that the type of word used in your answer choice corresponds to the type of words in the given pair. A general term in the given pair should be matched by a general term in the answer choice, a specific term in the given pair matched by a specific term in the answer choice, and a proper noun in the given pair matched by a proper noun in the answer choice.

TREE : MAPLE ::
(A) rose : American Beauty
(B) dog : cat
(C) Seattle Slew : thoroughbred
(D) dog : poodle
(E) shrub : plant

Answer: (D)

Tree is a general term, while *maple* is a specific term and, in fact, a specific kind of tree. You should be looking for an answer with a general term as the first word, and a specific term—probably something that is a species of the first word—as the second word. *Rose* is a specific term; you can, therefore, eliminate choice (A). *Seattle Slew* is a proper noun; you can, therefore, eliminate choice (C). Of the remaining three choices, all the first words are general terms, but only in choice (D) is the second word a specific term: "One type of *tree* is the *maple*, in the same way that one type of *dog* is the *poodle*."

BABE RUTH : BALLPLAYER ::
(A) Dr. Jekyll : Mr. Hyde
(B) collie : sheepdog
(C) All-American : star performer
(D) Patrick Henry : Virginian
(E) Mark Twain : author

Answer: (E)

In this question, the first term of the given pair is *Babe Ruth*, a proper noun that is the name of a particular person. The second term, *ballplayer,* is the specific occupation of that particular person. In choice A, *Dr. Jekyll* is the name of a particular person, but the term *Mr. Hyde* is the name of Dr. Jekyll's other personality, not a description of his occupation. In B, a *collie* is, by occupation, a *sheepdog,* but *collie* is not a proper noun that is the name of a particular person. *All-American,* in choice C, is not the name of a particular person, and *star performer* is not a word that describes a specific occupation. In choice D, *Patrick Henry* is the name of a particular person, but the term *Virginian* does not tell what Patrick Henry's occupation was; it tells only that he came from Virginia. In choice E, *Mark Twain* and *author* are, respectively, the name of a particular person, and the specific occupation of that particular person.

After examining all the choices, you can see that choice E is the correct answer, and that the formula statement is: "*Babe Ruth* was a *ballplayer* by occupation, in the same way that *Mark Twain* was an *author* by occupation.''

· Although the symbols between the words in the SAT analogy/word relationship questions are the same as those used between the terms of a mathematical ratio, do not use mathematical terminology when you are working on verbal analogies.

It is not helpful to say, "*Surgeon* is to *scalpel* as _____ is to _____," because this statement tells you nothing about the relationship between *surgeon* and *scalpel*. In fact, a ratio-like statement like the one just above short-circuits your thinking process.

It is helpful to say, "A *surgeon* uses a *scalpel* as a tool or instrument in the same way that _____," because such a statement expresses the relationship between *surgeon* and *scalpel* and prepares you to recognize which of the choices is most similar in relationship to the given pair.

· The statement you make about the relationship between the two given words must be a significant statement. In other words, your statement must express the most important aspect of the relationship between the two words.

If you find that more than one of the pairs of choices seem to be equally related to the given pair, you must reexamine your original statement to see whether or not you have been specific enough in expressing the relationship. It is also possible that you may have to reexamine your statements about your choices. Study the following question:

PITCHER : THROWS ::
    (A) miler : trains
    (B) baserunner : slides
    (C) gymnast : runs
    (D) skater : pirouettes
    (E) batter : swings

Answer: (E)

You would probably say, at first, "a *pitcher* (throws)." Unfortunately, you could then say that a *miler* trains, a *baserunner* slides, a *gymnast* runs, a *skater* pirouettes, and a *batter* swings. All the statements about the choices are similar to the statement about the given pair, except for one thing: in four of the five choices, the act described is not the most significant act that person performs. Milers train, but their important act is running. Similarly, baserunners may slide, but their significant act is running, and the skater's most significant act is skating. If you revise your original statement to say, "A *pitcher throws* a ball as his main activity," you are ready to make the truly analogous statement, which is, "A *batter swings* at the ball as his main activity." The formula statement would be:

"A *pitcher throws* the ball as his main activity in the same way that a *batter swings* at the ball as his main activity."

You may have noticed, in doing the sample questions above, that once you understood the nature of the relationship between the words in the given pair, it was much easier to select the correct answer. The relationships in these analogies fall into certain types or categories: The relationship between *hot* and *cold* was one of opposites; the one between *surgeon* and *scalpel* was one of function; the relationship between *Babe Ruth* and *ballplayer* was description or characterization; and the one between *pitcher* and *throws* was one of function, again. Fortunately for our purposes in this book, most analogy/word relationships fit into a comparatively small number of categories. Knowing those categories and being able to recognize into which of them a particular given pair belongs is a great help in solving the analogy question. The next portion of this book sets forth the various categories into which analogies fall and gives examples for each category.

CATEGORIES OF SAT ANALOGY/WORD RELATIONSHIP PROBLEMS

If you can quickly recognize that *pitcher* and *throws* form a function or use relationship, you will find it easier to select the correct answer from among the choices offered you, because the category tells you something important about the nature of the relationship of the two words in question. Listed below are a number of fairly common, very useful relationship categories, with examples and explanatory answers for each:

1. Synonymous Relationship

In the Synonymous Relationship category, as you might expect, the two words of the given pair are similar in meaning.

> THIN : SLIM ::
> (A) hot : heavy
> (B) bald : bold
> (C) grin : grim
> (D) stout : portly
> (E) lean : long
>
> Answer: (D)

Thin and *slim* both mean "slender" and are synonyms in the same way that *stout* and *portly* meaning "heavy or fat" are synonyms.

2. Degree of Difference Relationship

In the Degree of Difference Relationship, the two words of the given pair are similar in meaning, but one of the words is stronger, harsher, more intense, greater in degree, or weaker, milder, less intense, lesser in degree than the other word.

> NIP : CRUSH ::
> (A) rip : tear
> (B) tap : slam
> (C) crimp : cramp
> (D) bruise : brush
> (E) pound : pat
>
> Answer: (B)

Nip, which means "compress tightly," is similar to, but much less forceful an expression than *crush*, which means "press with a force that destroys," in the same way that *tap*, which means "hit lightly," is similar to, but much less forceful an expression than *slam*, which means "hit with violence."

Note that the first word of the given pair, *nip*, is not as strong as the second word. In the answer, too, the first word of the selected pair, *tap*, is not as strong as the second word. In choice (E) there is also a degree of difference between *pound* and *pat*, but the difference is in the wrong direction; the first word is more forceful than the second, instead of the other way around.

The degree of difference must always flow in the same direction in the given pair as it does in the answer pair.

Another important consideration in working on Degree of Difference analogies is that the degree of difference in a given pair must be relatively the same as the degree of difference in the answer pair.

FREQUENTLY : ALWAYS ::
    (A) seldom : never
    (B) shaky : stable
    (C) never : seldom
    (D) early : late
    (E) rarely : always

Answer: (A)

Frequently means "very often," but *always* means "every time," without exception. The degree of difference between the two words is not very great, but the second word is an absolute. *Seldom* means "infrequently," but *never* means "at no time," without exception. As in the given pair, the second word is an absolute. The formula statement would read, as follows: "*Frequently* differs in degree from *always* in the same way that *seldom* differs in degree from *never*."

Again, in this example, the second word is more intense than the first word in both the given pair and in the answer pair. If something happens more often than *frequently*, you would probably say that it happened "most of the time," and if it happened more often than that, you would say that it *always* happened. Similarly, if something happened less often than *seldom*, you would say that it happened *rarely*, and it could not happen less often than rarely, for then you would have to say that it *never* happened.

In choice (C), the intensity of the degree of difference flows in the wrong direction. In choice (E), the degree of difference is less intense than it is in the given pair. The words in choice (B) form an antonymous relationship, not a degree of difference relationship.

3. Antonymous Relationship

In this relationship category, the two words of the given pair are opposed to one another in meaning. Your task, of course, is to find the pair among the choices that is made up of words that are opposed to each other in meaning.

THIN : PORTLY ::
    (A) cold : light
    (B) plump : short
    (C) grin : shortly
    (D) wild : wooly
    (E) slim : stout

Answer: (E)

Thin is the opposite of *portly* in the same way that *slim* is the opposite of *stout*.

4. Cause and Effect Relationship

The Cause and Effect Relationship, as you might expect, is one in which the action of the first word results in the effect of the second word, or vice versa.

SHOOT : KILL ::
   (A) vex : angry
   (B) demobilize : arrive
   (C) capture : escape
   (D) insult : humiliate
   (E) skip : skid

Answer: (D)

If you *shoot* someone, you may *kill* him, in the same way that if you *insult* someone, you may *humiliate* him.

If you use the formula statement at all times, you will avoid choosing answers like choice (A), above. Using *vex* and *angry* in the formula statement gives you, "If you vex someone, you may angry him." However, if you are not careful in your formula statement and fail to make the statement parallel to the first half of the statement, you might wind up saying, "If you vex someone, you will make him angry." How do you avoid mistakes like that? Check to make sure that the parts of speech correspond. *Shoot* and *kill* are verbs. The two words in the answer need not necessarily be verbs, but they should both be the same part of speech. *Vex* is a verb, but *angry* is an adjective.

MOSQUITO : MALARIA ::
   (A) contact : cholera
   (B) dampness : dengue
   (C) asbestos : encephalitis
   (D) flea : itching
   (E) fly : sleeping sickness

Answer: (E)

The anopheles *mosquito* can infect man with *malaria*, in the same way that the tsetse *fly* can infect man with *sleeping sickness*.

While it is true that a *flea* can cause *itching*, that statement is not analogous to the one about *mosquito* and *malaria*. The *mosquito* infects man with *malaria*. The analogous statement would be: The flea infects man with itching. That is not an accurate statement.

5. Whole and Part, Part and Whole, and Part and Part Relationships

If the first word of the given pair represents something that is part of what the second word stands for, the category into which the analogy/word relationship falls is the Part and Whole Relationship. If the words are reversed and the second word of the pair represents something that is part of what the first word stands for, the category into which the relationships falls is the Whole and Part Relationship. A third, very similar category is the Part and Part Relationship.

AUTOMOBILE : WHEEL ::
- (A) violin : winds
- (B) sleigh : runner
- (C) fringe : carpet
- (D) thorn : tendril
- (E) bacon : eggs

Answer: (B)

A part of the undercarriage of an *automobile* is a *wheel* in the same way that a part of the undercarriage of a *sleigh* is a *runner*.

In the example above, the first word, *automobile,* represents a whole, while the second word, *wheel,* represents a part. You would, of course, look for the pair in which the first word represents the whole and the second word the part. In choice (C), the *fringe* is a part of the *carpet,* so the words are in the wrong order. In choices (D) and (E), both words represent parts: *thorn* and *tendril* are both parts of a plant, and *bacon* and *eggs* are both parts of a larger whole.

CONTROL COLUMN : AIRPLANE ::
- (A) deck : runabout
- (B) engine : locomotive
- (C) keel : sailboat
- (D) propeller : airplane
- (E) helm : sailboat

Answer: (E)

The *control column* is the part of the *airplane* that governs the rudder and turns the plane in the same way that the *helm* is the part of the *sailboat* that governs the rudder and turns the *sailboat*.

In the example just given, all of the choices fell into the Part and Whole category. To determine which of the choices was most similar to the given pair, you had to determine which part had a relationship to the whole that was most like the relationship between *control column* and *airplane*. In order to do that, you had to decide what the *control column* was like and then decide which other part functioned or looked most like the control column in its relationship to the *airplane*.

In addition to using function of a part, or appearance, to determine analogy, you can use position, location, or any other characteristic which most closely matches part and part, and whole and whole.

FENDER : TIRE ::
- (A) elevator : aileron
- (B) stool : chair
- (C) pistol : trigger
- (D) pocket : coat
- (E) pin : needle

Answer: (A)

Fender and *tire* are each part of an automobile in the same way that *elevator* and *aileron* are each part of an airplane.

6. Classification Relationship

In the Classification Relationship, the first word may be classified by the second word, or vice versa.

> HORSE : MAMMAL ::
> (A) gorilla : subhuman
> (B) cat : domestic
> (C) lobster : invertebrate
> (D) sole : flounder
> (E) eagle : mammal
>
> Answer: (C)

The *horse* can be classified as a *mammal* in the same way that the *lobster* can be classified as an *invertebrate*.

In choice (A), unlike the relationship in the given pair, the *gorilla* is not classified as *subhuman,* but rather, characterized. In choice (E), the only choice, aside from the correct answer, to attempt to classify the first word, the classification is factually incorrect. An *eagle* is not a *mammal.*

The Classification Relationship can also be thought of as the defining relationship. One word of the pair defines the other.

7. Function, Composition, Action, Etc., Relationships

This is a multipurpose category. In this category, we have several different types of analogies:
a) The first term describes the function of the second term.
b) The first term describes what the second term is made of.
c) The first term describes a tool used by the second term.

For instance, *sneakers* : *canvas* says that the relationship between the two words is that sneakers are made of canvas; *axe* : *cuts* tells you what the function of the axe is; *lion* : *hunts* describes what the lion does; *coffee* : *berry* states that coffee comes from a berry. This category also includes Associational Relationships, like *gourmet* : *truffles*. In the Associational Relationship category, you must use your intuition and your broad cultural background. An Associational Relationship is one where the two words go together as a pair simply on the basis of the fact that you recognize them as associated.

> AXE : WOOD ::
> (A) steamroller : flatten
> (B) scissors : fabric
> (C) knife : whittlings
> (D) marble : chisel
> (E) gun : hunt
>
> Answer: (B)

An *axe* is used to chop or cut *wood* in the same way that *scissors* are used to cut *fabric.*

GENERAL : COMMANDS ::
    (A) senator : filibusters
    (B) teacher : moralizes
    (C) senator : legislates
    (D) judge : condemns
    (E) waiter : orders

Answer: (C)

A *general*, as one of his main functions, *commands* his forces in the same way that a *senator*, as one of his main functions, *legislates*, that is, writes proposals for new laws. A senator *filibusters* on occasion, perhaps, but not as one of his main functions. Likewise, the main functions of a *judge* are to preside over trials, hearings, etc., and to deliver decisions.

It is always wise to consider carefully whether or not the relationship of the choice is really analogous to the relationship of the given pair. Always phrase your formula statements carefully to make sure that you are using the same terminology in both halves of the statement.

8. *Sequential Relationship*

In the Sequential Relationship category, the first word represents something that usually follows or is followed by what the second word stands for. This type of relationship is similar to the Cause and Effect Relationship, except that in this category, there is sequence without a causal relationship.

EIGHT : NINE ::
    (A) four : 2^2
    (B) 2^3 : 3^2
    (C) eight : eighty
    (D) ten : nine
    (E) six : twelve

Answer: (B)

Eight is followed by *nine* in the same way that 2^3, which is eight, is followed by 3^2, which is nine.

Note: *Hit* followed by *hurt* does not fall into the Sequential category because *hit* causes *hurt*.

9. *Characterization Relationship*

In the Characterization Relationship category, the first term characterizes or is characterized by the second term. The first term may be a person, place, or thing.

HOST : HOSPITABLE ::
    (A) artist : imitative
    (B) guest : rude
    (C) humanitarian : altruistic
    (D) idealist : cynical
    (E) Pollyanna : pessimistic

Answer: (C)

You would expect, as a matter of course, that a *host* would be *hospitable* in the same way that you would expect that a *humanitarian* would be *altruistic*, since a *humanitarian* is, by definition, concerned about the welfare of mankind, and *altruistic* means "unselfishly devoted to the welfare of others."

Sometimes, instead of finding that a person, place, or thing is properly characterized, you may find an opposite characterization. If you find an opposite characterization in the given pair, you will have to find an opposite characterization among the choices, too.

> DIPLOMAT : TACTLESS ::
> (A) starveling : weak
> (B) boor : offensive
> (C) charlatan : guileful
> (D) coward : intrepid
> (E) acrobat : agile
>
> Answer: (D)

You would not expect a *diplomat* to be *tactless*. Similarly, or in the same way, you would not expect a *coward* to be *intrepid* (fearless).

10. *Grammatical or Verbal Relationships*

In the Grammatical or Verbal Relationship category, the two words in the given pair may be related to one another by being different parts of speech with the same stem, or by being parts of the same conjugation, or they may be related in other, similar, ways: *neurotic* : *neurosis* :: psychotic : psychosis; *work* : *wrought* :: fight : fought. (The past participle of *work* is *wrought* in the same way that the past participle of *fight* is *fought*.)

WINNING STRATEGIES FOR SOLVING THE SAT ANALOGY/WORD RELATIONSHIP QUESTION

You will find the categories to be among the most important aids you have in dealing with the SAT Analogy/Word Relationship question. It is often much faster and easier to determine the category of a given pair than it is to construct your statement. Of course, the formula statement is a crucial part of your approach to the solution of the analogy question. Identifying the category will be an enormous help to you in constructing the formula statement. As soon as you have identified the category, whether it is before you make the statement or after you make the initial statement, you are in the advantageous position of knowing that you are looking for something specific—synonyms, antonyms, degrees of difference, or any of the other types—and that focuses your attention more sharply and permits you to solve the problem more effectively and efficiently.

If the given pair is made up of two words of the same part of speech, like two nouns or two verbs, then the words in your answer choice will also be two words that are both the same part of speech. However, the parts of speech of your choice need not necessarily be the same parts of speech as those in the given pair.

If the given pair is made up of two different parts of speech, like a noun and a verb, or a noun and an adjective, or any other combination of parts of speech, then the answer pair will almost inevitably consist of the same two parts of speech in the same order as in the given pair.

Keep your eyes peeled for such strong clues as words that are proper nouns, specific terms, general terms, function terms, etc. The corresponding word in your answer choice, too, will match the nature of those terms.

If you are unable to find a parallel pair among the answers, try one of the following: reexamine the relationship—you may have missed the significant aspect; take a fresh look at the given words—words have varieties of meanings, and you may be applying the wrong one in this case; restate the formula, trying a slightly different approach.

Last, but not least, remember that all relationships do not look the same to all people. The category approach is a highly useful one, but it is not a perfect one. Its use does permit you to see the problem in a structured way. However, if you cannot fit a given pair into a category, you still can make the formula statement. And the two halves of the formula statement, the one dealing with the given pair and the one dealing with the answer pair, should be phrased in almost exactly the same terms. If you can make such a structured formula statement, you are almost certain to have the right answer.

The SAT Sentence Completion Question

Before you can deal successfully with the SAT sentence completion question, you must familiarize yourself with the format of the question, read carefully the instructions that accompany the question, and understand the nature of the task that you must perform to answer the question correctly.

The instructions that follow may differ slightly from those on the actual test, but the overall meaning is just about the same. The sample question that appears below the instructions is given in the same format as that used in the actual test.

Directions: In each sentence below, blanks indicate where a word or set of words has been omitted. Following each sentence, lettered (A) through (E), are five choices of words or sets of words. Select the lettered choice which fills the blanks so as to complete the sentence correctly as to meaning, correct diction and usage, and appropriate expression.

The ancient city of Pompeii lay _____ in the shadow of Mount Vesuvius for more than 1700 years under a deep layer of volcanic _____.

(A) titled . . heat
(B) unconscious . . eruption
(C) buried . . debris
(D) sweltering . . lava
(E) despairing . . activity

Answer: (C)

As you can see by even a cursory examination of the sample question, the sentence above has two words missing. You are asked to select the lettered pair of words which will successfully complete the sentence so that the completed sentence makes perfect sense and so that the added words will be correct from the point of view of diction and usage.

The SAT sentence completion question tests your ability in several areas. First, the question tests your ability to grasp the context of a sentence even with some of the words missing; second, the question tests your knowledge of vocabulary as demonstrated by your ability to select the correct words to complete the given sentence so that it becomes a sound, logical, meaningful verbal statement of the sort that an educated English-speaking person would be expected to make; third, the question seeks to check your ability to recognize the interrelationships between various parts of a sentence.

Only one of the choices offered can fill in the blanks so that the finished sentence meets the criteria given above. However, you do not play guessing games when you answer the SAT sentence completion question. All the information you need to make the correct choice is contained in the incomplete sentence. Your task is to identify the information that is given and analyze it so that you select the correct answer.

In the sample question, the incomplete sentence informs you that for seventeen centuries the city of Pompeii has lain under a deep layer of something volcanic. The phrase "deep layer" is a significant one that helps you to eliminate some of the choices. Pompeii could not have lain under a deep layer of volcanic *heat*, volcanic *activity*, or volcanic *eruption*. Heat, activity, and eruption are not ordinarily described as forming layers, deep or otherwise. Pompeii might have lain under a deep layer of *debris* or *lava,* but not under a deep layer of "volcanic lava," since the word "volcanic" used with lava is redundant. Lava is, by definition, volcanic, and it would be incorrect to refer to it as volcanic lava.

Having determined that the second word of choice (C), *debris*, is the correct selection for the second blank in the complete sentence, you should now see whether or not the first word of choice (C), *buried,* is appropriate for the first blank. A quick perusal of the sentence affirms that Pompeii could properly be described as having lain buried if it was under a deep layer of volcanic debris. Choices (A) and (B) make no sense at all. As for choice (D), Pompeii could have lain *sweltering* under an oppressive climate, but not under the already discredited "volcanic lava." And, while the city might have lain *despairing* as a result of the impact of continuous volcanic activity, as you have already seen, there is no such thing as a deep layer of volcanic *activity*.

The completed sentence, then, reads as follows: "The ancient city of Pompeii lay *buried* in the shadow of Mount Vesuvius for more than 1700 years under a deep layer of volcanic *debris*."

APPROACHES TO THE SAT SENTENCE COMPLETION QUESTION

While the SAT sentence completion question does not lend itself to a single, simplified formula approach for solution, there are a number of ways of approaching each sentence so as to uncover clues more readily.

Contextual Clues.

To begin with, you should always examine each sentence for contextual clues, words, or phrases that tell you something about the setting for the sentence's action, or the nature of the subject, or the period of time that is being written about. In the following example, for instance, several of the words give you background information that leads you directly to the correct answer.

> Every year thousand of Moslems make a(n) _____ to the holy
>   city of Mecca.
> (A) expedition
> (B) tour
> (C) excursion
> (D) junket
> (E) pilgrimage
>
>   Answer: (E)

All the choices offered for the solution of this sentence are words that define some kind of trip. You should ask yourself: How do these trips differ, and who would make each kind of trip, and under what circumstances? Your examination of the sentence reveals two significant words: *Moslem* and *Mecca*. These two words give you a reasonable basis for deciding what kind of trip the people involved would be making . . . or taking. Since Mecca is the holy city of the Moslems, you can conclude that the thousands of Moslems are making a trip of a religious nature, or a pilgrimage.

You can conclude that the trip the Moslems are making is a pilgrimage, on the basis of the contextual clues, but you *must* conclude that it is a pilgrimage when you consider the linguistic structure of the sentence. People take tours, go on excursions and junkets, mount, launch, form, or organize expeditions, but of the five choices, the only kind of trip that people *make* is a pilgrimage. You might say: Make a tour of a place; you would not say: Make a tour to a place. The answer is choice (E).

Reversal Indicators.

Certain words that appear in sentence completion questions signal that one part of the sentence will be the reverse of what the other part of the sentence led you to expect. These words, some of which are listed below, may be thought of as reversal indicators:

although	nevertheless	notwithstanding
despite	however	still
but	yet	even though

Notice how the reversal indicator works in the following sample:

> His most recent novel was a commercial _____, even though the
>   leading critics of the literary establishment _____ him to the
>   skies for his glowing insights and masterful characterizations.

(A) failure . . extolled
(B) venture . . exposed
(C) success . . praised
(D) advertisement . . panned
(E) project . . launched

Answer: (A)

The words "even though" tell you that if his novel were a commercial success, it had to be despite the critics' praise. However, you would expect a book to succeed commercially if the critics praised it, and you would not say it succeeded, even though it was praised. On the contrary, the words "even though" tell you that if his book failed, it was despite the critics' praise. The clues in the second half of the sentence indicate that the critics praised him: They (blanked) him for his glowing insights and masterful characterizations, both obviously praiseworthy achievements. You must conclude, therefore, that his novel was a commercial *failure,* despite the fact that the critics *extolled* him to the skies.

Expectation Intensifiers.

Just as some words serve as reversal indicators, others act as expectation intensifiers. When you see intensifers in a sentence, they signal that what you expect is what you will get. Look for such words as:

therefore	since	consequently
as a result	because	

The following sentence completion question shows how expectation intensifiers can help you determine the answer.

He labored industriously at the job for long, weary hours, giving
_____ of his energy and loyalty, no matter how great the de-
mands; as a result, when the plant superintendent's position
fell vacant, he was _____ nominated by directors.
(A) grudgingly . . thoughtlessly
(B) sparingly . . almost
(C) some . . again
(D) unstintingly . . unanimously
(E) freely . . reluctantly

Answer: (D)

The words "as a result" tell you he will receive in the second part of the sentence whatever he deserves for what he did in the first part of the sentence. That he labored industriously for long, weary hours suggests that he gave either freely or unstintingly (without holding back) of his energy and loyalty, especially in the light of the words, "no matter how great the demands." As a result of working hard and giving *unstintingly* of his time, you can properly expect that he would be rewarded. There is certainly no evidence to indicate that the directors would have anything but a high opinion of him, and therefore (or as a result), he would be *unanimously* nominated for a promotion.

Stylistic Clues.

Very often, certain elements of style will help you to recognize the clues in a sentence completion question. For instance, the use of the colon can indicate that what follows will be a list, a series of similar things, an illustration of what has just been said, or an explanation of the statement prior to the colon. The following sentence illustrates this point:

> Fenton was an enigma to us: one moment smiling and telling funny stories, the next snarling and hurling insults; one day _____ and philosophical, the following, completely outgoing and hail-fellow-well-met; sometimes unfeeling and flinty, other times warmly _____ and giving.
> (A) pragmatic . . soft
> (B) withdrawn . . dramatic
> (C) introspective . . sympathetic
> (D) intellectual . . hostile
> (E) taciturn . . loquacious
>
> Answer: (C)

The colon should indicate to you that what is to come will illustrate the point that Fenton was an enigma (a puzzle or riddle). You should note, too, that the explanation comes in a series of remarks. The first of the series of remarks is a pair of contrasting descriptions of Fenton's behavior. You can assume that the next two remarks in the series will, to demonstrate that Fenton is an enigma, consist of contrasting statements. The opposite of "outgoing and hail-fellow-well-met" is (B) *withdrawn,* (C) *introspective,* or (E) *taciturn.* The opposite of "unfeeling and flinty" is (C) *sympathetic.* Choices (B) and (E) are not correct, since only the first term of each is appropriate. The answer is (C).

Some constructions indicate that the pairs of blanks must be opposed to one another, as in the following sentence:

> Although he is generally considered to be a highly opinionated person, he does not _____ but rather _____ those who, on principle, oppose his views.
> (A) despise . . admires
> (B) value . . compels
> (C) crush . . dazzles
> (D) single out . . isolates
> (E) attack . . reveals
>
> Answer: (A)

If you fill in the blanks with generalized words or words like "blank" or "something," you will find that your own sense of language will often clarify the problem in a sentence completion question. In the instance above, if you say to yourself: "He does not do *x* but rather *y,*" you will feel the opposing character of the two blanks. The only pair of words among the choices that are in opposition to one another are those in choice (A). When you try substituting them for the blanks in the sentence, you can see immediately that you have found the correct answer.

SUMMARIZING APPROACHES TO THE SAT SENTENCE COMPLETION QUESTION

You will find the preceding approaches to the SAT sentence completion question useful for a large percentage of the completion questions, but they cannot help you with all the sentence completions. You should always be aware of the need to look for contextual clues, reversal indicators, expectation intensifiers, and stylistic clues, but in addition, to check the correctness of your choice or even to help in selecting the correct answer, you should look carefully at the syntax of the sentence, the logic of the language, the vocabulary used in the sentence, and any other aspect of the sentence that offers itself for examination. Even so simple a thing as the preposition that a word takes can be a critical clue. For instance, if you try to fill in a blank with the word "concerned" and find that, in part, the sentence now reads, "He felt deeply concerned of the outcome . . . ," you can be sure that you have selected the wrong answer, because "concern" does not take the preposition "of."

You may find it helpful to try to fill in the blanks without referring to the choices first. Many people have a strongly enough developed sense of language to close the gaps in many sentence completions. However you arrive at your choice of an answer on the SAT sentence completion question, ask yourself these crucial questions:

· Does this sentence, with the blanks filled, make a meaningful statement?
· Is this sentence, with the blanks filled, correct as to grammar and syntax?
· Are the words that fill the blanks correct as to diction and usage?
· Is this sentence, with the blanks filled, the kind of sentence that an educated English-speaking person uses as standard written English?

If you cannot answer "yes," to each and all of these questions, you'd better take another look at the choices.

The SAT Reading Comprehension Question

Just as in dealing with any other type of question on the SAT, your first order of business in approaching the SAT reading comprehension question should be to familiarize yourself with the instructions for answering the question.

The directions immediately following are almost exactly the same as those on actual past SAT's:

Directions: Each of the reading passages below is followed by several questions about the contents of that passage. Select the correct answer based on what is *stated* or *implied* in the passage.

The wording of the actual test instructions may differ slightly from the one above, but the general sense will remain the same.

Note carefully that you are to judge the correctness of an answer on the basis of what is *stated* or *implied* in the passage. Even if the information in the passage runs counter to what you believe to be correct, base your answer on what the author says in the passage, *not* on what you have read elsewhere, *not* on what you believe to be true.

If you familiarize yourself with these instructions for the reading comprehension question beforehand, you will not have to wrestle with what they mean when you take the test. You will be able to use all your time for answering questions rather than for puzzling over instructions.

One word of caution: To be on the safe side, when you actually take the test, read the instructions to make sure that no changes have been made.

THE FORMAT OF THE SAT READING COMPREHENSION QUESTION

The format of the SAT reading comprehension question is straightforward: You are given a reading passage of from 300 to 550 words taken from published materials, and a series of questions about the contents of that passage. Some of the questions test your ability to understand directly stated information, some test your ability to recognize implications and draw inferences, some test your ability to identify the author's purpose, evaluate the author's style, or analyze the author's arguments, and some test your ability to recognize the main idea presented by the author, and to apply his viewpoint. In sum, then, the questions test your ability to read a passage and comprehend its meaning, showing that ability by selecting the correct answer from among the choices supplied.

A SAMPLE READING PASSAGE AND SOME SAMPLE QUESTIONS

The reading passages of the SAT are drawn from several areas. You will find, on the test, passages from:

> *Science*: biology, chemistry, physics, astronomy, botany, etc.
> *Social studies*: history, anthropology, sociology, government, etc.
> *Humanities*: art, music, literature, philosophy, etc.
> *Other prose writings*: polemical writings (argumentation), plays,
>   biographies, novels, essays, short stories, etc.

Although it is not important for you to identify the category from which a passage comes, this information will permit you to anticipate the kinds of passages you will find on the test. The important thing to remember is that you must answer the questions that are asked, and that your answers must be based on the contents of the passage.

In the vocabulary question, you are given a word, but *you* must supply the meaning from your own store of knowledge. In the reading comprehension question, all the information you need to answer any of the questions is in the passage, either stated clearly or implied (hinted at or suggested).

The sample passage which follows is shorter than the usual reading passage on the SAT, but otherwise it is typical of the easier passages you can expect to see on the test. In the practice tests you will find more difficult samples that will be illustrations of the various types of reading comprehension questions that you will encounter on the actual SAT.

Directions: The passage below is followed by several questions about the content of that passage. Select the correct answer to each of the questions, basing your response on what is *stated* or *implied* in the passage.

Just for good measure, and because your guess is apt to be as sound as mine, here are a few of the current theories about the origin of the Basques. Some of the professors who distill racial theories out of skulls and gutturals, believe them to be connected with those Berbers whom I mentioned several chapters ago as the possible descendants of one of the earliest tribes of prehistoric Europeans, the so-called Cromagnon race. Others claim that they are the survivors who saved themselves on the European continent when the romantic island of Atlantis disappeared beneath the waves of the ocean. Still others hold that they have always been where they are now and don't bother to ask where they came from. Whatever the truth, the Basques have shown remarkable ability in keeping themselves aloof from the rest of the world. They are very industrious. More than a hundred thousand of them have migrated to South America. They are excellent fishermen and sailors and iron workers and they mind their own business and keep off the front page of the newspapers.

1. Which of the following does the passage suggest is the correct origin of the Basques?
    (A) They can be traced to the survivors of Atlantis.
    (B) They are connected with the Berbers.
    (C) Their guttural language is like the skull people's.
    (D) They are descended from the Cromagnons.
    (E) The author admits to not knowing their origin.
2. The main purpose of the passage is to
    (A) explain the origin of the species
    (B) trace the ancestry of the Basques
    (C) characterize the Basques without concern for theoretical speculation as to their origin
    (D) establish the relationship between the Berbers and the Cromagnons
    (E) argue that Atlantis is not just a romantic myth
3. The word "distill," as used in the second sentence of the passage, most nearly means
    (A) vaporize and then condense, as for purification or concentration
    (B) obtain, extract or condense by or as if by distillation
    (C) infuse
    (D) instill
    (E) let fall in drops

AN APPROACH TO THE SAT READING COMPREHENSION QUESTION

Before we look at the sample questions above, let us consider how to approach the reading comprehension question overall. If you do not have a method which works for you, or if you feel insecure with the method you are now using, here is an approach that has been used with great success on reading comprehension questions:

Step No. 1. Read the questions quickly.

Skim over the questions at a moderately fast rate. Determine from this quick inspection which of the questions seem to deal with materials directly stated in the passage, which seem to call for the use of inference, which seem to ask you to make evaluations, and so on.

Read the questions quickly! Step No. 1 is a preliminary step. Don't spend too much time on it. You will be rereading the questions in a subsequent step.

The purpose of Step No. 1 is to give you some idea of what you should be looking for as you read the passage.

Step No. 2. Read the passage at your fastest rate.

Read the passage at your fastest rate of reading—short of skimming—without worrying about full comprehension at this point.

As you read, try to keep the questions in mind, and if you come across material that seems related to any of the questions, hold the place in the passage with your finger or mark it with a pencil, and go back to check the question's wording.

If the material seems applicable, (1) mark the question number in the margin of the passage alongside the relevant part, and (2) circle your provisional answer choice under the question.

Resume reading where you had left off and repeat the process outlined above.

Don't worry if you can't recall all the questions while you are doing this first reading!

Don't worry if you can't find materials relating to all of the questions during this first reading!

The purpose of Step No. 2 is to let you get an overview of the structure of the passage and to familiarize you with the relative position, in the passage, of key words, key facts, key ideas.

Step No. 3. Reread the questions at your best rate for comprehension, and check materials in known locations in the passage.

Reread the questions one at a time. This time, as you read, do so at your best rate of reading for comprehension. After you have read a question, if you have some idea of the location in the passage of material that answers that question, find that place and reread the material to see if it is relevant and answers the question. If it does, mark the answer in the appropriate place on your answer sheet.

If you have no idea as to the location in the passage of material that is relevant to that question, go on to the next question! Don't skim through the passage on "fishing expeditions" in search of answer material unless you have a fairly good idea of where that material is placed in the passage! Skimming without strong ideas as to the location of relevant materials is an uneconomical use of time!

Where you have already noted relevant material during Step No. 2, check the question and the applicable portion of the passage quickly and enter your answer on your answer sheet.

The purpose of Step No. 3 is to permit you to go through the more accessible questions quickly so that you may concentrate on the more taxing questions during the next two steps.

Step No. 4.   Reread the passage at your best, most comfortable rate of reading for comprehension.

This step will be your second and final complete reading of the passage. This time read the passage at your most comfortable rate of reading for comprehension, but don't backtrack as you read.

As you read, keep the unanswered questions in mind, following the same process as in Step No. 2: If you come across material that seems related to the question, hold the place in the passage with your finger or mark it with a pencil, and go back to check the question's wording.

If the material seems applicable, (1) mark the question number in the margin of the passage alongside the relevant part, and (2) circle the provisional answer choice under the question.

Resume reading where you had left off and repeat the process outlined above.

Resist the temptation to abandon this approach! Don't backtrack! Don't skim! Keep on reading!

The aim of Step No. 4 is different from that of Step No. 2. You already have some idea of the overall structure of the passage; your second, more thoughtful reading should permit you to pick up more subtle clues. Furthermore, you should now have fewer questions to concentrate on since you probably have already answered one or two in previous steps.

Step No. 5.   Reread those questions that are still unanswered, and proceed as in Step No. 3.

This step calls for a third rereading of the questions that you have not as yet succeeded in answering.

Follow the procedures in Step No. 3: After you have read a question, if you have some idea of the location in the passage of material relevant to the question, go to that location, reread the material to make sure that it is applicable and, if it is, enter the answer in the appropriate place on your answer sheet.

If you can't readily connect the question to material you can locate in the passage, don't start skimming in a random search.

Read on for further clues about answering SAT reading comprehension questions.

ADDITIONAL SUGGESTIONS FOR ANSWERING SAT READING COMPREHENSION QUESTIONS

The five steps above provide a structured basic approach to the reading comprehension question of the SAT, but there are other procedures, techniques, and approaches to the question that you should bear in mind.

Some examples of certain types of questions may better be answered after you have completed the five steps above: *main idea* questions; *best title* questions; *style* questions; *author's purpose* or *application of author's principles* questions; and certain *inference* questions. You will probably be able to answer easy and moderately difficult questions of the type mentioned, in the course of following the five-step basic approach, but you may have to try other approaches for the more resistant questions.

"Main idea" questions

Save consideration of "main idea" questions until you have gone through the five-step basic approach, then ask yourself one or both of the following questions: "In a short phrase or sentence, what is the *topic* of this passage?" or "How would I summarize this passage most succinctly, that is, in the fewest possible words?"

The answer to either of those two questions would provide a good clue to the SAT "main idea" question, which is usually phrased, "What is the main point of this passage?"

A point to remember when trying to determine the main point of the passage is that the answer choices will very often include statements that present minor or secondary points of the passage. Just because a choice may state a point that is contained in the passage does not make that choice correct. Ask yourself, "Does this choice correctly answer the question 'What is the *main point* of this passage?' "

Frequently, in passages that consist of several paragraphs, the answer choices offered for a "main idea" question will give the main point of one or another paragraphs. The main point of the passage has to include and encompass the main points of all the paragraphs combined, not just the main points of one or some of the paragraphs of the passage. To be the correct choice for the "main idea" question or, for that matter, any other question, the answer must be completely correct, not partially correct.

"Best title" questions

The "best title" type of question is another form of "main idea" question which often confuses SAT test takers, many of whom are not aware that the word "title," as used in this question, does not have the meaning that we usually attribute to this word—the name by which a book, play, story, essay, or other piece of writing is known.

As used in the SAT reading comprehension question, the word "title" means the phrase or sentence that best summarizes what the passage as a whole is about.

"Best title" questions are usually worded: "Which of the following would be the most appropriate title for the passage?" or, "Which of the titles below best describes the content of the passage?"

In either case, the question is not really concerned about a title in the sense of a catchy or interest-provoking name for the passage. Rather, the question seeks the answer to the unstated or implied question, "Which of the following phrases or sentences best summarizes what this passage, as a whole, is about?"

As in the "main idea" question, do not accept as an answer a sentence or phrase that tells what *part* of the passage is about. What is only partially true is, in this case, not an acceptable answer.

When deciding what the passage as a whole is about, be sure that you do not select a summary statement that sums up only a part of the passage. Select a statement, phrase, or sentence that sums up the *entire* passage.

Questions calling for information directly stated in the passage

A common type of question is one that asks you to identify or locate information that is directly stated in the passage. Questions that ask "Who?" "What?" "Where?" or "When?"—questions that ask for dates, places, names, and quantities—can usually be answered by locating and identifying information that is directly stated in the passage.

The fact that a question's answer is directly stated in the passage does not necessarily mean that finding that answer will always prove easy. You must be aware that the question may, very often, paraphrase what is in the passage, thus making identification of the information more difficult. For instance, if the question read:

> Which of the following personality traits was most highly regarded
>   by the ancient Greeks?
> (A) courtesy
> (B) cunning
> (C) generosity
> (D) loyalty
> (E) fortitude

You would be looking for the mention of those traits as you read the passage. However, you would be well advised to keep in mind the possibility that those traits might be mentioned through the use of paraphrase or synonym. Thus, unless you were watching for words or phrases that mean the same as "courtesy," "cunning," "generosity," "loyalty," or "fortitude," you might not be able to locate the answer to the question. In the passage, "courtesy" could be written as "politeness" or "civility" or "polite behavior." Similarly, "cunning" could be describe as "guile," "generosity" as "munificence," "loyalty" as "fidelity," or "fortitude" as "stoicism."

Be aware, then, that in looking for a particular key word you should be prepared to recognize the meaning of that word even when it is contained in the form of a paraphrase or a synonym.

As always, be sure to read the question carefully to be certain that your choice of an answer meets the demands of the question. A choice that offers a verbatim (word-for-word) piece of information from the passage is not necessarily the correct choice merely because it contains true statements. To be correct, the information in your selected answer must respond to the question.

Inference questions

Some of the questions in the reading comprehension portion of the SAT cannot be answered by referring to directly stated material in the reading passage but rather can be answered only by inference.

"Inference" is the process of arriving at a conclusion by indirect means: reading between the lines; using logical reasoning; linking circumstantial evidence together to build to a rational conclusion. Inference is the interpretation of indirect statements, hints, suggestions, and the like.

In some instances, indirect evidence is so strong that you can arrive at a conclusion that is as unmistakably correct as if the evidence had been directly stated. In other instances, you may only be able to say that you have arrived at a logical and probable conclusion, one that seems more nearly correct than any other. Remember, however, that instructions for SAT questions usually ask you to choose the best answer available even if that answer is not a perfect one.

Application of the author's principles questions

Some questions ask you to predict how the author of the passage would act, what position he would take, what his attitude or approach would be in a hypothetical (imaginary or conjectural) situation. You should assume that there is enough evidence in the passage to permit you to determine the author's attitudes, views, or beliefs so that you have a basis for concluding what his probable behavior would be in other situations.

If the author rhapsodizes about nature and the great outdoors, you can probably predict that, given a choice, he would prefer a backpacking vacation to one spent at the gaming tables of Las Vegas. If his passage is a tirade against rigid controls on personal freedoms, you can assume that he would favor the American or the British form of government to that run by a totalitarian elite.

To apply the author's principles, then, you must first determine from the evidence in the passage what he advocates in the concrete situation described, and then you can apply that knowledge to the hypothetical, or imaginary, situation. In a sense, the question that seeks to apply the author's principles is related to the inference question, since you must draw conclusions from indirect evidence.

Author's style or mood questions

Some reading comprehension questions ask you to identify the author's mood, attitude, or style. Such questions are best answered after you have completed the other questions, because your response must be based upon an overall understanding of the passage rather than on individual bits of evidence.

While it is true that an author may be very blunt about his attitude in a particular matter, very often the author's attitude or mood is revealed more subtly or indirectly. Read carefully and note value-packed words or sentence constructions.

In order to evaluate or determine an author's style of writing, you must be familiar with some of the words used to describe style—words like "formal," "informal," "florid," "understated," "scholarly," "hyperbolic," and so forth.

"Informal writing" is writing that employs colloquial expressions, idiomatic terms, everyday language, and comparatively uncomplicated sentence structure.

"Scholarly language" is formal writing that uses high-level vocabulary in complex sentence structures, technical terms, and carefully qualified statements.

A "florid" style is one that uses very ornate language, flowery adjectives, and literary-sounding figures of speech.

"Understated writing" is writing in which the author plays down what he is saying so that he sounds unexcited or cool.

"Hyperbole," on the other hand, is the use of great exaggeration, as in the expression, "I've told you a million times . . . " or "He hit the ball a mile."

ANSWERING THE SAMPLE QUESTIONS

Let us return to the sample passage on the Basques on page 35. After you have read the questions, as suggested in Step No. 1 of the suggested approach to the reading question, you start on Step No. 2, the first reading of the passage. If question 1 has stuck in your mind, the word "origin" in the first sentence should trigger a reaction. As soon as you see that word, you should look back at the question. You would probably quickly realize that the author is saying that although there are theories about the origin of the Basques, he doesn't know which of them is correct.

At any rate, you would, at the very least, put a number "1" in the margin next to the first sentence, and circle letter "E" as a tentative answer to the question.

Question 2 is an author's purpose question, and you should be able to answer it after you have completed Step No. 2 or Step No. 4. You probably would note after the first reading that (D) is only a distraction, since the passage deals mainly with Basques—the Berbers and Cromagnons being mentioned only in passing. Similarly, the reference to Atlantis is only marginal. You would know already, after having answered question 1, that the passage is not trying to trace the ancestry of the Basques, since the author has said that your guess is as good as his in deciding which theory is correct. Choice (A) is a deliberately misleading one, because the phrase, "the origin of the species," usually refers to Darwinian evolutionary theory, and the passage is not about evolution. We can conclude that the author considers most of the passage unimportant except the portion beginning, "Whatever the truth. . . . " The answer, therefore, is (C).

In question 3, you are given several dictionary meanings for the word "distill" and are asked which meaning applies in the context of the passage. That the professors "distill" theories out of "skulls and gutturals" implies that they start with bone structures and language sounds, and that from evidence about these, they arrive at their theories. Choice (A) gives a meaning that describes a physical process. Choice (B) gives a similar meaning but suggests that the word can be used figuratively, for it says, " . . . as if by distillation." You can see that the professors don't arrive at their theories by vaporizing bones and then condensing that vapor in a literal sense, but they could do so in a figurative sense. The answer to the question is choice (B).

Part III

Review of Mathematics
for the Scholastic
Aptitude Test

The mathematics section of the SAT deals mainly with problem-solving situations in the areas of arithmetic, algebra, and informal geometry.

The *arithmetic* includes the four basic operations on whole numbers, fractions, and decimals. It also stresses the properties of odd and even integers, prime numbers, factors of numbers, and averages.

The *algebra* includes signed numbers, formulas and linear equations, exponents and roots, and solution of verbal problems by algebraic techniques. Quadratic equations and negative or fractional exponents are generally avoided.

The *geometry* is informal in the sense that it does not stress postulational structure, proofs of theorems or constructions. The geometry includes angle relationships, right triangle relationships, parallel line theorems, and the mensurational aspects of area, volume, and perimeter.

The mathematics problems on the SAT frequently require a certain degree of insight or originality for their solution. There is a conscious attempt to avoid the more stereotyped kind of question requiring merely a routine solution.

About two-thirds of the mathematics test is made up of the conventional multiple-choice questions (five choices). However, one-third of the math section is made up of quantitative comparison questions, each of which has only four choices. These will be explained later in this review section.

The math review section will frequently cut across subject lines. For example, the topic of proportion will deal first with *arithmetic* proportion, then the use of proportion in *algebra* for problem-solving, and finally the application of proportion to triangles in *geometry*.

The math review section is followed by a practice exercise section which amply supplies problems related to all topics reviewed. Answer keys and explanatory answers accompany these problems.

The math review section goes over in detail all topics covered in the mathematics section of the SAT. If you find that you are having difficulty with any particular type of problem in the practice tests, review this type carefully in the math review section and work out the practice exercises related to this topic.

Fractions

· A <u>fraction</u> is an indicated division of two numbers. Thus, the fraction $\frac{9}{3}$ indicates $9 \div 3$. The top number, 9, is called the <u>numerator</u> and the bottom number, 3, is called the <u>denominator</u> of the fraction. The denominator indicates the number of equal parts into which the whole has been broken, and the numerator indicates how many of these parts are taken.

· A <u>simple</u> fraction (or common fraction) is one whose numerator and denominator are <u>whole</u> numbers. For example, $\frac{3}{4}$ is a simple fraction. If the numerator and/or denominator are also fractions, the fraction is called <u>complex</u>. Thus, the fraction $\frac{1/2}{3}$ is a complex fraction.

If the numerator of a fraction is less than the denominator, as in $\frac{3}{7}$, the fraction is called a <u>proper</u> fraction. If the numerator is equal to or greater than the denominator, as in $\frac{5}{5}$ or $\frac{8}{5}$, the fraction is called an <u>improper</u> fraction.

· A <u>mixed</u> number is a whole number plus a proper fraction. The mixed number $4 + \frac{2}{5}$ is usually written $4\frac{2}{5}$. An improper fraction may be written as a mixed number by carrying out the indicated division; thus, $\frac{9}{5} = 1 + \frac{4}{5} = 1\frac{4}{5}$ $\left(1 \text{ and } \frac{4}{5}\right)$.

The following principle is basic in working with fractions:
· The numerator and denominator of a fraction may both be multiplied (or divided) by the same number without changing the value of the fraction.

By means of this rule, we see that $\frac{9}{12}$ is equivalent in value to $\frac{3}{4}$.

$$\frac{9}{12} = \frac{9 \div 3}{12 \div 3} = \frac{3}{4} .$$

Since $\frac{3}{4}$ cannot be reduced further by division, we say the fraction is in lowest terms.

· <u>To reduce a fraction</u> to lowest terms, divide the numerator and denominator by their highest common factor (the largest number that goes into both).

<u>Example 1:</u>
Reduce $\frac{12}{30}$ to lowest terms.

<u>Solution:</u>
Six goes into 12 and 30.

$$\frac{12}{30} = \frac{12 \div 6}{30 \div 6} = \frac{2}{5} .$$

<u>Example 2:</u>
Reduce $\frac{12x}{15x}$ to lowest terms.

<u>Solution:</u>
Divide both terms by $3x$.

$$\frac{12x}{15x} = \frac{12x \div 3x}{15x \div 3x} = \frac{4}{5} .$$

· <u>To multiply fractions,</u>
1. reduce by cancellation (divide any number in the numerators and any number in the denominators by their highest common factor),
2. multiply numerators and denominators to get the numerator and denominator of the product.

Example 1:

Multiply: $\dfrac{4}{5} \times \dfrac{25}{6}$.

Solution:

$$\dfrac{\overset{2}{\cancel{4}}}{\underset{1}{\cancel{5}}} \times \dfrac{\overset{5}{\cancel{25}}}{\underset{3}{\cancel{6}}} = \dfrac{10}{3} = 3\dfrac{1}{3} .$$

Note that we have divided 25 and 5 by 5, and 4 and 6 by 2.

Example 2:

Multiply: $\dfrac{a^2}{6} \cdot \dfrac{9}{a}$.

Solution:

$$\dfrac{\overset{a}{\cancel{a^2}}}{\underset{2}{\cancel{6}}} \cdot \dfrac{\overset{3}{\cancel{9}}}{\underset{1}{\cancel{a}}} = \dfrac{3a}{2} .$$

Note that we have divided 6 and 9 by 3, and a^2 and a by a.

· To divide fractions, invert the divisor and multiply the resulting fractions.

Example:

Divide: $\dfrac{5}{8} \div \dfrac{15}{4}$.

Solution:

$$\dfrac{\overset{1}{\cancel{5}}}{\underset{2}{\cancel{8}}} \times \dfrac{\overset{1}{\cancel{4}}}{\underset{3}{\cancel{15}}} = \dfrac{1}{6} .$$

· To add or subtract like fractions (having the same denominator), add or subtract the numerators and keep the denominator.

Thus, $\dfrac{3}{7} + \dfrac{2}{7} = \dfrac{5}{7}$

$\dfrac{5}{8} - \dfrac{3}{8} = \dfrac{2}{8} = \dfrac{1}{4}$.

· To add unlike fractions (different denominators), we must first change all fractions to equivalent fractions with the same denominator (least common denominator).

Example 1:

$\dfrac{2}{3} + \dfrac{1}{2}$.

<u>Solution:</u>

Both denominators go into 6.

$$\frac{2}{3} = \frac{2 \cdot 2}{3 \cdot 2} = \frac{4}{6}$$

$$\frac{1}{2} = \frac{1 \cdot 3}{2 \cdot 3} = \frac{3}{6}$$

$$\frac{4}{6} + \frac{3}{6} = \frac{7}{6} = 1\frac{1}{6}.$$

<u>Example 2:</u>

$$\frac{m}{2} - \frac{m}{5}.$$

<u>Solution:</u>

$$\frac{m}{2} = \frac{m \cdot 5}{2 \cdot 5} = \frac{5m}{10}$$

$$\frac{m}{5} = \frac{m \cdot 2}{5 \cdot 2} = \frac{2m}{10}$$

$$\frac{5m}{10} - \frac{2m}{10} = \frac{3m}{10}.$$

· <u>To change a mixed number to an improper fraction,</u> treat the problem as the sum of two fractions.

Thus, $\quad 5\frac{2}{3} = \frac{5}{1} + \frac{2}{3}$

$$= \frac{15}{3} + \frac{2}{3} = \frac{17}{3}.$$

A simple rule is the following:

· To change a mixed number to an improper fraction, multiply the whole number by the denominator of the fraction and add its numerator. The result is the numerator of the improper fraction and the denominator remain unchanged.

Thus, $\quad 5\frac{2}{3} = \frac{5(3) + 2}{3} = \frac{15 + 2}{3} = \frac{17}{3}.$

· In performing arithmetic operations on mixed numbers, it is frequently more convenient to change them to improper fractions, and then use the rules for operating with fractions.

<u>Example:</u>

$$3\frac{3}{4} \times \frac{8}{5}.$$

Solution:

$$\frac{\overset{3}{\cancel{12}}}{\cancel{4}} \times \frac{\overset{2}{\cancel{8}}}{\cancel{2}} = \frac{6}{1} = 6.$$

Decimals and Signed Numbers

· A *decimal fraction* is a fraction whose denominator is some power of 10, such as 10, 100, 1000, 10,000, etc.

For example, $\frac{423}{1000}$ is a decimal fraction and is usually written .423. It may be thought of as $\frac{4}{10} + \frac{2}{100} + \frac{3}{1000}$.

As we continue to the right of the decimal point, the denominator is multiplied by 10 more. As a result, adding zeros to the right side of a decimal fraction does not alter its value. Thus, .42300 = .423.

We frequently refer to decimal fractions as simply decimals. A *mixed decimal* is merely a whole number plus a decimal fraction. Thus, 37.285 is a mixed decimal.

· To add or subtract decimals, write the numbers vertically, aligning them so the decimal points are directly beneath each other. Then, add or subtract as for whole numbers, and carry the decimal point directly below into the result.

Example 1:
    Add 5.78, 23.1 and 8.734.

Solution:

    5.78
    23.1
    8.734
    37.614.

Example 2:
    Subtract 9.3 from 21.78.

Solution:

    21.78
    − 9.3
    12.48.

Example 3:
    How much change does a man receive from a $10 bill if he buys a tie for $4.73?

Solution:

    $10.00
    − 4.73
    $ 5.27.

· To convert a decimal to a fraction, simply write out the numerator and denominator in full and reduce to lowest terms.

Example:
Change .15 to a fraction.

Solution:

$$.15 = \frac{15}{100} = \frac{15 \div 5}{100 \div 5} = \frac{3}{20}.$$

· To multiply two decimals,

1. multiply as though the numbers were whole numbers,
2. mark off as many decimal places in the product as there are decimal
   places in the factors together.

Example:
Multiply: 4.5 × 2.1.

Solution:

$$
\begin{array}{r}
4.5 \\
\times \quad 2.1 \\
\hline
45 \\
90 \quad \\
\hline
9.45
\end{array}
$$

When multiplying a decimal by a power of 10, move the decimal point
to the right one place for each zero in the power of 10. Thus,

3.875 × 100 = 387.5.

8.4 × 1000 = 8400.

In the last example, we had to add zeros to move the decimal point the
required number of places.

· To divide a number by a decimal,

1. multiply both divisor and dividend by the power of 10 that will make the
   divisor a whole number,
2. then carry out the division as with whole numbers, placing the decimal
   point in the quotient directly above the decimal point in the dividend.

Example:
Divide .045 by .25.

Solution:
Multiply the divisor by 100, making it 25. Multiply the dividend by 100,
making it 4.5 or 4.50. Thus,

$$
\begin{array}{r}
.18 \\
25 \overline{\smash{)}4.50} \\
\underline{2\,5} \quad \\
2\,00 \\
\underline{2\,00}
\end{array}
$$

When dividing a number by a power of 10, merely move the decimal
point one place to the left for each zero in the power of 10. Thus,

$$18.3 \div 100 = .183$$
$$8.5 \div 1000 = .0085.$$

· To convert a fraction to a decimal, merely divide the numerator by the denominator, adding zeros after the decimal point in the numerator when needed.

Example:
Write $\frac{3}{8}$ as a decimal.

Solution:
Write 3 as 3.000 and divide by 8:

$$
\begin{array}{r}
.375 \\
8\overline{)3.000} \\
\underline{24} \\
60 \\
\underline{56} \\
40
\end{array}
$$

Thus, $\frac{3}{8} = .375$.

· To add two signed decimals, use the basic rules for adding signed numbers:

1. To add numbers with *like* signs, add the absolute values (without signs) and prefix the sum with the common sign.
2. To add two numbers with *unlike* signs, find the difference between the absolute values and prefix the sign of the number with the greater absolute value.

Example 1:
Add -4.2 to -3.5.

Solution:

$$
\begin{array}{r}
-4.2 \\
\underline{-3.5} \\
-7.7.
\end{array}
$$

Example 2:
Add -5.4 and $+2.1$.

Solution:

$$
\begin{array}{r}
-5.4 \\
\underline{+2.1} \\
-3.3.
\end{array}
$$

· To subtract one signed number from another, change the sign of the *subtrahend* and proceed as in the addition of signed numbers.

Example:

$$(-5.4) - (+2.8).$$

Solution:
The subtrahend is $+2.8$.
Change it to -2.8, then add.

$$-5.4$$
$$\underline{-2.8}$$
$$-8.2.$$

· <u>To multiply two signed numbers</u>, multiply their absolute values and then use the following rules of signs:

1. The product of two numbers with like signs is positive.
2. The product of two numbers with unlike signs is negative.

<u>Example 1:</u>

$$(-5) \times (-8) = +40.$$

<u>Example 2:</u>

$$(+6) \times (-9) = -54.$$

· <u>To divide two signed numbers</u>, divide their absolute values and use the same rules of signs above as for multiplication.

<u>Example:</u>

$$(-50) \div (+5) = -10.$$

Percentage

· *Percent* simply means per hundred. Percentage deals with the group of decimal fractions whose denominators are 100, or fractions of two decimal places. The symbol for percent is %. Thus,

$$15\% = \frac{15}{100} = .15$$

$$4\% = \frac{4}{100} = .04.$$

· <u>To change any decimal to a percent</u>, multiply the decimal by 100 and add the % sign. Thus,

$$.45 = 45\%$$

$$.032 = 3.2\%$$

$$3.00 = 300\%.$$

· <u>To change a percent to a decimal</u>, drop the percent sign and move the decimal point two places to the left. Thus,

$$34\% = .34$$

$$4.7\% = .047$$

$$135\% = 1.35.$$

These decimal fractions may be changed to common fractions by writing the denominators as powers of 10 and reducing to lowest terms. Thus,

$$75\% = \frac{75}{100} = \frac{75 \div 25}{100 \div 25} = \frac{3}{4}.$$

· To change a fraction to a percent, change the fraction to a decimal by dividing the numerator by the denominator and then change the decimal to a percent, as shown above.

Example:

Change $\frac{7}{8}$ to a percent.

Solution:

Divide 7.00 by 8.

$$
\begin{array}{r}
.87 \\
8\overline{)7.00} \\
6\ 4 \\
\hline
60 \\
56 \\
\hline
\end{array}
$$

$$\frac{4}{8} = \frac{1}{2}$$

$$.87\frac{1}{2} = 87\frac{1}{2}\%.$$

It is frequently time-saving to remember the equivalent percents for some common fractions. Below is a list of some common ones.

$\frac{1}{2} = 50\%$	$\frac{1}{5} = 20\%$	$\frac{1}{8} = 12\frac{1}{2}\%$
$\frac{1}{3} = 33\frac{1}{3}\%$	$\frac{2}{5} = 40\%$	$\frac{3}{8} = 37\frac{1}{2}\%$
$\frac{2}{3} = 66\frac{2}{3}\%$	$\frac{3}{5} = 60\%$	$\frac{5}{8} = 62\frac{1}{2}\%$
$\frac{1}{4} = 25\%$	$\frac{4}{5} = 80\%$	$\frac{7}{8} = 87\frac{1}{2}\%$
$\frac{3}{4} = 75\%$		$\frac{1}{10} = 10\%$
		$\frac{3}{10} = 30\%,$ etc.

· To find a percent of a number, change the percent to a decimal or a common fraction and multiply it by the given number.

Example 1:

Find 8% of 45.

Solution:

Change 8% to .08 and multiply.

$$\times \begin{array}{r} 45 \\ \underline{.08} \\ 3.60 \end{array} \quad \text{(Ans.)}.$$

Example 2:

A salesman receives a $12\frac{1}{2}\%$ commission on a sale of $2560. How much commission did he receive?

Solution:

He received $12\frac{1}{2}\%$ of $2560. Change $12\frac{1}{2}\%$ to $\frac{1}{8}$ (from table above). Then

$$\frac{1}{8} \times \frac{\$2560}{1} = \$320 \quad \text{(Ans.)}.$$

· <u>To find what percent one number is of another</u>, find what fractional part the first number is of the other, and change the fraction to a percent.

Example:

40 is what percent of 60?

Solution:

Find what part 40 is of 60.

$$\frac{40}{60} = \frac{2}{3} = 66\frac{2}{3}\%.$$

An alternate solution is by proportion.

$$\frac{40}{60} = \frac{x}{100}$$

$$60x = 4000$$

$$x = 66\frac{2}{3}.$$

Thus, 40 is $66\frac{2}{3}\%$ of 60.

· A third type of percentage problem that frequently arises is exemplified by the following example:

Example:

30% of what number is 42?

Solution:

Let x = the number.

$.30x = 42.$

Multiply both sides by 100.

$30x = 4200.$

Divide both sides by 30.

$x = 140.$

30% of 140 is 42 (Ans.).

· To find a percent increase or decrease, determine what percent the increase or decrease is of the *original* amount.

Example:
   Coffee rises from $4.00 per lb. to $5.00 per pound. What is the percent increase?

Solution:
   The increase is $1.00 per lb. Find what percent $1.00 is of $4.00. ¼ = 25% increase (Ans.).

· Discount problems—In solving problems of this type, the basic relationship is

Amount of Discount = Original Price × Rate of Discount

Example 1:
   A man buys an $80 radio at a discount of 20%. How much does he pay?

Solution:
   80 × .20 = $16.00 (amt. of discount)

   $80 − $16 = $64   (amt. he pays).

Example 2:
   A woman pays $45 for a dress after a 25% discount. What was the original price of the dress?

Solution:

   Let x = the original price.

   $\frac{1}{4}x$ = amount of discount.

   $x - \frac{1}{4}x = 45.$

   Multiply both sides by 4.

   $4x - x = 180$

   $3x = 180$

   $x = \$60$ (original price).

Exponents and Roots

· The expression 5^3 means $5 \times 5 \times 5 = 125$. We say that 125 is the third *power* of 5. The *power* of a number is the number of times the number itself is to be taken as a factor.

In $5^3 = 125$, the number 125 is the power and 3 is called the *exponent* of the number 5. The exponent 3 indicates that the number 5, called the *base*, is to be raised to the third power. The first power of a number is the number itself. Thus, $7^1 = 7$.

In general, the expression b^n, where n is a positive integer greater than or equal to 1, represents the product of n factors, each factor equal to b; b is called the *base, n* the *exponent*, and b^n the *n*th power of b.

Thus, $3^4 = 3 \times 3 \times 3 \times 3 = 81$. We say 81 is the 4th power of 3. b^2 is read "*b* square" or "*b* to the second power." b^3 is read "*b* cube" or "*b* to the third power."

· The following are the basic *laws* governing operations with *exponents*:

1. $b^m \cdot b^n = b^{m+n}$.

2. $\dfrac{b^m}{b^n} = b^{m-n}$, $b \neq 0$, (since we cannot divide by 0).

3. $(b^m)^n = b^{mn}$.

4. $(ab)^n = a^n b^n$.

5. $\left(\dfrac{a}{b}\right)^n = \dfrac{a^n}{b^n}$.

Example 1:

$$\frac{7^8}{7^6} = 7^{8-6} = 7^2 = 49.$$

Example 2:

$$(-3)^2 = (-3)(-3) = 9.$$

Example 3:

$$(2^3)^2 = 2^6 = 64.$$

· In *scientific notation*, a number is written as the product of a number between 1 and 10 and an integral power of 10. It provides us with a convenient way of writing very large numbers. Thus, 1 light year = 5.87×10^{12} miles. To write this number in ordinary notation, we would move the decimal point 12 places to the right: 5,870,000,000,000.

· The *square root* of a given number is that number which when squared produces the given number. The square root of 25 is written $\sqrt{25}$, which must equal 5, since $5^2 = 25$.

It is convenient to remember some basic square roots: $\sqrt{1} = 1$, $\sqrt{4} = 2$, $\sqrt{9} = 3$, $\sqrt{16} = 4$, $\sqrt{25} = 5$, $\sqrt{36} = 6$, $\sqrt{49} = 7$, etc.

Remember that the square root of a number really has *two* values, one positive and one negative. Thus, the square root of 25 is -5 as well as $+5$, since $(-5)^2 = (-5)(-5) = 25$. However, when we use the square root symbol with no sign in front of it, we mean the positive value, so that $\sqrt{25} = +5$.

· *To simplify a square root*, we use the following basic relationship:

$$\sqrt{ab} = \sqrt{a}\,\sqrt{b}.$$

Example 1:

Simplify $\sqrt{300}$.

Solution:

Look for perfect square factors of the number under the radical. Thus,

$$\sqrt{300} = \sqrt{100 \cdot 3} = \sqrt{100}\,\sqrt{3} = 10\sqrt{3}.$$

We may add or subtract *like* radicals as shown by the following example:

Example 2:

$$\sqrt{75} + 2\sqrt{3} = ?$$

Solution:

$$\sqrt{75} = \sqrt{25 \cdot 3} = \sqrt{25} \cdot \sqrt{3} = 5\sqrt{3}$$

$$5\sqrt{3} + 2\sqrt{3} = 7\sqrt{3}.$$

We cannot add *unlike* radicals, such as $\sqrt{5}$ and the $\sqrt{3}$. A *cube root* of a given number is that number which when cubed produces the given number. Thus, the cube root of 27, written $\sqrt[3]{27}$, is 3 since $3^3 = 27$.

Operations with Algebraic Expressions

· Algebraic Language

In algebra, we use letters to represent sets of numbers; these letters are called *variables*, while fixed numerical values are called *constants*. In the expression $7x^2y$, we refer to the 7 as a constant and x and y as variables. Since there is no sign of operation between the number and letters, we consider the number and letters to be multiplied. The number and letters are then called the *factors* of the product. Thus, the factors of $7x^2y$ are 7, x, x and y. If we cannot factor these numbers and letters any further, we call these the *prime* factors of the expression.

Each factor of a particular product is called the *coefficient* of the other factors. In the expression $7x^2y$, 7 is the *numerical coefficient* of x^2y and x, x and y are the literal coefficients of 7. In general, when we refer to the coefficient of an algebraic product, we mean the *numerical* coefficient.

An algebraic term which is the product of numbers and letters is called a *monomial*. Examples of monomials are $7x^2y$, $3ab$, $9m$ and k^2.

An algebraic expression of two terms is called a *binomial*; it is the sum or difference of two monomials. Examples of binomials are $3r + 7s$, $a^2 - b^2$ and $7x^2y + 5$.

An algebraic expression of three terms is called a *trinomial*. The expression $5r^2 - 10rs + 4s^2$ is a trinomial. Monomials, binomials, and trinomials are all special cases of the more general set of *polynomials*.

· Adding and Subtracting Polynomials

Algebraic terms can be *combined* (added or subtracted) only if they are *similar*, or *like*, terms; that is, terms that have the same variables and these variables have the same exponents. For example, $9s^2t$ and $7s^2t$ are like terms. They can be added to give $16s^2t$. Likewise $12x - 8x = 4x$, just as 12 nuts − 8 nuts = 4 nuts.

Like terms are added or subtracted by adding or subtracting the *numerical coefficients* and placing the result in front of the common literal factor.

In adding or subtracting polynomials, we add or subtract the like terms only. Thus, to add

$$7m^2 + 2km - 3k^2 \quad \text{to}$$
$$3m^2 - 5km + 2k^2 \quad \text{we obtain}$$
$$10m^2 - 3km - k^2.$$

Lining up the like terms in vertical columns is a good way to avoid error.

· To multiply two monomials:

1. Multiply the numerical coefficients to form the coefficient of the product.
2. Multiply the literal symbols to form the literal part of the product.

Example:
Multiply $(-4x^3y)$ by $(3x^2y^2)$.

Solution:

$$(-4x^3y)(3x^2y^2) = (-4 \cdot 3)(x^3y \cdot x^2y^2)$$
$$= -12x^5y^3.$$

· To multiply a polynomial by a monomial, multiply each term of the polynomial by the monomial.

Example 1:

$$3a(2r - 5s) = 3a(2r) - 3a(5s)$$
$$= 6ar - 15as.$$

Example 2:

$$8x(x^2 - 5x + 2) = 8x(x^2) - 8x(5x) + 8x(2)$$
$$= 8x^3 - 40x^2 + 16x.$$

· To multiply two polynomials:

1. Multiply each term of one polynomial by each term of the other.
2. Add like terms algebraically.

Example 1:
Multiply $(2r - 3)$ by $(r^2 - 5rs)$.

Solution:

$$(2r - 3)(r^2 - 5rs) = 2r(r^2 - 5rs) - 3(r^2 - 5rs)$$

$$= 2r^3 - 10r^2s - 3r^2 + 15rs.$$

Example 2:

Multiply $(2y + 4)$ by $(3y - 5)$.

Solution:

$$(2y + 4)(3y - 5) = 2y(3y - 5) + 4(3y - 5)$$

$$= 6y^2 - 10y + 12y - 20$$

$$= 6y^2 + 2y - 20.$$

· To divide one monomial by another:

> 1. Divide the coefficients to find the coefficient of the quotient.
> 2. Divide the literal factors in the dividend by the literal factors in the divisor.

Example:

Divide $10x^2y^3z^5$ by $-5xy^2z^3$.

Solution:

$$\frac{10x^2y^3z^5}{-5xy^2z^3} = -\frac{10}{5} \cdot \frac{x^2}{x} \cdot \frac{y^3}{y^2} \cdot \frac{z^5}{z^3}$$

$$= -2xyz^2.$$

> To divide a polynomial by a monomial, divide each term of the polynomial by the monomial.

Example:

$$\frac{x^6 - 7x^5 + 4x^4}{x^2} = \frac{x^6}{x^2} - \frac{7x^5}{x^2} + \frac{4x^4}{x^2}$$

$$= x^4 - 7x^3 + 4x^2.$$

· Factoring Polynomials

The factors of a polynomial are two or more expressions which when multiplied together give the polynomial as a product. For example, $5p$ and $p^2 - 3$ are factors of $5p^3 - 15p$, since, $5p(p^2 - 3) = 5p^3 - 15p$.

The first step in factoring a polynomial is the removal of a common monomial factor, if there is one. For example, the expression $6x^2y - 9xy^2$ contains $3xy$ as a common factor in each term. Thus,

$$6x^2y - 9xy^2 = 3xy(2x - 3y).$$

A second type of factoring applies to a binomial which is the difference of two perfect squares, such as $r^2 - s^2$. To factor such an expression, find the square root of each term. The two factors are then the sum and the difference of the two square roots. Thus,

$$r^2 - s^2 = (r + s)(r - s).$$

Example:

$$9x^2 - 49 = (3x)^2 - 7^2$$
$$= (3x + 7)(3x - 7).$$

A third type of factoring applies to the factoring of trinomials into two binomials. We may illustrate this technique by the following examples:

Example 1:
  Factor $x^2 + 7x + 12$.

Solution:
  Make x and x the first term of each binomial factor. Then find two factors of 12 that add up to 7, coefficient of the middle term. These are, of course, 4 and 3. Then,

  $$x^2 + 7x + 12 = (x + 4)(x + 3).$$

Example 2:
  Factor $y^2 + 8y - 48$.

Solution:

  $$y^2 + 8y - 48 = (y + 12)(y - 4).$$

  Here we chose factors of -48 that add up to $+8$. These are, of course $+12$ and -4.

Ratio and Proportion

· A *ratio* is a comparison of two numbers or two measurements in the same unit. Thus, if a girl is 5 feet tall and a boy is 6 feet tall, the ratio of the girl's height to the boy's height would be 5 to 6. This ratio may be written 5 : 6 or the fraction $\frac{5}{6}$.

Example 1:
  In a class of 30 students, there are 20 boys and 10 girls. What is the ratio of (a) boys to girls, (b) boys to students, (c) girls to students?

Solution:

  (a) $\frac{20}{10} = \frac{2}{1} = 2$, or 2 : 1.

  (b) $\frac{20}{30} = \frac{2}{3}$, or 2 : 3.

(c) $\dfrac{10}{30} = \dfrac{1}{3}$, or 1 : 3.

Example 2:

A rod 14 meters long is divided in the ratio 3 : 4. What is the length of the smaller piece?

Solution:

Let $3x$ = length of smaller piece.

       $4x$ = length of larger piece.

Then, $3x + 4x = 14$

          $7x = 14$

           $x = 2$

        $3x = 3(2) = 6$ meters (Ans.).

A <u>proportion</u> is an equality between two ratios.

Thus, $\dfrac{4}{5} = \dfrac{8}{10}$ is a proportion.

The 5 and 8 are called the *means* and the 4 and 10 are called the *extremes* of the proportion.

In general, in the proportion

the means and extremes are as indicated.

> In a *proportion*, the product of the means is equal to the product of the extremes.

We call the operation using this rule *cross-multiplication*.

Example 1:

Solve the proportion:

$\dfrac{8}{x} = \dfrac{6}{21}$.

Solution:

Cross-multiply:

$\dfrac{8}{x} = \dfrac{6}{21}$

$6x = 168.$ Divide both sides by 6.

$x = 28$ (Ans.).

Example 2:

If 2 inches of snow fall in 5 hours, how many inches will fall in 8 hours, if snow continues to fall at the same rate?

<u>Solution:</u>

The words "at the same rate" indicate that the ratio of number of inches to number of hours remains the same. Thus,

let x = number of inches in 8 hours.

$$\frac{2 \text{ in.}}{5 \text{ hr.}} = \frac{x \text{ in.}}{8 \text{ hr.}} \quad \text{or} \quad \frac{2}{5} = \frac{x}{8} .$$

Cross-multiply: $5x = 16$

$$x = 3\frac{1}{5} \text{ in. (Ans.).}$$

· Example 2 above is an illustration of a *direct* proportion. An increase in the number of hours led to an increase in the number of inches.

The following problem is an example of an *inverse* proportion:

<u>Example 1:</u>

Four men do a job in 12 days. How many days does it take 6 men to do the job if all men work at the same rate?

<u>Solution:</u>

Here, an increase in the number of men produces a decrease in the number of days, resulting in an inverse proportion.

Let x = number of days for 6 men to do the job.

Then, $\dfrac{4 \text{ men}}{6 \text{ men}} = \dfrac{x \text{ days}}{12 \text{ days}}$. (Note inversion of second ratio.)

Cross-multiply: $6x = 48$

$$x = 8 \text{ days (Ans.).}$$

<u>Check</u>: Note that the ratio of the number of men $= \dfrac{4}{6} = \dfrac{2}{3}$ is the *inverse*

of the ratio of the number of corresponding days $= \dfrac{12}{8} = \dfrac{3}{2} .$

<u>Example 2:</u>

A large gear of diameter 5 inches drives a smaller gear of diameter 2 inches. When the large gear turns through 20 revolutions, how many revolutions does the smaller one turn through?

<u>Solution:</u>

Note that the smaller gear turns through a larger number of revolutions. Thus, an *inverse* proportion is required.

Let n = the number of revolutions by smaller gear.

Then, $\dfrac{5 \text{ in.}}{2 \text{ in.}} = \dfrac{n \text{ rev.}}{20 \text{ rev.}}$ or $\dfrac{5}{2} = \dfrac{n}{20} .$

Cross-multiply: $2n = 100$

$$n = 50 \text{ rev. (Ans.).}$$

· *Proportions* occur frequently in *geometric* problems. In similar polygons, corresponding sides are proportional.

Example:

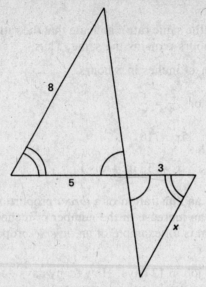

In the figure above, corresponding angles are equal as shown, and the lengths of given sides are shown. Find x.

Solution:

Since the triangles are similar, corresponding sides are in proportion.

$$\frac{8}{x} = \frac{5}{3}$$

Cross-multiply: $5x = 24$

$$x = 4\frac{4}{5} \text{ (Ans.)}.$$

Equations and Formulas

· An *equation* is a statement that two mathematical expressions are equal.

In the equation $2x - 5 = 7$, the 2, 5 and 7 are called *constants* and the letter x is a *variable*. In solving an equation, we try to find a numerical value (or values) of the variable that makes the equality true. In $2x - 5 = 7$, the value $x = 6$ would be a *solution*, or *root*, of the equation. Such an equation is called *first degree*, since the highest exponent of the variable is 1. It is also called a *linear* equation, since its graph is a straight line. An equation which also has a variable term with exponent 2 is called *second degree* or *quadratic*. The equation $x^2 - x + 6 = 0$ is a quadratic equation.

· The basic principle of solving equations is the following:

> Addition, subtraction, multiplication, or division of *both* sides of an equation by the same number results in an *equivalent* equation; that is, one with the same root or roots.

Example 1:
Solve: $3y - 4 = 11$.

Solution:
First, we add 4 to both sides.

$$
\begin{array}{rcl}
3y - 4 &=& 11 \\
+4 & & +4 \\
\hline
3y &=& 15.
\end{array}
$$

Now divide both sides by 3.

$$\frac{3y}{3} = \frac{15}{3}$$

$$y = 5 \text{ (Ans.)}.$$

Note that we are constantly trying to isolate the term with the variable.

Example 2:
Solve for t:

$$8t - 5 = 2t - 23.$$

Solution:
Add 5 to both sides and then subtract $2t$ from both sides.

$$
\begin{array}{rcl}
8t - 5 &=& 2t - 23 \\
-2t + 5 &=& -2t + 5 \\
\hline
6t &=& -18.
\end{array}
$$

Divide both sides by 6.

$$\frac{6t}{6} = \frac{-18}{6}$$

$$t = -3 \ \text{(Ans.)}.$$

· <u>To solve fractional equations</u>, first multiply both sides of the equation by the least common denominator to clear out fractions.

Example:
Solve the equation: $\dfrac{3p}{2} - \dfrac{2}{3} = \dfrac{p}{4} + 1$.

Solution:
Multiply each term by 12, the least common denominator.

$$\frac{3p}{2}(12) - \frac{2}{3}(12) = \frac{p}{4}(12) + 1(12)$$

$$
\begin{array}{rcl}
18p - 8 &=& 3p + 12 \\
-3p + 8 &=& -3p + 8 \\
\hline
15p &=& 20
\end{array}
$$

$$\frac{15p}{15} = \frac{20}{15}$$

$$p = \frac{4}{3} \text{ or } 1\frac{1}{3} \text{ (Ans.)}.$$

· A *literal* equation has literal expressions for its constants instead of numerical ones.

Example:
Solve for x: $ax - b = c$.

Solution:

$$ax - b = c$$
$$\underline{+ b + b}$$
$$ax \quad\quad = b + c$$

Divide by a: $\dfrac{ax}{a} = \dfrac{b + c}{a}$

$$x = \dfrac{b + c}{a} \text{ (Ans.).}$$

· An equation such as $x^2 = 49$ is called an *incomplete quadratic equation* since it lacks a first-degree term. To solve it, take the *square root* of both sides.

$$x^2 = 49$$

$$x = \pm\sqrt{49} = \pm 7.$$

Note that every quadratic equation has *two* roots, which may, in some cases, be equal.

Example:
Solve for r: $r^2 = 12$.

Solution:

$$r^2 = 12$$

$$r = \pm\sqrt{12}$$

$$r = \pm\sqrt{4 \cdot 3} = \pm\sqrt{4}\sqrt{3}$$

$$r = \pm 2\sqrt{3} \text{ (Ans.).}$$

We usually leave the roots in simplest radical form unless otherwise specified.

· A *formula* involves a relationship between several literal quantities. The area, A, of a triangle is given by the formula $A = \dfrac{1}{2}bh$, where b is the base and h the height.

Example:
Solve for b: $A = \dfrac{1}{2}bh$.

Solution:

Multiply both sides by 2.

$2A = bh.$

Divide both sides by h.

$$\frac{2A}{h} = \frac{bh}{h}$$

$$b = \frac{2A}{h} \text{ (Ans.).}$$

Motion Problems

The basic relationship in motion problems is the following:

$$\text{Distance} = \text{Rate} \times \text{Time.}$$

As a formula: $D = RT$.

If R is in miles per hour and T is in hours, then D is in miles. The formula may be written in two other forms:

$$R = \frac{D}{T} \quad \text{and} \quad T = \frac{D}{R},$$

giving the rate and time respectively.

Example 1:

A collegiate track star runs 1 mile in 4 minutes. What is his rate in miles per hour?

Solution:

Change 4 minutes to $\frac{4}{60} = \frac{1}{15}$ hour. Then

$$R = \frac{D}{T}$$

$$R = \frac{1}{\frac{1}{15}} = 1 \times \frac{15}{1} = 15 \text{ mph (Ans.).}$$

Example 2:

A man drives 120 miles in 2 hours and returns home in 3 hours. What is his average speed for the round trip?

Solution:

$$\text{Average rate} = \frac{\text{total distance}}{\text{total time}}$$

$$R = \frac{240 \text{ miles}}{5 \text{ hours}} = \frac{240}{5}$$

$$R = 48 \text{ mph (Ans.).}$$

Example 3:

A pilot flies his plane d miles at the rate of m miles per *minute*. How many hours does the flight take?

Solution:

Change m miles per minute to $60m$ miles per hour. Thus,

$$T = \frac{D}{R} = \frac{d}{60m} \text{ hours (Ans.)}.$$

· In doing more complex motion problems, a *diagram* frequently helps to see the relationship needed to form the equation for solving the problem.

Example 1:

Two cars started from the same town and traveled in opposite directions on a straight road, one at 50 mph and the other at 60 mph. In how many hours were they 495 miles apart?

Solution:

Make a diagram and let h = number of hours required.

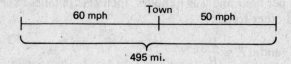

The slower car travels $50h$ miles. The faster car travels $60h$ miles. Then,

$$50h + 60h = 495$$

$$\frac{110h}{110} = \frac{495}{110}$$

$$h = 4\frac{1}{2} \text{ hours (Ans.)}.$$

Example 2:

A man leaves home and travels in his car at 40 mph. Thirty minutes later, his wife follows him at 50 mph. How many hours does she travel before she catches up with him?

Solution:

Let h = number of hours she travels.

Man ——— 40 mph ———→

Wife ——— 50 mph ———→

Let $h + \frac{1}{2}$ = number of hours he travels. Since they both travel the same distance,

$$50h = 40\left(h + \frac{1}{2}\right)$$

$$50h = 40h + 20$$
$$10h = 20$$
$$h = 2 \text{ hours.}$$

Average Problems

· The *average* of a set of quantities is the *sum* of the quantities divided by the *number* of quantities. If a student's grades on four tests were 76, 78, 82, and 87, the average is

$$\frac{76 + 78 + 82 + 87}{4} = \frac{323}{4} = 80\frac{3}{4} .$$

Example 1:

The temperatures one cold morning were recorded as follows: 12, 6, −4, 0, and −5. Find the average temperature for that morning.

Solution:

$$\text{Average} = \frac{12 + 6 + (−4) + 0 + (−5)}{5}$$

$$\text{Average} = \frac{9}{5} = 1\frac{4}{5}° .$$

Example 2:

Nancy gets grades of 77, 82, 86, and 88 in four of her subjects. What grade must she get in her fifth subject to average 85 in her five subjects?

Solution:

Let x = grade in her fifth subject.

$$\frac{77 + 82 + 86 + 88 + x}{5} = 85$$

$$333 + x = 425$$

$$x = 92 \text{ (Ans.).}$$

· In solving many average problems, it is frequently convenient to convert a given average back to a sum, as illustrated in the following problem:

Example:

In a class of 30 students, 20 average 78 on a test and 10 average 83. What is the class average?

Solution:

If 20 average 78, then the sum of these 20 scores is $78 \times 20 = 1560$. If 10 average 83, the sum of these 10 scores is $83 \times 10 = 830$. The sum of all 30 scores is $1560 + 830 = 2390$.

$$\text{Average} = \frac{2390}{30} = 79\frac{2}{3} \text{ (Ans.).}$$

Integer Problems

· The *set of integers* is made up of the set of *positive* and the set of *negative* *whole* numbers including *zero*.

Any integer with a factor of 2 is an *even* integer. An even integer may be designated as $2n$, where n is any integer. Any integer that is not even is an *odd* integer. An odd integer may be designated as $2n + 1$, where n is any integer. The numbers $-4, -2, 0, 2, 4$ are *consecutive even* integers. The numbers 3, 5, 7, 9 are *consecutive odd* integers. The numbers 6, 7, 8, 9, 10 are just called *consecutive* integers, since they follow in natural order.

If x is an integer divisible by another integer y, then y is said to be a *factor* of x, or x is said to be a multiple of y. A number that has no other factors but itself and 1 is called a *prime* number. Thus 7, 11 and 19 are examples of prime numbers. Numbers which are not prime are called *composite*. Thus 15 is a composite number since $15 = 1 \cdot 3 \cdot 5$.

The number 1 is not considered as a prime or composite number; the number 2 is the only even prime number.

· Let us examine some problems involving integers.

Example 1:
  If k is any integer, which of the following must also be an integer:

  (A) $\dfrac{k}{3}$

  (B) $\dfrac{k + 1}{3}$

  (C) $\dfrac{k + 2}{3}$

  (D) $\dfrac{3k - 1}{3}$

  (E) $\dfrac{3k + 3}{3}$

Solution:
  Substitute various integral values of k. $k = 7$ will rule out (A) and (B) as integers. $k = 5$ will rule out (C) and (D) as integers. Then, $\dfrac{3k + 3}{3}$ $= \dfrac{3(k + 1)}{3} = k + 1$. If k is an integer, then $k + 1$ must also be an integer. (E) is the answer.

Example 2:
  A haberdasher sells neckties for $7 each and shirts for $12 each. If he sells $95 worth of ties and shirts, what is the *least* amount of ties he could have sold?

  (A) 3

(B) 4

(C) 5

(D) 6

(E) 7

Solution:

The number of ties and the number of shirts must be positive integers. If he sells 3 ties ($21), it would leave $95 − 21 = $74, which is not divisible by 12. If he sells 4 ties ($28), it would leave $95 − 28 = $67, which is not divisible by 12. If he sells 5 ties ($35), it would leave $95 − 35 = $60, which is divisible by 12 (5 shirts). Similar reasoning would rule out (D) and (E) so that (C) is the answer.

· The *sum* or *difference* of two even integers is an *even* integer. The *sum* or *difference* of two *odd* integers is an even integer.

The *sum* or *difference* of an odd and an even integer is an *odd* integer.

The product of an *even* integer and any integer is an *even* integer. The product of two *odd* integers is an *odd* integer.

Example:

If *n* is any integer, which of the following must be an *even* integer?

(A) $2n + 3$

(B) $2n - 1$

(C) $3n$

(D) $2n + 4$

(E) $6n - 3$

Solution:

$2n$ is even and $2n + 3$ is odd; $2n - 1$ is odd; $3n$ could be even or odd; since $2n$ is even, $2n + 4$ is even; $6n$ is even and $6n - 3$ is odd. Answer is (D).

Angle Relationships

· Dealing with geometric problems frequently requires a knowledge of certain angle relationships.

If two sides of a triangle are equal, the angles opposite these sides are equal. (Base angles of an isosceles triangle are equal.)

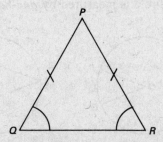

If $PQ = PR$, then angle Q = angle R

If two *parallel lines* are cut by a transversal, the *corresponding* angles and the *alternate interior* angles are equal.

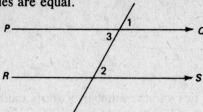

If *PQ* is parallel to *RS*, then $\angle 1 = \angle 2$ (corresponding angles) and $\angle 2 = \angle 3$ (alternate interior angles.)

The sum of the angles of a triangle is equal to one straight angle, or 180°.

Example 1:

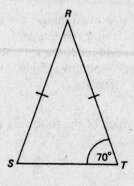

If *RS* = *RT* and angle *T* = 70°, find $\angle R$

Solution:

$\angle S = \angle T = 70°$

$\angle R = 180° - 70° - 70° = 40°$ (Ans.).

Each angle of an *equilateral* triangle is equal to 60°. The *acute* angles of a *right* triangle are complementary.

Example 2:

The acute angles of a right triangle are in the ratio 2:3. Find the smaller angle.

Solution:

Let the acute angles be $2x$ and $3x$. Then

$2x + 3x = 90°$

$5x = 90°$

$x = 18°, 2x = 36°$ (Ans.).

· A *central angle* of a circle is measured by its *intercepted* arc.

An *inscribed* angle in a circle is measured by *one-half* its *intercepted* arc.

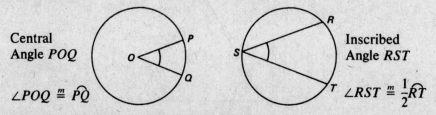

Central Angle *POQ*

$\angle POQ \overset{m}{=} \overset{\frown}{PQ}$

Inscribed Angle *RST*

$\angle RST \overset{m}{=} \frac{1}{2}\overset{\frown}{RT}$

An important special case of the inscribed angle theorem is the following:

An angle *inscribed* in a semicircle is a *right* angle.

<u>Example:</u>
In circle O, $\overset{\frown}{FG}$ = 130°. Find the value of x.

<u>Solution:</u>
Since GFH is a semicircle, $\overset{\frown}{FH}$ = 180° − 130° = 50°, then $x = \frac{1}{2}\overset{\frown}{FH}$

$= \frac{1}{2}(50)$ = 25 (Ans.).

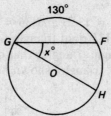

Right Triangle Relationships

· The basic relationship of the sides of a right triangle is the *Pythagorean Theorem*: The square of the hypotenuse of a right triangle is equal to the sum of the squares of the legs.

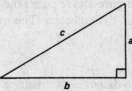

In the figure,

$$c^2 = a^2 + b^2.$$

Two *special* cases that occur frequently, where all three sides are integers, are shown below:

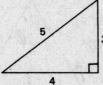 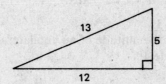

In general, if the legs of a right triangle are $3k$ and $4k$, the hypotenuse is $5k$. ($k > 0$). Or, if the legs are $5k$ and $12k$, the hypotenuse is $13k$.

Example 1:
A 39-foot ladder leaning against a building reaches a point 36 feet high on the building. How many feet is the foot of the ladder from the foot of the building?

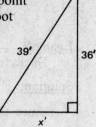

Solution:
Since $39 = 13(3)$ and $36 = 12(3)$, then $x = 5(3) = 15$. The triangle is a $5k$-$12k$-$13k$ right triangle with $k = 3$. Thus, $x = 15$ ft. (Ans.).

· Two *special* right triangles that occur frequently are the 30°-60°-90° triangle and the 45°-45°-90° triangle, shown below.

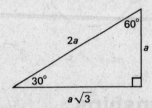

The diagrams show the relationships of the sides in these two triangles. In the figure on the left, the leg opposite the 30° angle (a) is one-half the hypotenuse ($2a$). It follows from the Pythagorean Theorem that the leg opposite the 60° angle is $a\sqrt{3}$.

In the right, isosceles triangle (figure above right) the legs are both represented by a. It then follows from the Pythagorean Theorem that the hypotenuse is $a\sqrt{2}$.

Example 2:
What is the length of the diagonal of a square of side 7?

Solution:
The diagonal divides the square into two right, isosceles triangles. Thus, $d = 7\sqrt{2}$ (Ans.).

Example 3:
Find the altitude of an equilateral triangle of side 10.

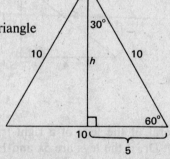

The altitude divides the figure into two 30°-60°-90° triangles.

Thus, $h = 5\sqrt{3}$ (Ans.).

Area Problems

· The *unit of area* is a square whose side is a unit of length; examples are the square inch, square yard, square meter, etc.

The *area of a surface* is the number of units of area it contains. The basic formulas for the areas of plane figures are shown below:

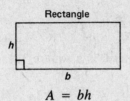

$$A = bh$$

Rectangle

$$A = s^2$$

Square

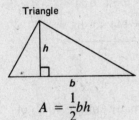

$$A = \frac{1}{2}bh$$

Triangle

$$A = \pi r^2$$

Circle

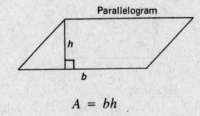

$$A = bh$$

Parallelogram

Example 1:
   Find the ratio of the area of a square of side 4 to the area of its inscribed circle.

Solution:
   From the figure, we see that the radius of the circle is 2.

   Area of square $= 4^2 = 16$.

   Area of circle $= \pi \cdot 2^2 = 4\pi$.

   Ratio $= \dfrac{16}{4\pi} = \dfrac{4}{\pi}$ (Ans.).

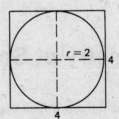

Example 2:

The area of a right, isosceles triangle is 50. Find its hypotenuse.

<u>Solution:</u>

$$\text{Area of triangle} = \frac{1}{2} \text{ base} \times \text{height}.$$

$$50 = \frac{1}{2}x \cdot x$$

$$50 = \frac{1}{2}x^2$$

$$x^2 = 100$$

$$x = 10.$$

$$\text{Hypotenuse} = 10\sqrt{2} \text{ (Ans.).}$$

· How many square feet in 1 sq. yd? Since 1 sq. yd. is a square 3 ft. on each side, its area is given by $A = 3^2 = 9$ sq. ft.

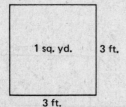

| Thus, 1 sq. yd. = 9 sq. ft. |
| and 1 sq. ft. = 144 sq. in. |

<u>Example:</u>
A living room is 20 ft. long and 14 ft. wide. How many *square yards* of carpeting are needed to cover the floor?

<u>Solution:</u>

$$\text{Area} = 20 \times 14 = 280 \text{ sq. ft.}$$

$$\frac{280}{9} = 31\frac{1}{9} \text{ sq. yd. (Ans.).}$$

Geometry of Solids

· The solid figure which appears most frequently about us is the *rectangular solid*; it has the shape of an ordinary box such as a brick.

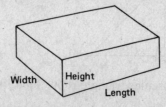

The rectangles which make up the top and bottom, front and back, and sides of the solid are called its *faces*. Note there are six faces.

The lines in which the rectangular faces meet are the *edges* of the solid. There are twelve such edges. The lengths of three of these edges meeting at a common vertex are the *dimensions* of the solid, referred to as the length, width, and height.

When the edges are all equal, the faces become congruent squares, and the rectangular solid is then a *cube*.

Cube

A cube 1 inch on an edge is a *cubic inch*. If the edge is 1 centimeter, the cube is a *cubic centimeter* (cc.), etc.

· The *volume* of a solid is the number of cubic units it contains. It is a measure of the amount of space within the solid figure.

The volume of a rectangular solid is the product of the length, width and height, if these dimensions are all in the same linear unit.

$$V = LWH$$

If the dimensions are in inches, the volume is in cubic inches; if they are in centimeters, the volume is in cubic centimeters (cc.), etc.

Example:
    How many cubic feet in the volume of a box 3 ft. long, 2 ft. wide and 18 in. high?

Solution:

Change 18 in. to $\frac{18}{12} = 1\frac{1}{2}$ ft.

$$V = LWH.$$

$$V = 3 \times 2 \times 1\frac{1}{2} = 3 \times 3 = 9 \text{ cu. ft. (Ans.).}$$

If a cube has edge e, its volume is

$V = e \times e \times e = e^3$.

Note that:

1 cu. yd.	=	3^3 = 27 cu. ft.
1 cu. ft.	=	12^3 = 1728 cu. in.

· The *surface area* of a rectangular solid is simply the sum of the areas of the six rectangular faces. The surface area, S, is thus measured in square units.

In the case of the cube of edge e, each face is a square of area e^2, so that

$$S = 6e^2$$

<u>Example:</u>
    Find the volume of a cube if its total surface area is 96 square centimeters.
<u>Solution:</u>

$$S = 6e^2$$

$$96 = 6e^2. \text{ Divide by 6.}$$

$$e^2 = 16$$

$$e = 4 \text{ cm.}$$

Then $V = e^3$

$$V = 4^3 = 64 \text{ cc. (Ans.).}$$

Coordinate Geometry

Coordinate geometry permits the use of algebra for the solution of many geometric problems. It makes use of a pair of perpendicular axes in a plane called the *x-axis* which is horizontal, and the *y-axis*, which is vertical. These two axes intersect at a point called the *origin*. This is shown below.

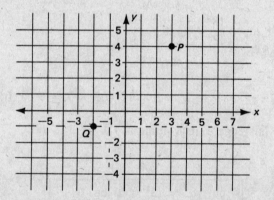

The *x*-axis is marked off in units; the origin *O* has the value zero; positive numbers are marked off to the right and negative values to the left. The *y*-axis is marked off in similar manner, positive values above the origin and negative values below it.

Every point in the plane is then represented by an *ordered number* pair. The first number, called the *x*-coordinate or *abscissa*, indicates how far to the right or left of the *y*-axis the point is located. The second number, called the *y*-coordinate or *ordinate*, indicates how far above or below the *x*-axis the point is located.

Thus, the point P above is designated by the coordinates $(3,4)$ and the point Q is designated by the coordinates $(-2,-1)$.

· The *distance formula* permits us to find the distance between any two points in the coordinate plane. Thus, if the coordinates of P are (x_1, y_1) and those of Q are (x_2, y_2), then,

$$PQ = \sqrt{(x_1 - x_2)^2 + (y_1 - y_2)^2}.$$

To find the coordinates of the midpoint of line segment PQ above, we use the midpoint formula:

$$\left(\frac{x_1 + x_2}{2}, \frac{y_1 + y_2}{2} \right).$$

Example:
    Find the distance PQ for the points P $(3,4)$ and Q $(-2,-1)$. Also find the coordinates of M, the midpoint of PQ.

Solution:

$$PQ = \sqrt{(x_1 - x_2)^2 + (y_1 - y_2)^2}$$

$$= \sqrt{[3 - (-2)]^2 + [4 - (-1)]^2}$$

$$= \sqrt{5^2 + 5^2}$$

$$= \sqrt{50} = 5\sqrt{2} \text{ (Ans.)}.$$

Coordinates of M are given by $\left(\dfrac{x_1 + x_2}{2}, \dfrac{y_1 + y_2}{2} \right)$

$$= \left(\frac{3 + (-2)}{2}, \frac{4 + (-1)}{2} \right)$$

$$= \left(\frac{1}{2}, \frac{3}{2} \right). \text{ (Ans.)}$$

· To find areas of figures in the coordinate plane, use the basic formulas for areas. Where a triangle has a horizontal or vertical base, this is a simple matter.

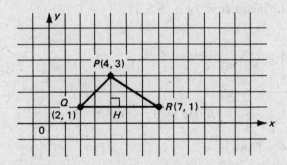

Find the area of the triangle in the figure with coordinates for its vertices as shown.

QR is parallel to the x-axis since the ordinates of Q and R are equal. Thus, $QR = 7 - 2 = 5$. The altitude PH is a vertical line and its length is $3 - 1 = 2$, so that the area of the triangle $= \frac{1}{2}bh = \frac{1}{2}(5)(2) = 5$ (Ans.).

If the triangle does not have a side parallel to either axis, it is necessary to draw lines parallel to the axes through its vertices so as to box it into a rectangle. Its area may then be found by adding or subtracting the areas of right triangles from the area of the rectangle.

Inequalities

· An *inequality* is simply a statement that one expression is not equal to ($\neq$) another expression. The inequality $5 > 2$($>$ is the symbol for "is greater than") merely states that 5 is greater than 2; it may also be written $2 < 5$ (2 is less than 5); ($<$ is the symbol for "is less than"). The expression $3x \geq 6$ states that $3x$ is greater than *or* equal to 6. The expression $2y \leq 5$ states that $2y$ is less than *or* equal to 5. These statements are all inequalities.

The inequality $3x > 6$ is satisfied for all values of x greater than 2. Thus, we say that all values of x greater than 2 give us the *solution set* for $3x > 6$.

To find the solution set for various inequalities, the following principles are helpful:

1. We may add or subtract the same quantity from both sides of an inequality without altering its solution set.
2. We may multiply or divide both sides of an inequality by the same *positive* quantity without altering its solution set.
3. We may multiply or divide both sides of an inequality by a *negative* number providing we reverse the sense of the inequality ($>$ becomes $<$ and $<$ becomes $>$).

Example 1:
   Solve the inequality: $3y + 5 > 17$.

Solution:

$$3y + 5 > 17. \quad \text{Subtract 5.}$$
$$\underline{-5 \qquad -5}$$
$$\frac{3y}{3} > \frac{12}{3}. \quad \text{Divide by 3.}$$
$$y > 4 \quad \text{(Ans.)}.$$

Example 2:
   Solve the inequality: $3t < 5t - 16$.

Solution:

$$3t < 5t - 16.$$

$$\underline{-5t \qquad -5t} \qquad \text{Subtract } 5t.$$

$$\frac{-2t}{-2} < \frac{-16}{-2}. \qquad \text{Divide by } -2.$$

↑

$t > 8$ (Reverse inequality sign.)

$t > 8$ (Ans.).

· Listed below are a number of *geometric* inequalities that are important:

1. The sum of any two sides of a triangle is greater than the third side.
2. If two sides of a triangle are unequal, the angles opposite these sides are unequal and the greater angle lies opposite the greater side; and conversely.

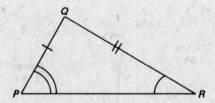

If $QR > PQ$, then angle $P >$ angle R.

3. The *exterior angle* of a triangle is greater than either remote interior angle.

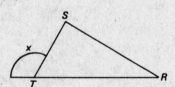

Thus, angle $x >$ angle R, and angle $x >$ angle S.

Example:

The two equal sides of an isosceles triangle are 5. What is the possible range of values of the third side?

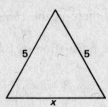

Solution:

Let $x =$ the length of third side. Then, $5 + 5 > x$, so that $x < 10$. Since x must be positive, $0 < x < 10$ (Ans.).

Interpretation of Data

· Organized data are presented in several different forms; table charts are sometimes used but graphs are frequently favored because of their easier readability. These may take the form of circle graphs, line graphs, bar graphs, pictographs, and others. Some of these are illustrated below with suggestions for interpreting the data presented.

· *Circle graphs* are commonly used to show some type of distribution.

Distribution of World Population, 1975

4.0 Billion = 100%

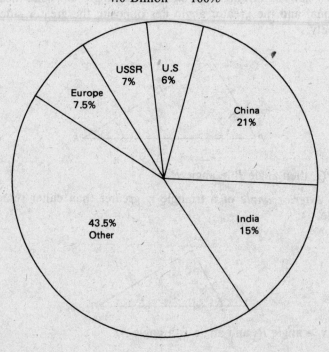

Questions:

1. How many more millions of people were there in China than in India in 1975?
2. How many degrees are there in the central angle of the sector for the U.S.?
3. What is the ratio of the population of Europe to the population of the U.S.?

Solutions

1. China has 21 − 15 = 6% more than India. 4,000 million × .06 = 240 million (Ans.).
2. Since the U.S. has 6% of the world population, its central angle = 6% of 360°. Thus 360 × .06 = 21.6 (about 22°) (Ans.).

3. The ratio $= \dfrac{7.5}{6.0} = \dfrac{75}{60} = \dfrac{5}{4}$ (Ans.).

Be sure to read carefully the title of the graph and the number represented by 100%.

· *Line graphs* are frequently used to represent change in a particular variable or variables.

Example:

Long-term Trends in World Population

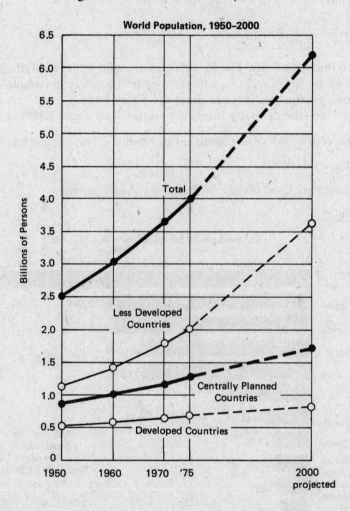

World Population, 1950–2000

Questions:

1. What was the world population, in billions, in 1975?
2. What was the percent increase in world population from 1950–1975?
3. In 1975, the less developed countries accounted for what percent of the world population?
4. What is the projected world population, in billions, for 1980?
5. In 1960, the centrally planned countries (China, U.S.S.R.) accounted for about what fractional part of world population?

Solutions:

1. The graph for total population indicates the population in 1975 to be 4.0 billion (Ans.).

2. In 1950, world population was 2.5 billion. By 1975, it increased 1.5 billion. Thus,

$$\frac{1.5}{2.5} = \frac{15}{25} = \frac{3}{5} = 60\% \text{ increase (Ans.).}$$

3. In 1975, the less developed countries had a population of 2.0 billion. Thus,

$$\frac{2.0}{4.0} = \frac{1}{2} = 50\% \text{ (Ans.).}$$

4. To find the vertical line for 1980, move as far to the right of 1975 as 1970 is to the left of it. Follow this line up to the projection graph (dotted) for total population. It reads about 4.4 billion (Ans.).

5. In 1960, the centrally planned countries had about 1 billion population out of a total world population of 3 billion. Thus, they had about $\frac{1}{3}$ of the total (Ans.).

· *Bar graphs* are used mainly for purposes of comparison.

Example:

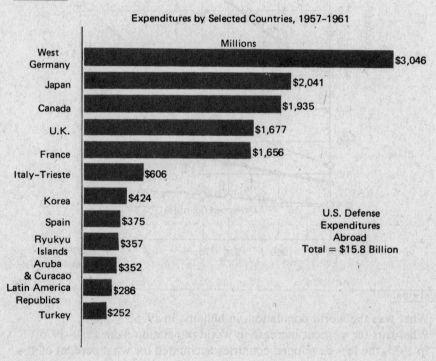

Expenditures by Selected Countries, 1957–1961

Questions:

1. The combined expenditures in West Germany and Japan were about what percent of the total expenditures?

<u>82</u> *How to Prepare for the Scholastic Aptitude Test (SAT)*

2. What was the approximate ratio of expenditures in West Germany to those in Italy?
3. The combined expenditures made in West Germany, Japan, Canada, U.K., and France were about what fractional part of total expenditures abroad?

Solutions:

1. The combined expenditures in Germany and Japan were about 5.1 billion dollars. Thus,

$$\frac{5.1}{15.8} = \frac{51}{158} = .32 \approx 32\% \text{ (Ans.).}$$

2. The approximate ratio of expenditures in Germany to those in Italy was

$$\frac{3000}{600} = \frac{5}{1} = 5 \text{ (Ans.).}$$

3. The combined expenditures made in the first five countries above add up to about 10.4 billion dollars. Thus,

$$\frac{10.4}{15.8} = \frac{104}{158} \approx \frac{2}{3} \text{ (Ans.).}$$

These numerical results are generally approximations. In making a selection from five multiple-choice answers, choose the one that is closest to the calculated answer. However, avoid lengthy calculations by making reasonably accurate approximations.

Quantitative Comparison Problems

· The quantitative comparison problem is a type of question that has been introduced in the SAT in recent years. These questions contain only four choices so that the (E) answer space should never be marked for these questions. The instructions and several illustrations are given below.

The following questions each consist of two quantities, one in Column A and one in Column B. Compare the two quantities and on the answer sheet blacken oval

A if the quantity in Column A is greater;
B if the quantity in Column B is greater;
C if the two quantities are equal;
D if the relationship cannot be determined from the information given.

All letters such as x, y and n represent real numbers. A symbol appearing in both columns represents the same quantity in Column A as it does in Column B.

In some questions, information concerning one or both of the quantities to be compared is centered above the two columns.

	Column A		Column B
Example 1:	$\dfrac{11}{25}$		$\dfrac{7}{13}$
Example 2:	$125 \times 18 \times 5$		$125 \times 30 \times 3$
Example 3:	p	$\dfrac{p}{q} = \dfrac{3}{5}$	q

Examples 4–6 refer to triangle *PQR*.

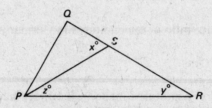

	Column A	Column B
Example 4:	PQ	PS
Example 5:	x	y
Example 6:	x	$y + z$

Solutions:

1. The answer is (B); $\dfrac{7}{13} > \dfrac{1}{2}$, since $\dfrac{6\frac{1}{2}}{13} = \dfrac{1}{2}$ and $\dfrac{11}{25} < \dfrac{1}{2}$, since $\dfrac{12\frac{1}{2}}{25} = \dfrac{1}{2}$

2. The answer is (C). Ignore the 125 in both columns, since it is common to both. Then compare 18×5 with 30×3. Since they are both equal to 90, the answer is (C).

3. The answer is (D). For $q > 0$, let $q = 5$. Then $p = 3$, so $p < q$ in that case.

   For $q < 0$, let $q = -5$. Then $p = -3$, so $p > q$. By definition, $q \neq 0$ since $\dfrac{p}{q} = \dfrac{3}{5}$. Thus, the answer is (D).

4. The answer is (D), since there is no information comparing PQ and PS. Do not assume any comparison from the diagram.

5. The answer is (A). In triangle *PRS*, angle x is an exterior angle and angle y is a remote interior angle, so that angle x is greater than angle y.

6. The answer is (C), since the exterior angle (x) is the sum of the two remote interior angles, y and z, in triangle *PRS*.

Some Suggestions

1. Do not do any more calculating than is necessary to make the comparison, as we saw in examples 1 and 2 above. In problems such as these two, where there are no *variables*, we may eliminate (D) as a possible answer choice.

2. Remember that negative numbers and zero are possible values of variables as well as positive numbers. This was illustrated in example 3 above. Remember also that the more negative a number becomes, the smaller it becomes.

3. Do not draw conclusions from the diagrams, as they are usually not drawn to scale. Sometimes, drawing a more accurate figure may give you a clue to the relationship you are seeking.

4. Remember that these questions do not take as much time as the standard type of question. You are expected to complete more of these in a given length of time.

Direct and Inverse Variation

Two algebraic functions are applied frequently in science problems; these are generally referred to as *variation* problems.

The variable y is said to vary *directly* as the variable x (or is directly proportional to x) if $y = kx$

in which k represents a constant value; k is usually called the constant of variation or *proportionality constant*. The graph of this relationship is a straight line passing through the origin; k is equal to the *slope* of the line where the slope refers to the ratio of the change in y to the change in x.

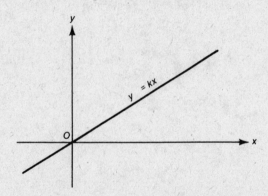

If the volume of an ideal gas is kept constant, the pressure varies *directly* with the temperature; $P = kT$. If one pair of values is given for T and P, k can then be determined. In many scientific formulas of this type, the units are frequently defined so as to make $k = 1$.

The variable y is said to vary *inversely* as x (or is inversely proportional to x) if

$$y = \frac{k}{x},$$

where k is a constant. For example, for several autos traveling the same distance, the time t in hours varies inversely as the rate r in miles per hour. In this case, the constant of variation is the distance in miles, since $t = d/r$.

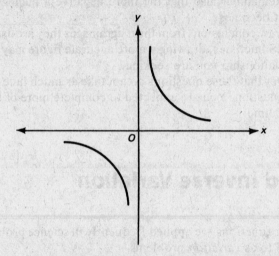

The variation $y = k/x$ may also be written $xy = k$. The graph of this relation is an equilateral hyperbola as shown in the figure. The specific hyperbola will depend on the value of k.

Direct and inverse variation may take several forms. If z varies directly as x and y, then $z = kxy$, where k is a constant. This is sometimes called *joint variation*.

If z varies directly as x and inversely as y, then $z = kx/y$ where k is a constant.

This section presents practice exercises in each of the mathematical topics reviewed in the preceding section. If you find that you are weak in a particular mathematical area, review the topic in the math review section and then work out the related practice exercises in this section.

The problems on any particular topic are followed by explanatory answers (starting on page 119). Check your results with the explanatory answer key. You may further wish to go back to the math review section and read the pages on this topic more thoroughly.

The topics in the practice exercise section are in the same sequence as those in the math review section. These topics are essentially the ones dealt with in the mathematical portion of the SAT.

Fractions

1. The fraction $\frac{24}{32}$ expressed in lowest terms is

   (A) $\frac{12}{16}$

   (B) $\frac{6}{8}$

   (C) $\frac{3}{4}$

   (D) $\frac{6}{16}$

   (E) $\frac{3}{8}$

2. Change $\frac{19}{5}$ to a mixed number.

   (A) $5\frac{1}{5}$

   (B) $3\frac{4}{5}$

   (C) $4\frac{4}{5}$

   (D) $15\frac{4}{5}$

   (E) $\frac{5}{19}$

3. 40 is what part of 64?

   (A) $\frac{3}{8}$

   (B) $\frac{5}{12}$

   (C) $\frac{7}{8}$

   (D) $\frac{5}{12}$

   (E) $\frac{5}{8}$

4. Change $9\frac{2}{3}$ to an improper fraction.

   (A) $\frac{14}{3}$

   (B) $\frac{21}{3}$

   (C) $\frac{21}{2}$

   (D) $\frac{29}{3}$

   (E) $\frac{54}{3}$

5. $\frac{2}{3} + \frac{3}{4} =$

(A) $1\frac{5}{12}$

(B) $\frac{5}{7}$

(C) $\frac{12}{17}$

(D) $\frac{5}{12}$

(E) $\frac{7}{12}$

6. $14\frac{1}{2} - 9\frac{2}{3} =$

(A) $5\frac{5}{6}$

(B) $5\frac{1}{3}$

(C) $4\frac{1}{3}$

(D) $3\frac{2}{3}$

(E) $4\frac{5}{6}$

7. 9 inches is what part of a foot?

(A) $\frac{2}{3}$

(B) $\frac{3}{4}$

(C) $\frac{7}{12}$

(D) $\frac{5}{6}$

(E) $\frac{4}{5}$

8. Divide 27 by $2\frac{1}{4}$.

(A) $60\frac{3}{4}$

(B) $13\frac{1}{2}$

(C) 12

(D) $12\frac{3}{4}$

(E) $13\frac{3}{4}$

9. A man owned $\frac{3}{8}$ of a business and sold $\frac{2}{3}$ of his share. What part of the entire business did he sell?

(A) $\frac{5}{11}$

(B) $\frac{5}{24}$

(C) $\frac{6}{11}$

(D) $\frac{1}{4}$

(E) $\frac{9}{16}$

10. $10\frac{2}{3}$ ounces is what fractional part of a pound?

(A) $\frac{2}{3}$

(B) $\frac{3}{4}$

(C) $\frac{5}{6}$

(D) $\frac{4}{7}$

(E) $\frac{5}{8}$

11. 81 is $\frac{3}{4}$ of what number?

(A) $60\frac{3}{4}$

(B) 112
(C) 102
(D) 108

(E) $90\frac{2}{3}$

12. A strip of metal $7\frac{1}{8}$ inches long is to be divided into 6 equal parts. How many inches in the length of each part?

(A) $1\frac{7}{48}$

(B) $1\frac{1}{6}$

(C) $\frac{11}{16}$

(D) $1\frac{3}{8}$

(E) $1\frac{3}{16}$

13. An oil tank is $\frac{5}{8}$ full. When 6 gallons of oil are removed, the tank is $\frac{1}{4}$ full. What is the total capacity of the tank in gallons?
(A) 14
(B) 16
(C) 18
(D) 20
(E) 24

14. $5\frac{2}{5} \times 6\frac{2}{3} =$
(A) 24
(B) 30
(C) 36
(D) 39
(E) 42

15. $\frac{5x}{8} - \frac{x}{2} =$

(A) $\frac{4x}{6}$

(B) $\frac{2x}{3}$

(C) $\frac{3x}{8}$

(D) $\frac{x}{8}$

(E) $\frac{x}{2}$

16. Reduce to lowest terms: $\frac{12k}{18k}$

(A) $\frac{2}{3}$

(B) $\frac{2k}{3}$

(C) $\frac{4}{6}$

(D) $\frac{6k}{9}$

(E) $\frac{3k}{4}$

17. $\frac{3}{4}$ is what fractional part of $1\frac{1}{8}$?

(A) $\frac{27}{32}$

(B) $\frac{5}{8}$

(C) $\frac{6}{11}$

(D) $\frac{7}{12}$

(E) $\frac{2}{3}$

18. A man completes $\frac{5}{8}$ of a job in 10 days. At this rate, how many more days will it take him to finish the job?
(A) 5
(B) 6
(C) 7

(D) $7\frac{1}{2}$

(E) 8

19. A boy spent $2.70, which was $\frac{5}{9}$ of what he had originally. How much did he have originally?
(A) $4.86
(B) $1.50
(C) $2.45
(D) $3.85
(E) $4.84

(A) $\frac{3y}{4}$

(B) $\frac{9y}{8}$

(C) $\frac{9y}{10}$

(D) $\frac{7y}{8}$

(E) $\frac{5y}{8}$

20. $\frac{7y}{4} - \frac{3y}{2} + \frac{5y}{8} =$

Decimals and Signed Numbers

1. A man's temperature rose one day from 98.6° to 102.4°. How many degrees did it rise?
(A) 2.2
(B) 2.4
(C) 3.4
(D) 3.8
(E) 4.2

2. $.0057 \times 1000 =$
(A) 57
(B) 5.7
(C) .57
(D) .057
(E) 570

3. Write the decimal .625 as a common fraction in *lowest* terms.

(A) $\frac{12}{100}$

(B) $\frac{625}{1000}$

(C) $\frac{62}{100}$

(D) $\frac{125}{200}$

(E) $\frac{5}{8}$

4. Write the fraction $\frac{7}{20}$ as a decimal.

(A) .35
(B) .7
(C) .27
(D) .53
(E) .72

5. Which of the following has the *largest* value?
(A) .3
(B) .33
(C) .303
(D) .033
(E) .333

6. Bill buys 8 rolls at 12¢ each, 4 lb. of beef at $1.12 per lb. and 3 qt. of milk at 47¢ per quart. How much change does he get from a 20 dollar bill?
(A) $6.85
(B) $8.42
(C) $13.15
(D) $14.12
(E) $14.87

7. $\frac{1}{3}$ is what *decimal* part of $\frac{5}{6}$?
(A) .28
(B) .32
(C) .36
(D) .40
(E) .56

8. Of the following, which is the closest approximation to the product

$$.51 \times .75 \times .375 \times .667$$

(A) $\frac{3}{32}$

(B) $\frac{3}{16}$

(C) $\frac{3}{4}$

(D) $\frac{7}{16}$

(E) $\frac{5}{16}$

9. Dividing by .04 is the same as multiplying by

(A) $\frac{1}{25}$

(B) $\frac{1}{4}$

(C) 4
(D) 25
(E) 400

10. $1.25 \times .60 =$
(A) .075

(B) $\frac{3}{4}$

(C) $\frac{4}{5}$

(D) 75

(E) $7\frac{1}{2}$

11. If a strip of metal is 0.28 feet long, its length in *inches* is
(A) less than 2

(B) between 2 and $2\frac{1}{2}$

(C) between $2\frac{1}{2}$ and 3

(D) between 3 and 4
(E) more than 4

12. If $\frac{13}{10}y = .039$, then $y =$
(A) .03
(B) .3
(C) 1.2
(D) 1.6
(E) 3

13. $\dfrac{7}{.7 \times .7} =$

(A) $\frac{7}{100}$

(B) $\frac{7}{10}$

(C) $\frac{100}{7}$

(D) 7
(E) 70

14. Solve for p: $.3p - 1.2 = 4.8$
(A) 2
(B) 20
(C) 200
(D) .2
(E) .02

15. $(-18.4) + (3.7) =$
(A) -14.7
(B) $+14.7$
(C) -1.47
(D) $+1.47$
(E) -22.1

16. If the temperature was $-27.5°$ yesterday and $+4.7°$ today, how much did the temperature rise?
(A) $3.22°$
(B) $32.2°$
(C) $22.8°$
(D) $2.28°$
(E) $31°$

17. What is the product of -8.7 and -3.4?
(A) -2.958
(B) $+2.958$
(C) -29.58
(D) $+29.58$
(E) -30

18. Divide -92.4 by $+4$
(A) $-.231$

(B) −2.31
(C) +2.31

(D) +23.1
(E) −23.1

Percentage

1. Find 30% of 42.
   (A) 126
   (B) 1.26
   (C) 12.6
   (D) 1260
   (E) .126

2. A team played 40 games one season and won 24 of them. What percent of the games played did it win?
   (A) 24
   (B) 32
   (C) 40
   (D) 48
   (E) 60

3. 75% equals how many twelfths?
   (A) 6
   (B) 7
   (C) 8
   (D) 9
   (E) 10

4. 120% of 40 =
   (A) 48
   (B) 50
   (C) 52
   (D) 54
   (E) 56

5. 15 is 60% of what number?
   (A) 22
   (B) 25
   (C) 28
   (D) 30
   (E) 32

6. The price of coffee dropped from $4.20 a pound to $3.15 a pound. What was the percent decrease?
   (A) 20
   (B) 23
   (C) 25
   (D) 27
   (E) 30

7. .8% is the same as 1 out of every
   (A) 90
   (B) 100
   (C) 110
   (D) 115
   (E) 125

8. In 1970, the rainfall in city X was 80% of normal. If the actual rainfall that year was 36 inches, how many inches of rainfall per year is normal for city X?
   (A) 30
   (B) 32
   (C) 34
   (D) 45
   (E) 48

9. What is 40% of $\frac{5}{6}$?

   (A) $\frac{1}{3}$

   (B) $\frac{4}{25}$

   (C) $\frac{5}{24}$

   (D) $\frac{10}{3}$

   (E) $\frac{100}{3}$

10. Eight ounces is what percent of 15 pounds?

    (A) $3\frac{1}{3}$

    (B) $18\frac{1}{3}$

    (C) 30

    (D) $33\frac{1}{3}$

    (E) $53\frac{1}{3}$

11. If x is 40% of y, then y is what percent of x?
    (A) 120
    (B) 130
    (C) 140
    (D) 210
    (E) 250

12. A tank contains 60 gallons of oil, which is 40% of its capacity. How many gallons can the tank hold?
    (A) 130
    (B) 150
    (C) 160
    (D) 180
    (E) 240

13. p is what percent of 25?

    (A) $\dfrac{p}{4}$

    (B) $\dfrac{p}{25}$

    (C) $4p$

    (D) $\dfrac{4p}{25}$

    (E) $\dfrac{p}{16}$

14. How many liters of pure acid are there in 8 liters of a 20% solution of acid?
    (A) 1.2
    (B) 1.4
    (C) 1.5
    (D) 1.6
    (E) 2.4

15. A man buys a $60 radio at a discount of 25%. How much does he pay for it?
    (A) $40
    (B) $45
    (C) $48
    (D) $50
    (E) $52

16. Beef loses 20% of its weight when roasted. How many pounds of raw beef must be roasted to yield 6 pounds of roast beef?
    (A) 6.5

(B) 6.8
(C) 7.2
(D) 7.5
(E) 8.2

17. If the ratio of nurses to doctors in a hospital is 7 to 1, what percent of the staff is made up of nurses?

    (A) $87\dfrac{1}{2}$

    (B) $83\dfrac{1}{3}$

    (C) 86

    (D) $83\dfrac{2}{3}$

    (E) 78

18. 2 is what percent of $4t$?

    (A) $\dfrac{t}{50}$

    (B) $\dfrac{50}{t}$

    (C) $2t$

    (D) $\dfrac{1}{2t}$

    (E) $200t$

19. An article costing C dollars is sold for a *gain* of $r\%$ on the *cost*. The selling price of the article is then

    (A) $\dfrac{rC}{100}$

    (B) $C(1 + r)$

    (C) $\dfrac{C(1 + r)}{100}$

    (D) $C\left(1 + \dfrac{r}{100}\right)$

    (E) $r + \dfrac{rC}{100}$

20. A 10-quart solution of alcohol and water is 30% alcohol. If 2 quarts of water are added, the percent of alcohol in the resulting solution is

(A) 20
(B) 24
(C) 25

(D) 26
(E) 30

Exponents and Roots

1. $r^3 \times r^5 =$
   (A) r^{15}
   (B) $2r^8$
   (C) r^{16}
   (D) r^8
   (E) $2r^8$

2. $(2p^2)^3 =$
   (A) $2p^6$
   (B) $8p^6$
   (C) $8p^5$
   (D) $2p^5$
   (E) $6p^6$

3. $2^8 \times 3^6$ is divisible by
   (A) $2^7 \times 3^7$
   (B) $2^6 \times 3^5$
   (C) $2^7 \times 3^9$
   (D) $2^4 \times 3^7$
   (E) $2^5 \times 3^8$

4. Divide $15c^6d^5$ by $-5c^2d^2$
   (A) $-3c^4d^3$
   (B) $-3c^3d^3$
   (C) $3c^4d^3$
   (D) $-3c^3d^4$
   (E) $-3c^4d$

5. $\sqrt{36r^5} =$
   (A) $6r^2$
   (B) $6r^3$
   (C) $6r^2\sqrt{r}$
   (D) $6r\sqrt{r}$
   (E) $6r^4\sqrt{r}$

6. $\sqrt[3]{-\dfrac{1}{8}} =$
   (A) $\dfrac{1}{2}$

   (B) $\dfrac{1}{4}$

   (C) $-\dfrac{1}{4}$

   (D) -2

   (E) $-\dfrac{1}{2}$

7. If 57 million $= 5.7 \times 10^n$, then $n =$
   (A) 5
   (B) 6
   (C) 7
   (D) 8
   (E) 9

8. $\sqrt{200} - \sqrt{50} =$
   (A) $\sqrt{150}$
   (B) 5
   (C) $\sqrt{40}$
   (D) $5\sqrt{2}$
   (E) 2

9. $\dfrac{(5r^2s^3)^3}{5r^2s^5} =$
   (A) r^4s^4
   (B) $25r^3s$
   (C) $25r^4s^4$
   (D) r^3s
   (E) $5r^3s$

10. If $2^p = q$, then $2^{p+1} =$
    (A) $q + 1$
    (B) $q + 2$
    (C) $2q$
    (D) q^2
    (E) $q^2 + 1$

Operations with Algebraic Expressions

1. Add $4x + 2y$ to $x - 4y$
   (A) $5x - 2y$
   (B) $5x + 2y$
   (C) $3x - 2y$
   (D) $3x + 2y$
   (E) $4x - 2y$

2. $(-5r^3s)(3rs^4) =$
   (A) $-15r^3s^4$
   (B) $-15r^4s^4$
   (C) $-15r^4s^5$
   (D) $15r^4s^5$
   (E) $15r^3s^4$

3. Divide $45x^3y^5$ by $-5x^2y^3$
   (A) $9xy^2$
   (B) $-9xy^2$
   (C) $-9y^2$
   (D) $-40xy^2$
   (E) $40xy^2$

4. Divide $(9x^3 - 6x^2 + 3x)$ by $3x$.
   (A) $6x^2 - 2x + 1$
   (B) $3x^2 - 3x + 1$
   (C) $3x^2 - 2x + 3$
   (D) $3x^2 - x$
   (E) $3x^2 - 2x + 1$

5. The sum of two binomials is $3x^2 - 5x$. If one of the binomials is $2x^2 - x$, what is the other?
   (A) $5x^2 - 6x$
   (B) $5x^2 - 4x$
   (C) $x^2 - 6x$
   (D) $x^2 - 4x$
   (E) $x^2 + 4x$

6. Factor: $x^2 - 36$
   (A) $(x + 6)(x - 6)$
   (B) $(x + 18)(x - 18)$
   (C) $(x - 6)(x - 6)$
   (D) $(x + 6)(x + 6)$
   (E) $(x - 9)(x + 4)$

7. Express as a trinomial: $(r - 1)(r + 2)$
   (A) $r^2 - 2$
   (B) $r^2 - r - 2$
   (C) $r^2 + r + 2$
   (D) $r^2 + r - 2$
   (E) $r^2 - 2r - 2$

8. Factor completely: $3y^2 - 48$
   (A) $3(y^2 - 16)$
   (B) $3(y - 4)(y + 4)$
   (C) $3(y - 4)(y - 4)$
   (D) $3(y + 4)(y + 4)$
   (E) $3(y + 8)(y - 8)$

9. Multiply $(2a - b)$ by $(2a + b)$.
   (A) $4a^2 - 2ab - b^2$
   (B) $4a^2 + 2ab - b^2$
   (C) $4a^2 - b^2$
   (D) $4a^2 + b^2$
   (E) $4a^2 - 4ab - b^2$

10. Express as a trinomial: $(2p + 1)(3p - 2)$
    (A) $6p^2 + p - 2$
    (B) $6p^2 + p + 2$
    (C) $6p^2 + 7p - 2$
    (D) $6p^2 - 7p - 2$
    (E) $6p^2 - p - 2$

11. Factor completely: $3ax + 3ay + 6a$
    (A) $3a(x + y + a)$
    (B) $3a(x + y + 2)$
    (C) $a(3x + 3y + 6a)$
    (D) $3(ax + ay + 2a)$
    (E) $3a(x + y + 3a)$

12. Factor completely: $m^2 + 5m - 24$
    (A) $(m - 8)(m - 3)$
    (B) $(m + 8)(m + 3)$
    (C) $(m + 12)(m - 2)$
    (D) $(m + 8)(m - 3)$
    (E) $(m - 8)(m + 3)$

Ratio and Proportion

1. What is the ratio of 9 inches to 2 feet?
   (A) 9:2
   (B) 2:9
   (C) 3:8
   (D) 8:3
   (E) 3:4

2. Two girls divide $1.60 in the ratio 5:3. How much more does one girl get than the other?
   (A) $.40
   (B) $.50
   (C) $.60
   (D) $.80
   (E) $1.00

3. The weight of 15 feet of wire is 6 pounds. How many pounds will 25 feet of this same wire weigh?
   (A) 8
   (B) 8.5
   (C) 9
   (D) 9.5
   (E) 10

4. At a certain time of day, a vertical yardstick casts a 20-inch shadow. How tall, in feet, is a flagpole that casts a shadow of 15 feet at the same time?
   (A) 20
   (B) 22
   (C) 25
   (D) 27
   (E) 30

5. A gear 12 cm. in diameter is turning a gear 18 cm. in diameter. When the smaller gear has made 42 revolutions, how many has the larger one made?
   (A) 24
   (B) 28
   (C) 50
   (D) 63
   (E) 72

6. An inch is to a foot as how many feet is to a yard?
   (A) 4
   (B) 3
   (C) $1\frac{1}{4}$
   (D) $\frac{5}{8}$
   (E) $\frac{1}{4}$

7. If 6 boys can paint their clubroom in 8 hours, how many hours would it take 10 boys working at the same rate?
   (A) $13\frac{1}{3}$
   (B) $8\frac{1}{4}$
   (C) $4\frac{4}{5}$
   (D) $4\frac{1}{2}$
   (E) $4\frac{1}{4}$

8.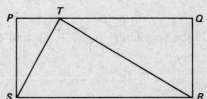

In the figure above, what is the ratio of the area of *triangle STR* to the area of *rectangle PQRS*?
   (A) 1:2
   (B) 1:3
   (C) 1:4
   (D) 1:1
   (E) 2:1

9. Of the following, which *cannot* be the ratio of the lengths of the sides of a triangle?
   (A) 3:4:5
   (B) 2:3:5
   (C) 3:3:4
   (D) 1:1:1
   (E) 6:7:8

10. If $r + s = 0$ and $r \neq 0$, what is the ratio of r to s?
    (A) 0
    (B) 1
    (C) $-\dfrac{1}{2}$
    (D) -1
    (E) It cannot be determined from the information given

11. If the ratio of p to q is 2 to 3 and the ratio of q to r is 1 to 2, then the ratio of p to r is
    (A) 1:1
    (B) 3:1
    (C) 1:2
    (D) 1:3
    (E) 2:5

12. A board is cut into three pieces whose lengths are in the ratio 3:4:5. If the piece of medium length is 10 feet long, what is the length in feet of the original board?
    (A) 28
    (B) 30
    (C) 32
    (D) 34
    (E) 36

Equations and Formulas

1. If $8x + 3 = 27$, then $x - 2 =$
   (A) 0
   (B) 1
   (C) 2
   (D) 3
   (E) 4

2. Solve for y: $2y + 7 = y - 9$
   (A) -2
   (B) $+2$
   (C) $+16$
   (D) -16
   (E) $-5\dfrac{1}{3}$

3. In the formula $F = \dfrac{9}{5}C + 32$, find C when $F = 77$.
   (A) 25
   (B) 45
   (C) 54
   (D) 60
   (E) 81

4. Solve for r:
   $$\frac{r}{3} + \frac{r}{4} = \frac{7}{12}$$
   (A) 0

   (B) 1
   (C) $1\dfrac{1}{4}$
   (D) $2\dfrac{1}{12}$
   (E) 3

5. Solve for x: $ax = 5 + bx$
   (A) $\dfrac{a - b}{5}$
   (B) $\dfrac{5}{a + b}$
   (C) $\dfrac{a}{b} - 5$
   (D) $\dfrac{a + b}{5}$
   (E) $\dfrac{5}{a - b}$

6. Solve for y: $3x - y = 30$
   $5x - 3y = 10$
   (A) 10
   (B) 20

(C) 30
(D) 40
(E) 50

(D) -2

(E) $\dfrac{2}{7}$

7. If $P = EI$ and $E = IR$, find P in terms of E and R.

(A) $\dfrac{E^2}{R}$

(B) E^2R

(C) $\dfrac{R}{E^2}$

(D) $\dfrac{E}{R}$

(E) $\dfrac{R}{E}$

9. If $5y = \dfrac{45}{y}$, then $y =$

(A) $+3$ only
(B) -3 only
(C) $+9$ only
(D) $+3$ or -3
(E) -9 only

10. The formula $h = 16t^2$ represents the distance h, in feet, that an object falls from rest after t seconds. In how many seconds will an object fall 400 ft.?
(A) 2
(B) 3
(C) $3\sqrt{2}$
(D) $2\sqrt{3}$
(E) 5

8. If $7p - 8 = 6 + 7q$, then $p - q =$
(A) 0
(B) 1
(C) 2

Motion Problems

1. A man drives 261 miles in $4\dfrac{1}{2}$ hours. What is his average speed in miles per hour?
(A) 50
(B) 52
(C) 54
(D) 56
(E) 58

(B) $1\dfrac{2}{3}$

(C) $1\dfrac{3}{4}$

(D) 2

(E) $2\dfrac{1}{4}$

2. A jet plane flies at 450 miles per hour from 2:30 p.m. to 6 p.m. How many miles does it fly?
(A) 1500
(B) 1540
(C) 1575
(D) 1600
(E) 1635

4. A plane flies k kilometers in h hours. What is its average speed in kilometers per hour?
(A) kh

(B) $\dfrac{h}{k}$

(C) $\dfrac{2k}{h}$

(D) $\dfrac{k}{h}$

(E) $\dfrac{2h}{k}$

3. How many minutes does it take to travel 1 mile at 45 miles per hour?

(A) $1\dfrac{1}{3}$

5. A boy is riding on his motorcycle at the rate of 45 miles per hour. What is his rate in feet per second? (5,280 feet = 1 mile).
   (A) 60
   (B) 66
   (C) 70
   (D) 76
   (E) 88

6. It takes Bill 14 minutes to bicycle 1 mile to school and 16 minutes to return. What is his average speed in miles per *hour* for the round trip?
   (A) 2
   (B) 3
   (C) 4
   (D) 5
   (E) 6

7. A bus travels a distance of 120 miles at 60 miles per hour and then returns at 40 miles per hour. What is the average speed in miles per hour for the round trip?
   (A) 42
   (B) 44
   (C) 46
   (D) 48
   (E) 50

8. Ralph runs 320 yards in 30 seconds. If he runs the first 200 yards in 20 seconds, what is his average speed, in yards per second, for the remainder of the distance?
   (A) 10
   (B) 11

(C) 12

(D) $12\frac{2}{3}$

(E) $13\frac{1}{4}$

9. Two planes leave the same airport at the same time and travel in opposite directions, one at 550 miles per hour and the other at 300 miles per hour. In how many hours will they be 2,550 miles apart?
   (A) 2.5
   (B) 3
   (C) 3.4
   (D) 3.8
   (E) 4

10. Jim started walking at 3 miles per hour. Helen started from the same place $2\frac{1}{2}$ hours later and traveled the same route by bicycle at 8 miles per hour. In how many hours did she overtake Jim?

   (A) $1\frac{1}{2}$

   (B) $1\frac{3}{4}$

   (C) 2

   (D) $2\frac{1}{4}$

   (E) $2\frac{1}{2}$

Average Problems

1. Arthur receives grades of 72, 77, 82, 83, and 91 in five subjects. What is his average?
   (A) 78
   (B) 79
   (C) 80
   (D) 81
   (E) 82

2. Temperature readings at a ski slope were taken every hour for six hours one afternoon. The readings were 12, 11, 7, 4, −2 and −8. What was the average temperature?
   (A) 3
   (B) $3\frac{1}{2}$

(C) 4

(D) $4\frac{1}{2}$

(E) 5

3. Marlene gets grades of 79, 83, 86, and 89 on four math tests. What grade must she get on her fifth test to average 85?
(A) 86

(B) $86\frac{2}{5}$

(C) 87

(D) $87\frac{1}{2}$

(E) 88

4. If a, b, c, d, and e are five consecutive odd numbers, their average is
(A) a
(B) b
(C) c
(D) d
(E) e

5. Fifty students had an average of 80%. Thirty other students had an average of 86%. Find the average of all the students.

(A) $81\frac{1}{4}$

(B) $81\frac{3}{4}$

(C) 82

(D) $82\frac{1}{4}$

(E) $83\frac{1}{2}$

6. Dan has 50 minutes to do 30 problems. He does the first 20 problems in 45 seconds each. What is the average number of minutes he can spend on each remaining problem?

(A) $1\frac{1}{4}$

(B) $2\frac{1}{3}$

(C) $2\frac{2}{3}$

(D) $3\frac{1}{2}$

(E) $3\frac{3}{4}$

7. What is the average of $n, n + 1, n + 2, n + 3, n + 4, n + 5$?
(A) $n + 2$

(B) $n + 2\frac{1}{2}$

(C) $n + 3$
(D) $6n + 15$

(E) $n + 3\frac{1}{2}$

8. If the average of r and s is 9, and $t = 18$, what is the average of r, s and t?
(A) 12

(B) $12\frac{1}{2}$

(C) $12\frac{2}{3}$

(D) 13

(E) $13\frac{1}{2}$

9. A class of 20 students has an average of p on a particular test. One student then has his grade raised by 10 points. What is the new class average?
(A) $p + 10$
(B) $p + 2$
(C) $p + 1$

(D) $p + \frac{1}{2}$

(E) $p + \frac{1}{4}$

10. The average of 10 scores is x and the average of another 20 scores is y. What is the average of all 30 scores?
(A) $10x + 20y$
(B) $x + 2y$

(C) $\dfrac{x + 2y}{30}$

(E) $\dfrac{x + 2y}{3}$

(D) $\dfrac{10x + 20y}{3}$

Integer Problems

1. If k is any integer, which of the following must also be an integer?

   (A) $\dfrac{k}{3}$

   (B) $\dfrac{k + 1}{3}$

   (C) $\dfrac{k + 3}{3}$

   (D) $\dfrac{3k - 1}{3}$

   (E) $\dfrac{3k + 3}{3}$

2. For any integer t, which of the following must be an even integer?
   (A) $2t + 2$
   (B) $2t + 1$
   (C) $2t - 1$
   (D) $2t + 3$
   (E) $t + 2$

3. If $p = \dfrac{2}{3}q$ and q is a positive integer, which of the following could be the value of p?

   (A) $\dfrac{3}{2}$

   (B) $\dfrac{4}{3}$

   (C) 3
   (D) 5

   (E) $2\dfrac{1}{2}$

4. Which of the following is a product of 17 and an integer?

   (A) 171
   (B) 1712
   (C) 1724
   (D) 1734
   (E) 1707

5. Which of the following is *not* the product of two consecutive odd integers?
   (A) 15
   (B) 63
   (C) 99
   (D) 143
   (E) 153

6. Which of the following *cannot* be written as the sum of two prime numbers?
   (A) 10
   (B) 14
   (C) 17
   (D) 20
   (E) 30

7. If p is a positive integer divisible by 6, which of the following must also be divisible by 6?
   (A) $p + 48$

   (B) $\dfrac{p}{6}$

   (C) $2p - 1$
   (D) $3p + 2$

   (E) $\dfrac{p}{3}$

8. For which of the following values of y will $36y^2 + 36y + 36$ be an integer?

   (A) $\dfrac{1}{4}$

   (B) $\dfrac{1}{3}$

(C) $\frac{1}{9}$

(D) $\frac{1}{5}$

(E) $\frac{1}{8}$

9. If a carton containing a dozen eggs is dropped, which of the following *cannot* be the *ratio* of broken eggs to whole eggs?
    (A) 2:1
    (B) 3:1

(C) 3:2
(D) 5:1
(E) 7:5

10. A salesman in a fruit store sells peaches for 15¢ each and oranges for 20¢ each. If he sells $3.00 worth of peaches and oranges, what is the *least* amount of peaches he could have sold?
    (A) 4
    (B) 5
    (C) 6
    (D) 7
    (E) 8

Angle Relationships

1. In triangle *RST, TR = TS* and angle *T* = 70°. What is the number of degrees in angle *R*?
    (A) 50
    (B) 55
    (C) 60
    (D) 65
    (E) 70

2. If the angles of a triangle are in the ratio 3:4:5, what is the difference in degrees between the largest and smallest angle?
    (A) 15
    (B) 22
    (C) 30
    (D) 35
    (E) 40

3. What is the number of degrees in the angle between the hands of a clock at 12:30?
    (A) 145
    (B) 150
    (C) 155
    (D) 160
    (E) 165

4. If a wheel has 24 spokes evenly spaced from one another, how many degrees in the angle between two consecutive spokes?
    (A) 15   (D) 22
    (B) 18   (E) 24
    (C) 20

5. A string 3π cm. long is laid along the circumference of a circle of radius 4 cm. How many degrees in the arc covered by the string?
    (A) 150
    (B) 135
    (C) 120
    (D) 105
    (E) 90

6. In a circle with center at *O*, arc *PQ* measures 100°. How many degrees in angle *PQO*?
    (A) 30
    (B) 37
    (C) 40
    (D) 45
    (E) 50

7.
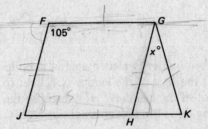

In the figure above, *FG = JH, JF = GH = GK;* ∠*F* = 105°; *x* =
(A) 25°

(B) 30°
(C) 35°
(D) 40°
(E) 45°

8. In parallelogram *RSTV*, angle *R* = 2*n*°. How many degrees in angle *S*?
(A) 90 + 2*n*
(B) 180 − *n*
(C) 180 + 2*n*
(D) 180 − 2*n*
(E) 4*n*

9.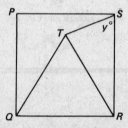

In the figure above, *PQRS* is a square and *QRT* is an equilateral triangle; then *y* =
(A) 55°
(B) 60°
(C) 65°
(D) 70°
(E) 75°

10.

World Population

In the circle graph above, how many degrees are there in the central angle of the sector for China?
(A) 68
(B) 70
(C) 72
(D) 74
(E) 76

Right Triangle Relationships

1. The diagonal of a rectangle is 26 feet and its height is 10 feet. Its base in feet is
(A) 21
(B) 22
(C) 23
(D) 24
(E) 25

2. A 20-foot ladder is placed against a building so that the foot of the ladder is 12 feet from the foot of the building. How high up the building does the ladder reach, in feet?
(A) 14
(B) 15
(C) 16
(D) 17
(E) 18

3. The perimeter of a square is 16. The length of a diagonal of the square is
(A) 4
(B) $4\sqrt{2}$
(C) $4\sqrt{3}$
(D) $2\sqrt{2}$
(E) $2\sqrt{3}$

4. In triangle *PQR*, *PQ* = *PR* = 17. Base *QR* = 16. Find the length of the altitude to base *QR*.
(A) 15
(B) $8\sqrt{2}$

(C) $8\sqrt{3}$

(D) $\sqrt{353}$

(E) 14

5. The legs of a right triangle are $\frac{3}{4}$ and 1. What is the length of the hypotenuse?

(A) $\sqrt{2}$

(B) 2

(C) $1\frac{1}{2}$

(D) $\frac{\sqrt{5}}{2}$

(E) $1\frac{1}{4}$

6. Point P is 25 inches from the center O of a circle of radius 7 inches. How many inches are there in the length of a tangent from P to the circle?

(A) $12\sqrt{2}$

(B) 20
(C) 22
(D) 24

(E) $10\sqrt{3}$

7. A ship sails 60 miles south, 90 miles east, and 60 miles south again. How many miles is it from its starting point?
(A) 120
(B) 135
(C) 150
(D) 160

(E) $100\sqrt{3}$

8. A 24-inch chord is drawn in a circle with a radius of 13 inches. How far, in inches, from the center of the circle is the chord?
(A) 5

(B) $5\sqrt{2}$

(C) $5\sqrt{3}$

(D) $6\sqrt{2}$

(E) 12

9.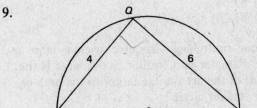

In semicircle PQR, $PQ = 4$ and $QR = 6$. The radius of the semicircle is

(A) $2\sqrt{13}$

(B) 8
(C) 4

(D) $\sqrt{13}$

(E) $\frac{1}{2}\sqrt{13}$

10. A square is inscribed in a circle of diameter 10 cm. What is the length in centimeters of the side of the square?

(A) $5\sqrt{3}$

(B) $5\sqrt{2}$

(C) 8

(D) $10\sqrt{2}$

(E) $4\sqrt{3}$

Area Problems

1. What is the price per square foot of carpet that sells for $10.80 per square yard?
   (A) $1.20
   (B) $1.80
   (C) $3.25
   (D) $3.50
   (E) $3.70

2. If one circle has a diameter twice as large as the diameter of a smaller circle, what is the ratio of the area of the larger to the area of the smaller circle?
   (A) 2:1
   (B) 4:1
   (C) 6:1
   (D) 3:2
   (E) 8:1

3. The length of a rectangle is 3 cm. more than its width. If the perimeter of the rectangle is 58 cm., how many square cm. in the area of the rectangle?
   (A) 104
   (B) 143
   (C) 162
   (D) 186
   (E) 208

4.

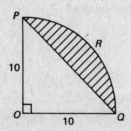

   In the figure above, arc PRQ is a quarter of a circle of radius 10. The area of the shaded portion is
   (A) $50 - 25\pi$
   (B) $50\pi - 50$
   (C) $25\pi - 50$
   (D) $50\pi - 100$
   (E) $50 - 50\pi$

5. If the area of a square is $49t^2$, the perimeter of the square is
   (A) $49t$
   (B) $36t$
   (C) $28t^2$
   (D) $28t$
   (E) $14t$

6.

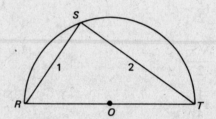

   In the figure above, RST is a semicircle with center O. The area of the semicircle is

   (A) $\dfrac{5\pi}{2}$

   (B) $\dfrac{5\pi}{4}$

   (C) $\dfrac{\pi\sqrt{5}}{2}$

   (D) $\dfrac{25\pi}{8}$

   (E) $\dfrac{5\pi}{8}$

7. The length and width of a rectangle are respectively 8 cm. larger and 4 cm. shorter than the side of a square of equal area. What is the length, in centimeters of the side of the square?
   (A) 4
   (B) 8
   (C) 12
   (D) 24
   (E) 40

8.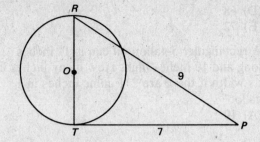

In the figure above, PT is tangent to circle O. $PT = 7$ and $PR = 9$. The area of circle O is

(A) 4π

(B) $\pi\sqrt{32}$

(C) 8π

(D) 16π

(E) 32π

9. A square has a side of p inches. Its sides are then increased by q inches each to form a new square. By how many square inches is the area of the original square increased?

(A) $q^2 + 2pq$

(B) q^2

(C) $q^2 - 2pq$

(D) pq

(E) $2p + 2q$

10. The base of a rectangle is increased by 20% and its height is increased by 10%. By what percent is its area increased?

(A) 15

(B) 24

(C) 30

(D) 32

(E) 40

Geometry of Solids

1. A truck can hold 3 cubic yards of sand. If a cubic foot of sand weighs 80 pounds, the weight of a truck load of sand in pounds, is

(A) 240

(B) 270

(C) 2160

(D) 6480

(E) 6820

2. A rectangular tank is 14 feet long, 7 feet wide, and 6 feet deep. How many cubic feet of water will it hold, if it is filled to within 6 inches from the top?

(A) 330

(B) 430

(C) 539

(D) 637

(E) 686

3. A coal bin is 8 feet long and 5 feet wide. How many feet deep must it be filled to hold 6 tons of coal if 1 ton of coal occupies 35 cubic feet?

(A) $5\frac{1}{4}$

(B) 6

(C) $6\frac{2}{7}$

(D) $6\frac{2}{3}$

(E) 7

4. If each dimension of a cube is doubled, its volume is multiplied by

(A) 2

(B) 3

(C) 4

(D) 6

(E) 8

5. A cube 3 inches on each edge is painted on all faces. If this cube is then cut into cubes 1 inch on each edge, how many of these 1-inch cubes will have paint on only one face?

(A) 4

(B) 6

(C) 8

(D) 10

(E) 12

6. What is the surface area, in square

---

centimeters, of a rectangular solid whose
dimensions are p cm., $2p$ cm. and $3p$ cm.?
(A) $11p^2$
(B) $14p^2$
(C) $6p^3$
(D) $20p^2$
(E) $22p^2$

7. The formula for the volume of a cone is $V =$
$\frac{1}{3}Bh$, where B represents the area of the
circular base and h represents the height of
the cone. If the volume is 96π and the height
is 8, find the radius of the circular base.
(A) 6
(B) 7
(C) $7\frac{1}{2}$
(D) 8
(E) 9

8. What is the surface area, in square inches, of
a cube whose volume is 27 cubic inches?
(A) 27
(B) 36
(C) 54

(D) 68
(E) 72

9. A rectangular 5-gallon oil can is 11 inches
long and 10 inches high. How many inches in
its width if there are 231 cubic inches in 1
gallon?
(A) 10
(B) $10\frac{1}{2}$
(C) 11
(D) $11\frac{1}{2}$
(E) 12

10. Cubes 1 inch on each edge were used to form
a cube 1 foot on each edge. How many of the
small cubes does the bottom layer of the large
cube contain?
(A) 12
(B) 24
(C) 48
(D) 144
(E) 152

Coordinate Geometry

1.

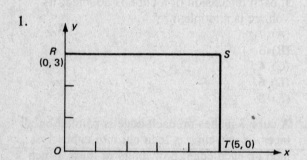

In the figure above, the perimeter of rectangle
$ORST$ is
(A) 16
(B) 14
(C) 11
(D) 8
(E) 6

2.

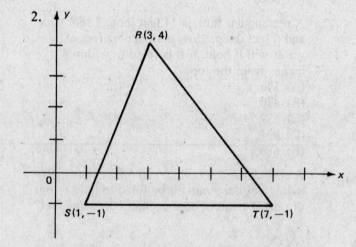

What is the area of triangle RST in the figure
above?

(A) 8
(B) 12
(C) 15
(D) 18
(E) 9

3. The *x*-axis is shifted to a new position such that the points *H, J, K* assume new coordinates as follows:

Point	Original Coordinates	New Coordinates
H	(3,5)	(3,2)
J	(4,2)	(4,−1)
K	(2,6)	(2,3)

If the original coordinates of *P* were (5,1), which of the following are the new coordinates of *P*?
(A) (2,−2)
(B) (5,4)
(C) (8,1)
(D) (8,−2)
(E) (5,−2)

4.

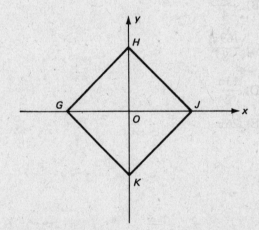

In the figure above, *GHJK* is a square of area 49. The coordinates of *K* are

(A) $\left(\frac{7}{2}\sqrt{2},0\right)$

(B) (7,0)

(C) $\left(0,\frac{7\sqrt{2}}{2}\right)$

(D) $\left(0,-\frac{7}{2}\sqrt{2}\right)$

(E) $(7\sqrt{2},0)$

5.

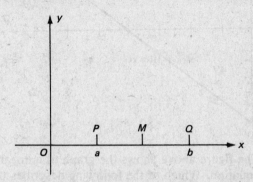

In the figure above, points *P* and *Q* are *a* and *b* units, respectively, from origin *O*. If *M* is the midpoint of *PQ*, how many units from the origin is point *M*?

(A) $\frac{a-b}{2}$

(B) $\frac{a+b}{2}$

(C) $\frac{b-a}{2}$

(D) $a + \frac{b}{2}$

(E) $b + \frac{a}{2}$

6. The coordinates of the vertices of a triangle are (0,5), (0,−3) and (4,3). What is the area of the triangle?
(A) 16
(B) 20
(C) 24
(D) 28
(E) 32

7. A straight line passes through the points *R*(0,8) and *S*(6,4). Through what point does it pass on the *x*-axis?
(A) (0,12)
(B) (9,0)
(C) (10,0)
(D) (11,0)
(E) (12,0)

8.

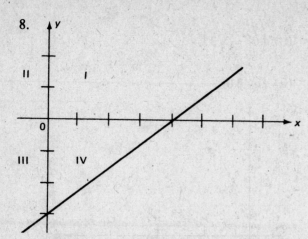

The figure above shows the graph of a linear equation. Which of the following describes the y-coordinates of those points on the graph in quadrant IV?
(A) $0 < y < 4$
(B) $-3 < y < 0$
(C) $y < 0$
(D) $y > -3$
(E) $-4 < y < 0$

9.

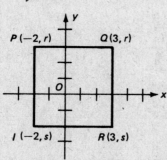

In the figure above, the area of PQRT is

(A) $5(r - s)$
(B) $5(r + s)$
(C) $3r + 2s$
(D) $3r - 2s$
(E) $r - s$

10.

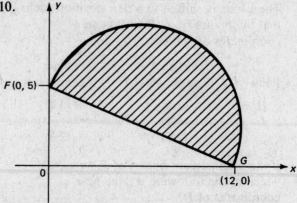

In the figure above, what is the area of the shaded semicircular region?

(A) $\dfrac{13\pi}{4}$

(B) $\dfrac{169\pi}{4}$

(C) $\dfrac{169\pi}{8}$

(D) $\dfrac{13\pi}{2}$

(E) 26π

Inequalities

1. If $2x + 2 > 10$, x must be
   (A) <8
   (B) <6
   (C) >4
   (D) >5
   (E) >6

2. If $9 < y^2 < 64$, then
   (A) $3 < y < 8$
   (B) $3 < y^2 < 8$

(C) $\dfrac{1}{8} < y^2 < \dfrac{1}{3}$

(D) $-8 < y^2 < -3$

(E) $\sqrt{3} < y < \sqrt{8}$

3. The inequality $\dfrac{p}{3} - 2 > 5$ is equivalent to

(A) $p > \dfrac{7}{3}$

(B) $p > \dfrac{5}{3}$

(C) $p > 9$
(D) $p > 15$
(E) $p > 21$

4. If p and q are integers and $2p - q > 2p + q$, then
(A) $q > 0$
(B) $q < 0$
(C) $p = q$
(D) $p > q$
(E) $q > p$

5.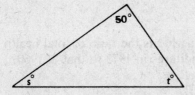

In the figure above, if $s < 50 < t$, then
(A) $t < 80$
(B) $s + t < 130$
(C) $50 < t < 80$
(D) $t > 80$
(E) $t > 100$

6. If $(r - s)^2 < r^2 + s^2$, then
(A) $r^2 < s^2$
(B) $s^2 < r^2$
(C) $r > s$
(D) $s > r$
(E) $rs > 0$

7. If n is an integer and $\dfrac{1}{5} < \dfrac{1}{n + 1} < \dfrac{1}{3}$, then

(A) $n < 4$
(B) $n > 4$
(C) $n = 3$

(D) $n = \dfrac{1}{4}$

(E) n cannot be determined from the information given

8. If $-4 < p < 5$ and $-2 < q < 0$, then, for all possible values of $(p - q)$
(A) $-6 < (p - q) < 5$
(B) $-4 < (p - q) < 5$
(C) $-2 < (p - q) < 5$
(D) $-6 < (p - q) < 7$
(E) $-4 < (p - q) < 7$

9.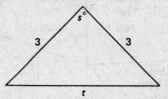

In the figure above, if $90 < s < 180$, then

(A) $0 < t < 3\sqrt{2}$

(B) $3 < t < 3\sqrt{2}$

(C) $6 < t < 6\sqrt{2}$

(D) $3\sqrt{2} < t < 6$

(E) $3 < t < 6$

10. If $0 < r < s < 1$, which of the following is true?
(A) $r + s > 1$

(B) $\dfrac{1}{r} > \dfrac{1}{s}$

(C) $r^2 + s^2 > 1$
(D) $rs > 1$
(E) $-s > -r$

Interpretation of Data

Questions 1–4 refer to the graph below.

Personal Income, 1975
$1,249.7 Billion = 100%

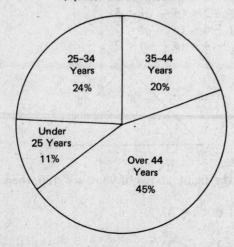

1. In 1975, what was the approximate personal income in billions of dollars, of the age group from 35–44 years?
   (A) 180
   (B) 220
   (C) 250
   (D) 280
   (E) 310

2. About how many degrees are there in the central angle of the sector devoted to the personal income of the age group under 25 years?
   (A) 31
   (B) 34
   (C) 37
   (D) 40
   (E) 43

3. What is the ratio of the personal income of the group over 44 years of age to that of the age group from 35–44 years?
   (A) 2:1
   (B) 3:2
   (C) 5:2
   (D) 8:5
   (E) 9:4

4. If total personal income in 1975 was 20% greater than it was in 1972, what was the approximate total personal income, in 1972, in billions of dollars?
   (A) 1100
   (B) 1040
   (C) 1000
   (D) 960
   (E) 900

Questions 5—9 refer to the bar graph on the facing page.

5. About what is the ratio of total health expenditures in 1973 to that in 1960?
   (A) 3:1
   (B) 4:1
   (C) 3:2
   (D) 7:3
   (E) 5:2

6. If the population of the U.S. was about 215 million in 1973, what was the approximate cost per capita for health and medical care that year?
   (A) $465
   (B) $510
   (C) $550
   (D) $590
   (E) $615

7. Approximately what was the Gross National Product, in billions of dollars in 1965?
   (A) 500
   (B) 550
   (C) 590
   (D) 630
   (E) 680

8. During what 3-year period did the proportion of the Gross National Product accounted for by health care expenditures remain steadiest?
   (A) 1965–67
   (B) 1967–69
   (C) 1969–1971
   (D) 1971–73
   (E) 1968–70

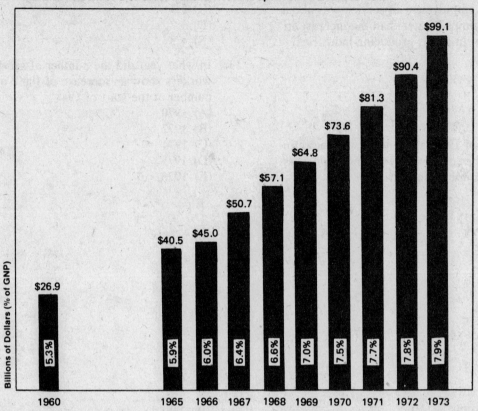

Total and Percent of U.S. Gross National Product Spent on Health 1960–1973

9. What was the percent increase in health care expenditures from 1972 to 1973?
   (A) 8.9
   (B) 9.6
   (C) 10.4
   (D) 11.2
   (E) 12.0

   Questions 10–13 refer to the line graph below.

10. At the end of 1965, about what was total employment, in millions, in both service and goods-producing industries?
    (A) 51
    (B) 54
    (C) 57
    (D) 60
    (E) 63

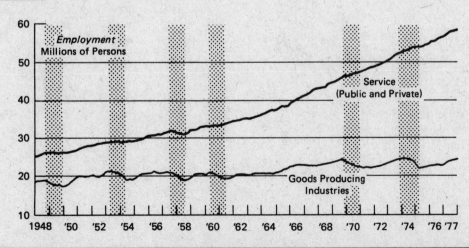

11. For the entire period shown in the graph, the increase in employment in service was about how many times greater than the increase in employment in goods-producing industries?
    (A) 2
    (B) 3
    (C) 4
    (D) 5
    (E) 7

12. At the end of 1970, about what was the ratio of the number of service workers to workers in goods-producing industries?
    (A) 2:1

(B) 3:2
(C) 5:3
(D) 5:2
(E) 4:3

13. In what year did the number of service workers show an increase of 100% over that number at the start of 1948?
    (A) 1970
    (B) 1972
    (C) 1974
    (D) 1975
    (E) 1976

Quantitative Comparison Problems

The following questions each consist of two quantities, one in Column A and one in Column B. Compare the two quantities and on the answer sheet blacken oval

A if the quantity in Column A is greater;
B if the quantity in Column B is greater;
C if the two quantities are equal;
D if the relationship cannot be determined from the information given.

All letters such as x, y and n represent real numbers. A symbol appearing in both columns represents the same quantity in Column A as it does in Column B.

In some questions, information concerning one or both of the quantities to be compared is centered above the two columns. Geometric figures may not be drawn to scale.

	Column A	Column B
1.	$2 \times 3 \times 4 \times 5$	110
2.	$(25)^2$	5^4
3.	$3y - 1$	$3y + 1$

4.
$$0 < p < q$$

	Column A	Column B
	$3p$	q

5.
$$r - 10 = 15$$

	Column A	Column B
	$r + 5$	30

6.

$L_1 \| L_2 \| L_3$

	Column A	Column B
	n	112
7.	0.05	$\sqrt{0.05}$

	Column A		Column B

8.

t is the smallest of
9 consecutive numbers

The average of
the 9 numbers $t + 4$

---

9. $\sqrt{9.14}$ $\sqrt[3]{26.8}$

10.

$$3s = 2$$

s^2 s

11.

$$M^2 = 36$$

M 6

12.

p 5

13.

$$0 < m + n < 1$$

n 1

---

14. $\dfrac{1}{3} - \dfrac{1}{6}$ $\dfrac{1}{6} - \dfrac{1}{12}$

---

15. Area of a square

with side $\dfrac{3}{4}k$ Area of a circle

               with diameter k

---

16. $3\sqrt{11}$ 11

17.

$$5r = 4k, \quad 4s = 3k$$

r s

18.

QR PR

Column A		Column B
19.	g and h are positive numbers	
$\dfrac{gh-3}{gh}$		$\dfrac{g-\dfrac{3}{h}}{g}$

20.

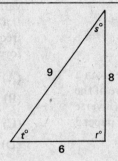

r		$s+t$

Direct and Inverse Variation

1. If y varies directly as x, and $y = 12$ when $x = 3$, find y when $x = 10$.

   (A) 30
   (B) 35
   (C) 40
   (D) 45
   (E) 50

2. If y varies inversely as x, and $y = 8$ when $x = 3$, find y when $x = 10$.

   (A) 1.8
   (B) 2.0
   (C) 2.2
   (D) 2.4
   (E) 2.8

3. According to Hooke's law, the amount x that a spring is stretched is directly proportional to the force F applied. If a force of 10g stretches a spring 3 cm., how large a force will stretch the spring 8 cm.?

   (A) 25g
   (B) 26 2/3g
   (C) 27g
   (D) 27 1/2g
   (E) 28g

4. According to Boyle's law, the volume, V, of an ideal gas at a fixed temperature varies inversely as the pressure P applied to it. If such a gas occupies 20 cu. in. when under a pressure of 12 lb. per sq. in., what pressure will result in a volume of 30 cu. in? (in lb. per sq. in.)

   (A) 6

   (B) 6.5

   (C) 7

   (D) 7.5

   (E) 8

5. At a fixed voltage, the current, I, in a DC electric circuit varies inversely as the resistance R of the circuit. If the resistance is tripled, the current is

   (A) tripled

   (B) doubled

   (C) divided by 3

   (D) divided by 2

   (E) decreased by 3

6. When an object is dropped from a position above ground, the vertical distance s it falls varies directly as the square of the time t it takes to fall. In 10 seconds, an object falls 1,600 ft. Write a formula expressing s in terms of t.
   (A) $s = 16t^2$
   (B) $t = 16s^2$
   (C) $s = 16t$
   (D) $t = 16s$
   (E) $s = 4t^2$

7. The intensity of illumination on a surface from a source of light varies inversely as the square of the distance of the surface from the source (inverse square law). The effect of moving a piece of paper 3 times as far from the source is to
   (A) divide the intensity by 3
   (B) multiply the intensity by 3
   (C) divide the intensity by 9
   (D) multiply the intensity by 9
   (E) decrease the intensity by 3

8. The frequency of vibration (f) of a pendulum varies inversely as the length (L) of the pendulum. If a pendulum with a length of one foot produces a frequency of one vibration per second, write a formula relating f to L.
   (A) $f = L$
   (B) $f = \dfrac{1}{L}$
   (C) $f = 2L$
   (D) $f = \dfrac{2}{L}$
   (E) $f = L + 1$

Explanatory Answers

FRACTIONS

1. **C.** $\dfrac{24}{32} = \dfrac{24 \div 8}{32 \div 8} = \dfrac{3}{4}$.

2. **B.** Divide 19 by 5. Thus,

   $\dfrac{19}{5} = 19 \div 5 = 3\dfrac{4}{5}$.

3. **E.** $\dfrac{40}{64} = \dfrac{40 \div 8}{64 \div 8} = \dfrac{5}{8}$.

4. **D.** Multiply 9 by 3 and add 2.

   Thus, $9\dfrac{2}{3} = \dfrac{9 \cdot 3 + 2}{3} = \dfrac{29}{3}$.

5. **A.** $\dfrac{2}{3} + \dfrac{3}{4} = \dfrac{2 \cdot 4}{3 \cdot 4} + \dfrac{3 \cdot 3}{4 \cdot 3}$

   $= \dfrac{8}{12} + \dfrac{9}{12} = \dfrac{17}{12} = 1\dfrac{5}{12}$.

6. **E** Since $\dfrac{2}{3}$ cannot be subtracted from $\dfrac{1}{2}$ with a positive difference, we borrow $1 = \dfrac{2}{2}$ from 14. Thus, we get

   $13\dfrac{3}{2} - 9\dfrac{2}{3} = 13\dfrac{9}{6} - 9\dfrac{4}{6}$

   $= 4\dfrac{5}{6}$.

7. **B.** There are 12 inches in 1 foot.

   $\dfrac{9}{12} = \dfrac{3 \cdot 3}{3 \cdot 4} = \dfrac{3}{4}$.

8. **C.** $27 \div 2\dfrac{1}{4} = 27 \div \dfrac{9}{4}$

   $= \dfrac{\overset{3}{\cancel{27}}}{1} \times \dfrac{4}{\underset{1}{\cancel{9}}} = \dfrac{12}{1} = 12$.

9. **D.** $\dfrac{\overset{1}{\cancel{2}}}{\underset{1}{\cancel{3}}} \times \dfrac{\overset{1}{\cancel{3}}}{\underset{4}{\cancel{8}}} = \dfrac{1}{4}$.

10. **A.** There are 16 ounces in a pound.

    $\dfrac{10\dfrac{2}{3}}{16} = \dfrac{32}{3} \div \dfrac{16}{1}$

    $= \dfrac{32}{3} \times \dfrac{1}{\underset{1}{\cancel{16}}}^{\,2} = \dfrac{2}{3}$.

11. **D.** $81 = \dfrac{3}{4}x$

    $x = 81 \div \dfrac{3}{4}$

    $= \dfrac{\overset{27}{\cancel{81}}}{1} \times \dfrac{4}{\cancel{3}} = 108$.

12. **E.** $7\dfrac{1}{8} \div 6 = \dfrac{57}{8} \div \dfrac{6}{1}$

    $= \dfrac{\overset{19}{\cancel{57}}}{8} \times \dfrac{1}{\underset{2}{\cancel{6}}} = \dfrac{19}{16} = 1\dfrac{3}{16}$.

13. **B.** Let x = capacity of tank in gallons.

    $\dfrac{5}{8}x - 6 = \dfrac{1}{4}x$. Multiply both sides by 8.

    $5x - 48 = 2x$

    $5x - 2x = 48$

    $3x = 48$

    $x = 16$.

14. **C.** $5\dfrac{2}{5} \times 6\dfrac{2}{3} = \dfrac{\overset{9}{\cancel{27}}}{\cancel{5}} \times \dfrac{\overset{4}{\cancel{20}}}{\cancel{3}}$

$$= \dfrac{36}{1} = 36.$$

15. **D.** $\dfrac{5x}{8} - \dfrac{x}{2}$. The LCD is 8.

$$\dfrac{5x}{8} - \dfrac{4x}{8} = \dfrac{x}{8}.$$

16. **A.** $\dfrac{12k}{18k} = \dfrac{12k \div 6k}{18k \div 6k}$

$$= \dfrac{2}{3}.$$

17. **E.** $\dfrac{\dfrac{3}{4}}{1\dfrac{1}{8}} = \dfrac{3}{4} \div \dfrac{9}{8}$

$$= \dfrac{\overset{1}{\cancel{3}}}{\cancel{4}} \times \dfrac{\overset{2}{\cancel{8}}}{\underset{3}{\cancel{9}}} = \dfrac{2}{3}.$$

18. **B.** If he does $\dfrac{5}{8}$ of a job in 10 days, then he does $\dfrac{1}{8}$ of the job in $\dfrac{10}{5} = 2$ days. To perform the remaining $\dfrac{3}{8}$ of the job will take him $3 \times 2 = 6$ days.

19. **A.** Let $x =$ original amount, then

$\dfrac{5}{9}x = 2.70$. Divide both sides by $\dfrac{5}{9}$.

$$x = 2.70 \div \dfrac{5}{9}$$

$$= \dfrac{\overset{.54}{\cancel{2.70}}}{1} \times \dfrac{9}{\cancel{5}} = \$4.86.$$

20. **D.** $\dfrac{7y}{4} - \dfrac{3y}{2} + \dfrac{5y}{8}$; LCD $= 8$

$$= \dfrac{14y}{8} - \dfrac{12y}{8} + \dfrac{5y}{8}$$

$$= \dfrac{14y - 12y + 5y}{8} = \dfrac{7y}{8}.$$

DECIMALS AND SIGNED NUMBERS

1. **D.**
$$\begin{array}{r} 102.4 \\ -\ 98.6 \\ \hline 3.8. \end{array}$$

2. **B.** $.0057 \times 1000$.

Move decimal point in .0057 three places to the right, giving 5.7.

3. **E.** $.625 = \dfrac{625}{1000} = \dfrac{625 \div 5}{1000 \div 5}$

$$= \dfrac{125}{200} = \dfrac{125 \div 25}{200 \div 25} = \dfrac{5}{8}.$$

4. **A.** $\dfrac{7}{20} = \dfrac{7 \times 5}{20 \times 5} = \dfrac{35}{100} = .35,$

or $\begin{array}{r} .35 \\ 20\overline{)7.00} \\ \underline{6\ 0} \\ 1\ 00 \\ \underline{1\ 00} \end{array}$

5. **E.** $.3 = \dfrac{3}{10} = \dfrac{300}{1000}$

$.33 = \dfrac{33}{100} = \dfrac{330}{1000}$

$.303 = \dfrac{303}{1000}$

$.033 = \dfrac{33}{1000}$

$.333 = \dfrac{333}{1000}$ (largest).

6. **C.**
$$8 \times .12 = .96$$
$$4 \times 1.12 = 4.48$$
$$3 \times .47 = \frac{1.41}{6.85}$$

$$\begin{array}{r} \$20.00 \\ - \ 6.85 \\ \hline \$13.15 \end{array} \text{ (Ans.).}$$

7. **D.**
$$\dfrac{\overset{1}{\cancel{3}}}{\underset{6}{\cancel{5}}} = \dfrac{1}{\cancel{3}} \times \dfrac{\overset{2}{\cancel{6}}}{5} = \dfrac{2}{5}$$

$$= \frac{2 \times 20}{5 \times 20} = \frac{40}{100} = .40.$$

8. **A.** $.51 \times .75 \times .375 \times .667$

$$\approx \frac{1}{\cancel{2}} \times \frac{\overset{1}{\cancel{3}}}{4} \times \frac{3}{8} \times \frac{\overset{1}{\cancel{2}}}{\underset{1}{\cancel{3}}}$$

$$\approx \frac{3}{32}.$$

9. **D.** Dividing by .04 is equivalent to dividing by $\dfrac{4}{100} = \dfrac{1}{25}$, or the same as multiplying by 25.

10. **B.** $1.25 \times .60 = .750 = .75 = \dfrac{3}{4}.$

11. **D.** .28 ft. = .28 × 12 in. = 3.36 in., which is between 3 and 4.

12. **A.** $\dfrac{13}{10}y = .039.$

Multiply both sides by 10.

$13y = .39$. Divide by 13.

$y = .03.$

13. **C.** $\dfrac{7}{.7 \times .7} = \dfrac{70}{7 \times .7} = \dfrac{10}{.7} = \dfrac{100}{7}.$

14. **B.** $.3p - 1.2 = 4.8$

Multiply all terms of the equation by 10.

$$3p - 12 = 48.$$

Add 12 to both sides.

$$3p = 60.$$

Divide both sides by three.

$$p = 20.$$

15. **A.**
$$\begin{array}{r} -18.4 \\ + \ 3.7 \\ \hline -14.7. \end{array}$$

16. **B.**
$$\begin{array}{r} + \ 4.7 \\ +27.5 \\ \hline +32.2°. \end{array}$$

17. **D.**
$$\begin{array}{r} -8.7 \\ \times \ -3.4 \\ \hline 348 \\ 261 \\ \hline +29.58. \end{array}$$

18. **E.** $\dfrac{-92.4}{+4} = -23.1.$

PERCENTAGE

1. **C.** $30\% = .30 = .3$

$.3(42) = 12.6.$

2. **E.** 24 is what % of 40?

$$\frac{24}{40} = \frac{6}{10} = 60\%.$$

3. **D.** $75\% = \dfrac{3}{4} = \dfrac{3 \times 3}{4 \times 3} = \dfrac{9}{12},$

so that $75\% = 9$ twelfths.

4. **A.** $120\% = 1.20 = 1.2$

$$1.2(40) = 48.$$

5. **B.** Let $x =$ the number, then

$15 = .6x$. Multiply both sides by 10.

$150 = 6x$. Divide both sides by 6.

$x = 25.$

6. **C.** The price decreased $4.20 - $3.15 = $1.05 per lb.

$$\frac{1.05}{4.20} = \frac{105}{420} = \frac{1}{4} = 25\% \text{ decrease.}$$

7. **E.** $.8\% = \frac{.8}{100} = \frac{8}{1000} = \frac{1}{125}$,

so that .8% is the same as 1 out of every 125.

8. **D.** Let x = normal rainfall in inches, then

$.8x = 36.$ Multiply both sides by 10.

$8x = 360.$ Divide both sides by 8.

$x = 45.$

9. **A.** $40\% = \frac{40}{100} = \frac{2}{5}$

$$\frac{\cancel{2}^{1}}{\cancel{5}_{1}} \times \frac{\cancel{5}^{1}}{\cancel{6}_{3}} = \frac{1}{3}.$$

10. **A.** 15 lb. = 15 × 16 = 240 oz.

$$\frac{8}{240} = \frac{1}{30} = \frac{x}{100} \text{ where } x\% = \frac{1}{30}$$

$30x = 100$

$x = 3\frac{1}{3}.$

11. **E.** $x = .4y$

$x = \frac{2}{5}y.$ Multiply both sides by $\frac{5}{2}$.

$\frac{5}{2}x = y,$

or $y = 2.5x = 250\%x,$

so that 250% is the answer.

12. **B.** Let n = total no. of gallons tank holds.

Then $.4n = 60.$ Multiply both sides by 10.

$4n = 600.$ Divide both sides by 4.

$n = 150.$

13. **C.** $\frac{p}{25} = \frac{x}{100}$ where x is percent desired.

$25x = 100p.$ Divide both sides by 25.

$x = 4p.$

14. **D.** The amount of pure acid is 20% of 8 liters.

$.2(8) = 1.6.$

15. **B.** $25\% = \frac{1}{4}$

$\frac{1}{4} \times \$60 = \$15$ (amount of discount).

$60 - 15 = \$45$ (sale price).

16. **D.** Let r = no. of lb. of raw beef.
If 20% is lost, then 80% remains.

$.8r = 6.$ Multiply both sides by 10.

$8r = 60.$ Divide both sides by 8.

$r = 7.5.$

17. **A.** Out of every 8 staff members, 7 are nurses.

$\frac{7}{8} = \frac{x}{100}$

$8x = 700$

$x = 87\frac{1}{2}\%.$

18. **B.** $\frac{2}{4t} = \frac{x}{100}$

$4tx = 200.$ Divide both sides by $4t$.

$x = \frac{200}{4t} = \frac{50}{t}\%.$

19. **D.** The gain $= \frac{r}{100}C = \frac{rC}{100}$.

Selling price $= C + \frac{rC}{100}$. Factor this.

$= C\left(1 + \frac{r}{100}\right).$

20. **C.** 30% of 10 is the number of quarts of pure alcohol.

$.3(10) = 3$ quarts.

If 2 quarts of water are added, there will be 12 quarts of solution containing the original 3 quarts of alcohol. Thus,

$$\frac{3}{12} = \frac{1}{4} = 25\%.$$

EXPONENTS AND ROOTS

1. **D.** $r^3 \times r^5 = r^{3+5} = r^8$.

2. **B.** $(2p^2)^3 = 2^3 \times p^6$

   $= 8p^6$.

3. **B.** In order for $2^8 \times 3^6$ to be divisible by one of the choices, the divisor must have exponents of 2 and 3 that are less than or equal to 8 and 6 respectively. (B) is the only such choice; that is,

   $$\frac{2^8 \times 3^6}{2^6 \times 3^5} = 2^2 \times 3^1 = 12.$$

4. **A.** $\dfrac{15c^6d^5}{-5c^2d^2} = -3c^4d^3$.

5. **C.** $\sqrt{36r^5} = \sqrt{36r^4} \cdot \sqrt{r}$

   $= 6r^2\sqrt{r}$.

6. **E.** $\sqrt[3]{-\dfrac{1}{8}} = -\dfrac{1}{2}$,

since $\left(-\dfrac{1}{2}\right)^3$

$= \left(-\dfrac{1}{2}\right)\left(-\dfrac{1}{2}\right)\left(-\dfrac{1}{2}\right) = -\dfrac{1}{8}$.

7. **C.** $57{,}000{,}000 = 5.7 \times 10^7$,

   so that $n = 7$.

8. **D.** $\sqrt{200} - \sqrt{50} = \sqrt{100}\sqrt{2} - \sqrt{25}\sqrt{2}$

   $= 10\sqrt{2} - 5\sqrt{2}$

   $= 5\sqrt{2}$.

9. **C.** $\dfrac{(5r^2s^3)^3}{5r^2s^5} = \dfrac{125r^6s^9}{5r^2s^5}$

   $= 25r^4s^4$.

10. **C.** $2^{p+1} = 2^p \cdot 2^1 = 2 \cdot 2^p$

   $= 2q$.

OPERATIONS WITH ALGEBRAIC EXPRESSIONS

1. **A.** $4x + 2y$
   $x - 4y$
   $\overline{5x - 2y}.$

2. **C.** $(-5r^3s)(3rs^4) = (-5)(3)r^3 \cdot r \cdot s \cdot s^4$

   $= -15r^4s^5$.

3. **B.** $\dfrac{45x^3y^5}{-5x^2y^3} = \dfrac{45}{-5} \cdot \dfrac{x^3}{x^2} \cdot \dfrac{y^5}{y^3}$

   $= -9xy^2$.

4. **E.** $\dfrac{9x^3 - 6x^2 + 3x}{3x} = \dfrac{9x^3}{3x} - \dfrac{6x^2}{3x} + \dfrac{3x}{3x}$

   $= 3x^2 - 2x + 1$.

5. **D.** From $3x^2 - 5x$, subtract $2x^2 - x$.

   $3x^2 - 5x$
   $\underline{2x^2 - x}$
   $x^2 - 4x.$

6. **A.** $x^2 - 36$ is a difference of two squares.

   $x^2 - 36 = x^2 - 6^2 = (x + 6)(x - 6)$.

7. D. $(r - 1)(r + 2) = r(r + 2) - 1(r + 2)$

$\qquad = r^2 + 2r - r - 2$

$\qquad = r^2 + r - 2.$

8. B. $3y^2 - 48 = 3(y^2 - 16)$

$\qquad = 3(y - 4)(y + 4).$

9. C. $(2a - b)(2a + b) = 2a(2a + b) - b(2a + b)$

$\qquad = 4a^2 + 2ab - 2ab - b^2$

$\qquad = 4a^2 - b^2$

10. E. $(2p + 1)(3p - 2) = 2p(3p - 2) + 1(3p - 2)$

$\qquad = 6p^2 - 4p + 3p - 2$

$\qquad = 6p^2 - p - 2.$

11. B. $3ax + 3ay + 6a = 3a(x + y + 2).$

12. D. $m^2 + 5m - 24.$

Seek two factors of -24 that add up to $+5$. These are, of course, $+8$ and -3. The factors are $(m + 8)(m - 3).$

RATIO AND PROPORTION

1. C. 2 feet $= 2 \times 12 = 24$ inches.

$\dfrac{9}{24} = \dfrac{3 \times \cancel{3}}{8 \times \cancel{3}} = \dfrac{3}{8}$, or 3:8.

2. A. Let $3x =$ amount one girl gets in \$.

$\qquad 5x =$ amount other girl gets in \$.

$3x + 5x = 1.60$

$8x = 1.60$

$x = .20$

$3x = .60$

$5x = 1.00$

$5x - 3x = \$.40$ (Ans.)

3. E. Let $w =$ weight of 25 pounds of wire,

then $\dfrac{15}{6} = \dfrac{25}{w}$. Cross-multiply.

$15w = 150$

$w = 10$ lb. (Ans.).

4. D. The shadows are in the same ratio as the corresponding vertical heights.

Let $h =$ height of flagpole in feet.

then $\dfrac{36}{20} = \dfrac{x}{15}$. Cross-multiply.

$20x = 540$. Divide both sides by 20.

$x = 27$ feet (Ans.).

5. B. The diameter of the gear is *inversely* proportional to the number of revolutions. Let $n =$ number of revolutions of larger gear,

then $\dfrac{12}{18} = \dfrac{n}{42}$. Reduce left side to lowest terms.

$\dfrac{2}{3} = \dfrac{n}{42}$. Cross-multiply.

$3n = 84$. Divide both sides by 3.

$n = 28$ revolutions (Ans.).

6. E. 1 foot $= 12$ inches; 1 yard $= 3$ ft.

$\dfrac{1}{12} = \dfrac{x}{3}$. Cross-multiply.

$12x = 3$. Divide both sides by 12.

$x = \dfrac{3}{12} = \dfrac{1}{4}$ (Ans.).

7. C. The number of boys is *inversely* proportional to the number of hours.

Let $t =$ no. of hours it takes 10 boys,

then $\dfrac{6}{10} = \dfrac{t}{8}$. Cross-multiply.

$10t = 48$. Divide both sides by 10.

$t = 4\dfrac{4}{5}$ hours (Ans.).

8. A. The triangle and the rectangle have the

same base and equal altitudes. Area of $\triangle STR = \frac{1}{2}bh$, area of rectangle $PQRS = bh$. Thus, the ratio of the areas = 1:2.

9. **B.** The sum of any two sides of a triangle must be greater than the third side. Thus, the sides of a triangle *cannot* be in the ratio 2:3:5, since the sum of the first two would *equal* the third. Hence, the answer is (B).

10. **D.** $r + s = 0$. Add $-s$ to both sides.

   $r = -s$. Divide both sides by s.

   $\frac{r}{s} = -1$ (Ans.).

11. **D.** $\frac{p}{q} = \frac{2}{3}, \frac{q}{r} = \frac{1}{2}$.

   Multiply the left members of both equations and the right members of both equations.

$$\frac{p}{\cancel{q}} \times \frac{\cancel{q}}{r} = \frac{\cancel{2}}{3} \times \frac{1}{\cancel{2}}$$

$$\frac{p}{r} = \frac{1}{3} = 1:3 \text{ (Ans.)}.$$

12. **B.** Let the lengths of the three pieces be $3x$, $4x$ and $5x$ feet. Then the total length is $12x$.

   $4x = 10$

   $x = 2\frac{1}{2}$

   $12x = 12 \times 2\frac{1}{2}$

$$= \frac{\cancel{12}^{6}}{1} \times \frac{5}{\cancel{2}_{1}} = 30 \text{ feet (Ans.)}.$$

EQUATIONS AND FORMULAS

1. **B.** $8x + 3 = 27$. Add -3 to both sides.

   $8x = 24$. Divide both sides by 8.

   $x = 3$

   $3 - 2 = 1$ (Ans.).

2. **D.** $2y + 7 = y - 9$. Add $-y$ to both sides.

   $y + 7 = -9$. Add -7 to both sides.

   $y = -16$ (Ans.).

3. **A.** $F = \frac{9}{5}C + 32$

   $77 = \frac{9}{5}C + 32$. Add -32 to both sides.

   $45 = \frac{9}{5}C$. Multiply both sides by $\frac{5}{9}$.

   $C = \frac{5}{\cancel{9}} \times \frac{\cancel{45}^{5}}{1} = 25$ (Ans.).

4. **B.** $\frac{r}{3} + \frac{r}{4} = \frac{7}{12}$. Multiply both sides by 12.

   $4r + 3r = 7$

   $7r = 7$. Divide both sides by 7.

   $r = 1$. (Ans.)

5. **E.** $ax = 5 + bx$. Add $-bx$ to both sides.

   $ax - bx = 5$. Factor out x.

   $x(a - b) = 5$. Divide both sides by $(a - b)$.

   $x = \frac{5}{a - b}$ (Ans.).

6. **C.** $3x - y = 30$

   $5x - 3y = 10$. Multiply first equation by -3

   $\underline{-9x + 3y = -90}$ Add both equations.

   $-4x = -80$. Divide both sides by -4.

   $x = 20$. Substitute in first equation.

   $3(20) - y = 30$

   $60 - y = 30$. Add y and -30 to both sides.

   $60 - 30 = y$

   $y = 30$ (Ans.).

7. **A.** $P = EI, E = IR$.
Solve the second equation for I and substitute this value of I in the first equation.

$$I = \frac{E}{R}$$

$$P = \frac{E}{I} \times \frac{E}{R}$$

$$P = \frac{E^2}{R} \text{ (Ans.)}.$$

8. **C.** $7p - 8 = 6 + 7q$.
Add $-7q$ and $+8$ to both sides.

$7p - 7q = 6 + 8$. Factor left side.

$7(p - q) = 14$. Divide both sides by 7.

$p - q = 2$ (Ans.).

9. **D.** $5y = \dfrac{45}{y}$. Multiply both sides by y.

$5y^2 = 45$. Divide both sides by 5.

$y^2 = 9$. Take square root of both sides.

$y = \pm 3$.

10. **E.** $h = 16t^2$. Substitute $h = 400$.

$400 = 16t^2$. Divide both sides by 16.

$\dfrac{400}{16} = t^2$.

$t^2 = 25$. Take square root of both sides.

$t = \pm 5$. Reject -5 since it is time.

$t = +5$ feet (Ans.).

MOTION PROBLEMS

1. **E.** $\text{Rate} = \dfrac{\text{Distance}}{\text{Time}} = \dfrac{261}{4\frac{1}{2}}$

$$= 261 \div \frac{9}{2} = \frac{\overset{29}{\cancel{261}}}{1} \times \frac{2}{\underset{1}{\cancel{9}}}$$

$$= 58 \text{ mph (Ans.)}.$$

2. **C.** 6 p.m. $-$ 2:30 p.m. $= 3\frac{1}{2}$ hours.

$$D = RT$$

$$D = 450 \times 3\frac{1}{2}$$

$$= \frac{\overset{225}{\cancel{450}}}{1} \times \frac{7}{\underset{1}{\cancel{2}}} = 1575 \text{ miles (Ans.)}.$$

3. **A.** $T = \dfrac{D}{R} = \dfrac{1}{45}$ hour

$$\frac{1}{\underset{3}{\cancel{45}}} \times \frac{\overset{4}{\cancel{60}}}{1} = \frac{4}{3} = 1\frac{1}{3} \text{ minutes (Ans.)}.$$

4. **D.** $R = \dfrac{D}{T} = \dfrac{k}{h}$ kilometers per hour (Ans.).

5. **B.** 45 miles per hour $= 45 \times 5280$ feet per hour

$$\frac{\overset{1}{\cancel{45}} \times \overset{66}{\cancel{5280}}}{\underset{\underset{1}{\cancel{8}}}{\cancel{3600}}} = 66 \text{ ft. per second (Ans.)}.$$

6. **C.** $\text{Average rate} = \dfrac{\text{total distance}}{\text{total time}}$

$$= \frac{2 \text{ miles}}{30 \text{ minutes}}$$

$$= \frac{2 \text{ miles}}{\frac{1}{2} \text{ hour}}$$

$$= \frac{2}{1} \times \frac{2}{1}$$

$$= 4 \text{ mph (Ans.)}.$$

7. D.

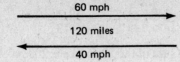

Time going $= \dfrac{120}{60} = 2$ hours.

Time returning $= \dfrac{120}{40} = 3$ hours.

Total time $= 5$ hours.

Av. rate $= \dfrac{240}{5} = 48$ mph (Ans.).

8. C.

He must do the remaining 120 yards in 10 seconds.

$$R = \frac{D}{T} = \frac{120}{10}$$

$$= 12 \text{ yards per second (Ans.)}$$

9. B.

Let h = no. of hours to be 2550 miles apart, then $300 h + 550h = 2550$

$$850h = 2550$$

$$h = 3 \text{ hours (Ans.).}$$

10. A.

Jim ——————— 3 mph ———————→
Helen ——————— 8 mph ———————→

Let x = no. of hours Helen travels,

then $\quad x + 2\dfrac{1}{2}$ = no. of hours Jim travels

$$3\left(x + 2\frac{1}{2}\right) = 8x$$

$$3x + \frac{15}{2} = 8x$$

$$\frac{15}{2} = 5x$$

$$x = \frac{3}{2}$$

$$= 1\frac{1}{2} \text{ hours (Ans.).}$$

AVERAGE PROBLEMS

1. D. Av. $= \dfrac{72 + 77 + 82 + 83 + 91}{5}$

$$= \frac{405}{5} = 81.$$

2. C. Av. $= \dfrac{12 + 11 + 7 + 4 - 2 - 8}{6}$

$$= \frac{24}{6} = 4°.$$

3. E. Let x = her grade on fifth test.

$$\frac{79 + 83 + 86 + 89 + x}{5} = 85$$

$$\frac{337 + x}{5} = 85$$

$$337 + x = 425.$$

$$x = 88.$$

4. C. Since all five numbers are evenly spaced, the average must be equal to the middle one, c.

5. D. $\quad 50 \times 80 = 4000$

$$30 \times 86 = 2580$$

Total $= 6580$

Average $= \dfrac{6580}{80} = \dfrac{658}{8} = 82\dfrac{1}{4}.$

6. **D.** He has to do the remaining 10 problems in 35 minutes, since he used $20 \times \frac{3}{4} = 15$ minutes for the first 20 problems. Thus, $\frac{35}{10} = 3\frac{1}{2}$ minutes per problem.

7. **B.** The sum of the six numbers is $6n + 15$.

   $$\text{Average} = \frac{6n + 15}{6} = n + 2\frac{1}{2}.$$

8. **A.** $\frac{r + s}{2} = 9$

   $r + s = 18, t = 18.$

$$\text{Av.} = \frac{r + s + t}{3} = \frac{18 + 18}{3} = \frac{36}{3} = 12.$$

9. **D.** The sum of the 20 scores is $20p$. If one score is raised 10 points, the sum becomes $20p + 10$. Then,

   $$\text{Average} = \frac{20p + 10}{20} = p + \frac{1}{2}.$$

10. **E.** The sum of first 10 scores is $10x$. The sum of next 20 scores is $20y$.

   $$\text{Av.} = \frac{10x + 20y}{30} = \frac{10(x + 2y)}{30}$$

   $$= \frac{x + 2y}{3}.$$

INTEGER PROBLEMS

1. **E.** $\frac{3k + 3}{3} = \frac{3(k + 1)}{3} = k + 1.$

   Since k is an integer, $k + 1$ is also an integer. Substitution of values will show that the other choices will not always yield integers.

2. **A.** $2t + 2 = 2(t + 1).$
   If t is an integer, $t + 1$ is an integer. Therefore, $2(t + 1)$ is an even integer. Substitution of values will eliminate the other possible choices.

3. **B.** If $p = \frac{2}{3}q$, then $q = \frac{3}{2}p.$

   Substitute the choices for p. If $p = \frac{4}{3}$, then $q = \frac{3}{2}\left(\frac{4}{3}\right) = 2.$ The other choices of values for p do not make q an integer.

4. **D.** Divide each choice by 17. $\frac{1734}{17} = 102.$
   Since there is no remainder, 1734 is divisible by 17. The other choices always leave a remainder.

5. **E.** $15 = 5(3); 63 = 7(9); 99 = 9(11); 143 = 11(13); 153$ cannot be written as the product of two consecutive odd numbers.

6. **C.** $10 = 7 + 3; 14 = 11 + 3; 20 = 17 + 3;$ $30 = 23 + 7; 17$ cannot be written as the sum of two prime numbers.

7. **A.** Let $p = 6k$, where k is an integer. Then, $p + 48 = 6k + 48 = 6(k + 8)$, which is divisible by 6. This is not true of the other choices.

8. **B.** Substitute each choice for y in $36(y^2 + y + 1)$. For $y = \frac{1}{4}$, the polynomial $= 36\left(\frac{1}{16} + \frac{1}{4} + 1\right)$, which is not an integer.

   For $y = \frac{1}{3}$, the polynomial $= 36\left(\frac{1}{9} + \frac{1}{3} + 1\right) = 4 + 12 + 1 = 17$, which is an integer. This is not true for the other choices.

9. **C.** For the number of whole or broken eggs to be an integer, the sum of the two numbers in the ratio must divide evenly into 12. This is true for all choices but (C), since $3 + 2 = 5$, which is not a divisor of 12.

10. **A.** Try each choice. If he buys 4 peaches, they cost 60¢, leaving $2.40 for the oranges. Thus (A) is a solution, since 2.40 is divisible by 20. The only other choice possible is 8, but 4 is the least number.

ANGLE RELATIONSHIPS

1. **B.** Since $TR = TS$, angle R = angle S. If $T = 70°$, then $R + S = 180 - 70 = 110$; $\angle R = \dfrac{110}{2} = 55°$.

2. **C.** Let the angles $= 3x$, $4x$ and $5x$. Then

$$3x + 4x + 5x = 180$$
$$12x = 180$$
$$x = 15$$
$$5x = 5(15) = 75$$
$$3x = 3(15) = 45$$
$$5x - 3x = 75 - 45 = 30°.$$

3. **E.** At 12 o'clock, the hands are together. Between every two numbers on a clock, there are $\dfrac{360}{12} = 30°$. At 12:30, the big hand is on the 6 and the small hand is half-way between the 12 and 1. It moved $\dfrac{30}{2} = 15°$. The angle between the hands is $180 - 15 = 165.°$

4. **A.** $\dfrac{360}{24} = 15°$.

5. **B.** The circumference $= 2\pi(4) = 8\pi$.

The arc $\dfrac{3\pi}{8\pi} = \dfrac{3}{8}$ of the circle

$\dfrac{3}{8} \times 360 = 135°.$

6. **C.**

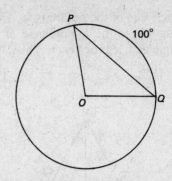

$\angle POQ = 100°$. Since $PO = OQ$,

$$\angle P = \angle Q = \frac{180 - 100}{2} = \frac{80}{2} = 40°.$$

7. **B.** Since $FGHJ$ is a parallelogram, $\angle JHG = \angle F = 105°$, then $\angle GHK = 180° - 105° = 75° = \angle K$. Then $x = 180 - 2(75) = 180 - 150 = 30°$.

8. **D.** $\angle R$ and $\angle S$ are supplementary, so that $\angle S = 180 - 2n$.

9. **E.** $\angle QRS = 90°$ and $\angle QRT = 60°$, so that $\angle TRS = 90 - 60 = 30°$. Since $RT = RQ = RS$, then $\angle RTS = y°$. Thus, $\angle TRS = 180 - 2y = 30$; $2y = 150°$ and $y = 75°$.

10. **C.** The central angle of the sector $= \dfrac{1}{5} \times 360 = 72°$.

RIGHT TRIANGLE RELATIONSHIPS

1. **D.** Let b = the length of the base in feet. The diagonal is the hypotenuse of a right triangle with the base and height as legs. Since the hypotenuse is $26 = 13 \cdot 2$ and one leg is $10 = 5 \cdot 2$, the other leg must be $12 \cdot 2 = 24$ feet. They form a 5-12-13 right triangle, with all sides multiplied by 2.

2. **C.** $20 = 4(5)$, $12 = 4(3)$; so that we have a 3- 4-5 right triangle, all multiplied by 4, so that $h = 4(4) = 16$ feet.

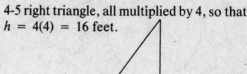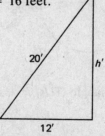

3. B. Each side of the square is $16 \div 4 = 4$. The diagonal is the hypotenuse of a right triangle with legs of 4 each. Thus, the diagonal $= 4\sqrt{2}$.

4. A.

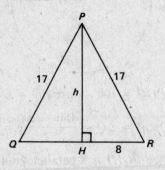

$HR = \frac{1}{2}(QR) = \frac{1}{2}(16) = 8$.

Thus, $h^2 + 8^2 = 17^2$

$h^2 + 64 = 289$

$h^2 = 225$

$h = 15$.

5. E.

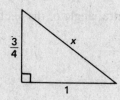

The legs are $\frac{3}{4}$ and $1 = \frac{4}{4}$. Thus, the triangle is a 3-4-5 right triangle with each side divided by 4. So that $x = \frac{5}{4} = 1\frac{1}{4}$.

6. D.

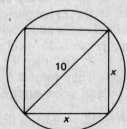

In triangle OTP, $7^2 + x^2 = 25^2$

$49 + x^2 = 625$

$x^2 = 576$

$x = \sqrt{576}$

$= 24$ inches.

7. C.

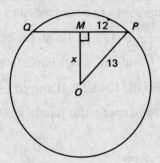

$RM = MS = \frac{90}{2} = 45$.

In $\triangle PRM$, $RM = 45 = 15(3)$, $PR = 15(4)$ and $x = PM = 15(5) = 75$. Thus, $PQ = 2x = 2(75) = 150$ miles.

8. A.

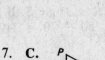

$PM = \frac{1}{2}PQ = \frac{1}{2}(24) = 12$.

$\triangle OPM$ is a 5-12-13 right triangle, so that $x = 5$ inches.

9. D. Angle PQR is a right angle since it is inscribed in a semicircle. Thus,

$(PR)^2 = 4^2 + 6^2 = 16 + 36 = 52$.

$PR = \sqrt{52} = \sqrt{4 \cdot 13} = 2\sqrt{13}$.

Radius $= \frac{1}{2}(PR) = \frac{1}{2}(2\sqrt{13}) = \sqrt{13}$.

10. B.

$$x^2 + x^2 = 100$$

$$2x^2 = 100$$

$$x^2 = 50$$

$$x = \sqrt{50} = \sqrt{25 \cdot 2}$$

$$x = 5\sqrt{2}$$

AREA PROBLEMS

1. **A.** 1 square yard = 9 square feet.
   $10.80 ÷ 9 = $1.20.

2. **B.** Let the radius of the smaller circle be 1 and the radius of the larger circle is then 2. The area of the larger circle = $\pi(2^2) = 4\pi$. The area of the smaller circle = $\pi(1^2) = \pi$.
   Ratio = $\dfrac{4\pi}{\pi} = \dfrac{4}{1}$ = 4:1.

3. **E.** Let x = width in cm. of the rectangle; then $x + 3$ = length in cm. of the rectangle.
   $$2x + 2(x + 3) = 58$$
   $$2x + 2x + 6 = 58$$
   $$4x = 52$$
   $$x = 13 \text{ (width)}$$
   $$x + 3 = 16 \text{ (length)}$$
   Area = 16(13) = 208 sq. cm.

4. **C.** Area of sector $OPRQ = \dfrac{1}{4}(100\pi) = 25\pi$
   Area of triangle $OPQ = \dfrac{1}{2}(10)(10) = 50$.
   Shaded area = $25\pi - 50$.

5. **D.** Side of square = $\sqrt{49t^2} = 7t$.
   Perimeter of square = 4(7t) = 28t.

6. **E.** Angle RST is a right angle since it is inscribed in a semicircle. Therefore, $(RT)^2 = 1^2 + 2^2 = 5$
   $RT = \sqrt{5}$ and $OT = r = \dfrac{1}{2}\sqrt{5}$.
   Area of semicircle = $\dfrac{1}{2}\pi\left(\dfrac{\sqrt{5}}{2}\right)^2$
   $$= \dfrac{\pi}{2}\left(\dfrac{5}{4}\right) = \dfrac{5\pi}{8}.$$

7. **B.** Let x = length of side of square in cm. Thus,
   $$x^2 = (x + 8)(x - 4)$$
   $$x^2 = x^2 + 4x - 32$$
   $$4x = 32$$
   $$x = 8 \text{ cm.}$$

8. **C.** $(RT)^2 = 9^2 - 7^2$ in right triangle RTP
   $$(RT)^2 = 81 - 49 = 32$$
   $$RT = \sqrt{32} = \sqrt{4 \cdot 3} = 2\sqrt{8}$$
   $$r = OT = \dfrac{1}{2}(2\sqrt{8}) = \sqrt{8}$$
   $$= \sqrt{4}\sqrt{2} = 2\sqrt{2}.$$
   Area of circle = $\pi(\sqrt{8})^2 = 8\pi$.

9. **A.** Area of original square = p^2.
   Area of new square = $(p + q)^2$
   $$= p^2 + 2pq + q^2$$
   Increase in area = $p^2 + 2pq + q^2 - p^2$
   $$= q^2 + 2pq.$$

10. **D.** Let the original base and height be 10 each. The original area is then 100. The base of the new rectangle is 10 + .2(10) = 10 + 2 = 12. The height of the new rectangle is 10 + .1(10) = 10 + 1 = 11. Area of new rectangle = 12(11) = 132. Increase in area = 132 − 100 = 32.
   % Increase = $\dfrac{32}{100}$ = 32%.

GEOMETRY OF SOLIDS

1. **D.** 1 cubic yard = 27 cu. ft.
   3 cubic yards = 3 × 27 = 81 cu. ft.
   Weight of sand = 80 × 81 = 6480 pounds.

2. **C.** The depth of water = $5\frac{1}{2}$ feet.

   Volume of water = $14 \times 7 \times 5\frac{1}{2}$

   $$= \overset{7}{\cancel{14}} \times 7 \times \frac{11}{\underset{1}{\cancel{2}}}$$

   $$= 49 \times 11 = 539 \text{ cu. ft.}$$

3. **A.** 6 tons occupies 6 × 35 = 210 cu. ft.
   Let h = height of coal in feet.
   (8)(5)h = 210
   40h = 210
   $h = 5\frac{1}{4}$ feet.

4. **E.** $V = e^3$ where e = edge of cube.
   If e is doubled, the volume V is multiplied
   by $2^3 = 8$.

5. **B.**

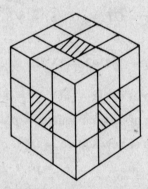

The diagram above shows the cubes with
only one painted face. Three more such
cubes are in the three faces we cannot see.

Thus, there are 6 cubes with only one
painted face.

6. **E.** The surface area = sum of areas of 6 faces.

   $S = 2[p(2p) + p(3p) + 2p(3p)]$

   $S = 2[2p^2 + 3p^2 + 6p^2]$

   $S = 2(11p^2) = 22p^2$ sq. cm.

7. **A.** $V = \frac{1}{3}Bh$

   $96\pi = \frac{1}{3}B(8)$. Divide both sides by 8.

   $12\pi = \frac{1}{3}B$

   $B = 36\pi$

   $\pi r^2 = 36\pi$

   $r = 6$.

8. **C.** $V = e^3 = 27$

   $e = 3$ in.

   $S = 6e^2 = 6(3)^2$

   $= 6(9) = 54$ sq. in.

9. **B.** 5 gallons = 5(231) = 1155 cu. in.
   $V = LWH = 11(10)w$
   $1155 = 110w$
   $W = 10\frac{1}{2}$ in.

10. **D.** A cube 1 foot on each edge must have 12
    inches on each edge. The bottom layer
    would thus have 12 × 12 = 144 cubes 1
    inch on each edge.

COORDINATE GEOMETRY

1. **A.** The base of the rectangle is 5.
   The height of the rectangle is 3.

   Perimeter = $2(b + h) = 2(5 + 3)$

   $= 2(8) = 16$.

2. **C.** b = base = $ST = 7 - 1 = 6$

   h = height = $4 - (-1) = 5$

   Area = $\frac{1}{2}bh = \frac{1}{2}(6)(5) = 15$.

3. **E.** Note that in each case, the ordinate of each point is reduced by 3. Thus, $(5,1)$ becomes $(5,-2)$.

4. **D.** Since the area of the square is 49, each side is 7. Thus, in right, isosceles triangle *JHK*,

$HK = 7\sqrt{2}.$

OK is then $\dfrac{7\sqrt{2}}{2}$. So that the coordinates

of K are $\left(0, \dfrac{-7\sqrt{2}}{2}\right).$

5. **B.** The distance OM is the average of the distances OP and OQ. Thus,

$OM = \dfrac{a+b}{2}.$

6. **A.** The base of the triangle is on the *y*-axis.

$b = 5 - (-3) = 8$

$h = 4.$

$\text{Area} = \dfrac{1}{2}bh = \dfrac{1}{2}(8)(4) = 16.$

7. **E.**

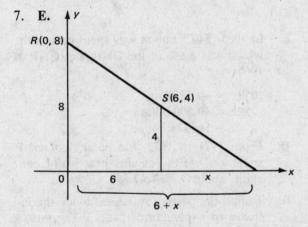

Due to similar triangles,

$\dfrac{8}{4} = \dfrac{6+x}{x}$

$8x = 24 + 4x$

$4x = 24$

$x = 6$

$6 + x = 12.$

Coordinates of *x*-intercept are $(12,0)$.

8. **B.** In quadrant IV, the ordinates of points on the line vary from 0 to -3. Thus, $-3 < y < 0$.

9. **A.** Base of rectangle $PQRT = 3 - (-2) = 3 + 2 = 5$.
Height of rectangle $PQRT = r - s$
Area of rectangle $PQRT = 5(r - s)$.

10. **C.** In right triangle *OFG*, the legs are 5 and 12 and so $FG = 13$. The radius of the semi-circle is $\dfrac{13}{2}$.

$\text{Area of semicircle} = \dfrac{1}{2}\pi\left(\dfrac{13}{2}\right)^2$

$= \dfrac{1}{2}\pi\,\dfrac{169}{4}$

$= \dfrac{169\pi}{8}.$

INEQUALITIES

1. **C.** $2x + 2 > 10$
$\dfrac{-2 - 2}{2x > 8}$
   $x > 4.$

2. **A.** $9 < y^2 < 64$. Take square root of all
$3 < y < 8.$ terms. Use positive square root only

3. **E.** $\dfrac{p}{3} - 2 > 5$

$$\underline{+2+2}$$

$\dfrac{p}{3} > 7.$ Multiply by 3.

$p > 21.$

4. **B.** $2p - q > 2p + q$

$$\underline{-2p - 2p}$$

$-q > q.$ Add q to both sides.

$$\underline{+q + q}$$

$0 > 2q.$ Divide by 2.

$0 > q,$ or $q < 0.$

5. **D.** $s + t + 50 = 180$

$s + t = 130.$

Since $s < 50,$ t must be greater than 80.

$t > 80.$

6. **E.** $(r - s)^2 < r^2 + s^2$

$r^2 - 2rs + s^2 < r^2 + s^2.$ Subtract $r^2 + s^2.$

$-2rs < 0.$ Divide by $-2.$

$rs > 0.$

7. **C.** $\dfrac{1}{5} < \dfrac{1}{n + 1} < \dfrac{1}{3}.$ Invert all fractions.

$5 > n + 1 > 3.$ Subtract 1 from all terms.

$4 > n > 2.$

Since n is an integer, $n = 3.$

8. **E.** $-4 < p < 5$ and $-2 < q < 0.$ The least possible value of $(p - q)$ is $-4 - 0 = -4.$ The greatest possible value of $(p - q)$ is $5 - (-2) = 7.$ Thus, $-4 < (p - q) < 7.$

9. **D.** If s were equal to 90, then t would be $3\sqrt{2}.$ Since $s > 90,$ $t > 3\sqrt{2}.$ Also, $3 + 3 > t,$ or $t < 6.$ So that $3\sqrt{2} < t < 6.$

10. **B.** Since r and s are positive, we may invert them and reverse the inequality.

$r < s$

$\dfrac{1}{r} > \dfrac{1}{s}.$

Since r and s are less than 1, the other inequalities do not hold true in all cases.

INTERPRETATION OF DATA

1. **C.** 20% of 1250 = .2 (1250)

= \$250 billion.

2. **D.** 11% of 360 = .11 (360)

= 39.6 $\approx$ 40°.

3. **E.** Since we are taking percents of the same total, we need only take the ratio of the percents in each sector

$\dfrac{45}{20} = \dfrac{9}{4} = 9{:}4.$

4. **B.** Let $x =$ total personal income, in billions, in 1972.

$x + .2x = 1250$

$1.2x = 1250$

$x = \$1040$ billion.

5. **B.** $\dfrac{99.1}{26.9} \approx \dfrac{99}{27} \approx \dfrac{4}{1} = 4{:}1.$

6. **A.** $\dfrac{\$99.1 \text{ billion}}{215 \text{ million}} \approx \dfrac{\$100{,}000}{215} = \dfrac{20{,}000}{43} \approx \$465.$

7. **E.** In 1965, \$40.5 billion was spent on health, which was 5.9% of the GNP. Let GNP in 1965 = $x.$

$.059x = 40.5$ billion

$59x = 40{,}500$ billion

$x \approx \$680$ billion.

8. **D.** From 1971 to 1973, the percent of GNP spent on health remains practically constant, about 7.7% to 7.8%.

9. **B.** To find the percent increase, divide the increase in expenditures from 1972 to 1973 (\$8.7 billion) by the expenditures in 1972 (\$90.4 billion):

$\dfrac{8.7}{90.4} \approx 9.6\%$

10. **E.** Employment in service at end of 1965 = 40 million. Employment in goods production at the end of 1965 = 23 million. Total = 63 million.

11. **D.** Increase in service employment = 58 − 25 = 33 million. Increase in goods-production employment = 25 − 18 = 7 million.

Increase in service employment was about 5 times as great.

12. **A.** At end of 1970, there were about 47 million workers in service and about 23 million workers in goods-producing industries, about twice as many.

13. **B.** At start of 1948, there were 25 million service workers. An increase of 100% would result in 50 million service workers. It reached this figure in 1972.

QUANTITATIVE COMPARISON PROBLEMS

1. **A.** $2 \times 3 \times 4 \times 5 = 120 > 110$.

2. **C.** $(25)^2 = (5^2)^2 = 5^4$.

3. **B.** $3y + 1$ is 1 more than $3y$.
   $3y - 1$ is less than $3y$.
   Regardless of the value or sign of $3y$,
   $3y + 1 > 3y - 1$.

4. **D.** If p were 1 and q were 2, $3p$ would be greater than q. However, if p were 1 and q were 5, $3p$ would be less than q. Hence, the relationship cannot be determined.

5. **C.** $r - 10 = 15$
   $r = 25$
   $r + 5 = 30$.

6. **A.** n is supplementary to $48°$. Thus,
   $n + 48 = 180$
   $n = 132$
   $n > 112$.

7. **B.** $\sqrt{.05}$ is slightly more than $.2$, since $(.2)^2 = .04$. Hence $\sqrt{.05} > .05$.

8. **C.** The numbers in order are $t, t + 1, t + 2, \ldots, t + 8$. The average of these 9 numbers is the middle one, or the fifth in order; namely, $t + 4$.

9. **A.** $\sqrt{9.14}$ is slightly more than $\sqrt{9} = 3$.
   $\sqrt[3]{26.8} < \sqrt[3]{27} = 3$,
   so that $\sqrt{9.14} > \sqrt[3]{26.8}$.

10. **B.** $3s = 2$
   $s = \dfrac{2}{3} = \dfrac{6}{9}$

$s^2 = \dfrac{4}{9}$.

Thus, $s > s^2$.

11. **D.** $M^2 = 36$
   $M = \pm 6$.
   Since there are two possible value of M, we cannot determine the relationship.

12. **B.** $p^2 + 11^2 = 12^2$
   $p^2 + 121 = 144$
   $p^2 = 23$
   $p = \sqrt{23} < 5$.

13. **D.** m and n can have both positive and negative values as long as their sum remains between 0 and 1. For example, m may equal 1 and n may equal $-\dfrac{1}{4}$. These values may also be reversed. Thus, we cannot determine the relationship between n and 1.

14. **A.** $\dfrac{1}{3} - \dfrac{1}{6} = \dfrac{2}{6} - \dfrac{1}{6} = \dfrac{1}{6} = \dfrac{2}{12}$
   $\dfrac{1}{6} - \dfrac{1}{12} = \dfrac{2}{12} - \dfrac{1}{12} = \dfrac{1}{12}$.

Thus, $\dfrac{1}{6} > \dfrac{1}{12}$.

15. **B.** Area of square $= \left(\dfrac{3k}{4}\right)^2 = \dfrac{9k^2}{16}$.

Area of circle $= \pi \left(\dfrac{k}{2}\right)^2 = \dfrac{\pi k^2}{4} = \dfrac{3.14k^2}{4}$.

Since k^2 is positive, we need only compare

$\frac{9}{16}$ with $\frac{3.14}{4}$; since $\frac{3.14}{4}$ is more than $\frac{12}{16}$, it follows that the circle is greater in area.

16. **B.** 11 may be written $\sqrt{11}\,\sqrt{11}$.

Since $\sqrt{11} > 3$, it follows that

$\sqrt{11}\,\sqrt{11} > 3\sqrt{11}$

$11 > 3\sqrt{11}$.

17. **D.** $5r = 4k$, $r = \frac{4k}{5}$

$4s = 3k$, $s = \frac{3}{4}k$.

It is true that $\frac{4}{5} > \frac{3}{4}$, since $.80 > .75$

However, since we do not know if $k > 0$ or less than 0 or equal to 0, we cannot make the comparison.

18. **A.** $n = 180 - (65 + 55) = 180 - 120$
$n = 60$.
Greater angle, $QR > PR$.

19. **C.** $\dfrac{g - \dfrac{3}{h}}{g} = \dfrac{gh - 3}{gh}$ by multiplying numerator and denominator by h.

20. **B.** If the triangle were a right triangle, the hypotenuse would be 10. Since the hypotenuse is less than 10, the angle r, which is opposite the hypotenuse, is less than 90°. Therefore, $s + t$ must be more than 90°, so that $s + t > r$.

DIRECT AND INVERSE VARIATION

1. **C.**
$y = kx$ $y = 4x$
$12 = 3k$ $y = 4(10)$
$k = 4$ $y = 40$(Ans.)

2. **D.**
$y = \dfrac{k}{x}$ $y = \dfrac{24}{x}$

$8 = \dfrac{k}{3}$ $y = \dfrac{24}{10}$

$k = 24$ $y = 2.4$

3. **B.**
$F = kx$ $F = \dfrac{10}{3}x$

$10 = 3k$

$k = \dfrac{10}{3}$ $F = \dfrac{10}{3}(8) = \dfrac{80}{3}$

$F = 26\frac{2}{3}g$ (Ans.)

4. **E.**
$V = \dfrac{k}{P}$ $V = \dfrac{240}{P}$

$20 = \dfrac{k}{12}$ $30 = \dfrac{240}{P}$

$k = 240$ $30P = 240$

$P = 8$ lb. per sq. in.

5. **C.**
$I = \dfrac{k}{R}$

$I' = \dfrac{k}{3R} = \dfrac{1}{3}\left(\dfrac{k}{R}\right)$

Replace $\dfrac{k}{R}$ by I.

$I' = \dfrac{1}{3}$ $I = \dfrac{I}{3}$

The current is divided by 3. (Ans.)

6. **A.**
$s = kt^2$
$1600 = k \cdot 10^2 = 100k$
$k = 16$
$s = 16t^2$ (Ans.)

7. **C.**
$I = \dfrac{k}{d^2}$

$I' = \dfrac{k}{(3d)^2} = \dfrac{k}{9d^2} = \dfrac{1}{9}\left(\dfrac{k}{d^2}\right)$

Replace $\dfrac{k}{d^2}$ by I.

$I' = \dfrac{1}{9}$ $I = \dfrac{I}{9}$

The effect is to divide the intensity by 9. (Ans.)

8. **B.**
$f = \dfrac{k}{L}$

$1 = \dfrac{k}{1}$

$k = 1$

$f = \dfrac{1}{L}$ (Ans.)

PART

Vocabulary Study List
for the Scholastic
Aptitude Test

Each vocabulary word is followed by its synonyms. Antonyms, if there are any, appear below the synonyms.

Abaft. (*Naut.*) behind; to the rear of; aft of; astern. *Ant.*: Afore; forward; ahead; in front of.

Abeam. (*Naut.*) to the side of; on right angles to a ship's keel.

Abhorrence. Repugnance; destestation; loathing. *Ant.*: Adoration; idolatry.

Abnegation. Self-denial; relinquishment; rejection.

Aborigine. Original inhabitant; primitive tribesman (especially of Australia).

Abrogate. Nullify; abolish. *Ant.*: Enact; put into effect; establish.

Absolve. Pardon; exculpate; clear. *Ant.*: Implicate; incriminate; involve; imply.

Abstain. Refrain voluntarily; refrain from voting. *Ant.*: Indulge; yield to desire; gratify one's self.

Abstemious. Sparing; moderate; abstinent. *Ant.*: Gluttonous; voracious; insatiable.

Abstinent. Abstemious; self-denying.

Abstruse. Recondite; esoteric; profoundly difficult. *Ant.*: Rudimentary; elementary.

Accelerate. Speed up. *Ant.*: Decelerate; slow down.

Acetic. Vinegary.

Acquiescing. Agreeing; going along; favoring. *Ant.*: Averse; opposed; loath; unwilling.

Acrimony. Sharpness; harshness or bitterness of nature, speech, disposition.

Acrophobia. Pathological fear of high places.

Acumen. Superior mental acuteness; keen insight. *Ant.*: Credulity; gullibility.

Adamant. Unyielding; harsh; stubborn. *Ant.*: Relenting; bending; yielding; giving in.

Adroit. Dexterous; deft; adept; clever. *Ant.*: Inept; clumsy; bungling; ungainly.

Adulation. Servile flattery; excessive devotion. *Ant.*: Disparagement; belittling; deprecation; slighting; revilement; abusing verbally.

Aesthetic. Having a sense of the beautiful; a love of beauty.

Affinity. Having a natural attraction to. *Ant.*: Antipathy; aversion; repugnance.

Affluent. Prosperous; wealthy. *Ant.*: Indigent; impoverished; destitute; penurious.

Aggressive. Boldly assertive; taking the offensive. *Ant.*: Submissive; compliant; subdued; resigned; obedient; yielding.

Alchemy. Magic.

Alert. Keen; vigilantly attentive. *Ant.*: Lethargic; drowsy; sluggish; apathetic.

Alien. Strange; not native. *Ant.*: Indigenous; native to.

Allusive. Implying things; suggesting.

Alluvial. Pertaining to sandy soil.

Alms. Money or other donation to the poor.

Alpinism. Mountain climbing. *Ant.*: Spelunking; cave exploring.

Altruism. Selfless concern for others. *Ant.*: Egoism; selfishness; self-interest.

Ambiguous. Indefinite; unclear. *Ant.*: Explicit; definite; clearly expressed.

Ambivalent. Having opposing feelings or desires. *Ant.*: Single-minded.

Amenable. Tractable; agreeable; answerable. *Ant.*: Opposed; averse; unwilling.

Amphibian. Living/operating on land and in water. *Ant.*: Aquatic (living in water); terrestrial (living on land); arboreal (living in trees); aerial (in air).

Ample. Adequate or more than adequate in size. *Ant.*: Meager; scanty.

Anachronistic. Set in the wrong time; misdated.

Analogous. Similar; parallel; corresponding. *Ant.*: Disparate; dissimilar; incongruous.

Anathema. A curse; a thing accursed; a formal ecclesiastical curse involving excommunication.

Anile. Like a weak old woman. Senile (not an antonym) refers to loss of faculties due to old age.

Animated. Lively; spirited.
   Ant.: Lethargic; sluggish.

Animosity. Ill will; hostility; antagonism.
   Ant.: Amity; friendship; harmony.

Anneal. Toughen; temper.

Annihilate. Ruin; destroy utterly.

Annular. Ring-shaped.

Anodyne. Pain reliever.

Antipathy. Aversion; basic or habitual repugnance.
   Ant.: Affinity; natural attraction.

Apathetic. Impassive; unresponsive.
   Ant.: Responsive; ardent; excited; concerned.

Apiary. A bee house containing a number of bee-hives.

Aplomb. Great poise; imperturbable self-possession.
   Ant.: Perturbation; nervousness; agitation; excitability.

Apocalyptic. Revelatory; prophetic.

Apogee. The point in a satellite's orbit farthest from earth.
   Ant.: Perigee; closest point.

Apostate. One who deserts his religion or principles.

Aquiline. Hooked; eagle-like.

Ardor. Fervor; zeal; passion.
   Ant.: Apathy; indifference.

Ascetic. Austere; rigorously abstinent; one who practices extreme self-denial or self-mortification.
   Ant.: Hedonist; one who devotes himself to pleasure.

Assiduity. Diligence; industry.
   Ant.: Sloth; indolence; laziness.

Assuage. Appease; satisfy; mollify.
   Ant.: Perturb; irritate; agitate.

Astute. Sagacious; shrewd; ingenious.
   Ant.: Injudicious; ill-advised; asinine; foolish.

Asunder. In pieces; apart.

Attentuate. Weaken; make slender; reduce in force.
   Ant.: Enlarge; expand; amplify.

Audacious. Brazen; impudent; extremely bold.

   Ant.: Timorous; fearful; apprehensive.

Auspicious. Favorable; propitious.
   Ant.: Sinister; unfavorable; malevolent.

Austral. Southern.
   Ant.: Boreal; northern.

Autarchy. Absolute sovereignty; autocratic government; self-sufficiency.

Authoritarian. Domineering; autocratic; favoring complete subjection to authority.

Autocrat. Domineering person; one who exercises complete power.

Avarice. Greed; inordinate desire to gain and hoard wealth.

Averse. Antipathetic; opposed.
   Ant.: Acquiescing.

Avuncular. Pertaining to uncles; behaving like an uncle.

Azure. Sky-blue; the blue of a clear, unclouded sky.

Banal. Hackneyed; trite; commonplace; insipid; inane.
   Ant.: Original; creative.

Batten. Thrive; grow fat; fatten; cover to make watertight.

Beatific. Blissful; saintly.

Bedeck. Adorn; deck out; ornament.

Bedizen. Adorn in showy, gaudy, vulgar manner.

Bellicose. Pugnacious; ready to fight.
   Ant.: Pacific; peaceful.

Benefactor. Kindly helper; one who confers a benefit; one who makes an endowment or bequest.
   Ant.: Malefactor; culprit; criminal; evil-doer.

Beneficial. Helpful; advantageous; conferring benefits.
   Ant.: Deleterious; harmful.

Benevolent. Kind-hearted; benign; charitable.
   Ant.: Rancorous; intensely malignant.

Benign. Gracious; favorable; kindly; salubrious.
   Ant.: Malignant; dangerous; harmful malevolent.

Bifurcate. Forked; divided into two branches.

Biota. Animal and plant life of a region.

Blackbirding. Kidnapping for selling into slavery.

Blasphemer. Impious one; irreverent one; one who speaks evil.

Blunt. Gruff; bluff; brusque; dull; insensitive; obtuse.
Ant.: Keen; sharp; perceptive.

Blurt. Utter suddenly, inadvertently.

Boorish. Rude; crude; loutish; oafish; rustic; unmannerly.
Ant.: Urbane; suave; polished; sophisticated; elegant.

Bovine. Stolid; dull; oxlike; cowlike; cow or ox.

Boycott. To abstain from buying or using; to combine in abstaining as a means of coercion.

Brusque. Blunt; unceremonious; abrupt in manner.
Ant.: Suave.

Bucolic. Pastoral; idyllically rural.

Bumble. Bungle; blunder; muddle; stumble; botch; mumble.

Bumptious. Offensively aggressive.
Ant.: Diffident; timid; shy; self-effacing.

Cabal. Clique; group of plotters.

Cacophonous. Harsh; discordant.
Ant.: Mellifluous; sweet-sounding; honeyed.

Cadaver. Dead body; corpse (especially one used for dissection).

Caliber. Degree of merit, competence, or importance; diameter of the bore of a gun.

Calibrate. Mark with gradations or graduations; check the graduation of an instrument giving quantitative measurements.

Calumny. Slander; defamation.
Ant.: Panegyric; formal commendation; eulogy.

Candid. Frank; outspoken; open; sincere.
Ant.: Disingenuous; insincere; deceitful.

Canine. Of or like a dog; a dog; a cuspid or eyetooth.

Canon. Church law; criterion; the body of works of an author; body of principles; officially recognized set of sacred books; fugal musical composition.

Captious. Fault-finding; exaggerating trivial defects.

Cardiac. Pertaining to the heart.

Cardinal. Of prime importance.

Carnal. Fleshly; sensual; worldly.
Ant.: Spiritual; incorporeal; other-worldly.

Carnivore. Flesh-eater: dogs, cats, lions, etc.

Carom. Strike and rebound.

Carping. Captious; petulant; faultfinding.

Castigate. Correct by punishing; criticize severely.
Ant.: Extol; glorify; exalt.

Catholic. Universal; wide-ranging; all encompassing.
Ant.: Provincial; parochial; narrow; illiberal; unsophisticated.

Caustic. Severely critical/sarcastic; capable of burning, corroding, destroying living tissue.
Ant.: Emollient; soothing to living tissue.

Cauterize. Burn for curative purposes with iron, fire, or caustic.

Cavalier. Haughty, disdainful; unceremonious; supercilious.

Cavil. Carp; nitpick; raise inconsequential objections.

Censure. Reprimand vehemently; reproach harshly; express strong disapproval.
Ant.: Commend; approve; applaud; praise.

Chaff. Mock; tease; banter; husks separated from grain during threshing; worthless matter; refuse.

Chagrin. Vexation from humiliation or disappointment.

Charlatan. Quack; imposter; mountebank; fraud.

Chasm. Gorge; abyss; fissure; interruption or gap.

Chaste. Decent; undefiled; stainless; virtuous; not obscene.
Ant.: Salacious.

Chastise. Discipline; punish.
Ant.: Commend; applaud; reward.

Chauvinist. Zealous, belligerent patriot; prejudiced devotee of any attitude or cause.

Chiaroscuro. Distribution of light and shade in a picture.

Chide. Scold; rebuke; find fault.
Ant.: Approve; esteem; acclaim; credit.

Chiromancy. The art of divination by analyzing the appearance of the hand; palmistry.

Chromatic. In music, progressing by semitones; pertaining to color.

Circumspect. Discreet; cautious; prudent.
Ant.: Indecorous; indiscreet; unseemly; improper.

Clarify. To make clear.
Ant.: Obfuscate.

Coalesce. Unite; blend; fuse; grow into one.
Ant.: Disintegrate; disjoin; separate; decompose.

Codicil. Supplement to a will; any similar supplement; an appendix; clause with change or modification.
Ant.: Deletion; removal; erasure; eradication.

Coercion. Intimidation by threat or duress; forceful compulsion.
Ant.: Persuasion; inducing belief through appeal to reason and understanding.

Coeval. Of the same age or duration; contemporary with.

Cogent. To the point; relevant.
Ant.: Irrelevant; not pertinent.

Cohort. Companion; associate.

Comatose. In a coma; lethargic; lacking energy.

Comely. Pretty; fair; pleasing in appearance.
Ant.: Unattractive; plain; unpretentious; not beautiful.

Commodious. Spacious; roomy.
Ant.: Cramped; confined; contracted; narrow.

Compunction. Contrition; uneasiness about the rightness of an action; remorse for wrongdoing.
Ant.: Remorseless; unscrupulous; conscienceless.

Concatenation. A linking together.
Ant.: Discontinuity; unlinked; gap or break.

Conciliatory. Placatory; propitiating; pacific.
Ant.: Contentious; disputatious.

Concise. Succinct; terse.
Ant.: Prolix; long-winded; wordy; verbose.

Concur. Agree; coincide; work together.
Ant.: Demur; object (esp. on grounds of scruples); take exception.

Conflagration. Large, destructive fire.

Conflagrative. Combustible; flammable, inflammable (note that these two words both have the same meaning).
Ant.: Incombustible; *not* flammable.

Connoisseur. Expert in art, the fine arts, and/or in matters of taste.

Consonant. In agreement; corresponding in sound; in harmony.
Ant.: Dissonant; discordant; disagreeing; harsh in sound; out of harmony.

Contentious. Quarrelsome; disputatious.
Ant.: Conciliatory.

Continent. Restrained in regard to desires or passions.
Ant.: Lustful; unrestrained in regard to sexual desires, etc.; motivated by lust, greed or the like.

Contumacious. Contrary; refractory; stubbornly perverse; obstinately rebellious or disobedient.
Ant.: Pliant; unresisting; compliant; obedient.

Coolie. Unskilled low-paid laborer in or from the Orient.

Cooper. Barrel-maker.

Copious. Abundant; fullness (as of thoughts and words).
Ant.: Scanty; inadequate; meager; insufficient.

Coronary. Relating to the heart (with respect to health); crownlike.

Corroborate. Confirm; substantiate; certify; make more certain.
Ant.: Contradict; gainsay; dispute; controvert; deny directly and categorically.

Coruscate. Sparkle; scintillate; gleam; emit vivid flashes of light.

Cosmopolitan. Belonging to all the world; free from local, provincial, or national ideas, prejudices, or attachments; a citizen of the world.
Ant.: Provincial; narrow; illiberal; unsophisticated.

Coterie. Clique; set; group of associates who are close because of common social purposes or interests.

Covetous. Greedy; grasping; avaricious.

Credulity. Gullibility; readiness to believe without

proper evidence.
Ant.: Acumen.

Crescendo. Gradual increase in force, volume, loudness.
Ant.: Diminuendo; gradual decrease in force, volume, loudness.

Crestfallen. Dejected; disspirited; depressed.
Ant.: Exuberant; abounding in vitality.

Cuneiform. Wedge-shaped; wedge-shaped writing of the Assyrians and Babylonians.

Cupidity. Avarice; greed; covetousness.
Ant.: Unselfishness; liberality; magnaminity.

Curmudgeon. Churl; irascible person.

Cynosure. Center of interest; something that strongly attracts attention by its brilliance, interest, etc.

Dearth. Scarcity; shortage; lack; famine.
Ant.: Plenitude; abundance; fullness; adequacy.

Debacle. Sudden collapse; general breakup; violent rush of waters or ice.

Decalogue. Ten Commandments.

Decelerate. Slow down.

Deciduous. Shedding leaves annually; transitory; not permanent.
Ant.: Coniferous; not leaf shedders; evergreen cone bearers.

Decorous. Proper; seemly; sedate; characterized by propriety.
Ant.: Unseemly; inappropriate; unbecoming.

Decry. Belittle; disparage; discredit.
Ant.: Praise; commend.

Delete. Erase; remove; expunge.
Ant.: Insert; put in.

Deleterious. Hurtful; harmful; injurious.
Ant.: *See* **Beneficial**.

Deluge. Flood; downpour; great flood; anything that overwhelms like a flood.

Demur. *See* **Concur**.

Deplete. Exhaust or seriously decrease.

Deploy. Spread out or array strategically.

Despondent. Morose; depressed; low-spirited.
Ant.: *See* **Ebullient**.

Destitute. Indigent; poor; without means of subsistence.
Ant.: *See* **Affluent**.

Desultory. Disconnected; fitful; random; lacking in order.
Ant.: Concatenate; link together.

Dexterous. Skillful; adept.
Ant.: Inept; clumsy; unskilled.

Diametrical. Direct; absolute; complete; pertaining to or along the diameter.

Diatribe. Tirade; bitter, abusive denunciation.
Ant.: Panegyric; oration in praise.

Didactic. Intended for instruction; too inclined to teach, preach, lecture, moralize.

Diffident. Timid; shy; lacking in self-confidence.
Ant.: Bold; resolute; self-assured; confident.

Diffuse. Spread out; scatter widely; disseminate.
Ant.: Focus; concentrate.

Dilatory. Delaying; procrastinating; tardy; slow.
Ant.: Expeditious; prompt; quick; speeded-up.

Dilemma. Perplexing problem; situation requiring a choice between equally undesirable alternatives.

Dilettante. Dabbler; one who takes up an art, activity, etc., merely for amusement, rather than seriously; a lover of an art, esp. a fine art or science.

Diminuendo. *See* **Crescendo**.

Disburse. Expend; pay out; distribute.

Disconsolate. Inconsolable; cheerless; gloomy; sad; melancholy; miserable.

Discreet. Judicious; circumspect; tactful; diplomatic.

Discrete. Separate; distinct; detached from others; discontinuous.
Ant.: *See* **Integral**.

Disingenuous. *See* **Candid**.

Disparagement. *See* **Adulation**.

Disparate. *See* **Analogous**.

Disport. To display oneself; to divert or amuse oneself.

Dissonant. *See* **Consonant**.

Dissuade. Persuade not to do something.
Ant.: Persuade.

Doldrums. State of inactivity or stagnation; low spirits; a dull, listless, depressed mood.

Dolt. Blockhead; dull, stupid person.

Doting. Bestowing excessive love or fondness on.

Doughty. Steadfastly courageous and resolute.
Ant.: See **Pusillanimous**.

Dregs. Lees; grounds; a small remnant; the least valuable parts of anything.

Duplicity. Deceitfulness; double-dealing; a double state or quantity of something.
Ant.: Straightforwardness; honesty; lack of deceit.

Duress. Coercion; constraint; forcible restraint; compulsion by threat.

Ebullient. High-spirited; overflowing with enthusiasm; boiling up.
Ant.: See **Despondent**.

Eccentric. Person with unusual or odd personality, set of beliefs, or behavior pattern; something unusual, peculiar, or odd.

Ecclesiastical. Clerical (as opposed to lay); of the church or clergy.
Ant.: Laic; not clerical.

Ecstatic. Rapturous; delightful.

Educe. Infer; deduce; draw forth; bring out.

Effeminate. *See* **Virile**.

Effete. Decadent; lacking in wholesome vigor; worn out; unable to produce; sterile.
Ant.: See **Puissant**.

Effulgent. Radiant; shining forth brilliantly.

Effusive. Unduly demonstrative; pouring out; overflowing.
Ant.: Reserved; reticent; distant; cold; self-restrained.

Egregious. Flagrant; notorious; remarkable in some bad way.

Élan. Dash; impetuous ardor.

Elation. Great joy or gladness; high spirits; exultant gladness.
Ant.: Somberness; gloom; depression; extreme gravity.

Elegy. A lament for the dead.

Emanate. Emit; send forth; flow out; issue forth.

Emancipate. Free from bondage; free from restraint or influence.
Ant.: Enslave; put into bondage; to make a slave of.

Emollient. *See* **Caustic**.

Empathy. Identification with or vicarious experiencing of the feelings, thoughts, etc., of another.

Encomium. Formal expression of high praise; eulogy.
Ant.: See **Slander**.

Encumber. Impede; hinder; hamper; retard; burden or weigh down.

Enervate. Weaken; enfeeble; exhaust; deprive of strength; destroy the vigor of.

Enigma. A puzzle; a person of contradictory traits.

Enjoin. Direct or order someone to do something.

Ennui. Boredom; weariness or discontent stemming from satiety or lack of interest.

Enslavement. *See* **Manumission**.

Ephemeral. Transitory; short-lived; fleeting.
Ant.: Enduring; long-lasting.

Equine. Relating to horses; a horse; horselike.

Equinox. Time of equal day and night: occurs about March 21 or September 21.

Equitable. Reasonable; just and right.
Ant.: Unfair; inequitable.

Eradicate. To root out; remove completely; annihilate.

Erudite. Learned; scholarly.
Ant.: Unlettered; uneducated; illiterate; ignorant.

Esoteric. Recondite; known only to a few.
Ant.: Commonplace; ordinary.

Espouse. To adopt or make one's own (as a cause); to take in marriage.

Essence. Core; soul; intrinsic nature.

Estivate. To spend the summer, as at a specific place; (*zool.*) to pass the summer in a torpid state.
Ant.: See **Hibernate**.

Ethereal. Light; airy; tenuous; heavenly; celestial; extremely delicate or refined; of the upper regions of space.

Ant.: Earthy; robust; practical; coarse; unrefined.

Eulogy. High praise; encomium; speech or writing that praises.

Evanescent. Vanishing; fleeting; tending to become imperceptible. *See also* **Ephemeral**.
Ant.: Enduring; long-lasting.

Evoke. Elicit; summon; call up.

Exacerbate. *See* **Mollify**.

Exculpate. Absolve; vindicate; free from blame.
Ant.: Incriminate; involve.

Exemplar. Model; pattern; typical example or instance.

Exhort. Urge; advise; admonish.

Exhume. Disinter; bring to light; revive.
Ant.: *See* **Inter**.

Exigency. Emergency; something that needs prompt attention.

Exiguous. Scanty; meager; small.

Exodus. Departure; emigration (usually of a large number of people); second book of the Bible; the departure of the Israelites from Egypt.

Exonerate. Free from blame; exculpate. *See also* **Absolve**.
Ant.: Incriminate.

Expectoration. Spitting; hawking phlegm.

Expedite. Hasten; dispatch; quicken; accelerate; hurry; to speed up the progress of.
Ant.: Delay; hold back; retard; defer; postpone.

Expiration. Termination; ending; breathing out; emission of air from the lungs.

Explicate. Explain; interpret; unfold; make plain; to develop a theory or principle.
Ant.: Obfuscate; make obscure; muddle; perplex; cloud.

Expunge. Erase; efface; wipe out; destroy; blot out.

Extemporize. To improvise; to deliver impromptu; to do in a makeshift way.

Extol. *See* **Castigate; Objurgate**.

Extricate. Disengage; liberate from combination; to free from entanglement.

Extrinsic. Extraneous; external.
Ant.: *See* **Intrinsic**.

Exuberant. *See* **Crestfallen**.

Exultation. Triumphant joy; jubilation.

Fabulous. Incredible; almost unbelievable; marvelous; superb; known through myths and legends.
Ant.: Historical; of history, as opposed to legend or fiction.

Fallible. Liable to err.
Ant.: Infallible; exempt from error; unfailingly effective.

Fathom. Understand fully; measure by sound; six-foot unit of measure.

Fatuous. Inane; silly; illusory; complacently foolish.
Ant.: Judicious; characterized by good judgment; wise; sensible.

Fealty. Sworn allegiance to a lord; fidelity.

Feasible. Workable; practicable; suitable.

Feckless. Feeble; ineffective; worthless; lazy; valueless.

Fecund. Creative; fruitful; fertile; productive.

Feign. Simulate; affect; concoct; pretend.

Ferment. Seethe with agitation or excitement; inflame or foment; biochemical change brought on by yeasts, molds, enzymes, bacteria, etc.

Fervor. Ardor; intensity; passion.
Ant.: Gravity; sobriety; restrained behavior.

Fetid. Stinking; having an offensive odor.

Fetish. Amulet; object believed to have magical power.

Fidelity. Accuracy; faithfulness; loyalty.
Ant.: Perfidy; faithlessness; a deliberate breach of trust.

Fission. Cleaving or splitting into parts.

Flag. Diminish in vigor; droop; pave with flagstones.

Flagellate. Whip; scourge; flog; lash.

Flaunt. Parade or display ostentatiously.

Flock. Animals keeping together in large numbers such as birds, sheep, and goats. Terms used for other animal groups: pack of wolves; gaggle of geese; herd of elephants; bevy of quail; covey of partridge; exaltation of larks; shoal of fish; pod of whales; swarm of bees, etc.

Flora. Plants of a particular region or period.

Flout. Treat with disdain, scorn, or contempt; scoff at; mock.

Flux. Continuous change; instability; fusion.
  Ant.: Stability; permanence; resistance to change.

Foment. Instigate; foster (rebellion, etc.).

Footpad. Robber who goes on foot.

Foreboding. Presentiment; portent.

Fortissimo. (*Mus.*) very loud.
  Ant.: (*Mus.*) pianissimo—very soft.

Frippery. Gewgaws; trifles; empty display; ostentation.

Frivolous. Lack of seriousness or sense; paltry; trivial.
  Ant.: *See* **Grave**.

Furtive. Stealthy; sly; shifty.

Fusion. Uniting by melting together; a blending or merging as if by melting.

Galvanize. Startle into sudden activity; to coat with zinc.

Gamut. Entire scale or range.

Garrulous. Verbose; wordy; excessively talkative.
  Ant.: Reticent; taciturn; reserved in speech.

Gauche. Awkward; tactless; lacking social grace.

Gauge. Appraise; estimate; measure; device for measuring; distance between wheels on an axle.

Geegaw. Bauble; trifle.

Germane. Relevant; pertinent.

Glutton. Excessive eater; one with great capacity for doing something (work).

Gondola. Venetian boat powered by single oarsman in stern; car of a dirigible.

Gourmand. Gourmet; epicure; glutton.

Gourmet. Connoisseur of fine food and wine; epicure.

Grave. Solemn; serious; sedate; dignified; staid.
  Ant.: *See* **Frivolous**.

Graven. Carved; deeply impressed; firmly fixed.

Gregarious. Sociable; fond of company.

Halcyon. Peaceful; calm; tranquil; joyful; carefree; wealthy; prosperous.
  Ant.: Tumultuous; turbulent; state of agitation; ill-omened; unlucky.

Hallucinate. Experience something sensorily that does not exist outside the mind.

Harbinger. Herald; omen; a foreshadow; advance man.

Harking. Listening; hearing.

Hauteur. Haughtiness.

Hedonist. *See* **Ascetic**.

Heinous. Hateful; odious; abominable; totally reprehensible.

Herbivorous. Feeding on plants. *See* **Carnivore**.

Heretic. A professed believer who holds opinions contrary to those of his church; anyone who does not conform with an established attitude, doctrine, or principle.
  Ant.: Orthodox; conforming to attitudes, doctrines, or principles that are generally approved.

Hiatus. Gap; missing part; break in continuity; lacuna.

Hibernate. To spend the winter in a dormant state; to withdraw to seclusion; to retire.
  Ant.: *See* **Estivate**.

Hierarchy. Any system of persons or things rated one above the other.

Hieroglyphic. Pictographic script, esp. ancient Egyptian; hard to decipher.

Hip. (Slang); informed; knowledgeable; up on the latest.

Histrionics. Acting; theatricals; artificial behavior or speech done for effect.

Hodgepodge. Jumble; heterogeneous mixture.

Holocaust. Devastation; a sacrifice totally consumed by fire.

Homely. Unattractive; plain; unpretentious; not beautiful.

Homologous. Corresponding; same or similar relation.

Hone. Sharpen.

Hubbub. Tumult; uproar; loud confused noise or disturbance.

Humble. Modest; courteously respectful; unpretentious.
Ant.: See **Pompous**.

Hurly-burly. Uproar; tumult; commotion.

Hyperbola. Curve with two distinct and similar branches.

Hyperbole. Intentional or obvious exaggeration; excess.
Ant.: Understatement; less strong expression than the facts would bear out; expressed in restrained or weak terms.

Hypercritical. Captiously critical; excessively fault-finding.

Iconoclast. Attacker of traditions; destroyer of images or idols.
Ant.: Iconolater—worshipper of idols or traditions.

Idol. Favorite; pet; any person or thing devotedly or excessively admired; an image or object worshipped as a deity.

Idolater. Hero worshipper; worshipper of idols; devotee.

Illicit. Unlicensed; unlawful.
Ant.: Legal; licit; permitted by law.

Imago. An adult insect.

Imbroglio. Bitter disagreement; confused state of affairs.

Immiscible. Incapable of being mixed.
Ant.: Mixable.

Immutable. Unchangeable; unalterable; changeless.

Impeccable. Faultless; irreproachable; not liable to sin.

Impermeable. Impenetrable; impassable.

Impervious. Incapable of being impaired; impermeable.

Implicate. *See* **Absolve**.

Imply. Hint; indicate without express statement.

Impolitic. Unwise; inexpedient; injudicious. *See also* **Fatuous**.
Ant.: Judicious.

Impress. Force (into public service); seize (for public use).

Impromptu. Extemporaneous; improvised; unprepared; made or done without previous preparation.
Ant.: Planned.

Imprudent. Improvident; not wise; indiscreet.
Ant.: See **Judicious**.

Impudent. Rude; saucy; presumptuous; brazen; bold; shameless.
Ant.: Courteous.

Inadvertent. Heedless; unintentional; negligent; thoughtlessness.
Ant.: Provident; proceeding from foresight; acting with prudence.

Inane. Pointless; silly; foolish.

Incarcerate. Imprison; confine; enclose; constrict.

Incarnadine. Blood-red; crimson; flesh color; pale pink.

Inception. Outset; start; origin; beginning.

Inchoate. Rudimentary; incipient; not organized.

Incinerate. Burn; reduce to ashes.

Incipient. Initial; beginning.

Incite. Foment; provoke; goad; arouse.
Ant.: Discourage.

Incombustible. *See* **Conflagrative**.

Incorporeal. Unsubstantial; not material.

Incorrigible. Bad beyond reform; uncorrectible; impervious to punishment.

Incorruptible. Incapable of being bribed or perverted.
Ant.: See **Venal**.

Incriminate. Inculpate; implicate; accuse; charge with a crime or fault.
Ant.: See **Exculpate**.

Incumbent (upon). Obligatory; holder of an office; leaning upon.

Indecorous. *See* **Circumspect.**

Indigenous. Native; natural; innate; aboriginal; inherent.
Ant.: Alien; strange; noncitizen; not native.

Indigent. Destitute; impoverished; needy.

Indisputable. Incontrovertible; incontestable; undeniable.
Ant.: *See* **Moot.**

Ineffable. Inexpressible; unutterable; indescribable.

Ineluctable. Inescapable; incapable of being evaded.

Inept. *See* **Dexterous.**

Inexorable. Implacable; relentless; unyielding.
Ant.: Flexible; merciful.

Infallible. *See* **Fallible.**

Infamous. Disreputable; notorious; scandalous; nefarious.

Infer. Conclude or deduce from evidence.

Ingenious. Bright; gifted; able; inventive.

Ingenuous. Artless; innocent; naive; candid.

Inherent. Innate; native; inbred; ingrained.

Iniquitous. Sinful; wicked; nefarious; base.

Injudicious. *See* **Judicious** and **Imprudent.**
Ant.: *See* **Astute.**

Inordinate. Immoderate; disproportionate.
Ant.: Reasonable.

Insidious. Crafty; wily; deceitful; intended to beguile.

Insipid. Pointless; vapid; flat; dull.

Inspiration. Inhalation; taking of air into lungs; stimulus.

Insular. Detached; isolated; illiberal; of an island.

Insulated. Covered; surrounded; separated with nonconducting material; isolated.

Intangible. Incorporeal; incapable of being perceived through the sense of touch.
Ant.: *See* **Tactile.**

Integral. Entire; whole; essential.
Ant.: *See* **Discrete.**

Inter. Bury.

Ant.: *See* **Exhume.**

Interdiction. Prohibition; prevention from participation in certain sacred acts.

Intern. Restrict; confine; impound; apprentice.

Intrepid. Fearless; dauntless.
Ant.: Timorous; fearful; timid; pusillanimous.

Intrinsic. Innate; true; natural.
Ant.: Extrinsic; extraneous; external.

Inundation. Deluge; flood; anything overwhelming.

Inure. Toughen; harden; habituate.

Invertebrate. Without a backbone; spineless; without strength of character.

Invidious. Offensive; injurious.

Irascible. Testy; touchy; irritable; choleric.

Irreconcilable. Firmly opposed; incapable of being made to compromise.
Ant.: *See* **Placable.**

Jayhawker. Plundering marauder.

Jejune. Immature; juvenile; dull; dry; insipid.

Jubilation. Exultation; rejoicing.

Judicious. Prudent; wise; sagacious; reasonable.
Ant.: *See* **Imprudent.**

Kleptomania. Irresistible impulse to steal.

Kudos. Praise; glory.

Labial. Of the lips.

Laconic. Concise; terse; succinct; expressing much in few words.
Ant.: Wordy; voluble; verbose.

Lacuna. Gap; hiatus.

Laic. Not clerical.
Ant.: *See* **Ecclesiastical.**

Lariat. Lasso; long, noosed rope.

Larva. Immature stage of an insect; any animal in an analogous immature form.

Lascivious. Lewd, wanton; arousing sexual desire.

Laud. Praise; extol.

Lax. Careless; negligent; loose; vague; not rigid.

Leeward. The side toward which the wind blows; the sheltered side.
  Ant.: Windward; the side from which the wind blows; toward that direction.

Leonine. Of or about lions; resembling a lion.

Lethargic. Drowsy; sluggish; apathetic.
  Ant.: Alert; keen; vigilantly attentive.

Levity. Lightness of character, mind, or behavior.

Lewd. Obscene; vulgar; low; characterized by lust.

Libel. Written defamation; anything defamatory.

Limpid. Clear; transparent (as water or air); pellucid; lucid; completely calm.

Lipid. Fat; other esters with analogous properties.

Lissome. Supple; nimble; agile; limber.

Lithe. Pliant; flexible; easily bent.

Loquacious. Talkative; garrulous.
  Ant.: *See* **Laconic.**

Low. Mean; base; to moo; calling sound of cattle; deficient in vital energy.

Lucid. Clear; bright; shining; pellucid; easily understood.

Ludicrous. Laughable; ridiculous; laughably incongruous.

Lugubrious. Mournful; dismal; gloomy; excessively sorrowful (sometimes feigned).

Lustful. Lecherous; zestful; passionately yearning; motivated by greed or sexual appetite.

Machete. Heavy knife used in cutting undergrowth or cane.

Macroscopic. Large enough to be observed by the human eye.
  Ant.: Microscopic.

Malefactor. Criminal; evil-doer; offender; culprit.
  Ant.: *See* **Benefactor.**

Malfeasance. Wrongdoing; official misconduct; illegal deed.

Malign. Defame; vilify; calumniate; slander; having an evil disposition; sinister; baleful.
  Ant.: *See* **Benign.**

Malignant. Harmful dangerous; malevolent.
  Ant.: Benign.

Malingering. Shirking; avoiding duty through pretense of illness.

Mandate. Command; authorize; fiat; injunction; decree.

Manumission. Freeing; release; releasing from slavery.
  Ant.: Enslavement.

Marital. Connubial; conjugal; of or about marriage.

Marrow. Inmost or essential part; tissue in the inner cavity of bones.

Marsupial. Pertaining to a pouch; any mammal that nurses or carries young in a marsupium.

Martial. Warlike; soldierly; pertaining to war.

Mature. Fully developed in mind and body; ripe; fully aged.
  Ant.: Puerile; immature.

Maudlin. Mawkish; tearfully sentimental from too much liquor; effusively sentimental.

Meager. Sparse; scanty; spare; exiguous; lacking richness.
  Ant.: Opulent; rich; affluent; abundant.

Medieval. Of the Middle Ages.

Mercenary. Venal; acquisitive; covetous; hired for service; acting only for a reward; a professional soldier serving in a foreign army solely for pay.
  Ant.: *See* **Altruism.**

Mercurial. Active; lively; sprightly; volatile; changeable; fickle; flightly; erratic.
  Ant.: *See* **Stolid.**

Meridian. Highest point; midday; period of greatest splendor or prosperity; great circle of the earth, passing through the poles and any other given point.

Mete. Dole; measure out; parcel out; deal; allot; boundary; limiting mark.

Miasma. Noxious exhalations (from putrescent organic matter); foreboding influences.

Microscopic. Too small to be seen by the unassisted human eye.
  Ant.: Macroscopic.

Millenium. Thousand years; period of general happiness (esp. in the indefinite future).

Mellifluous. Honeyed; sweet-sounding.
Ant.: Cacophonous.

Misanthropy. Hatred or distrust of mankind.

Miscegenation. Marriage between those of different races.

Misogamy. Hatred of marriage.

Misogynist. Woman-hater.

Mixable. Able to be mixed.
Ant.: See **Immiscible.**

Mollify. Pacify; appease; mitigate; reduce.
Ant.: Exacerbate; aggravate.

Moot. Doubtful; debatable; hypothetical; purely academic; unsettled.
Ant.: Indisputable; incontrovertible; incontestable; undeniable.

Moraine. A deposit of gravel and other materials carried by a glacier.

Morass. Marsh; bog.

Morbid. Gruesome; grisly; unwholesomely gloomy; pertaining to diseased parts.
Ant.: Wholesome.

Mordant. Sarcastic; caustic.

Moribund. Dying; stagnant; on the verge of extinction.

Mufti. Civilian dress as worn by one who usually wears a uniform; religious head of a Muslim community.

Mummer. Actor; pantomimist.

Mundane. Common; ordinary; banal; of everyday concerns of the world.

Munificent. Very generous.
Ant.: Parsimonious; stingy.

Mystical. Occult; mysterious; spiritually symbolic.

Nadir. Lowest point.
Ant.: Zenith—highest point.

Naive. Unsophisticated; ingenuous; lacking experience.
Ant.: Sophisticated; worldly-wise; deceptive; misleading; complex; intricate.

Nebulous. Hazy; vague; indistinct.

Necromancy. Magic; witchcraft; conjuration; divination through communication with the dead.

Nefarious. Iniquitous; extremely wicked; heinous; vile.

Nepotism. Favoritism or patronage based upon family relationship.

Nescient. Ignorant; agnostic.

Neurotic. One affected with an emotional disorder involving anxiety, compulsion, etc.

Niggardly. Stingy.

Noisome. Offensive; disgusting; harmful; noxious; stinking.
Ant.: Healthful; salubrious.

Nonfeasance. Omission of some act which ought to have been performed.

Nostrum. Quack medicine; pet scheme; favorite remedy; panacea.

Notorious. Widely but unfavorably known; recognized.

Nugatory. Trifling; trivial; frivolous; useless; ineffective.
Ant.: Significant; important; weighty; momentous.

Numismatist. Collector of coins and medals.

Obdurate. Stubborn; unyielding; unmovable; persistently impenitent.
Ant.: Relenting.

Obedient. *See* **Obstreperous.**

Obese. Corpulent; overweight; excessively fat.

Obfuscate. Confuse; cloud; make obscure; stupefy.
Ant.: Clarify; make clear.

Objurgate. Berate sharply; reproach vehemently.
Ant.: Extol; glorify; exalt.

Obliterate. Destroy completely; expunge; efface; remove all traces.

Obloquy. Bad repute; reproach; aspersion; disgrace.

Obsequious. Fawning; servilely deferential; sycophantic.

Obstreperous. Unruly; clamorous; boisterous; uncontrolled.

Ant.: Obedient; compliant; tractable; docile; willing.

Obtuse. Dull.
Ant.: *See* **Perspicacious**.

Officious. Meddling; interfering; objectionably forward in offering unrequested help or advice.
Ant.: Retiring; shy; withdrawing.

Olfactory. Of the sense of smell.

Oligarchy. Government by the few, or by a dominant clique.

Ominous. Threatening; portentous; portending evil or harm.
Ant.: Propitious; auspicious; favorable.

Omniscient. All-knowing.

Omnivore. One who eats both animal and plant food; taking in everything indiscriminately, as with the intellect.

Opalescent. Having a milky irridescence.

Opaque. Not transmitting light; dull; impenetrable; hard to understand.
Ant.: Transparent; easily seen through; transmitting light so that bodies situated beyond or behind can be distinctly seen.

Ophthalmic. Pertaining to the functions and diseases of the eye.

Opprobrium. Infamy; disgrace resulting from outrageously shameful conduct.

Opulent. *See* **Meager**.

Ordain. Decree; destine; prescribe; confer holy orders upon.

Ornithologist. One who studies birds.

Orthodox. *See* **Heretic**.

Ostracism. Banishment; exile; exclusion from society, privileges, etc., by general consent.

Otiose. Indolent; futile; superfluous; ineffective; leisured; slothful.

Paean. A song of praise, joy, or triumph; a hymn of thanksgiving.
Ant.: *See* **Tirade**.

Palmistry. *See* **Chiromancy**.

Panegyric. Encomium; formal eulogy or commendation.

Parabola. A conic section, the intersection of a cone with a plane parallel to its side; something bowl-shaped.

Paradigm. Model; pattern; standard; touchstone; paragon; a set of forms containing the same element.

Paradox. Seeming self-contradiction which may be true; a statement contrary to accepted opinion.

Pariah. Outcast; person despised by society; member of a low Indian caste.

Parochial. *See* **Catholic**.

Parricide. Murder of one's parent.

Parsimonious. Stingy; penurious; frugal to excess.
Ant.: *See* **Munificent**.

Parvenu. Upstart; one with recently acquired wealth or position who lacks the "proper" social qualifications.

Pathos. Pity; evoking pity or compassion.

Patrician. Aristocrat; noble; of high birth.
Ant.: *See* **Plebeian**.

Patrimony. Heritage from one's father or other ancestor.

Pecuniary. Financial; monetary; relating to money.

Pedantry. Slavish attention to details; didacticism; excessive formalism; ostentatious display of learning.

Pelage. Hair, fur, wool, or other soft covering of a mammal.

Pelt. Hide or skin of an animal; attack; assail; beat; pound; throw; hurry.

Pensive. Reflective; meditative; dreamily or wistfully thoughtful.

Penurious. *See* **Affluent**.

Peremptory. Arbitrary; dogmatic; arrogant; incontrovertible; imperious; decisive; leaving no chance for refusal or denial.

Perfidy. *See* **Fidelity**.

Perigee. *See* **Apogee**.

Peripatetic. Wandering; roving; vagrant; itinerant;

pertaining to the Aristotelian school of philosophy.

Peripheral. External; outside; superficial; not concerned with the essential.
Ant.: Central; at the core.

Perjure. Swear falsely; lie under oath.

Perquisites. Fringe benefits or bonuses granted an employee; incidental gain additional to regular wages.

Perspicacious. Shrewd; discerning; perceptive; acute; astute.
Ant.: Obtuse; dull.

Peruse. Read; read critically or thoroughly.
Ant.: Skim; to read in a cursory way.

Pessimistic. Gloomy; hopeless; anticipating only the worse.
Ant.: *See* **Sanguine**.

Pewter. Any alloy having tin as its chief constituent.

Philatelist. One who collects and studies stamps.

Philogyny. Fondness for women.
Ant.: Misogyny; hatred of women.

Physiognomy. The face; external aspect; countenance.

Pianissimo. (*Mus.*) very soft.
Ant.: (Mus.) fortissimo—very loud.

Pious. Devout; reverent; godly.
Ant.: *See* **Sanctimonious**.

Piquant. Pungent; spicy; intriguing; provocative; pleasantly sharp or tart.
Ant.: Insipid; pointless; vapid; flat; dull.

Pique. Offense; dudgeon; fit of resentment; provoke; nettle; challenge; goad; arouse resentment.

Pisces. Class of vertebrates comprising fish; twelfth sign of the Zodiac—the Fish.

Piscine. Of or like fish.

Pithy. Concise; substantial; succinct; tersely cogent.
Ant.: Verbose; garrulous. *See* **Prolix**.

Placable. Conciliatory; forgiving; appeasable.
Ant.: *See* **Irreconcilable**.

Placebo. Substance, having no pharmaceutical effect, given to soothe or appease the patient.

Plebeian. Common; vulgar; commonplace; belonging to the common people.
Ant.: *See* **Patrician**.

Plenitude. Abundance; fullness; adequacy.
Ant.: *See* **Dearth**.

Plethora. Excess; abundance; state of being overfull.
Ant.: *See* **Dearth**.

Pliant. Unresisting; compliant; obedient.
Ant.: *See* **Contumacious**.

Pompous. Showy; ostentatious; self-important.
Ant.: *See* **Humble**.

Portentous. Ominous; momentous; significant; inauspicious.
Ant.: Propitious; favorable.

Poser. Puzzle; baffling question; one who poses.

Practicable. Possible; feasible; usable; capable of being put into practice.

Pragmatism. Philosophy stressing practical consequences and values; character which stresses practicality.

Predatory. Rapacious; living by plunder; preying upon other animals.

Preemptive. Appropriating; usurping; acquiring before someone else.

Presto. Rapid; immediately; at a rapid tempo.

Primeval. Primordial; of the first ages (of the earth).

Proboscis. An elephant's trunk; any long, flexible snout.

Procrastination. Deferring; delaying; putting off till another time.

Prodigal. Spendthrift; profligate; wastefully extravagant; wastrel; waster.
Ant.: Thrifty; parsimonious.

Prodigy. One with extraordinary talent or ability; something wonderful; something monstrous.

Prognosticate. Forecast; foretoken; prophecy.

Proliferation. Excessive rapid spread.

Prolix. Long-winded; wordy; verbose.
Ant.: *See* **Concise**.

Propitious. Favorable; auspicious.
Ant.: *See* **Ominous**.

Proscribe. Denounce; condemn; prohibit; outlaw.

Prosthetic. An artificial part to supply a defect of the body.

Protean. Variable; readily assuming different shapes.

Provident. Proceeding from foresight; acting with prudence.
  Ant.: See **Inadvertent**.

Provincial. Narrow; illiberal.
  Ant.: See **Catholic**.

Prudery. Excessive modesty.

Psychotic. Person with a severe mental disorder, or having a disease affecting the total personality.

Puce. Dark or brownish purple.

Puerile. Childishly foolish; boyish; juvenile.
  Ant.: See **Mature**.

Pugnacious. Quarrelsome; argumentative; contentious; excessively inclined to fight.
  Ant.: Agreeable; peaceable.

Puissant. Powerful; might; potent.
  Ant.: See **Effete**.

Pullulate. Sprout; teem; breed; multiply; swarm; germinate.

Pulmonary. Of the lungs.

Pulverize. Demolish; crush; reduce to dust; pound or grind.

Pupa. Stage between larva and imago in an insect.

Purblind. Dim-sighted; partially blind; slow in imagination, understanding, vision.

Purveyance. Act of supplying provisions.

Purview. Range of authority; scope; range of vision, sight, or understanding.

Pusillanimous. Cowardly in spirit; timorous; fearful.
  Ant.: See **Intrepid**; **Doughty**.

Pyromania. Compulsion to set things on fire.

Quack. Charlatan; fraudulent pretender to medical skill.

Quaff. Drink copiously and heartily.

Quagmire. A bog; a situation from which extrication is very difficult.

Qualm. Misgiving; compunction; pang of conscience; sudden onset of illness (esp. nausea).

Quarter. Region or district; one-fourth; one of the four principal points of the compass; to lodge and feed; mercy or indulgence; to traverse ground from left to right and right to left while advancing.

Quell. Suppress; vanquish; subdue; extinguish.

Quench. Slake, satisfy, or allay thirst, hunger, passions, etc.; extinguish; cool suddenly; overcome.

Querulous. Complaining; peevish; petulant; testy.

Quirk. Peculiarity; evasion; sudden twist or turn; mannerism.

Quotidian. Daily; everyday; ordinary; recurring daily.

Raconteur. One skilled in telling tales or anecdotes.

Raillery. Banter; badinage; satirical pleasantry; good-humored ridicule.

Rallentando. (*Mus.*) gradually slowing tempo.

Rancorous. Intensely malignant; vehemently antagonistic; filled with spite or ill-will; full of enmity.
  Ant.: Benign. *See also* **Benevolent**.

Reata. *See* **Lariat**.

Rebuke. Reprove; reprimand; censure; admonish.

Recalcitrant. Rebellious; opposed; resistant; refractory.

Recidivism. Repeated or habitual relapse; chronic tendency toward repeated criminal or antisocial behavior patterns.
  Ant.: **Rehabilitation**; restoration of good reputation and or standing; restoration to a condition of good health or the like.

Recondite. Abstruse; deep; difficult; profound; obscure; little known; beyond ordinary understanding; esoteric; secret.
  Ant.: Commonplace. *See* **Abstruse**; **Esoteric**.

Redemption. Deliverance; rescue; repurchase; salvation; recovery of something pledged; conversion.

Regicide. Killing of a king; killer of a king.

Rejuvenate. Restore to youthful vigor; refresh; renew.

Relinquish. Renounce; surrender; yield: resign; abdicate.

Remonstrate. Object; expostulate; plead in protest.

Repine. Grumble; fret; complain.

Replenish. Supply with fresh fuel; refill.

Reprehend. Rebuke; censure; blame; reproach; admonish; chide; upbraid.

Repugnance. Aversion; objection; antipathy.
Ant.: Attraction.

Rescind. Abrogate; annul; revoke; repeal; invalidate by later action.

Resuscitation. Revival, especially from apparent death.

Retiring. Shy; withdrawing.
Ant.: Forward. *See* **Officious**.

Revilement. Verbal abuse.
Ant.: *See* **Adulation**.

Rickshaw. Jinrikisha; a small two-wheeled passenger vehicle formerly drawn by one man on foot, currently drawn by a man on a bicycle.

Roister. Revel noisily; swagger boisterously.

Ruminant. Contemplative; cud-chewing; any even-toed, cloven-hoofed, cud-chewing quadruped.

Sagacious. Wise; sage; discerning; showing acute mental discernment.
Ant.: Injudicious. *See also* **Astute; Impolitic**.

Salacious. Lustful; lecherous; obscene; grossly indecent; pornographic.
Ant.: *See* **Chaste**.

Salubrious. Healthful; wholesome; favorable to health.
Ant.: *See* **Noisome**.

Salutatory. Greeting; welcoming address at a commencement.

Samisen. Guitarlike Japanese stringed musical instrument.

Sanctimonious. Hypocritical; pietistic; hypocritical show of piety or righteousness.
Ant.: *See* **Pious**.

Sanction. Authorize; approve; allow; ratify; confirm; enact as a penalty for disobedience, or as a reward for obedience.

Sanguinary. Bloodthirsty; characterized by bloodshed.

Sanguine. Cheerful; hopeful; confident; reddish; ruddy.
Ant.: *See* **Pessimistic**.

Sardonic. Biting; mordant; contemptuous; characterized by scornful derision.

Sartorial. Of or about tailors or tailoring.

Saturnine. Gloomy; sluggish in temperament; suffering from lead poisoning.

Satyr. A lecher; a lascivious man; a woodland deity, part human, part goat.

Savanna. Grassland with scattered trees; a plain with coarse grasses, usually in tropical or subtropical regions.

Scathing. Injurious; searingly harmful; bitterly severe.

Scavenger. Animals that feed on dead organic matter; a street cleaner.

Scepter. A rod; emblem of regal power; sovereignty.

Scintilla. Minute trace; jot; a spark; a minute particle.

Scour. Range over; move rapidly; cleanse or polish by rubbing; remove dirt.

Scourge. Whip; lash; punish; chastise; criticize severely; the cause of affliction or calamity.

Scruple. Qualm; compunction; a very small amount—an apothecary's unit of weight; moral or ethical restriction that acts as a restraining force.

Seething. Surging; foaming; boiling; steeping; soaking; act of being agitated or excited; frothing.

Senile. Referring to loss of faculties due to old age.

Servile. Obsequious; fawning; cringing; sycophantic; slavishly submissive.
Ant.: *See* **Aggressive**.

Significant. Important; weighty; momentous.
Ant.: *See* **Nugatory**.

Similitude. Likeness; resemblance; semblance; comparison; parable or allegory.

Sinister. Portending evil; threatening; malevolent; on the left; unfavorable.
Ant.: Auspicious; favorable; propitious.

Sitar. Lute of India.

Skim. Glance over; read in a cursory way.
  Ant.: *See* **Peruse**.

Slander. Defame orally; defamation; calumny.
  Ant.: *See* **Encomium**.

Sloth. Indolence; laziness; habitual disinclination to exertion; a sluggish arboreal animal.

Slough. Swamp; mire; marshy pool; condition of degradation; the outer layer of the skin of a snake; a discard; get rid of; dispose of; shed; molt.

Sobriety. Restrained behavior.
  Ant.: *See* **Fervor**.

Solecism. Breach of good manners or etiquette; error in propriety or consistency; substandard grammatical usage.

Soliloquy. Talking as if alone; utterance by a person talking to himself.

Somber. Grave; gloomily dark; shadowy; dull; murky; sunless; melancholy.
  Ant.: Exuberant; extremely joyful; jubilant.

Sophisticated. Worldly-wise; complex or intricate; deceptive; misleading.
  Ant.: *See* **Naive**.

Soporific. Causing sleep; of or about sleep; drowsy.

Sordid. Dirty; squalid; wretchedly poor; morally ignoble or base; vile; degraded; self-seeking; mercenary.
  Ant.: Honorable; cheerful; generous; clean.

Sororicide. Killing of one's sister; one who kills one's own sister.

Spectrum. An ordered array of entities; an array; band of colors produced when sunlight is passed through a prism; a broad range of varied but related ideas.

Squall. To cry; to scream violently; a sudden disturbance or commotion; a sudden violent wind, accompanied by snow, or sleet.

Stability. Permanence; resistance to change.
  Ant.: *See* **Flux**.

Stable. Reliable; steady; enduring; permanent; resistant to sudden change or deterioration.
  Ant.: *See* **Volatile**.

Steer. A castrated bull.

Stigmatize. Mark with a brand; set a mark of disgrace upon; characterize in marked manner as unfavorable; to produce stigmata, marks, etc.

Stoical. Impassive; imperturbable; characterized by calm, austere fortitude.

Stolid. Unemotional; immovable; dull; stupid; phlegmatic; not easily stirred.
  Ant.: Mercurial; lively; sprightly; volatile; fickle; flighty; erratic.

Stratum. Layer; level; single bed of sedimentary rock; one of a number of parallel levels.

Stringent. Strict; severe; compelling; urgent; forceful; exacting; rigorously binding.
  Ant.: Lax; slack; not rigid; lenient.

Strop. Sharpen; strip of leather used for sharpening razors.

Suavity. Sophistication; worldliness; smoothly agreeable manners.

Sumptuous. Splendid; superb; luxuriously fine; entailing great expense.

Supine. Inactive; passive; lying on the back; inert.

Supplant. Replace; remove; succeed; overthrow.

Suppliant. Petitioner; supplicant.

Surreptitious. Stealthy; sneaky; clandestine; secret; unauthorized; underhanded.

Tacit. Unspoken; silent; implicit; indicated.
  Ant.: Explicit; unequivocal; fully and clearly expressed; leaving nothing merely implied.

Taciturn. Uncommunicative; reticent; dour; stern; habitually silent.
  Ant.: Loquacious; talkative; verbose; garrulous; wordy; voluble.

Tactile. Tangible; perceptible to the touch; or about touch.
  Ant.: Intangible; incorporeal; incapable of being perceived through the sense of touch.

Tangential. Divergent; digressive; erratic; merely contiguous; only slightly connected.

Tedium. Boredom; ennui; tediousness; irksomeness.

Teem. Be prolific; abound; produce; to empty; to pour out; to discharge.

Teleology. The belief that designs are apparent in nature, and that final causes exist.

Temerity. Audacity; effrontery; check; hardihood; rashness; nerve; unreasonable contempt for danger.

Temporal. Secular; transitory; civil or political (as opposed to religious); of or limited by time; pertaining to the present life, or this world.

Tendentious. Showing a definite tendency, bias, or purpose.

Tendril. A shoot; a sprout; a leafless organ of climbing plants.

Tepid. Lukewarm; moderately warm.

Terrain. Milieu; environment; a tract of land, (esp. with reference to its natural features, military advantages, etc.).

Terrestrial. Living/operating on land.

Tetrahedron. A solid figure: a triangular pyramid.

Therapeutic. Curative; treatment and curing of disease.

Thrifty. Frugal; sparing; saving; thriving.
Ant.: See **Prodigal.**

Timorous. Fearful; timid; cowardly.
Ant.: See **Intrepid.**

Tirade. Harangue; diatribe; long vehement speech; bitter outspoken denunciation.
Ant.: Paean; song of praise, joy, or triumph.

Tithe. A tenth part or small part of anything; a tenth part set aside as an offering to God, for works of mercy, or the like; any tax levy, or the like, or one-tenth.

Tittle. Jot; whit; a particle.

Tonsure. The shaven crown or patch worn by monks or ecclesiasts; the act of cutting the hair; the act of shaving the head, or some part of it, as a religious practice or rite.

Torpid. Lethargic; dull; inert; stupid; apathetic; sluggish; dormant.

Torque. That which produces rotation or torsion.

Totem. A natural object assumed as the emblem of a clan or group; an object with which a clan or

sib considers itself closely related.

Toxicology. Study of poisons and antidotes.

Tractable. Obedient; docile; malleable; easily controlled.
Ant.: See **Recalcitrant.**

Transitory. Short-lived; fleeting.
Ant.: Enduring; long-lasting.

Transparent. Easily seen through; transmitting light so that bodies situated beyond or behind can be distinctly seen.
Ant.: See **Opaque.**

Triptych. A picture or carving in three compartments or panels, side by side.

Truculent. Savage; cruel; fierce.
Ant.: Gentle.

Turbid. Muddy; roiled; clouded; having the sediment disturbed.

Turbulent. Tumultuous; boisterous; disorderly; rambunctious; rowdy.

Turncoat. Renegade; traitor; apostate.

Tyrannical. Despotic; oppressive; dictatorial; imperious; domineering; unjustly severe in government.

Tyro. Novice; amateur; beginner in learning.

Ukase. Edict; proclamation; imperial order; official decree.

Ululate. Howl; wail; hoot, as an owl.

Unctuous. Suave; smug; oily; greasy; excessively pious; excessively smooth; oily or soapy to the touch.
Ant.: Sincere.

Ungulate. Hooflike; of or about hoofed mammals; any of the hoofed mammals.

Unique. Unequalled; matchless; single; sole; strange.

Unlettered. Uneducated; illiterate; ignorant.
Ant.: See **Erudite.**

Urban. Polished; citified; of or comprising a city or a town; relating to cities.
Ant.: Rustic; simple; artless; unsophisticated; countrified.

Urbane. Suave; smooth; polished; reflecting elegance and sophistication.
Ant.: Rude; crude; loutish; oafish; rustic; unmannerly.

Ursine. Bearlike; of or about bears.

Usury. The lending of money with an excessive charge for its use; unconscionable or exorbitant amount of interest.

Valedictory. A farewell; an occasion of leave-taking; a farewell address or oration.

Vapid. Insipid; spiritless; inane; having lost life or zest.
Ant.: *See* **Spirited**.

Vehement. Forceful; impetuous; furious; ardent; eager; impassioned; deeply felt.

Venal. Mercenary; corruptible; open to corrupt influence or bribery; capable of being bought.
Ant.: *See* **Incorruptible**.

Vendetta. Feud; rivalry; contention.

Venial. Excusable; trifling; minor; capable of being forgiven.

Verbose. Wordy; loquacious; talkative; prolix.
Ant.: *See* **Taciturn**; **Laconic**.

Vilify. Defame; slander; calumniate; disparage; malign.
Ant.: Commend; praise; laud.

Vindicate. Exculpate; defend; avenge; punish; justify; sustain; exonerate.

Virago. A shrew; an ill-tempered, scolding woman.

Virile. Vigorous; masculine; characteristic of, and befitting, a man.
Ant.: Effeminate—characterized by an unmanly softness and delicacy.

Vivacious. Lively; animated; sprightly.

Volatile. Changeable; fickle; evaporating rapidly.
Ant.: *See* **Stable**.

Voracious. Gluttonous; rapacious; ravenous; insatiable; immoderate; greedy.

Vulpine. Cunning; crafty; foxlike; of or about foxes.

Wane. Diminish; abate; decrease, as the waning of the moon from the full moon to the new moon.
Ant.: Wax; to grow; increase; enlarge; dilate.

Windward. Toward the direction from which the wind blows; the side from which the wind blows.
Ant.: *See* **Leeward**.

Whence. From what place; source; origin; cause.

Wholesome. Salubrious; healthful; salutary; beneficial.
Ant.: *See* **Noisome**.

Zealot. Fanatic; bigot; excessively zealous person.

Zenith. Acme; pinnacle; highest point.
Ant.: *See* **Nadir**.

PART **VI**

Sample Tests Explained
Question by Question

SAMPLE TESTS EXPLAINED QUESTION BY QUESTION

The sample tests in this section are designed as a transitional phase for you.

In parts II, III, and IV of this book you were offered many techniques for coping with the various types of questions that you are likely to encounter on the SAT. Learning the techniques requires that you practice them under "drill" conditions, without the stress of meeting the stringent time restraints imposed during the actual exam.

Thus, the suggested procedure for this section is for you to try to answer each question without additional help. Once you have tried your best, then refer back to the previous sections if there are still problems that you do not understand. If you encounter words that are unfamiliar to you, refer once again to the Vocabulary Study List in the preceding section. In these ways you will be able to verify that the correct response has been chosen and that you fully understand each and every question.

It is only after mastering these sample tests completely that you will be ready to proceed to the practice SAT tests under "battle" conditions.

Sample Test A—Verbal Section

Antonyms

Choose which of the five word or phrase choices is *most nearly opposite* in meaning to the word in capital letters. Fill in the appropriate letter space on the answer sheet. Consider all choices, since some are very similar in meaning.

1. TRITE
   A. verbose   B. futile   C. useful   D. innovative
   E. characteristic

   Explanation: If you know the meaning of *trite*, the root *nova* ("new") should have been enough to indicate the correct answer. If you didn't know the meaning, take a moment right now to look it up in the word list. However, you could have made an educated guess by recognizing that *futile* and *useful* are opposites. Since we know that none of the response choices mean the same as the given word, all sets of antonyms are eliminated as possible choices for the antonym of the given word. Thus, we have eliminated two possible answers. Answer (**D**)

2. BRAVE
   A. generous   B. avaricious   C. mature   D. timid
   E. philanthropic

   Explanation: First, look up any words you don't know in the word list or a dictionary. Now, look at the response choices. *Generous* and *philanthropic* are response choices. *Avaricious* is an antonym of both. Therefore, according to our rules, (A), (B), and (E) are eliminated from consideration. Our etymology shows *philo*—"love," and *anthro*—"man." Answer (**D**)

3. VETERAN
   A. servant   B. soldier   C. neophyte   D. antique
   E. master

   Explanation: *Servant* and *master* can be eliminated as being antonyms. If you have learned your prefixes, you know that *neo-* means "current" or "new." A *veteran* has obviously been around for a while.

Soldier is thrown in as a tempting wrong choice. Answer (**C**)

4. PROCEED
   A. reveal   B. conceal   C. defeat
   D. misunderstand   E. discontinue

   Explanation: This question is designed as an etymological workout. The given word has an "up" prefix, while each of the response choices has a "down" prefix. However, if we cover the prefixes in the response choices, we see that *continue* and *proceed* are synonyms, thus making *dis- continue* the antonym. Answer (**E**)

5. STABLE
   A. mercurial   B. specific   C. native
   D. inseparable   E. emblematic

   Explanation: The first step is to recognize that *stable* is not used as a noun ("horse barn"). This should be fairly obvious from an examination of the response choices, which are all adjectives. Once the adjectival meaning of *stable* is known, choices (B), (C), and (D) can be eliminated. In *mercurial*, the *mercury* signifies instability, since mercury is a liquid and will not maintain a given shape. Answer (**A**)

6. INFLEXIBLE
   A. primitive   B. yielding   C. elementary
   D. accede   E. avert

   Explanation: Here, the negative prefix *in-*, meaning "not," can be covered over, giving us the word *flexible*. Even if the meaning of *flexible* isn't known, you can eliminate *primitive* (A) and *elementary* (C) as possibilities, as they are too much alike in their meanings. *Accede* (D) could be the right answer except that it is a verb, while the given word is an adjective. *Avert* (E) has a negative prefix, (*a-*) and can be discarded, since two words with negative prefixes will seldom be opposites. Answer (**B**)

7. SYNTHETIC
A. plastic   B. viscous   C. natural   D. mass-produced   E. atomic

Explanation: If you were up on your etymology, you knew that *syn-* means "together," and *synthetic* means "something that is put together," or something man-made. This eliminated (A) and (D) as possibilities. Thus, even if you didn't know the meaning of *viscous*, you could have guessed with the guessing advantage. This is a question that should be omitted if you have no hint of the meaning of the given word. Answer (C)

8. IMPERMANENT
A. indifferent   B. tardy   C. unchangeable
D. perfect   E. flawless

Explanation: This question is designed to teach you that no rule is without its exceptions. You must be aware that the test-makers "know their onions" and their etymology very well indeed. In question 6 we stated that two words with negative prefixes will seldom be antonyms. However, the English language being as versatile as it is can produce almost anything. If we cover over the negative *im-* in the given word, we see that we are searching for a synonym of *permanent*. The best choice here, *unchangeable*, also has a negative prefix. Even if you were mislead by our rule, you should have been able to eliminate *perfect* and *flawless* as possibilities, since they mean the same thing. Answer (C)

9. MINUTE
A. week   B. second   C. hour   D. day   E. huge

Explanation: This is a test-maker's attempt to trick you into using the primary noun meaning of this given word by offering four choices that will fit in with that primary meaning. The correct choice is left for last so that the test-taker will be further tempted. As a matter of fact, once you realize that there is a second meaning ("very small") for the given word, only one choice is possible. As we have stated before, when several answers seem equally good or bad, search for a secondary meaning for the given word. Answer (E)

10. DISCORD
A. tenor   B. alto   C. harmony   D. soprano
E. melody

Explanation: Here, all five response choices have to do with music, so we know the given word is musically related. Since (A), (B), and (D) are each a range of the human voice, they are similar enough in meaning to be eliminated as possible choices. *Harmony* is a better choice than *melody*, since it infers more than one voice, singing together. *Discord* would also require more than one voice. Answer (C)

11. OBSOLETE
A. automobile   B. fancy   C. free   D. current
E. airplane

Explanation: Answers (A) and (E) can be eliminated, since they are examples of things that are not obsolete, not synonyms of the word itself. In addition, being nouns, they are the wrong part of speech for the given word, which is an adjective. With the guessing advantage thus obtained, you could have guessed that *current* was correct, since its adjectival meaning is that of "up-to-date," the opposite of *obsolete*, or "out-of-date." Answer (D)

12. ALIEN
A. pleasant   B. comfortable   C. American
D. native   E. Russian

Explanation: (A) and (B) can be eliminated as being too close together in their meanings. (C) and (E) are included as a choice to throw you off the track. Obviously, to us a Russian is an alien, but so is an American an alien to a Russian. This, logically, eliminates both as possibilities. Answer (D)

13. UNLIKELY
A. haughty   B. humble   C. denounce   D. apt
E. praise

Explanation: The prefix *un-* means "not." If we are looking for the opposite of *unlikely*, we are looking for a synonym of *likely*. This is a secondary meaning of *apt* as used in the sentence, "He is apt to be angry if we call him." Furthermore, if you are aware that the other four choices are two sets of antonyms, you will realize that (D) is the only possible answer. Answer (D)

14. SOCIABLE
A. hermit   B. kind   C. reserved   D. charitable
E. dictatorial

Explanation: (A) can be ruled out immediately, as it is a noun and you are looking for an adjective. At this point, a guess would have the guessing advantage. (B) and (D) are more or less synonyms and, thus, neither one will probably be correct. The test-maker hopes that you will confuse *sociable* with "socialism" and be taken in by (E). Answer (**C**)

15. PASSIVE
    A. active B. immoral C. candid D. aromatic
    E. fragrant

Explanation: (D) and (E) are synonyms and can be ruled out. This allows you to guess. Certainly, two words with the same endings should be considered as possible antonyms, since we know by the rules of the test that none of the choices can be synonyms of the given word. If we conceal the *-ive* endings, we remain with *pass-* and *act-*. Even if you didn't know the meaning of these roots, *pass-* and *act-* should get your guess as being very different in meaning. Answer (**A**)

16. IMMUNE
    A. commune B. susceptible C. inoculate
    D. inject E. virus

Explanation: (C) and (D) are eliminated, since they are verbs, and the given word is a noun or adjective, depending on usage. (A) is a detractor and may trap those who are relying on the relationship of the prefix *im-* to *com-*. They are, indeed, contrary in meaning, but do not, in this case, yield the best answer. No technique is perfect. But, then again, you don't have to get them all correct. Answer (**B**)

17. TERRESTRIAL
    A. calm B. cloudy C. rough D. subway
    E. nautical

Explanation: It is possible to eliminate (A) and (C),

Sentence Completions

Each sentence has one or two blanks. There are five choices of words or groups of words listed below the sentence. Choose the word or group of words which *best* completes the meaning of the entire sentence.

21. The _____ of the invariable routine created _____ among the workers on the assembly line.

since they are antonyms. If you knew the root *terra-* means "land," you should have no difficulty in selecting *nautical*, meaning "having to do with sailors or ships," as the answer. Answer (**E**)

18. ACUTE
    A. depressed B. dull C. ugly D. dishonest
    E. fragile

Explanation: Since all the response choices are "down" words, we cannot make any distinctions on that basis. Furthermore, there are no synonyms, antonyms, or etymological limits in the response choices. This question, as in others on the SAT, will yield to none of the test-taker's tips that this book has offered. You just have to know it—or omit it. There is no logical way to eliminate any answers unless you know the meaning of the given word. Answer (**B**)

19. COY
    A. manage B. pier C. healthy D. frantic
    E. brazen

Explanation: (A) and (B) can be eliminated, since they are the wrong parts of speech. At this point, a guess will give the advantage. *Coy* or "bashful" is the opposite of *brazen* or "bold." Answer (**E**)

20. PREVIOUS
    A. concurrent B. together C. subsequent
    D. temporary E. transient

Explanation: (D) and (E) mean approximately the same and, thus, can be eliminated as choices. Using your etymology, it should be clear that the prefixes *pre-* and *sub-* are more nearly opposed in meaning than *pre-* and *con-*. In addition, (A) and (B) are also synonyms. The upshot of all of this shows that, logically, you can isolate the answer by using the techniques given in this book. Answer (**C**)

A. tedium . . . interest
B. monotony . . . boredom
C. flatness . . . variety
D. similarity . . . piquancy
E. equability . . . diversity

Explanation: Here the operational phrase is "invariable routine." It carries negative connotations, so we expect the second word to be something more or less unpleasant, since it was "created" by the first word. Thus, we eliminate (A) and (C) because *interest* and *variety* are generally positive terms. *Diversity* (E) is unlikely to result from unvaried routine, but *boredom* is. *Monotony* properly completes the sentence, and (B) is the correct answer. (D) is completely irrelevant. Answer (**B**)

22. When he recalled his war experiences, they seemed like terrible _____ or dark _____ from a nightmare world.
    A. hallucinations . . . phantasms
    B. images . . . dreams
    C. mirages . . . passages
    D. visions . . . illuminations
    E. supports . . . stimulants

Explanation: Here the operational words are "terrible" and "dark." The transitional word "or" informs us that both blanks are similar in meaning. (C), (D), and (E) are eliminated because we do not think of those words as terrible things, nor are they synonyms. Dreams can be good or bad (B), but phantasms and hallucinations are always bad, so (A) is the best answer. Answer (**A**)

23. He was not guilty of any serious moral _____; however, he did have occasional human _____ from absolute virtue.
    A. infractions . . . lapses
    B. offenses . . . ravines
    C. turbulence . . . corruptions
    D. outrages . . . abuses
    E. malevolence . . . abominations

Explanation: "However" is one of the key words here. Since the first clause indicates that he was not guilty, "however" will suggest some qualification of that statement and will imply that he is somehow guilty. We will not expect him to be guilty of anything too serious though, since we do not want a complete contradiction. *Ravines* is completely irrelevant; *abominations* and *abuses* are too severe. *Infractions* and *lapses* fit the blanks best. Answer (**A**)

24. The mythological _____ were a combination of a horse's lower body with a man's head and _____.

    A. satyrs . . . hooves
    B. ogres . . . trunk
    C. Cyclops . . . arms
    D. giants . . . tails
    E. centaurs . . . torso

Explanation: Though this question requires some knowledge of satyrs and centaurs, you can still eliminate several answers by recognizing that the second word will have to be part of the *human* body. Thus (A) and (C) are incorrect. The Cyclops was a one-eyed giant and did not have a horse's body; nor did ogres. Thus (E) is correct. Answer (**E**)

25. Because of the noisy, _____ behavior of the bluejay family, one slang description of a person who is loudly _____ is "a jay."
    A. raucous . . . talkative
    B. demure . . . garrulous
    C. blatant . . . taciturn
    D. modest . . . argumentative
    E. inquisitive . . . prudent

Explanation: "Because" indicates a cause-effect relation will appear. The first word somehow complements "noisy" in describing "behavior," and the second word will reinforce the noisiness. (Thus we have two blanks similar in meaning.) Since *taciturn* and *prudent* do not imply loudness, (E) and (C) are incorrect. For the same reason *demure* and *modest* (B) and (D) are eliminated. *Raucous* and *talkative* (A) is the proper answer, since they are the only choices which are similar in meaning. Answer (**A**)

26. Frequent signs warned against _____ in the hallways; nevertheless, the corridors were full of _____.
    A. expectorating . . . transients
    B. loitering . . . dawdlers
    C. soliciting . . . pedestrians
    D. noctambulating . . . spectators
    E. littering . . . idlers

Explanation: "Nevertheless" tips us off that the signs are not being obeyed, so the second blank should describe people who perform the action warned against in the first blank. *Transients* do not expectorate ("spit"); they come and go. *Dawdlers* do loiter, though; thus (B) is the proper answer. None of the other pairs work. Answer (**B**)

27. Bertrand Russell's razor-sharp intellect was _____ by contact with the _____ minds of the century.
    A. dulled . . . brightest
    B. pitched . . . devious
    C. honed . . . keenest
    D. increased . . . biggest
    E. magnified . . . microscopic

Explanation: Sometimes certain words are used almost exclusively with only one or two other words. When you see such combinations, regard them closely. *Honed* is reserved for blades—one hones or sharpens a blade. Thus *honed* works well with "razor-sharp intellect," and *keenest* properly completes the sentence. In any event, we would expect the two answers to complement each other. His mind will be sharpened by sharp intellects or dulled by dull ones. This makes (C) a better answer than (D), which also makes sense. Answer (C)

28. His parents considered his wanderings merely a (an) _____ way of life, while he felt himself to be a modern _____ in a positive sense of that word.
    A. ephemeral . . . hobo
    B. derelict . . . nomad
    C. stolid . . . herd
    D. bohemian . . . precursor
    E. fixed . . . turmoil

Explanation: "Merely" indicates a word of insubstantial or negative connotations, and "while" implies a contradiction of those connotations. "Wanderings" describes his activity for us. Hobos and nomads wander, so we can narrow the answer to (A) or (B). *Derelict* has appropriately negative connotations, and *ephemeral* does not, so (B) is the answer. Answer (B)

29. The _____ theory of the creation of language _____ that words are formed to imitate or mirror the sounds of nature.
    A. demonstrative . . . ventures
    B. ecumenical . . . pontificates
    C. valid . . . proves
    D. romance . . . proposes
    E. echoic . . . theorizes

Explanation: The theory is about imitation or mirroring, so our first word should reflect that concept. Only *echoic* ("echo") does that, and (E) is the

correct answer. Answer (E)

30. Horace defended the golden _____ for human behavior as avoiding extremes of action and choosing a _____ middle ground.
    A. path . . . devious   D. tablets . . . balanced
    B. rod . . . rash   E. road . . . mediocre
    C. mean . . . prudent

Explanation: "Defender" is the operational word here. He is unlikely to defend a *devious, rash,* or *mediocre* middle ground, so we may eliminate (A), (B), and (E). Since in mathematics a mean is akin to the average, *mean* is a likely choice for a word that implies avoiding extremes and choosing a middle ground, and (C) is indeed the correct answer. Additional reinforcement of the correct answer can be provided by recognizing that the transitional word "as" signifies that the second part of the sentence is a definition of the first part. Thus "golden _____" must be defined as "_____ middle ground." Answer (C)

31. When the evangelist preached _____ under the threat of wholesale _____, the congregation shuddered in an ecstasy of fear.
    A. vividly . . . salvation
    B. repentance . . . damnation
    C. gratuitously . . . perdition
    D. thunderously . . . happiness
    E. docilely . . . suffering

Explanation: "Threat" is a key word here. *Damnation, perdition,* and *suffering* can be threats, but *salvation* and *happiness* cannot; so (A) and (D) are eliminated and a guess can be attempted. Of the remaining choices, only *repentance* fills the first blank meaningfully. Answer (B)

32. His friends considered him a person of courage, character, and _____; his enemies were forced to _____.
    A. cowardice . . . coordinate
    B. mettle . . . agree
    C. craven . . . demur
    D. indecision . . . concur
    E. calumny . . . silence

Explanation: The first blank must be filled by a word of praise, similar to "courage" and "character." Since the enemies are *forced*, we may assume that they too are compelled to praise him. Only *agree*, *silence*, and *concur* are appropriate for the second blank, so our choice is between (B) and (D). Even if you did not know that *mettle* means "strength of character," you can eliminate (D), because *indecision* does not complement "courage" and "character." If you didn't know that *calumny* means "slander," you might have been fooled by (E). Answer (**B**)

33. The Kamchatka Peninsula in northeastern Siberia is the _____ homeland of a small number of _____ Aleuts and adventurers.
    A. desolate . . . nomadic   D. vernal . . . capricious
    B. verdant . . . hunting   E. populous . . . whaling
    C. primeval . . . mystical

Explanation: All of the choices for the second word fit, though *capricious* ("whimsical") is somewhat dubious. Since Siberia is near the Arctic Circle, it is unlikely to flourish with vegetation; thus *verdant* ("heavily vegetated") and *vernal* ("spring-like") are eliminated. "Homeland of a small number" indicates that it is not heavily populated, or *populous*. *Primeval* refers to ancient historical times, usually before mankind existed. Thus, it too is eliminated, and *desolate* is the proper answer. Answer (**A**)

34. In contrast to the sexual _____ of the Victorian era, the sexual liberalism of Edwardian England seemed _____.
    A. permissiveness . . . lecherous
    B. austerity . . . restrained
    C. abstinence . . . coy
    D. repression . . . promiscuous
    E. conservatism . . . abundant

Explanation: Even if you are unaware of the Victorian age's reputation for being ultraconservative in matters of sex, you could figure out that fact by realizing that, according to the sentence, it is in contrast (transition word) to Edwardian "liberalism." Furthermore, the liberalism will seem exaggerated by the comparison. Consequently, the liberalism may appear *lecherous*, *promiscuous*, or *abundant*, but not *restrained* or *coy* ("shy"). Thus (B) and (C) are eliminated. The Victorian era may have been repressive or conservative about sex, but not permissive, as (A) too is eliminated. Because *promiscuous* is a term frequently used in the context of discussing sex, it is the best answer. (E) fits, but it is not as good an answer as (D). Answer (**D**)

35. The judge was forced to uphold the anti-_____ statutes even though his conscience was _____ by this type of racism.
    A. segregation . . . appeased
    B. busing . . . titilated
    C. lynching . . . mollified
    D. miscegenation . . . disturbed
    E. evolutionary . . . violated

Explanation: A close reading of the sentence reveals that an "anti-_____" is a form of racism. Further, that the judge is "forced" to uphold the statute implies that he does not approve of it. So the second word will be negative, and the first will involve anything racial. We may eliminate (A), (B), and (C) because their second words are positive. *Evolutionary* has nothing to do with race, so we may also eliminate (E). *Miscegenation* is the mixing of the race (the root *gen* means "race"). Thus, an anti-miscegenation statute would prohibit mixing of the races and would, for example, forbid interracial marriage. Answer (**D**)

36. Many people dislike traveling by bus because of the _____ and _____ companions whom they meet along the way.
    A. loquacious . . . insensitive
    B. garrulous . . . austere
    C. taciturn . . . prying
    D. reserved . . . discreet
    E. friendly . . . patronizing

Explanation: Both words here must describe unpleasant people, since they are disliked by many people. We may readily eliminate (E) and (D) because *friendly* and *reserved* are not generally negative traits. Though *prying* is unpleasant, being *taciturn*, or quiet, is not. *Garrulous* and *loquacious* both mean "talkative." *Austere* means "very simple and plain." That is not a negative trait, but insensitivity is. Although a good case could be made for (C), (A) is probably the better answer. On the SAT you just have to pick from two answers which seem to have the same chance of being correct. Answer (**A**)

37. Even though he hoped he had outgrown his _____ attitudes, whenever he returned to his parent's home he felt himself _____ to earlier patterns of behavior.
    A. adolescent . . . ascending

B. immature . . . protruding
C. childish . . . retaining
D. interim . . . projecting
E. puerile . . . regressing

Explanation: "Even though" and "outgrown" are the key words. The return to earlier patterns which had been outgrown is a step backward, and "even though" indicates we are looking for the opposite of "outgrown." Of the possibilities for the second blank only *regressing* indicates that movement backward. *Puerile* means "childish," and so it is appropriate for the first blank. Answer (**E**)

38. Despite the coach's _____ attempts to encourage the team's morale, the squad _____ in their bid for the league championship.
   A. laconic . . . floundered
   B. sincere . . . excelled
   C. histrionic . . . failed
   D. genuine . . . triumphed
   E. vigorous . . . decimated

Explanation: "Despite" indicates that the coach's efforts did not succeed and that the team lost. We may thus eliminate (B) and (D) because they suggest the team won. The team may "have *been* decimated," but they didn't *decimated*, so (E) too is eliminated (wrong tense). We must choose between (A) and (C). *Laconic* means "silent," or "short and to the point." *Histrionic* means "dramatic." In the context, we may assume that the coach was more histrionic than laconic. Answer (**C**)

39. Many historical landmarks in Chicago have been _____ to allow for urban development; as a result, concerned citizens have petitioned for a (an)

_____ on new construction in the Loop.
   A. erected . . . prohibition
   B. designed . . . hindrance
   C. cataloged . . . amendment
   D. razed . . . moratorium
   E. demolished . . . incentive

Explanation: We should gather from the sentence that something bad has happened to the historical landmarks and that as a result concerned citizens are trying to keep it from happening again. The first words in (A), (B), and (C) indicate positive or neutral things, so those alternatives may be eliminated. Since the landmarks have been *demolished* to make way for new building, we may conclude that the concerned citizens do not want incentives for new construction. They want an end, or *moratorium*, on new construction in The Loop. As in "razor," *razed* means "cut down completely." *Moratorium* means "delay" or "halt." Answer (**D**)

40. By studying the principles of classical _____, the orator hoped to transform his style of speaking from staccato to _____.
   A. logic . . . terse
   B. obloquy . . . concise
   C. rhetoric . . . euphonious
   D. eulogies . . . cacophonous
   E. form . . . cadent

Explanation: Since he is an orator, we may assume that he is concerned with public speaking and that he wants to sound pleasant. *Euphonious* means literally "good sound," and *rhetoric* deals with speech, so (C) is the answer (*eu-* means "good"; *caco-* means "bad"; *phono-* means "sound"). Answer (**C**)

Analogies

Each question contains a pair of related words or phrases. There are five choices of words or phrases following each of the given pairs. Choose the word or phrase which *best* expresses a relationship which is similar to that expressed in the given pair.

41. CRITERIA : CRITERION : :
   A. hen : roosters
   B. mademoiselle : madame
   C. geese : goose
   D. data : alumnae
   E. thesis : theses

Explanation: The relationship here is fairly simple to recognize: plural-singular. *Thesis : theses* is incorrect because that relationship is singular-plural. The proper answer is *geese : goose* (C). Answer (**C**)

42. WINE : GOBLET : :
   A. whiskey : cask
   B. tea : pot
   C. grapes : china
   D. glass : decanter
   E. coffee : demitasse

Explanation: The test sentence might be "Wine is drunk from a goblet." Though whiskey is aged or contained in a cask, it is not drunk from one. Coffee is drunk from a demitasse or small cup, so that is a better answer. Answer (**E**)

43. BICUSPID : CUSPID : :
    A. dental : hygiene   D. canine : feline
    B. teeth : spine   E. molar : incisor
    C. filling : orthodontist

Explanation: The test sentence might be "Bicuspid : cuspid are two classes of teeth." The relationship is duplicated in (E), since a molar belongs to the bicuspid class, and the incisor to the cuspid. Answer (**E**)

44. RADIATION : X-RAYS : :
    A. color : red   D. recession : inefficiency
    B. vitamins : digestion   E. infrared : ultraviolet
    C. battery : starter

Explanation: This question is tricky unless you recognize that X-rays are simply one form of radiation (test sentence). The relationship then is a class : member and it is duplicated in *color : red*. Answer (**A**)

45. PALLID : LIVID : :
    A. pale : anemic   D. ghostly : specter
    B. rosy : ruddy   E. chill : tropics
    C. wan : flushed

Explanation: *Pallid* ("pale") and *livid* ("flushed") are simple opposites, and the correct answer is (C). (E) is eliminated because while *pallid* and *livid* are both adjectives, *chill* and *tropics* are nouns. Answer (**C**)

46. TUSK : TRUNK : :
    A. elephant : rhinoceros   D. boar : sow
    B. snout : hoof   E. bill : webbed
    C. carnivore : lioness

Explanation: *Tusk* and *trunk* are parts of the same whole—an elephant. *Snout* and *hoof* are also parts of the same whole—a horse. *Bill : webbed* is eliminated because *webbed* is an adjective, not a noun. Had it been "webbed feet" that relationship would have been correct too, since both are parts of a duck. Answer (**B**)

47. SCAVENGER : VULTURE : :
    A. hyena : coyote   D. carrion : buzzard
    B. crow : grain   E. predator : prey
    C. carnivore : lioness

Explanation: "A vulture is a kind of scavenger" (member-class). A coyote is not a kind of hyena; grain is not a kind of crow; buzzard is not a kind of carrion; and prey is not a kind of predator. A lioness, though, is a kind of carnivore (flesh-eater). Sometimes using simple sentences like these is useful. Answer (**C**)

48. OXIDATION : RUST : :
    A. hydrogen : water
    B. fluoridation : decay
    C. corrosion : deteriorated
    D. maturity : senility
    E. exertion : fatigue

Explanation: Test sentence: "Rust is an intense form of oxidation." *Corrosion : deteriorated* is a tempting answer, but *deteriorated* is the wrong part of speech. An intense form of corrosion is, perhaps, *deterioration*, but not *deteriorated*. The relationship is that of degree. Answer (**D**)

49. SOPHISTICATED : RUSTIC : :
    A. urbane : bucolic
    B. droll : comic
    C. polished : dapper
    D. witty : concise
    E. knowledgeable : worldly

Explanation: *Sophisticated* and *rustic* are opposites, and since we tend to associate sophistication with city life and innocence with rustic or rural life, *urbane* also implies sophistication (the root *urb* means city). *Bucolic* means *rustic*. So (A) is the answer. If you do not know the meaning of the head pair, you may recognize that (B), (C), and (E) all express nearly identical relationships, so the answer is unlikely to be any of those. Answer (**A**)

50. MEAN : MAGNANIMOUS : :
    A. cruel : treacherous
    B. stingy : parsimonious
    C. taciturn : loquacious
    D. miserly : cupidity
    E. compromising : unfaithful

Explanation: *Mean* and *magnanimous* ("generous") are opposites; so we must seek another pair of antonyms (the root *magni-* means "large"). We can eliminate (D) because both words must be adjectives, and *cupidity* is a noun. If you do not know the meaning of *magnanimous*, you can still recognize that (A), (B), and (E) all express nearly the same relationship (synonyms), so they are probably incorrect. Thus (C) remains. *Taciturn* is "quiet," and *loquacious* is "talkative." Answer (**C**)

51. EGG : OVOID : :
    A. globe : spherical   D. pyramid : square
    B. ham : slice   E. plane : rhomboid
    C. fence : periphery

Explanation: Even if you do not know that *ovoid* describes the three-dimensional shape of an egg, you can recognize it as an adjective. Only in (A) and (D) are the second words adjectives. Since a globe is spherical, (A) is the answer. Answer (**A**)

52. BRAID : STRANDS : :
    A. hair : ribbons   D. curry : favor
    B. join : merge   E. weave : fabric
    C. splice : wire

Explanation: This question is tricky. We may immediately eliminate (B) because *merge* is a verb and does not agree with the noun, *strands*. The relationship is verb to object. We braid strands. We do not hair ribbons, so (A) is eliminated. We do, however, splice wire, curry favor ("solicit" favor), and weave fabric. A closer examination of the head pair shows that strands are the material that is used to produce the final result; they are not, however, the result of the braiding. Fabric is the end result of weaving, and favor is the desired end result of currying, so those answers are wrong. Wires are the things spliced and are not the result of the splicing, so (C) is the correct answer. Answer (**C**)

53. DIVULGE : REVEAL : :
    A. conceal : demonstrate   D. perceive : apprehend
    B. divest : approve   E. advance : stall
    C. renounce : perform

Explanation: *Divulge* and *reveal* are synonymous, and so are *perceive* and *apprehend*. Note again that among the choices several opposite relationships exist, but only one synonymous one. Thus, the synonymous relationship is the likely choice, even if you do not know what the head pair means. Answer (**D**)

54. OAKEN : GRAIN : :
    A. bucket : malt   D. linen : flax
    B. cotton : cloth   E. tree : whiskey
    C. tweed : texture

Explanation: The relationship is adjective-noun. We eliminate (A) and (E) because *bucket* and *tree* are nouns, not adjectives. Though *linen* can sometimes act as an adjective, it cannot modify *flax* (the plant from which linen is made). We can, however, have a *cotton* cloth or a *tweed* texture. At this point, we turn to the meanings of the head words. Since *texture* has more in common with *grain* than does *cloth*, (C) is the answer. Answer (**C**)

55. GREECE : CLASSICAL : :
    A. Italy : Rome   D. France : Romance
    B. India : Maharajah   E. Trojan : Ionic
    C. America : patriotic

Explanation: The relationship is a proper noun-adjective. We eliminate (A) and (B) because *Rome* and *Maharajah* are not adjectives. We eliminate (E) because *Trojan* is not a noun (*Troy* is the appropriate noun form). *Romance* may be either a noun ("love") or an adjective (deriving from Rome: French is a Romance language). Patriotism is not a concept uniquely linked with America, but classicism is technically defined by ancient Greece, and Romanticism is closely associated with France. The final choice between (C) and (D) is admittedly difficult, but (D) is the better answer. Answer (**D**)

56. ROW : OAR : :
    A. canoe : canvas   D. tow : barge
    B. dinghy : steamship   E. scull : river
    C. punt : pole

Explanation: The relationship is verb-noun, and we may find useful the sample sentence "Row with an oar." We eliminate (B) because *dinghy* is not a verb. Though a towboat tows a barge, it does not tow *with* a barge, and we do not scull with a river ("sculling" is a way of propelling a boat by moving the rudder). So we also eliminate (D) and (E). Nor do we canoe with a canvas, so (A) is also eliminated. To *punt* not only means "to kick a football," it also refers to propelling a boat by pushing a long pole against the river or canal bottom. Thus, we can punt with a pole. Answer (C)

57. TRUANT : ATTENTIVE : :
   A. vagrant : affluence   D. wandering : observant
   B. officer : secretary   E. stolid : polite
   C. peace : plenty

Explanation: *Truant* can be either noun or adjective, but *attentive* is always an adjective. We eliminate (A), (B), and (C) because *affluence*, *secretary*, and *plenty* are nouns. *Truant* means "absent," so the head relationship is one of opposites. (D) comes closest to replicating that relationship. Answer (D)

58. DRILL : TOOTH : :
   A. cap : crown   D. dynamite : mine
   B. plank : chisel   E. punch : leather
   C. polish : silverware

Explanation: The relationship here is verb-object. We can drill a tooth, polish silverware, dynamite a mine, punch leather, and cap a crown. But we cannot plank a chisel, so (B) is eliminated. Since all of the choices share the same relationship as the head pair, we must turn to a more precise test sentence. To drill is to make a hole in a tooth. Dynamiting and punching also make holes, but capping and polishing do not, so eliminate (A) and (C). The distinction between (D) and (E) is perhaps subtle. Dynamiting is a less controlled and more massive procedure than either drilling or punching; so *punch* proves to be the best answer. Answer (E)

59. STAG : BOW : :
   A. hunting : deer   D. sporting : arrow
   B. doe : fawn   E. antler : ribbon
   C. whale : harpoon

Explanation: The relationsip is noun-noun, thus we eliminate (D) because *sporting* is not a noun. The relationship is basically object-tool. We can kill a stag with a bow (and arrow), but we cannot kill hunting with a deer, kill a doe with a fawn, or kill an antler with a ribbon. We may, however, kill a whale with a harpoon. Answer (C)

60. ANXIETY : ULCERS : :
   A. tension : fear
   B. cholesterol : diabetes
   C. wind : rain
   D. exposure : shock
   E. indifference : indigestion

Explanation: The relationship expresses cause and effect between two nouns. Anxiety causes ulcers. Fear may cause tension, but tension does not cause fear; cholesterol may contribute to heart disease, but not to diabetes; wind does not cause rain; and indifference does not cause indigestion. So (D) remains the answer. Exposure to the elements may cause the body to enter a state of shock. Answer (D)

61. BILL : WING : :
   A. snout : sow   D. duck : drake
   B. beak : aviary   E. lading : tail
   C. muzzle : hoof

Explanation: We must recognize the relationship as part-part. *Bill* and *wing* are parts of the same whole, the bird. Even if you are not sure of all the vocabulary, you can eliminate those relationships you know are not part-part and seek out one that is. A snout is a part of a pig, but a sow is the entire female pig; thus (A) is incorrect. A duck is not a part, so (D) too is eliminated. The beak is part of a bird. However, the muzzle and hoof are both parts of a horse, so (C) is the answer. Answer (C)

62. GORILLA : APE : :
   A. thug : intimidate   D. roar : mimic
   B. spider : arachnid   E. gibbon : anthropoid
   C. monkey : orangutan

Explanation: Though this question requires some special knowledge of biology, we can nonetheless make an intelligent response. This noun-noun relationship is basically part-whole. A gorilla is a kind of ape. Eliminate (A) and (D) because *intimidate* and *mimic* are not nouns. Monkey is not a class of orangutan, so (C) is eliminated too. Spiders are kinds of arachnids (those familiar with mythology may recall the story of Athena and Arachne), and gibbons are kinds of anthropoids. (E) is the better choice because *anthropoid* is more closely aligned in meaning to *ape* than *arachnid*. Both *anthropoid* and *ape* refer to primates that resemble humans. Answer (E)

63. CUFF : HEM
    A. hit : haw
    B. shirt : collar
    C. solid : stripe
    D. pocket : sleeve
    E. vest : suit

Explanation: The relationship here, though perhaps not readily obvious, is part-part. *Cuff* and *hem* are parts of the same shirt. (A) plays on secondary meanings of the head words. To cuff can mean to hit, and to hem and haw means to stall. But *hit : haw* is not an appropriate answer. (B) represents a whole-part relationship, and (E) depicts a part-whole relationship. But *pocket* and *sleeve* are parts of the same shirt, so (D) is correct; (C) is irrelevant. Answer (**D**)

64. GOBBLE : TURKEY : :
    A. cackle : fishwife
    B. bleat : toad
    C. horn : honk
    D. giggle : ascetic
    E. pizzicato : violin

Explanation: The relationship is action-doer: a turkey gobbles. We may eliminate (C) and (E) because *horn* and *pizzicato* are not verbs. Toads do not bleat, sheep do; and ascetics, people who deprive themselves of sensual pleasure, are not known for their giggling. Thus (B) and (D) are also eliminated. In nineteenth-century fiction, fishwives, the little old ladies who sell fish by the pier, frequently laugh in an eerie way known as cackling. Answer (**A**)

65. HYPOCHONDRIAC : MALINGER : :
    A. shrew : scold
    B. hermit : indulge
    C. fling : gauntlet
    D. illness : invent
    E. hypocrite : candid

Explanation: Even if you do not know the meanings of the head words, you can probably identify them as noun-verb. Thus you may eliminate (C) and (E) because *gauntlet* ("glove") and *candid* ("frank" or "honest") are not verbs. Furthermore, if the *-ac* ending on *hypochondriac* indicates to you that the word is a label for a kind of person, you may also eliminate (D), since illness is not a person. Thus, you have improved considerably your guessing advantage. A shrew (an ill-tempered woman) scolds, and a hermit does the opposite of indulge. Since a hypochondriac is one who imagines he is sick, and to malinger is to feign sickness to avoid work, (A) fits the analogy best. Answer (**A**)

Reading Comprehension

Each passage is followed by a series of questions. All questions should be answered on the basis of what is stated or implied in that passage.

The first series of paragraphs and questions are diagnostic exercises; these will help the test-taker through the mental processes necessary to answer the most common forms of reading comprehension questions on the SAT.

Title Questions

66. All sounds are caused by mechanical motion of some kind—hands clapping, a door banging, vocal chords vibrating, etc. The object pushes the air around it and sets the air vibrating (or oscillating). The vibration in air then moves outward from the source as a sound wave.

    The most suitable title would be
    A. The Sound of Silence.
    B. The Physical Laws of Oscillation.
    C. Mechanical Motion.
    D. Hands, Doors, and Vocal Chords.
    E. Vibration and Sound Waves.

    The title which is *inappropriate* because it is illogical is _____.
    The title which is *inappropriate* because it is too technical is _____.
    The title which is *inappropriate* because it merely lists supporting examples is _____.
    The title which is *inappropriate* because it is too general is _____.
    The title which is *most suitable* is _____.

67. The nonviolent resisters can summarize their message in the following simple terms: We will take direct action against injustice without waiting for other agencies to act. We will not obey unjust laws or submit to unjust practices. We will do this peacefully, openly, cheerfully because our aim is to persuade. We adopt the means of nonviolence because our end is a community at peace with itself.

We will try to persuade with our words, but if our words fail, we will try to persuade with our acts. We will always be willing to talk and seek fair compromise, but we are ready to suffer when necessary and even to risk our lives to become witnesses to the truth as we see it.

The most appropriate title is
A. Obedience to Unjust Laws.
B. A Community at Peace.
C. A Code of Nonviolent Resistance.
D. The Civil Rights Movement.
E. A Philosopher Speaks.

The title which is *unsuitable* because it decribes a general historical expression of the main idea is _____.

The title which is *unsuitable* because it describes only one specific aim of the whole selection is _____.

The title which is *unsuitable* because it refers to an unmentioned author is _____.

The title which is *unsuitable* because it contradicts the message of the selection is _____.

The title which is *most appropriate* is _____.

68. Larger astronomical telescopes are of the reflecting type. That is, they have a curved mirror at the lower end which gathers and focuses the light from the object being viewed. There are two ways of getting this image out of the telescope tube. One way is to use a small curved mirror centered in the upper end of the tube which completes the focusing and throws the concentrated beam of light out through a small hole in the center of the curved mirror. The other method is to use a flat mirror tilted at an angle so that the light forming the image can pass out through the side of the telescope tube.

The most suitable title is
A. The Wonders of Astronomy.
B. The Telescopic Tube.
C. Planetarium Construction.
D. Types of Reflecting Telescopes.
E. Curved Versus Flat Mirrors.

The title which is *not* appropriate because it deals with one specific contrasting detail is _____.

The title which is *not* appropriate because the subject is not discussed in the selection is _____.

The title which is *not* appropriate because it could be the topic for an entire book is _____.

The title which is *not* appropriate because it uses too general a name for the obejct being discussed is _____.

The title which is *most appropriate* is _____.

69. I wish the bald eagle had not been chosen as the representative of our country; he is a bird of bad moral character; he does not get his living honestly; you may have seen him perched on some dead tree, where, too lazy to fish for himself, he watches the labor of the fish-hawk; and, when that diligent bird has at length taken a fish and is bearing it to his nest for the support of his mate and young ones, the bald eagle pursues him and takes it from him. With all this injustice he is never in good case; but, like those among men who live by sharping and robbing, he is generally poor, and often very lousy.

The best title would be
A. The Enemy of the Fish-Hawk.
B. The Bad Moral Character of the Bald Eagle.
C. The Generally Poor and Often Very Lousy.
D. Audubon's Bad Boy.
E. A Proud American Symbol.

The title which is *wrong* because it merely quotes a general description that could be applied to many things is _____.

The title which is *wrong* because it describes only one aspect of the main subject's character is _____.

The title which is *wrong* because it mentions a famous naturalist who is never discussed in the paragraph is _____.

The title which is *wrong* because it describes the subject positively is _____.

The *best* title is _____.

70. Of course, the most impressive part of a thunderstorm is the lightning and thunder. Time was when people were terrified by them. The Greeks thought angry Zeus, king of the gods, was hurling thunderbolts forged for him by the lame smith Hephaestus. Nowadays everybody knows that lightning is just a huge electric spark. Everybody knows that thunder is just a noise. It is the sound made by rapidly expanding air when lightning passes through it and heats it. The lightning is extremely hot—perhaps 1,500° C. After it tears the atmosphere apart, the air comes together with a bang.

The most suitable title is

A. Zeus and His Thunderbolts.
B. Hephaestus's Smithy.
C. Meteorological Disturbances.
D. Greek War Heroes.
E. Thunderstorms: Myths and Facts.

The title which is *inappropriate* because it is too broad is _____.

The title which is *inappropriate* because it is not discussed in the selection is _____.

The titles which are *inappropriate* because they deal with specific details and not the main idea are _____ and _____.

The title which is *most suitable* is _____.

Implications

71. Within the nucleus are very tiny bodies called *chromosomes*. They are so small that their fine structure can be seen clearly only by using an electron microscope, which provides much greater magnification than the most powerful optical microscope. Since all cells seem so much alike, how is it that a geranium cell will always make a geranium plant and a cat cell will always make a cat? The chromosomes bear the fundamental units of heredity, known as the *genes*, which may be called the "cell memory." The genes in the cell of a geranium plant "remember" that the cell came from a geranium, and they activate the cell to build a geranium and nothing else.

It may be assumed from the information given in the passage that
A. the nucleus is contained within the genes.
B. geraniums and cats are genetically interchangeable.
C. units of heredity are equivalent to the cell memory.
D. chromosomes are visible to the naked eye.
E. an electron microscope is an optical microscope.

The answer which is *wrong* because one is more powerful than the other is _____.

The answer which is *wrong* because one is too small to be seen is _____.

The answer which is *wrong* because the greater cannot fit within the smaller is _____.

The answer which is *wrong* because different examples are assumed to be identical is _____.

The *correct* answer is _____.

Children were endangered by trucks and other automobiles when they gathered in the middle of streets to hear and watch the organ-grinders. Also, the simple, sentimental hurdy-gurdy man had become a victim of a racket. My sentimental correspondents did not realize that the Italians' instruments were rented to them by padrones at exorbitant fees. Their licenses from the city were in reality licenses to beg. About a year before I banned the organ-grinders, I had terminated the contracts with musicians on city ferry boats on the grounds that these were merely licenses to beg issued by the city.

72. It can be inferred that the main thing the author is opposed to is
A. children's enjoyment.
B. truck traffic.
C. sentimentality.
D. begging.
E. city ferry boats.

The answer which mentions something the author wishes to safeguard is _____.

The answers which mention modes of transportation to which the author is not opposed are _____ and _____.

The second best answer which mentions a quality of the writer's opponents is _____.

The *best* answer is _____.

73. One could deduce from the passage that the author is most probably a(n)
A. padrone.
B. construction engineer.
C. concerned parent.
D. organ-grinder.
E. city official.

The answer which is *wrong* because it is a Mafia figure is _____.

The answer which is *wrong* because it represents the individual being denied a license is _____.

The answer which is wrong because it is unrelated to the issues is _____.

The answer which is *wrong* because it probably would represent one of the sentimental correspondents is _____.

The *best* answer is _____.

Smuts of wheat, oats, onions, spinach, and sunflowers plague farmers. There are some 400 species of smuts, and perhaps the only good one is the one which attacks spinach! All are hard to control, as the spores may live for a long time until they have the opportunity to grow. A single diseased plant can infect a whole field. Perhaps in the distant past these fungi were less obnoxious. But as man developed agriculture, grains and fruits became important, and the very nature of farms and gardens made it easier for the fungus to spread and destroy crops.

74. It may be assumed that all of the following worry the farmer *except*
   A. the smuts of sunflowers.
   B. the spores of smuts.
   C. the long life of smut spores.
   D. smuts of spinach.
   E. smuts of acorns.

   The answer which is *wrong* because it is not mentioned at all is _____.
   The answers which are *wrong* because they refer to the qualities which make smuts hard to eliminate are _____ and _____.
   The answer which is *wrong* because it mentions one destructive type is _____.
   The *best* answer is _____.

75. It is implied that the growth of agriculture
   A. decreased smut destruction.
   B. made smuts less obnoxious.
   C. provided more crops for the smut to damage.
   D. dates back to a matriarchal culture.
   E. started with 400 species.

   The answer which is *wrong* because it is not mentioned in the passage is _____.
   The answer which is *wrong* because it takes a statistic out of context is _____.
   The answers which are *wrong* because they are contradicted by the facts given in the passage are _____ and _____.
   The *right* answer is _____.

Writing Techniques

Questions 76–78

If human nature were not base, but thoroughly honorable, we would in every debate have no other aim than the discovery of truth; we should not in the least care whether the truth proved to be in favor of the opinion which we had begun by expressing, or of the opinion of our adversary. That we should regard as a matter of no moment, or, at any rate, of very secondary consequence, but, as things are, it is the main concern. Our innate vanity, which is particularly sensitive in reference to our intellectual powers, will not suffer us to allow that our first position was wrong and our adversary's right. The way out of this difficulty would be simply to take the trouble always to form a correct judgment. For this a man would have to think before he spoke. But with most men, innate vanity is accompanied by loquacity and innate dishonesty. They speak before they think, and even though they may afterward perceive that they are wrong, and that what they assert is false, they want it to seem the contrary.

76. The writer would probably agree with which of the following descriptions of human nature:

      I. Base
     II. Honorable
    III. Vain
    IV. Dishonest
   A. I
   B. II
   C. I and III
   D. II and III
   E. I, III, and IV

   The answer which is *wrong* because it would only agree with the pursuit of truth is _____.
   The answer which is *right* is _____.

77. The approach of the author is essentially
   A. logical.
   B. emotional.
   C. poetic.
   D. historical.
   E. irrational.

   The answer which is *wrong* because the author does not use any figurative language is _____.
   The answer which is *wrong* because the author does not appeal to the reader's feelings is _____.
   The answer which is *wrong* because the author does not support his view with incidents from the past is _____.
   The answer which is *wrong* because the author uses a reasoned approach to his subject is _____.
   The *right* answer is _____.

78. One may infer from the passage that the author's view of mankind is
A. optimistic.
B. humorous.
C. hopeful.
D. vain.
E. cynical.

The answers which are *wrong* because they give too positive an interpretation of the writer's view are _____ and _____.

The answer which is *wrong* because it describes the author's opinion of human motives and not the author himself is _____.

The answer which is *wrong* because the writer's tone is generally serious is _____.

The *right* answer is _____.

Words in Context

Questions 79–81

For historians ought to be precise, truthful, and quite unprejudiced, and neither interest nor fear, hatred nor affection, should cause them to swerve from the path of truth, whose mother is history, the rival of time, the depository of great actions, the witness of what is past, the example and instruction to the present, and monitor to the future.

79. The author's view of historians is which of the following?

I. Unbiased
II. Critical
III. Detached
A. I
B. II
C. III
D. All of the above
E. None of the above

The answer which is *incorrect* because the author never comments on the defects of historians is _____.

The answers which are *incorrect* because the author presents a one-sided picture of historians are _____, _____, and _____.

The *best* answer is _____.

80. When the author symbolizes history as the mother of truth, he is being

A. clinical.
B. accurate.
C. metaphorical.
D. impersonal.
E. righteous.

The answer which is *wrong* because it refers to a moral issue is _____.

The answer which is *wrong* because it refers to a detached, physician-like attitude is _____.

The answer which is *wrong* because it is a term more appropriate to facts or statistics is _____.

The answer which is *wrong* because the author is introducing his own personal views into the passage is _____.

The *best* answer to describe the comparison is _____.

81. When the author claims that history should be the "monitor to the future" (last phrase), he means it should act as a

A. clerk.
B. watchman.
C. king.
D. janitor.
E. secretary.

The answer which is *incorrect* because it suggests a position of complete control is _____.

The answer which is *incorrect* because it suggests too menial a role is _____.

The answers which are *incorrect* because they suggest a more recording function are _____ and _____.

The answer which *best* suggests the idea of a guard is _____.

Facts

Questions 82–83

The general must know how to get his men their rations and every other kind of stores needed for war. He must have imagination to originate plans and practical sense and energy to carry them through. He must be observant, untiring, shrewd; kindly and cruel; simple and crafty; a watchman and a robber; lavish and miserly; generous and stingy; rash and conservative. All these and many other qualities, natural and acquired, he must have. He should also, as a matter of course, know his tactics; for a disorderly mob is no more an army than a heap of building materials is a house.

82. According to the passage the qualities of a general include all of the following *except*
    A. lavish.
    B. untiring.
    C. conservative.
    D. wise.
    E. miserly.

    Since a general should reward his troops generously when they fight well, the answer which is *wrong* is _____.
    Since a general should be cautious in risking the lives of his men, the answer which is *wrong* is _____.
    Since a general should have a tremendous supply of energy, the answer which is *wrong* is _____.
    Since a general should be stingy with his supplies, the answer which is *wrong* is _____.
    The only quality which seems like a good common-sense answer, but which is *not* directly listed in the paragraph is _____.

83. According to the selection, tactics are important to a general because
    A. he is a watchman and a robber.
    B. he must know how to build a house.
    C. he is kindly and cruel.
    D. he has learned them at the military academy.
    E. he needs to know how to organize his forces effectively.

    The answer which is *wrong* because it mistakes a symbolic comparison for a literal fact is _____.
    The answer which is *wrong* because it is not mentioned in the passage is _____.
    The answers which are *wrong* because they are descriptions applying to other sections of the passage are _____ and _____.
    The *best* answer is _____.

Questions 84–85

Electrolysis is one of the chemist's major tools for creating new materials. Aluminum is made by electrolysis from the mineral bauxite. Magnesium is made by electrolysis from chemicals in sea water. Copper is often separated from other metals and refined by electrolysis. Sodium and chlorine are also produced industrially in this manner.

84. The element "refined" by electrolysis is
    A. bauxite.
    B. magnesium.
    C. aluminum.
    D. copper.
    E. fluoride.

    The answers which are *wrong* because they are produced or made by electrolysis, not "refined" by it, are _____ and _____.
    The answer which is *wrong* because it is never mentioned in the selection is _____.
    The answer which is *wrong* because it is the source for another mineral is _____.
    The *best* answer is _____.

85. Electrolysis is used on all of the following raw materials to produce the elements listed in the passage.

    I. sea water
    II. other metals
    III. bauxite
    A. I
    B. II
    C. III
    D. I and III
    E. All of the above

    The answer which is *incorrect* because it produces only magnesium is _____.
    The answer which is *incorrect* because it produces only copper is _____.
    The answer which is *incorrect* because it produces only aluminum is _____.

Answer Key—Reading Comprehension

66. A, B, D, C, E
67. D, B, E, A, C
68. E, C, D, A, B
69. C, A, D, E, B
70. C, D, A, B, E
71. E, D, A, B, C
72. A, B, E, C, D
73. A, D, B, C, E
74. E, B, C, A, D
75. D, E, B, A, C

76. B, E
77. C, B, D, E, A
78. A, C, D, B, E
79. A, C, D, E, B
80. E, A, B, D, C
81. C, D, A, E, B
82. E, C, B, A, D
83. B, D, A, C, E
84. B, C, E, A, D
85. A, B, C

Reading Comprehension Passages

The following passages are comparable to those you will encounter on the SAT. Answers and explanations are given after each set of questions. It is suggested that all questions relating to a given paragraph be attempted before referring to the answers and explanations. By doing this, the continuity of the reading selection will not be broken.

Questions 86–90

Brother, you say there is but one way to worship and serve the Great Spirit. If there is but one religion, why do you white people differ so much about it? Why not all agreed, as you can all read the Book?

Brother, we do not understand these things. We are told that your religion was given to your forefathers and has been handed down from father to son. We also have a religion which was given to our forefathers and has been handed down to us, their children. We worship in that way. It teaches us to be thankful for all the favors we receive, to love each other, and to be united. We never quarrel about religion.

Brother, the Great Spirit has made us all, but He has made a great difference between His white and His red children. He has given us different complexions and different customs. To you He has given the arts. To these He has not opened our eyes. We know these things to be true. Since He has made so great a difference between us in other things, why may we not conclude that He has given us a different religion according to our understanding? The Great Spirit does right. He knows what is best for His children; we are satisfied.

Brother, we do not wish to destroy your religion or take it from you. We only want to enjoy our own.

Brother, you say you have not come to get our land or our money, but to enlighten our minds. I will now tell you that I have been at your meetings and saw you collect money from the meeting. I cannot tell what this money was intended for, but suppose that it was for your minister; and, if we should conform to your way of thinking, perhaps you may want some from us.

Brother, we are told that you have been preaching to the white people in this place. These people are our neighbors. We are acquainted with them. We will wait a little while and see what effect your preaching has upon them. If we find it does them good, makes them honest, and less disposed to cheat Indians, we will then consider again of what you have said.

86. The author of this passage is probably
   A. a missionary.
   B. a land agent.
   C. a governmental cabinet minister.
   D. an actor.
   E. a chief.

87. The author of this selection is protesting
   A. the warfare which has destroyed his family.
   B. the arts of the conquerors.
   C. the plan of the Great Spirit.
   D. the imposition of a foreign system of belief.
   E. the duplicity of treaties written by government agents.

88. The passage proceeds by
   A. enumerating logical contradictions.
   B. emotional demands for political equality.
   C. cause and effect organization.
   D. sophistical reasoning.
   E. cataloging economic grievances.

89. Which of the following paradoxes may *not* be inferred from the passage?
   A. The disagreement among Christians over points of scripture
   B. The mixing of spiritual and material goals
   C. The conflict between lip service and religious practice
   D. The variation in religion according to cultural differences
   E. The desire to destroy others' beliefs instead of tolerating them

90. This passage is most probably addressed to
   A. the Great Spirit.
   B. a political convention.
   C. a tax collector.
   D. a missionary.
   E. an Indian emissary.

Answers and Explanations

86. Answer (**E**)
   Explanation: Most people would have little trouble recognizing from the speaker's use of such phrases as "Great Spirit" that he is an Indian chief.

87. **Answer (D)**

Explanation: Since the general topic concerns religion, the answer should be somehow related to religion. In particular, the chief is objecting to the attempt of the white men to impose their religious beliefs on the Indian culture. Thus, (D) is the answer.

88. **Answer (A)**

Explanation: The chief is particularly effective at demonstrating failures and inconsistencies in the white man's religion. He notes in the first paragraph the dissension among various sects of Christianity. He questions in the fifth paragraph why money is collected at services, when he has been told that it is not the purpose of the religion to gather funds. Finally, in the last paragraph he points out discrepancies between what the white men preach in their religion and what they practice in their treatment of Indians. Thus, his argument proceeds by enumerating logical contradictions.

89. **Answer (D)**

Explanation: We must consider each answer until we find one that is not implied in the passage. (A) is implied in the first paragraph, where the chief wonders why the white people disagree so much if they all read the same Book (Book = Scriptures). The collection of money in paragraph five represents the mixing of operational and material goals (B). The failure of whites to treat Indians properly indicates one conflict between lip service and religious practice (C), and the white man's failure to tolerate the Indians' religion is indicated in the third paragraph (E). No mention is made, however, of variations in religion according to cultural differences.

90. **Answer (D)**

Explanation: Obviously, the chief is addressing someone who wants to convert him to another religion. Of the choices, only a missionary (D) is a likely answer.

Questions 91–95

I advise you to make your will in the following manner: Take care that if written on several separate sheets of paper, they are all fastened together and that the pages are numbered. Sign your name at the bottom of each sheet, and state at the end of your will of how many pages your will consists. If there are any erasures or interlineations, put your initials in the margin opposite to them, and notice them in the attestation. The attestation should be already written at the end of the will. . . .

The two persons intended to be the witnesses should be called in and told that you desire them to witness your will, and then you should sign your name in their presence, and desire them each to look at the signature. Your signature should follow your will but should precede the signatures of the witnesses, for if you were to sign after they have signed, your will would be void. When, therefore, you have signed, they should sign their names and residences at the foot of the attestation. You will observe, that according to the attestation, neither of the witnesses, although he has signed the attestation, should leave the room until the other witness has signed also. Remember that they must both sign in your presence, and therefore you should not allow them to go into another room to sign, or even into any recess, or any other part of the same room where it is possible that you may not be able to see them sign. If, therefore, you do not choose them to sign after you at the same table or desk, have a table placed close to you before they come into the room, so as to create no confusion, at which they can and ought to sign before leaving the room.

If you were to send your servant, who happened to be one of the intended witnesses, out of the room, even for a table, he must leave the room before you sign. If after your death a question were to arise upon the fact of your having signed in the presence of both the witnesses present at the same time, the man would of course admit that he left the room before you did sign, and then imagine what reliance would be placed upon that fact in cross-examination, and in the address to the jury. The precaution which I recommend would prevent this difficulty from arising.

91. A good title for this selection might be
   A. Legacies: Myth or Legend.
   B. Witnesses and Signatures.
   C. Inheritance and Avoiding Probate.
   D. The Handwritten Document.
   E. How to Execute a Will.

92. The suggestion for assembling a will which the author does *not* include is that
   A. the individual pages of the will should be filed separately.
   B. each sheet should be signed.
   C. corrections should be initialed.
   D. the pages of the will should be numbered.
   E. erasures should be listed in the attestation.

93. According to the passage the attestation
    A. precedes the body of the will.
    B. lists the property to be bequeathed.
    C. must be signed by a servant.
    D. should contain the addresses of the witnesses.
    E. is an optional section of the will.

94. All of the following must be observed in the signing of the will *except*:
    A. The witnesses must examine the signature.
    B. The witnesses must not ever leave the room.
    C. Each witness must be present when the other witness signs.
    D. The maker of the will must observe the witnesses signing the attestation.
    E. The witness cannot sign before the maker of the will.

95. It may be inferred that the discussion of the technical formalities of the signing of the will are outlined in order to
    A. create legalistic confusion in the mind of the reader.
    B. demonstrate the necessity for professional aid in preparing this kind of paper.
    C. prevent a contest of an improperly prepared document.
    D. ensure that a fair hearing will be held after the maker's death.
    E. avoid tricky procedures on the part of the witnesses.

Answers and Explanations

91. Answer (**B**)
    Explanation: Eliminate (A) because it is too general. Usually the most general and most restricted titles will be incorrect choices. Though the "how to" aspect of (E) seems appealing at first, we must eliminate it because the passage concerns signing the will, not executing it (putting it into force). Likewise, eliminate (C) because no specific mention is given to inheritance or probate. Eliminate (D) as too general also, since the term "handwritten document" can refer to many things in addition to wills.

92. Answer (**A**)
    Explanation: When asked what the passage does *not* include, the best procedure is to skim through the text looking for each of the possibilities, choosing the one possibility that does not appear. Here, all the

possibilities appear in the first paragraph. The passage states that the pages should be fastened together, a procedure that prevents their being filed separately. Common sense, too, should indicate the foolishness of filing each page of the document separately.

93. Answer (**D**)
    Explanation: Close reading of the passage is required to arrive at the proper answer, but common sense can eliminate a few erroneous answers. It is an unlikely requirement that a will *must* be signed by a servant. Also, given the very strict nature of the process, it is unlikely that the attestation will be optional. So, eliminate (C) and (E). In the middle of the second paragraph is a statement indicating that the addresses of the witnesses must appear in the attestation.

94. Answer (**B**)
    Explanation: Even if you do not completely understand the passage, you can eliminate several answers on the basis of common sense. If the purpose of the witnesses is to verify the signature, then they ought to examine it (A). They obviously cannot sign their verification before the maker has himself signed the will (E). But the witnesses may leave the room and return *before* the maker has signed, so (B) is correct.

95. Answer (**C**)
    Explanation: Eliminate (A), since the author is unlikely to want to create confusion. Eliminate (B), since the purpose of the passage is to provide the necessary procedures for preparing a will. Be suspicious of adjectives like "tricky"; they are usually too informal for this kind of writing. Thus, eliminate (E). Of the remaining choices, (C) is better because it addresses more directly the issue of how well the will is prepared.

Questions 96–100

Optimism is a good characteristic, but if carried to an excess it becomes foolishness. We are prone to speak of the resources of this country as inexhaustible; this is not so. The mineral wealth of the country, the coal, iron, oil, gas, and the like, does not reproduce itself and therefore is certain to be exhausted ultimately; and wastefulness in dealing with it today means that our descendants will feel the exhaustion a generation or two before they otherwise would. But there are certain other forms of waste which could be entirely stopped—the waste of soil by washing, for instance, which is among the most dangerous of all wastes now in progress in the United States, is easily preventable, so that this present enormous loss of fertility is entirely unnecessary. The preservation or replacement of the forests is one of the most important means of preventing this loss. We have made a beginning in forest preservation, but . . . so rapid has been the rate of exhaustion of timber in the United States in the past, and so rapidly is the remainder being exhausted, that the country is unquestionably on the verge of a timber famine which will be felt in every household in the land. . . . The present annual consumption of lumber is certainly three times as great as the annual growth; and if the consumption and growth continue unchanged, practically all our lumber will be exhausted in another generation, while long before the limit to complete exhaustion is reached the growing scarcity will make itself felt in many blighting ways upon our national welfare. About twenty percent of our forested territory is now reserved in national forests; but these do not include the most valuable timberlands, and in any event the proportion is too small to expect that the reserves can accomplish more than a mitigation of the trouble which is ahead for the nation.

96. The author of this passage is likely to be a(n):
    A. economist.
    B. capitalist.
    C. laborer.
    D. novelist.
    E. conservationist.

97. According to the passage waste may be categorized into
    A. recycled and unrecycled by-products.
    B. animal, vegetable, and mineral products.
    C. fertile and infertile wastes.
    D. preventable and nonpreventable exhaustion of resources.
    E. proportional and mitigated blights on the environment.

98. It may be inferred that the author of the passage views the exhaustion of America's nonreproductive wealth as
    A. reversible.
    B. welcome.
    C. inevitable.
    D. contemptible.
    E. sanctioned.

99. The author is most concerned about the exhaustion of lumber as a resource because
    A. optimism prevents him from acting.
    B. mineral wealth will be sufficient.
    C. soil erosion cannot be prevented.
    D. forest preservation is an intense public concern.
    E. it is being consumed faster than it can be grown.

100. According to the passage the author feels that national forests
    A. are an unnecessary bureaucratic expense.
    B. create a healthy environment for American recreation.
    C. are holding their own against soil erosion.
    D. were not created out of the best timberland.
    E. should represent fifty percent of the nation's timberland.

Answers and Explanations

96. Answer (**E**)
    Explanation: The passage concerns the use of our natural resources, especially forests. Thus, the author will be someone who is concerned with natural resources. Economists and laborers are not identified with resources; nor are novelists or capitalists, though they may sometimes show an interest in resources. But conservationists conserve resources.

97. Answer (**D**)
    Explanation: "According to the passage" means that the answer must be stated explicitly in the text. Be wary of popular-sounding answers that are not in the text. Even though recycling is currently a well-publicized way of preserving resources, it is not mentioned in the passage. Also, be skeptical of words that are intended to sound especially scientific or that are intended to be impressive in other ways. "Proportional and mitigated blights" (**E**) are such words. A reading of the passage reveals that the author speaks of preventable and nonpreventable exhaustion of resources.

98. Answer (**C**)
    Explanation: "Inferred" means that the answer will not be stated explicitly in the passage, so do not waste time looking for it.
    The author is unlikely to be happy about the exhaustion of resources, so we may eliminate (B). By definition "nonreproductive" means nonreplaceable;

as the exhaustion of such wealth must come sooner or later. It is not reversible (A); it is inevitable (C).

99. Answer (E)

Explanation: Common sense will eliminate (A) as ridiculous. Likewise. if mineral wealth will be sufficient, then the author will have no cause for concern; so we eliminate (B) too. For the same reason, we can eliminate (D). Public concern about forest preservation is unlikely to be the reason for the author's concern. So only (C) and (E) make sense as possible answers. The passage speaks specifically of how we are consuming lumber faster than we replace it; so (E) is correct.

100. Answer (D)

Explanation: Here too common sense will eliminate some answers. A conservationist will support national forests; he will not consider them an unnecessary bureaucratic expense. His concern about the exhaustion of resources should contradict the statement that the national forests are holding their own against soil erosion. So we eliminate (A) and (C). (B), (D), and (E) are all things he might have said, though (E) seems somewhat overstated. In fact, he states in the last sentence that national forests were not made from the best timberland.

Questions 101–105

First of all, my readers should know that the ancient astronomical hypotheses of Ptolemy, in the fashion in which they have been unfolded in the *Theoricae* of Purbach and by the other writers of epitomes, are to be completely removed from this discussion and cast out of the mind. For they do not convey the true layout of the bodies of the world and the polity of the movements.

Although I cannot do otherwise than to put solely Copernicus' opinion concerning the world in the place of those hypotheses and, if that were possible, to persuade everyone of it; but because the thing is still new among the mass of the intelligentsia (*apud vulgus studiosorum*), and the doctrine that the Earth is one of the planets and moves among the stars around a motionless sun sounds very absurd to the ears of most of them: therefore those who are shocked by the unfamiliarity of this opinion should know that these harmonical speculations are possible even with the hypotheses of Tycho Brahe—because that author holds, in common with Copernicus, everything else which pertains to the layout of the bodies

and the tempering of the movements, and transfers solely the Copernican annual movement of the Earth to the whole system of planetary spheres and to the sun, which occupies the center of that system, in the opinion of both authors. For after this transference of movement it is nevertheless true that in Brahe the Earth occupies at any time the same place that Copernicus gives it, if not in the very vast and measureless region of the fixed stars, at least in the system of the planetary world. And accordingly, just as he who draws a circle on paper makes the writing-foot of the compass or stylus motionless; so too, in the case of Copernicus, the Earth, by the real movement of its body, measures out a circle revolving midway between the circle of Mars on the outside and that of Venus on the inside; but in the case of Tycho Brahe, the whole planetary system (wherein among the rest the circles of Mars and Venus are round) revolves like a tablet on a lathe and applies to the motionless Earth, or to the stylus on the lathe, the midspace between the circles of Mars and Venus; and it comes about from this movement of the system that the Earth within it, although remaining motionless, marks out the same circle around the sun and midway between Mars and Venus, which in Copernicus it marks out by the real movement of its body while the system is at rest. Therefore, since harmonic speculation considers the eccentric movements of the planets, as if seen from the sun, you may easily understand that if any observer were stationed on a sun as much in motion as you please, nevertheless for him, the Earth, although at rest (as a concession to Brahe), would seem to describe the annual circle midway between the planets and in an intermediate length of time. Wherefore, if there is any man of such feeble wit that he cannot grasp the movement of the Earth among the stars, nevertheless he can take pleasure in the most excellent spectacle of this most divine construction, if he applies to their image in the sun whatever he hears concerning the daily movements of the Earth in its eccentric—such an image as Tycho Brahe exhibits, with the Earth at rest.

101. It may be assumed that the author challenges "the feeble wit" of his readers because
    A. the theory he is defending is feeble.
    B. Copernicus had a reputation for being backward.
    C. ancient astronomers were held in such low esteem in his day.
    D. he is propagandizing ideas that are new and shocking.
    E. he is in complete accord with Tycho Brahe.

102. It may be inferred that "harmonic speculation" is
    A. solely the subject of the writer of epitomes.
    B. based on the relation of the circles of the planets.
    C. a vulgar study of the intelligentsia.
    D. based on an earth standard of mathematics.
    E. independent of astronomical facts.

103. It can be inferred that the author of this passage is
    A. a peer of Ptolemy.
    B. roughly contemporary with Copernicus.
    C. sympathetic to the *Theoricae* of Purbach.
    D. convinced of a geocentric system.
    E. a crank astronomer.

104. Copernicus and Tycho Brahe agree in their theories that
    A. we live in a heliocentric system.
    B. the Earth is motionless.
    C. the moon turns like a lathe.
    D. the annual circle of the sun is diminishing.
    E. the Earth is placed inside of Mars and Venus.

105. The author's strongest argument for a sun-centered universe
    A. contradicts Aristarchus of Samos.
    B. is based on Ptolemy's theories.
    C. positions an observer stationed on the sun who witnesses the movements of all the planets.
    D. depends on the analogy of a tablet on a lathe.
    E. concurs with Tycho Brahe's viewpoint.

Answers and Explanations

101. Answer (**D**)
Explanation: Written in an archaic style and not well organized, the passage is particularly difficult to follow. Nonetheless, you can make intelligent responses even if you have not comprehended the passage too well. Eliminate (A) because the quotation says "The feeble wit of his reader," not the feebleness of his theory. Further, it is unlikely that he will refer to his theory as feeble. The answer must somehow indicate a situation in which readers are likely to resist accepting the theory, hence the necessity to insult their wit. Of the remaining possibilities, new and shocking ideas are most likely to be resisted, and (D) is, in fact, correct. If you are familiar with Copernicus, you will know that (B) and (C) are factually incorrect.

102. Answer (**B**)
Explanation: Given the general nature of the passage, we may reasonably infer that any technical term will be related to science or mathematics. Thus, (A) and (C) are unlikely answers because they do not deal directly with science. For the remaining answers we must consult the passage. "Harmonic speculation" is mentioned twice: once toward the beginning and once in the second-to-last sentence. In the latter instance we are told that harmonic speculation "considers the eccentric movement of the planets." Since only answer (B) mentions the planets, it is correct.

103. Answer (**B**)
Explanation: Answers like (E), which use very informal and demeaning language, can be eliminated immediately. Be wary of technical-sounding answers; more often than not they are incorrect. Thus (C) is probably incorrect too. (A) and (B) both deal with the notion of the author's being a peer of someone. Because the possibility appears twice, one of those answers is probably correct. Indeed, his discussion of Copernicus' *Theories* as though they are new indicates that (B) is correct.

104. Answer (**A**)
Explanation: Eliminate (E) because it is an absurd answer. All of the remaining answers are at least possible given the general subject of the passage, though (C) too should seem somewhat strange. Question 105, which talks about a sun-centered universe, should help direct us to the correct answer here (A). The root *-centric* means "centered," *helio-* means "sun" and *geo-* means "earth." Thus *heliocentric* means "sun centered," and *geocentric* means "earth centered."

105. Answer (**C**)
Explanation: Eliminate (A) because no one named Aristarchus of Samos is ever mentioned in the passage. You should have realized by now that the author agrees with Copernicus and disagrees with Ptolemy (the two most significant figures in pre-twentieth century astronomy). Thus (B) is incorrect too. Though the author is sympathetic to Tycho Brahe, his argument for a heliocentric universe is based on the positions of an observer stationed on the sun.

Each one has his reasons: for one, art is a flight; for another, a means of conquering. But one can flee into a hermitage, into madness, into death. One can conquer by arms. Why does it have to be *writing*, why does one have to manage his escapes and conquests by *writing*? Because, behind the various aims of authors, there is a deeper and more immediate choice which is common to all of us. We shall try to elucidate this choice, and we shall see whether it is not in the name of this very choice of writing that the engagement of writers must be required.

Each of our perceptions is accompanied by the consciousness that human reality is a "revealer"; that is, it is through human reality that "there is" being, or, to put it differently, that man is the means by which things are manifested. It is our presence in the world which multiplies relations. It is we who set up a relationship between this tree and that bit of sky. Thanks to us, that star which has been dead for millennia, that quarter moon, and that dark river are disclosed in the unity of landscape. It is the speed of our auto and our airplane which organizes the great masses of the earth. With each of our acts, the world reveals to us a new face. But, if we know that we are directors of being, we also know that we are not its producers. If we turn away from this landscape, it will sink back into its dark permanence. At least, it will sink back; there is no one mad enough to think that it is going to be annihilated. It is we who shall be annihilated, and the earth will remain in its lethargy until another consciousness comes along to awaken it. Thus, to our inner certainty of being "revealers" is added that of being inessential in relation to the thing revealed.

One of the chief motives of artistic creation is certainly the need of feeling that we are essential in relationship to the world. If I fix on canvas or in writing a certain aspect of the fields or the sea or a look on someone's face which I have disclosed, I am conscious of having produced them by condensing relationship, by introducing order where there was none, by imposing the unity of mind on the diversity of things. That is, I feel myself essential in relation to my creation. But this time it is the created object which escapes me; I cannot reveal and produce at the same time. The creation becomes inessential in relation to the creative activity. First of all, even if it appears to others as definitive, the created object always seems to us in a state of suspension; we can always change this line, that shade, that word. Thus, it never *forces itself*. A novice painter asked his teacher, "When should I consider my painting finished?" And the teacher answered, "When you can look at it in amazement and say to yourself 'I'm the one who did that!'"

106. A good title for this passage might be
    A. The Landscape of the Mind.
    B. Man's Flight out of the World.
    C. The Artist As Revealer of Reality.
    D. The Painter's and the Writer's Escape.
    E. Writer vs. Artist.

107. When the author claims that without the human consciousness the landscape "will sink back into its dark permanence," he does *not* imply that
    A. the observer reveals relationships.
    B. man organizes individual experiences into unity.
    C. humans are the producers of being.
    D. we cannot annihilate reality.
    E. man is inessential in relation to the thing revealed.

108. One of the satisfactions of the artist, it is implied, is
    A. a flight into a hermitage.
    B. the lethargy of consciousness.
    C. the initiation of an artistic project.
    D. indulging in a state of suspension.
    E. the imposition of unity on diversity.

109. It can be inferred that the difference between revealing and producing is that
    A. man acts in the former case, but is acted upon in the latter.
    B. one is the act of the writer, the other of the painter.
    C. man is inessential in one and essential in the other.
    D. of the intensity of the force of the object.
    E. one requires a teacher, while the other does not.

110. The author takes the attitude of a(an)
    A. satirist.
    B. anthropologist.
    C. philosopher.
    D. pedant.
    E. sentimentalist.

Answers and Explanations

106. Answer **(C)**

Explanation: In general, when asked to find a title of a passage, eliminate the most general and most restrictive answers. Also, eliminate answers that attempt to sound very poetic, technical, or fancy. Here, we may eliminate (A) as too general. None of the other answers is especially restrictive. (B) sounds a little too fancy and has little to do with the passage. (E) is also too general, compared to (D) and (C). Furthermore, the passage is not really comparing writers and artists—both types of creators are called artists. The philosophic tone suggests that (C) is the most appropriate answer, and indeed much of the passage involves the artist's relationship to reality.

107. Answer (C)

Explanation: To those unused to speculation about the arts, this passage too may be difficult to follow Nonetheless, if you simply observe the answers you can sometimes pinpoint the correct choice without too much difficulty. Here, we are looking for the one statement that the passage *does not* imply. If we can discover a statement that is clearly false, then we will probably do very well by choosing it, since no author is going to weaken his case by basing it on something that everyone recognizes as false. Thus, (C) is correct, for humans clearly are not the producers of being, no matter what their relation to reality may be.

108. Answer (E)

Explanation: Eliminate (A) because it is obviously a statement true of only a few artists, and it has little to do with artistic satisfaction. Likewise, (D) is too mystical sounding for the serious nature of this passage. Nor would the author likely promote lethargy as a satisfaction (B). (C) and (E), then, are possible answers. (E) is explicitly stated in the middle of the third paragraph.

109. Answer (C)

Explanation: Eliminate (E) because the only mention of a teacher in the passage is as part of an anecdote. (B) fails to regard both writers and painters as artists; both reveal reality in their separate ways. (D) does not really make sense. No mention is ever made of "force of an object," and the sentence as stated is too vague. Thus, (A) and (C) remain. The answer, (C), is given in the middle of the third paragraph.

110. Answer (C)

Explanation: The abstract consideration of such subjects as "being" and "reality" should point immediately to the correct answer, (C). Certainly, there is no satire, because there is no humor. Nor is the subject matter proper for an anthropologist. The passage further lacks sentimentality and shows no signs of pedantry.

Questions 111–115

The communities of ants are sometimes very large, numbering even up to 500,000 individuals; and it is a lesson to us that no one has ever yet seen a quarrel between any two ants belonging to the same community. On the other hand, it must be admitted that they are in hostility not only with most other insects, including ants of different species, but even with those of the same species if belonging to different communities. I have over and over again introduced ants from one of my nests into another nest of the same species; and they were invariably attacked, seized by a leg or an antenna, and dragged out.

It is evident, therefore, that the ants of each community all recognize one another, which is very remarkable. But more than this, I several times divided a nest into two halves and found that even after separation of a year and nine months they recognized one another and were perfectly friendly, while they at once attacked ants from a different nest, although of the same species.

It has been suggested that the ants of each nest have some sign or password by which they recognize one another. To test this I made some insensible. First I tried chloroform; but this was fatal to them, and . . . I did not consider the test satisfactory. I decided therefore to intoxicate them. This was less easy than I had expected. None of my ants would voluntarily degrade themselves by getting drunk. However, I got over the difficulty by putting them into whiskey for a few moments. I took fifty specimens—twenty-five percent from one nest and twenty-five percent from another—made them dead drunk, marked each with a spot of paint, and put them on a table close to where other ants from one of the nests were feeding. The table was surrounded as usual with a moat of water to prevent them from straying. The ants which were feeding soon noticed those which I had made drunk. They seemed quite astonished to find their comrades in such a disgraceful condition, and as much at a loss to know what to do with their drunkards as we were. After awhile, however, they carried them all away; the strangers they took to the edge of the moat and dropped into the water, while they bore their friends home into the nest, where by degrees they slept off the effects of the spirits. Thus it is evident that they know their friends even when incapable of giving any sign or password.

111. A good title for this passage might be
    A. Nature's Mysteries.
    B. Human Qualities in the Insect World.
    C. Drunken Ants.
    D. Communication in Ant Communities.
    E. Species of Password Development.

112. Attitudes of ants toward strangers of the same species may be categorized as
    A. indifferent.
    B. curious.
    C. hostile.
    D. passive.
    E. intoxicated.

113. The author's anecdotes of the inebriated ants would support all the following inductions *except* the statement that
    A. ants take unwillingly to intoxicants.
    B. ants aid comrades in distress.
    C. ants have invariable recognition of their community members.
    D. ants refuse to help strangers.
    E. ants recognize their comrades by a mysterious password.

114. According to the passage chloroform was less successful than alcohol for inhibiting communication because of
    A. its expense.
    B. its unpredictable side effects.
    C. its unavailability.
    D. its habit-forming qualities.
    E. its fatality.

115. Although the author is a scientist, his style of writing also exhibits a quality of
    A. sophistry.
    B. whimsy.

C. hypocrisy.
D. tragedy.
E. practicality.

Answers and Explanations

111. Answer (**D**)
    Explanation: Eliminate (A) and (E) as the most general and specific choices. Eliminate (C) because it is too informal. Since the true subject of the paper is the investigation of how ants communicate, (D) is correct.

112. Answer (**C**)
    Explanation: Eliminate (E) because "intoxicated" is not an attitude; it is a state of being. (A) and (B) form a pair of opposites, as do (C) and (D). In the second paragraph we are told that ants will attack members of the same species, so (C) is correct.

113. Answer (**E**)
    Explanation: This question requires an understanding of the passage. The purpose of the experiment with the drunken ants was to make them too inebriated to give a password, if one existed. That their comrades recognized them anyway indicates that no password was necessary for recognition. Thus, (E) is correct.

114. Answer (**E**)
    Explanation: Eliminate (D) because it is unlikely that the scientist will worry about habit-forming qualities, since he, not the ants, controls how much they receive. The other answers are plausible, but we are told that chloroform kills the ants; so (E) is correct.

115. Answer (**B**)
    Explanation: The word *although* indicates that his style will reveal something not usually associated with scientific writing. Thus we eliminate (E). There is no sense of tragedy or hypocrisy in this account of the ants. Sophistry is distorted logic, and that too is absent. But the scientist does maintain an unusual comic perspective on his subject, and (B) is correct.

In this section solve each problem, using any available space on the page for scratch work. Then indicate the *one* correct answer in the appropriate space on the answer sheet.

The following information is for your reference in solving some of the problems.

Circle of radius r: Area $= \pi r^2$
Circumference $= 2\pi r$

The number of degrees of arc in a circle is 360.

The measure in degrees of a straight angle is 180.

Definitions of symbols:

$<$ is less than	$\leq$ is less than or equal to
$>$ is greater than	$\geq$ is greater than or equal to
$\perp$ is perpendicular to	$\parallel$ is parallel to

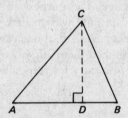

Triangle: The sum of the measures in degrees of the angles of a triangle is 180.

If $\angle CDA$ is a right angle, then
(1) Area of $\triangle ABC$
$= \dfrac{AB \times CD}{2}$;
(2) $AC^2 = AD^2 + DC^2$.

NOTE: Figures which accompany problems in this test are intended to provide information useful in solving the problems. They are drawn as accurately as possible *except* when it is stated in a specific problem that its figure is not drawn to scale. All figures lie in a plane unless otherwise indicated. All numbers used are real numbers.

1. $5 + 6 \cdot 2 + 8 = ?$
   (A) 25   (B) 30   (C) 68   (D) 110   (E) 65

2. If 1 inch equals 2.54 centimeters, then 2.54 inches equal _____ cm.

(A) 1   (B) 2.589   (C) .622   (D) 12   (E) None of these

3. The diameter of a circle is 40 inches. Two chords, $\overline{AB}$ and $\overline{CD}$ are 10 inches and 17 inches from the center of the circle respectively. It is true that
(A) $AB < CD$ (B) $AB > CD$ (C) $AD > BC$
(D) $AB - CD = 7$ (E) $CD - AB = 7$

4.

$$\frac{\dfrac{4}{5} + 3 + \dfrac{5}{8}}{\dfrac{8}{5} + 6\dfrac{5}{4}} =$$

(A) 1/4   (B) 1/2   (C) 1/8   (D) 1/6   (E) 17/40

5. Find the number of degrees in the angle made by the hour and minute hands of a clock at 3:30.
   (A) 90°   (B) 60°   (C) 75°   (D) 100°   (E) 82 1/2°

6. If $A > B$, then which of the following statements must be true?
   (A) $AC > BD$ for all values of C
   (B) $\dfrac{A}{C} > \dfrac{B}{C}$ for all values of C
   (C) $A + B > 0$
   (D) $AB > 0$
   (E) $A - B > 0$

7. How many 2-inch cubes can be put in a box 8 inches long, 2 inches wide, and 5 inches tall?
   (A) 8   (B) 9   (C) 10   (D) 11   (E) 12

8. Find the area of the shaded region if the radius of the circle is 6.

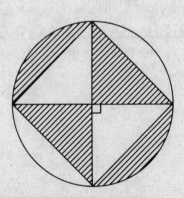

(A) 36π (B) 18π
(C) 24π (D) 16π
(E) 9π

9. One-half of a number is 7 more than one-third of that number. Find the number.
(A) 72   (B) 63   (C) 54   (D) 42   (E) 84

10.

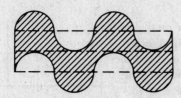

The figure above is constructed by drawing eight semicircles upon a rectangle as shown. If the diameter of the semicircles is D, find the area of the shaded region.
(A) $2\pi D$ (B) $4\pi D$ (C) $4D^2$ (D) $8D^2$
(E) $4D^2 + 2\pi D$

11. What percent of 5 is 50% of 50?
(A) 5   (B) 50   (C) 500   (D) 25   (E) 250

12. $(42 \cdot 143) + (37 \cdot 143) + (143 \cdot 31) =$
(A) 15,730   (B) 16,730   (C) 15,630   (D) 16,330
(E) None of these

13. Mr. Jones left half of his estate to his wife, half of the remainder to his older son, half of the new remainder to his younger son, and the last $5,000 to the Loyal Order of Water Buffalo. What was the total amount of Mr. Jones' estate?
(A) $5,000   (B) $15,000   (C) $20,000
(D) $40,000   (E) $80,000

14. Which is the largest of the following fractions?
(A) $\frac{1}{3}$ (B) $\frac{3}{10}$ (C) $\frac{5}{14}$ (D) $\frac{10}{27}$ (E) $\frac{17}{50}$

15. Find the sum of the measures of angles B, C, D, and E in the figure at right.

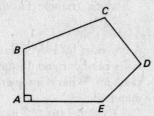

(A) $360°$ (B) $540°$ (C) $270°$ (D) $450°$ (E) $630°$

16. If every dimension of a rectangular box is doubled, by what number is the volume multiplied?
(A) 2   (B) 3   (C) 4   (D) 6   (E) 8

17. 17% of 200 =
(A) 22   (B) 34   (C) 8.5   (D) 17   (E) 51

18. If $\frac{3}{4}X - \frac{3}{4} = 0$, then $5x = ?$
(A) 5   (B) 1   (C) 0   (D) 15/4   (E) 20/3

19.

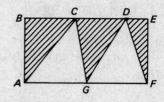

$AB = EF = 6$

$BC = CD = 5$

$AG = GF = 6$

$DE = 2$

Figure $ABEF$ is a parallelogram.
Find the area of the shaded region.
(A) 30   (B) 32   (C) 36   (D) 48   (E) Cannot be determined

20. An isosceles right triangle has hypotenuse of 8. Find its area.

(A) 4   (B) 8   (C) 16   (D) 32   (E) 48

21. A pipe has an outer diameter of 1.55 inches and an inside diameter of 1 1/4 inches. Find the thickness, assuming that the pipe is of equal thickness throughout.
(A) .30 inches   (B) .03 inches   (C) .15 inches
(D) .20 inches   (E) .25 inches

22. Mary's average on two tests is 65. What score does she need in the third test in order to raise her average to 70?
(A) 75
(B) $78\frac{2}{3}$
(C) 80
(D) $83\frac{1}{3}$
(E) 85

23. In the figure at right, how many different downward paths can be taken from point *A* to point *B*?

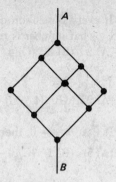

(A) 2 (B) 3 (C) 4 (D) 6 (E) 12

24. 100 is what percent of *P*?
(A) 100 (B) *P* (C) 100*P* (D) 100/*P*
(E) 10,000/*P*

25. A garbage disposal can handle 3 lbs of refuse in 6 minutes. How many minutes will it need for 6 lbs of refuse?
(A) 3 (B) 6 (C) 9 (D) 12 (E) 15

26. 20 pounds of laundry need 20 minutes to dry on a clothesline. How many minutes are needed to dry 50 lbs of laundry under similar conditions on another clothesline?
(A) 20 (B) 50 (C) 100 (D) 250 (E) 500

27. For which of the following pairs of numbers is the operation of exponentiation commutative (that is, $X^Y = Y^X$)?
(A) 1 and 2 (B) 1 and 3 (C) 2 and 3 (D) 2 and 4 (E) 3 and 4

28. $15 + 16 + 17 + \cdots + 22 + 23 + 24 = ?$
(A) 188 (B) 193 (C) 195 (D) 201 (E) None of these

29. By what number is the area of a circle multiplied if its diameter is doubled?
(A) 2 (B) 4 (C) 2π (D) 4π (E) $2\pi r$

30. If 1 foop = 3 zats and 1 zat = 3 doons, 27 doons = _____ foops.
(A) 1/3 (B) 1/9 (C) 1 (D) 9 (E) 3

31. A contractor can paint a house in 5 days by using 6 men. If he actually uses 4 men and 2 of the men work only half-days, how many days will it take to do this job?
(A) $2\frac{1}{2}$ (B) $3\frac{1}{4}$ (C) 5 (D) $7\frac{1}{2}$ (E) 10

32. (?) cubic feet = $\frac{1}{3}$ cubic yard
(A) 9 (B) 3 (C) 1 (D) 2/3 (E) 4/3

33. $\frac{0.5}{7} + \frac{0.2}{7} =$
(A) 1 (B) 7 (C) 1/10 (D) 1/100 (E) 10

34. What is $\frac{1}{3}$ of $\frac{3}{5}$ of $\frac{7}{8}$ of $\frac{5}{7}$ of 32?
(A) 2 (B) 4 (C) 5/8 (D) 35/48 (E) 16

35. The figure on the right is made up of congruent squares. Find the area of the figure if its perimeter is 48.

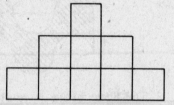

(A) 72 (B) 81 (C) 108 (D) 126 (E) None of these

36. What is the greatest number of pieces into which a pie can be cut with three straight cuts of a knife?
(A) 3 (B) 4 (C) 6 (D) 7 (E) 9

37. The figure below is a parallelogram with *N* = the midpoint of *BC* and *M* is any other point in *BN*. Determine which of the following triangles has the greatest area.

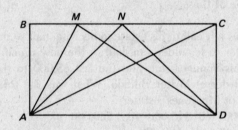

(A) *AMD*
(B) *AND*
(C) *ACD*
(D) All three triangles have equal areas.
(E) There is not enough information to determine which triangle has the greatest area.

38. A boy rides his bicycle for 10 minutes at a rate of 15 miles per hour and 15 minutes at a rate of 10 miles per hour. What is his average speed for the entire 25 minutes?
(A) 12 mph (B) $12\frac{1}{2}$ mph (C) 13 mph (D) $13\frac{1}{2}$ mph (E) None of these

39. What percent of the multiples of 5 between 101 and 600 are also multiples of 3?
(A) $\frac{1}{15}$ (B) $\frac{1}{3}$ (C) 50 (D) 20 (E) $33\frac{1}{3}$

40.

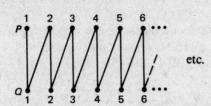

etc.

According to the figure above, which of the following pairs of points is(are) not connected by a little line segment?
   I. P_{11} and P_{12}
   II. Q_{11} and Q_{12}
   III. P_{21} and Q_{22}
   IV. Q_{27} and P_{28}
(A) I only
(B) I and II only
(C) IV only
(D) I, II, and III only
(E) I, II, III, and IV

41. Which of the following is not a prime number?
(A) 23 (B) 17 (C) 41 (D) 101 (E) 111

42. A grape weighs 2/3 of its weight plus 2/3 of an ounce. What is its weight in ounces?
(A) 2 (B) 1 2/3 (C) 2 2/3 (D) 1 (E) 1 1/3

43. If $1 + 2 + 3 + \cdots + 8 + 9 + 10 = 55$, then $341 + 342 + \cdots + 349 + 350 = ?$
(A) 3,455 (B) 3,355 (C) 3,555 (D) 3,505
(E) 3,405

44. A hen and one-half lays an egg and one-half in a day and one-half. How many eggs will three hens lay in three days?
(A) 3 (B) 4 1/2 (C) 6 (D) 1 1/2 (E) 9

45.

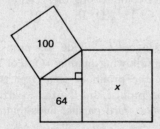

In the diagram above, the areas of the squares are 64, 100, and x. The value of x is

(A) 164 (B) 200 (C) 136 (D) 196 (E) 216

46. Which of the following *must* be an odd number?
   I. $n + 1$
   II. $2n + 1$
   III. $3n + 1$
(A) I only
(B) II only
(C) III only
(D) I and II only
(E) I, II, and III

47. When first-class postage rates were raised from 8¢ to 10¢, the rate of the increase was
(A) 2% (B) 10% (C) 16% (D) 20% (E) 25%

48. 15 is $12\frac{1}{2}$% of what number?
(A) 45 (B) 60 (C) 80 (D) 120 (E) 125

49. $\dfrac{15 \cdot 24 \cdot 15}{12 \cdot 5 \cdot 30} =$
(A) 1/5 (B) 45 (C) 3 (D) 1 (E) 1/15

50.

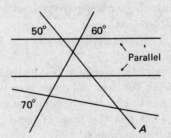

If each of the integers from 1 to 9 is placed in one of the boxes on the figure above in such a manner that the sum of the three integers in any row, or the three integers in any column, or the three integers in any diagonal is always 15, then the sum of the two integers needed to replace the x and y is
(A) 15 (B) 12 (C) 17 (D) 13 (E) 9

51.

What is the measure of angle A in the figure above?
(A) 30° (B) 40° (C) 50° (D) 60° (E) 70°

52. If $x + y$ is 60 more than $x - y$, then $y =$
(A) 30 (B) 15 (C) 60 (D) 40 (E) Cannot be determined

53. For what value of x is $x + 5$ equal to $(3x + 7)/3$?
(A) No value
(B) All values
(C) 0 only
(D) All natural numbers
(E) Cannot be determined

54. The average of four numbers is 6; the average of six other numbers is 4. What is the average of all ten numbers?
(A) 5 (B) 5.2 (C) 5.5 (D) 4.8 (E) 5.1

55.

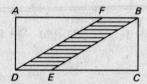

ABCD is a rectangle of dimensions 3 by 8. If $AF = EC = 5$, then the area of the shaded region is
(A) 6 (B) 8 (C) 9 (D) 10 (E) 12

56. If each of four numbers is doubled, their average is
(A) multiplied by 2.
(B) multiplied by 4.
(C) multiplied by 8.
(D) multiplied by 12.
(E) multiplied by 16.

57.

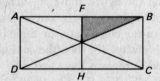

The area of rectangle ABCD is 24, and F and H are the midpoints of their respective sides. Find the area of the shaded region.
(A) 8 (B) 6 (C) 4 (D) 3 (E) 2

58. The inner diameter of a pipe is 2 inches. A pipe of inner diameter 4 inches will allow how many times as much water to flow through per unit of time?
(A) 2 (B) 4 (C) 8 (D) None of these
(E) Cannot be determined

59. How many 15-cent stamps can be purchased with P cents?
(A) $15P$ (B) $15/P$ (C) $P/15$ (D) $100P/15$
(E) $150/P$

60. A 600-foot-long fence has wooden posts spaced 40 feet apart. How many posts are there?
(A) 13 (B) 14 (C) 15 (D) 16 (E) 17

61.

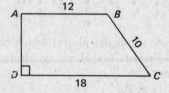

What is the area of trapezoid ABCD?
(A) 120 (B) 150 (C) 160 (D) 170 (E) 180

62. How many positive two-digit integers are there?
(A) 80 (B) 81 (C) 89 (D) 90 (E) 91

63. If twice the value of a certain integer is increased by 9, the result is 21. What is the value of the number?
(A) 2 (B) 4 (C) 6 (D) 12 (E) $\frac{21}{9} - 2$

64. What is the smallest positive integer that will leave a remainder of 1 when divided by 2, 3, 4, 5, or 6?
(A) 61 (B) 26 (C) 181 (D) 721 (E) 121

65.

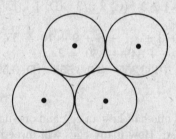

Four circles, each of the area 9π, are placed as shown in the figure above. Find the perimeter of the figure obtained by connecting their center points.
(A) 3 (B) 6 (C) 12 (D) 18 (E) 24

66. Three partners agree to divide the profits from a business in the following manner: One of the partners takes half the profits, a second partner takes one-third of the profits, and the third partner takes what is left. If the third partner finds that he is left

with half as much as the second partner, what was the total amount of profit they were dividing?

(A) $12,000 (B) $6,000 (C) $10,000 (D) $24,000
(E) Cannot be determined from the given data

67. Rearrange A, B, and C in descending order if $2A = 5B = 3C$ and $A > 0$.
(A) A, B, C (B) A, C, B (C) B, C, A (D) B, A, C
(E) C, A, B

68. The supplement of $\angle A$ is how many degrees greater than the complement of $\angle A$? ($\angle A$ is acute.)
(A) 90 (B) 90 - A (C) 180 - 2 A (D) 180 - A
(E) 90 - 1/2 A

69. Which of the following is the closest approximation to the value of $.499 \cdot .667 \cdot .375$?

(A) 5/9 (B) 3/8 (C) 1/9 (D) 1/8 (E) 8/9

70.

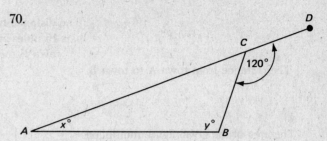

In the diagram above, AD is a straight line. $x + y = ?$
(A) 60 (B) 120 (C) 90 (D) 80 (E) Cannot be determined from the given data

Questions 71–100

Directions:
Each problem consists of two quantities, one in Column A and one in Column B. You are to compare the two quantities and choose

A if the quantity in Column A is greater;
B if the quantity in Column B is greater;
C if the two quantities are equal;
D if there is not enough information given to determine the relationship.

COLUMN A	COLUMN B
	$x > 0$
	$y > 0$
71. $x \cdot y$	$x + y$
72. The sum of the integers 1 through 10	$5 \cdot (10 + 1)$
73. $2 \cdot 4 \cdot 6 \cdot 8$	$2 \cdot (1 \cdot 2 \cdot 3 \cdot 4)$
74. A, if $1/2 A = 7$	2B, if $B = 7$

The area of $\triangle ABD$ equals the area of $\triangle BDC$

COLUMN A	COLUMN B
75. AD	DC
76. $52x$	$315x$

	Column A	Column B

77.

The distance from town A to town B
is 16 miles and the distance from
town B to town C is 14 miles

The distance from town A to town B   The distance from town A to town C

78.

The area of the given figure multiplied
times two

The area of a figure similar to the
figure given but with sides twice as
long

79. $5 + 3 \cdot 2$ 16

80. $|x| \neq x$

x $-x$

81. $2x < y$

x y

82.

A distance measured in feet   A distance measured in yards and
divided by 3

83.   The cube of twice a number   Eight times the cube of the same
number

84.

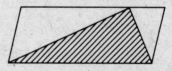

The area of the shaded region   The area of the unshaded region

85.   X, Y, and Z are 3 non-collinear points

$XY + XZ$ YZ

86. $\dfrac{153}{947}$ $\dfrac{153}{974}$

87. $P^2 + Q^2$ $(P + Q)^2$

Column A		Column B

$$AC = BC$$

88.

AB, if $m \angle C = 30°$ AB, if $m \angle C = 40°$

89.   The area of an equilateral triangle   12.5
with sides = 5

90.

$$\angle A < \angle B < \angle C$$

                 AB   AC

91. x^2 x^3

92.   3, 8, 15, 24, 35, . . .

The next term in the sequence above   49

93.   A, if $A = B + C$ B, if $A = B + C$

94.   The average of five numbers is 17

The sum of the five numbers   85

95.

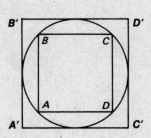

The area of square $A'B'C'D'$ Twice the area of square $ABCD$

96.   An even number greater than 5   An odd number less than 7

	Column A	**Column B**
97.	$\dfrac{1 + 3 + 5 + 7}{4}$	$\dfrac{2 + 4 + 6}{3}$
98.	$17^2 + 43^2$	$3,600$

99.

$$x > y$$

	Column A	Column B
	$x + y$	$x - 2y$

100. The sum of the first five odd natural numbers

The sum of the first five even natural numbers, decreased by 1

1. <u>M</u>y <u>D</u>ear <u>A</u>unt <u>S</u>ally
Use the above mnemonic device to help you remember the order in which operations are performed when there are no parentheses:

   - Multiplications and divisions first
   (left to right)
   - Additions and subtractions second
   (also left to right)

   If you answered (B), you were caught by the "expected" distractor. This distractor was produced by making the most common type of mistake and carrying it through the remaining steps in the problem.

   The correct choice is (A), and the correct way to work this problem follows:

   $$5 + 6 \cdot 2 + 8 =$$
   $$5 + 12 + 8 = 25$$

2. Choice (A) has a "1" to catch those who, not being sure of what operation to use, might be misled into dividing.

   The best approach to correctly determine what operation to use is to change the problem so that it represents a more obvious situation. For example:

   1 nickel = 5 pennies .

   5 nickels = _____ pennies .

   The correct answer to the above problem is, obviously, 25, and the operation needed to solve the original problem must be the same—multiplication.

   Time can sometimes be saved by *estimating* the answer. In the case presented here, the number 2.54 can be changed to either 2 or 3. If the answer is estimated by using 2 or 3 as an approximation, the result is either 4 or 9. Since none of the choices has a value in that range, it is safe to assume that the correct choice is (E) (None of these). If there were one or more choices with values in the appropriate range, the solution would have to be worked out exactly, instead of estimating it.

3. In problems that require you to visualize a situation or a figure, it is very important that you draw a diagram, if one is not furnished as part of the question.

   Let's consider a situation similar to the one described in the problem, but grossly exaggerated:

   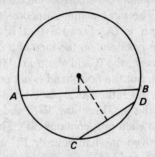

   From the above picture it should be evident that the chord nearer to the center of the circle is longer than the one farther away. The correct choice is (B) ($\overline{AB}$ is nearer to the center of the circle, so $AB > CD$).

   Choice (D) was offered as a distractor for those who felt they could predict the exact difference in lengths: the difference in lengths is not so easily determined, and one choice has already been identified as correct. Remember, there is only one correct choice for each problem. Thus, if, in fact $AB > CD$, then that *must* be the correct answer, and any exact numerical value *must* be wrong.

4. One correct approach to this problem would be to work out the numerator and the denominator independently and to then divide (invert and multiply) the demoniator into the numerator, *but this method is too slow.*

   A better method would be to multiply each entry by 40 (the least common denominator) yielding:

   $$\frac{32 + 120 + 25}{64 + 240 + 50} = \frac{177}{354} = \frac{1}{2}.$$

   This method is faster.

   Often, the test-makers build a pattern into the question, hopefully to be discovered by the better students and missed by the rest. This is done often enough to warrant considering first. *The best ap-*

proach, is to first look for a pattern. In this problem, for example, every entry in the denominator is twice as large as a corresponding entry in the numerator. Thus, if the sum of the quantities in the numerator is x, then the sum of the quantities in the denominator must be $2x$ and

$\dfrac{x}{2x}$ reduces to $\dfrac{1}{2}$, the correct answer (B) .

5. This problem illustrates how the best distractors are often placed before the correct choice to confuse the test-taker. The most common incorrect response to this question is (A) because that is the way we imagine the positions on the face of a clock.

   Sure enough, the 3 and the 6 are 90° apart on a clock's face, but the hour hand is not pointing at the 3 anymore, but rather, to a place midpoint between the 3 and the 4. There are 360° and 12 one-hour intervals, so each one contains 30°. The hour hand has then moved one-half-hour or 15° and the angle is $90° - 15° = 75°$.

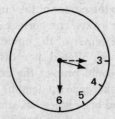

The correct choice is (C).

6. This problem can be classified as a "time-waster." This, and most other problems which direct you to make decisions about each of the choices are only designed with one purpose—wasting time. To this end, the correct answer is usually placed at one of the latter choices, (D) or (E), so that the test-taker will waste time considering several other choices before reaching the correct one. *This type of problem should be done backwards*; that is, the choices should be considered in reverse order—(E), (D), (C), (B) and (A). This problem also makes for easier guessing, since there is a very good chance that the correct answer is (D) or (E).

   Considering (E) first, we find that it is correct:

$$A - B > 0$$
$$\underline{+B + B}$$
$$A > B$$

Since there can be only one correct answer, we need not check the other responses.

WARNING: Occasionally, on the first part of a test, the author will place correct answers on the earlier responses.

7. *Caveat emptor*, . . . or, don't buy a used camel from a stranger!

   If you answered (C), don't feel lonesome, you have a lot of company. More people are caught by this wrong answer than by any other wrong answer to any other problem. The solution becomes apparent when a picture of the situation described in the problem is drawn:

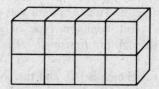

The arrangement shown is already 8″ × 2″ × 4″ and since the box is 8″ × 2″ × 5″, there is only 1″ left of height. No cubes can be put into this last inch without cutting the cube, so the extra space will remain wasted. The correct answer is 8, choice (A).

8. With a mental "scissors" we can imagine cutting up the figure and rearranging it as follows:

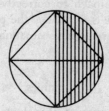

Thus, we can see that the shaded area is one-half of the area of the circle.

$$\tfrac{1}{2}(\pi r^2) = \tfrac{1}{2}(\pi \cdot 36) = 18\pi.$$

The correct choice is (B).

9. In reading math problems, the word "of" usually indicates a multiplication operation. The word "is" usually stands for equals. Thus the problem sets up as: $\tfrac{1}{2}$ of (means "times") × (the unknown number) is (means "equals") $\tfrac{1}{3}$ × (the unknown number) + 7. The equation reads mathematically as: $\tfrac{1}{2}x = \tfrac{1}{3}x + 7$.

Whenever solving equations with fractions, it is easier to get rid of the fractions first. This is most easily accomplished by multiplying *through* by the lowest common denominator, in this case, 6:

$$6(\tfrac{1}{2}x) = 6(\tfrac{1}{3}x) + 6(7)$$
$$3x = 2x + 42$$
$$x = 42$$

(D) is the correct choice.

10. It's time to use those mental "scissors" again (see problem No. 8). Each "bump" can be cut (along the dotted line) and made to fit into a "dip," filling it completely. The resulting figure will look like this:

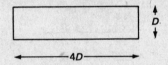

with area = $4D^2$, choice (C).

11. This problem was purposely written to sound like a riddle, to lure you into picking a "cute" answer—such as (A).

The problem is done correctly by first finding 50% of 50 (25) and then finding what percent of 5 is 25. Use the following formula:

$$\frac{\%}{100} = \frac{\text{"is"}}{\text{"of"}}.$$

In this case,

$$\frac{x}{100} = \frac{25}{5}$$
$$x = 500.$$

The correct choice is (C).

Again, by using our code words, we can set up an equation.

"What" = x,   "Of" = Times,

"Is" = Equals .

Thus,

$$(x\%) \cdot 5 = 50\% \cdot 50$$
$$(x\%) \cdot 5 = {}^{50}\!/_{100} \cdot 50, \text{ or } 25$$
$$(x\%) \cdot 5 = 25$$

$$(x/100) \cdot 5 = 25$$
$$5x/100 = 25$$
$$5x = 2500$$
$$x = 500$$

12. Factoring 143 from each term we get:

$$143 \cdot (42 + 37 + 31) =$$
$$143 \cdot (110) =$$
$$= 15{,}730$$

Choice (A) is the right answer.

13. *Work this one backwards!* (or plug in the answer) That is, pick one of the choices and take it through the steps. For example:

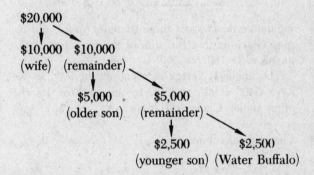

Since the quantity thus obtained for the Water Buffalo is one-half of that described in the problem, we should answer (D), which starts out with $40,000, twice as much.

14. Comparing (C) and (D), we can multiply (C) by 2, thus obtaining the same numerator. (C) then equals 10/28, which is smaller than (D) 10/27. 3/10 is less than 1/3, and the other three quantities are greater than 1/3, so choices (A), 1/3, and (B), 3/10, may be eliminated from further consideration. The best way to compare the rest of the fractions is, two at a time, to multiply across by each other's denominator as shown:

$$27 \cdot 5 \qquad 14 \cdot 10$$
$$\frac{5}{14} \qquad \frac{10}{27}$$

Since $27 \cdot 5 = 135$ is less than $10 \cdot 14 = 140$, we may conclude that 5/14 is also less than 10/27 and may eliminate it. This leaves us 10/27 and 17/50. Repeating the process:

$$500 \qquad 459$$

$$\frac{10}{27} \qquad \frac{17}{50}$$

This establishes that 10/27 is greater than 17/50, leaving no other choice but (D).

... Remember what we said about *time-waster* problems? ...

15. Dividing the figure into triangles,

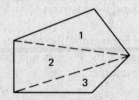

we notice that we get three triangles (min.), and we may conclude that the sum of the measures of the angles is $3 \cdot 180° = 540°$.

The angle at vertex A accounts for 90°, so we have $540° - 90° = 450°$ to account for by the other angles. Choice (D) is correct.

16. The original volume was:

$$V = L \cdot W \cdot H$$

The new volume is:

$$V' = 2L \cdot 2W \cdot 2H$$
$$= 8 \cdot L \cdot W \cdot H,$$

or eight times the original volume. Choice (A) was meant to catch those who did not realize the relationship (volume) was cubic. Choice (E) is correct.

In general, for similar figures:
If the ratio of corresponding *lengths* is $A : B$,
then the ratio of corresponding *areas* is $A^2 : B^2$
and the ratio of corresponding *volumes* is $A^3 : B^3$.

17. Change the problem to read: 200% of 17 = (?).

This is an easier problem to solve, since we know 200% of 17 is $2 \cdot 17 = 34$. (B) is the correct answer.

Generally, percent problems of the type $A\%$ of B = (?) can be rewritten as $B\%$ of A = (?). Do this if it results in a simplification of the problem; often enough, the test-makers pick a problem which is greatly simplified by such an inversion.

18. The only way for the statement to equal zero is for $3/4x$ to equal $3/4$. Thus, x must equal 1.

Multiplying through by 4 (see problem No. 4) will result in:

$$3x - 3 = 0$$

or, $\qquad\qquad x = 1$

so, $\qquad\qquad 5x = 5$

(A) is the correct response to this problem.

19. For a single triangle in a parallelogram:

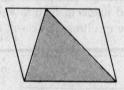

$$A \ \square = B \cdot H$$
$$A \ \triangle = \tfrac{1}{2}B \cdot H$$

This holds true for more than one triangle as long as, together, they cover the entire base of the parallelogram and each one reaches the full height.

The area of the parallelogram is $12 \cdot 6 = 72$, so the combined area of the unshaded triangles is half this figure (36), and the shaded area must be the other half (36). The correct choice is (C).

20. The figure given in the problem is one-fourth of the figure below (see shaded region).
So its area is:

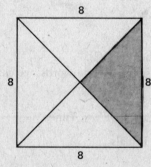

$$\tfrac{1}{4}(8 \cdot 8) = \tfrac{1}{4}(64) = 16.$$

(C) is the correct choice.

21. The difference $1.55 - 1.25 = .30$ accounts for two times the thickness (see figure).

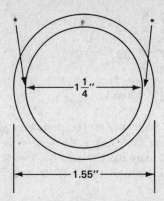

The thickness is $\frac{1}{2}(.30) = .15$ inches. (C) is the correct choice, and (A) is the most expected wrong answer.

22. Consider the following: In each of two tests Mary has a 65 and wants a 70. Thus, she is 5 points short in each of two tests, and on the third test she must make the 70 she wants *plus* the 10 points that she was short. . . . She must then make 80 points (C).

23. Label the points with numbers representing the number of ways of reaching that point, starting with 1. When two paths come together, the numbers they are "carrying" from the previous points are added together. See the figure below.

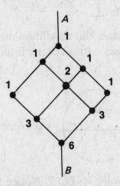

According to the figure, there are six different paths that may be taken from A to B. (D) is the correct choice.

Choice (E), 12, was used because in this problem large numbers become very attractive, and someone may be inclined to choose the largest answer rather than figure out how to do the problem.

24. Use the formula (see problem No. 11):

$$\frac{\%}{100} = \frac{\text{"is"}}{\text{"of"}}$$

$$\frac{x}{100} = \frac{100}{P}$$

$$x = \frac{10,000}{P}$$

The correct answer is (E), even though it seems the most unlikely choice. Choices (C) and (D) are prettier, but incorrect. Logically, we know that 100 is 100% of P if $P = 100$. Therefore, if we substitute 100 in the responses, the result equals 100. This yields (E) as the answer.

25. If you double the amount of trash, you will need to double the time. (D), 12, is the correct choice.

This problem seems almost too easy to be worth including in a test, but its real value lies in how effectively it can mislead you in the next problem (No. 26). This problem was, in fact, only designed as a lead-in to the next problem. . . .

26. Hopefully, problem No. 25 caused most people to miss this problem by picking (B), which is incorrect. Since the conditions (including spacing, temperature, wind, etc.) are the same, we can expect the drying time to remain the same, 20 minutes (A).

27. An odd integer raised to any power will result in an odd integer; an even integer raised to any power will result in an even integer.

In order for the operation to be commutative, the integers must be either both odd or both even. This leaves only two choices, (B) and (D), which may then be checked by plugging the numbers into the formula

$$x^y = y^x$$

We should have also recognized this problem as a *time-waster* (see problem No. 6).

28. There are ten numbers $(24 - 14 = 10)$, and their average value is 19.5

$$\frac{15 + 24}{2} = 19.5.$$

Their sum is:

$$10 \cdot (19.5) = 195,$$

which is choice (C).

29. See problem No. 16.

Since area is a "square" relationship, multiplying the diameter (length) by 2 will multiply the area by $2^2 (= 4)$. The correct answer is (B).

30. If 1 foop = 3 zats and 1 zat = 3 doons, then 1 foop = $3 \cdot 3$ (9) doons.

Factoring $27 = 3 \cdot 9$, we can see that 27 doons = $3 \cdot 9$ doons = 3 foops. (E) is right!

$$1 \text{ foop} = 9 \text{ doons}$$

$$? \text{ foops} = 27 \text{ doons}$$

31. He uses 4 men for 2 full-days and 2 half-days. The 2 half-day workers can be counted as 1 full-day worker and so he has, in effect, 3 full-day workers.

6 workers take 5 days, so half as many workers should take twice as many days. (E), 10, is the correct answer.

The inverse relationship (more men = fewer days) problems can be solved easily by imagining paying $1 per day per worker:

6 men for 5 days earn $30 this way; 3 men need 10 days to earn the same $30.

32. *Et tu, Brute?* . . . (which loosely translates as "Join the happy crowd!").

Think about this: 1 cubic yard *does not equal* 3 cubic feet.

$$1 \text{ } cubic \text{ yard} = 27 \text{ } cubic \text{ feet } .$$

So,

$$\tfrac{1}{3} \text{yd}^3 = \tfrac{1}{3}(27 \text{ ft}^3) = 9 \text{ ft}^3,$$

and this answer is in choice (A).

33. This problem is quite straightforward:

$$\frac{0.5}{7} + \frac{0.2}{7} = \frac{0.7}{7}.$$

Now, multiply both numerator and denominator by 10 (to eliminate the decimal) and get:

$$\frac{0.7}{7} = \frac{7}{70} = \frac{1}{10}.$$

(C) is the correct choice.

34. Substitute the word "of" for a multiplication sign, and reduce:

$$\frac{1}{3} \cdot \frac{3}{5} \cdot \frac{7}{8} \cdot \frac{5}{7} \cdot 32 =$$

$$\frac{\cancel{1}}{\cancel{3}} \cdot \frac{\cancel{3}}{\cancel{5}} \cdot \frac{7}{8} \cdot \frac{\cancel{5}}{7} \cdot \frac{32}{1} = 4$$

Choice (B) is correct.

35. Count the segments on the perimeter. There are 16 segments, so each one is $48 \div 16 = 3$. This means that each square has the area $3 \cdot 3 = 9$. There are 9 squares, so the total area is $9 \cdot 9 = 81$, choice (B).

36. Consider the following "cuts":

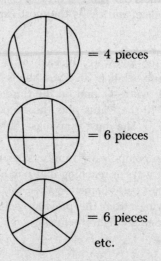

The way to obtain the maximum number of pieces is to draw the lines with as many intersection points as possible.

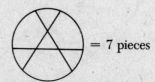

The correct choice is (D), 7. Notice that (C) is a very attractive answer, particularly if you don't know the trick just used.

37. See problem No. 19. Triangles *AMD*, *AND*, and *ACD* all have an area equal to one-half the area of the parallelogram (*ABCD*), since they all have the same base and equal height. Their areas are equal, and (D) is correct.

38. Logically, he rides for a greater time at 10 mph than at 15 mph. Therefore, the average speed should be closer to 10 than to 15. Thus, (A) and (E) are the only

possibilities. It would be very nice if we could just average 10 and 15 to get $12\frac{1}{2}$. (B) is a very good distractor but, unfortunately, incorrect.

Since the boy rode for different lengths of time at each of the two speeds, their average should be *weighted*: the 10 mph should be weighted by a factor of 15, and the 15 mph by a factor of 10.

$$\text{Rate} \times \text{Time} = \text{Distance}$$

$$\text{Average Rate} = \frac{\text{Total Distance}}{\text{Total Time}}$$

$$= \frac{15 \cdot 10 + 10 \cdot 15}{25} = \frac{300}{25} = 12.$$

The answer is (A).

39. Let's list the multiples of 5 and, of these, circle those that are also multiples of 3:

$$\boxed{105} \quad 110 \quad 115 \quad \boxed{120} \quad 125 \quad 130$$
$$\boxed{135} \quad \cdots$$

We see that every third one is circled, so the fraction is 1/3 and the *percentage* is 33⅓% (E).

40. The following pairs of points *are* connected by a single line segment:

1. Any number P with the same number Q
2. Any number Q with the next number P

According to the two rules above, only IV represents a pair of "connected" points, so I, II, and III constitute the right answer (those "not connected"). The correct choice is (D).

The correct answer to this type of problem *usually* involves *1 less than the number of choices*. This problem contains four choices (I, II, III, and IV), so we would expect the correct answer to involve three of these four choices, and it does!

41. Any "prime number" question usually concerns itself with testing the knowledge of one of two facts:

A. 1 is neither prime nor composite.
B. Rule for determining divisibility by 3:
If the sum of the digits of a number is divisible by 3, then so is the number itself.

In this problem, the digits of the numeral 111 add up to 3 (1 + 1 + 1 = 3), so 111 is divisible by 3 and, therefore, not prime. (E) is the right answer.

This problem is also a time-waster; see the com-

ment in the explanation of problem No. 6 regarding that type of problem.

42. Let x be the weight of the grape. Then:

$$x = \frac{2}{3}x + \frac{2}{3}$$

Multiplying *through* by 3 (see problem No. 9), we get:

$$3x = 2x + 2$$
$$x = 2$$

The grape weighs 2 ounces (A).

43. This problem can be done by the method of problem No. 28. However, *there is a better way*:

$$341 = 340 + 1$$
$$342 = 340 + 2$$
$$343 = 340 + 3$$
$$\downarrow \qquad \downarrow \qquad \downarrow$$
$$349 = 340 + 9$$
$$\underline{350 = 340 + 10}$$

Total: $3400 + 55 = 3{,}455$

(A) is the correct choice.

44. Doubling the number of hens will double the number of eggs laid. Doubling the length of time will also cause the number of eggs laid to be doubled, so we get:

$$1\frac{1}{2} \text{ eggs} \cdot 2 \cdot 2 = 6 \text{ eggs}$$

Choice (C) is correct.

45. Consider the following diagram:

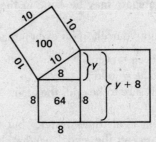

By using Pythagoras' theorem ($C^2 = A^2 + B^2$), we get:

$$10^2 = 8^2 + Y^2$$

$$100 = 64 + Y^2$$

$$36 = Y^2$$

$$6 = Y$$

Thus, the side of square X is $Y + 8$ or $6 + 8 = 14$, and its area is $14 \cdot 14 = 196$, choice (D).

Some very commonly used *Pythagorean ratios* are given below:

3–4–5,   6–8–10,   9–12–15, etc.

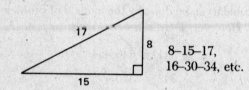

8–15–17, 16–30–34, etc.

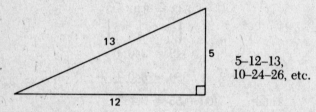

5–12–13, 10–24–26, etc.

 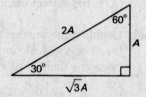

By having these ratios memorized, you can save time and effort by not having to compute the values for Pythagoras' theorem.

46. Problems which involve the identification of "odd" and "even" integers may be done in the following way:

1. First assure yourself of an even integer ($2n$).

2. Even + even = even.
   Even + odd = odd.

Thus, only II is sure to be odd; the others we cannot be sure about.

This problem is a "time-waster," but it did not have its answer at the end. . . . What happened?

Some exceptions have to be included—to keep test-takers honest. (B) is the correct answer.

47. Percents are always computed from the *original* (not the final) *value*. This problem asks what percent of 8 is 2 (the increase). Using the formula:

$$\frac{\%}{100} = \frac{\text{"is"}}{\text{"of"}}$$

$$\frac{x}{100} = \frac{2}{8}$$

$$x = \frac{200}{8} = 25\%$$

25% (E) is the correct choice.

48. This problem could also have been worked out using the % formula:

$$\frac{\%}{100} = \frac{\text{"is"}}{\text{"of"}}$$

$$\frac{12.5}{100} = \frac{15}{x} \Rightarrow x = 120 \qquad \text{(D)}$$

One other way to do this problem is to change the $12\frac{1}{2}\%$ to a fraction (1/8) and solve the equation:

$$15 = \frac{1}{8}x$$

SOME COMMON %—FRACTION—DECIMAL EQUIVALENCIES ARE LISTED BELOW:

$1 = 1.0 = 100\%$	$1/8 = .125 = 12\frac{1}{2}\%$
$1/2 = .5 = 50\%$	$3/8 = .375 = 37\frac{1}{2}\%$
$1/4 = .25 = 25\%$	$5/8 = .625 = 62\frac{1}{2}\%$
$3/4 = .75 = 75\%$	$7/8 = .875 = 87\frac{1}{2}$
$1/3 = .\overline{3} = 33\frac{1}{3}\%$	
$2/3 = .\overline{6} = 66\frac{2}{3}\%$	

There are only 10 of these and they are certainly worth memorizing!

49. Reduce first!

$$\frac{15 \cdot 24 \cdot 15}{12 \cdot 5 \cdot 30} = \frac{3}{1} = 3$$

(C) is the correct choice.

50. The figure given in this problem is known as a "magic square." The best approach is to look for any row, column, or diagonal which already has two entries, add them and subtract from 15 (to get the third entry). The completed square will look like this:

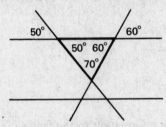

$$x + y = 8 + 9 = 17 \quad (C).$$

51. This problem has too much extra "junk." Remember that vertical angles are equal. Simplify first:

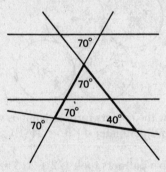

In the top (darkened) triangle, the missing angle is 70°, since all three angles must add up to 180°.

In the bottom triangle, the missing angle must be 40°. (B) is the right answer.

52. Write an equation:

$$x + y = 60 + x - y.$$

Eliminate the x's and get

$$y = 60 - y$$
$$2y = 60$$
$$y = 30$$

Choice (A) is correct. Choice (E) might tempt some people, since it is known that an equation with two unknowns cannot be *completely* solved. Sure enough, the x is unsolvable, but we were able to solve for y.

53. Set up the equation:

$$x + 5 = \frac{1}{3}(3x + 7)$$
$$x + 5 = x + \frac{7}{3}.$$

Eliminate the x's:

$$5 = \frac{7}{3}.$$

A contradiction such as this indicates the equation has no solution. (A) is the correct choice.

54. Another *weighted average* problem (see problem No. 38).

$$\frac{4 \cdot 6 + 6 \cdot 4}{10} =$$
$$\frac{24 + 24}{10} = \frac{48}{10} = 4.8$$

The correct answer is (D). Choice (A), 5, was used here to catch those who worked out the problem in the "natural" (and incorrect) way. Since more numbers average 4 than 6, the total average must be closer to 4 than 6. Therefore, only (D) can be the answer.

55. Figure *DEBF* is a parallelogram with base $8 - 5 = 3$ and height 3, so its area is $3 \cdot 3 = 9$ (C).

56. To discover the general rule, make a simpler problem for yourself:

The average of 1, 2, 3, and 4 is 2.5. The average of double the pevious numbers (2, 4, 6, and 8) is 5. So we see that doubling each of the numbers simply doubles their average. (A) is the right answer.

57. A line is missing in order to make eight *equal* parts:

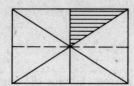

So, the shaded region is 1/8 of the total. Its area is 1/8 of 24, or 3. (D) is correct.

Choice (C) should have caught those who did not realize a line was missing and divided the total area by 6.

58. The cross-sectional *area* determines the rate of flow. Area is a "square" relationship and, therefore, varies directly with the square of the diameter (see problem No. 16). Thus, if the diameter is multiplied by 2, the area is multiplied by $2^2 = 4$.

The new pipe will allow 4 times as much water to flow through (B).

59. How many 15-cent stamps can be bought with 30 cents? Two.

$$\frac{30}{15} = 2$$

The above simpification of the given problem can serve as guide to determine what operation to use: *Division*. The correct choice is (C) $(P/15)$.

60. $600 \div 40 = 15$, so how come this answer is not correct?

There is one *extra* pole, the first pole, making the correct answer 16 poles (D).

Watch out for hidden "extras"!

61. Add a segment to the figure as follows:

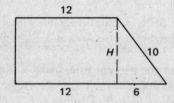

The height is 8 (using Pythagoras' theorem; see problem No. 45).

The area can now be found either by the formula for the area of a trapezoid $[A = \frac{1}{2}(B + b)H]$, or by separating the figure into a rectangle and a triangle. In either case, the area is 120 (A).

62. Here is another problem with a "hidden extra" (see problem No. 60). $99 - 10 = 89$, but this count does not include the number 10 itself. The correct choice is (D) 90. 89 (C) was also one of the choices, and, sadly probably distracted many people from the right answer.

63. Set up and solve the equation:

$$2x + 9 = 21$$
$$2x = 12$$
$$x = 6$$

(C) is the correct answer.

64. Find the smallest positive integer that 2, 3, 4, 5, and 6 divide evenly (*least common multiple*): 60. Then add 1 to it, $60 + 1 = 61$. The right answer is choice (A).

65. If the area of a circle is 9π, then its radius is 3:

$$A = \pi r^2$$
$$9\pi = 9\pi r^2$$
$$9 = r^2$$
$$3 = r$$

Adding this information to the figure,

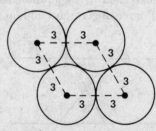

we see that the centers form a rhombus with sides of length 6 and perimeter $4 \cdot 6 = 24$ (E).

66. The first two partners took $1/2 + 1/3 = 5/6$ of the profits, leaving the third partner 1/6 of the profits.

For *any amount* of profit, 1/6 is always half of 1/3. The data given is not sufficient to solve the problem; (E) is the correct choice.

67. For positive-value variables, as in this problem, the one with the smallest coefficient is largest in value, and vice versa. $A > C > B$, and (B) is the right answer.

68. The supplement of A is $180° - A$.
The complement of A is $90° - A$.
The difference between these two is:

$$(180 - A) - (90 - A) =$$

$$180 - A - 90 + A = 90 \quad \text{(A)}$$

Logically, the supplement of any acute angle must be 90° greater than its complement.

69. $.499 \approx .500 = 1/2$

$.667 \approx .\overline{6} = 2/3 \quad$ (See problem No. 48.)

$.375 = 3/8$

So we can change the problem

$$(.499)(.667)(.375),$$

into (approximately),

$$\frac{1}{2} \times \frac{2}{3} \times \frac{3}{8} = \frac{1}{8} \quad \text{(D)}.$$

70. $\angle\, ACB = 60°$ and $x° + y° + 60° = 180°$, so $x + y = 120$. (B) is the correct choice.

71. If $x = 1$ and $y = 2$, then

$$x \cdot y = 2 \quad \text{and} \quad x + y = 3.$$

However, if $x = 4$ and $y = 3$, then

$$x \cdot y = 12 \quad \text{and} \quad x + y = 7.$$

For some values, the value of Column A is greater than the value of Column B, while for some other values the situation reverses. We do not have sufficient information to determine the relationship (D).

72. The sum of the integers 1 through 10 equals 55 (see No. 28).

$$5(10 + 1) =$$

$$5(11) = 55.$$

Since the two quantities are equal, (C) is the correct choice.

73. Multiplication may be distributive over addition, but it is not distributive over another multiplication.

$$2 \cdot 4 \cdot 6 \cdot 8 \qquad 2 \cdot 1 \cdot 2 \cdot 3 \cdot 4$$

Cancelling equal values on both sides, we are left with:

$$8 \qquad\qquad 1$$

With Column A unmistakably greater than Column B, the answer is (A).

74. If $\frac{1}{2}A = 7$, then \quad If $B = 7$, then
$A = 14$. \qquad\qquad $2B = 14$.

Both columns have the same value, and (C) is the correct answer.

75. Since the areas of the two triangles are equal and they have equal height, then they must have equal bases. Choice (C) is correct.

76. Most people should be misled into answering (B). However, since the value of x is unknown (could be 0 or negative), we cannot tell which is larger, $52x$ or $315x$.

(D) is the correct response to this problem. When comparing two unknowns, *always* consider fractional, negative, and zero values.

77. The distance from A to B is always 16 miles.

The distance from A to C may be as little as 2 miles:

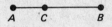

or as much as 30 miles:

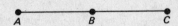

or any value in between.

In the first case, the value of Column B is greater; in the second case, the value of Column A is greater. There is not enough information to pinpoint the relationship with any more accuracy, so the answer is (D).

78. Doubling the length of each side quadruples the area. This is a "square" relationship (see No. 16). The correct answer is (B).

79. $5 + 3 \cdot 2 = 11$, not 16.

The proper order to perform operations if there is no parenthesis is: M–D–A–S (see problem No. 1). (B) is the right answer.

80. $|x| \neq x$ if and only if x is negative. If x is negative, $-x$ is positive and $-x > x$ (B).

81. An exception to the expected result occurs sometimes when $x > 2x$ (negative values of x).

Consider the following situation: $x = -5$ and $y = -7$. Then,

$2x$ or (-10) is less than y or (-7)

but

x or (-5) is greater than y or (-7).

(D) is the correct choice. When comparing two unknowns, *always* consider fractional, negative, and zero values.

82. Consider a distance of 18 feet (6 yards). For this distance the value of Column A is 18, and the value of Column B is 2. (A) is correct

This is a trap to see if you are really reading the question. To avoid error, substitute a value and work out the problem.

83. The cube of twice a number: $(2N)^3 = 8N^3$. Eight times the cube of the same number: $= 8N^3$. They are equal: (C) is the correct choice.

84. The area of the shaded region is one-half the total area of the parallelogram. The area of the unshaded region must be the other half (see problem No. 19), and the values of the quantities in both columns are equal. The right answer is (C).

85

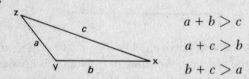

$a + b > c$

$a + c > b$

$b + c > a$

The sum of the lengths of any two sides of a triangle must be greater than the length of the third side. (A) is the correct choice.

86. If two fractions have equal numerators, the one with the smaller denominator is larger. (A) is correct.

87. $(P + Q)^2 = P^2 + 2PQ + Q^2$. Whether this quantity is greater than, equal to, or smaller than $P^2 + Q^2$ depends only on the middle term $(2PQ)$:

—If it is positive, $(P + Q)^2$ is greater.
—If it is 0, then they are equal.
—If it is negative, $P^2 + Q^2$ is greater.

We are not told enough to determine the nature of the middle term, so the answer is (D).

88. Imagine a compass (used for drawing circles); the more the angle between the legs is open, the greater that the radius of the circle will be (opposite side). Answer (B) is right.

89.

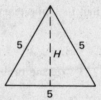

Consider the triangle above: H is less than 5. If the value of H were 5, the area of the triangle would be:

$A = \frac{1}{2}BH$

$A = \frac{1}{2}(5)(5)$

$A = 12\frac{1}{2}$

Since the height is, in effect, less than 5, the area is also less than $12\frac{1}{2}$. (B) is the correct choice.

90. For the given problem, AB is the longest side (A). The longest side of a triangle is always opposite to the largest angle, and the shortest side is opposite to the smallest angle (and vice versa).

91. If $x > 1$, then $x^3 > x^2$.

If $x = 0$ or $x = 1$, then $x^3 = x^2$.

If $0 < x < 1$, then $x^3 < x^2$.

(D) is the correct choice because we are not given sufficient information to determine which of the above cases is present. When comparing two unknowns, *always* consider fractional, negative, and zero values.

92. Find differences between consecutive terms:

3   8   15   24   35   48
  5   7   9   11   13

Since the differences show a pattern (odd integers), we may conjecture that the next difference must be 13 and the next term, $35 + 13 = 48$.

(B) is the correct choice because 49 is greater than the number just found.

93. The value of C is not known. If C were positive, $A > B$; if C were negative, $A < B$ and if C were 0, $A = B$.

(D) is the answer to this problem. When comparing two unknowns, *always* consider fractional, negative, and zero values.

94. If the average of five numbers is 17, then we can treat the numbers as if they all were 17s and find their sum to be $5 \cdot 17 = 85$.

The quantities in both columns are equal, and (C) is the correct choice.

95.

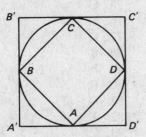

In the figure above, we have rotated square $ABCD$ to make the point easier to illustrate.

Let $A'D' = 2x$, then $AD' = x$ and $D'D = x$. Using Pythagoras' theorem,

$$(AD)^2 = x^2 + x^2$$
$$(AD)^2 = 2x^2$$
$$AD = \sqrt{2}\,x$$

And now, knowing the lengths (relative) of the sides, we can find their relative areas:

$$\text{Area of } ABCD = (\sqrt{2}\,x)(\sqrt{2}\,x)$$
$$= 2x^2$$
$$\text{Area of } A'B'C'D' = (2x)(2x)$$
$$= 4x^2$$

Thus, we see that the area of $A'B'C'D'$ is twice that of $ABCD$, and the quantities in the two columns are equal. The correct answer is (C). Two or three of these super-difficult problems are usually included in the PSAT to challenge the super student. Don't fret if you can't even begin to solve it. Chalk it off; don't waste time, and go to the next one.

96. An even number greater than 5 must be at least 6. An odd number less than 7 must be at most 5. The quantity in Column A is greater (A).

97. The average of 1, 3, 5, and 7 is 4 (the midpoint). The average of 2, 4, and 6 is also 4 (the midpoint). The two quantities are equal, and (C) is the correct answer.

98. Compare this problem with No. 87.

$$17^2 + 43^2 \qquad (17 + 43)^2$$

Since $2(17)(43) > 0$, the quantity in Column B is greater than the quantity in Column A. The correct answer is (B).

This problem could have also been done by squaring 17, square 43, and adding the two results to compare this with 3,600.

99. Try $x = 100$ and $y = 2$:

$$102 \qquad\qquad 96$$

Now, try $x = 100$ and $y = -2$.

$$98 \qquad\qquad 104$$

There is not enough information given to determine which of the above cases is at hand. (D) is the correct choice. When comparing two unknowns, *always* consider fractional, negative, and zero values.

100.

$$1 + 3 + 5 + 7 + 9 \qquad (2 + 4 + 6 + 8 + 10) - 1$$
$$5 \cdot 5 = 25 \qquad\qquad 5 \cdot 6 - 1 = 29$$

(See No. 94; number of terms $\cdot$ average $=$ total.)

As can be seen, the quantity in Column B is greater (B).

Answer Key—Mathematics Section

1.	A	35.	B	68.	A
2.	E	36.	D	69.	D
3.	B	37.	D	70.	B
4.	B	38.	A	71.	D
5.	C	39.	E	72.	C
6.	E	40.	D	73.	A
7.	A	41.	E	74.	C
8.	B	42.	A	75.	C
9.	D	43.	A	76.	D
10.	C	44.	C	77.	D
11.	C	45.	D	78.	B
12.	A	46.	B	79.	B
13.	D	47.	E	80.	B
14.	D	48.	D	81.	D
15.	D	49.	C	82.	A
16.	E	50.	C	83.	C
17.	B	51.	B	84.	C
18.	A	52.	A	85.	A
19.	C	53.	A	86.	A
20.	C	54.	D	87.	D
21.	C	55.	B	88.	B
22.	C	56.	A	89.	B
23.	D	57.	D	90.	A
24.	E	58.	B	91.	D
25.	D	59.	C	92.	B
26.	A	60.	D	93.	D
27.	D	61.	A	94.	C
28.	C	62.	D	95.	C
29.	B	63.	C	96.	A
30.	E	64.	A	97.	C
31.	E	65.	E	98.	B
32.	A	66.	E	99.	D
33.	C	67.	B	100.	B
34.	B				

Sample Test B—Verbal Section

Antonyms

Choose which of the five word or phrase choices is *most nearly opposite* in meaning to the word in capital letters. Fill in the appropriate letter space on the answer sheet. Consider all choices, since some are very similar in meaning.

1. OMNIPOTENT
   A. miserable B. colony C. obey D. feeble
   E. benevolent

   Explanation: The given word is an adjective. Choice (B) is a noun. Choice (C) is a verb. They are, therefore, eliminated as choices. The prefix *omni-* means "all" and *potent* means "powerful." The opposite of "all-powerful" would be *feeble*. *Benevolent* means "kind," which may or may not be true of an all-powerful person. In the same way he/she may or may not be *miserable*. Answer (D)

2. MAJORITY
   A. democratic B. popular C. clique
   D. monarchy E. nobility

   Explanation: A *clique* is a small group of people. This is the opposite of a *majority*, which is more than one-half of a total group. While it is true that a *monarchy* or *nobility* might be less than a majority, this is not necessarily so. Answer (C)

3. DEVASTATE
   A. honor B. rebuild C. award D. deteriorate
   E. deviate

   Explanation: The prefix *de-* in the given word denotes a negative or "down" meaning. Thus, we are looking for an "up" word as our antonym. Choices (D) and (E) are probably eliminated, since their prefix *de-* also denotes a "down" word. Of the three remaining choices, the prefix *re-* in *rebuild*, if known, would suggest a definition of "build back" or "build again." You might also consider the fact that *honor* and *award* are fairly close in meaning and thus are probably not correct. Answer (B)

4. SANCTIFY
   A. cure B. desecrate C. salvage D. infect E. demerit

   Explanation: There are a number of clues that should guide the test-taker. First, (E) is the wrong part of speech. We are looking for a verb, and *demerit* is a noun. (A) and (D) are antonyms and, hence, neither one can be the answer. *Sanct-*, the root of the given word, means "holy," and *sanctify* means "to make holy." *Desecrate* means "to make unholy" or "to profane." The roots *sancti-* and *sacri-* are two ways to indicate "holy." Answer (B)

5. GALLOP
   A. trot B. canter C. walk D. gait E. jump

   Explanation: The question requires some knowledge of horses. A *gallop* is a horse's fastest *gait* or manner of movement. A *walk* is its slowest *gait*. A *trot* and a *canter* are intermediate gaits. Answer (C).

6. MALCONTENT
   A. island B. continent C. isthmus D. satisfied
   E. peninsula

   Explanation: The test-maker attempts to deceive the test-taker by indicating four responses as geographical in nature. Thus, he hopes to lure you into choosing (B), since *cont* is contained in both the given word and the choice. However, if you recognize the prefix *mal* as meaning "not," you realize we are looking for a synonym of "content." This is, of course, *satisfied*. Answer (D)

7. FETTER
   A. unlock B. uncoil C. unbolt D. unzip E. unhook

   Explanation: No help here unless you know the meaning of the given word, which is to lock up a person by means of a chain around his or her ankles. Answer (A)

8. FEARLESSNESS
   A. latitude B. refugee C. kinship D. victim E. cowardice

   Explanation: This is an exercise in suffixes, which do not come into play too often, but are very helpful when they do. If we take the given word apart we have the suffix *-ness*, meaning "the state of," the suffix *-less*, meaning "the absence or the lack of," and the root *fear*. Putting it all together, we have "the state of having a lack of fear." The opposite of this, of course, is to show fear. This defines *cowardice*, choice (E). Answer (E)

9. SIGHTED
   A. deaf B. mute C. blind D. hidden E. unseen

   Explanation: The clues to this question involve recognition of tense and a secondary meaning. If the primary meaning of the given word is used, "to sight," meaning "the act of seeing," then the antonym must be in the past tense, since *sighted* is the past tense of the verb "to sight." Since all of the choices are adjectives, we must be dealing with an adjectival meaning of *sighted*. In fact, this adjectival meaning is "to have sight," the opposite of being *blind*. At any rate, you should have been able to eliminate choices (A) and (B), as they are obviously not the opposite of the given word. Answer (C)

10. INTOXICATED
    A. repaired B. remedy C. celebrate D. sober E. cured

    Explanation: The root *toxic* means "poisonous." Logically, therefore, *intoxicated* should mean "poisoned." However, the English language is not static, and from the root *poisoned*, *intoxicated* has come to mean "drunk." *Sober* started out to mean "serious" or "sedate," but, in addition, has taken on the meaning "not drunk." Several of the choices are geared to mislead anyone taking the word at its literal meaning. Answer (D)

11. POLLUTE
    A. clear B. scrub C. washed D. cleaned E. purify

    Explanation: All the response choices are more or less opposed in meaning to the original word. However, since there can be only one correct answer, you must look for the best choice. *Purify* means "to get rid of impurities." Since to *pollute* is to "introduce impurities," these two are the most opposed in meaning. In addition, choices (C) and (D) are the wrong tense, being past instead of present. Answer (E)

12. ANTIPATHY
    A. candor B. love C. empathy D. respect E. felicity

    Explanation: The given word is composed of the prefix *anti-*, meaning "against," and the root *path*, meaning "feeling." Thus *antipathy* is a "feeling against" or a "strong dislike." The opposite of that is *love*. *Empathy* is a "feeling of identification or unity with another person." It would be a good choice if (B) were not one of the choices. Answer (B)

13. CORPULENT
    A. skeleton B. skinny C. starving D. poor E. decent

    Explanation: The root *corp* in the given word refers to "body," and the suffix *-lent* means "having." "Having body" evolved to "very fat," which is the meaning of *corpulent*. Thus, *skinny* is the opposite. Choice (A) is the wrong part of speech. (C) and (D) reflect a meaning opposed to *corpulent* but are not as totally descriptive as the correct choice. (E) is totally irrelevant. Answer (B)

14. EMBRYONIC
    A. fully developed B. partly developed C. experimental D. leading E. laconic

    Explanation: An embryo is an early stage of the human fetus in the mother's body or an early stage of development of an idea, a project, etc. The best antonym is *fully developed*. Answer (A)

15. JUDICIOUS
    A. calm B. criminal C. partly D. unfair E. aroused

    Explanation: Choices (A) and (E) can be eliminated, since they are antonyms, and no set of antonyms can be the correct response. Remember, according to the PSAT rules none of the choices can be synonyms of the given word. When two antonyms are among the choices, one of them would have to be a synonym of the given word if the other word were the correct antonym. Being *unfair* is more nearly opposite *judicious* than *criminal*. If someone is not judicious, he is not necessarily criminal. Answer (**D**)

16. EMANCIPATION

A. confederacy B. torture C. servant
D. enslavement E. inquisition

Explanation: You should know that the Emancipation Proclamation freed the slaves during the Civil War. While the Confederacy upheld slavery, it is not the opposite of freeing the slaves. Its opposite is enslavement, which means "making people slaves." (B) and (E) were prevalent during slavery days but are not good choices. Answer (**D**)

17. SCION

A. reap B. niece C. sow D. nephew E. parent

Explanation: (A) and (C) are antonyms and are therefore eliminated. *Scion* means "offspring" or "child." *Niece* and *nephew* are clear enough in meaning so that it is highly unlikely that either one will be the correct response. Answer (**E**)

18. WARY

A. dauntless B. witless C. carefree D. vigilant
E. vapid

Explanation: There isn't much help for the test-taker in this question unless he or she knows the meaning of the given word. *Wary* means "cautious" or "careful." Its antonym is "carefree," or "free of care." This is the type of question that should be omitted if the meaning of the given word isn't known, since none of our methods of gaining the guessing advantage seem to work. Answer (**C**)

19. RAVENOUS

A. pale B. sated C. awake D. evolve
E. helpful

Explanation: Choice (D) can be eliminated, since it is in a verb form and the given word is an adjective. The suffix *-ous* will give you that much information even if you don't know the meaning of the given word. With just this one response choice eliminated, you now have the guessing advantage and should guess at the answer, even if you have no further clues. Actually, *ravenous* means "extremely hungry," which is the opposite of *sated*, which means "satisfied." Answer (**B**)

20. MALEDICTION

A. diction B. dictation C. dictator
D. dictionary E. benediction

Explanation: Here is another etymological workout based on the Latin root *dict*, meaning "to speak." The given word combines the prefix *mal-*, meaning "bad," with this root. The meaning "to speak badly" has evolved to mean "curse." Choice (A), *diction*, combines the root *dict* with the suffix *-ion*, meaning "the act or condition of." Thus *diction* becomes "the act of speaking" and has evolved to mean "the manner of expression." The suffix *-ate* means "to form or to provide." Thus *dictator* is the one who "provides speech" and has come to mean "a ruler or tyrant with absolute power." *Dictation* is "the act of forming speech" (*-tion* is a suffix meaning "the act of") and has come to mean "telling a secretary what to say." A *dictionary* is "a place to" (*-ary*) find "diction" (*speech*). *Benediction* uses the prefix *bene*, meaning "good," with *diction* to give the derivation "good speaking." This has been changed to "blessing." Thus, it is the opposite of the given word *malediction*, or "curse." Answer (**E**)

Sentence Completions

Each sentence has one or two blanks. There are five choices of words or groups of words listed below the sentence. Choose the word or group of words which best completes the meaning of the entire sentence.

21. Janus, the Roman god of doorways, was _____ as having two faces, one countenance symbolizing the beginnings of things, the other their _____.
   A. portrayed . . . initiations
   B. depicted . . . culminations
   C. sculpted . . . progress
   D. created . . . finalizations
   E. delineated . . . origins

Explanation: Though the relationship is not explicit, the inference we are to make is that the second face will depict the endings of things. All of the choices for the first word are appropriate, but only (B) and (D) suggest an ending in their second word. Since a god cannot be created, we can also eliminate (D). Technically, "final" is an adjective, and though one can make arrangements final, he cannot "finalize" them, since that word does not exist in proper English. Nor does the term *finalizations*. Thus, *culminations* is the proper choice, (B). This question is a reminder to the test-taker that sentences on the SAT are based on proper written usage of English and do not normally use slang or improper derivations. Answer (**B**)

22. In a _____ culture such as that of Iceland, minority problems lack the _____ they have in the multicultural United States.
    A. heterogeneous . . . appeal
    B. heterodox . . . dogma
    C. diversified . . . idolatry
    D. homogeneous . . . immediacy
    E. variegated . . . coercion

Explanation: Iceland is being contrasted to the U.S. The U.S. is described as multicultural, so we may infer that Iceland is not. Hence, its culture will not be *heterogeneous* ("mixed"), *diversified*, or *variegated* ("varied"). *Heterodox*, which refers to unorthodox ideas, is entirely out of place in this context, but *homogeneous*, which means "of one kind," is appropriate. In such a society minority problems would indeed lack *immediacy*. This question offers a good workout in etymology. Answer (**D**)

23. Recently, various systems of meditation have each been _____ as the single _____ for human anxiety.
    A. languished . . . cure
    B. moderated . . . remedy
    C. temporized . . . bane
    D. evaluated . . . myth
    E. promoted . . . panacea

Explanation: Most people are aware that meditation has been offered as a cure for anxiety, so we need here words that mean "offered" and "cure." Eliminating (C) and (D) because *myth* and *bane* do not mean "cure," we recognize that only *promoted* resembles "to offer." Answer (**E**)

24. Although the giant panda, _____ to the Himalayas, is _____ referred to as a bear, in reality this animal is more closely related to the raccoon family.
    A. pandemic . . . vulgarly
    B. indigenous . . . commonly
    C. native . . . judiciously
    D. belonging . . . incorrectly
    E. herbivorous . . . ordinarily

Explanation: The sentence states that pandas are not bears, so we may eliminate (C) because referring to them as bears would not be *judicious*, or wise. If the author had intended to use *incorrectly* as a word choice, she probably would not have begun the sentence with "although," since the phrase "in reality" serves the same purpose of indicating a shift in the direction of thought; so (D) too is incorrect. Of the remaining choices, the first word must be capable of being followed by "to." We cannot say "pandemic to" (*pandemic* means "universal"); nor do we say "herbivorous to" (*herbivorous* means "plant-eating"). We do, however, say "indigenous to" ("native to"), and (B) is correct. Answer (**B**)

25. The southern border of Brazil features many dramatic _____, spectacular waterfalls and other natural formations as yet _____ as tourist attractions.
    A. escarpments . . . developed
    B. fissures . . . touted
    C. cascades . . . unexploited
    D. dungeons . . . publicized
    E. glaciers . . . exploited

Explanation: The first word is part of a list including spectacular waterfalls and natural formations, and it should therefore be similar to those. The transition "as yet" suggests that the second word indicates that they are not yet tourist attractions. Only *unexploited* suggests that the formations have not become tourist attractions yet; so (C) is correct. We also may eliminate (D) and (E) because *dungeons* is not a natural formation and *glaciers* are unlikely in Brazil. Answer (**C**)

26. The _____ of gardenia blossoms was _____ by the sea breezes to our hotel terrace.
    A. pungency . . . blown   D. trace . . . induced
    B. smell . . . lavished   E. scent . . . wafted
    C. odor . . . carried

Explanation: The second word should indicate that the smell was transported. All the choices except (D) do that. The first word should indicate smell and should be appropriate to the sweet mildness of gardenias. *Pungency* and *odor* are too harsh and have negative "vibes." *Scent* is the most appropriate answer. Answer (**E**)

27. When a poisonous substance has been _____, most authorities advise administering a(n) _____ such as mustard diluted in water.
    A. inhaled . . . cathartic   D. incurred . . . antidote
    B. ingested . . . emetic   E. inferred . . . dose
    C. imbibed . . . purgative

Explanation: Some outside knowledge may be necessary for this question. The proper procedure in many, but not all, instances when someone has taken a poison is to induce vomiting. Mustard in water is one way of producing that effect. The second word, therefore, should be something that brings about vomiting. We thus eliminate (D) and (E). *Cathartic, emetic,* and *purgative* are all words for substances that purge the body, usually through vomiting. The first word should show that the poison has been taken. Though all three choices work, *ingested* is the most comprehensive, since it refers to either eating, drinking, or breathing, while *inhaled* refers only to gases. *Imbibed* refers only to liquids. Answer (**B**)

28. The legislator proposed that a(n) _____ study should be made to _____ the practicality of the reform measure.
    A. financial . . . undo
    B. statutory . . . determine
    C. ad hoc . . . reverse
    D. feasibility . . . assess
    E. kangaroo . . . demonstrate

Explanation: The key word is "practicality"—will the measure work or not in any realistic way. The first word should thus reflect practicality, and the second word should indicate some way of determining the practicality. We may eliminate (A) and (C) on the basis of the second word. (E), *kangaroo*, is completely irrelevant. *Statutory* refers to laws, and *feasibility* refers to something's ability to work properly. Thus (D) best reflects the concept of practicality. Answer (**D**)

29. The _____ of the feudal system depended on

the ability of the overlords to maintain the _____ of their vassals.
    A. success . . . fealty
    B. strength . . . villainy
    C. cohesion . . . antagonism
    D. practicality . . . whims
    E. structure . . . politics

Explanation: "Maintain" is an important word here. Even if you know nothing about the feudal system you can infer that overlords are unlikely to try to maintain the *villainy, antagonism,* or *whims* of their vassals, since they are more likely to maintain something positive toward themselves than negative. One does not usually maintain someone else's politics, so (E) is a weak answer. *Fealty* means "loyalty," so (A) is the correct answer, since "overlords" would want the loyalty of their "vassals," or slaves. Answer (**A**)

30. Even though he professed a(n) _____ belief in religion, he was a(n) _____ practitioner of good works toward his fellow man.
    A. zealous . . . rabid
    B. enthusiastic . . . cheerful
    C. fervent . . . lukewarm
    D. strong . . . intense
    E. prejudiced . . . biased

Explanation: "Even though" suggests that the two blanks will be opposites. Of the choices, only (C) reflects an opposite relationship between the words, and indeed (C) is correct. Answer (**C**)

31. Florida is a paradise for con men eager to _____ a(n) _____ public.
    A. hoodwink . . . gullible
    B. dupe . . . shrewd
    C. fool . . . canny
    D. aid . . . sophisticated
    E. fleece . . . knowledgeable

Explanation: Con men will try to take advantage of a public that is easily tricked. Certainly, a con man's paradise or heaven would contain many easily tricked people. Answer (**A**)

32. The right of _____, which once protected refugees from arrest in holy places, is now merely a historical _____.
    A. sacrilege . . . anachronism
    B. knighthood . . . relic

C. sanctuary . . . curiosity
D. ordination . . . memory
E. hierarchy . . . tale

Explanation: All of the choices for the second word fit the context, though *relic* usually refers to objects and not to rights. The key phrase is "protected refugees." Of the choices, only a *sanctuary* provides protection, and indeed, in earlier times, people were immune to arrest while they remained in a church. Answer (**C**)

33. The dew on the flowers acted like a(n) _____ reflecting a(n) _____ of color in the garden.
    A. mirror . . . condensation
    B. prism . . . kaleidoscope
    C. lens . . . telescope
    D. opaque . . . myriad
    E. centrifuge . . . spectrum

Explanation: Of the choices for the second word, we may eliminate (A), (C), and (D) because we do not speak of a *condensation*, *telescope*, or *myriad* of color (there may be a myriad of colors, but not of color). The first word must be a noun, and *opaque* is an adjective, thus (B) remains. A *prism* does reflect a *kaleidoscope* of color. Answer (**B**)

34. The disease appears to have impaired his _____ system; consequently, he _____ slightly to one side when he walks.
    A. alimentary . . . tilts
    B. pedestrian . . . falters
    C. nervous . . . staggers
    D. locomotive . . . lists
    E. digestive . . . waddles

Explanation: Though *waddles* is not a particularly good choice, any of the choices for the second word is acceptable. The context asks for the bodily system that controls walking. That system is the *locomotive* system. A *pedestrian* (B) is a person who walks, not a system of the body. Answer (**D**)

35. The Spanish galleons of the fifteenth and sixteenth centuries had a(n) _____ function; they _____ as battleships and trading vessels.
    A. multiple . . . acted
    B. dual . . . served
    C. single . . . stood
    D. latent . . . sailed

E. political . . . malingered

Explanation: Of the second words, we may eliminate (E), since galleons did not *malinger* as battleships. Since the vessels perform two functions, we must choose between (A) and (B). Both choices indicate more than one function, but since *dual* refers to exactly two functions and only two functions are mentioned, it is the better answer. Answer (**B**)

36. The act of burying the _____ was symbolic of putting away _____ in order to establish peace.
    A. dead . . . corpses
    B. hatchet . . . antagonisms
    C. entrails . . . greed
    D. arrow . . . flight
    E. ego . . . resentments

Explanations: Burying the *dead* is a literal, not symbolic, way of putting away *corpses*. To establish peace, people would be unlikely to put away *flight*, so eliminate (D) too. We cannot physically bury an ego, so eliminate (E). The proper expression is "burying the hatchet." Answer (**B**)

37. His parents tried to make him stop _____ in order to _____ a more dignified posture as he walked.
    A. loping . . . elevate   D. shuffling . . . adopt
    B. prancing . . . mask   E. vibrating . . . hold
    C. careening . . . carry

Explanation: One does not *elevate* a posture. Of the remaining choices, the first word must be something negative that distorts posture; thus we eliminate (B) and (C). *Vibrating* is not a realistic choice, but *shuffling* is. Answer (**D**)

38. Some educators believe that printed communication will become _____ with the growth of electronic _____.
    A. obsolete . . . media
    B. futuristic . . . graphics
    C. anachronistic . . . transport
    D. powerful . . . forms
    E. primitive . . . technology

Explanation: The fear is that print will be replaced by forms of electric communication devices. Things either are or are not *primitive*; they do not *become* primitive. They may, however, become *obsolete*, and

(A) is correct. The other choices are obviously inappropriate in one of the word choices. Answer (A)

39. The counselor evaluated her state of mind as _____ and unhealthy because of the death of her mother; he advised _____ activities to distract her mind from its grief.
    A. sound . . . leisure
    B. sorry . . . extracurricular
    C. mundane . . . ordinary
    D. fey . . . sports
    E. morbid . . . diversionary

Explanation: The second word should describe activities meant to divert her thoughts. We may eliminate (C) and (D), and we should be especially impressed by *diversionary*. Of the first word choices we eliminate *sound* and *mundane* because they do not complement "unhealthy." *Morbid* is an appropriate choice, though, and (E) is correct, although a case probably could be made for (B). However, we are looking for the best answer, and (E) clearly is better than (B). Answer (E)

40. The hero of the novel *Tom Jones* is a _____ lad whose good heart but _____ morals get him involved in many dangerous adventures.
    A. roguish . . . lax   D. merry . . . prudent
    B. villainous . . . strict   E. heretical . . . sloppy
    C. fortunate . . . hearty

Explanation: "But" indicates that Tom's morals will be in contrast to his good heart. Thus we eliminate (B), (C), and (D). *Sloppy* does not properly modify "morals," and *heretical* is too harsh a word for the book's hero. He is a *roguish* lad with *lax* morals. Answer (A)

Analogies

Each question contains a pair of related words or phrases. There are five choices of words or phrases following each of the given pairs. Choose the word or phrase which *best* expresses a relationship which is similar to that expressed in the given pair.

41. HURL : CHALLENGE : :
    A. offer : amends   D. cast : shadow
    B. throw : plaudits   E. incite : invitation
    C. fling : gauntlet

Explanation: The action-object relationship is duplicated by all the answers except (E). One does not *incite* an *invitation*. Thus, from the four remaining answers we must now match the meanings as closely as possible. *Offering amends* is the opposite of *hurling* a *challenge*, as is *throwing plaudits*. But to *fling* a *gauntlet* ("glove") was once a way of challenging someone to a duel. (C) is correct. Answer (C)

42. TALKATIVE : LOQUACIOUS : :
    A. veracious : voluminous
    B. concise : terse
    C. garrulous : laconic
    D. philanthropic : misanthropic
    E. saturnine : jovial

Explanation: If you do not know that *loquacious* means "talkative," and if you do not identify the *loq* root as being associated with speech, you can still eliminate responses if you are familiar with the vocabulary. *Veracious* means "truthfulness" (not to be confused with *voracious*, which means "insatiable." The root *ver* means "truth"). Thus no relationship exists at all between *veracious* and *voluminous*. *Concise* and *terse* are synonymous, and all the other relationships depict opposites (*philo-* and *mis-* are always opposites: "love" and "hate"). In this situation the logical response is to guess the one synonymous relationship. However, if none of the vocabulary's familiar to you, this would be a good question to omit on the exam. Answer (B)

43. ENCOURAGE : COERCE : :
    A. aggregate : group   D. relish : intimidate
    B. fade : bleach   E. vilify : criticize
    C. candid : honest

Explanation: Because both lead words are verbs, we may eliminate (A) and (C). *Coercion* is an intense form of *encouragement*, so the relationship is that of degree. *Vilify* is a stronger form of *criticize*, but the order is wrong, stronger-weaker. *Relish* is not a weaker form of *intimidate*, but *bleach* is indeed a more intense form of *fade*. Answer (**B**)

44. SHUN : AVOID : :
    A. close : open
    B. shuttle : press
    C. criticize : excommunicate
    D. exclaim : declare
    E. frisk : gambol

Explanation: Even if you do not know that *shun* is a more intense form of *avoid*, you can eliminate (B), since no relationship at all exists between *shuttle* and *press*. (A) represents opposites, (E) synonyms, (C) weaker-stronger, and (D) stronger-weaker. SHUN : AVOID is a stronger-weaker relationship, so (D) is correct. Answer (**D**)

45. GLIMPSE : EXPOSURE : :
    A. glib : articulate   D. hallow : berate
    B. hint : revelation   E. film : camera
    C. gleam : diminution

Explanation: *Glimpse* can be either noun or verb, but *exposure* is always a noun, so we eliminate (A) and (D) because their second words are verbs. *Exposure* is a more intense form of *glimpse*, and a *revelation* is a more intense form of *hint*; so (B) is correct. Answer (**B**)

46. FUTURE : PAST : :
    A. science fiction : autobiography
    B. prediction : now
    C. will : was
    D. modern : ancient
    E. embryo : generation

Explanation: The relationship of opposites is indicated by (C) and (D). *Modern*, however, refers more to the present than to the future, but *will* refers explicitly to the future. Thus, (C) is the better answer. Answer (**C**)

47. MACARONI : WHEAT : :
    A. lye : soap   D. porridge : oats
    B. bread : dough   E. cob : corn
    C. wine : barley

Explanation: *Macaroni* is made from *wheat*. *Lye* is not made from *soap*; *bread* is made from *dough*; *wine* is not made from *barley*; *porridge* is made from

oats; and *cob* is not made from *corn*. Thus, only (B) and (D) replicate the relationship expressed by the head pair. Both wheat and oats are grains that appear in nature, but dough is man-made. Thus (D) is the better answer. Answer (**D**)

48. PUEBLO : HOPI : :
    A. village : Indian   D. agricultural : pastoral
    B. market : Apache   E. Zuni : rain
    C. peaceful : southwest

Explanation: If you know that *Hopis* are *Indians* who sometimes live in *pueblos*, then you will recognize that (A) is correct. If you do not know that Hopis are Indians but could nonetheless recognize the word to be a noun, you could eliminate (C) and (D). If you further recognize the likelihood that *Zuni* will correspond to *Hopi*, then you can see that it is out of order and thus eliminate (E) too. Answer (**A**)

49. ASSEMBLY : STUDENTS : :
    A. meeting : chairmen
    B. convocation : anthems
    C. reveille : bugles
    D. sarcophagus : people
    E. congregation : laity

Explanation: A group of *students* may constitute an *assembly*. A group of *chairmen* does not constitute a *meeting*; a group of *anthems* does not constitute a *convocation*; a group of *bugles* does not constitute a *reveille*; a group of *people* does not constitute a *sarcophagus* (a stone coffin); but a group of *laity* ("nonordained people") may constitute a *congregation*. Answer (**E**)

50. PANE : S\SH : :
    A. glass : automobile   D. bicycle : hub
    B. bar : saloon   E. window : lower
    C. knob : hinge

Explanation: *Pane* and *sash* are parts of the same whole: a window. We immediately eliminate (E) because *lower* is not a noun. Only (C) also represents a part-part relationship. *Knob* and *hinge* are parts of the same door. Answer (**C**)

51. LOCAL : INTERNATIONAL : :
    A. town : country
    B. region : urbanity
    C. rustic : bucolic

D. American : European
E. indigenous : cosmopolitan

Explanation: Though this is perhaps not a very straightforward analogy, we may eliminate (A) and (B) because they represent noun-noun instead of adjective-adjective relationships. We are seeking opposites; so we eliminate (C), which presents a synonymous relationship. *American* and *European* may or may not be regarded as opposites. *Indigenous* means "native to" and *cosmopolitan* means "sophisticated and well traveled" which would have the connotation of being *international*. Though neither answer is a particularly strong fit, (E) is the better answer. Answer (**E**)

52. MYSTERY : BAFFLE : :
    A. riddle : rhyme   D. clue : detective
    B. conundrum : amuse   E. difficulty : hard
    C. puzzle : elucidate

Explanation: The relationship is cause-effect. A *mystery baffles*. We eliminate (D) and (E) because the second words are not verbs. *Riddles* do not necessarily *rhyme*, and *puzzles* do not *elucidate* ("make clear"). But *conundrums* ("riddles") do *amuse*. A good vocabulary is very helpful on this one. Answer (**B**)

53. NERVOUS : FIDGET : :
    A. hungry : mastication   D. poetic : symbolism
    B. famous : fly   E. musician : compose
    C. philosophic : muse

Explanation: This condition-action relationship is best treated in a sample sentence. A *nervous* person (condition) *fidgets* (action). We eliminate (A) and (D) because the second words are not verbs. We eliminate (E) because *musician* is not an adjective. *Famous* people do not necessarily *fly*, but *philosophic* people do *muse* ("contemplate"). Answer (**C**)

54. MUM : SILENT : :
    A. wild : relentless   D. skew : balance
    B. mummy : tomb   E. fond : lazy
    C. glib : smooth

Explanation: Mum and *silent* are synonymous adjectives. We eliminate (B) and (D) because they include nonadjectives. Neither (A) nor (E) depict synony-

mous relationships, but *glib* means "in a smooth, casual manner." Answer (**C**)

55. OBSERVATORY : STARS : :
    A. laboratory : tubes   D. archive : documents
    B. telescope : heavens   E. university : professors
    C. library : catalogs

Explanation: The sample sentence here is "we go to an *observatory* to study the *stars*." We do not usually go to a *laboratory* to study *tubes* or to a *library* to study *catalogs*, though we may study what is inside the tube or what is listed in the catalogs. So (A) and (C) are eliminated. We also eliminate (B) because a *telescope* is not a place. At a *university* we do not study *professors*; we study with them. But at an *archive*, a place where documents are kept, we do indeed study *documents*. This analogy shows how precise shades of meaning may be in a well-constructed analogy. Answer (**D**)

56. COARSE : FINE : :
    A. chopped : diced   D. crude : unmannered
    B. meal : grain   E. wild : reckless
    C. rude : sophisticated

Explanation: The relationship is clearly one of antonyms. Further, both words must be adjectives. We eliminate (B) because *meal* and *grain* are nouns. (D) and (E) represent synonymous relationships; only (C) reflects an antonymous relationship. Answer (**C**)

57. SCENT : OLFACTORY : :
    A. smell : touch   D. hearing : auditory
    B. grimace : gustatory   E. ductile : tactile
    C. tactile : touch

Explanation: The noun-adjective relationship reveals sensation-sensory system. We eliminate (C) and (E) because *tactile* and *ductile* are adjectives. *Smell* is not related to the system, and *grimace* is not related to the *gustatory* system, but *hearing* is the appropriate sensation for the *auditory* system. Answer (**D**.)

58. OURS : WE : :
    A. theirs : them   D. hers : she
    B. I : mine   E. its : yours
    C. his : him

Explanation: The relationship between pronouns requires a knowledge of cases. *Ours* is the reflexive possessive, and *we* is the subjective case; both words are plural. Only (D) duplicates that relationship, in the singular. If the approach seems difficult, you can always create a sample sentence and substitute the choices. "*We* lost the book that was *ours.*" We cannot say, "*Them* lost," "*mine* lost," "*him* lost," or "*its* lost." We can, however, say "*she* lost the book that was *hers.*" Answer (D)

59. ADAMANT : DOCILE : :
    A. rocky : lewd   D. mellow : aged
    B. adroit : ignorant   E. firm : yielding
    C. stern : austere

Explanation: All relationships are adjective-adjective. No meaningful relationship exists between *rocky* and *lewd* or between *adroit* and *ignorant*. At this point, you have the guessing advantage. If you do not recognize *adamant* and *docile* as antonyms, you can nonetheless see that (C) and (D) depict synonymous relationships and that (E) depicts opposites. Given that situation, you should guess the pair of opposites. Answer (E)

60. ARID : IRRIGATE : :
    A. sand : oasis
    B. drought : monsoon
    C. roast : moisture
    D. parched : water
    E. desert : vegetate

Explanation: The trial sentence is "we *irrigate* an area to eliminate its *arid* condition." The relationship is adjective-verb. Only (D) and (E) provide that relationship, and (E) would not make sense. We *irrigate arid* land, and we *water parched* land. Answer (D)

61. PILOT : MARITIME : :
    A. steward : aviation
    B. captain : navigator
    C. guide : expeditionary
    D. plane : circumnavigating
    E. general : corporal

Explanation: The first word must be a kind of person; the second word is an adjective. Thus we eliminate (A), (B), and (E) (second word is noun), and (D) (a *plane* is not a person). A ship's *pilot* operates in a *maritime* situation; a *guide* operates in an *expeditionary* situation. Answer (C)

62. MYSTIC : VISIONS : :
    A. hermit : hermaphrodites
    B. ascetic : deprivations
    C. monk : monasteries
    D. diabolist : purifications
    E. mythologist : verities

Explanations: A *mystic* experiences *visions*. A *hermit* does not experience *hermaphrodites*; a *monk* does not experience *monasteries*; a *diabolist* does not experience *purifications* (*diabol* refers to "devil"); and a *mythologist* does not experience *verities* ("truths"). But an *ascetic* does experience *deprivations* (he deprives himself of sensual pleasure). Answer (B)

63. SCYTHE : REAPER : :
    A. plow : dairyman   D. plumb bob : fisherman
    B. horn : fox   E. harrow : farmer
    C. sportsman : hounds

Explanation: The first word is a tool; the second word is a person. A *reaper* uses a *scythe*. Eliminate (C) because a *sportsman* is not a tool, and (B) because a *fox* is not a person. A *dairyman* does not use a *plow*; a *fisherman* does not use a *plumb bob* (a carpenter's tool); but a *farmer* does use a *harrow* (an instrument for plowing). Answer (E)

64. BERRY : BUSH : :
    A. tea : pod   D. coffee : vine
    B. apple : shrub   E. olive : oil
    C. coconut : palm

Explanation: *Berries* grow on *bushes*; *apples* do not grow on *shrubs*; *coffee* does not grow on *vines*; *olives* do not grow on *oil*; but *coconuts* do grow on *palms*. Answer (C)

65. DETOUR : ROUTE : :
    A. rest : cure   D. elongate : traveler
    B. stop : go   E. curry : favor
    C. evasion : answer

Explanation: Our trial sentence might be: "A deviation from a *route* is called a *detour.*" The noun-noun relationship is one in which the first word is a deviation from the second. Eliminate (B), (D), and (E) because those are not noun-noun relations. A *rest* is not a deviation from a *cure*, but an *evasion* is a deviation from an *answer*. Answer (C)

Reading Comprehension

Each passage is followed by a series of questions. All questions should be answered on the basis of what is stated or implied in that passage.

The first series of paragraphs and questions are diagnostic exercises; these will help you understand the mental processes necessary to answer the most common forms of reading comprehension questions on the SAT.

Title Questions

66. Human nature is such that if A. and B. are engaged in thinking in common and are communicating their opinions to one another on any subject, so long as it is not a mere fact of history, and A. perceives that B.'s thoughts on one and the same subject are not the same as his own, he does not begin by revising his own process of thinking, so as to discover any mistake which he may have made, but he assumes that the mistake has occurred in B.'s. In other words, man is naturally obstinate.

The most appropriate title is
A. Conflicts Between A. and B.
B. Human Nature.
C. Obstinacy.
D. Irrational Factors in Communication.
E. How to Succeed in Everyday Life.

The title which is *not* suitable because it offers a solution to a problem not treated in the paragraph is _____.
The title which is *not* suitable because it uses symbols which cannot be easily understood is _____.
The title which is *not* suitable because it describes only one specific human trait mentioned by the author is _____.
The title which is *not* suitable because it is far too general is _____.
The title which is *most appropriate* is _____.

67. Cloth is not only a shelter against weather but also the most important means of adornment. It is natural that the desire for good clothes created a large demand for silk, since silk is one of the most beautiful cloths that we are able to make. But the demand is larger than the supply. Chemists solved this problem by producing an imitation silk called nylon. It is made synthetically from coal, air, and water and forced through minute holes under great pressure. The process forms fine threads which feel and look somewhat like silk. Chemists have also created other artificial fibers which are stronger than natural fibers. Some are wrinkle-resistant and retain creases even when wet.

The best title would be
A. Water-Resistant Fabrics.
B. A Shelter Against the Weather.
C. Silk: The Queen of Fabrics.
D. The Chemical Industry.
E. Developments in Cloth Production.

The title which is *wrong* because it focuses on one example of the general theme is _____.
The title which is *wrong* because it could apply to an umbrella as well as to the topic of the paragraph is _____.
The title which is *wrong* because it mentions too specific an example is _____.
The title which is *wrong* because it mentions a broad subject only vaguely associated with the main topic is _____.
The *best* title is _____.

68. Make a count of your teeth and you'll see that you have two pairs, in each jaw, of incisor teeth—your front teeth, used for cutting and tearing. On each side of these there is a long, sharp cuspid, or "dog" tooth. Then come the premolar teeth for light grinding, and at the back of the mouth are the heavy molars for a thorough chewing.

The most appropriate title would be
A. Grinding and Chewing.
B. The Function of Your Teeth.
C. A Visit to the Dentist.
D. Incisors: The Canine Teeth.
E. The Human Mouth.

The title which is *inappropriate* because it is too broad is _____.
The title which is *inappropriate* because it describes an experience which is not given in the paragraph is _____.
The title which is *inappropriate* because it deals with a pair of activities which are merely examples is _____.
The title which is *inappropriate* because it focuses on just one type of the general class being discussed is _____.

The title which is *most suitable* is _____.

69. Those who say that old men can do nothing useful completely miss the point—for all the world like those who think the pilot has no part in the sailing of the ship. For he sits quietly in the stern merely holding the tiller, while other men are climbing the masts, running about the gangways or manning the pumps. He may not be doing the work of the young men, but what he does is better and more important. The big things are not done by muscle or speed or physical dexterity but by careful thought, force of character, and sound judgment. In these qualities old age is usually not only not lacking but even better equipped.

The most suitable title would be
A. The Value of Aging.
B. The Pilot and His Ship.
C. The Importance of Physical Dexterity.
D. Forced Retirement.
E. Youth Is Not All It Is Cracked Up to Be.

The title which is *not* suitable because it implies an aspect of the topic which is not discussed is

_____.

The title which is *not* suitable because it uses a symbol for the subject which is too vague _____.

The title which is *not* suitable because it contradicts the argument made in the paragraph is

_____.

The title which is *not* suitable because it is expressed in too informal language is _____.
The *most suitable* title is _____.

70. In the field of modern business, so rich in opportunity for the exercise of man's finest and most varied mental faculties and moral qualities, mere money-making cannot be regarded as the legitimate end. Neither can mere growth in bulk or power be admitted as a worthy ambition. Nor can a man nobly mindful of his serious responsibilities to society, view business as a game; since with the conduct of business human happiness or misery is inextricably interwoven.

The author's primary concern is
A. to defend money-making.
B. to describe business as a complicated game.
C. to argue that business offers mental and moral challenges.

D. to justify the charging of modest rates of interest.
E. to show the causes of human happiness and misery.

The summary which is *wrong* because it is too broad is _____.
The summary which is *wrong* because it is not mentioned in the passage is _____.
The summary which is *wrong* because it contradicts the viewpoint of the author is _____.
The summary which is *wrong* because the author goes beyond this concept is _____.
The summary which expresses the *main* idea of the selection is _____.

Implications

Questions 71–72

I arrange my subject as I want it, then I go ahead and paint it, like a child. I want a red to be sonorous, to sound like a bell; if it doesn't turn out that way, I add more reds and other colors until I get it. I am no cleverer than that. I have no rules and no methods; anyone can look at my materials or watch how I paint—he will see that I have no secrets. I look at a nude; there are myriad tiny tints. I must find the ones that will make the flesh on my canvas live and quiver. Nowadays they want to explain everything. But if they could explain a picture, it wouldn't be art. Shall I tell you what I think are the two qualities of art? It must be indescribable and it must be inimitable.

71. The author of this passage is most likely to be
A. an art historian.
B. a professor of fine arts.
C. a photographer.
D. a child.
E. a famous painter.

The answer which is *wrong* because it takes a comparison literally is _____.
The answers which are *wrong* because the approaches of these individuals would be too intellectual are _____ and _____.
The answer which is *wrong* because this field is not discussed in the selection is _____.
The *correct* answer is _____.

72. From the context of the passage one could assume that "myriad" (sentence 5) probably means
A. two.

B. dull.
C. bright.
D. millions.
E. ordinary.

The author implies that there are many tints to choose from in order to make the canvas "live and quiver"; therefore, the best answer would be _____.

73. *Fluorides* may be the easiest of all the air pollutants to recognize by the damage they cause to plants. Leaves damaged by fluorides may show spots, streaks, blotches, or margins of dead tissue like little lifeless islands surrounded by healthy plant tissue. This damage can stunt the growth of trees, cause loss of leaves, and reduce the production of fruit crops. Some plants are injured by only one part per *billion* of fluoride in the air around them. Others can build up large concentrations without showing ill effects.

Of the following, the statement best supported by the passage is
A. some pollutants show less visible damage to plants than do fluorides.
B. areas of dead leaf tissue show chloride damage.
C. production of fruit crops is increased by fluorides.
D. all plants are susceptible to one part per billion fluoride damage.
E. fluorides injure the root systems of plants.

The answer which is *wrong* because it suggests the opposite effect from what occurs is _____.
The answer which is *wrong* because it mentions a chemical not discussed in the passage is _____.
The answer which is *wrong* because it suggests a broader category than is discussed in the selection is _____.
The answer which is *wrong* because it mentions damage to a part of the plant not discussed in the passage is _____.
The *best* answer is _____.

Questions 74–75

A shadow has fallen upon the scenes so lately lighted by the Allied victory. Nobody knows what Soviet Russia and its Communist international organization intend to do in the immediate future, or what are the limits, if any, to their expansive and proselytizing tendencies. I have a strong admiration and regard for the valiant Russian people and for my wartime comrade, Marshal Stalin. There is deep sympathy and goodwill in Britain—and I doubt not here also—toward the peoples of all the Russias and a resolve to persevere through many differences and rebuffs in establishing lasting friendships. We understand the Russian need to be secure on her western frontiers by the removal of all possibility of German aggression. We welcome Russia to her rightful place among the leading nations of the world.

74. It can be inferred that the author is likely to be

    I. American
    II. Russian
    III. British
    IV. a contemporary of Stalin
    V. a Communist

A. I and V
B. II and V
C. III and V
D. III and IV
E. II and IV

The answers which are *wrong* because the author is a spokesman for the "goodwill in Britain" are _____ and _____.
The answer which is *wrong* because the author is negative about the "expansive and proselytizing tendencies" of the Russians is _____.
The *right* answers are _____ and _____.

75. Considered in context, "rebuffs" (sentence 4, this passage) is most likely to mean
A. encouragements.
B. replies.
C. rejections.
D. inventions.
E. courtesies.

The answers which are *wrong* because they are positive are _____ and _____.
The answer which is *wrong* because it is too neutral is _____.
The answer which is *wrong* because it does not apply is _____.
The *best* answer is _____.

Questions 76–78

But notes are missing from Manhattan's symphony. We whose homes are on it can go from spring to spring without once hearing the neighborly, communal music of a lawnmower. We never have a chance to stand at sundown, hose in hand, and water the brave beds of nasturtiums and phlox and blue delphiniums which we ourselves have planted. We don't even know the names of the nice-looking people next door, and it does not matter much because before long the moving vans will back up callously for their furniture—or ours. For above all we have no yesterdays, no reminders from one day's dawn to the next that ever folk have walked before in the streets where now we walk. Here we are today, indeed. But in our cramped and hurried habitations there is no murmur of a year gone by to suggest a little hopefully that here we may also be tomorrow.

76. When the author describes "Manhattan's symphony," he is probably referring to
    A. the orchestra that plays at Carnegie Hall.
    B. the neighborhood musicians practicing their instruments.
    C. a youth choir at a nearby church.
    D. the assorted everyday sounds of the city.
    E. the rumble of a furniture moving van.

    The answer which is *wrong* because it takes a symbolic description literally is _____.
    The answers which are *wrong* because, although they mention musical activities, they are too limited are _____ and _____.
    The answer which is *wrong* because it mentions only one particular discordant sound is _____.
    The *best* general answer is _____.

77. It is implied that the author misses certain experiences because he lives in Manhattan; one type of activity which is *not* mentioned in the passage but one that the author probably misses as well would be
    A. the accessibility of large department stores.
    B. the cultural activities of a big city.
    C. rapid transit systems.
    D. library and research opportunities.
    E. waking up to the song of a bird.

    The answer which is *wrong* because it is too scholarly is _____.

The answers which are *wrong* because they refer to things available in Manhattan are _____ and _____ and _____.
The *best* answer is _____.

78. When the author describes the sound of a lawnmower as "neighborly, communal," he is
    A. merely being illogical.
    B. indulging in a mathematical equivalent.
    C. contradicting himself.
    D. acting like a reporter.
    E. personifying the sound or describing it as though it were human.

    The answers which are *wrong* because they suggest that the author is not consistent are _____ and _____.
    The answer which is *wrong* because it suggests the passage sounds like a newspaper report is _____.
    The answer which is *wrong* because it tries to place symbolic language in a numerical category is _____.
    The *best* answer is _____.

Questions 79–81

There are five stages of meditation. The first is the meditation of love in which thou must so adjust thy heart that thou longest for the weal and welfare of all beings, including happiness of thine enemies.

The second meditation is the meditation of pity, in which thou thinkest of all beings in distress, vividly representing in thine imagination their sorrows and anxieties so as to arouse a deep compassion for them in thy soul.

Thy third meditation is the meditation of joy, in which thou thinkest of the prosperity of others and rejoicest with their rejoicing.

The fourth meditation is the meditation on impurity, in which thou considerest the evil consequences of corruption, the effects of wrongs and evils. How trivial is the pleasure of the moment and how fatal are its consequences of corruption, the effects of wrongs and evils.

The fifth meditation is the meditation on serenity, in which thou risest above love and hate, tyranny and thralldom, wealth and want, and regardest thine own fate with impartial calmness and perfect tranquility.

79. The author probably uses the old-fashioned "thou" and "thy" to create an effect of

A. piety. D. lightness.
B. humor. E. factuality.
C. obscurity.

The answer which is *wrong* because the author is not concerned with material reality is _____.

The answer which is *wrong* because the author is not trying to confuse the reader is _____.

The answers which are *wrong* because the author is not trying for a comic effect are _____ and _____.

The *best* answer to suggest the religious tone of the passage is _____.

80. In the context of the passage the term "weal" (sentence 2) is most likely to mean
A. courage. D. injury.
B. well-being. E. bravery.
C. downfall.

The answers which you would *reject* because they have negative meanings are _____ and _____.

The answers which you would *reject* because they are associated with fighting are _____ and _____.

The *best* synonym for *welfare* is _____.

81. In the fourth meditation the author discusses the "evil consequences of corruption." The best *opposite* for *corrupt* would be
A. voilent. D. sane.
B. balanced. E. pure.
C. evil.

The answer which is *wrong* because it is the opposite of *mad* is _____.

The answer which is *wrong* because it is the opposite of *peaceful* is _____.

The answer which is *wrong* because it is the opposite of *unstable* is _____.

The answer which is *wrong* because it means the same as *corrupt* is _____.

The *best* antonym is _____.

Questions 82–83

When the artist sees new things, or relates things together in a new way, the rest of us gasp with recognition. It is quite obvious that he is telling the truth. We can wish only that we had seen what he has shown us. But the scientist cannot communicate in this intuitive way. To

tell his insights, he must start with what is already known and then proceed logically, step by step, to demonstrate the unknown.

82. According to the passage, when an artist relates things in a new way the viewer responds with
A. logic.
B. intuition.
C. distrust.
D. recognition.
E. indifference.

The answer which is *wrong* because it is too negative a reaction is _____.

The answer which is *wrong* because it is too neutral a reaction is _____.

The answer which is *wrong* because it describes the artist's approach and not the viewer's reaction is _____.

The answer which is *wrong* because it describes the methods of the scientist is _____.

The *best* answer is _____.

83. The scientist's method is different from the artist's in that he
A. begins with the unknown.
B. depends most strongly on intuition.
C. makes the audience gasp with amazement.
D. is limited by the facilities of his laboratory.
E. starts from known facts.

The answer which is *incorrect* because it describes the response to the artist is _____.

The answer which is *incorrect* because it mentions the setting for the scientist's work, which is ignored in the passage, is _____.

The answer which is *incorrect* because it describes the approach of the artist is _____.

The answer which is *incorrect* because it describes the opposite procedure to that of the scientist is _____.

The *best* choice is _____.

Questions 84–85

Some cloth is a mixture of cotton, wool, linen, and manmade fibers. The microscope is useful for finding out what fibers have been mixed together in weaving the cloth. Each kind of fiber has a different structure, which is clearly visible under the microscope. For example, wool fibers are kinky and short; cotton fibers are straight and long.

84. The tool most helpful for analyzing the type of fiber in cloth would be
    A. a telescope.
    B. a textbook on cloth.
    C. a microscope.
    D. a chart of atomic structures.
    E. a mill.

The answer which is *wrong* because it describes the place where the cloth is made is _____.

The answer which is *wrong* because it mentions an instrument used to study the heavens is _____.

The answer which is *wrong* because it is merely a book is _____.

The answer which is *wrong* because it is a table is _____.

The *best* answer is _____.

85. Fibers which are kinky and long would probably be
    A. wool.
    B. cotton.
    C. acrylic.
    D. a blend of cotton and wool.
    E. linen.

The answer which is *incorrect* because these fibers are short is _____.

The answer which is *incorrect* because these fibers are straight is _____.

The answers which are *incorrect* because the structure of these fibers are never described are _____ and _____.

The *best* answer is _____.

Answer Key—Reading Comprehension

66. E, A, C, B, D
67. C, B, D, A, E
68. E, C, A, D, B
69. D, B, C, E, A
70. E, D, A, B, C
71. D, A, B, C, E
72. D
73. C, B, A, E, D
74. A, B, E, C, D
75. A, E, B, D, C

76. A, B, C, E, D
77. D, A, B, C ,E
78. A, C, D, B, E
79. E, C, B, D, A
80. C, D, A, E, B
81. D, A, B, C, E
82. C, E, B, A, D
83. C, D, B, A, E
84. E, A, B, D, C
85. A, B, C, E, D

Reading Comprehension Passages

The following passages are comparable to those you will encounter on the SAT. Answers and explanations are given after each set of questions. It is suggested that all questions relating to a given paragraph be attempted before referring to the answers and explanations. By doing this, the continuity of the reading selections will not be broken.

Questions 86–90

The life cycle of the committee is so basic to our knowledge of current affairs that it is surprising more attention has not been paid to the science of comitology. The first and most elementary principle of this science is that a committee is organic rather than mechanical in its nature: it is not a structure but a plant. It takes root and grows, it flowers, wilts, and dies, scattering the seed from which other committees will bloom in their turn. Only those who bear this principle in mind can make real headway in understanding the structure and history of modern government.

Committees, it is nowadays accepted, fall broadly into two categories, those (A) from which the individual member has something to gain; and those (B) to which the individual member merely has something to contribute. Examples of the B group, however, are relatively unimportant for our purpose; indeed some people doubt whether they are committees at all. It is from the more robust A group that we can learn most readily the principles which are common (with modifications) to all. Of the A group the most deeply rooted and luxuriant committees are those which confer the most power and prestige upon their members. In most parts of the world these committees are called cabinets. This chapter is based on an extensive study of national cabinets, over space and time.

When first examined under the microscope, the cabinet council usually appears—to comitologists, historians, and even to the people who appoint cabinets—to consist ideally of five. With that number the plant is viable, allowing for two members to be absent or sick at any one time. Five members are easy to collect and, when collected, can act with competence, secrecy, and speed. Of these original members four may well be versed, respectively, in finance, foreign policy, defense, and law. The fifth, who has failed to master any of these subjects usually becomes the chairman or prime minister.

86. A good title for this selection might be

A. Life Cycles.
B. The Flowering Plant of Human Cooperation.
C. Group A and Group B Organization.
D. Committees.
E. Five Members: The Science of Comitology.

87. It can be inferred that the author compares committees to plants because

A. all forms of modern government are organic units functioning in harmony.
B. committees reproduce and proliferate.
C. the microscope reveals their inner structure.
D. five is an organic number.
E. committees are mechanical in nature.

88. According to the passage Group B committees are unimportant because

A. their members have something to gain.
B. they are more robust than Group A.
C. they muster more power and prestige.
D. they are sometimes called cabinets.
E. they have something to contribute.

89. According to the passage the cabinet council is *not* constituted to

A. act with complete secrecy.
B. function competently.
C. contain a member versed in foreign policy.
D. be governed by the most able member.
E. function with three members.

90. The tone of the passage is

A. balanced.
B. prosaic.
C. biased.
D. legalistic.
E. satiric.

Answers and Explanations

86. Answer (D)
Explanation: Eliminate (A) as too general, (E) as to specific and too technical sounding, and (B) as too poetic sounding. (C), too, is at once too particular and imprecise, since it does not identify what Group A and B are. Thus (D) remains.

87. Answer (B)

Explanation: Eliminate (C) because it is impossible to scrutinize a committee with a microscope. Eliminate (E) because plants are not mechanical in nature. Eliminate (D), because it too makes no sense. Numbers cannot be organic or inorganic; furthermore, the statement reveals no similarity between committees and plants. (B) is stated directly in the passage.

88. Answer (E)
Explanation: Whereas the two questions above could be answered with little or no actual familiarity with the passage itself, this question requires some knowledge of the text. Eliminate (C) because it is unlikely that a committee will be considered unimportant because it musters power and prestige. In the second paragraph the author categorizes committees into those in which the members have something to gain and those in which they only have something to contribute. He quickly dismisses the latter, speculating that they might not even exist at all.

89. Answer (D)
Explanation: We must also consult the passage to answer this question. The last paragraph discusses the cabinet. We can see quickly that the cabinet is constituted to function competently, to act with secrecy, to function with three members, and to contain a member versed in foreign policy. But, we are told that the chairman will be the one who has failed to acquire expertise in any field. Thus the committee is not governed by the most able member.

90. Answer (E)
Explanation: The author's skeptical observations that Group B committees may not exist and that cabinets are run by the least able person indicate his generally satiric tone. Eliminate (D) because no legalistic jargon appears; eliminate (C) because he is not taking a stand for or against anything and thus has no opportunity to reveal bias.

Questions 91–95

Asceticism is one of the abiding ills of modern music. Asceticism and music do not go together. Music is a spontaneous, uninhibited expression of feeling. Without feeling there can be no music. Asceticism is opposed to the expression of feeling and the indulgence of the senses.

This is why ascetic faiths and philosophies have no music and why, in certain austere faiths, music is associated with evil.

It is in the opera house that the ascetic character of modern music is most keenly felt. A symphony without song may deceive by its thematic workmanship and the skill and ingenuity of its orchestration. In the opera house, with attention diverted from the orchestra to the stage, the absence of song is insupportable. For there is less music in the declamation of modern opera than in the spoken lines of the modern theater.

The kind of declamation or *parlando recitative* now fashionable in modern opera defeats rather than assists the musical objective. By restricting the voice to arbitrary pitches in a manner incompatible with the melodic-structural character of song, the composer puts the singer in an emotional straitjacket. The vocal line to which he is constrained offers less opportunity for melodic expression than the flattest sort of speech.

Nothing has been written in the opera since the end of World War I that could compare as music with any Shakespearean speech, even as delivered by a third-rate actor. Thus it is that modern opera reveals the full calamity of serious music. An art that originated as the creative extension of the rudimentary music of speech has ended, in the more radical of its present forms, by being less musical than the gurgle of a newborn babe.

There is little, as usual, that the composer can do about it, even if he recognizes the fact. If he tries to write musically he ends, like Krenek twenty years ago, in a no-man's land between serious and popular music, or like Menotti today, somewhere between the present and Puccini. Or he finds, as did Weill, that he can compete successfully with the really popular composers, and does so. In either case he ceases to be taken seriously as a serious composer. If he continues in directions still taken seriously he may make a reputation, but he will hardly make money. Certainly he will not make music.

Music still lives in the theater. It probably always will. But it lives in the theater today, in America, at least, in the music of Gershwin, Kern, Rodgers, Porter, Schwartz, and Berlin. Their shows have never been fully recognized as opera. But it is not what a thing is called that counts. It is what it is. If opera is the extension of the theater in song, then these shows are operas, regardless of the spoken dialogue and regardless of who does the orchestration.

By the same definition most modern opera is not.

91. The author considers asceticism a negative force because it

A. encourages the indulgence of the senses.
B. contributes emotions to modern music.
C. inhibits feelings necessary to music.
D. comes from a philosophical conviction.
E. is evil.

92. The phrase *parlando recitative* probably means
    A. a symphonic tone poem.
    B. an expression of an austere faith.
    C. a spontaneous melodic expression.
    D. a technique of orchestration in modern opera.
    E. a speaking in arbitrary pitches.

93. When the author compares modern music with Shakespearean speech, he intends to
    A. praise the efforts of contemporary composers.
    B. show the emotional strength of modern music.
    C. demonstrate that World War I began a creative era in music.
    D. show that modern compositions are less musical than the rhythms of speech.
    E. celebrate the complexity of the gurgle of a baby.

94. The author considers the music of Irving Berlin to be
    A. inferior to modern classical opera.
    B. similar to Puccini.
    C. superior to Schwartz's work.
    D. in a no-man's land like Weill.
    E. theater in song.

95. It may be inferred that the author's general attitude toward traditional forms of modern opera is
    A. deferential.
    B. snobbish.
    C. equivocating.
    D. critical.
    E. tolerant.

Answers and Explanations

91. Answer (C)
    Explanation: If you know that "asceticism" means the deprivation of sensual pleasure, then you can immediately eliminate (A) and (B), and you will be directed to the correct answer, (C). Even if you do not know what "asceticism" means and if you are unsure about the meaning of the passage, you should perceive from the term "negative force" that the answer will be something negative. On that basis you could probably eliminate (B) and (D). (E) is too simplistic to be convincing.

92. Answer (E)
    Explanation: If you know that a "recitative" is a spoken passage in opera, then you can choose the correct answer, (E), immediately. Otherwise, by referring to the passage you can see the term italicized (because it is a foreign phrase) in the third paragraph. It is called there a "declamation," which is a kind of outright statement.

93. Answer (D)
    Explanation: The general tone of the passage should suggest that the author is critical of modern music (see question 95). Thus, the comparison to Shakespeare will not be meant in praise of modern musicians. Eliminate, then, (A), (B), and (C). Statement (E) is completely irrelevant, and statement (D) is critical of modern composers; so (D) is the proper choice.

94. Answer (E)
    Explanation: Eliminate (A) because that statement is inconsistent with the general criticism of modern music. In glancing quickly through the passage, we see Berlin mentioned in the final paragraph along with other writers of theater music. Therefore, the expression "theater in song" is indeed used to refer to Berlin's music.

95. Answer (D)
    Explanation: The first sentence, which mentions "the abiding ills of modern music," sets the tone for the passage. The passage abounds with negative terms describing modern music. The *parlando recitative*, for example, is said to "defeat" the musical objective and place the singer in "an emotional straitjacket." Thus, through vocabulary as well as through the meaning, we can sense the author's critical attitude.

Questions 96–100

Character is a Greek word, but it did not mean to the Greeks what it means to us. To them it stood first for the mark stamped upon the coin, and then for the impress of this or that quality upon a man, as Euripides speaks of the stamp—character—of valor upon Hercules, man the coin, valor the mark imprinted on him. To us a man's character is that which is peculiarly his own; it distinguishes each one from the rest. To the Greeks it was a man's share in qualities all men partake of; it united each one to the rest. We are interested in people's special characteristics, the things in this or that person which are different from the general. The Greeks, on the contrary, thought what was important in a man were precisely the qualities he shared with all mankind.

The distinction is a vital one. Our way is to consider each separate thing alone by itself; the Greeks always saw things as parts of a whole, and this habit of mind is stamped upon everything they did. It is the underlying cause of the difference between their art and ours. Architecture, perhaps, is the clearest illustration. The greatest buildings since Greek days, the cathedrals of the Middle Ages, were built, it would seem, without any regard to their situation, placed haphazardly, wherever it was convenient. Almost invariably a cathedral stands low down in the midst of a huddle of houses, often as old or older, where it is marked by its incongruity with the surroundings. The situation of the building did not enter into the architects' plans. They were concerned only with the cathedral itself. The idea never occurred to them to think of it in relation to what was around it. It was not part of a whole to them; it was the whole. But to the Greek architect the setting of his temple was all-important. He planned it, seeing it in clear outline against sea or sky, determining its size by its situation on plain hilltop or the wide plateau of an acropolis. It dominated the scene, indeed; it became through his genius the most important feature in it, but it was always a part of it. He did not think of it in and for itself, as just the building he was making; he conceived of it in relation to the hills and the seas and the arch of the sky.

96. Of the following, which is the most appropriate title for the passage?
   A. Greek Coins
   B. Cathedrals Versus Temples
   C. Architecture in Ancient Greece and the West
   D. The Individual and Society
   E. Character and the Greeks

97. To the Greeks the human qualities that were most important were
   A. the distinguishing ones.
   B. the ones marking out a man as valorous.
   C. the special characteristics which defined the individual.
   D. the general qualities shared in common with mankind.
   E. the aesthetic qualities which enable man to appreciate beauty.

98. The secondary meaning of character to the Greeks was
   A. the mark stamped upon the coin.
   B. the peculiarities of individual natures.
   C. the impress of this or that quality upon a man.
   D. the relation of a thing in terms of its setting.
   E. the whole of a thing.

99. Western architecture differs from the Greek in that the Westerner
   A. saw things as parts of a whole.
   B. considered the setting in relation to the artistic center.
   C. was concerned with the building alone.
   D. made the cathedral dominate the scene.
   E. conceived of the cathedral in relation to the hills and the arch of the sky.

100. The passage claims that the Greek architect thought the all-important thing was
   A. the classic proportions of the temple.
   B. the setting.
   C. the quality of the materials and the workmanship involved.
   D. the convenience of the location to the populace.
   E. the incongruity of the temple with its surroundings.

Answers and Explanations

96. Answer (E)
Explanation: Choice (D) can be eliminated, since it is too broad a title and covers too much ground. (A) can be eliminated, since the example of courage is only incidental to the main idea. Similarly, architecture (C) is used only as an example. The comparison between cathedrals and temples (B) is broader in scope but still is only a method of illustrating the main point, which is the interpretation that the Greeks put in the idea of character. (E) is the correct answer.

97. Answer (D)
Explanation: The correct answer, (D), is indicated in the middle of the first paragraph. (C) is specifically indicated as a modern definition of character. The other possibilities do not make sense.

98. Answer (C)

Explanation: The correct answer, (C), is almost a word-for-word repetition of a portion of the second sentence. (A) is designated as the primary meaning in the same sentence. This question and the previous one show the heavy emphasis that test-makers place on material presented in the first paragraph of the selection. Both questions can be answered if the test-taker has read only that paragraph.

99. Answer (**C**)

Explanation: The correct answer is (C) and is indicated in the sentence "they were concerned only with the cathedral itself" located in the middle of the second paragraph. (D) misses the point, while (A) and (B) are similar in meaning but apply to the Greeks rather than to Westerners. (E) is nowhere alluded to in the passage.

100. Answer (**B**)

Explanation: The correct answer, (B), is repeated almost word for word in the passage. "But to the Greek architect, the setting of his temple was all-important." Recognition of this sentence eliminates all the other possibilities, which, incidentally, are nowhere mentioned in the selection.

Questions 101–105

There is a homely proverb, which speaks a shrewd truth, that whoever the devil finds idle he will employ. And what but habitual idleness can hereditary wealth and titles produce? For man is so constituted that he can only attain a proper use of his faculties by exercising them and will not exercise them unless necessity of some kind first sets the wheels in motion. Virtue likewise can only be acquired by the discharge of relative duties; but the importance of these sacred duties will scarcely be felt by the being who is cajoled out of his humanity by the flattery of sycophants. There must be more equality established in society, or morality will never gain ground, and this virtuous equality will not rest firmly even when founded on a rock, if one-half of mankind be chained to its bottom by fate, for they will be continually undermining it through ignorance or pride.

It is vain to expect virtue from women till they are in some degree independent of men; nay, it is vain to expect that strength of natural affection which would make them good wives and mothers. Whilst they are absolutely dependent on their husbands they will be cunning, mean, and selfish, and the men who can be gratified by the fawning fondness of spaniel-like affection have not much delicacy, for love is not to be bought, in any sense of the words; its silken wings are instantly shrivelled up when anything besides a return in kind is sought. Yet whilst wealth enervates men, and women live, as it were, by their personal charms, how can we expect them to discharge those ennobling duties which equally require exertion and self-denial? Hereditary property sophisticates the mind, and the unfortunate victims to it, if I may so express myself, swathed from their birth, seldom exert the locomotive faculty of body or mind; and, thus viewing everything through one medium, and that a false one, they are unable to discern in what true merit and happiness consist. False, indeed, must be the light when the drapery of situation hides the man and makes him stalk in masquerade, dragging from one scene of dissipation to another the nerveless limbs that hang with stupid listlessness, and rolling round the vacant eye which plainly tells us that there is no mind at home.

I mean, therefore, to infer that the society is not properly organized which does not compel men and women to discharge their respective duties by making it the only way to acquire that countenance from their fellow-creatures which every human being wishes some way to attain. The respect, consequently, which is paid to wealth and mere personal charms is a true north-east blast that blights the tender blossoms of affection and virtue. Nature has wisely attached affections to duties to sweeten toil and to give that vigor to the exertions of reason which only the heart can give. But the affection which is put on merely because it is the appropriated insignia of a certain character, when its duties are not fulfilled, is one of the empty compliments which vice and folly are obliged to pay to virtue and the real nature of things.

101. The author uses the proverb about idleness and the devil to demonstrate that
   A. hereditary wealth produces energy.
   B. aristocratic position is the best teacher of homely virtues.
   C. the devil is a concrete reality.
   D. idleness prevents a man from proper exercise of his faculties.
   E. natural affection is a vain tool.

102. The author believes that morality can be firmly established in society only if
   A. the flattery of sycophants is introduced.
   B. hereditary wealth and titles remain stable.

C. equality is achieved.

D. relative duties are not discharged.

E. one-half of mankind is chained to its bottom by fate.

103. The author claims that women will remain cunning and selfish as long as

A. they are the devil's employees.

B. they are good wives and mothers.

C. they are dependent on men.

D. they are aware of their sacred duties.

E. they discharge ennobling duties.

104. From the context of the first paragraph the term "sycophants" probably means

A. wealthy individuals.

B. flattering subordinates.

C. disdainful superiors.

D. virtuous cajolers.

E. philosophers committed to an ideal of equality.

105. It can be inferred that the author believes that living by hereditary wealth or personal charm makes an individual

A. strive to perfect the interior life.

B. isolated from the energetic realities of life.

C. blossom to affection and virtue.

D. value self-denial.

E. respected by his fellow creatures.

Answers and Explanations

101. Answer (D)

Explanation: This question again demonstrates the emphasis the test-makers place on the first sentences of a reading passage. In fact, the entire premise upon which the selection is based is clearly and distinctly given in the first few lines. Understanding these sentences shows that only (D) can be the correct answer.

102. Answer (C)

Explanation: If we look for words in the passage which are the same as or similar to the words in a comprehension question, we will usually find the answer. Thus, we find the words "established in society" and "morality" toward the end of the first paragraph. The passage statement "there must be more equality established in society, or morality will never gain ground" clearly indicates that (C) is the correct answer.

103. Answer (C)

Explanation: The words "cunning" and "selfish" are the key words in the questions. If we can find them in the passage, we probably have a clear shot at the answer without being forced to read the entire passage. Sure enough, we find those words in the second sentence of the second paragraph. This sentence clearly paraphrases the correct answer, (C).

104. Answer (B)

Explanation: Since sycophants flatter, according to the passage and flattering is used in one of the response choices, we could certainly hazard a guess that (B) is the correct answer, even if the meaning of "sycophant" is not known. Actually, a sycophant is one who seeks the favor of the wealthy by flattering them.

105. Answer (B)

Explanation: Since the entire tone of the passage indicates that the author looks with disfavor on people who live by hereditary wealth or personal charm, we should be able to infer that he will reject any good results that could happen from living in this manner. Thus choices (A), (C), (D), and (E) can all be eliminated, since they indicate positive results. The only negative choice is (B), which is the correct answer. The bias of the writer is clearly revealed in the first few sentences. As a matter of fact, this entire set of questions can be answered by a thorough reading of the first paragraph and by the location in the passage of a few key words in the questions. This is not meant to discourage test-takers from reading an entire passage if time permits. However, all too often, there just isn't enough time to do that. In these circumstances, reading the first paragraph and using the questions to locate the answers can often produce good results in a very small period of time.

Questions 106–110

1. The story of a play must be the story of what happens within the mind or heart of a man or woman. It cannot deal primarily with external events. The external events are only symbolic of what goes on within.

2. The story of a play must be conflict and, specifically, a conflict between the forces of good and evil within a single person. The good and evil to be defined, of course, as the audience wants to see them.

3. The protagonist of a play must represent the forces

of good and must win, or, if he has been evil, must yield to the forces of the good, and know himself defeated.

4. The protagonist of a play cannot be a perfect person. If he were he could not improve, and he must come out at the end of the play a more admirable human being than he went in.

5. The protagonist of a play must be an exceptional person. He or she cannot be run-of-the-mill. The man in the street simply will not do as the hero of a play. If a man be picked from the street to occupy the center of your stage, he must be so presented as to epitomize qualities which the audience can admire. Or he must indicate how admirable human qualities can be wasted or perverted—must define an ideal by falling short of it, or become symbolic of a whole class of men who are blocked by circumstances from achieving excellence in their lives.

6. Excellence on the stage is always moral excellence. A struggle on the part of a hero to better his material circumstances is of no interest in a play unless his character is somehow tried in the fire, and unless he comes out of his trial a better man.

7. The moral atmosphere of a play must be healthy. An audience will not endure the triumph of evil on the stage.

8. There are human qualities for which the race has a special liking on the stage: in a man, positive character, strength of conviction not shaken by opposition; in a woman, fidelity, passionate faith. There are qualities which are especially disliked on the stage: in a man, cowardice, any refusal to fight for a belief; in a woman, an inclination toward the Cressid.

106. Of the following which is the most appropriate title?
A. Broadway Success Story
B. Plot and Action
C. Some Rules for Playwriting
D. A Playwright Speaks Out
E. Drama and Unity

107. The author of the selection would agree with all of the following *except*
A. events are symbolic of inner conflict.
B. conflict is essential in drama.
C. the story of a drama should focus on external events.
D. the protagonist represents the forces of good.
E. the protagonist should not be perfect.

108. The author feels that the protagonist cannot simply be the man in the street because
A. the protagonist should not be imperfect.

B. the protagonist should be run of the mill.
C. the protagonist must yield to the forces of evil.
D. the protagonist should be an exceptional person.
E. the protagonist should not epitomize a conflict.

109. If an ordinary man is used as a hero, however, the author would agree with the following:

I. He must epitomize qualities considered admirable by the audience.
II. He must be symbolic of a class of men.
III. He defines an ideal by falling short of it.
IV. He shows how character can be developed without suffering.

A. I and II
B. II and III
C. II and IV
D. I, II and III
E. All of the above.

110. In the context of paragraph 8 when the author refers to a "Cressid" he most probably means
A. a cowardly woman.
B. a woman of moral strength.
C. a timid woman without energy.
D. an unsympathetic nagger of her husband.
E. an unfaithful, uncommitted woman.

Answers and Explanations

106. Answer (**C**)
Explanation: Choices (B) and (E) can be ruled out as being too general. Also, there are no particular references in the text to unity or action. (A) does not seem to be a likely answer, since Broadway is not mentioned or even referred to in the reading selection. There are many other centers where plays are presented. The choice thus becomes one between (C) and (D). While it is obvious that playwriting is the subject of the passage, it is not at all clear that a playwright is the author. The passage could just as easily have been written by a critic, or even a member of the audience. In addition, the outline-like listing of the paragraphs fits into the idea of a list of rules. (C) becomes the only possible answer.

107. Answer (**C**)
Explanation: The best approach to this question is to try to find each of the response choices in the paragraph. Obviously, since only *one* is omitted, if it cannot be found then that choice is the answer and

we need look no further. The test-makers realize that this technique might be used and will tend to make you use more time by usually placing the correct answer as one of the later choices. We advise starting the elimination process with choice (E) so as to counteract this tendency, if present. Choice (E) is indicated in paragraph 4; choice (D) is represented in paragraph 3. Choice (C) is obviously not the feeling of the outline, as the author specifically contradicts it in paragraph 1, where he states that "it cannot deal primarily with external events." This question can be answered without reading the entire passage.

108. Answer **(D)**

Explanation: This answer is clearly given in paragraph 5. Here again, the test-taker need not read the entire passage to find the answer. If he or she merely looks for the words "man in the street" in the passage, he or she will be given a free ride to the correct answer. (B) is obviously wrong, since it merely contradicts the thought of the question. The other choices are merely the opposite of points stated in the passage.

109. Answer **(D)**

Explanation: Here again, we must search through the passage to see if any of the statements can be eliminated. Statement I is shown in paragraph 5. Statement II is also indicated in paragraph 5, toward the end. Statement III is in the same sentence as statement II. The idea of suffering as part of character development is presented in paragraph 6. Thus, statement IV contradicts that paragraph and would not represent the author's point of view.

110. Answer **(E)**

Explanation: Since the test-makers direct your attention to paragraph 8, you know that the answer to this question will be found in that paragraph. Thus, there is no need to read the balance of the passage in order to find the answer. As demonstrated in this and other questions, it often pays off to scan over the questions before reading the passage. Of course, if you have the time, reading the entire passage is helpful. But, if you don't, you may be surprised at how well you can do by picking out certain key sentences or phrases. In this question, the qualities liked in a woman are enumerated—"fidelity, passionate faith." Thus qualities disliked would be opposed to these.

The physician of the future will not be a "scientist" of the orthodox type, a man with the technique of laboratories at his finger ends, and with the aim in his mind of elucidating the phenomena of life in terms of chemistry or physics. Rather, he will be a humanist, a man with the widest possible knowledge of human nature, and the deepest possible understanding of human motives. He will be a cultured man, ripe in intellectual attainments but not lacking in emotional sympathy, a lover of the arts as well as a student of the sciences. This is, indeed, no more than a projection into the future of a gracious figure of the past—for the great physicians of other days were all, likewise, great citizens of humanity. I look forward to the time when the practice of medicine will include within its scope every influence of known potency over the human spirit and when the practitioner, like Pygmalion, will look on his work and see, not disease and death, but the glowing lineaments of life.

The science of medicine is the science of life, of humanity. The whole universe of knowledge, of emotion and of reaction is included in this tremendous ambit. There is nothing which man has ever thought or felt which cannot be used for his preservation or his healing—and which, therefore, does not concern his physician. The mind of man with its powerful memory is a storehouse of things felt and experienced and of things imagined. It is nature's whip in a man's own hands, by means of which he is able to stimulate himself to overcome nature.

Here is the doctor's most splendid field of effort and enterprise. The doctor of tomorrow will certainly till it. Realizing that man owes all that he is to his power of self-stimulation by thought, he will perceive that no limit can be set to the extension of this process, and that, under guidance, men and women may indeed be evolved mentally and spiritually in a manner not yet generally dreamed of. This feeble structure, the body, is yet an instrument capable of celestial music when played upon by rich stimuli of the mind, stimuli derived all of them from nature as the pigments of the artists are derived from common stuff, or the notes of the musician from the voices of wind and tide; but stimuli evolved and perfected and, by most cunning and secret process of the spirit, endowed with the qualities of life itself. What a piece of work may not a man become when his physicians have learned that his mind is indeed the key, not only to his dominance of nature but also to his dominance of his own flesh!

111. A possible title for this selection would be

A. The Humanistic Science of Medicine.
B. Laboratory Art.
C. Physicians.
D. A Splended Enterprise.
E. The Instrument of Celestial Music: A Doctor Examines His Patient.

112. The author defines the term "humanist" as a man with the deepest understanding of
A. self-stimulation by thought.
B. stimuli evolved and perfected.
C. the phenomena of life.
D. the laboratory of mankind.
E. man's nature and motives.

113. The author might be considered reactionary in that he looks forward to a time when
A. society is all one class.
B. physicians imitate the great healers of the past.
C. death is made obsolete.
D. material substances are totally analyzed.
E. laboratory facilities are expanded to their right-ful importance.

114. The author is primarily concerned with
A. the ability of mind over matter.
B. the subservience of the spiritual element.
C. the control of the mind through hypnosis by the physician.
D. the limitation of human thought.
E. Pygmalion as a symbol of submission.

115. The tone of the passage is
A. somber and restrained.
B. factual and informative.
C. halting and stiff.
D. celestial and fleshly.
E. optimistic and lyrical.

Answers and Explanations

111. Answer (A)
Explanation: Answers (C) and (D) can be eliminated as possibilities, since they are so broad that they could apply to many different passages having noth-ing to do with the subject. At this point, if there is no time to go further, the guessing advantage is with you, and a guess could be attempted. Laboratories are mentioned only fleetingly, so (B) is inappropri-ate. In fact, the article points away from the labora-tory. The musical metaphor is, likewise, used only in passing and would not support titling the passage in

that way. The first sentence of the second paragraph really gives the best clue.

112. Answer (E)
Explanation: When the question states "the author defines," the test-taker knows that the definition lies within the passage. The best way to find it is to locate the given word and to examine what sur-rounds it. Here we find "humanist" in the second sentence of the first paragraph followed by the author's definition. The words "human nature" and "motives" appear in that definition, so the test-taker need look no further.

113. Answer (B)
Explanation: The key words in the question are "looks forward to a time." We find those words in the last sentence of the first paragraph. While not precisely stated, the respect the author shows for the great healers of the past is obvious in the preceding sentence. The other response choices are not men-tioned in the material surrounding the key words, if at all. Once again we can arrive at the correct response without reading the entire passage.

114. Answer (A)
Explanation: The idea of "mind over matter" is clearly communicated in the final sentence of the passage. Often, the final sentence will attempt to distill the basic idea of a passage into one clear, final sentence. Choices (B) and (D) more or less contra-dict the tone of the passage. (E) is irrelevant and untrue. Nowhere is hypnosis (C) mentioned in the passage. This passage demonstrates the importance of reading key portions of the passage thoroughly: the first paragraph, the first sentence of all subse-quent paragraphs, and the final sentence of the selection. In this series of questions, three out of five are contained in these areas.

115. Answer (E)
Explanation: There is no way to define the tone of a passage without reading and understanding it. If pressed for time, this question should be omitted. Certainly, it is anything but stiff and restrained. (A) and (C). It may be informative but does not contain very many facts (B). There is a real choice between (D) and (E) but "fleshly" really doesn't describe the tone as well as "lyrical." However, even if you could reduce the choices to these two, you have a fifty-fifty chance of being correct if you guess.

Sample Test B—Mathematics Section

In this section solve each problem, using any available space on the page for scratch work. Then indicate the *one* correct answer in the appropriate space on the answer sheet.

The following information is for your reference in solving some of the problems.

Circle of radius r: Area $= \pi r^2$
            Circumference $= 2\pi r$

The number of degrees of arc in a circle is 360.

The measure in degrees of a straight angle is 180.

Definitions of symbols:
$<$ is less than $\leq$ is less than or equal to
$>$ is greater than $\geq$ is greater than or equal to
$\perp$ is perpendicular to $\parallel$ is parallel to

Triangle: The sum of the degree measures of the angles of a triangle is 180.

If $\angle CDA$ is a right angle, then
(1) Area of $ABC = \dfrac{AB \cdot CD}{2}$
(2) $AC^2 = AD^2 + DC^2$

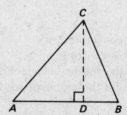

NOTE: Figures which accompany problems in this test are intended to provide information useful in solving the problems. They are drawn as accurately as possible *except* when it is stated in a specific problem that its figure is not drawn to scale. All figures lie in a plane unless otherwise indicated. All numbers used are real numbers.

1. If x is less than 3 and y is less than 7, we may conclude that
   (A) y is greater than x.
   (B) $y - x = 4$.
   (C) y is greater than $2x$.
   (D) $x + y$ is less than 10.
   (E) x is greater than y.

2. Half the average of two numbers is equal to how many times their sum?
   (A) $\frac{1}{4}$ (B) $\frac{1}{2}$ (C) 1   (D) 2   (E) 4

3. What is the value of

if $\boxed{N} = N^2$ and $\textcircled{Q} = Q^3$?
(A) 6   (B) 12   (C) 108   (D) 2,916   (E) 5,832

4. What is the area of a square whose perimeter is 1?
   (A) 1   (B) .25   (C) .50   (D) .0625   (E) .125

5.

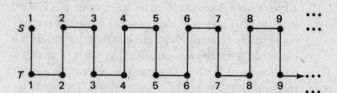

According to the figure above, which of the following pairs of points are connected by a single line segment?

    I. S_{35} and T_{35}
    II. S_{14} and S_{15}
    III. T_{174} and T_{175}

(A) I only
(B) I and II only
(C) I and III only
(D) II and III only
(E) I, II, and III

6. A pirate treasure map has the following directions:

"From the Bent Tree walk 20 paces east to the Rock Formation, then 120 paces south to the Bottomless Pit, 200 paces east to Alligator Bay, 20 paces north to the Old Wreck, and 20 paces east to where the treasure is buried." How far from the Bent Tree is the treasure if we walk in a straight line?
(A) 240 paces
(B) 253.2 paces
(C) 260 paces
(D) 220.2 paces
(E) 280 paces

7. $5 \cdot 3 + 2 \cdot 2 =$
  (A) 34 (B) 50 (C) 60 (D) 14 (E) None of these

8. How much interest will be earned on a $10,000 deposit at an interest rate of 5% per annum, compounded yearly, for a period of three years?
(A) $1,500 (B) $11,500 (C) $1,576.25
(D) $11,575.25 (E) $1,575.25

9. The winner of a 400-mile auto race averaged 160 miles per hour, and the second-place car averaged 150 miles per hour. How many miles back was the second-place car when the winner crossed the finish line?
(A) 20
(B) $23\frac{1}{3}$
(C) $24\frac{2}{3}$
(D) 25
(E) None of these

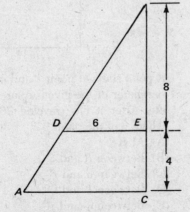

10. In the figure below left, $\overline{DE}$ is parallel to $\overline{AC}$. $AC = $?
(A) 8 (B) 12 (C) 9
(D) 7 (E) 10

11. What is the smallest positive integer value of P that will make the expression $2 \cdot 2 \cdot 2 \cdot 3 \cdot 3 \cdot P$ a perfect square?
(A) 2 (B) 3 (C) 6 (D) 12 (E) 18

12. If

$$A \,\#\, B = \frac{A}{B} + \frac{B}{A}$$

for all nonzero values of A and B, what is $x \,\#\, x$ if $x \neq 0$?

(A) 2 (B) $2x$ (C) x^2 (D) $\dfrac{2x}{x^2}$ (E) $\dfrac{x^2}{2x}$

13. Find the average of the integers 1 through 21.
(A) 22 (B) 10 (C) 10.5 (D) 11 (E) 12

14.

$$f(x) = \begin{cases} x, & \text{if } x \text{ is even} \\ 2x, & \text{if } x \text{ is odd} \end{cases}$$

and

$$g(x) = \begin{cases} x, & \text{if } x \text{ is odd} \\ x + 1, & \text{if } x \text{ is even} \end{cases}$$

Find $f(g(2))$.
(A) 4 (B) 6 (C) 3 (D) 2 (E) 8

15. How many pieces are obtained if a pie is cut with 12 straight cuts from the center?
(A) 10 (B) 11 (C) 12 (D) 13 (E) 24

16. Find the sum of the integers 74, 75, 76, 77, 78, 79, and 80.
(A) 539 (B) 580 (C) 556 (D) 565 (E) 559

17.

The area of the parallelogram above is 46, the base is 24 and is divided into three equal parts by points M and N. Find the area of the shaded region.
(A) 46/3 (B) 23 (C) 92/3 (D) 24 (E) $34\frac{1}{2}$

18.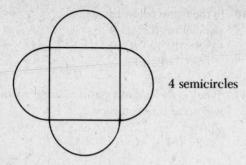

4 semicircles

Find the perimeter of the figure above if the area of the square is 36.
(A) 3π (B) 4π (C) 6π (D) 9π (E) 12π

19. K is 20% of
(A) $K/20$ (B) $5K$ (C) $20K$ (D) $K/5$ (E) None of these

20.

x	7	3	−1	?
y	0	1	2	3

(A) 3 (B) 2 (C) −2 (D) −4 (E) −5

21. The equation $x + 3 = \frac{1}{2}(2x + 6)$ is satisfied for
(A) $x = +3$ only.
(B) $x = -3$ only.
(C) $x = \pm 3$ only.
(D) All values of x.
(E) No values of x.

22. An increase of 500 is an increase of _____ %.
(A) 50 (B) 5 (C) 500 (D) 50,000 (E) Cannot be determined

23. The base of an isosceles triangle is 12, and each of the equal sides is 10. Find the area of the triangle.
(A) 24 (B) 48 (C) 96 (D) 36 (E) 72

24. 25% of 80 is one-half of _____.
(A) 40 (B) 160 (C) 10 (D) 50 (E) 60

25.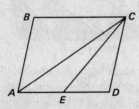

ABCD is a parallelogram, and $AE = ED$. What is the ratio of the area of triangle ACE to the area of the parallelogram?
(A) $1 : 2$ (B) $1 : 4$ (C) $1 : 3$ (D) $1 : 1$
(E) Cannot be determined

26. Points $(1,4)$, $(x,6)$ and $(3,5)$ lie on the same line. $x = ?$
(A) 2 (B) 3 (C) 4 (D) 5 (E) 6

27. A fish has a head 10 inches long. The tail is equal to the length of the head plus half the length of the tail. The body is equal to the length of the head plus the length of the tail plus half the length of the body. How long (in inches) is the entire fish?
(A) 90 (B) 50 (C) 45 (D) 80 (E) 120

28. A man left a $90,000 estate to be distributed among his three children in a $5 : 3 : 1$ ratio. What is the largest share?
(A) $45,000 (B) $30,000 (C) $50,000
(D) $80,000 (E) $60,000

29. One acute angle of a right triangle measures $27°$. Find the measure of the other acute angle.
(A) $73°$ (B) $81°$ (C) $54°$ (D) $27°$
(E) None of these

30. Find the three-digit number for which: The first and third digit are equal, the middle digit is twice the sum of the first and the third, and the sum of the digits is 6.
(A) 121 (B) 363 (C) 141 (D) 282 (E) 161

31.

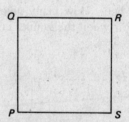

A point starts at point P and moves clockwise on the perimeter of the given square from P to Q, Q to R, etc. After it has traveled 767% of the perimeter, where will the point be?
(A) At R
(B) Between R and S
(C) Between S and P
(D) Between P and Q
(E) Between Q and R

32. In a line of people, John is fifth from either end. How many are there in the line?
(A) 5   (B) 9   (C) 10   (D) 11   (E) 25

33. Of the following, which is greatest?
(A) $\frac{20}{42}$ (B) $\frac{15}{35}$ (C) $\frac{3}{7}$ (D) $\frac{27}{63}$ (E) $\frac{63}{147}$

34. The minor base of a 45° isosceles trapezoid is 10, and the altitude is 7. Find the length of the major base.
(A) 13   (B) 17   (C) 21   (D) 24   (E) 39

35.

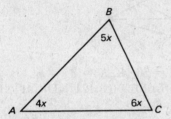

What is the measure of angle A?
(A) 48°   (B) 60°   (C) 62°   (D) 72°   (E) 84°

36.

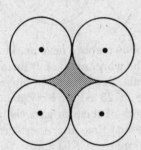

The area of each of the four circles in the figure above is 25π and the centers are the corners of a square. Find the area of the shaded region.
(A) $25\pi - 25$ (B) $80 - 25\pi$ (C) 100
(D) $10\pi - 10$ (E) $100 - 25\pi$

37.

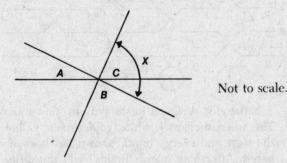

Not to scale.

Angles A, B, and C are in a $1 : 3 : 5$ ratio. Find the value of $\frac{1}{2}x$.
(A) 40°   (B) 50°   (C) 60°   (D) 70°   (E) 80°

38. The area of a square is 72. Find the length of its diagonal.
(A) 6   (B) $6\sqrt{2}$ (C) 12   (D) $12\sqrt{2}$ (E) $6\sqrt{6}$

39. Which of the following weights (in ounces) can be used to make all integral weights in ounces from 1 to 7 ounces?
(A) 1, 2, 5   (B) 1, 3, 4   (C) 1, 3, 3   (D) 1, 2, 4
(E) 1, 2, 3

40. At which of the following times do the hands of a clock make a 90° angle?
(A) 3:30   (B) 12:15   (C) 12:45   (D) 9:00
(E) All of the above

41.

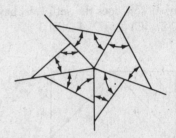

What is the sum of the degree measures of the angles marked above?
(A) 180°   (B) 225°   (C) 270°   (D) 360°   (E) 540°

42. There is a duck in front of a duck and a duck in back of a duck. What is the least number of ducks for which the above statement holds true?
(A) 2   (B) 3   (C) 4   (D) 5   (E) Cannot be determined

43. In a small school 25 students take science and 32 take math. 18 students take both science and math. What is the ratio of the students taking only math to the students taking only science?
(A) 1 : 2   (B) 1 : 1   (C) 5 : 7   (D) 7 : 5   (E) 2 : 1

44. What is the area of the quadrilateral passing through the points (0,4), (4,0), (0,− 4) and (− 4, 0)?
(A) 16   (B) 24   (C) 32   (D) 64   (E) Cannot be determined

45. John is 20 years old and Tom is 2 years old. In n years John will be twice as old as Tom. Find n.
(A) 12   (B) 16   (C) 18   (D) 20   (E) 24

46. In a group of 143 students there are 13 more girls than boys. What part of the group are the boys?
(A) 5/6   (B) 5/13   (C) 6/13   (D) 11/143
(E) None of these

47. Suppose a "belt" were made to fit snugly around the earth's equator and 10 feet were added to its length (circumference). The slack caused in the belt (if any) is evenly distributed all around the length of the belt. Then,
(A) a man can walk under it upright.
(B) a man can crawl under it, but not walk under it upright.
(C) a mouse can run under it, but a man cannot crawl under it.
(D) a coin could be passed under it, but a mouse could not run under it.
(E) there would be no slack at all.

48. How many subsets does the set $\{A, B\}$ have?
(A) 1   (B) 2   (C) 3   (D) 4   (E) 5

49.

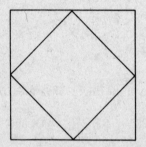

If a square is constructed inside another square, as shown, and if the area of the outside square is 50, then the area of the inside square is:
(A) 25   (B) $25\sqrt{2}$ (C) $25\sqrt{3}$ (D) $10\sqrt{2}$
(E) $10\sqrt{5}$

50. A die has been "doctored" so that it rolls only 3s and 5s. Which of the following cannot be the sum of the results of several rolls?
(A) 17   (B) 23   (C) 13   (D) 19   (E) 7

51. In the figures below, "I" can be drawn with a single trace of a pencil without lifting it off the paper, while "II" cannot be so drawn.

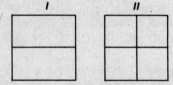

Which one of the following figures cannot be drawn with a single trace in the manner described above?

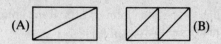

52. If $77 \cdot 88 = 56 \cdot K$, $K = $?
(A) 100   (B) 101   (C) 121   (D) 141   (E) 161

53.

The two wheels shown above have markings at their tops as shown. The wheel on the left turns clockwise at 15 RPM, while the wheel on the right turns counterclockwise at 25 RPM. How many minutes will it take for both of them to have their markings at the top for the first time after they start turning?
(A) 3 min.   (B) 5 min.   (C) 10 min.   (D) 15 min.
(E) None of these

54.

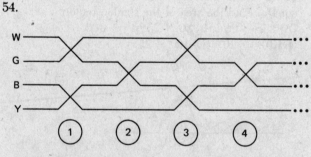

A hatband is designed in the pattern shown above. The order of colors is white, gold, brown, yellow at the start and every "braid" shown has been numbered. After how many "braids" will the order of colors be white, brown, yellow, and gold?
(A) Never   (B) 13   (C) 16   (D) 28   (E) Some number other than those above

55. $2x = 3y$, $\frac{1}{4}y = \frac{1}{2}z$ and $x > 0$. Arrange the variables in descending order.
(A) xyz (B) yxz (C) xzy (D) zxy (E) zyx

56. In 5 years Tina will be twice as old as she was 3 years ago. How old is Tina now?
(A) 5 (B) 7 (C) 8 (D) 11 (E) 16

57.

Find the perimeter of the figure above if each circle has radius 2.
(A) 8π (B) 12π (C) 16π (D) 18π (E) 24π

58. If $a = 3x + 5$, then $6x - 5 =$
(A) $a - 10$
(B) $2a - 10$
(C) $2a - 5$
(D) $a - 5$
(E) $2a - 15$

59. The product of three consecutive integers is always
(A) a multiple of 3.
(B) even.
(C) a multiple of 6.
(D) All of the above
(E) None of the above

60. $\sqrt{90.26} =$
(A) 0.95 (B) 8.5 (C) 9.5 (D) 10.5 (E) 85

61. Find the midpoint of the segment from $(0,5)$ to $(6,-3)$.
(A) $(6,2)$ (B) $(3,4)$ (C) $(3,2)$ (D) $(3,1)$ (E) $(6,4)$

62. Which of the following represents a whole number?
(A) $\frac{1}{2} \div \frac{1}{3}$ (B) $\frac{1}{2} \cdot \frac{1}{2}$ (C) $\frac{3}{4} + \frac{3}{4}$ (D) $\frac{3}{7} \div \frac{1}{7}$
(E) $\left(\frac{1}{4}\right)^4$

63.

In the figure above, each of the two curves is a semicircle of diameter 6. Find the area of the figure.
(A) 18 (B) 36 (C) 6π (D) 9π (E) 12π

64. It takes 4 seconds for a grandfather clock to strike 3 o'clock, beginning at 3 o'clock sharp. How long will it take the same clock to strike 12 o'clock if the strikings are uniformly spaced?
(A) 12 seconds (B) 11 seconds (C) 13 seconds
(D) 22 seconds (E) 16 seconds

65. The sum of two numbers is 12, and their product is 6. What is the sum of their reciprocals?
(A) 1 (B) 2 (C) 6 (D) $\frac{1}{2}$ (E) 3

66.

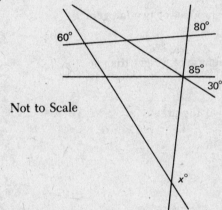

Not to Scale

Find the value of x.
(A) $120°$ (B) $160°$ (C) $140°$ (D) $100°$ (E) $70°$

67. What is the probability of drawing two hearts in a row from a standard deck of 52 cards?
(A) $\frac{4}{52} \times \frac{3}{51}$ (B) $\frac{1}{12} \times \frac{1}{11}$ (C) $\frac{12}{52} \times \frac{11}{51}$
(D) $\frac{13}{52} \times \frac{12}{51}$
(E) None of these

68. How much is $\frac{1}{3}$ of $\frac{x}{3}$?
(A) x (B) $\frac{x}{9}$ (C) $\frac{9}{x}$ (D) $9x$ (E) $\frac{1}{x}$

69.

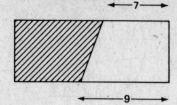

In the figure above, the rectangle has length 16 and width 6. Find the area of the shaded region.
(A) 45   (B) 52   (C) 48   (D) 64   (E) 72

70. Which of the figures below has the greatest area?

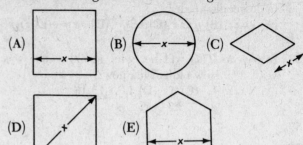

Questions 71–100

Directions:

Each problem consists of two quantities, one in Column A and one in Column B. You are to compare the two quantities and choose

A   if the quantity in Column A is greater;
B   if the quantity in Column B is greater;
C   if the two quantities are equal;
D   if there is not enough information given to determine the relationship.

COLUMN A	COLUMN B

71. Twice the product of two integers

The product of double each of the same two integers

72. The hypotenuse of a right triangle

The sum of the two legs of the same right triangle

73. A

$\sqrt{A}$

74.

$$2x = 3y$$

x

y

75. $(.03)^{17}$

$(.03)^{23}$

76.

In triangle ABC, $\overline{AC}$ is the longest side

$\angle A$

$\angle B$

77.

x is negative

$x^2 + 1$

$(x - 1)^2$

78.

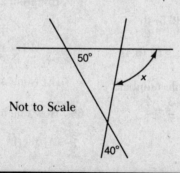

Not to Scale

$m \angle x$

$100°$

	Column A		Column B

79. **ABDE is a parallelogram**

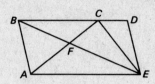

The area of triangle *ABF*   The area of triangle *FCE*

80. Twice the average of two numbers   The sum of the same two numbers

81. $x < y$

    $|x|$ $|y|$

82. $A > -B$

   $\dfrac{A + B}{2}$ $\dfrac{A + B}{3}$

83.   1, 1, 2, 3, 5, 8, 13, _____

The next term in the sequence above   21

84. $\dfrac{8}{23}$ $\dfrac{17}{50}$

85. $\dfrac{A + B}{3} > A$

   A B

86. Half the sum of two numbers   Their average

87. $\dfrac{n}{2}$ $\dfrac{2}{n}$

88. $1 + 2 + 3 + \ldots + 9 + 10$ $5 + 6 + 7 + \cdots + 10 + 11$

89. $\dfrac{x}{y} > 1$

   x y

90. 32% of 25   8

91.   *A, B,* and *C* are collinear

Distance *AC* plus distance *CB*   Distance *AB* plus distance *BC*

92. 50^2 $25^2 + 25^2$

93.   *A, B,* and *C* are consecutive integers,
                   in order: $A < B < C$

   $\dfrac{1}{3}(A + B + C)$ B

94. $2^7 + 2^7$ 2^8

95. 19% of 21   21% of 23

Column A		Column B
96. $\lvert x \rvert$		$-x$

97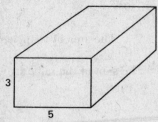

3
5

Figure not drawn to scale.

Column A		Column B
The volume of the rectangular box above		The volume of the rectangular box above
98. The sum of the integers 1 through 40		800
99. $3x$		$-5x$
100.	$2x > x$	
x		0

1. This problem is a *time-waster* and there is a good chance that the correct answer is near the end. It is.

$$x < 3$$
$$\underline{+y < 7}$$
$$x + y < 10 \quad \text{(D)}$$

2. The average of two numbers $= \frac{1}{2}$ their sum.

$\frac{1}{2}$ the average $= \frac{1}{2}$ of $\frac{1}{2}$ their sum

$\qquad\qquad = \frac{1}{4}$ their sum.

The correct choice is (A).

3. The required operations are performed, starting with the innermost one:

$$\boxed{2 \cdot ③} = \boxed{2 \cdot 3^3} = \boxed{2 \cdot 27}$$

$$= \boxed{54}$$

$$= 54^2$$

$$= 2,916 \quad \text{(D)}$$

4. If the perimeter is 1, then *its side has length $\frac{1}{4}$, or .25* (beware of strangers bearing gifts ... the problem would have been too nice if the length of the side were 1).

Its area is:

$$A = s^2 = \left(\tfrac{1}{4}\right)^2 = 1/16 = .0625 \quad \text{(D)}$$

5. *Look for patterns.* Let's list first the points that are connected as required:
(A) Any number S with the same number T
(B) T's are connected odd-to-even
(C) S's are connected even-to-odd

and no other way. I fits pattern (A), II fits pattern (C), while III goes against pattern (B). (B) is the correct choice (I and II only).

6. Draw a picture.

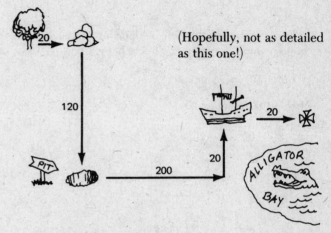

(Hopefully, not as detailed as this one!)

Or better yet, simplify the problem by combining all the north-south directions separate from the east-west directions obtaining:

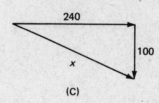

(C)

The triangle to the left is equivalent to a 5–12–13 right triangle (which is a very commonly used ratio and should be memorized),

therefore $x = 260$.

7. My Dear Aunt Sally
    The above mnemonic device should help you remember the order in which operations are performed when there are no parentheses:
(1) Multiplication
(2) Division
(3) Addition
(4) Subtraction

Then

$$5 \cdot 3 + 2 \cdot 2 = 15 + 4 = 19 \quad \text{(E)}.$$

8. The important phrase here is "compounded yearly."
Then:

$$10,000 \rightarrow 10,500 \rightarrow 11,025 \rightarrow 11,576.25$$

$$\underline{-10,000.00}$$

$$1,576.25 \quad \text{(C)}.$$

9. The winner finished in

$$\frac{400}{160} = 2\frac{1}{2} \text{ hours}.$$

The second-place car fell behind the winner by 10 miles every hour, so in $2\frac{1}{2}$ hours he will be

$$(2\tfrac{1}{2})(10) = 25 \text{ miles}$$

behind the winner (D).

10. $$\frac{8}{6} = \frac{12}{x} \quad (8 + 4)$$

$$8x = 72$$

$$x = 9 \quad \text{(C)}.$$

11. Discard "paired" numbers, since they already make perfect squares.

$$2 \cdot 2 \cdot 2 \cdot 3 \cdot 3 \cdot P$$

This leaves only $2P$, and the easiest way to make $2P$ a perfect square is to let $P = 2$ (A).

12. Substitute x into the formula:

$$x \ \# \ x = \frac{x}{x} + \frac{x}{x} = 1 + 1 = 2 \quad \text{(A)}.$$

13. Find, instead, the average of 1 *and* 21:

$$\frac{1 + 21}{2} = \frac{22}{2} = 11 \quad \text{(D)}.$$

14. $f(g(2))$
First, find $g(2) : g(2) = 2 + 1 = 3$. Then, find $f(g(2)) = f(3) = 2 \cdot 3 = 6$ (B).

15. Draw some examples:

1 cut _____ 1 piece

2 cuts _____ 2 pieces

3 cuts _____ 3 pieces

etc.
So, 12 cuts will yield 12 pieces (C).

16. First find their average (*midpoint*). This is 77:

$$74 \quad 75 \quad 76 \quad 77 \quad 78 \quad 79 \quad 80$$

The sum $= 7 \cdot 77 = 539$ (A).
You could eliminate all choices but (A) and (E) by adding last digits, which equal 9.

17. The area of the shaded region is half the total area. The three triangles have the same total base as the parallelogram and each triangle has the same height as the parellelogram.

$$\tfrac{1}{2}(46) = 23 \quad \text{(B)}.$$

18. The area of the square $= 36$ makes each side $= 6$ and the radius of each semicircle $= 3$.

$$\text{Circumference} = 2\pi r$$

$$= 2\pi(3) = 6\pi$$

$$4 \text{ semicircles} = 2 \text{ circles}$$

$$\text{Perimeter} = 2 \cdot \text{circumference}$$

$$= 2 \cdot 6\pi = 12\pi \quad \text{(E)}.$$

19. $20\% = .20 = 1/5$, and K is $1/5$ of $5K$ (B).

20. Notice the pattern:
While y increases by 1, x decreases by 4. The next value of x (corresponding to the next value of y) must be $-1 - 4 = -5$ (E).

21. Multiply both sides by 2:

$$2x + 6 = 2x + 6$$

This is an identity and will be satisfied by all real values of x. Choice (D) is the correct answer.

22. An increase of 500 over *what*?

    The basis of the increase must be known or else the problem cannot be worked out (E).

23. Draw the figure:

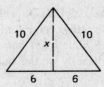

    The height, x, must be 8 (6–8–10 right triangle).
    Or use Pythagorean Theorem—

    $$6^2 + x^2 = 10^2$$
    $$36 + x^2 = 100$$
    $$x^2 = 64$$
    $$x = 8.$$

    The area is:

    $$A = \tfrac{1}{2}BH = \tfrac{1}{2}(12)(8) = 48 \qquad (B).$$

24. 25% of 80 = $\tfrac{1}{4}$ of 80 = 20. 20 is $\tfrac{1}{2}$ of 40 (A).

25. $\triangle ACD$ has half the area of $\square ABCD$ and
    $\triangle ACE$ has half the area of $\triangle ACD$. Therefore,
    $\triangle ACE$ has one-fourth the area of $\square ABCD$. (B) is the right answer to this problem.

26. The slope must be the same on all parts of the line.

    $$\text{Slope} = \frac{\text{change in } y}{\text{change in } x}$$

    $$\frac{6-4}{x-1} = \frac{5-4}{3-1}$$

    $$\frac{2}{x-1} \diagdown\diagup \frac{1}{2}$$

    $$4 = x - 1$$
    $$5 = x \qquad (D).$$

27. $\underline{H = 10}$

    $T = H + \tfrac{1}{2}T = 10 + \tfrac{1}{2}T$; so, $\underline{T = 20}$.

    $B = H + T + \tfrac{1}{2}B = 30 + \tfrac{1}{2}B$; so, $\underline{B = 60}$.

Therefore, the total length of the fish is 10 + 20 + 60 = 90 (A). This makes a great fish story!

28. The shares are $\tfrac{5}{9}$, $\tfrac{3}{9}$, and $\tfrac{1}{9}$ (they add up to $\tfrac{9}{9} =$ the total).

    The largest share is $\tfrac{5}{9}$ of \$90,000, or \$50,000 (C).

29. The sum of the three angles of any triangle is 180°.

    The sum of the two acute angles of a right triangle is 90°. So:

    $$90° - 27° = 63° \qquad (E).$$

30. 141 is the only one of the answers for which all three conditions are met. Choice (C) is correct.

31. 700% of the perimeter (or any multiple of 100%) will return the point to its starting position at P.

    We only need to consider the remaining 67%; this will place the point better than half-way around, at a place between R and S (B).

32. See the figure below.

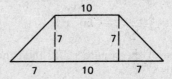

    There are 9 people in the line (B).

33. Reduce first:

    (A)$\dfrac{10}{21}$ (B)$\dfrac{3}{7}$ (C)$\dfrac{3}{7}$ (D)$\dfrac{3}{7}$ (E)$\dfrac{3}{7}$

    Since there can be only one right answer, choices (B), (C), (D), and (E) must be eliminated. (A) is the right answer.

34. Draw the figure (remember, the legs of the 45° – 45° – 90° right triangle are congruent):

    The length of the major base is 24 (D).

35. The sum of the measures of the three angles is 180°.

    $$4x + 5x + 6x = 180$$
    $$15x = 180$$

$$x = 12.$$

The measure of $\angle A$ is $4x$ or $4(12) = 48°$. The right answer is (A).

36. Add auxiliary lines:

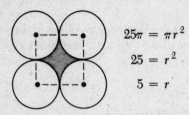

$$25\pi = \pi r^2$$
$$25 = r^2$$
$$5 = r$$

It can be seen that the shaded area equals the area of the dotted square minus the area of one circle (four quarter-circles). This is:

$$10^2 - 25\pi = 100 - 25\pi \qquad (E).$$

37. Since $m \angle A + m \angle B + m \angle C = 180°$,

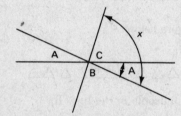

and they are on a $1 : 3 : 5$ ratio, we have

$$1y + 3y + 5y = 180$$
$$9y = 180$$
$$y = 20$$

and

$$m \angle x = m \angle A + m \angle C$$
$$= y + 5y = 6y = 6(20) = 120°.$$

Then, $\frac{1}{2}x = \frac{1}{2}(120°) = 60°$ (C).

38. If the area of the square is 72, then the length of each side is $\sqrt{72}$.

Drawing only half of the square (a $45° - 45° - 90°$ right triangle):

and $\sqrt{72}\sqrt{2} = \sqrt{144} = 12$ (C).

39. This is a time-waster; we should check the last choices first.

Only (D) works, so it must be the right answer.

40. The hands of the clock make a $90°$ angle only at 9:00. At all the other given times we have to consider that the hour hand has moved and is no longer pointing exactly at the numeral. (D) is the correct choice.

41. Counting the "central" angles, we have five complete triangles, and the sum of the measures of their angles is:

$$5(180°) = 900°.$$

Subtracting the sum of the measures of the "central" angles (which make a circle) leaves:

$$900° - 360° = 540° \qquad (E).$$

42. We need only two ducks:

(A) is the right answer.

43. See the Venn diagrams below:

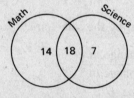

$$\frac{\text{only math}}{\text{only science}} = \frac{14}{7} = \frac{2}{1} \qquad (E).$$

44. The quadrilateral described in the problem could be:

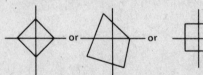

Its area cannot be determined without additional information (E).

45. John is 18 years older than Tom. When Tom is 18, John will be 36 (twice as old). This will happen in 16 years ($36 - 20$). The right answer is (B). (Plug in the answers, starting with the middle option. See what the result is. Decide whether you need a smaller or larger number and proceed to plug in the next smaller or larger answer.)

46. If we set aside the 13 extra girls, we are left with a group of 130, which is evenly divided between boys and girls $65 : 65$. Then there are 65 boys and $65 + 13 = 78$ girls.

   The boys are $65/143$ of the total group. (E) is the correct answer.

47. The original circumference is:

   $$C = 2\pi R$$

   The circumference after the increase is:

   $$C + 10 = 2\pi(R + r)$$
   $$C + 10 = 2\pi R + 2\pi r.$$

   Subtracting the original circumference leaves:

   $$C + 10 = 2\pi R + 2\pi r$$
   $$\underline{-C = (2\pi R)}$$
   $$10 = 2\pi r.$$

   And the difference in radii is:

   $$\frac{10}{2\pi} = r,$$

   or, approximately 1.6 feet. A man can then crawl under the belt (B).

48. $\{A\}$, $\{B\}$, $\{A, B\}$, and $\varnothing$ are all the subsets of the given set (D).

   In general, a set with n elements has 2^n subsets.

49. Adding the necessary auxiliary lines we see:

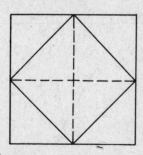

that the area of the inside square is half the area of the outside (total) square, 25 (A).

50. In this question we are asked which of the given numbers cannot be made up by adding 3s and 5s. Since the problem is a time-waster, we should start checking from the end. 7 does not work, so (E) has to be the right choice.

51. I can be drawn in the prescribed manner, and we should notice that:
   —only two points have an odd number of lines converging on them;
   —we needed to start at one of these "odd" points and end at the other one.

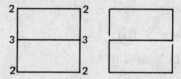

II has four (more than two) "odd" points and cannot be drawn as described.

Since this problem is a time-waster, we should start checking the choices from the end. Figure (D) also has four "odd" points, so it must be the one which cannot be drawn as described.

52. $77 \cdot 88 = 7 \cdot 11 \cdot 8 \cdot 11 = 56 \cdot 11^2 = 56 \cdot 121$, and K must be 121 (C).

53. Each wheel will have its marking at the top after every revolution. At the end of 1 minute, both wheels will have their markings at the top (and this will have happened at the end of every 1/5 minute).

   None of the choices offered as answers is correct, and so we must choose (E).

54. From the pattern in the figure we see that the white (W) and the yellow (Y) strands are either both inside

or else both outside. The question calls for determining when the white strand will be outside and the yellow strand inside—this will never happen (A).

55. Of two positive variables, the one with the smaller coefficient is larger.

$$2x = 3y \Rightarrow x > y$$

$$\tfrac{1}{4}y = \tfrac{1}{2}z \Rightarrow y > z$$

And so, $x > y > z$ (A).

56. Set up the equation:

$$x + 5 = 2(x - 3)$$

$$x + 5 = 2x - 6$$

$$11 = x \qquad (D).$$

(See No. 45. Start with 8.)

57. Two-thirds of the circumference of each circle is "exposed" or on the perimeter.

The perimeter is:

$$P = 6(2/3C) \text{ and } C = 2\pi r$$

$$= 2\pi(2)$$

$$= 4\pi.$$

$$P = 6(2/3)(4\pi) = 16\pi \qquad (C).$$

58. $A = 3x + 5$ and $2A = 6x + 10$.
$6x - 5$ is 15 less than $6x + 10$, so it equals $2A - 15$ (E).

59. $(x)(x + 1)(x + 2)$.
One of the three consecutive numbers must be a multiple of 3 and at least one must also be even. Therefore, their product must be an even multiple of 3 (i.e., a multiple of 6), and the correct choice is (D).

60. $9^2 = 81$ and $10^2 = 100$.
90.25 must be between 9 and 10. The only possible answer is 9.5 (C).

61. The midpoint is best found by averaging the x-values and the y-values of the two points.

$$\text{Midpoint} = \left(\frac{0 + 6}{2}, \frac{5 - 3}{2}\right) = (3, 1) \qquad (D).$$

62. This is another time-waster, and we should check the choices starting from the end.

$$\text{Choice (D)}, \frac{3}{7} \div \frac{1}{7} = \frac{3}{7} \times \frac{7}{1} = 3, \text{ is right}.$$

63. The semicircle on the left fills in the space on the right, as shown below.
Relocate the semicircular region in the following way:

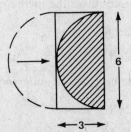

We can then see that the area is $6 \cdot 3 = 18$ (A).

64. The first strike does not count—time is measured from its sound. It takes 4 seconds for $2(3 - 1)$ strikes or 2 seconds per strike.
At 12 o'clock, only 11 strikes count, and it takes $11 \cdot 2 = 22$ seconds. (D) is the right choice.

65. $x + y = 12$ and $xy = 6$,
so,

$$\frac{1}{x} + \frac{1}{y} = \frac{y + x}{xy} = \frac{12}{6} = 2 \qquad (B).$$

66. Disregarding the unnecessary lines, we get:

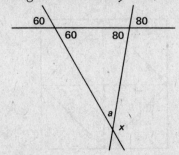

Since $\angle a$ must measure $40°$, $\angle x$ must measure $180° - 40° = 140°$ (C).

67. There are 13 hearts, so the probability for the first heart is 13/52.

The probability for the second heart is 12/51.
The combined probability for both events is:

$$\frac{13}{52} \cdot \frac{12}{51} \quad (D).$$

68. Exchange the word "of" for the multiplication symbol:

$$\frac{1}{3} \text{ of } \frac{x}{3} = \frac{1}{3} \times \frac{x}{3} = \frac{x}{9} \quad (B).$$

69. If you notice,

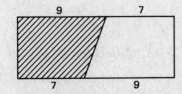

the two regions in the figure are congruent. Each has half the area of the original figure:

$$\tfrac{1}{2}(6 \cdot 16) = 48 \quad (C).$$

70. Figure (B) fits inside figure (A), while figure (D) fits inside figure (B):

From the above, we see that $(A) > (B) > (D)$ and can eliminate (B) and (D). Figure (C) is like figure (A), but distorted, and thus has less area.

The choice between (A) and (E) can be made easier if we draw figure (B) in the interior of each of them. Since (E) has less "wasted" area, (A) must be larger.

71.

Column A	Column B
$2xy$	$(2x)(2y) = 4xy$

At first glance it would seem that the quantity in Column B is greater, but we do not know whether xy is positive, negative, or zero, and so we really do not have enough information to determine which is greater. Choice (D) is correct.

72. (B) is the right answer. The sum of the lengths of any two sides of a triangle must always be longer than the third side (the shortest distance between two points lies along a straight-line path).

73. Although it would seem that $A > \sqrt{A}$, we really do not have enough information. The value of A could be positive, negative, or zero, and the answer would be different for each of the above situations. The correct choice is (D).

74. There is not enough information to determine the answer to this problem:

If $x > 0$, then $x > y$.

If $x = 0$, then $x = y$.

The correct answer is (D).

75. Fractions between 0 and 1 are very special—the value of their powers decrease as the exponents increase:

For example, $\frac{1}{2} > \frac{1}{2}^2 > \frac{1}{2}^3 > \frac{1}{2}^4$, etc.

The correct answer is (A).

76. In any triangle, the largest angle is always opposite to the longest side. The longest side is $\overline{AC}$ and $\angle B$ is opposite to it. (B) is the right choice.

77.

Column A	Column B
$x^2 + 1$	$(x-1)^2 = x^2 - 2x + 1$

The expression in Column B has an extra "$-2x$", whose value is positive if the value of x is negative. The quantity in Column B is greater (Plug in a negative number.)

78.

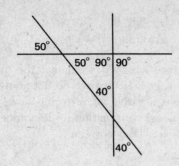

$m \angle x = 90°$, and this is less than 100°. The correct answer is (B).

79.

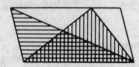

The two shaded regions are equal in area (they each have half the area of the parallelogram).

If the double-shaded region is discarded from both of the above equal areas, the remaining areas must be equal (C).

80. Twice the average equals the sum. The quantities in the two columns are equal (C).

81. There is not enough information to determine the relationship (D). See the examples below.

$$3 < 5 \quad \text{and} \quad |3| < |5|$$
$$-7 < 7 \quad \text{and} \quad |-7| > |5|$$
$$-5 < 5 \quad \text{and} \quad |-5| = |5|$$

82. If we knew nothing about the values of A and B, we would have to choose (D). We are, however, given some information:

$$A > -B$$

This means that:

$$A + B > 0 \quad \text{(adding } B \text{ to both sides)}.$$

If the numerators are equal and positive, the fraction with the smaller denominator is greater (A).

83. To find the next term, find the difference between consecutive terms, and try to discover a pattern:

1		1		2		3		5		8		13		<u>21</u>
	1		1		2		3		5		8			

The differences repeat the original series, and thus we can see that the last difference is 8, and the missing number is $13 + 8 = 21$.

The quantities in both columns are equal (C).

84. To compare two fractions, *cross-multiply* as shown below.

$$\frac{8}{23} \diagdown \!\!\!\!\! \diagup \frac{17}{50}$$

Since $400 > 391$, then $8/23 > 17/50$, and (A) is the right answer.

85. Let us start simplifying the given information and see where it takes us:

$$\frac{A + B}{3} > A$$

$$A + B > 3A \quad \text{(multiplying both by 3)}$$

$$B > 2A \quad \text{(subtracting } A \text{ from both)}$$

But $B > 2A$ does not necessarily mean that B is greater than A. Consider the example below:

Let $A = -3$ and $B = -5$

then $-5 > -6$,

or, $B > 2A$, but $B < A$ in this case.

The correct answer is (D).

86. Half the sum of two numbers equals their average (C).

87. We do not know the value of n and cannot determine the relationship between the two quantities (D).

88. Discarding the numbers which repeat in both columns, we are left with:

Column A	Column B
$1 + 2 + 3 + 4$	11

We can then see that the quantity in Column B (11)

is greater than the quantity in Column A (10). The correct choice is (B).

89. Multiplying both sides by y, we get $x > y$ (unless y is negative). Since we have no information about the nature of y, we have to choose (D).

90. Instead of 32% of 25, we could find 25% of 32 and get the same answer:

$$25\% \text{ of } 32 = \tfrac{1}{4}(32) - 8$$

The quantities in the two columns are equal, and the correct choice is (C).

91. We are not told which point is between the other two, and without that information we cannot determine which quantity is greater (D).

92.

Column A	Column B
50^2	$25^2 + 25^2$
$= 2,500$	$= 625 + 625$
	$= 1,250$

Choice (A) is the right answer to this problem.

93. If the numbers are evenly distributed, their average equals their midpoint (C).

94. $2^7 + 2^7 = 128 + 128 = 256.$

$2^8 = 256.$

The quantities in both columns are equal (C).

95. Reverse one of the two expressions:

Column A	Column B
21% of 19	21% of 23

Since both columns *now* have 21%, we can discard it, leaving us the integers 19 and 23 to compare. Obviously, the quantity in Column B is greater.

96. We do not know whether x is positive, negative, or zero (D).

97. We cannot assume that the missing dimensions are equal in both figures (D).

98. To find the sum of the integers 1 through 40, first find their average:

$$\frac{40 + 1}{2} = 20.5$$

and then multiply this average times how many numbers are involved (in this case 40).

$$(20.5)(40) = 820$$

(A) is the right answer to this problem.

99. We are not given whether x is positive, zero, or negative (D).

100. If $2x > x$, then $x > 0$ (subtract x from both sides). The answer is (A).

Answer Key—Mathematics

1.	D	35.	A	68.	B
2.	A	36.	E	69.	C
3.	D	37.	C	70.	A
4.	D	38.	C	71.	D
5.	B	39.	D	72.	B
6.	C	40.	D	73.	D
7.	E	41.	E	74.	D
8.	C	42.	A	75.	A
9.	D	43.	E	76.	B
10.	C	44.	E	77.	B
11.	A	45.	B	78.	B
12.	A	46.	E	79.	C
13.	D	47.	B	80.	C
14.	B	48.	D	81.	D
15.	C	49.	A	82.	A
16.	A	50.	E	83.	C
17.	B	51.	D	84.	A
18.	E	52.	C	85.	D
19.	B	53.	E	86.	C
20.	E	54.	A	87.	D
21.	D	55.	A	88.	B
22.	E	56.	D	89.	D
23.	B	57.	C	90.	C
24.	A	58.	E	91.	D
25.	B	59.	D	92.	A
26.	D	60.	C	93.	C
27.	A	61.	D	94.	C
28.	C	62.	D	95.	B
29.	E	63.	A	96.	D
30.	C	64.	D	97.	D
31.	B	65.	B	98.	A
32.	B	66.	C	99.	D
33.	A	67.	D	100.	A
34.	D				

PART  VII

Four Practice Tests
for the Scholastic
Aptitude Test

In this part of the book, there are four practice tests that are similar in form, content, and level of difficulty to the actual SAT. Take these tests under actual examination conditions, allowing yourself the time indicated for each section.

When you have completed a test, check your answers with the answer key at the end of the test, and determine your *raw* score in accordance with the scoring instructions on page 2. Then study the explanatory answers that follow the answer key for the questions that you did incorrectly. You may evaluate your raw score for each test by looking at the self-appraisal chart following practice test one.

If you are having difficulty with a particular mathematical topic, study this topic in Part III of this book and then do the corresponding exercises in Part IV. If you are having difficulty with any particular verbal portion of the test, study Part II of this book more carefully.

Going through these tests in the manner described will help you become more familiar with the SAT and can help you toward continuous improvement of your SAT score.

Before starting the practice tests, look over the following suggestions for test-taking.

Test-Taking Suggestions

· Remember that each section of the SAT is limited in time. Try to develop a pace that will permit you to finish each section without loss of accuracy. Do not spend too much time on any single question; make a notation of those you find difficult and return to them if and when you finish the section.

· Make sure you read and understand the directions thoroughly. In doing the sample tests, you will become familiar with the directions for each type of question asked on the SAT, but make sure they are the same when you are taking the actual test.

· Since there is a penalty for a wrong answer as against an omitted answer, try to avoid guessing when you know nothing about the question. If you can eliminate one or more answers, take an educated guess.

· Make sure that the number of each question matches the corresponding number on the answer sheet. On the answer sheet, the number of answer spaces may be more than the number of questions in a particular section, but ignore the excess. If you erase an answer, do it thoroughly.

· Avoid using time unnecessarily. It is wise not to check problems in a mathematics section until you have finished it. Make quick, simple diagrams and figures if they are helpful in solving a problem. If the diagram for a particular problem accompanies the problem, write directly on it; do not start drawing another diagram.

· Do not become alarmed if you cannot answer some questions or if you do not finish every section. You may still achieve a good score on the SAT. Statistics indicate that a student getting a raw score equal to about half the number of questions would be above average on the 200 to 800 scale. Recent average scores are about 430 for the verbal and about 470 for the math.

· It is a good idea to bring a watch with you to check your pace from time to time. In some sections, the easier questions come first, so you should be doing these more rapidly in order to conserve time for the more difficult questions that come later.

SAT Practice Test 1

ANSWER SHEET

When you have chosen your answer to any question, blacken the corresponding space on the answer sheet below. Make sure your marking completely fills the answer space. If you change an answer, erase the previous marking completely.

Section I—Verbal

1 Ⓐ Ⓑ Ⓒ Ⓓ Ⓔ	13 Ⓐ Ⓑ Ⓒ Ⓓ Ⓔ	24 Ⓐ Ⓑ Ⓒ Ⓓ Ⓔ	35 Ⓐ Ⓑ Ⓒ Ⓓ Ⓔ
2 Ⓐ Ⓑ Ⓒ Ⓓ Ⓔ	14 Ⓐ Ⓑ Ⓒ Ⓓ Ⓔ	25 Ⓐ Ⓑ Ⓒ Ⓓ Ⓔ	36 Ⓐ Ⓑ Ⓒ Ⓓ Ⓔ
3 Ⓐ Ⓑ Ⓒ Ⓓ Ⓔ	15 Ⓐ Ⓑ Ⓒ Ⓓ Ⓔ	26 Ⓐ Ⓑ Ⓒ Ⓓ Ⓔ	37 Ⓐ Ⓑ Ⓒ Ⓓ Ⓔ
4 Ⓐ Ⓑ Ⓒ Ⓓ Ⓔ	16 Ⓐ Ⓑ Ⓒ Ⓓ Ⓔ	27 Ⓐ Ⓑ Ⓒ Ⓓ Ⓔ	38 Ⓐ Ⓑ Ⓒ Ⓓ Ⓔ
5 Ⓐ Ⓑ Ⓒ Ⓓ Ⓔ	17 Ⓐ Ⓑ Ⓒ Ⓓ Ⓔ	28 Ⓐ Ⓑ Ⓒ Ⓓ Ⓔ	39 Ⓐ Ⓑ Ⓒ Ⓓ Ⓔ
6 Ⓐ Ⓑ Ⓒ Ⓓ Ⓔ	18 Ⓐ Ⓑ Ⓒ Ⓓ Ⓔ	29 Ⓐ Ⓑ Ⓒ Ⓓ Ⓔ	40 Ⓐ Ⓑ Ⓒ Ⓓ Ⓔ
7 Ⓐ Ⓑ Ⓒ Ⓓ Ⓔ	19 Ⓐ Ⓑ Ⓒ Ⓓ Ⓔ	30 Ⓐ Ⓑ Ⓒ Ⓓ Ⓔ	41 Ⓐ Ⓑ Ⓒ Ⓓ Ⓔ
8 Ⓐ Ⓑ Ⓒ Ⓓ Ⓔ	20 Ⓐ Ⓑ Ⓒ Ⓓ Ⓔ	31 Ⓐ Ⓑ Ⓒ Ⓓ Ⓔ	42 Ⓐ Ⓑ Ⓒ Ⓓ Ⓔ
9 Ⓐ Ⓑ Ⓒ Ⓓ Ⓔ	21 Ⓐ Ⓑ Ⓒ Ⓓ Ⓔ	32 Ⓐ Ⓑ Ⓒ Ⓓ Ⓔ	43 Ⓐ Ⓑ Ⓒ Ⓓ Ⓔ
10 Ⓐ Ⓑ Ⓒ Ⓓ Ⓔ	22 Ⓐ Ⓑ Ⓒ Ⓓ Ⓔ	33 Ⓐ Ⓑ Ⓒ Ⓓ Ⓔ	44 Ⓐ Ⓑ Ⓒ Ⓓ Ⓔ
11 Ⓐ Ⓑ Ⓒ Ⓓ Ⓔ	23 Ⓐ Ⓑ Ⓒ Ⓓ Ⓔ	34 Ⓐ Ⓑ Ⓒ Ⓓ Ⓔ	45 Ⓐ Ⓑ Ⓒ Ⓓ Ⓔ
12 Ⓐ Ⓑ Ⓒ Ⓓ Ⓔ			

Section II—Verbal

1 Ⓐ Ⓑ Ⓒ Ⓓ Ⓔ	11 Ⓐ Ⓑ Ⓒ Ⓓ Ⓔ	21 Ⓐ Ⓑ Ⓒ Ⓓ Ⓔ	31 Ⓐ Ⓑ Ⓒ Ⓓ Ⓔ
2 Ⓐ Ⓑ Ⓒ Ⓓ Ⓔ	12 Ⓐ Ⓑ Ⓒ Ⓓ Ⓔ	22 Ⓐ Ⓑ Ⓒ Ⓓ Ⓔ	32 Ⓐ Ⓑ Ⓒ Ⓓ Ⓔ
3 Ⓐ Ⓑ Ⓒ Ⓓ Ⓔ	13 Ⓐ Ⓑ Ⓒ Ⓓ Ⓔ	23 Ⓐ Ⓑ Ⓒ Ⓓ Ⓔ	33 Ⓐ Ⓑ Ⓒ Ⓓ Ⓔ
4 Ⓐ Ⓑ Ⓒ Ⓓ Ⓔ	14 Ⓐ Ⓑ Ⓒ Ⓓ Ⓔ	24 Ⓐ Ⓑ Ⓒ Ⓓ Ⓔ	34 Ⓐ Ⓑ Ⓒ Ⓓ Ⓔ
5 Ⓐ Ⓑ Ⓒ Ⓓ Ⓔ	15 Ⓐ Ⓑ Ⓒ Ⓓ Ⓔ	25 Ⓐ Ⓑ Ⓒ Ⓓ Ⓔ	35 Ⓐ Ⓑ Ⓒ Ⓓ Ⓔ
6 Ⓐ Ⓑ Ⓒ Ⓓ Ⓔ	16 Ⓐ Ⓑ Ⓒ Ⓓ Ⓔ	26 Ⓐ Ⓑ Ⓒ Ⓓ Ⓔ	36 Ⓐ Ⓑ Ⓒ Ⓓ Ⓔ
7 Ⓐ Ⓑ Ⓒ Ⓓ Ⓔ	17 Ⓐ Ⓑ Ⓒ Ⓓ Ⓔ	27 Ⓐ Ⓑ Ⓒ Ⓓ Ⓔ	37 Ⓐ Ⓑ Ⓒ Ⓓ Ⓔ
8 Ⓐ Ⓑ Ⓒ Ⓓ Ⓔ	18 Ⓐ Ⓑ Ⓒ Ⓓ Ⓔ	28 Ⓐ Ⓑ Ⓒ Ⓓ Ⓔ	38 Ⓐ Ⓑ Ⓒ Ⓓ Ⓔ
9 Ⓐ Ⓑ Ⓒ Ⓓ Ⓔ	19 Ⓐ Ⓑ Ⓒ Ⓓ Ⓔ	29 Ⓐ Ⓑ Ⓒ Ⓓ Ⓔ	39 Ⓐ Ⓑ Ⓒ Ⓓ Ⓔ
10 Ⓐ Ⓑ Ⓒ Ⓓ Ⓔ	20 Ⓐ Ⓑ Ⓒ Ⓓ Ⓔ	30 Ⓐ Ⓑ Ⓒ Ⓓ Ⓔ	40 Ⓐ Ⓑ Ⓒ Ⓓ Ⓔ

Section III—Mathematical

1 Ⓐ Ⓑ Ⓒ Ⓓ Ⓔ	8 Ⓐ Ⓑ Ⓒ Ⓓ Ⓔ	14 Ⓐ Ⓑ Ⓒ Ⓓ Ⓔ	20 Ⓐ Ⓑ Ⓒ Ⓓ Ⓔ
2 Ⓐ Ⓑ Ⓒ Ⓓ Ⓔ	9 Ⓐ Ⓑ Ⓒ Ⓓ Ⓔ	15 Ⓐ Ⓑ Ⓒ Ⓓ Ⓔ	21 Ⓐ Ⓑ Ⓒ Ⓓ Ⓔ
3 Ⓐ Ⓑ Ⓒ Ⓓ Ⓔ	10 Ⓐ Ⓑ Ⓒ Ⓓ Ⓔ	16 Ⓐ Ⓑ Ⓒ Ⓓ Ⓔ	22 Ⓐ Ⓑ Ⓒ Ⓓ Ⓔ
4 Ⓐ Ⓑ Ⓒ Ⓓ Ⓔ	11 Ⓐ Ⓑ Ⓒ Ⓓ Ⓔ	17 Ⓐ Ⓑ Ⓒ Ⓓ Ⓔ	23 Ⓐ Ⓑ Ⓒ Ⓓ Ⓔ
5 Ⓐ Ⓑ Ⓒ Ⓓ Ⓔ	12 Ⓐ Ⓑ Ⓒ Ⓓ Ⓔ	18 Ⓐ Ⓑ Ⓒ Ⓓ Ⓔ	24 Ⓐ Ⓑ Ⓒ Ⓓ Ⓔ
6 Ⓐ Ⓑ Ⓒ Ⓓ Ⓔ	13 Ⓐ Ⓑ Ⓒ Ⓓ Ⓔ	19 Ⓐ Ⓑ Ⓒ Ⓓ Ⓔ	25 Ⓐ Ⓑ Ⓒ Ⓓ Ⓔ
7 Ⓐ Ⓑ Ⓒ Ⓓ Ⓔ			

Section IV—Mathematical

1 Ⓐ Ⓑ Ⓒ Ⓓ Ⓔ	10 Ⓐ Ⓑ Ⓒ Ⓓ Ⓔ	19 Ⓐ Ⓑ Ⓒ Ⓓ	28 Ⓐ Ⓑ Ⓒ Ⓓ
2 Ⓐ Ⓑ Ⓒ Ⓓ Ⓔ	11 Ⓐ Ⓑ Ⓒ Ⓓ Ⓔ	20 Ⓐ Ⓑ Ⓒ Ⓓ	29 Ⓐ Ⓑ Ⓒ Ⓓ
3 Ⓐ Ⓑ Ⓒ Ⓓ Ⓔ	12 Ⓐ Ⓑ Ⓒ Ⓓ Ⓔ	21 Ⓐ Ⓑ Ⓒ Ⓓ	30 Ⓐ Ⓑ Ⓒ Ⓓ
4 Ⓐ Ⓑ Ⓒ Ⓓ Ⓔ	13 Ⓐ Ⓑ Ⓒ Ⓓ Ⓔ	22 Ⓐ Ⓑ Ⓒ Ⓓ	31 Ⓐ Ⓑ Ⓒ Ⓓ
5 Ⓐ Ⓑ Ⓒ Ⓓ Ⓔ	14 Ⓐ Ⓑ Ⓒ Ⓓ Ⓔ	23 Ⓐ Ⓑ Ⓒ Ⓓ	32 Ⓐ Ⓑ Ⓒ Ⓓ
6 Ⓐ Ⓑ Ⓒ Ⓓ Ⓔ	15 Ⓐ Ⓑ Ⓒ Ⓓ Ⓔ	24 Ⓐ Ⓑ Ⓒ Ⓓ	33 Ⓐ Ⓑ Ⓒ Ⓓ
7 Ⓐ Ⓑ Ⓒ Ⓓ Ⓔ	16 Ⓐ Ⓑ Ⓒ Ⓓ Ⓔ	25 Ⓐ Ⓑ Ⓒ Ⓓ	34 Ⓐ Ⓑ Ⓒ Ⓓ
8 Ⓐ Ⓑ Ⓒ Ⓓ Ⓔ	17 Ⓐ Ⓑ Ⓒ Ⓓ Ⓔ	26 Ⓐ Ⓑ Ⓒ Ⓓ	35 Ⓐ Ⓑ Ⓒ Ⓓ
9 Ⓐ Ⓑ Ⓒ Ⓓ Ⓔ	18 Ⓐ Ⓑ Ⓒ Ⓓ	27 Ⓐ Ⓑ Ⓒ Ⓓ	

Section V—Mathematical

1 Ⓐ Ⓑ Ⓒ Ⓓ Ⓔ	8 Ⓐ Ⓑ Ⓒ Ⓓ Ⓔ	14 Ⓐ Ⓑ Ⓒ Ⓓ Ⓔ	20 Ⓐ Ⓑ Ⓒ Ⓓ Ⓔ
2 Ⓐ Ⓑ Ⓒ Ⓓ Ⓔ	9 Ⓐ Ⓑ Ⓒ Ⓓ Ⓔ	15 Ⓐ Ⓑ Ⓒ Ⓓ Ⓔ	21 Ⓐ Ⓑ Ⓒ Ⓓ Ⓔ
3 Ⓐ Ⓑ Ⓒ Ⓓ Ⓔ	10 Ⓐ Ⓑ Ⓒ Ⓓ Ⓔ	16 Ⓐ Ⓑ Ⓒ Ⓓ Ⓔ	22 Ⓐ Ⓑ Ⓒ Ⓓ Ⓔ
4 Ⓐ Ⓑ Ⓒ Ⓓ Ⓔ	11 Ⓐ Ⓑ Ⓒ Ⓓ Ⓔ	17 Ⓐ Ⓑ Ⓒ Ⓓ Ⓔ	23 Ⓐ Ⓑ Ⓒ Ⓓ Ⓔ
5 Ⓐ Ⓑ Ⓒ Ⓓ Ⓔ	12 Ⓐ Ⓑ Ⓒ Ⓓ Ⓔ	18 Ⓐ Ⓑ Ⓒ Ⓓ Ⓔ	24 Ⓐ Ⓑ Ⓒ Ⓓ Ⓔ
6 Ⓐ Ⓑ Ⓒ Ⓓ Ⓔ	13 Ⓐ Ⓑ Ⓒ Ⓓ Ⓔ	19 Ⓐ Ⓑ Ⓒ Ⓓ Ⓔ	25 Ⓐ Ⓑ Ⓒ Ⓓ Ⓔ
7 Ⓐ Ⓑ Ⓒ Ⓓ Ⓔ			

Section VI—Written English

1 Ⓐ Ⓑ Ⓒ Ⓓ Ⓔ	14 Ⓐ Ⓑ Ⓒ Ⓓ Ⓔ	27 Ⓐ Ⓑ Ⓒ Ⓓ Ⓔ	39 Ⓐ Ⓑ Ⓒ Ⓓ Ⓔ
2 Ⓐ Ⓑ Ⓒ Ⓓ Ⓔ	15 Ⓐ Ⓑ Ⓒ Ⓓ Ⓔ	28 Ⓐ Ⓑ Ⓒ Ⓓ Ⓔ	40 Ⓐ Ⓑ Ⓒ Ⓓ Ⓔ
3 Ⓐ Ⓑ Ⓒ Ⓓ Ⓔ	16 Ⓐ Ⓑ Ⓒ Ⓓ Ⓔ	29 Ⓐ Ⓑ Ⓒ Ⓓ Ⓔ	41 Ⓐ Ⓑ Ⓒ Ⓓ Ⓔ
4 Ⓐ Ⓑ Ⓒ Ⓓ Ⓔ	17 Ⓐ Ⓑ Ⓒ Ⓓ Ⓔ	30 Ⓐ Ⓑ Ⓒ Ⓓ Ⓔ	42 Ⓐ Ⓑ Ⓒ Ⓓ Ⓔ
5 Ⓐ Ⓑ Ⓒ Ⓓ Ⓔ	18 Ⓐ Ⓑ Ⓒ Ⓓ Ⓔ	31 Ⓐ Ⓑ Ⓒ Ⓓ Ⓔ	43 Ⓐ Ⓑ Ⓒ Ⓓ Ⓔ
6 Ⓐ Ⓑ Ⓒ Ⓓ Ⓔ	19 Ⓐ Ⓑ Ⓒ Ⓓ Ⓔ	32 Ⓐ Ⓑ Ⓒ Ⓓ Ⓔ	44 Ⓐ Ⓑ Ⓒ Ⓓ Ⓔ
7 Ⓐ Ⓑ Ⓒ Ⓓ Ⓔ	20 Ⓐ Ⓑ Ⓒ Ⓓ Ⓔ	33 Ⓐ Ⓑ Ⓒ Ⓓ Ⓔ	45 Ⓐ Ⓑ Ⓒ Ⓓ Ⓔ
8 Ⓐ Ⓑ Ⓒ Ⓓ Ⓔ	21 Ⓐ Ⓑ Ⓒ Ⓓ Ⓔ	34 Ⓐ Ⓑ Ⓒ Ⓓ Ⓔ	46 Ⓐ Ⓑ Ⓒ Ⓓ Ⓔ
9 Ⓐ Ⓑ Ⓒ Ⓓ Ⓔ	22 Ⓐ Ⓑ Ⓒ Ⓓ Ⓔ	35 Ⓐ Ⓑ Ⓒ Ⓓ Ⓔ	47 Ⓐ Ⓑ Ⓒ Ⓓ Ⓔ
10 Ⓐ Ⓑ Ⓒ Ⓓ Ⓔ	23 Ⓐ Ⓑ Ⓒ Ⓓ Ⓔ	36 Ⓐ Ⓑ Ⓒ Ⓓ Ⓔ	48 Ⓐ Ⓑ Ⓒ Ⓓ Ⓔ
11 Ⓐ Ⓑ Ⓒ Ⓓ Ⓔ	24 Ⓐ Ⓑ Ⓒ Ⓓ Ⓔ	37 Ⓐ Ⓑ Ⓒ Ⓓ Ⓔ	49 Ⓐ Ⓑ Ⓒ Ⓓ Ⓔ
12 Ⓐ Ⓑ Ⓒ Ⓓ Ⓔ	25 Ⓐ Ⓑ Ⓒ Ⓓ Ⓔ	38 Ⓐ Ⓑ Ⓒ Ⓓ Ⓔ	50 Ⓐ Ⓑ Ⓒ Ⓓ Ⓔ
13 Ⓐ Ⓑ Ⓒ Ⓓ Ⓔ	26 Ⓐ Ⓑ Ⓒ Ⓓ Ⓔ		

SAT Practice Test 1

Section I

Time—30 minutes

45 Questions

For each of the numbered questions in this section, choose the best answer according to the instructions, and blacken the corresponding blank space on the answer sheet.

In each of the questions below, a capitalized word is followed by five words or phrases lettered (A) through (E). Select the word or phrase *most nearly opposite* in meaning to the capitalized word.

Since some of the questions require that you distinguish fine shades of meaning, consider all choices carefully before you select your answer.

1. ACCELERATE:
   (A) downshift
   (B) slow down
   (C) speed up
   (D) exhilarate
   (E) devalue

2. INCITE:
   (A) discourage
   (B) locate
   (C) enhance
   (D) submit
   (E) contrite

3. BUMBLE:
   (A) utter noisily
   (B) flitter about
   (C) butcher
   (D) perform adroitly
   (E) fall under

4. STRINGENT:
   (A) pungent
   (B) austere
   (C) corrupt
   (D) flexible
   (E) inexorable

5. FURTIVE:
   (A) inert
   (B) contrary
   (C) aboveboard
   (D) concealed
   (E) unintentional

6. DECRY:
   (A) convey
   (B) descry
   (C) uncover
   (D) derogate
   (E) esteem

7. ZEALOT:
   (A) harlot
   (B) moderate
   (C) contemporary
   (D) hothead
   (E) veteran

8. CIRCUMSPECT:
   (A) guarded
   (B) indiscreet
   (C) direct
   (D) proper
   (E) punctilious

9. PARSIMONIOUS:
   (A) grammatical
   (B) egotistical
   (C) unstinting
   (D) close
   (E) constrained

10. TRUCULENT:
    (A) juicy
    (B) desiccated
    (C) determined
    (D) diffident
    (E) gentle

11. IMPLACABLE:
    (A) relentless
    (B) appeasable
    (C) minatory
    (D) voracious
    (E) lovable

12. QUARTER:
    (A) appointment
    (B) section
    (C) anger
    (D) incarcerate
    (E) ruthlessness

13. JUDICIOUS:
    (A) thoughtful
    (B) criminal
    (C) foolish
    (D) plausible
    (E) impulsive

14. MENDACITY:
    (A) veracity
    (B) boldness
    (C) diffidence
    (D) concern
    (E) adequacy

15. USURP:
    (A) revise
    (B) abdicate
    (C) coerce
    (D) reversion
    (E) divisor

Each of the sentences below has one or more blank spaces indicating where a word (or words) has been omitted. Each sentence is followed by five words or sets of words lettered from (A) through (E). Select the lettered word or set of words which, when inserted to replace the blanks, *best* fits in with and completes the meaning of the sentence as a whole.

16. Though Slim Somerset was, at least for a time, a lawman, he was _____ as a gunfighter, gambler, and brawler.
    (A) reputed
    (B) mistaken
    (C) famous
    (D) notorious
    (E) known

17. When it was young, the earth took a much shorter time—perhaps only about four hours—to make a complete _____ of its _____; today it takes about twenty-four hours.
    (A) reversal . . position
    (B) circuit . . orbit
    (C) rotation . . axis
    (D) change . . tides
    (E) transit . . ellipse

18. Strangely enough, a ship passing from the Atlantic end of the Panama Canal through to the Pacific end leaves the Canal _____ of where it entered.
    (A) west

(B) opposite
(C) regardless
(D) short
(E) east

19. The movement of so many thousands of feet throws up such dense and _____ clouds of dust that one who has not witnessed the phenomenon will find it difficult to imagine it in all its vastness and nuisance.
    (A) fulsome
    (B) fulminating
    (C) portentous
    (D) prodigious
    (E) prohibitive

20. Our basic freedoms are not as _____ as we like to think, just as our passion for individualism is not as _____ as we suppose.
    (A) vital . . rigorous
    (B) incisive . . consuming
    (C) broad . . invidious
    (D) inclusive . . profound
    (E) basic . . passionate

21. The most brilliantly colored reef fishes, by nature fish with small populations, are often _____ types rather than abundant _____ types.
    (A) solitary . . schooling
    (B) sterile . . fertile
    (C) phosphorescent . . fluorescent
    (D) invertebrate . . vertebrate
    (E) cold-blooded . . warm-blooded

22. Although records on the practice of medicine by women in ancient times are _____, enough evidence remains from literary and archeological sources to draw acceptable _____.
    (A) frugal . . data
    (B) buried . . impressions
    (C) scant . . conclusions
    (D) uncertain . . diagrams
    (E) biased . . references

23. Pure methane gas has a _____ value of about 1000 British Thermal Units (Btu) per foot— and 5 cubic feet of methane provides enough _____ to boil a half-gallon of water and keep it bubbling for 20 minutes.
    (A) pecuniary . . wherewithal
    (B) full . . thermite
    (C) total . . value
    (D) heat . . energy
    (E) cloud chamber . . radiation

24. Tree-dwelling bats tend to remain _____ from other members of their species, while bats whose resting hours are spent in caves tend to _____.
    (A) contiguous . . extricate
    (B) isolated . . cluster
    (C) restricted . . segregate
    (D) reciprocal . . diverge
    (E) juxtaposed . . converge

25. While desert plants do not have to _____, as forest vegetation does, against other plants for light and space, they do have to struggle to obtain sufficient water to _____.
    (A) strive . . bloom
    (B) compete . . survive
    (C) conspire . . inspire
    (D) exert . . drink
    (E) expand . . retract

In each of the questions below, a related pair of words or phrases, in capital letters, is followed by five pairs of words or phrases lettered from (A) to (E). Select that lettered pair which expresses a relationship that is *most* similar to that of the capitalized pair.

26. LAW : CRIME ::
    (A) rules : game
    (B) game : foul
    (C) legal code : sin
    (D) society : crime
    (E) religious code : sin

27. DIFFUSE : PITHY ::
    (A) sacred : profane
    (B) falling : trees
    (C) decisive : terse
    (D) permanent : everlasting
    (E) foliage : greenery

28. CARELESSNESS : ERROR ::
    (A) groan : pain
    (B) bricks : building
    (C) trial : blunder
    (D) simplicity : naiveté
    (E) starvation : atrophy

29. VERSIFICATION : POETRY ::
    (A) symptoms : illness
    (B) facts : fancies
    (C) gestures : acting
    (D) wolf : mammal
    (E) techniques : craft

30. TEPID : BOILING ::
    (A) tranquil : frenzied
    (B) cool : freezing
    (C) viscous : syrup
    (D) timid : timorous
    (E) cold : frigid

31. DILIGENT : ASSIDUOUS ::
    (A) mortal : hostile
    (B) halcyon : bellicose
    (C) pacific : peace
    (D) fictitious : imaginary
    (E) liquid : solid

32. DEARTH : PLENITUDE ::
    (A) scarcity : shortage
    (B) fact : idea
    (C) fact : fiction
    (D) death : famine
    (E) abundance : scarcity

33. SHIP : HELMSMAN ::
    (A) conduct : conscience
    (B) victory : leader
    (C) trail : spoor
    (D) patriot : nation
    (E) state : army

34. COTERIE : UNRESTRICTED ::
    (A) destroy : restore
    (B) exclusive : circle
    (C) fiery : chill
    (D) mercenary : altruistic
    (E) delinquent : deliquescent

35. INSTIGATE : INCITE ::
    (A) explicit : equivocal
    (B) investigate : insight
    (C) encumber : cucumber
    (D) obdurate : adamant
    (E) foment : vinegar

Each of the reading passages below is followed by several questions about the contents of the passage. In answering the questions, base your responses on what is *stated* or *implied* in the passage.

As operations on land, at sea, and in the skies became increasingly risky, American scientists and engineers were forced to develop advanced satellites that could see, hear, and "sense" what was happening on terra firma. Once or twice a month, a secret Discoverer or SAMOS spy-in-the-sky satellite is launched from Vandenberg Air Force Base into a polar orbit to circle the globe every 90 minutes at altitudes of 86 to 114 miles, carrying cameras that can spot, on the earth's surface, an object as small as a basketball.

Some years ago, U.S. spy satellites, after a number of passes over the Soviet Union and mainland China, would eject a package at a predetermined time and position over the Pacific. Air Force cargo planes equipped with skyhooks would snare the falling package as it slowly parachuted earthward. The package would be rushed to a nearby military base and its valuable film developed for analysis by photo interpreters.

Now all of that is old hat. Satellites launched in the 1970s transmit telemetry that ground stations convert to videotape images, which can be projected or printed as high-resolution photos. "Sensing" satellites like the Vela and MIDAS spy satellites, orbiting at an altitude of 55,000 miles from earth, pick up various signals: infrared (heat) rays given off by a blast furnace, a launched missile, a fleet of trucks, trains, ships, and even crops; also concentrations of gamma rays, X rays, neutrons, and large electromagnetic fields—indications of nuclear-bomb fallout .

Satellites have replaced the Distant Early Warning (DEW) line and Ballistic Missile Early Warning System of the 1950s and 1960s—those football-field-sized masses of steel, wire mesh, cables, and plastic domes along the Arctic Circle. Today, the United States has surveillance satellites that eavesdrop on transmissions throughout the world and relay voice and code messages back to earth where high-speed computers take over and distill and file potential intelligence information.

36. Which of the following is not stated or implied to be a purpose of the "sensing" satellites?
   (A) Spot nuclear fallout
   (B) Identify major troop movements
   (C) Locate major industrial targets
   (D) Transmit international cultural events
   (E) Locate major agricultural centers

37. Camera-equipped spy satellites orbit around the
   (A) earth
   (B) moon
   (C) sun
   (D) South and North poles
   (E) moon and earth

38. Which of the following sentences in the passage best illustrates the adage: "Necessity is the mother of invention"?
   (A) Paragraph 3, "Now all of that is old hat."
   (B) Paragraph 4, last sentence, "Today, the United States has . . ."
   (C) Paragraph 1, first sentence, "As operations . . ."
   (D) Paragraph 2, sentence 1, "Some years ago, . . ."
   (E) Paragraph 4, sentence 1, "Satellites have replaced . . ."

39. Implied in the use of quotation marks around the word "sensing" is the understanding that
   (A) the ability of the satellite to sense is uncertain
   (B) mechanical and electronic equipment is not deemed capable of sensing in the usual meaning of the word
   (C) this equipment is more sensitive than that of the past
   (D) sensory neurons are very delicate
   (E) satellites, though sophisticated, have little sense

40. Which of the following is (are) true of the more recent satellites such as the SAMOS or the MIDAS, but not of those of some years ago?
   I. They all orbit at an altitude of under 200 miles.
   II. Their information is transmitted to ground stations, which record the telemetry and convert it to videotape images.
   III. They can pick up concentrations of gamma rays.
   (A) I only
   (B) II only
   (C) III only
   (D) II and III only
   (E) I, II, and III

The continuum of changing dominance from the robin's acre to the barnyard pecking order has been duplicated in the human experience. The urban concentration has come to present as its conventional prize not dominance over space but dominance over men. It is the status struggle—that rat race which rats under natural conditions do their best to avoid. Territory lingers, but as a symbol of status, and not as a prize in itself. For comfort's sake we seek a large apartment, but were comfort all, then we should not worry about the fashionable address. It is a symbol of status and, while presenting a degree of territorial security, commands through size and location its far more pressing symbolic contribution to rank. Similarly, the size of a man's office offers no functional value whatsoever except as an advertisement of status. Dominance relates little to space but almost exclusively to dominance over our fellows.

The ambiguity of the automobile in urban life bears fascinated if morbid inspection. It is a mobile territory without doubt, confirmed by the readiness to defend it emotionally on the part of both the driver and the dog beside him. The territorial boundaries of bumpers and fenders likewise separate proprietors so that even in a standstill traffic jam one confronts a territorial mosaic in which proprietors, aside from fleeting rage, acknowledge not at all each other's existence. Perhaps the car is a tender subconscious keepsake from a time when we walked beneath trees that were our own. Yet in urban life the car is a monstrosity. While it provides for the proprietor a tiny area of spatial privacy and a carpet on which to fly away, still, in the city, it exposes him to human density at its worst. As a territorial prize worth gaining, the car could not exist. Only its value as a symbol of status converts the urban automobile from prison to prize.

41. Which of the following is (are) important indicators of status as regards a person's apartment in an urban concentration?
   I. The apartment is comfortable and airy.
   II. The apartment is located close to the fashion industry.
   III. The apartment is large.
   (A) II only
   (B) I and III only
   (C) I only
   (D) III only
   (E) I, II, and III

42. The author terms the automobile a monstrosity in urban life because
   (A) it takes up an inordinate amount of space
   (B) it emits pollutants into the air we breathe
   (C) it provides only a tiny area of spatial privacy
   (D) its use brings its owner into contact with the most severe conditions of human density
   (E) its value lies only in the status it bestows

43. Which of the following is (are) statements that define the territoriality of the automobile?
   I. The car exposes the driver to population density.
   II. The driver is willing to defend his car.

III. The bumpers and fenders are the boundaries of the car.
   (A) III only
   (B) I only
   (C) II and III only
   (D) I and II only
   (E) I, II, and III

44. Which of the following statements is expressed or implied by the author in the passage?
   (A) Cars are a prized possession in an urban setting.
   (B) Cars are the ideal satisfaction of man's territorial urge.
   (C) Cars are important to people only as a means of transportation.
   (D) Traffic jams bring people closer together.
   (E) The car as a status symbol is a reflection of the ambiguity of man's self-consciousness.

45. The word "ambiguity" as used in the first line of the second paragraph most nearly means
   (A) uncertain value
   (B) validity
   (C) worthlessness
   (D) utility
   (E) strangeness

STOP
WORK ONLY ON THIS SECTION UNTIL THE TIME ALLOTTED IS OVER.

SECTION II

Time—30 minutes

40 Questions

For each of the numbered questions in this section, choose the best answer according to the instructions, and blacken the corresponding blank space on the answer sheet.

In each of the questions below, a capitalized word is followed by five words or phrases lettered (A) through (E). Select the word or phrase *most nearly opposite* in meaning to the capitalized word.

Since some of the questions require that you distinguish fine shades of meaning, consider all choices carefully before you select your answer.

1. ENDURABLE:
   (A) fragile
   (B) industrious
   (C) tolerant
   (D) doughty
   (E) intolerable

2. TEEMING:
   (A) devising
   (B) wanting
   (C) pouring
   (D) denying
   (E) suffering

3. MERCENARY:
   (A) altruist
   (B) nursemaid
   (C) rifleman
   (D) agent
   (E) miser

4. FERVOR:
   (A) normal
   (B) ardor
   (C) apathy
   (D) disservice
   (E) cautious

5. ILLICIT:
   (A) safe
   (B) authorized
   (C) satisfactory
   (D) natural
   (E) unadulterated

6. TEMERITY:
   (A) crassness
   (B) solidity
   (C) frigidity
   (D) wariness
   (E) élan

7. INDIGENT:
   (A) affluent
   (B) alien
   (C) concerned
   (D) lustrous
   (E) laudatory

8. EPHEMERAL:
   (A) masculine
   (B) intransigent
   (C) asleep
   (D) penetrable
   (E) permanent

9. OBTUSE:
   (A) flat
   (B) perceptive
   (C) similar
   (D) unobserved
   (E) blunt

10. ABSTRUSE:
    (A) banal
    (B) sensitive
    (C) venial
    (D) concrete
    (E) elementary

Each of the reading passages below is followed by several questions about the contents of the passage. In answering the questions, base your responses on what is *stated* or *implied* in the passage.

Rice is the main food for half the world's population. There are thousands of varieties of rice. All are crops of warm climates and only a few new types produce well where the mean temperature is 70°F (or higher) for less than four months of the year.

In the United States, rice culture began in South Carolina in 1694, but almost all of our rice is now grown in limited regions of Arkansas, California, Louisiana, Mississippi, and Texas. The nutritive value of milled rice is about that of potatoes, but in the rough, or unhulled, form at everyday temperatures, rice can keep for several years—much longer than raw potatoes.

Yields around the world vary widely, from only 1,000 pounds per acre on unfertilized plots dependent on fluctuating rainfall to more than 6,000 pounds per acre where plant variety is matched to optimum conditions of soil, water, and temperature. United States production in 1976 was nearly 13 billion pounds from 2.8 million acres, for an average yield of 4,600 pounds per acre. More than half of our production is exported—major customers include South Korea, South Africa, the Arab countries of the Mideast, and some western European nations.

In the United States, commercial production is energy-intensive and usually employs chemical aids. Rice seed is either sown by airplane in flooded fields or planted with grain drills in fields drained for planting and subsequently flooded. Weed-control herbicides such as 2,4-D are commonly applied by airplane. Fields are drained again before harvest and allowed to dry sufficiently for combines to be used. Rice is hulled in centrally located mills—the largest process as much as a billion pounds a year. Milling nowadays is often preceded by special processing, which first places rough rice under a vacuum to remove air from the hull and kernel, then steams it under high pressure. This practice, akin to parboiling, drives some vitamins and minerals from the rice hull into the kernel, thereby producing a more nutritious, longer-lasting final product. Milled rice is often further enriched with vitamins and minerals before being packaged for distribution to markets.

11. The author's primary purpose in this passage is to
    (A) advocate an agricultural policy
    (B) compare farming in the United States with farming in South Korea and South Africa
    (C) provide some general information about rice and rice farming
    (D) propose that rice be made more nutritious through special processing
    (E) advocate an increase in rice production in the U.S.

12. In writing of the nutritive value of rice, the author says that
(A) milled rice has the same food value as potatoes but lasts longer
(B) rough, unhulled rice has greater nutritive value than raw potatoes
(C) steaming rice drives some of the vitamins and minerals out
(D) milled rice is often fortified with vitamins and minerals
(E) the nutritive value of rice depends upon fluctuating rainfall

13. Which of the following statements is (are) true of rice production in the United States?
  I. Rice culture is greatest in South Carolina.
  II. Commercial production in the U.S. is energy-intensive.
  III. Yields of rice vary from 1,000 to 6,000 pounds per acre.
  IV. The largest American mills process up to a billion pounds per year.
  V. Less than half of U.S. rice production is kept for domestic use.
(A) I, II, III, IV, and V
(B) IV and V only
(C) III and V only
(D) II, IV, and V only
(E) II, III, and IV only

14. Which of the following statements is neither expressed nor implied in this passage?
(A) Rice is grown in flooded fields.
(B) Canada and Finland would probably not be favorable areas for rice production.
(C) The average yield per acre for rice grown in the U.S. is greater than the average yield world-wide.
(D) Almost all rice grown in the United States is grown in only five of the states.
(E) Unhulled rice can be stored for several years at everyday temperatures.

15. Of the following statements, which is (are) true according to the passage?
  I. All varieties of rice are warm weather crops.
  II. Rice crop yields are dependent on fertilization.
  III. Rainfall is an important factor in rice production.
(A) II only
(B) III only
(C) I and II only
(D) II and III only
(E) I, II, and III

By the turn of the century, the fishing industry had become well established as a group of small, family enterprises. Typical upper lakes ports might support half a dozen fishing families, and because these were mostly small towns, the fishermen of each community knew each other well. They competed for fish on the lakes and for markets on shore, but they also had to live together, and this produced a kind of extended family held together by a mutually competitive spirit and daily use of a common market-place and a common fishing ground. Consequently, once commercial fishing became established, it also became a very stable social institution. In this small town push and shove, nobody got rich, but fishing families thrived, outsiders were kept out, and gaining the respect of other fishermen was a goal worthy of a life's work.

A member of such a clan had to have a wide range of practical knowledge and skills. He had to be skilled in construction, handling, management, and repair of boats. He had to know his lake intimately. He had to be storekeeper, salesman, and market manager. And he had to be a weatherman. Fogs, blizzards, and ice storms sweep off the shores and across these lakes with blinding speed, and someone preoccupied with nets and lines can suddenly find himself locked in a small, white, very angry room. At that point the brainpan must call forth from memory a highly detailed chart of the entire area surrounding the boat, including islands, shoals, channels, and the nearest safe haven.

One fisherman from Saginaw Bay recalled a story about an old-timer, a one-armed fisherman named Harvey Dutcher, who took a gathering of local youngsters on his small, sail-powered fishing boat one Fourth of July and dropped them on an island a dozen miles out in the bay. They would have a picnic while he fished, and he would pick them up on his return. But in the afternoon a storm came up and fog blanketed the bay. Soon, worried parents gathered at the dock, where visibility was zero. The world around them was nothing but howling white walls. Darkness fell and anxiety rose. Toward nine that evening the wind dropped, but seas in that dishpan bay remained violent. Suddenly, near midnight, without sound or warning, Dutcher's little vessel, loaded with kids and tugged along by one small sail, eased out of the fog and snuggled up next to the pier. A collective sigh of relief rose from the parents, but Dutcher himself shrugged off his pinpoint landing as routine. "Jest listen to the shore sounds," he said, "and watch the water under you. Hell, that ain't much to do. You'll always get home."

16. The fishing industry of the upper lakes was
    (A) part of a group of large-scale industrialized activities
    (B) well established by the start of the last quarter of the nineteenth century
    (C) owned by outsiders but operated by local people
    (D) established as a group of small, family enterprises
    (E) highly competitive, and few fishing families thrived

17. Of the following, which are (is) part of the profile of skills and practical knowledge needed by an upper lakes fisherman?
    I. Familiarity with boatbuilding and maintenance
    II. Competitive spirit and common fishing grounds
    III. Knowledge of navigation, and familiarity with the geography of the lake
    IV. Knowledge of weather systems
    V. Keeping occupied with fishing nets and lines
    (A) I, II, and IV only
    (B) I and III only

(C) I only
(D) I, III, and V only
(E) I, III, and IV only

18. When the author refers to a "small, white, very angry room," in paragraph 2, he means
    (A) the cabin of a small fishing boat
    (B) Davey Jones's locker
    (C) a padded cell for violent psychopathic sailors
    (D) the brig
    (E) being in the boat in a violent storm, enveloped by fog or snow

19. The parents of the youngsters were concerned because
    (A) Harvey Dutcher was physically handicapped
    (B) their children were on a picnic on an isolated island unsupervised
    (C) they were fearful that Harvey Dutcher's small boat might come to grief in the storm
    (D) the boat did not return home until after dark
    (E) the wind had dropped, but the seas in the bay continued to be violent

20. Harvey Dutcher's advice on how to get back to shore safely can be summed up as follows:
    (A) Guide yourself by listening for familiar sounds, and avoid shoals.
    (B) Use ship-to-shore communication.
    (C) Just keep heading in the same direction and you must reach shore sooner or later.
    (D) Common sense and the use of pinpoints will get you home.
    (E) Follow normal routines. There isn't much else to do.

The world, like an ore-bearing mountain, is veined with every possible kind of significance. We are all miners and quarrymen, tunneling, cutting, extracting. An artist is a man equipped with better tools than those of common men—sometimes, too, with a divining rod by whose aid he discovers, in the dark chaotic mass, veins of hitherto unsuspected treasure—new meanings and values. He opens our eyes for us, and we follow in a kind of gold rush. The whole world seems all at once to glitter with the nuggets which he first taught us to see. What was empty of significance becomes, after his passage, suddenly full—and full of *his* significance. Nature, as Oscar Wilde insists in one of the best of his essays, is always imitating art, is perpetually creating men and things in art's image. How imperfectly did mountains exist before Wordsworth! How dim, before Constable, was English pastoral landscape! Yes, and how dim, for that matter, before the epoch-making discoveries of Shakespeare and Chaucer were even men and women!

Nations are to a very large extent invented by their poets and novelists. The inadequacy of German drama and the German novel perhaps explains the curious uncertainty and artificiality of character displayed by so many of the Germans whom one meets in daily life.

Thanks to a long succession of admirable dramatists and novelists, Frenchmen and Englishmen know exactly how they ought to behave. Lacking these, the Germans are at a loss. It is a good art that makes us natural.

21. The author implies that
    (A) our understanding of human nature and the motivation of people is corrupted by the insight of the artist
    (B) he agrees with Wilde's idea that life imitates art
    (C) the artist is better equipped than the average man for quarrying and building tunnels
    (D) achieving success is like mining for gold
    (E) Wordsworth explored the mountains of England

22. In the second sentence, the author is saying, in effect, that
    (A) we all have our places in the scheme of things regardless of the mode of our employment
    (B) miners and quarrymen are honeycombing our mountains
    (C) we are each, regardless of occupation, concerned with understanding the world around us
    (D) to understand the world better, we ought to have closer contact with the more fundamental activities of the world
    (E) under the seeming significance of our world lies nothing but stone and marble

23. According to the author, the German character is flawed because
    (A) Germans have no literary models that adequately demonstrate for them how they should behave
    (B) drama and literature in Germany are filled with artificial characters
    (C) the Germans do not agree that life imitates art
    (D) Germany has no writers comparable to Wilde or Wordsworth
    (E) Germans are better technicians than miners or quarrymen

24. The author depends heavily upon
    (A) detail
    (B) illustration and example
    (C) understatement
    (D) figurative language
    (E) logical marshaling of fact.

25. In the last sentence of the first paragraph, the author is saying, in effect, that
    (A) before Shakespeare and Chaucer, most authors wrote allegories
    (B) Shakespeare and Chaucer understood human nature so well that their writings have helped us, their readers, to understand human nature better
    (C) Shakespeare's discoveries brightened English drama
    (D) we would know nothing about the epochs of Chaucer or Shakespeare were it not for their writings
    (E) men and women were somewhat dimwitted in the days before Shakespeare and Chaucer

Each of the sentences below has one or more blank spaces indicating where a word (or words) has been omitted. Each sentence is followed by five words or sets of words lettered from (A) through (E). Select the lettered word or set of words which, inserted to replace the blanks, *best* fits in with and completes the meaning of the sentence as a whole.

26. Beethoven was a composer of such _____ genius that his work is a benchmark against which to _____ that of all who have come after him.
    (A) exorbitant . . judge
    (B) exuberant . . extol
    (C) extraordinary . . measure
    (D) tempestuous . . seat
    (E) temperamental . . weigh

27. Tradition is merely custom that has _____ long enough for people to forget that it was ever _____.
    (A) subsided . . habit
    (B) hardened . . attitude
    (C) endured . . history
    (D) subsisted . . thus
    (E) survived . . innovation

28. At Hopeville, the river _____ at eleven feet, but forty miles below, where the surging waters of the Elf joined the swollen torrents, the river was at eighteen feet and _____.
    (A) rippled . . freezing

    (B) crested . . rising
    (C) arrived . . going
    (D) dipped . . cresting
    (E) rested . . falling

29. He could identify some of the _____ trees like the oaks and the maples by the shapes of their leaves, but he could not identify any of the _____ except the hemlocks.
    (A) shade . . deciduous
    (B) ornamental . . shrubs
    (C) deciduous . . conifers
    (D) fruit . . evergreens
    (E) dwarf . . giants

30. Augustus John is _____ for his work as a portraitist, but _____ for his bohemian life style.
    (A) famous . . infamous
    (B) renowned . . revered
    (C) known . . famous
    (D) renowned . . notorious
    (E) reviled . . despised

In each of the questions below, a related pair of words or phrases, in capital letters, is followed by five pairs of words or phrases lettered from (A) to (E). Select that lettered pair which expresses a relationship that is *most* similar to that of the capitalized pair.

31. YEAR : MONTH ::
    (A) annuity : perpetuity
    (B) hour : second
    (C) week : day
    (D) eternal : annual
    (E) minute : hour

32. EROSION : RAVINE ::
    (A) hunger : food
    (B) happiness : misfortune
    (C) overeating : obesity
    (D) fight : recurrence
    (E) persistence : intermittence

33. LARVA : IMAGO ::
    (A) quanta : tempo
    (B) volcano : photo
    (C) warp : woof
    (D) crawler : stinger
    (E) caterpillar : butterfly

34. ENERVATE : EXHAUST ::
    (A) strengthen : use up
    (B) enfeeble : deplete
    (C) invigorate : drain
    (D) support : abandon
    (E) culminate : critical

35. SKIM : PERUSE ::
    (A) note : detect
    (B) summarize : minimize
    (C) defect : abscond
    (D) glance over : scrutinize
    (E) slim : lissome

36. SACRILEGE : WORSHIP ::
    (A) conviction : persuasion
    (B) stimulus : response
    (C) voodoo : sacrifice
    (D) heresy : idol
    (E) treason : patriotism

37. CHEMIST : SODIUM ::
    (A) architect : building
    (B) ancestor : descendants
    (C) botanist : plant
    (D) geologist : quartz
    (E) anthropologist : ape

38. COACH : TEAM ::
    (A) Dodge : V-8
    (B) dray : sleigh
    (C) rickshaw : coolie
    (D) wagon : Shetland
    (E) coupe : sedan

39. NEUROSIS : NEUROTIC ::
    (A) schizophrenia : schizoid
    (B) sanity : insanity
    (C) prisoner : imprisonment
    (D) maniacal : mania
    (E) Freud : analysis

40. CARPENTER : MITER BOX ::
    (A) plumber : pipe
    (B) bricklayer : mortar
    (C) builder : level
    (D) peddler : cart
    (E) baker : dough

STOP
WORK ONLY ON THIS SECTION UNTIL THE TIME ALLOTTED IS OVER.

Time—30 minutes

25 Questions

In the mathematical sections, use any available space on the page for scratchwork in solving problems. Then indicate the *one* correct answer by darkening the appropriate oval on the answer sheet.

You may wish to refer to the following formulas and relationships in solving some of the problems.

Triangle:
The sum of the angles of any triangle is one straight angle, or 180 degrees.

The area of a triangle $= \frac{1}{2}$ (base $\times$ altitude).

In a right triangle, the square of the hypotenuse = the sum of the squares of the legs.

Circle of radius *r*:
Area $= \pi r^2$
Circumference $= 2\pi r$
There are 360 degrees of arc in a circle.

Definitions of Symbols

$=$ is equal to	$\leqq$ is less than or equal to
$\neq$ is unequal to	$\geqq$ is greater than or equal to
$\approx$ nearly equal to	$\parallel$ is parallel to
$<$ is less than	$\perp$ is perpendicular to
$>$ is greater than	

Note: Figures are drawn as accurately as possible *except* when it is stated in a specific problem that its figure is not drawn to scale. All figures lie in a plane unless otherwise indicated. All numbers used in this test are real numbers.

1. 12 is what percent of 300?
   (A) 2
   (B) 4
   (C) 6
   (D) 8
   (E) 12

2. If $\frac{3}{4}$ of a certain number is $\frac{2}{3}$, what is $\frac{3}{8}$ of the number?

(A) $\frac{1}{3}$

(B) $\frac{2}{3}$

(C) $\frac{1}{4}$

(D) $\frac{5}{8}$

(E) $\frac{4}{9}$

3. The altitude to the hypotenuse of a right triangle
(A) is also a median
(B) is also an angle bisector
(C) divides the triangle into two equal areas
(D) divides the triangle into two similar triangles
(E) divides the triangle into two congruent triangles

4. If $y = \dfrac{mx}{p - x}$, then $x =$

(A) $\dfrac{py}{m - y}$

(B) $\dfrac{py}{m - 1}$

(C) $\dfrac{py}{m + 1}$

(D) $\dfrac{p}{m}$

(E) $\dfrac{py}{m + y}$

5. A taxi service charges 50¢ for the first quarter-mile of a ride and 20¢ for each additional quarter of a mile. What is the fare in cents for a trip of n miles, where n is greater than $\frac{1}{4}$ mile?

(A) $40 + 2n$

(B) $50 + 20(n - 1)$

(C) $50n + 20\left(n - \dfrac{1}{4}\right)$

(D) $50 + 20(4n - 1)$

(E) $50 + 20\left(n - \dfrac{1}{4}\right)$

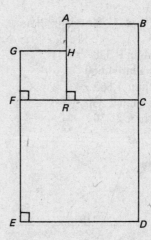

6. In the figure above, all the quadrilaterals are squares. The area of *HGFR* is 4 and the area of *ABCR* is 9. The area of *CDEF* is
(A) 16
(B) 20
(C) 25
(D) 30
(E) 36

7. If $\frac{5}{3} y = \frac{5}{3}$, then $1 - y =$

(A) $-\dfrac{5}{3}$

(B) $-\dfrac{4}{5}$

(C) $\dfrac{1}{2}$

(D) $-\dfrac{1}{2}$

(E) 0

8. In a class of 20 students, the class average for a certain test was p. Two students then had their grades raised 10 points each. The class average then became
(A) $p + 1$
(B) $p + 2$
(C) $p - 1$
(D) $p - 2$
(E) $2p + 10$

9. $\left(\dfrac{17}{36} + \dfrac{23}{50}\right) \times 4{,}660$ is slightly
(A) less than 9,320
(B) more than 4,660
(C) less than 4,660
(D) more than 2,330
(E) less than 2,330

10.

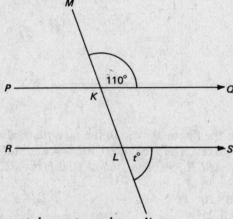

Figure not drawn to scale.

In the figure above $PQ \parallel RS$. Then $t =$
(A) 60
(B) 70
(C) 75
(D) 80
(E) 110

11. $\dfrac{8}{0.2 \times 0.2} =$

(A) 200
(B) 20
(C) 2

(D) $\dfrac{1}{20}$

(E) $\dfrac{1}{200}$

12. If the volume of a cube is 125, then the total surface area of the cube is
(A) 100
(B) 125
(C) 150
(D) 175
(E) 200

13.

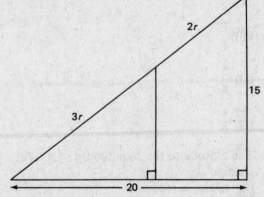

In the triangle above, $r =$
(A) 3
(B) 4
(C) 10
(D) 6
(E) 5

14. If $p + q$ is 150% of q, then p is what percent of q?
(A) 10%
(B) 15%
(C) 25%
(D) 50%
(E) 75%

15.

In the figure above, if the hand turns 560° counterclockwise, between what two numbers will it point?
(A) 4 and 5
(B) 5 and 6
(C) 6 and 7
(D) 7 and 8
(E) 8 and 9

16. If a theater ticket, including a 12% tax, costs $5.60, then the amount of the tax is
(A) $.60
(B) $.67
(C) $.75
(D) $.82
(E) $.88

17. If the area of a circle of radius x is five times that of a circle of radius y, then x equals
(A) $5y$

(B) $y\sqrt{5}$

(C) $\dfrac{y}{\sqrt{5}}$

(D) $5y^2$
(E) $25y$

18. A man does one-sixth of a job in h hours. If he continues to work at the same rate, how many *more* hours will he need to complete *half* the job?
(A) h

(B) $\dfrac{h}{2}$

(C) $\dfrac{2h}{3}$

(D) $3h$
(E) $2h$

19. A bicycle wheel with a radius of 14 inches travels one mile (5,280 feet). Approximately how many revolutions does the wheel make?
(A) 780
(B) 740
(C) 720
(D) 560
(E) 48

20. If a carton containing a dozen eggs is dropped, which one of the following *cannot* be the ratio of broken eggs to whole eggs?
(A) 1:2
(B) 1:3
(C) 5:7
(D) 1:4
(E) 1:5

21.

In the figure above $\angle KPG = 90°$, $\angle KPH = 40°$, and $\angle GPJ = 65°$. How many degrees in $\angle HPJ$?
(A) 15
(B) 18
(C) 20
(D) 23
(E) 26

22. For any integer n, which of the following must be an odd integer?
   I. $2n + 1$
   II. $2n + 4$
   III. $2n - 3$
(A) I only
(B) II only
(C) III only
(D) I and II only
(E) I and III only

Questions 23–25 refer to the following table:

U.S. Population 1950–75						
Year	1950	1955	1960	1965	1970	1975
Population in Millions	152	166	181	196	205	213

23. What is the percent increase in population in the U.S. from 1950 to 1975?
(A) 30
(B) 34
(C) 37
(D) 40
(E) 44

24. During which five-year period did the U.S. have the lowest percent increase in population?
    (A) 1950–55
    (B) 1955–60
    (C) 1960–65
    (D) 1965–70
    (E) 1970–75

25. If the population continues to grow uniformly at the same rate that it grew from 1970–75, what is the projected population in millions for 1980?
    (A) 215
    (B) 218
    (C) 221
    (D) 224
    (E) 227

STOP
WORK ONLY ON THIS SECTION UNTIL THE TIME ALLOTTED IS OVER.

SECTION IV

Time—30 minutes

35 Questions

1. If $8{,}787 = 87p$, then $p =$
   (A) 11
   (B) 10
   (C) 87
   (D) 111
   (E) 101

2. If t is a whole number greater than 5 and less than 14, how many different values could t have?
   (A) 7
   (B) 8
   (C) 9
   (D) 10
   (E) 11

3. If $\dfrac{2}{3} + \dfrac{1}{4} + y = 1$, then $y =$
   (A) $\dfrac{4}{7}$
   (B) $\dfrac{5}{6}$
   (C) $\dfrac{1}{12}$
   (D) $\dfrac{1}{3}$
   (E) $\dfrac{2}{5}$

4.

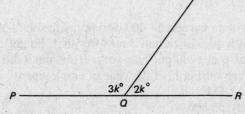

In the figure above, PQR is a straight line; $k =$
   (A) 36
   (B) 45
   (C) 64
   (D) 72
   (E) 80

5. A boy runs 780 yards in one minute. What is his rate in feet per second?
   (A) 13
   (B) 15
   (C) 24
   (D) 39
   (E) 48

6. If the average of p and q is 7 and $r = 13$, what is the average of p, q, and r?
   (A) 10
   (B) $6\dfrac{2}{3}$
   (C) 8
   (D) 7
   (E) 9

7. Which of the following *cannot* represent the sides of a triangle?
   (A) 4, 10, 11
   (B) 10, 8, 16
   (C) 11, 5, 17
   (D) 5, 10, 8
   (E) 8, 6, 7

8. Which of the following is (are) equal to $45y$?
   (I) $40y + 5y$
   II. $80\left(\dfrac{y}{2} + \dfrac{y}{16}\right)$
   III. $50y + 4y$

   (A) I only
   (B) II only
   (C) I and III only
   (D) I and II only
   (E) I, II, and III

9. What is 25% of $\dfrac{4}{7}$?
   (A) $\dfrac{1}{7}$
   (B) $\dfrac{4}{35}$
   (C) $\dfrac{4}{175}$
   (D) $\dfrac{16}{7}$
   (E) $\dfrac{100}{7}$

10.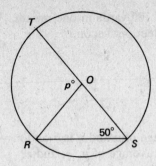

In the circle above with center O, $p =$
(A) 25
(B) 50
(C) 75
(D) 100
(E) 125

11. A car left town A at 10:30 a.m. and arrived in town B, 130 miles away, at 1:45 p.m. the same day. What was the average speed of the car in miles per hour on this trip?
(A) 30
(B) 35
(C) 40
(D) 45
(E) 50

12. If n is a positive integer and $18n$ is the cube of an integer, what is the least value of n?
(A) 6
(B) 8
(C) 10
(D) 12
(E) 14

13.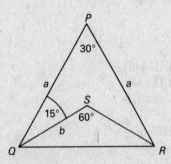

In the figure above, sides and angles are as shown. Express the perimeter of quadrilateral $PQSR$ in terms of a and b.
(A) $2a + b$
(B) $2a + 2b$
(C) $2a + 3b$
(D) $2a + b\sqrt{3}$
(E) $a + 2b$

14. If $0 < s < r$ and s is equal to the difference between r and s, then $s =$
(A) 1
(B) $\dfrac{1}{2}$
(C) $\dfrac{r}{s}$
(D) $\dfrac{r}{3}$
(E) $\dfrac{r}{2}$

15. If $p = 1$, find the value of $3 + 3^p + 3^{p+2}$.
(A) 9
(B) 12
(C) 15
(D) 18
(E) 33

16.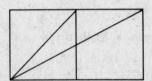

Two congruent squares are placed next to each other as shown in the figure above. What is the ratio of the length of the diagonal of the square to that of the diagonal of the rectangle formed?

(A) $\sqrt{2} : \sqrt{5}$
(B) $\sqrt{2} : \sqrt{3}$
(C) $1 : 2$
(D) $2 : 3$
(E) $\sqrt{3} : \sqrt{5}$

17. A man earned $4,000 during his first half-year of work. Each half-year after that, he got a raise of $200 per half-year. How much did he earn during his fifth year of employment?
(A) $11,400.
(B) $5,800.
(C) $5,600.
(D) $11,200.
(E) $12,000.

Questions 18–35 each consist of two quantities, one in Column A and one in Column B. Compare the two quantities and on the answer sheet blacken oval

A if the quantity in Column A is greater;
B if the quantity in Column B is greater;
C if the two quantities are equal;
D if the relationship cannot be determined from the information given.

All letters such as x, y and n represent real numbers. A symbol appearing in both columns represents the same quantity in Column A as it does in Column B.

In some questions, information concerning one or both of the quantities to be compared is centered above the two columns.

Column A	Column B
18. The average of $(60 + 3)$ and $(60 - 3)$	The average of 58, 59, 60, 61, 62
19. 3×97	$300 - 8$

20. $3y + 2$ $\qquad 6y + 4 = 14 \qquad$ $\dfrac{20}{3}$

Column A	Column B
21. The area of a square with a side of 3	The area of a triangle with a base of 3

22. $\dfrac{\sqrt{5}}{5}$ $\qquad\qquad\qquad\qquad$ $\dfrac{1}{\sqrt{5}}$

23. $1 + \dfrac{x}{y}$ $\qquad x, y = 0 \qquad$ $1 + \dfrac{y}{x}$

24. 6% of 80 $\qquad\qquad\qquad$ 10% of 50

25.

A = area of circle
d = diameter
r = radius

$\dfrac{A}{d}$ $\qquad\qquad\qquad\qquad$ $\dfrac{A}{r}$

26. p $\qquad\qquad p \cdot q = 0 \qquad$ q

	Column A		Column B

27. 5k $\qquad$ $\dfrac{k}{3} = \dfrac{m}{5}$ $\qquad$ 3m

---

28. $2\sqrt{5}$ $\qquad\qquad\qquad\qquad\qquad\qquad\qquad$ 5

29.

C = circumference of circle
A = area of circle

A $\qquad\qquad\qquad\qquad\qquad\qquad\qquad\qquad\qquad$ C

30.

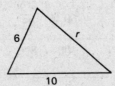 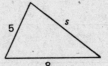

The minimum possible value of r $\qquad\qquad\qquad$ The minimum possible value of s

---

31. Percent increase in the size of a class that was raised from 30 to 36 students $\qquad\qquad$ Percent decrease in the size of a class that was reduced from 36 to 30

---

32. u $\qquad\qquad$ $u^2 = 9$ $\qquad\qquad$ 3

33.

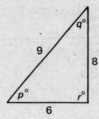

Figure is not drawn to scale

$p + q$ $\qquad\qquad\qquad\qquad\qquad\qquad\qquad$ r

Column A		Column B

34. $f - g$ $f > o, g > o, f \neq g$ $\dfrac{f^2 - g^2}{f - g}$

35.

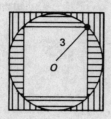

Area shaded vertically

$\left(\;||||\; \right)$

Area shaded
horizontally $\left(\equiv \right)$

STOP
WORK ONLY ON THIS SECTION UNTIL THE TIME ALLOTTED IS OVER.

1. Which of the following is a product of 13 and an integer?
   - (A) 131
   - (B) 1314
   - (C) 1323
   - (D) 1326
   - (E) 1303

2. $(4r^2s^3)^3 =$
   - (A) $16r^6s^9$
   - (B) $64r^6s^9$
   - (C) $64r^5s^6$
   - (D) $64r^5s^9$
   - (E) $16r^6s^6$

3. Which of the following fractions is greater than $\frac{1}{4}$ and less than $\frac{1}{3}$?
   - (A) $\frac{3}{8}$
   - (B) $\frac{1}{5}$
   - (C) $\frac{3}{10}$
   - (D) $\frac{4}{7}$
   - (E) $\frac{4}{9}$

4. If $x = -1$, which of the following is the greatest?
   - (A) $x^2 - 1$
   - (B) $-\frac{1}{x}$
   - (C) $1 + x$
   - (D) $\frac{1}{x}$
   - (E) $1 - x$

5. What is the volume of a cube with a surface area of $54t^2$?
   - (A) $27t^3$
   - (B) $9t^2$
   - (C) $27t^2$
   - (D) $9t^3$
   - (E) $54t^3$

6. If a 19-cup mixture of powder and water contains 1 cup of powder, how many cups of powder must be added to get a mixture having powder and water in the ratio of 1:2?
   - (A) 6
   - (B) 8
   - (C) 17
   - (D) 19
   - (E) 24

7. What is the maximum number of books, each $\frac{5}{6}$ inch thick, that can be placed upright on a shelf 4 feet long?
   - (A) 57
   - (B) 58
   - (C) 60
   - (D) 4
   - (E) 5

8. A motorist wishes to cover a certain distance in 40% less time than he usually does. To do this, he increases his overall average speed by $r\%$. Then $r =$
   - (A) 40
   - (B) 50
   - (C) 60
   - (D) $62\frac{1}{2}$
   - (E) $66\frac{2}{3}$

9. What is the largest number of cubic blocks, 3 cm. on an edge, that can fit into a box that is 16 cm. long, 13 cm. wide and 20 cm. high?
   - (A) 158
   - (B) 154
   - (C) 142
   - (D) 131
   - (E) 120

10. If it takes 10 men 9 days to do a certain job, how many *more* men will it take to do the job in 6 days, if all men work at the same rate?
    (A) 3
    (B) 4
    (C) 5
    (D) 6
    (E) None of these

11.

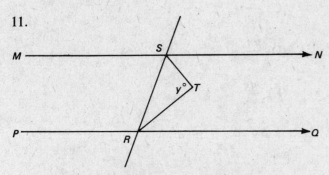

This figure is not drawn to scale.

In the figure above, *MN* is parallel to *PQ*, *ST* bisects angle *NSR* and *RT* bisects angle *SRQ*. Then *y* =
    (A) 83
    (B) 90
    (C) 95
    (D) 100
    (E) The measure of the angle cannot be determined from the information given

12. What must be added to $(r^2 + s^2)$ to equal $(r + s)^2$?
    (A) 0
    (B) *rs*
    (C) $-rs$
    (D) $-2rs$
    (E) $2rs$

13. Troop A is 11 miles south of a fire tower and troop B is 15 miles east of the tower. Troop A travels at a rate of 2 miles an hour and troop B travels at a rate of 3 miles an hour. If both travel toward the tower for one hour, how many miles apart will they then be?
    (A) 13
    (B) 14
    (C) 15
    (D) 16
    (E) It cannot be determined from the information given

14.

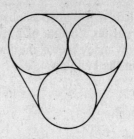

The above diagram represents three circular garbage cans, each of diameter 2 feet. The three cans are all touching as shown. Find, in feet, the perimeter of the rope encompassing the three cans.
    (A) 8
    (B) $6 + 2\pi$
    (C) 6π
    (D) $8 + 2\pi$
    (E) $6 + 4\pi$

15. If $\dfrac{2x + 6}{x^3 + 6x^2 + 5x} = 0$, then $x =$
    (A) -3
    (B) 3
    (C) 0
    (D) -5
    (E) -1

16. If $p = 2q$ and $q = 3r$, find the value of *r* in terms of *p*.
    (A) $\dfrac{3p}{2}$
    (B) $3p$
    (C) $6p$
    (D) $\dfrac{2p}{3}$
    (E) $\dfrac{p}{6}$

17. If a student has an average of 76% on his first two tests and has an average of 85% on the next four tests, what is his final average on all six tests?
    (A) 82.0%
    (B) 80.5%
    (C) 82.5%
    (D) 81.3%
    (E) 81.6%

18. A 26-foot ladder is placed against a building so that it reaches a height of 24 feet from the ground. How many feet is the foot of the ladder from the building?
(A) 5 √2
(B) 5
(C) 4
(D) 10
(E) 2 √313

19.

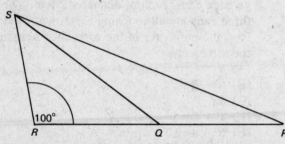

In the figure above, $PQ = QS$, $QR = RS$, and angle $SRQ = 100°$, how many degrees in angle QPS?
(A) 10
(B) 15
(C) 20
(D) 25
(E) 30

20.

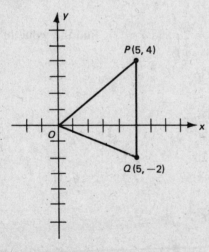

In the figure above, what is the area in square units of triangle OPQ?
(A) 5
(B) 8
(C) 10
(D) 13
(E) 15

21. A car averages m miles on g gallons of gasoline. At the same rate, how many miles will the car travel on n gallons?

(A) $\dfrac{mn}{g}$

(B) $\dfrac{n}{mg}$

(C) $\dfrac{g}{mn}$

(D) $\dfrac{gn}{m}$

(E) $\dfrac{mg}{n}$

22. If $y = \dfrac{rs}{1 + x}$, then $x =$

(A) $\dfrac{rs}{y} - y$

(B) $\dfrac{rs - y}{r}$

(C) $\dfrac{y}{rs} - 1$

(D) $\dfrac{rs - 1}{y}$

(E) $\dfrac{rs}{y} - 1$

23. A piece of a square metal shaft p cm on a side is ground down on a lathe into a cylindrical shaft p cm in diameter, its length remaining the same. What fractional part of the original shaft is cut away?

(A) $\dfrac{4 - \pi}{\pi}$

(B) $\dfrac{1}{2}$

(C) $\dfrac{\pi}{4}$

(D) $\dfrac{4 - \pi}{4}$

(E) $\dfrac{1 - \pi}{4}$

Questions 24–25 refer to the following circle graph.

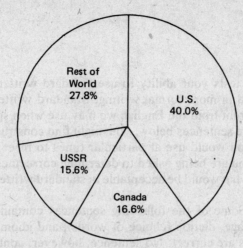

World Production of Aluminum—1958

24. How many degrees in the central angle of the sector of the circle representing U.S.?
(A) 112
(B) 124
(C) 135
(D) 144
(E) 150

25. If Canada produced .581 million metric tons of aluminum in 1958, what was the world production of aluminum in millions of metric tons in that year?
(A) 2.5
(B) 2.8
(C) 3.0
(D) 3.2
(E) 3.5

STOP
WORK ONLY ON THIS SECTION UNTIL THE TIME ALLOTTED IS OVER.

SECTION VI

Time—30 minutes

50 Questions

This section tests your ability to use standard written English, the kind used in more formal writing. Standard written English is quite different from the English we may use when speaking to friends. In the sentences below, you might find constructions and forms that you would use at particular times to meet particular needs, but you are being asked to determine correctness only on the basis of what would be acceptable in standard written English.

<u>Directions:</u> Some of the following sentences contain errors in grammar, usage, diction (choice of words), and idiom. Some of the sentences are correct. No sentence, however, contains more than one error. If a sentence has an error, it will be in one of the lettered and underlined words or phrases. Assume there are no errors in the parts of the sentence that are not underlined. *If there is an error in any underlined part, note the letter under it, and blacken the corresponding space on the answer sheet. If the sentence is free of errors, blacken answer space (E). Follow the guidelines for standard written English when determining the answer.*

1. <u>Casting cautiously</u> from the slippery <u>rocks,</u> he caught two large speckled
         A   B
    trout <u>with the new bait</u> <u>which he fried for breakfast</u>. <u>No error</u>
              C   D   E

2. <u>We girls</u> <u>had ought to be</u> prepared for a <u>long delay</u> in the event that the
      A   B   C
    game goes <u>into overtime</u>. <u>No error</u>
           D   E

3. There was a moment of complete silence as he <u>ended his address;</u> <u>then,</u> as
                                            A   B

    if by prearrangement, everybody in the audience <u>raised up</u> in testimony of
                                               C

    their admiration and <u>respect for</u> his lifetime of achievement. <u>No error</u>
                      D   E

4. In their <u>report,</u> the detectives noted that the body had apparently <u>lain</u>
           A   B
    <u>in the copse</u> for several hours before <u>being discovered</u>. <u>No error</u>
      C   D   E

5. I <u>urged</u> Jane to come to the camp <u>reunion because</u> it <u>would not</u> be the
        A   B   C
    same without <u>Jim and she</u>. <u>No error</u>
               D   E

6. As part of <u>their</u> daily <u>rounds</u>, the <u>internes study</u> the chart
            A   B   C
<u>of each patient who</u> the doctor examines. <u>No error</u>
        D   E

7. <u>Neither</u> the <u>teacher nor the</u> guidance counselor <u>were</u> available when
    A   B   C
Susan's parents arrived for their meeting. <u>No error</u>
    D   E

8. <u>Between you and I</u>, I think <u>the reason he gave</u> for <u>missing the party</u> <u>was</u>
       A   B   C   D
just an excuse. <u>No error</u>
              E

9. I know <u>that the</u> book was <u>returned;</u> Mrs. Brown, <u>the librarian,</u> took it
         A   B   C
<u>from myself</u> when I entered. <u>No error</u>
   D   E

10. The member of the council <u>who</u> was most disliked was <u>the one who</u>
                          A   B
<u>continuously</u> boasted of <u>his</u> accomplishments. <u>No error</u>
   C   D   E

11. <u>Besides</u> the line of stalled cars <u>stood</u> two policemen engaged in casual
    A   B
conversation, <u>making</u> no effort to get <u>the traffic moving</u>. <u>No error</u>
            C   D   E

12. Anyone in the class <u>who has</u> not completed the <u>course</u> requirements
                       A   B
<u>should</u> make an appointment to see <u>their</u> advisor. <u>No error</u>
  C   D   E

13. Insisting that it could not <u>have been he</u> who stole the <u>bonds,</u> the prisoner
                            A   B
continued <u>to maintain</u> that <u>he was innocent</u> of the crime. <u>No error</u>
         C   D   E

14. Mother refused to permit <u>us girls</u> to <u>subscribe to that</u> magazine; <u>she</u>
                    A   B   C
always was opposed <u>to these kind of publication</u>. <u>No error</u>
                  D   E

15. <u>Although</u> we tried to avoid the encounter, <u>Mrs. Smith</u> spotted us and
    A   B
hastened over to demand: "Why <u>haven't</u> you visited my <u>sister and I</u>?"
                             C   D
<u>No error</u>
  E

16. When the tallies <u>were</u> completed, <u>it appeared that</u> Mark <u>had swam</u> the
              A   B   C
distance <u>in record time</u>. <u>No error</u>
       D   E

17. Each district <u>affected</u> by the constraints imposed by the State Assembly
<u>A</u>

must try to influence <u>its</u> legislator <u>if any</u> relief is <u>to be forthcoming</u>.
B   C   D

<u>No error</u>
E

18. It <u>was</u> only after the driver had managed <u>to thread</u> through the onrushing
A   B

streams of traffic to the safety of the <u>road's</u> shoulder that he discovered
C

that the radiator <u>had sprang</u> a leak. <u>No error</u>
D   E

19. <u>Being that</u> we <u>had reached</u> our destination earlier than we <u>had planned</u>,
A   B   C

the <u>girls and I</u> decided to explore the house before the agent got there. <u>No error</u>
D   E

20. Please do not feel <u>badly</u> about the <u>outcome</u>; we all know that
A   B

circumstances <u>beyond your control</u> made it difficult
C

<u>for you to do your best</u>. <u>No error</u>
D   E

21. How disappointed <u>we were</u> to discover, <u>after</u> our long afternoon of berry-
A   B

picking anticipation, that the <u>tiny, gem-like</u> fruits tasted <u>bitterly</u>. <u>No error</u>
C   D   E

22. The judges finally <u>ruled Betty</u> the <u>prettiest</u> of the two finalists although for
A   B

several minutes it <u>had seemed</u> that the result <u>would be</u> a tie. <u>No error</u>
C   D   E

23. <u>Since</u> his daughters were both at the hospital <u>awaiting</u> the results of the
A   B

operation, Mr. Benton had to depend upon his <u>son-in-laws</u> to drive him
C

<u>into town</u>. <u>No error</u>
D   E

24. <u>Hardly no one</u> in the audience heard the <u>slip, but</u> the speaker became
A   B

<u>so rattled</u> that he could not <u>regain his equilibrium</u>. <u>No error</u>
C   D   E

25. <u>Scarcely pausing</u> for <u>thought</u>, the moderator summarized the agreements
A   B

and differences <u>among</u> the five panelists, and then <u>asking</u> them for their
C   D

final statements. <u>No error</u>
E

Directions: In each of the sentences below, a part or the whole of the sentence is underlined. Following each sentence will be five different ways of writing the underlined segment—the first is an exact repeat of the underlined original, the other four are different. If you think the underlined segment is correct as it stands, you will select choice (A) as your answer. *If you think the underlined segment is incorrect as it stands, select the one of the remaining lettered choices that you think makes the sentence correct.* For whichever of the five lettered choices you select as correct, blacken the corresponding space on your answer sheet.

This portion of the examination tests your ability to determine correctness and effectiveness of expression according to the requirements of standard written English. You are to take into account grammar, diction (choice of words), sentence construction, and punctuation. *Do not select a version that changes the original sense of the sentence as given.* Choose the version that offers the clearest, most precise sentence according to the guidelines imposed.

26. Although the windows were closed, the children shouted excitedly to the brown bear they spotted driving through the state park.
    (A) they spotted driving through
    (B) they spotted, driving through
    (C) they spotted as they were driving through
    (D) they spotted which was driving through
    (E) they noticed driving through

27. Our new convertible, which we had ordered some nine weeks before, was finally delivered without the power steering or air conditioning we had specified.
    (A) convertible, which we had ordered some nine weeks before,
    (B) convertible which we had ordered some nine weeks before
    (C) convertible, which we ordered some nine weeks before,
    (D) convertible, which we had ordered some nine weeks earlier,
    (E) convertible, which we had ordered over nine weeks before,

28. It is fairly certain that the infant has an immune system when newly born and then you develop susceptibility to disease.
    (A) and then you develop susceptibility to disease
    (B) and then you would develop susceptibility to disease
    (C) and then it develops susceptibility to disease
    (D) and, then you develop susceptibility to disease
    (E) and then you might develop susceptibility to disease

29. We have extended every effort to improve the situation and hoping these efforts will bear fruit.
    (A) and hoping these efforts
    (B) and hope these efforts
    (C) and, hoping these efforts
    (D) and in hoping these efforts
    (E) and in the hoping these efforts

30. In the first years of his research and experimentation, Pasteur concentrated on finding the causes of various diseases, <u>but in later years focusing</u> on preventative measures.
    (A) but in later years focusing
    (B) but later concentrating
    (C) but, later on focusing
    (D) but in future years focusing
    (E) but in later years focused

31. It is better to have that tooth treated now <u>than putting treatment off</u> until later.
    (A) than putting treatment off
    (B) then putting treatment off
    (C) than to put treatment off
    (D) then to put treatment off
    (E) than to wait

32. <u>Each student who has not completed his registration</u> should go at once to the Registrar's Office.
    (A) Each student who has not completed his registration
    (B) Each student, who has not completed his registration
    (C) Each student who has not completed their registration
    (D) Each student not having completed his registration
    (E) Students whose registration have not been completed

33. I have always <u>been interested and stimulated by</u> the arguments raised in political debates.
    (A) been interested and stimulated by
    (B) been interested in and stimulated by
    (C) seemed interested and stimulated by
    (D) been both interested and stimulated by
    (E) shown interest in and stimulation by

34. <u>Hopefully, our</u> point of view will be considered.
    (A) Hopefully, our
    (B) Hopefully our
    (C) It is hopeful our
    (D) We hope our
    (E) Hoping our

35. It is too early to expect a <u>decision, the jury has just begun</u> its deliberations.
    (A) decision, the jury has just begun
    (B) decision; the jury has just begun
    (C) decision, the jury had just begun
    (D) decision, since the jury just begun
    (E) decision the jury has just begun

36. <u>Lady's handbags and children's clothing were both</u> sold in the same store.
    (A) Lady's handbags and children's clothing were both
    (B) Lady's handbags and children's clothing both were
    (C) Lady's handbags and childrens' clothing were both
    (D) Ladies' handbags and children's clothing were both
    (E) Ladies' handbags and childrens' clothing were both

---

37. Jean and I were both looking forward to seeing all our old classmates and their spouses at our High School's homecoming ball.
    (A) and their spouses at our High School's homecoming ball
    (B) and, their spouses at our High School's homecoming ball
    (C) and their spouses at our High Schools homecoming ball
    (D) and their spouse's at our High School's homecoming ball
    (E) and their spouses at our high school's homecoming ball

38. If George and Helene had only known you were coming, they would of stayed.
    (A) had only known you were coming, they would of stayed
    (B) had only known of your coming, they would of stayed
    (C) had only known you were coming they would of stayed
    (D) had only known you were coming, they would have stayed
    (E) had only known you were coming, they might of stayed

39. He had been seen at the scene of the crime at just about the moment that the coroner had ascertained to be the time of the victim's murder.
    (A) had ascertained to be the time of the victim's murder
    (B) had ascertained was the time of the victim's murder
    (C) had ascertained to be the time of the victims murder
    (D) ascertained the time of the victim's murder
    (E) had ascertained the time of the victim's murder

40. Hopkins late as usual went directly to his seat near the fifty-yard line.
    (A) Hopkins late as usual went directly
    (B) Hopkins, late as usual, went directly
    (C) Hopkins late as usual went straight
    (D) Hopkins late, as usual, went directly
    (E) Hopkins late as usual went direct

GO ON TO THE NEXT PAGE

Directions: Some of the following sentences contain errors in grammar, usage, diction (choice of words), and idiom. Some of the sentences are correct. No sentence, however, contains more than one error. If a sentence has an error, it will be in one of the lettered and underlined words or phrases. Assume there are no errors in the parts of the sentence that are not underlined. *If there is an error in any underlined part, note the letter under it, and blacken the corresponding space on the answer sheet. If the sentence is free of errors, blacken answer space (E).* Follow the guidelines for standard written English when determining the answer.

41. He responded to his adversary's clever taunts just like an eager trout rises
      A   B   C
to a skillfully cast fly. No error
      D   E

42. Dad thundered, "Either you or Bill is responsible for damaging the tennis
                                       A
court, and whoever did it will have to pay to repair it!" No error
   B   C   D   E

43. The flowers smelled so sweetly that the meadow in which we lay
                             A   B   C
seemed perfumed. No error
      D   E

44. The course that we have just completed helped us to learn more about the
earth and its resources, and in understanding that we must conserve those
             A   B   C
resources for posterity. No error
              D   E

45. Although Gloria is probably a better scholar than myself, I have earned
                                                       A   B
higher grades than she. No error
      C   D   E

46. The very people which we were trying to help turned away from us when
        A   B   C
we sought their testimony. No error
      D   E

47. Beside himself with grief, the bereaved father ran wildly into the street,
      A   B
chasing after the ambulance until he fell, exhausted. No error
         C   D   E

48. After investigating various types of machines, Lindbergh chose the
                                        A
monoplane, considering it more serviceable than the biplane because its
      B   C   D
reduced head resistance provided a greater cruising range. No error
                                                              E

49. <u>During the summer months</u>, several unusual exhibits <u>were showed</u> at the
            A   B

   museum as part of the <u>city's</u> effort <u>to attract</u> <u>people to</u> the downtown
                     C   D

   area. <u>No error</u>
        E

50. In the continuing <u>debate over</u> school <u>financing</u>, it is unclear <u>whom</u> will
                   A   B   C

   bear the responsibility for meeting <u>students'</u> needs. <u>No error</u>
                                      D   E

STOP
WORK ONLY ON THIS SECTION UNTIL THE TIME ALLOTTED IS OVER.

Answer Key—SAT Practice Test 1

Section I

1.	B	13.	C	24.	B	35.	D
2.	A	14.	A	25.	B	36.	D
3.	D	15.	B	26.	E	37.	D
4.	D	16.	D	27.	A	38.	C
5.	C	17.	C	28.	E	39.	B
6.	E	18.	E	29.	C	40.	D
7.	B	19.	D	30.	B	41.	D
8.	B	20.	E	31.	D	42.	D
9.	C	21.	A	32.	C	43.	C
10.	E	22.	C	33.	A	44.	A
11.	B	23.	D	34.	D	45.	A
12.	E						

Section II

1.	E	11.	C	21.	B	31.	C
2.	B	12.	D	22.	C	32.	C
3.	A	13.	D	23.	A	33.	E
4.	C	14.	C	24.	D	34.	B
5.	B	15.	E	25.	B	35.	D
6.	D	16.	D	26.	C	36.	E
7.	A	17.	E	27.	E	37.	D
8.	E	18.	E	28.	B	38.	C
9.	B	19.	C	29.	C	39.	A
10.	E	20.	A	30.	D	40.	C

Section III

1.	B	8.	A	14.	D	20.	D
2.	A	9.	C	15.	D	21.	A
3.	D	10.	B	16.	A	22.	E
4.	E	11.	A	17.	B	23.	D
5.	D	12.	C	18.	E	24.	E
6.	C	13.	E	19.	C	25.	C
7.	E						

Section IV

1.	E	10.	D	19.	B	28.	B
2.	B	11.	C	20.	A	29.	A
3.	C	12.	D	21.	D	30.	A
4.	A	13.	B	22.	C	31.	A
5.	D	14.	E	23.	D	32.	D
6.	E	15.	E	24.	B	33.	A
7.	C	16.	A	25.	B	34.	B
8.	D	17.	A	26.	D	35.	B
9.	A	18.	C	27.	C		

Section V

1.	D	8.	E	14.	B	20.	E
2.	B	9.	E	15.	A	21.	A
3.	C	10.	C	16.	E	22.	E
4.	E	11.	B	17.	A	23.	D
5.	A	12.	E	18.	D	24.	D
6.	B	13.	C	19.	C	25.	E
7.	A						

Section VI

1.	C	14.	D	27.	A	39.	A
2.	B	15.	D	28.	C	40.	B
3.	C	16.	C	29.	B	41.	B
4.	E	17.	E	30.	E	42.	E
5.	D	18.	D	31.	C	43.	A
6.	D	19.	A	32.	A	44.	B
7.	C	20.	A	33.	B	45.	A
8.	A	21.	D	34.	D	46.	B
9.	D	22.	B	35.	B	47.	E
10.	C	23.	C	36.	D	48.	E
11.	A	24.	A	37.	E	49.	B
12.	D	25.	D	38.	D	50.	C
13.	E	26.	C				

Explanatory Answers
Practice Test 1

SECTION I

1. **B.** *Accelerate*: speed up.
   Opposite: *slow down*.

2. **A.** *Incite*: urge on.
   Opposite: *discourage*.

3. **D.** *Bumble*: bungle.
   Opposite: *perform adroitly*.

4. **D.** *Stringent*: exacting and restrictive.
   Opposite: *flexible*.

5. **C.** *Furtive*: stealthy, or secret.
   Opposite: *aboveboard*.

6. **E.** *Decry*: belittle.
   Opposite: *esteem*.

7. **B.** *Zealot*: fanatic.
   Opposite: *moderate*.

8. **B.** *Circumspect*: discreet.
   Opposite: *indiscreet*.

9. **C.** *Parsimonious*: stingy.
   Opposite: *unstinting*.

10. **E.** *Truculent*: brutally harsh.
    Opposite: *gentle*.

11. **B.** *Implacable*: inexorable, relentless.
    Opposite: *appeasable*.

12. **E.** *Quarter*: mercy.
    Opposite: *ruthlessness*.

13. **C.** *Judicious*: wise.
    Opposite: *foolish*.

14. **A.** *Mendacity*: untruthfulness.
    Opposite: *veracity*.

15. **B.** *Usurp*: Seize power without legal right.
    Opposite: *abdicate*.

16. **D.** The word "Though" at the beginning of the sentence lets us know that Slim Somerset's early reputation as a lawman was probably reversed. The word *notorious*, which means widely but unfavorably known, completes the reversal implied at the beginning.

17. **C.** Whatever the earth now does in twenty-four hours is what it did earlier in four hours, and that is a *rotation* of its *axis*.

18. **E.** To complete the implication of "Strangely enough . . . " the word *east* is needed. It is indeed strange that a passage from the Atlantic Ocean to the Pacific Ocean would result in someone's arriving at a spot east of where he began. None of the other options is strange or correct.

19. **D.** What kind of clouds are vast and a nuisance? *Prodigious* clouds!

20. **E.** Choices (A) and (D) both make some sense, but (E), *basic* and *passionate*, not only completes the sense of the sentence, it also fits in stylistically as deliberate repetition.

21. **A.** The expression " . . . rather than . . . " between "_____ types" and "abundant _____ types," leads us to look for an answer with a pair of words which are opposite in meaning. However, four of the choices are pairs of opposites, and so we must look for additional evidence of correctness. Choice (B) is wrong because if the fish were *sterile*, they would cease to exist as species. The answer must relate in some way to the word "abundant." The only answer that applies is choice (A), *solitary* and *schooling*.

22. **C.** When we deal with evidence, we usually expect to draw conclusions from what we have found. *Scant . . conclusions*.

23. **D.** Since "Thermal" has in it the root word "therm," meaning heat, we can see that *heat* satisfies the first blank, and *energy* the second.

24. **B.** Only *isolated* or *restricted* could precede the preposition "from," but only *cluster* can successfully complete the sentence, since the word "while" implies that tree-dwelling bats have quite different habits from cave-dwelling bats.

25. **B.** Both choice (A) and choice (B) can complete this sentence, but the implication of struggling to obtain sufficient water leads us to expect that the plant is struggling for something more vital than mere blooming, that the answer is, rather, *compete . . survive.*

26. **E.** *Law* and *crime* are associated in the following statement: Violating the law is a crime. A similar statement is: Violating the *religious code* is a *sin*.

27. **A.** *Diffuse* means the opposite of *pithy*, which means concise or terse. Similarly, *sacred*, which means venerable or holy, is the opposite of *profane*, which means unholy.

28. **E.** *Carelessness* can lead to *error*, just as *starvation* can cause *atrophy*. "Bricks" cannot lead to "building." "Trial" may just as easily lead to success as to error or "blunder."

29. **C.** Just as *versification* is one of the elements of *poetry*, so, too, *gestures* are employed as one of the elements of *acting*.

30. **B.** *Tepid*, which means moderately warm, is a much lower degree of heat than *boiling*. They are alike in being levels of heat, but there is a degree of difference, the second being more intense. Similarly, *cool* means moderately cold, while *freezing* is more intensely cold than cool.

31. **D.** *Diligent* and *assiduous* are synonyms that mean hardworking. *Fictitious* and *imaginary* are synonyms that mean created by the imagination. "Pacific" is an adjective meaning peaceful; it cannot be synonymous with "peace," which is a noun.

32. **C.** *Dearth* and *plenitude*,which mean, respectively, scarcity and abundance, are opposites, as are *fact* and *fiction*, the former meaning "an actuality," while the latter means "a product of the imagination." The

choices in (E) are opposites, but the order of the words is wrong in that "dearth" and "abundance", the first words of the given pair and of the option, are opposites.

33. **A.** The *ship* is guided or steered by the *helmsman*—the crew member who is at the wheel or tiller, just as *conduct* is guided or steered or directed by *conscience*. *Victory* is not guided or steered by the *leader*, but rather, a nation or an army is guided by the leader (to victory).

34. **D.** A *coterie*, or clique, cannot be characterized as *unrestricted*, and a *mercenary*, one who fights for a cause solely for pay, cannot be characterized as altruistic, or unselfishly concerned for the welfare of others.

35. **D.** *Instigate* and *incite* are synonyms meaning provoke or foment; similarly, *obdurate* and *adamant* are synonyms meaning utterly unyielding.

36. **D.** The passage does not mention or even imply that the satellites' purpose is to transmit information about cultural events. The other four purposes are mentioned in the last sentence of paragraph 3.

37. **D.** The polar orbit of the satellites is mentioned in the last sentence of paragraph 1.

38. **C.** Sentence 1 says that the scientists were forced to develop the new satellites because it was too risky to continue with the old types. The adage means that when circumstances force us to, or when an old method of doing something of necessity to us fails, we somehow find a new way to get the job done.

39. **B.** Real sensing can only be accomplished by use of sensory organs of living beings. The quotation marks indicate that there is a difference between what the satellite's instruments do and what a human's sensory organs do.

40. **D.** The Discoverer or SAMOS satellites orbit at under an altitude of 200 miles, but the Vela and MIDAS orbit at 55,000 miles from earth. Item II is covered in sentence 2 of paragraph 3. Item III is covered in the last sentence of the same paragraph.

41. **D.** The passage says that size and location of an apartment act as advertisement of rank, which is but saying "symbol of status."

42. **D.** Toward the end of paragraph 2, sentences 5 and 6 specifically indicate that (D) is the answer.

43. **C.** Sentences 2 and 3 of paragraph 2 confirm statements II and III as descriptions that define territoriality. Statement I does not refer to territoriality.

44. **A.** According to the passage, only one thing makes the urban automobile a prize, and that is its status as a symbol. However, it *is*, the last sentence says, a prize.

45. **A.** The second paragraph calls the automobile an ambiguous possession because it has advantages and disadvantages and, therefore, its value is uncertain.

SECTION II

1. **E.** *Endurable*: tolerable.
   Opposite: *intolerable*.

2. **B.** *Teeming*: abounding.
   Opposite: *wanting*, or lacking.

3. **A.** *Mercenary*: one who works solely for pay, for a cause.
   Opposite: one who is unselfishly devoted to the welfare of others, or *altruist*.

4. **C.** *Fervor*: warmth and earnestness of feeling.
   Opposite: *apathy*, or lack of concern.

5. **B.** *Illicit*: unauthorized.
   Opposite: *authorized*.

6. **D.** *Temerity*: rashness.
   Opposite: *wariness*.

7. **A.** *Indigent*: impoverished.
   Opposite: *affluent*, or wealthy.

8. **E.** *Ephemeral*: transient, or fleeting.
   Opposite: *permanent*.

9. **B.** *Obtuse*: dull in perception or feeling.
   Opposite: *perceptive*.

10. **E.** *Abstruse*: recondite, hard to understand.
    Opposite: *elementary*.

11. **C.** The passage merely tells us about rice and rice farming without advocating or proposing anything.

12. **D.** Unhulled rice lasts longer than potatoes. The passage says nothing about how long milled rice lasts in storage, nor does it say anything about the nutritive value of unhulled rice. Steaming rice drives some vitamins and minerals into the kernel. The yield per acre depends, to some extent, on the amount of rainfall. The last sentence in the passage confirms that (D) is the answer.

13. **D.** Sentence 1 of paragraph 2 tells us I is wrong. Sentence 1, paragraph 4 says that II is right. Sentence 1, paragraph 3 tells us about yields around the world, not about U.S. yields. Sentence 5, paragraph 4 says that IV is right. The last sentence in paragraph 3 tells us that V is right.

14. **C.** The passage does not state the average yield per acre, world-wide, nor can we infer that figure from the data given.

15. **E.** Sentence 3, paragraph one confirms item I. Sentence 1, paragraph 3, confirms that fertilization (item II) and rainfall (item III) are factors that affect rice yields.

16. **D.** The answer is directly stated in sentence 1, paragraph 1.

17. **E.** Paragraph 2 lists the skills needed to be an upper lakes fisherman. For item I, see sentence 2; for item III, see sentence 3 and the last sentence; for item IV, see sentence 5.

18. **E.** The sentence which contains the phrase, "small, white, very angry room," refers to fogs, blizzards, and ice storms. Since the storms come up quickly, a person who is preoccupied with other matters might not notice what had happened until he found himself in the storm, fogged in, the sea becoming violent, and the wind beginning to blow fiercely. Figuratively speaking, then,

he would feel as if he were in a "small, white, very angry room."

19. **C.** Since the parents gathered soon after the storm came up, we can infer that they were worried about the safety of the boat in the storm.

20. **A.** The sentence third from last implies that the boatman would recognize the shore sounds and that watching the water under you would mean being wary of shallows.

21. **B.** The author says, " . . . as Oscar Wilde insists," nature imitates art, which implies not merely that he himself holds this view, but that he and Wilde are in agreement. As to (C), the author says that artists are equipped with better tools for the discovery of new meanings and values, not for quarrying and building tunnels.

22. **C.** The author compares the world to an ore-bearing mountain, except that the world's veins of ore are filled with the deep significance, or meaning, of life. Miners and quarrymen extract metallic ore from an ore-bearing mountain, while all of us, like miners in a sense, work at trying to extract meaning from the world.

23. **A.** The last two paragraphs explain (A) but, more specifically, sentences 1 and 2 of the last paragraph make the point.

24. **D.** The author says the world is like an ore-bearing mountain (simile); that we are miners (metaphor); that we follow in . . . gold rush; and that the world glitters with nuggets (metaphors). These and other phrases are figures of speech.

25. **B.** Shakespeare and Chaucer so clearly and perceptively portrayed people that their contemporaries and all who came after them had a basis for understanding people better.

26. **C.** A benchmark is a marked point of known elevation. It serves as a point of reference for measuring other heights. Beethoven's *extraordinary* genius is a reference point against which to *measure* the genius of others.

27. **E.** Solve this problem by asking: What was custom before it became custom? If something *survived* long enough, we would forget that it had to be an *innovation* at one time, before it became custom.

28. **B.** The "but" implies that the river was acting quite differently at Hopeville than it was forty miles below. The river *crested*, (reached its highest point), but below, where the Elf added its swollen torrents, the river was still *rising*.

29. **C.** Oaks and maples are *deciduous*, losing their leaves in autumn. Hemlocks are *conifers*; they bear cones, similar to pine cones.

30. **D.** The "but" implies contrast in the description of John's reputation as a portraitist as against the description of his personal reputation. Choice (A) is not as good a choice as (D) because *infamous*, which connotes an evil reputation, is too harsh a word to apply to a bohemian (unconventional) life style. Rather, he is *renowned* as a portraitist, but *notorious* as a bohemian—*notorious* meaning widely but unfavorably known. In choice (B), the two words are not contrasting. Similarly, the words in choices (C) and (E) are not contrasting.

31. **C.** *Year* is the whole, and *month* is a part of that whole, just as *week* is the whole, and *day* is a part of that whole. In each case, the second word is a part of the first and, in addition, the next smaller component. In choice (B), while *second* is a part of the whole, or *hour*, it is not the next smaller component. *Minute* would be the next smaller component, not *second*.

32. **C.** *Erosion* can result in the formation of a *ravine*, just as *overeating* can result in *obesity*.

33. **E.** *Larva* is the immature, wingless form of an insect; the *imago* is the adult insect. The *caterpillar* is the larva of the *butterfly*, which is the adult insect, or imago.

34. **B.** *Enervate* expresses a thought similar to *exhaust*, but to a lesser degree. In the same fashion, *enfeeble* is similar to *deplete*, but to a lesser degree. In addition, the two

35. **D.** *Skim* and *peruse* express a degree of difference relationship. To *skim* means to *glance over* or read cursorily, while *peruse* means to read with thoroughness, or *scrutinize*. Choice (D) is synonymous with the given pair.

36. **E.** *Sacrilege*, the violation of something sacred, is the opposite of *worship*; *treason* is the opposite of *patriotism*.

37. **D.** A *chemist* might work with a specific chemical such as *sodium*; a *geologist* might work with a specific mineral such as *quartz*. In (C) the word *plant* is a general term.

words in choice (B) are each, respectively, the synonyms of the two given words.

38. **C.** A *coach*, or carriage, is drawn by a *team*, just as a *rickshaw*, or small, two-wheeled passenger vehicle, is drawn by a *coolie*, or cheaply employed Oriental laborer.

39. **A.** A person with a *neurosis* is characterized as *neurotic*; a person with *schizophrenia* is characterized as *schizoid*.

40. **C.** A *carpenter* uses a *miter box* to guide his saw in making an angled cut; a *builder* uses a *level* to guide himself in making level foundations, square corners, etc. In both instances, the article of the second term is used as a tool or instrument for determining angles.

SECTION III

1. **B.** $\frac{12}{300} = \frac{4}{100} = 4\%.$

2. **A.** Let n = the number,

then $\frac{3}{4}n = \frac{2}{3}$

$n = \frac{2}{3} \cdot \frac{4}{3} = \frac{8}{9}$

$\frac{3}{8} \cdot \frac{8}{9} = \frac{1}{3}.$

3. **D.** The altitude to the hypotenuse of a right triangle divides the figure into two right triangles that are similar to the given triangle and are, therefore, similar to each other.

4. **E.** $y = \frac{mx}{p - x}$

$py - xy = mx$

$py = mx + xy$

$py = x(m + y)$

$x = \frac{py}{m + y}.$

5. **D.** n miles = $4n$ quarter-miles.

After paying for the first quarter-mile, there are $(4n - 1)$ quarter-miles to be paid for at the rate of 20¢ each. Thus,

Fare = $50 + 20(4n - 1)$.

6. **C.** $FR = \sqrt{4} = 2$

$RC = \sqrt{9} = 3$

$FC = FR + RC$

$= 2 + 3 = 5$

Area of $CDEF = (\overline{FC})^2 = 5^2 = 25.$

7. **E.** $\frac{5}{3}y = \frac{5}{3}.$

Divide both sides by $\frac{5}{3}$, giving

$y = 1,$

then $1 - y = 0.$

8. **A.** If the average score for 20 students was p, then the sum of all 20 scores was $20p$. When 2 students had their scores raised 10 points each, the total score became $20p + 20$.

Thus,

average score = $\frac{20p + 20}{20} = p + 1.$

9. **C.** $\frac{17}{36}$ and $\frac{23}{50}$ are each slightly less than $\frac{1}{2}$

$\left(\text{since } \frac{18}{36} \text{ and } \frac{25}{50} \text{ each equal } \frac{1}{2}\right)$. Thus,

$\left(\frac{17}{36} + \frac{23}{50}\right)$ is slightly less than 1 and

$\left(\frac{17}{36} + \frac{23}{50}\right) \times 4{,}660$ is slightly less than

4,660.

10. **B.** $\angle KLS = \angle MKQ = 110°$ (corresponding angles).
$\angle SLN$ is supplementary to $\angle KLS$, so that $t = 180 - 110 = 70$.

11. **A.** $\dfrac{8}{.2 \times .2} = \dfrac{8}{.04} = \dfrac{800}{4} = 200$.

12. **C.** $e = \text{edge of cube} = \sqrt[3]{125} = 5$,

then $S = 6e^2$

$\qquad = 6(5)^2$

$\qquad = 150$.

13. **E.** Since the legs of the large right triangle are 15 and 20, the triangle is a 3-4-5 right triangle with all sides multiplied by 5. Hence, the hypotenuse is 25. Thus,

$3r + 2r = 25$

$\qquad 5r = 25$

$\qquad r = 5$.

14. **D.** $p + q = 1.5q$

$\qquad p = .5q$

$\qquad p$ is 50% of q.

15. **D.** Since there are ten equal arcs, each arc measures $\dfrac{360}{10} = 36°$. If the dial makes $1\frac{1}{2}$ turns (540°), it ends up on the 8. It must now move another 20° counterclockwise and will thus be between the 7 and 8.

16. **A.** Let x = cost of the ticket in dollars before tax,

then $.12x$ = tax in dollars

$x + .12x = 5.60$

$\qquad 1.12x = 5.60$

$\qquad 112x = 560$

$\qquad\qquad x = \$5.00$.

Thus, tax = \$.60.

17. **B.** $\pi x^2 = 5\pi y^2$

$\qquad x^2 = 5y^2$

$\qquad x = y\sqrt{5}$.

18. **E.** If he does $\dfrac{1}{6}$ of the job in h hours, he will do $\dfrac{3}{6}$ or half the job in $3h$ hours. Thus, he will need $2h$ *more* hours.

19. **C.** $\qquad C = 2\pi r$

$\qquad\quad = 2 \cdot \dfrac{22}{7}\,(14)$

$\qquad\quad = 88$ inches,

or $C = \dfrac{88}{12}$ feet.

No. of revolutions $= 5280 \div \dfrac{88}{12}$

$\qquad = 5280 \times \dfrac{12}{88}$

$\qquad = 720$.

20. **D.** The number of broken eggs (or whole eggs) must be a whole number. The sum of 1 and 4 is 5 and, since 12 is not divisible by 5, we cannot find two whole numbers in the ratio 1:4 that add up to 12. It is possible to find two such numbers in the four other cases.

21. **A.** Let y = no. of degrees in $\angle HPJ$,

then $\angle KPJ = 40 - y$

$\angle GPJ + \angle KPJ = 90°$

$\qquad 65 + (40 - y) = 90°$

$\qquad\qquad 40 - y = 25°$

$\qquad\qquad\qquad y = 15°$.

22. **E.** $2n + 1$ must be odd since $2n$ is even and 1 more than an even number is odd. $2n + 4 = 2(n + 2)$ and is thus an even number. $2n - 3$ must be odd since $2n$ is even and 3 less than an even number is odd. Thus I and III are odd integers.

23. **D.** The population increased from 152 to 213, an increase of 61 million. Thus the percent increase $= \dfrac{61}{152} \times 100\% = .40 \times 100\% = 40\%$.

24. **E.** The increase from 1970 to 1975 was 8. Percent increase $= \dfrac{8}{205}$, which is less than 4%.

From 1965 to 1970, the increase was 9 million. Percent increase $= \dfrac{9}{196} > \dfrac{9}{200}$, about $4\frac{1}{2}\%$. The other percent increases are larger, so that (E) is the lowest percent increase.

25. **C.** The percent increase from 1970 to 1975 was less than 4%. Based on 213 in 1975, less than 4% would be about 8. Thus the population (in millions) in 1980 would be $213 + 8 = 221$.

SECTION IV

1. **E.** $87p = 8787$.
Divide both sides by 87, yielding $p = 101$.

2. **B.** $14 - 5 = 9$.
There are 9 integers from 6 to 14 inclusive. Thus, there are 8 integers from 6 to 13 inclusive.

3. **C.** $\dfrac{2}{3} + \dfrac{1}{4} + y = 1$.

Multiply both sides by 12. (LCD).

$8 + 3 + 12y = 12$

$12y = 1$

$y = \dfrac{1}{12}$.

4. **A.** The two angles shown are supplementary.

$3k + 2k = 180°$

$5k = 180°$.

$k = 36°$.

5. **D.** $780 \times 3 = 2340$ feet in one minute.

$\dfrac{2340}{60} = 39$ feet per second.

6. **E.** $\dfrac{p + q}{2} = 7$

$p + q = 14$.

Average of p, q, and r

$= \dfrac{p + q + r}{3}$

$= \dfrac{14 + 13}{3} = \dfrac{27}{3} = 9$.

7. **C.** The sum of any two sides of a triangle is greater than the third side. This is true in (A), (B), (D) and (E) but not in (C), since $11 + 5 < 17$.

8. **D.** In I, $40y + 5y = 45y$.

In II, $80 \left(\dfrac{y}{2} + \dfrac{y}{10} \right) = 40y + 5y = 45y$.

In III, $50y + 4y = 54y$.

Hence I and II only is the correct answer.

9. **A.** 25% of $\dfrac{4}{7} = \dfrac{1}{4} \times \dfrac{4}{7} = \dfrac{1}{7}$.

10. **D.** Since OR and OS are radii, $OR = OS$ and $\angle R = \angle S = 50°$; $\angle ROT$ is an exterior angle of the triangle and is thus equal to $\angle R + \angle S = 100°$. Thus $p = 100°$.

11. **C.** The time for the trip is $13:45 - 10:30$ which is 3:15 or $3\frac{1}{4}$ hours.

$$\text{Rate} = \frac{\text{Distance}}{\text{Time}}$$

$$\text{Rate} = 130 \div 3\frac{1}{4}$$

$$130 \times \frac{4}{13} = 40 \text{ mph.}$$

12. **D.** $18n = 3 \cdot 3 \cdot 2n$.
To make $18n$ the cube of an integer, n must be at least $3 \cdot 2 \cdot 2 = 12$. If $n = 12$, $18n = 3 \cdot 3 \cdot 2 \cdot 3 \cdot 2 \cdot 2$ so that $18n = (3 \cdot 2)^3 = 6^3$.

13. **B.** Since triangle PQR is isosceles, $\angle PQR = \angle PRQ$. Since $\angle P = 30°$, $\angle PQR + \angle PRQ = 150°$, so that each angle is equal to $75°$. Then $\angle SQR = 75° - 15° = 60°$. Triangle SQR is, therefore, equilateral and $SQ = SR = b$. Thus, the perimeter of quadrilateral $PQSR = 2a + 2b$.

14. **E.** $s = r - s$

$2s = r$

$s = \dfrac{r}{2}$.

15. **E.** $3 + 3^p + 3^{p+2}$

$3 + 3^1 + 3^3$

$3 + 3 + 27 = 33$.

16. **A.** Consider the side of each square as 1. The diagonal of the square is then the hypotenuse of a right, isosceles triangle with legs equal to 1; so that the diagonal $= \sqrt{2}$. The base of the rectangle is then 2 and its altitude 1. The diagonal of the rectangle is then $\sqrt{2^2 + 1^2} = \sqrt{5}$. The ratio of the lengths is $\sqrt{2} : \sqrt{5}$.

17. **A.** There are nine half-years after the first. Thus he earned $4,000 + 9(200) = 4,000 + 1,800 = 5,800$ during the last half-year and 5,600 during the first half-year of the fifth year of employment. So that he earned $5,600 + 5,800 = \$11,400$.

18. **C.** Both averages equal 60 and are therefore equal.

19. **B.** $3 \times 97 = 291$ and $300 - 8 = 292$. Hence

the item in Column B is greater.

20. **A.** $6y + 4 = 14$.
Divide both sides by 2. $3y + 2 = 7$ and $\dfrac{20}{3} = 6\dfrac{2}{3}$. Thus Column A is greater.

21. **D.** The area of a triangle $= \dfrac{1}{2}bh$. Since we do not know the value of h, we cannot determine its area.

22. **C.** Rationalize the denominator in Column B.

$$\frac{1}{\sqrt{5}} \cdot \frac{\sqrt{5}}{\sqrt{5}} = \frac{\sqrt{5}}{5}.$$

The items in both columns are equal.

23. **D.** We cannot compare the two quantities without knowing the values of x and y.

24. **B.** 6% of $80 = .06(80) = 4.8$.

10% of $50 = .10(50) = 5.0$.

So that the item in Column B is greater.

25. **B.** Since $d = 2r$, the denominator of $\dfrac{A}{d}$ is greater than that in $\dfrac{A}{r}$ and, therefore, $\dfrac{A}{d} < \dfrac{A}{r}$.

26. **D.** If $pq = 0$, we know only that p or q or both are zero. Since we do not know whether either p or q is positive or negative, we cannot compare them.

27. **C.** $\dfrac{k}{3} = \dfrac{m}{5}$. Cross-multiply,

$5k = 3m$.

28. **B.** $\sqrt{5}$ is slightly more than 2.

$\sqrt{5} > 2$.

Multiply both sides by $\sqrt{5}$.

$\sqrt{5} \cdot \sqrt{5} > 2\sqrt{5}$

$5 > 2\sqrt{5}$.

29. **A.** $C = 2\pi r = 2\pi(3) = 6\pi$.

$A = \pi r^2 = \pi(3)^2 = 9\pi.$
Thus, $A > C.$

30. **A.** The sum of any two sides of a triangle is greater than the third side.
In Column A, $r > 4.$
In Column B, $s > 3.$
So that the minimum possible value of r is greater than the minimum possible value of $s.$

31. **A.** Increase in class size is $36 - 30 = 6.$

$\%$ increase $= \dfrac{6}{30} = \dfrac{1}{5} = 20\%.$

Decrease in class size is $36 - 30 = 6.$

$\%$ decrease $= \dfrac{6}{36} = \dfrac{1}{6} = 16\dfrac{2}{3}\%.$

So that item in Column A is greater.

32. **D.** If $u^2 = 9$, then u may equal $+3$ or -3. So that we cannot compare the two quantities in both columns.

33. **A.** If the side opposite r were 10, the triangle would be a 6-8-10 or 3-4-5 right triangle, and $\angle r$ would equal $90°$. Since the side op-

posite r is less than 10, $r < 90°$ and thus $p + q > 90°$. So that $p + q > r.$

34. **B.** $\dfrac{f^2 - g^2}{f - g} = \dfrac{(f + g)(f - g)}{(f - g)}$

$= f + g.$

Since f and g are positive quantities,

$f + g > f - g.$

35. **B.** Vertical shaded area = Large Square − Circle.
The large square has a side equal to the diameter of the circle; so its area $= 6^2 = 36.$
The area of the circle $= \pi \cdot 3^2 = 9\pi \approx 28.$
Vertical shaded area $\approx 36 - 28 = 8.$
Horizontal shaded area = Circle − Small Square.

The small square is equal in area to $\dfrac{1}{2}$ the

product of its diagonals $= \dfrac{1}{2} \cdot 6 \cdot 6 = 18.$

Horizontal shaded area $\approx 28 - 18 = 10.$
Thus, the horizontally shaded area is the greater.

SECTION V

1. **D.** Divide each choice by 13 and find the one with an integral quotient.

$\dfrac{1326}{13} = 102.$

The other four choices all have remainders.

2. **B.** $(4r^2s^3)^3 = 4^3(r^2)^3(s^3)^3$

$= 64r^6s^9.$

3. **C.** $\dfrac{1}{4} = .25$ and $\dfrac{1}{3} = .33\dfrac{1}{3}.$

Look for the fraction that has a decimal value between these two values. Since $\dfrac{3}{10} = .30$, this choice is the desired answer.

4. **E.** Substitute -1 for x in each choice.
$1 - x = 1 - (-1) = 1 + 1 = 2.$

The other choices yield 0, 1, or -1 so that 2 is the greatest value.

5. **A.** The surface area of a cube is given by $S = 6e^2$ where e is the edge of the cube.

Then, $54t^2 = 6e^2$

$9t^2 = e^2$

$e = 3t$

$V = e^3 = (3t)^3$

$V = 27t^3.$

6. **B.** The mixture has 1 cup of powder to 18 cups of water. To get a ratio of 1:2 for powder to water, there must be $\dfrac{1}{2}$ of $18 = 9$ cups of powder. Hence, 8 cups of powder must be added.

7. A. 4 feet = 4 × 12 = 48 inches,

$$48 \div \frac{5}{6} = 48 \times \frac{6}{5} = 57\frac{3}{5}.$$

Thus, 57 is the maximum number of books.

8. E. Let his original speed be

$$r = \frac{d}{t}.$$

If t is decreased by 40%, then his new time for distance d is $t - .4t = .6t$.
Let r' be his increased speed. Then,

$$r' = \frac{d}{.6t} = \frac{10d}{6t} = \frac{5}{3}\frac{d}{t} = \left(1 + \frac{2}{3}\right)\frac{d}{t}$$

$$r' = \frac{d}{t} + \frac{2}{3}\frac{d}{t}.$$

Replace $\frac{d}{t}$ by r, giving

$$r' = r + \frac{2}{3}r,$$

so that the speed r has been increased by $66\frac{2}{3}\%$.

9. E. Only 5 blocks 3 cm. on an edge can be placed along the 16 cm. length, since 16 ÷ 3 = 5+. Likewise, only 4 blocks can be placed along the 13 cm. width and 6 blocks along the 20 cm. height. Thus, the largest number of blocks is 5 × 4 × 6 = 120.

10. C. The number of men is inversely proportional to the number of days.

$$\frac{10}{x} = \frac{6}{9}$$

$$6x = 90$$

$$x = 15.$$

It thus requires 5 more men.

11. B. Since $MN \parallel PQ$, $\angle NSR + \angle SRQ = 180°$. Dividing both sides of this equation by 2, we get

$$\frac{1}{2}\angle NSR + \frac{1}{2}\angle SRQ = \frac{1}{2} \cdot 180°,$$

or $\angle TSR + \angle SRT = 90°$.

In triangle RST, since the sum of two angles is 90°, the third angle is also 90°. Thus, $y = 90°$.

12. E. $(r + s)^2 = (r + s)(r + s)$

$$= r^2 + 2rs + s^2.$$

Thus, $2rs$ must be added to $r^2 + s^2$ to equal $(r + s)^2$.

13. C.

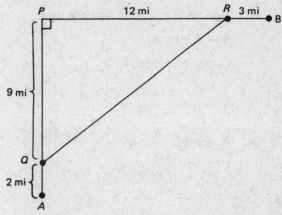

The above figure shows the positions of A and B after traveling for one hour. A moves to Q and B moves to R, so that triangle PQR has legs of 9 and 12 miles. It is a 3-4-5 triangle, with sides multiplied by 3; so that $QR = 15$.

14. B.

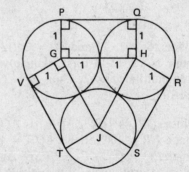

In the above figure, the length of the rope is $PQ + \overset{\frown}{PV} + VT + \overset{\frown}{TS} + SR + \overset{\frown}{QR} = 3PQ + 3VP$. From rectangle $PQHG$, $PQ = GH = 2$. Since triangle GHJ is equilateral, $\angle HGJ = 60°$. Angles PGH and VGJ are each 90°, so that angle $PGV = 360 - 180 - 60 = 120°$. Thus, arc $\overset{\frown}{PV} = \frac{1}{3}$ circumference $= \frac{1}{3}(2\pi)$ and $\overset{\frown}{3PV} = 2\pi$. Thus the length of the rope is $2\pi + 6$.

15. **A.** If $\dfrac{2x + 6}{x^3 + 6x^2 + 54} = 0$, then

$$2x + 6 = 0$$

$$x = -3.$$

16. **E.** $p = 2q, q = 3r.$

Substitute $q = 3r$ in first equation:

$p = 2(3r) = 6r.$

Divide both sides by 6.

$$r = \frac{p}{6}.$$

17. **A.** Average $= \dfrac{76 + 76 + 85 + 85 + 85 + 85}{6}$

$$= 82.0\%.$$

18. **D.**

Since $26 = 2 \cdot 13$ and $24 = 2 \cdot 12$, the triangle is a 5-12-13 right triangle with each side multiplied by 2. Thus, $x = 2 \cdot 5 = 10$ feet.

19. **C.** Since $QR = QS$, $\angle SQR = \angle QSR$ and, since $\angle R = 100°$, then $\angle SQR = 40°$. Also, since $PQ = QS$, $\angle P = \angle PSQ$. Angle SQR is an exterior angle of triangle PQS and is therefore equal to $\angle P + \angle SPQ = 2\angle P$. Thus $\angle P = 20°$.

20. **E.** $PQ = 4 - (-2) = 4 + 2 = 6.$

$OR = 5.$

Area of triangle $OPQ = \dfrac{1}{2} \cdot PQ \cdot OR$

$$= \frac{1}{2} \cdot 6 \cdot 5$$

$$= 15.$$

21. **A.** The car travels $\dfrac{m}{g}$ miles per gallon. On n gallons, it travels

$$\left(\frac{m}{g}\right)n = \frac{mn}{g}.$$

22. **E.** $$y = \frac{rs}{1 + x}$$

$$y(1 + x) = rs$$

$$y + xy = rs$$

$$xy = rs - y$$

$$x = \frac{rs - y}{y} = \frac{rs}{y} - 1.$$

23. **D.**

Cross-section of shaft Cut away

Original cross-section area $= p^2$

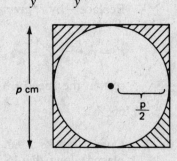

Final cross-section area $= \pi \left(\dfrac{p}{2}\right)^2$

$$= \frac{\pi p^2}{4}$$

Area cut away $= p^2 - \dfrac{\pi p^2}{4}$

$$= p^2\left(1 - \frac{\pi}{4}\right)$$

Fractional part cut away $= \dfrac{p^2\left(1 - \dfrac{\pi}{4}\right)}{p^2}$

$$= 1 - \frac{\pi}{4}$$

$$= \frac{4 - \pi}{4}.$$

24. **D.** Central angle = 40% of 360°

$$= .4(360) = 144°.$$

25. **E.** Let x = no. of millions of metric tons in world production,

then 16.6% of x = .581

$$\frac{1}{6}x = .581 \text{ (approx.)}$$

$$x = 3.486 = 3.5 \text{ (approx.)}.$$

SECTION VI

1. **C.** "With the new bait" should follow "Casting cautiously." The error in the sentence as it stands is that "which he fried for breakfast" modifies "with the new bait" instead of modifying "two large speckled trout."

2. **B.** Omit the auxiliary verb "had."

3. **C.** Error in diction. Use "arose" instead of "raised up."

4. **E.** No error.

5. **D.** Replace "she" with "her," since "without" is a preposition and takes an objective pronoun.

6. **D.** Use "whom" instead of "who" in this case. The word is the object of "examines."

7. **C.** Verbs agree in number with the closer of two subjects separated by "nor." Replace "were" with "was."

8. **A.** The preposition "Between" takes the objective case. Replace "I" with "me."

9. **D.** The librarian took the book from "me," not from "myself." "Myself" is a reflexive pronoun and, when used as an object, would refer to "I."

10. **C.** "Continuously" should be replaced by "continually." The former means "without interruption," while the latter means "frequently or closely repeated."

11. **A.** Error in diction. "Besides" means "in addition to." The word needed here is "beside," which means "alongside of."

12. **D.** Error in agreement of number. "Their" should be replaced by "his" or "her," since the pronoun referred to is "anyone," which is singular.

13. **E.** No error.

14. **D.** Error in agreement and in diction. The demonstrative pronoun should agree in number with the word "kind." The correct word should have been "that" instead of "these."

15. **D.** Error in grammar. The object of "visited" should have been "me" instead of "I."

16. **C.** Error in grammar. The correct past participle of "swim" is "swum."

17. **E.** No error.

18. **D.** Error in grammar. The correct past participle of "spring" is "sprung."

19. **A.** "Being that" is an illiterate substitute for the appropriate subordinating conjunction "since."

20. **A.** Error in diction. The predicate adjective "bad" should be used instead of the adverb "badly."

21. **D.** Error in diction. Same as above. Use "bitter" instead of "bitterly."

22. **B.** As between two contestants, use the comparative form, "prettier," rather than the superlative form, "prettiest, which would be used to compare three or more."

23. **C.** Error in diction. The plural of "son-in-law" is "sons-in-law."

24. **A.** "Hardly" is a negative and should not be used with "no one." Replace "no one" with "anyone."

25. **D.** Lack of parallel construction. Since the moderator "summarized" the agreements, he should have "asked" them for their final statements. The two constructions should have been similar.

26. **C.** Dangling modifier. The sentence as given states that the bear was driving through the park. The correction shows that "they," the children, were driving through the park.

27. **A.** The sentence is correct as given.

28. **C.** Error resulting from shift of person as subject. "Infant" is third person, while "you" is second person.

29. **B.** Verb shift. We have extended every effort . . . , and (we) hope . . .

30. **E.** Lack of parallel construction. Pasteur "concentrated"; Pasteur "focused."

31. **C.** Use of infinitive: "to have that tooth treated," must be matched by use of infinitive: "than to put treatment off.'

32. **A.** The sentence is correct as given.

33. **B.** The two passive verbs, "interested" and "stimulated" each takes a different preposition, and each preposition must be used in the sentence immediately following the respective verbs.

34. **D.** Although "hopefully" is accepted in informal use in the construction here employed, the construction in choice (D) is preferred in standard written English.

35. **B.** Run-on sentence. Two main clauses should not be separated by a comma. Use a semicolon or a coordinating conjunction, or make a separate sentence of each clause.

36. **D.** The handbags spoken of in this sentence are in the plural, and they are used by la-

dies, not a single lady. The word "Lady's" should, therefore, be replaced by the plural possessive form, "Ladies'."

37. **E.** Error in capitalization. The words "high school" are common nouns and should not be capitalized.

38. **D.** "Would of" is an illiterate substitute for "would have."

39. **A.** The sentence is correct as given.

40. **B.** The phrase, "late as usual," is a parenthetical remark and should, therefore, be set off by commas.

41. **B.** The conjunction that introduces clauses of comparison is "as."

42. **E.** The sentence is correct as given.

43. **A.** The correct construction in this case would be the use of the predicate adjective "sweet," rather than the adverb "sweetly."

44. **B.** Substitute "to understand" for "understanding," and that will give the correct parallelism.

45. **A.** "Myself" is a reflexive pronoun, and "than" is a conjunction. The conjunction introduces a verbless clause that should read "than I," not "than me" or "than myself."

46. **B.** "Which" is used to refer to things or to groups of people used impersonally. The correct pronoun here would be "whom."

47. **E.** The sentence is correct as given.

48. **E.** The sentence is correct as given.

49. **B.** Error in grammar. The correct past participle of "show" is "shown."

50. **C.** Error in grammar. The subject of the clause should be the nominative form of the pronoun, "who."

Conversion of Raw Scores to SAT Scaled Scores

In part I, page two, the method of determining your raw scores is explained. However, when you receive your SAT scores, you will find that your mathematical and verbal scores are scaled within a range of 200 to 800 and the TSWE score is scaled within a range of 20 to 60.

The scaled score is based on a statistical determination and varies somewhat from one test to another. The table below gives a conversion based on results over the past few years.

To use this table, determine your verbal raw score from sections 1 and 2 of the practice test, your mathematical raw score from sections 4 and 5, and your TSWE raw score from section 6. These raw scores may then be converted to scaled scores by using the table below as a guide.

This table may be used for all practice tests in this book.

Raw Score	Scaled Verbal Score	Scaled Math Score	Scaled TSWE Score
85	800		
83	785		
81	770		
79	740		
77	730		
75	720		
73	710		
71	700		
69	670		
67	660		
65	650		
63	640		
61	620		
60	610	800	
58	600	785	
56	590	770	
54	570	740	
52	555	720	
50	540	705	60+
48	530	690	59
46	520	670	58+
44	500	650	58
42	485	620	56
40	470	610	55
38	450	600	53
36	430	580	51
34	420	560	47
32	410	540	45
30	400	530	43
28	390	520	42
26	370	490	40
24	350	470	37
22	340	450	34
20	330	440	33
18	320	430	32
16	310	410	29
14	280	390	26
12	270	370	25
10	260	360	24
8	250	350	23
6	240	330	22
4	220	300	21
2	210	285	20
0	200	270	20

SAT Practice Test 2

ANSWER SHEET

When you have chosen your answer to any question, blacken the corresponding space on the answer sheet below. Make sure your marking completely fills the answer space. If you change an answer, erase the previous marking completely.

Section I—Verbal

1 Ⓐ Ⓑ Ⓒ Ⓓ Ⓔ	13 Ⓐ Ⓑ Ⓒ Ⓓ Ⓔ	24 Ⓐ Ⓑ Ⓒ Ⓓ Ⓔ	35 Ⓐ Ⓑ Ⓒ Ⓓ Ⓔ
2 Ⓐ Ⓑ Ⓒ Ⓓ Ⓔ	14 Ⓐ Ⓑ Ⓒ Ⓓ Ⓔ	25 Ⓐ Ⓑ Ⓒ Ⓓ Ⓔ	36 Ⓐ Ⓑ Ⓒ Ⓓ Ⓔ
3 Ⓐ Ⓑ Ⓒ Ⓓ Ⓔ	15 Ⓐ Ⓑ Ⓒ Ⓓ Ⓔ	26 Ⓐ Ⓑ Ⓒ Ⓓ Ⓔ	37 Ⓐ Ⓑ Ⓒ Ⓓ Ⓔ
4 Ⓐ Ⓑ Ⓒ Ⓓ Ⓔ	16 Ⓐ Ⓑ Ⓒ Ⓓ Ⓔ	27 Ⓐ Ⓑ Ⓒ Ⓓ Ⓔ	38 Ⓐ Ⓑ Ⓒ Ⓓ Ⓔ
5 Ⓐ Ⓑ Ⓒ Ⓓ Ⓔ	17 Ⓐ Ⓑ Ⓒ Ⓓ Ⓔ	28 Ⓐ Ⓑ Ⓒ Ⓓ Ⓔ	39 Ⓐ Ⓑ Ⓒ Ⓓ Ⓔ
6 Ⓐ Ⓑ Ⓒ Ⓓ Ⓔ	18 Ⓐ Ⓑ Ⓒ Ⓓ Ⓔ	29 Ⓐ Ⓑ Ⓒ Ⓓ Ⓔ	40 Ⓐ Ⓑ Ⓒ Ⓓ Ⓔ
7 Ⓐ Ⓑ Ⓒ Ⓓ Ⓔ	19 Ⓐ Ⓑ Ⓒ Ⓓ Ⓔ	30 Ⓐ Ⓑ Ⓒ Ⓓ Ⓔ	41 Ⓐ Ⓑ Ⓒ Ⓓ Ⓔ
8 Ⓐ Ⓑ Ⓒ Ⓓ Ⓔ	20 Ⓐ Ⓑ Ⓒ Ⓓ Ⓔ	31 Ⓐ Ⓑ Ⓒ Ⓓ Ⓔ	42 Ⓐ Ⓑ Ⓒ Ⓓ Ⓔ
9 Ⓐ Ⓑ Ⓒ Ⓓ Ⓔ	21 Ⓐ Ⓑ Ⓒ Ⓓ Ⓔ	32 Ⓐ Ⓑ Ⓒ Ⓓ Ⓔ	43 Ⓐ Ⓑ Ⓒ Ⓓ Ⓔ
10 Ⓐ Ⓑ Ⓒ Ⓓ Ⓔ	22 Ⓐ Ⓑ Ⓒ Ⓓ Ⓔ	33 Ⓐ Ⓑ Ⓒ Ⓓ Ⓔ	44 Ⓐ Ⓑ Ⓒ Ⓓ Ⓔ
11 Ⓐ Ⓑ Ⓒ Ⓓ Ⓔ	23 Ⓐ Ⓑ Ⓒ Ⓓ Ⓔ	34 Ⓐ Ⓑ Ⓒ Ⓓ Ⓔ	45 Ⓐ Ⓑ Ⓒ Ⓓ Ⓔ
12 Ⓐ Ⓑ Ⓒ Ⓓ Ⓔ			

Section II—Verbal

1 Ⓐ Ⓑ Ⓒ Ⓓ Ⓔ	11 Ⓐ Ⓑ Ⓒ Ⓓ Ⓔ	21 Ⓐ Ⓑ Ⓒ Ⓓ Ⓔ	31 Ⓐ Ⓑ Ⓒ Ⓓ Ⓔ
2 Ⓐ Ⓑ Ⓒ Ⓓ Ⓔ	12 Ⓐ Ⓑ Ⓒ Ⓓ Ⓔ	22 Ⓐ Ⓑ Ⓒ Ⓓ Ⓔ	32 Ⓐ Ⓑ Ⓒ Ⓓ Ⓔ
3 Ⓐ Ⓑ Ⓒ Ⓓ Ⓔ	13 Ⓐ Ⓑ Ⓒ Ⓓ Ⓔ	23 Ⓐ Ⓑ Ⓒ Ⓓ Ⓔ	33 Ⓐ Ⓑ Ⓒ Ⓓ Ⓔ
4 Ⓐ Ⓑ Ⓒ Ⓓ Ⓔ	14 Ⓐ Ⓑ Ⓒ Ⓓ Ⓔ	24 Ⓐ Ⓑ Ⓒ Ⓓ Ⓔ	34 Ⓐ Ⓑ Ⓒ Ⓓ Ⓔ
5 Ⓐ Ⓑ Ⓒ Ⓓ Ⓔ	15 Ⓐ Ⓑ Ⓒ Ⓓ Ⓔ	25 Ⓐ Ⓑ Ⓒ Ⓓ Ⓔ	35 Ⓐ Ⓑ Ⓒ Ⓓ Ⓔ
6 Ⓐ Ⓑ Ⓒ Ⓓ Ⓔ	16 Ⓐ Ⓑ Ⓒ Ⓓ Ⓔ	26 Ⓐ Ⓑ Ⓒ Ⓓ Ⓔ	36 Ⓐ Ⓑ Ⓒ Ⓓ Ⓔ
7 Ⓐ Ⓑ Ⓒ Ⓓ Ⓔ	17 Ⓐ Ⓑ Ⓒ Ⓓ Ⓔ	27 Ⓐ Ⓑ Ⓒ Ⓓ Ⓔ	37 Ⓐ Ⓑ Ⓒ Ⓓ Ⓔ
8 Ⓐ Ⓑ Ⓒ Ⓓ Ⓔ	18 Ⓐ Ⓑ Ⓒ Ⓓ Ⓔ	28 Ⓐ Ⓑ Ⓒ Ⓓ Ⓔ	38 Ⓐ Ⓑ Ⓒ Ⓓ Ⓔ
9 Ⓐ Ⓑ Ⓒ Ⓓ Ⓔ	19 Ⓐ Ⓑ Ⓒ Ⓓ Ⓔ	29 Ⓐ Ⓑ Ⓒ Ⓓ Ⓔ	39 Ⓐ Ⓑ Ⓒ Ⓓ Ⓔ
10 Ⓐ Ⓑ Ⓒ Ⓓ Ⓔ	20 Ⓐ Ⓑ Ⓒ Ⓓ Ⓔ	30 Ⓐ Ⓑ Ⓒ Ⓓ Ⓔ	40 Ⓐ Ⓑ Ⓒ Ⓓ Ⓔ

Section III—Verbal

1 Ⓐ Ⓑ Ⓒ Ⓓ Ⓔ	11 Ⓐ Ⓑ Ⓒ Ⓓ Ⓔ	21 Ⓐ Ⓑ Ⓒ Ⓓ Ⓔ	31 Ⓐ Ⓑ Ⓒ Ⓓ Ⓔ
2 Ⓐ Ⓑ Ⓒ Ⓓ Ⓔ	12 Ⓐ Ⓑ Ⓒ Ⓓ Ⓔ	22 Ⓐ Ⓑ Ⓒ Ⓓ Ⓔ	32 Ⓐ Ⓑ Ⓒ Ⓓ Ⓔ
3 Ⓐ Ⓑ Ⓒ Ⓓ Ⓔ	13 Ⓐ Ⓑ Ⓒ Ⓓ Ⓔ	23 Ⓐ Ⓑ Ⓒ Ⓓ Ⓔ	33 Ⓐ Ⓑ Ⓒ Ⓓ Ⓔ
4 Ⓐ Ⓑ Ⓒ Ⓓ Ⓔ	14 Ⓐ Ⓑ Ⓒ Ⓓ Ⓔ	24 Ⓐ Ⓑ Ⓒ Ⓓ Ⓔ	34 Ⓐ Ⓑ Ⓒ Ⓓ Ⓔ
5 Ⓐ Ⓑ Ⓒ Ⓓ Ⓔ	15 Ⓐ Ⓑ Ⓒ Ⓓ Ⓔ	25 Ⓐ Ⓑ Ⓒ Ⓓ Ⓔ	35 Ⓐ Ⓑ Ⓒ Ⓓ Ⓔ
6 Ⓐ Ⓑ Ⓒ Ⓓ Ⓔ	16 Ⓐ Ⓑ Ⓒ Ⓓ Ⓔ	26 Ⓐ Ⓑ Ⓒ Ⓓ Ⓔ	36 Ⓐ Ⓑ Ⓒ Ⓓ Ⓔ
7 Ⓐ Ⓑ Ⓒ Ⓓ Ⓔ	17 Ⓐ Ⓑ Ⓒ Ⓓ Ⓔ	27 Ⓐ Ⓑ Ⓒ Ⓓ Ⓔ	37 Ⓐ Ⓑ Ⓒ Ⓓ Ⓔ
8 Ⓐ Ⓑ Ⓒ Ⓓ Ⓔ	18 Ⓐ Ⓑ Ⓒ Ⓓ Ⓔ	28 Ⓐ Ⓑ Ⓒ Ⓓ Ⓔ	38 Ⓐ Ⓑ Ⓒ Ⓓ Ⓔ
9 Ⓐ Ⓑ Ⓒ Ⓓ Ⓔ	19 Ⓐ Ⓑ Ⓒ Ⓓ Ⓔ	29 Ⓐ Ⓑ Ⓒ Ⓓ Ⓔ	39 Ⓐ Ⓑ Ⓒ Ⓓ Ⓔ
10 Ⓐ Ⓑ Ⓒ Ⓓ Ⓔ	20 Ⓐ Ⓑ Ⓒ Ⓓ Ⓔ	30 Ⓐ Ⓑ Ⓒ Ⓓ Ⓔ	40 Ⓐ Ⓑ Ⓒ Ⓓ Ⓔ

Section IV—Mathematical

1 (A) (B) (C) (D) (E)	10 (A) (B) (C) (D) (E)	19 (A) (B) (C) (D)	28 (A) (B) (C) (D)
2 (A) (B) (C) (D) (E)	11 (A) (B) (C) (D) (E)	20 (A) (B) (C) (D)	29 (A) (B) (C) (D)
3 (A) (B) (C) (D) (E)	12 (A) (B) (C) (D) (E)	21 (A) (B) (C) (D)	30 (A) (B) (C) (D)
4 (A) (B) (C) (D) (E)	13 (A) (B) (C) (D) (E)	22 (A) (B) (C) (D)	31 (A) (B) (C) (D)
5 (A) (B) (C) (D) (E)	14 (A) (B) (C) (D) (E)	23 (A) (B) (C) (D)	32 (A) (B) (C) (D)
6 (A) (B) (C) (D) (E)	15 (A) (B) (C) (D) (E)	24 (A) (B) (C) (D)	33 (A) (B) (C) (D)
7 (A) (B) (C) (D) (E)	16 (A) (B) (C) (D) (E)	25 (A) (B) (C) (D)	34 (A) (B) (C) (D)
8 (A) (B) (C) (D) (E)	17 (A) (B) (C) (D) (E)	26 (A) (B) (C) (D)	35 (A) (B) (C) (D)
9 (A) (B) (C) (D) (E)	18 (A) (B) (C) (D)	27 (A) (B) (C) (D)	

Section V—Mathematical

1 (A) (B) (C) (D) (E)	8 (A) (B) (C) (D) (E)	14 (A) (B) (C) (D) (E)	20 (A) (B) (C) (D) (E)
2 (A) (B) (C) (D) (E)	9 (A) (B) (C) (D) (E)	15 (A) (B) (C) (D) (E)	21 (A) (B) (C) (D) (E)
3 (A) (B) (C) (D) (E)	10 (A) (B) (C) (D) (E)	16 (A) (B) (C) (D) (E)	22 (A) (B) (C) (D) (E)
4 (A) (B) (C) (D) (E)	11 (A) (B) (C) (D) (E)	17 (A) (B) (C) (D) (E)	23 (A) (B) (C) (D) (E)
5 (A) (B) (C) (D) (E)	12 (A) (B) (C) (D) (E)	18 (A) (B) (C) (D) (E)	24 (A) (B) (C) (D) (E)
6 (A) (B) (C) (D) (E)	13 (A) (B) (C) (D) (E)	19 (A) (B) (C) (D) (E)	25 (A) (B) (C) (D) (E)
7 (A) (B) (C) (D) (E)			

Section VI—Written English

1 (A) (B) (C) (D) (E)	14 (A) (B) (C) (D) (E)	27 (A) (B) (C) (D) (E)	39 (A) (B) (C) (D) (E)
2 (A) (B) (C) (D) (E)	15 (A) (B) (C) (D) (E)	28 (A) (B) (C) (D) (E)	40 (A) (B) (C) (D) (E)
3 (A) (B) (C) (D) (E)	16 (A) (B) (C) (D) (E)	29 (A) (B) (C) (D) (E)	41 (A) (B) (C) (D) (E)
4 (A) (B) (C) (D) (E)	17 (A) (B) (C) (D) (E)	30 (A) (B) (C) (D) (E)	42 (A) (B) (C) (D) (E)
5 (A) (B) (C) (D) (E)	18 (A) (B) (C) (D) (E)	31 (A) (B) (C) (D) (E)	43 (A) (B) (C) (D) (E)
6 (A) (B) (C) (D) (E)	19 (A) (B) (C) (D) (E)	32 (A) (B) (C) (D) (E)	44 (A) (B) (C) (D) (E)
7 (A) (B) (C) (D) (E)	20 (A) (B) (C) (D) (E)	33 (A) (B) (C) (D) (E)	45 (A) (B) (C) (D) (E)
8 (A) (B) (C) (D) (E)	21 (A) (B) (C) (D) (E)	34 (A) (B) (C) (D) (E)	46 (A) (B) (C) (D) (E)
9 (A) (B) (C) (D) (E)	22 (A) (B) (C) (D) (E)	35 (A) (B) (C) (D) (E)	47 (A) (B) (C) (D) (E)
10 (A) (B) (C) (D) (E)	23 (A) (B) (C) (D) (E)	36 (A) (B) (C) (D) (E)	48 (A) (B) (C) (D) (E)
11 (A) (B) (C) (D) (E)	24 (A) (B) (C) (D) (E)	37 (A) (B) (C) (D) (E)	49 (A) (B) (C) (D) (E)
12 (A) (B) (C) (D) (E)	25 (A) (B) (C) (D) (E)	38 (A) (B) (C) (D) (E)	50 (A) (B) (C) (D) (E)
13 (A) (B) (C) (D) (E)	26 (A) (B) (C) (D) (E)		

SAT Practice Test 2

SECTION I

Time—30 minutes

45 Questions

For each of the numbered questions in this section, choose the best answer according to the instructions, and blacken the corresponding blank space on the answer sheet.

In each of the questions below, a capitalized word is followed by five words or phrases lettered (A) through (E). Select the word or phrase *most nearly opposite* in meaning to the capitalized word.

Since some of the questions require that you distinguish fine shades of meaning, consider all choices carefully before you select your answer.

1. GRAVE:
   (A) drunk
   (B) inherent
   (C) frivolous
   (D) curdled
   (E) vacuous

2. MEAGER:
   (A) abandoned
   (B) profuse
   (C) supplied
   (D) forgotten
   (E) restrained

3. PRECEDE:
   (A) yield
   (B) ensue
   (C) revert
   (D) step back
   (E) lead

4. MARTIAL:
   (A) unwed
   (B) undisciplined
   (C) pacific
   (D) military
   (E) brassy

5. EXTOL:
   (A) ring out
   (B) assess
   (C) admit
   (D) castigate
   (E) recant

6. IMPLICATE:
   (A) bless
   (B) simple
   (C) absolve
   (D) hint at
   (E) state clearly

7. ABHORRENCE:
   (A) adoration
   (B) idiosyncrasy
   (C) vengeance
   (D) fearlessness
   (E) serenity

8. MUNIFICENT:
   (A) penurious
   (B) disarming
   (C) inventive
   (D) demented
   (E) penultimate

9. OBDURATE:
   (A) redeemed
   (B) relenting
   (C) resenting
   (D) rejoicing
   (E) whisper

10. HEINOUS:
    (A) untoward
    (B) outmoded
    (C) admirable
    (D) courteous
    (E) chivalrous

11. CREDULOUS:
    (A) skeptical
    (B) tyrannical
    (C) brusque
    (D) doubtless
    (E) redoubtable

12. VINDICTIVE:
    (A) surly
    (B) pensive
    (C) forgiving
    (D) profound
    (E) arrogant

13. RIGOROUS:
    (A) flimsy
    (B) relaxed
    (C) angry
    (D) anxious
    (E) harsh

14. BIZARRE:
    (A) unwieldy
    (B) bothersome
    (C) crusty
    (D) normal
    (E) questionable

15. PARTIAL:
    (A) denture
    (B) component
    (C) uninterested
    (D) disinterested
    (E) biased

Each of the sentences below has one or more blank spaces indicating where a word (or words) has been omitted. Each sentence is followed by five words or sets of words lettered from (A) through (E). Select the lettered word or set of words which, inserted to replace the blanks, *best* fits in with and completes the meaning of the sentence as a whole.

16. To his great disappointment, Edmundson contracted a _____ disease which incapacitated him to such an extent that he was forced to _____ his participation in the jungle campaign.
    (A) malevolent . . suspend
    (B) virulent . . curtail
    (C) mystical . . limit
    (D) topical . . renew
    (E) congenital . . cease

17. The process of digesting lean meat and other _____ is an exothermic one; that is, _____ is actually given off during digestion.
    (A) carbohydrates . . moisture
    (B) proteins . . acid
    (C) fats . . energy
    (D) proteins . . heat
    (E) enzymes . . condensation

18. The propaganda of a nation at war is designed to _____ the energy of its citizens and their will to win, and to _____ them with an overwhelming sense of the justice of their cause.
    (A) incorporate . . inflame
    (B) harness . . include
    (C) sap . . fill
    (D) stimulate . . imbue
    (E) nurture . . arouse

19. The report indicated that while many of the difficulties faced by the colonists were indeed substantial and even, perhaps, ineradicable, many others were mere _____.
    (A) concerns
    (B) conjectures
    (C) apprehensions
    (D) replications
    (E) precipitations

20. Since the _____ of the fish extract oxygen from the water to pass on to the bloodstream, the fish must, in order to _____, remain underwater.
    (A) dorsals . . retaliate
    (B) gills . . breathe
    (C) lungs . . mature
    (D) maxillae . . oxidize
    (E) capillaries . . resist

21. While Isadora Duncan encouraged the notion that her art welled up _____, it is apparent that her "natural" movements were the result of great _____.
(A) emotionally . . logic
(B) empathetically . . tension
(C) spontaneously . . discipline
(D) sporadically . . planning
(E) unintentionally . . coincidences

22. The enemies of Israel contradict themselves, _____ the land for themselves by reason of prior occupation, but _____ it to the Israelis who, in turn, occupied it even earlier.
(A) defending . . granting
(B) commanding . . remanding
(C) taking . . giving
(D) claiming . . denying
(E) seizing . . expropriating

23. Mr. Marquette's cutting remarks and sharp rejoinders _____ Caldwell's feelings.
(A) mauled
(B) hurt
(C) injured
(D) lacerated
(E) bruised

24. Most of the younger generation had _____ forth into the great world, but they _____ returned to the land of their fathers.
(A) departed . . weren't
(B) fared . . always
(C) sallied . . never
(D) not gone . . seldom
(E) meandered . . stolidly

25. Even in winter when we do not seem to perspire at all, we have what is called insensible _____, and our skins give up to the air by _____ nearly a quart of perspiration every twenty-four hours.
(A) perspiration . . evaporation
(B) dryness . . repetition
(C) mucous . . nasality
(D) wetness . . contact
(E) feelings . . osmosis

In each of the questions below, a related pair of words or phrases, in capital letters, is followed by five pairs of words or phrases lettered from (A) to (E). Select that lettered pair which expresses a relationship that is *most* similar to that of the capitalized pair.

26. SATURDAY : SUNDAY ::
(A) temper : rage
(B) sugar : sweeten
(C) affront : apology
(D) eve : holiday
(E) torrid : humid

27. SPY : SECRETIVE ::
(A) entirely : wholly
(B) pathos : pathetic
(C) fan : partisan
(D) elephant : heavy
(E) candidate : bipartisan

28. GLUTTON : FOOD ::
(A) aesthete : art
(B) miser : money
(C) liberal : philosophy
(D) cupidity : money
(E) leader : decisions

29. SAINT : CANONIZATION ::
(A) sinner : expiation
(B) child : confirmation
(C) youth : graduation
(D) priest : parishioner
(E) king : coronation

30. PRUDERY : MODESTY ::
(A) reserve : shyness
(B) freedom : license
(C) introvert : extrovert
(D) pedantry : scholarship
(E) conviction : belief

31. BRAGGART : HUMILITY ::
(A) traitor : repentance
(B) amiss : aright
(C) heretic : religion
(D) prolix : bore
(E) rebel : conventionality

32. SAW : LOG ::
   (A) jackknife : whittlings
   (B) millstone : grindings
   (C) thresher : husks
   (D) scissors : cloth
   (E) potter : wheel

33. STORM : SUBSIDE ::
   (A) temperature : raise
   (B) energy : flag
   (C) rebellion : quell
   (D) treason : execution
   (E) Dublin : Belfast

34. ROOSEVELT : TRUMAN ::
   (A) Washington : Adams
   (B) Eisenhower : Kennedy
   (C) Johnson : Nixon
   (D) Lincoln : Johnson
   (E) Ford : Rockefeller

35. PORT : STORM ::
   (A) embarkation : tempest
   (B) homecoming : disaster
   (C) hurricane : palm tree
   (D) storm : stormcellar
   (E) haven : oppression

Each of the reading passages below is followed by several questions about the contents of the passage. In answering the questions, base your responses on what is *stated* or *implied* in the passage.

It had been a clear night with no wind, but several times we heard the low boom of thunder in the west. Were there storms over in Harris Bay? Sometimes the individual fjords have their own weather systems. No storms—it was a calving glacier miles distant at the head of Aialak Bay.

We headed up that way, picking our course carefully through the floating ice, and came up to within less than a half-mile of the face of Aialak Glacier. It must have been about that far; it could have been only a few hundred yards, except that the large seabirds flying between us and the glacier appeared no larger than gnats. Many birds were working in the area near the glacial front, and dozens of harbor seals were lying on ice floes not far from the forbidding ice cliffs. This is surely fertile water, rich in both classes of plankton. Of what effect is the infusion of fresh water with its rock flour and attendant wealth of minerals? No matter; the winged and finned hunters know. Mineral-rich waters nourish plankton blooms, the plankton nourish shrimp, the shrimp bring fish, the fish draw seals and kittiwakes and other gulls. These are the apices of their respective food pyramids, and we find them in abundance at the face of every glacier.

Engines silent, we could hear the voices of the glacier. They were myriad and awesome. There were long running sighs like hidden rivers deep in the ice, and mighty creaks and groans that passed through the body of ice as if the glacier were an immense animal suffering under its own weight. There was that rumble again, that muted thunder, as a section of ice broke away from the glacial face. It poured down with a roar from the blue-white heights, pushing a swell of water far out into the bay and rocking our boat so that even at half a mile we were unable to compose pictures with longer lenses. The seals were undisturbed.

Another roar as a mass of ice calved into the sea. The sound, rather than the size of the icefall, gave some perspective of the glacier's dimension. An insignificant dribble of ice had flaked away from the glacial face, pouring down in slow motion, and then a stentorian rumble reached us and we could see a ground swell rising and coming on. The icefall stirred a burst of activity among the seabirds; they whirled in a cloud above a house-sized mass of ice as it broached from the fjord, gray water pouring from its flanks.

36. What caused the thunderous sound that was mentioned in the first sentence of the passage?
    (A) The collision of two glaciers some miles away
    (B) A storm over in Harris Bay
    (C) The crashing of plankton
    (D) The voice of the glacier
    (E) The breaking off of sections of the glacial face

37. The food chain described in the passage follows an established order which is that
    (A) plankton add minerals to the water; shrimp and fish are attracted by the minerals; gulls eat fish and are eaten by seals
    (B) seals and gulls and kittiwakes eat fish, which eat shrimp, which eat plankton, which in turn flourish in mineral-rich water fed by glacial ice
    (C) gulls and seals feed on glacial calves and plankton
    (D) fresh water, rock flour, plankton, and shrimp are at the apex of the food pyramid
    (E) plankton nourishes shrimp, which are eaten by humans

38. In the last paragraph, the word "stentorian" as used means most nearly
    (A) distant
    (B) quiet
    (C) intermittent
    (D) very loud
    (E) barely audible

39. The voices of the glacier, referred to in paragraph 3, are
    I. the bellowings of an immense seal suffering
    II. the squeaks of the gulls and the shrimp
    III. the muted thunder of ice pouring down the glacial face
    IV. creaks and groans caused by internal expansion and contractions of the heavy glacier
    (A) II and III only
    (B) III and IV only
    (C) II and IV only
    (D) IV only
    (E) I, III, and IV only

40. "Calving" as used in this passage most nearly means
    (A) collapsing, a variant spelling of caving
    (B) giving birth to
    (C) decreasing in size
    (D) bellowing loudly, like a calf
    (E) breaking up or splintering

GO ON TO THE NEXT PAGE

Franz Liszt, the incomparable pianist, the highly distinguished composer, is the very embodiment of the romantic spirit in his fantastic life as well as in his art. His biography reads like highly colored fiction, for his triumphal success as a virtuoso made him perhaps the most universally admired and celebrated man of his time. We are concerned here only with the manner in which he fashioned the romantic ideas of his age to his particular individual needs. His manifold achievements were of the greatest importance for the cause of progress in music, sending stimulating impulses in many directions. Dispute is possible as to the lasting artistic value and the ultimate perfection of his music but not as to his inventiveness in finding new technical means of expression or as to his wonderful sense of sound and color. From Berlioz he took over the ideas of orchestral tone color and program music, developing them in a very individual manner. From Chopin he inherited the sensitive new chromatic harmony, which he enriched in many ways, handing over to Wagner an admirably perfected tool to be used in *Tristan und Isolde*. In the matter of musical form he applied for the first time the principle of "cyclic" construction, evolving all the various themes of a symphonic or sonata-like work in several movements from a few fundamental motives, which through rhythmical or melodic transformations could be made to assume numerous changes of impression. César Franck, Vincent d'Indy, and the modern French and Russian schools later adopted this *principe cyclique* of Liszt's. Here we see a particularly striking musical application of the dominant romantic idea of evolution. In his various "symphonic poems," his *Faust* and *Dante* symphonies, and his concertos, Liszt has brilliantly demonstrated the possibilities of this principle of organic structure. The cyclic method had been widely employed in music of the seventeenth century, but had been forgotten in the eighteenth century. Probably, however, Liszt knew nothing at all of these two-hundred-year-old ancestors of his method. It is probable that he elaborated it from his studies of the last Beethoven sonatas and quartets, where a very ingenious and complex use is made of a similar transformation of motives.

41. According to the author, there can be no dispute about Franz Liszt's musical achievements *except* as to
(A) his inventiveness in finding new technical means of expression
(B) the degree of his pianistic virtuosity
(C) the ultimate perfection of his music
(D) his sense of sound and color
(E) the extent to which they influenced others

42. The passage speaks of musical ideas and developments being transmitted from
(A) Liszt to Berlioz to Chopin
(B) Chopin to Liszt to Wagner
(C) Chopin to Wagner to Franck
(D) Berlioz to Liszt to Chopin
(E) Wagner to Berlioz to d'Indy

43. Liszt is credited with the development of the *principe cyclique*. Which of the statements below is (are) true as relates to this principle?
   I. Liszt used this organic structure in only his "Faust" and "Dante" symphonies.
   II. Liszt was the first composer to use the cyclic method
   III. Liszt probably based his idea for the *principe cyclique* on a similar construction in Beethoven's late sonatas and quartets.
(A) I only
(B) II and III only
(C) I and III only
(D) III only
(E) I, II, and III

44. We can infer from this passage that the term "cyclic" construction was applied to Liszt's important musical development because
(A) the music repeated the romantic cycle of the past
(B) he used a few fundamental musical motives with rhythmic or melodic transformations to evolve all the themes of a large-scale musical work
(C) he used the new chromatic harmony
(D) he took Berlioz's ideas of orchestral color and reworked them
(E) he stimulated new developments in all areas of music

45. It is most likely that the author of this passage is a
(A) biographer
(B) contemporary of Liszt
(C) newspaper feature writer
(D) musicologist
(E) a conductor

STOP
WORK ONLY ON THIS SECTION UNTIL THE TIME ALLOTTED IS OVER.

Time—30 minutes

40 Questions

For each of the numbered questions in this section, choose the best answer according to the instructions, and blacken the corresponding blank space on the answer sheet.

In each of the questions below, a capitalized word is followed by five words or phrases lettered (A) through (E). Select the word or phrase *most nearly opposite* in meaning to the capitalized word.

Since some of the questions require that you distinguish fine shades of meaning, consider all choices carefully before you select your answer.

1. RAPTURE:
   (A) intent
   (B) coma
   (C) conniption
   (D) satisfaction
   (E) depression

2. APATHY:
   (A) pity
   (B) opposition
   (C) corruption
   (D) enthusiasm
   (E) tenderness

3. SECRETE:
   (A) nectar
   (B) flaunt
   (C) stimulate
   (D) convey
   (E) exhort

4. SAGACIOUS:
   (A) foolish
   (B) arrow-shaped
   (C) candid
   (D) pugnacious
   (E) unprepared

5. QUESTIONABLE:
   (A) shady
   (B) respective
   (C) concentrated
   (D) insupportable
   (E) authoritative

6. HONE:
   (A) intensify
   (B) curtail
   (C) dull
   (D) classify
   (E) condemn

7. EXPUNGE:
   (A) retaliate
   (B) absorb
   (C) restore
   (D) re-edit
   (E) relieve

8. GARRULOUS:
   (A) condescending
   (B) exhausting
   (C) surly
   (D) taciturn
   (E) voluble

9. TENDENTIOUS:
   (A) blasé
   (B) nonchalant
   (C) unbiased
   (D) competitive
   (E) aggressive

10. EFFULGENT:
    (A) murky
    (B) revered
    (C) catatonic
    (D) unresponsive
    (E) unknown

Each of the reading passages below is followed by several questions about the contents of the passage. In answering the questions, base your responses on what is *stated* or *implied* in the passage.

Most milestones in the auto industry are occasion for celebration. When the fifty thousandth car comes off the line, the hundred thousandth transmission, the first this, or the last that, Detroit indulges in a little ritual of celebration and self-congratulation.

There is one milestone, however, that passed unobserved by the auto firms—the tenth anniversary of the National Highway Traffic Safety Act. The Act, effective September 1966, created a new government agency—the National Highway Traffic Safety Administration—empowered to force car producers to recall and repair defective automobiles.

This piece of legislation has humbled and humiliated the car companies, caused a few auto execs to lose their jobs or suffer demotion and, the deepest hurt of all, cost carmakers untold millions, perhaps billions, of dollars.

In the first ten years that NHTSA watchdogged Detroit, carmakers have recalled 41,292,109 U.S.-made cars and 7,786,205 foreign vehicles.

How can one industry go wrong so often? Who's responsible for the blunders? How do they happen? Why do they happen?

From the time an auto company or supplier receives the raw materials until the finished product is shipped to a dealer, there are millions of opportunities for error. The companies make mistakes in design and engineering, in the fabrication process, in the assembly process, in preproduction testing. Workers make mistakes in putting the pieces together. Production equipment can malfunction, testing equipment can go haywire. One small part can have as many as one hundred specifications. Multiply that by the fifteen thousand parts in a car and the chances for error become astronomical.

In addition to human error and the unforeseen, recalls also result from carmakers' being penny-wise and pound-foolish. If you use twelve washers to a car and can use a washer costing six-tenths of a cent instead of a penny, and can freeze the design of the washer so the same item can be used over several model years, you're talking big savings. But if the washer fails, leading to a recall, the company is in big trouble.

The companies won't release cost figures on recalls, but there are some ballpark numbers available. A minor recall can cost $5 million to $10 million; a major recall, $25 million to $50 million. And recalls are embarrassing. Although a company may recall only 50,000 cars out of a production of 1,000,000, the 50,000 callbacks reflect unfavorably on the 950,000 good cars. Most people remember the name of the company that manufactured a lemon—Acme Motors—and not the name of the particular Acme model recalled.

11. Of the statements below, the one that is not a stated or implied effect of the National Highway Traffic Safety Act is
   (A) recalls have cost car manufacturers huge sums of money
   (B) government is under attack for interfering in private enterprise
   (C) some Detroit bigwigs have lost their positions
   (D) car manufacturers have had to admit mistakes
   (E) recalls hurt manufacturers' reputations

12. The approximate number of vehicles recalled during the first ten years under NHTSA was
   (A) 42 million
   (B) 49 million
   (C) 100,000
   (D) 7 million
   (E) millions, perhaps billions

13. The phrase "penny-wise and pound-foolish" used in paragraph 7 means
   (A) instead of costing six-tenths of a cent, a washer costs a penny
   (B) a foolish and petty economy may result in a large loss
   (C) instead of twelve washers, carmakers should use a pound
   (D) recall of washing machines costs as much as recall of autos
   (E) carmakers are very wise to economize

14. A recall can cost from
    (A) $5 million to $10 million
    (B) $100 to $15,000
    (C) $50,000 to $1,000,000
    (D) $50,000 to $950,000
    (E) $5 million to $50 million

15. The reason that the tenth anniversary of the NHTSA was not celebrated by the carmakers is that
    (A) automakers were too busy with new regulations
    (B) the cost of recalls made a celebration too expensive
    (C) it conflicted with the milestone of the hundred thousandth transmission
    (D) automakers were stung for millions, perhaps billions in costs for recalls under this legislation
    (E) car buyers questioned the effectiveness of the Act

Those who wield the thunder of the state may have more confidence in the efficacy of arms. But I confess, possibly for want of this knowledge, my opinion is much more in favor of prudent management, than of force; considering force not as an odious but a feeble instrument for preserving a people so numerous, so active, so growing, so spirited as this, in profitable and subordinate connection with us.

First, Sir, permit me to observe, that the use of force alone is but temporary. It may subdue for a moment; but it does not remove the necessity of subduing again: and a nation is not governed, which is perpetually to be conquered.

My next objection is uncertainty. Terror is not always the effect of force; and an armament is not a victory. If you do not succeed, you are without resource; for, conciliation failing, force remains; but force failing, no further hope of reconciliation is left.

A further objection to force is, that you impair the object by your very endeavors to preserve it. The thing you fought for is not the thing which you recover; but depreciated, sunk, wasted, and consumed in the contest. Nothing less will content me than whole America. I do not choose to consume its strength along with our own; because in all parts it is the British strength that I consume.

Lastly, we have no sort of experience in favor of force as an instrument in the rule of our colonies. Their growth and their utility has been owing to methods altogether different. These, Sir, are my reason for not entertaining that high opinion of untried force, by which many gentlemen, for whose sentiments in other particulars I have great respect, seem to be so greatly captivated.

16. An argument not stated or implied by the author is that
    (A) the use of force destroys that which it would attain
    (B) force may have to be used over and over again
    (C) the use of force is spiritually and morally offensive
    (D) the use of force leaves no hope for reconciliation
    (E) force does not always succeed as a deterrent

17. The author's purpose in this passage seems to be
    (A) to suggest modifications in the terms of a peace treaty
    (B) to persuade the British to surrender
    (C) to bring about reconciliation through negotiation
    (D) to advocate the use of economic sanctions rather than force
    (E) to imply, by presenting them disdainfully, that the arguments against force are not valid

18. It can be inferred from this passage that the author would have
    (A) approved a policy of armed intervention in Vietnam
    (B) opposed the establishment of the United Nations
    (C) advocated the occupation of Cuba to depose Castro
    (D) proposed the saturation bombing of Belfast to end Irish terrorist activities in England
    (E) favored direct confrontation of Middle East peace problems through face-to-face negotiations

19. In the last sentence of the passage, the author is saying
(A) he has a high opinion of those who favor force
(B) he has great respect for sentiment
(C) that force can be applied only by gentlemen
(D) that although he may respect their views in other matters, he cannot accept the position of those who advocate force
(E) that those who oppose him are the captives of the Americans, who consume British strength

20. In setting forth his argument, the author uses an approach that can best be described as
(A) satirical
(B) judgmental
(C) hostile
(D) pragmatic
(E) apologetic

At Altamira and in the painted caves of the Dordogne there are paleolithic bisons that might have been drawn by Degas. On the walls of the rock shelters of a later age there are neolithic figures that might have been drawn by a child of seven. And yet all the evidence conclusively shows that the men of the New Stone Age were incomparably more intelligent and accomplished than their Magdalenian ancestors. The seeming degeneration of neolithic art is in fact an advance. For it marks an increase in the power of generalization. When he drew his bisons, the paleolithic medicine man was simply putting an outline round his visual memories. The neolithic artist worked in a different way. What he set down was a set of hieroglyphical symbols, each representing an intellectual abstraction. A circle—that stood for Head; an egg for Body; four lines for Arms and Legs.

Neolithic man, it is evident, had learned to think mainly in words—real conceptual words, not mere noises expressive of emotional states. Apes have emotional noises, but no names for classes of objects. The language of paleolithic man was probably not very unlike the language of apes. He must have found it difficult to make noises when

emotionally calm. (An unexcited dog cannot bark.) Noises that were intellectual abstractions—these he was only just learning to make. His power of generalization was therefore extremely feeble. He thought in terms of particular images. Hence the snapshot realism of his bisons—a realism which is only recaptured when men, grown very highly civilized, discover a technique for forgetting that art of abstraction, which made civilization possible, and learn to look at the world again with the unprejudiced eyes of beings who do not yet know how to speak. Nature, then, does not change; but the outlines that man sees in nature, the tunes he hears, the eternities he imaginatively apprehends—these, within certain limits, are continuously changing.

21. According to the author,
(A) the realism of paleolithic man's art showed him to be more advanced than neolithic man
(B) dogs cannot bark
(C) the power of generalization stems from conceptual language
(D) the language of neolithic man does not differ from that of the apes
(E) the art of abstraction has been forgotten

22. The author attempts to convince the reader of the primitive state of paleolithic man's development by
(A) citing the realism of paleolithic man's art as evidence of his inability to generalize
(B) adducing proof that apes have successfully employed conceptual language
(C) comparing the art of modern man with that of neolithic man
(D) saying that paleolithic man was too emotional to develop conceptual language
(E) implying that the gains of neolithic man were lost with the emergence of paleolithic man

23. The author's purpose in contrasting the art of paleolithic man with that of neolithic man is
    (A) to show that neolithic man's art had regressed
    (B) to show that neolithic man had the skill of a child of seven
    (C) to prove that paleolithic man was capable of generalization
    (D) to show that neolithic man was capable of abstraction and generalization
    (E) to show that Degas was influenced by the cave paintings at Altamira

24. With which of the following statements would the author most likely be in disagreement?
    (A) The nature of a people's art reveals the level of development of that people.
    (B) Man constantly revises his vision of Nature.
    (C) The ability of man to generalize was an important upward change in his development.
    (D) Neolithic man stood in the same relationship to paleolithic man as paleolithic man did to the ape.
    (E) The ability of man to think in particular images marks his highest level of development since it permitted him to understand Nature and the eternities.

25. The last sentence would support the conclusion that
    (A) Beethoven's music is superior to Chopin's
    (B) the author would prefer Rembrandt to Picasso
    (C) even the most abstract modern painting is a valid expression of man's view of the universe
    (D) modern art is far inferior to the art of the old masters
    (E) contemporary art cannot be condoned since it depicts a changing universe, and Nature does not change

Each of the sentences below has one or more blank spaces indicating where a word (or words) has been omitted. Each sentence is followed by five words or sets of words lettered from (A) to (E). Select the lettered word or set of words which, inserted to replace the blanks, *best* fits in with and completes the meaning of the sentence as a whole.

26. Don Carlos and his contemporaries _____ left their mountain _____ valley, even for a trip to La Paz.
    (A) hurriedly . . green
    (B) frequently . . clouded
    (C) deliberately . . trapped
    (D) seldom . . girded
    (E) never . . cluttered

27. Euphemistically called "inventory losses" by most department stores, _____ by employees continues as one of the major problems _____ retailers everywhere.
    (A) arbitrage . . offending
    (B) absenteeism . . hurting
    (C) vandalism . . obstructing
    (D) purchasing . . affecting
    (E) pilferage . . plaguing

28. His reputation for probity was such that his testimony, though it was _____ by that of others, was considered by most to be _____.
    (A) overturned . . one-sided
    (B) corroborated . . unacceptable
    (C) contradicted . . ineffable
    (D) refuted . . incontrovertible
    (E) substantiated . . libelous

29. The law can _____ be said to be the belated ratification of a coup, secretly devised by a cabal; _____, it represents the result of our full bicameral procedures.
    (A) in due measure . . truly
    (B) hardly . . for which reason
    (C) by no means . . rather
    (D) absolutely . . therefore
    (E) perhaps . . consequently

30. Some believe that crime is caused by economic disadvantage, but this belief is not _____ with the findings of research; studies have shown the poor to be as observant of the law as _____.

(A) consonant . . the well-to-do
(B) supported . . the average
(C) in disagreement . . felons
(D) in accord . . ever
(E) responsive . . their peers

In each of the questions below, a related pair of words or phrases, in capital letters, is followed by five pairs of words or phrases lettered from (A) to (E). Select that lettered pair which expresses a relationship that is *most* similar to that of the capitalized pair.

31. HAT : BRIM ::
(A) seam : dress
(B) coat : lapel
(C) crown : jewel
(D) pocket : flap
(E) cap : gown

32. CRUMPLE : FOLD ::
(A) wrinkle : dirty
(B) fall : push
(C) scissors : knife
(D) tear : cut
(E) rankle : rumble

33. WHITHER : WHENCE ::
(A) destination : origin
(B) going : coming
(C) if : unless
(D) hereafter : heretofore
(E) since : before

34. PILLAR : CEILING ::
(A) trunk : tree
(B) comfort : grief
(C) corroboration : alibi
(D) pride : accomplishment
(E) tension : tranquility

35. RUBBER : ELASTICITY ::
(A) iron : pliability
(B) helium : flexibility
(C) steel : rigidity
(D) synthetics : artificiality
(E) wood : plasticity

36. RAISIN : PRUNE ::
(A) grape : plum
(B) apricot : currant
(C) orange : grapefruit
(D) kumquat : mango
(E) orange : marmalade

37. SCORE : MOZART ::
(A) virtuosity : Cliburn
(B) cello : Casals
(C) script : playwright
(D) blueprint : architect
(E) painting : Picasso

38. SAFETY VALVE : BOILER ::
(A) fuse : motor
(B) house : wire
(C) jack : tire
(D) brake : automobile
(E) extinguisher : fire

39. LORD : FEUDALISM ::
(A) laissez-faire : tariff
(B) conservative : radical
(C) child : parent
(D) entrepreneur : capitalism
(E) castle : farm

40. GOURMET : FINE FOOD ::
(A) numismatist : stamps
(B) lepidopterist : butterfly
(C) painter : canvas
(D) mycologist : germs
(E) entomologist : words

STOP
WOR'. ONLY ON THIS SECTION UNTIL THE TIME ALLOTTED IS OVER.

SECTION III

Time—30 minutes

40 Questions

For each of the numbered questions in this section, choose the best answer according to the instructions, and blacken the corresponding blank space on the answer sheet.

In each of the questions below, a capitalized word is followed by five words or phrases lettered (A) through (E). Select the word or phrase *most nearly opposite* in meaning to the capitalized word.

Since some of the questions require that you distinguish fine shades of meaning, consider all choices carefully before you select your answer.

1. SLANDER:
   (A) glorify
   (B) expand
   (C) disdain
   (D) categorize
   (E) empathize

2. FIDELITY:
   (A) volume
   (B) dispersion
   (C) heterodoxy
   (D) reality
   (E) perfidy

3. NEGLIGIBLE:
   (A) picayune
   (B) careless
   (C) significant
   (D) liable
   (E) reliable

4. BOORISH:
   (A) interesting
   (B) urbane
   (C) jejune
   (D) loutish
   (E) corpulent

5. FORTIFY:
   (A) enfeeble
   (B) besiege
   (C) strengthen
   (D) quarter
   (E) accentuate

6. EQUITABLE:
   (A) variable
   (B) unfair
   (C) imperturbable
   (D) undecided
   (E) unshakable

7. NEBULOUS:
   (A) galactic
   (B) vapid
   (C) ambiguous
   (D) distinct
   (E) viscous

8. CLANDESTINE:
   (A) glowing
   (B) confined
   (C) unsung
   (D) overt
   (E) indirect

9. LACONIC:
   (A) intemperate
   (B) stoic
   (C) epicurean
   (D) heterosexual
   (E) verbose

10. IMMISCIBLE:
    (A) returnable
    (B) mixable
    (C) redeemable
    (D) sorted
    (E) corruptible

Each of the sentences below has one or more blank spaces indicating where a word (or words) has been omitted. Each sentence is followed by five words or sets of words lettered from (A) through (E). Select the lettered word or set of words which, inserted to replace the blanks, *best* fits in with and completes the meaning of the sentence as a whole.

11. Faraday had two qualities that more than made up for his _____ of education: fantastic intuition, and independence and _____ of mind.
(A) excellence . . sterility
(B) lack . . originality
(C) abhorrence . . inflexibility
(D) scorn . . ambiguity
(E) want . . vacuity

12. When beings become biologically dependent on the group, and existence is impossible without the _____ of one's fellows, then the _____ resolution of natural disagreement becomes a form of suicide as emphatic as the migration of the lemmings.
(A) knowledge . . ideological
(B) gratification . . final
(C) sympathy . . futile
(D) cooperation . . violent
(E) concurrence . . fatal

13. While adolescents feel an overwhelming need for escaping family to achieve _____, they also experience a vast and urgent need for personal _____.
(A) independence . . security
(B) self-realization . . success
(C) the heights . . debasement
(D) understanding . . reminiscence
(E) isolation . . solitude

14. Some economists believe that America is running out of the resources we need to build a prosperous and dynamic future, contending that we have _____ our natural _____ by wasteful and extravagant practices in the past.
(A) undermined . . future
(B) mortgaged . . wonders
(C) stripped . . splendor
(D) manifested . . destiny
(E) squandered . . patrimony

15. A formal summary is a _____ restatement of a passage, without comment and with nothing _____ that is essential to the development of the ideas in the passage.
(A) short . . precluded
(B) concise . . omitted
(C) verbatim . . added
(D) verbose . . implied
(E) figurative . . included

16. The only purpose for which _____ can be rightfully exercised over any member of a _____ community, against his will, is to prevent harm to others.
(A) threats . . rural
(B) a writ . . foreign
(C) power . . civilized
(D) authorization . . free
(E) forbearance . . cooperative

17. The basis on which good repute in any highly organized industrial community ultimately rests is _____ strength; and the means of showing pecuniary strength are leisure and a _____ consumption of goods.
(A) moral . . minimal
(B) not . . complete
(C) peculiar . . perspicuous
(D) pecuniary . . conspicuous
(E) physical . . violent

18. The simplicity of the theory of making corrugated boxes and sheets is _____ belied by the _____ of the huge machines which make them.
(A) perversely . . complexity
(B) rather . . cumbersomeness
(C) not . . fragility
(D) forthrightly . . efficiency
(E) horribly . . fearsomeness

19. Because we are a civilized nation, we presume all people innocent of crime unless proven guilty, but I would not rely on that _____ if I were you and found myself in a courtroom accused of crime.
    (A) sentiment
    (B) outcome
    (C) presumption
    (D) supposition
    (E) hope

20. John Milton, the Puritan poet, was complex in character: dogmatic in certain matters, flexible in others; diffident yet _____ ; _____ at home, catholic abroad.
    (A) irreverent . . parochial
    (B) unoriginal . . irreligious
    (C) cantankerous . . sardonic
    (D) arrogant . . provincial
    (E) pertinacious . . provocative

In each of the questions below, a related pair of words or phrases, in capital letters, is followed by five pairs of words or phrases lettered from (A) to (E). Select that lettered pair which expresses a relationship that is *most* similar to that of the capitalized pair.

21. COTTON : FABRIC ::
    (A) flower : aster
    (B) chestnut : wood
    (C) glass : vase
    (D) telephone : communication
    (E) horse : carriage

22. TOOTH : FILLING ::
    (A) bone : graft
    (B) eyes : spectacles
    (C) puncture : patch
    (D) fracture : crutch
    (E) pothole : bump

23. PITCHER : BALL ::
    (A) fielder : throw
    (B) quarterback : pass
    (C) forward : shoot
    (D) lineman : block
    (E) batter : strike

24. NEMESIS : RETRIBUTION ::
    (A) liar : mendicancy
    (B) advocate : renunciation
    (C) referee : partiality
    (D) benefactor : assistance
    (E) nitwit : wisdom

25. AMUSEMENT : HILARITY ::
    (A) indignation : fury
    (B) sorrow : sadness
    (C) futility : uselessness
    (D) cough : sneeze
    (E) joke : jest

26. INCORRIGIBLE : REFORMED ::
    (A) harsh : bitter
    (B) coarse : rough
    (C) untenable : defended
    (D) crusty : lovable
    (E) surreptitious : sneaky

27. CONSTANTINOPLE : ISTANBUL ::
    (A) Paris : Lyons
    (B) London : New London
    (C) Troy : Aleppo
    (D) Turkey : Turkestan
    (E) Petrograd : Leningrad

28. PTARMIGAN : GNAT ::
    (A) bird : bee
    (B) reed : rood
    (C) column : aplomb
    (D) bred : bread
    (E) breadth : breath

29. GENERAL : COMMANDS ::
    (A) ransom : demands
    (B) soldier : salutes
    (C) skater : glides
    (D) diplomat : quibbles
    (E) senator : legislates

30. AMBIGUOUS : EQUIVOCAL ::
    (A) sanctimonious : hypocritical
    (B) doubtful : indubitable
    (C) effervescent : evanescent
    (D) inflammable : incombustible
    (E) animated : enervated

Each of the reading passages below is followed by several questions about the contents of the passage. In answering the questions, base your responses on what is *stated* or *implied* in the passage.

In short, like the medieval guildsman, the Great Lakes fisherman has secret knowledge. He holds a bounty of natural wisdom locked in his head, some passed on from his father, some drawn from even earlier generations. By contrast, anyone who ever came to this business with no background did so at a severe and dangerous disadvantage. Fish are a cash crop and fishermen must live on their daily income, so an outsider who does not know the territory or the fish could starve before he is well started in the business. All of this produces in the survivors a central vein of blunt practicality and an absolutely undentable core of personal independence.

This practicality shows up in the boats these men designed for their work. Virtually all these boats are different, yet most are much alike in their appearance. And nothing beats a 1930s Great Lakes gill net fish tug for ugliness. They look like thirty-nine-foot outhouses plunked down lopsided on forty-foot dishpans. They perch so high on the water you expect them to turn turtle at the first puff of wind. Their small, beady-eyed windows look out suspiciously on the lakes, as though glaring at ancient enemies. As a class, they have gathered more scales over the years than all the fish they seek. When painted, which is seldom, the color is inevitably a gray not found on any color chart; when repaired, which is often, the standard materials are pie tins and tar or tar paper and roofing nails or window glass and plywood. And they are durable.

But looks are one thing and work is another. For use in commercial fishing, these tough little boats incorporate a full range of practical virtues. Although perched high on the water, they are amazingly stable craft. Sleet and snow cannot ice the nets stored inside. A five-ton following sea slapping that blunt stern simply means a faster passage home. The small windows and durable materials are inexpensive and long lasting. And no fisherman was ever expected to love his boat for its looks. What he designed and built was what he needed for his work, and it is a tribute to the canny ways of his forebears that the design of the twenties and thirties is still used in the few steel tugs now being built.

31. A serious disadvantage for an outsider entering the Great Lakes fishery is that
(A) he does not have natural wisdom locked in his head
(B) fish are a cash crop, and a newcomer would not have enough credit
(C) fishermen live on what they catch and sell each day, and a newcomer could starve while he was learning where to fish, and how.
(D) the other fishermen come from a better background
(E) he would have to develop the kind of blunt practicality which was passed on to the others by earlier generations

32. Of the following statements, which is (are) true of the Great Lakes gill net fish tug?
   I. Though ugly, virtually all these boats are the same in basic design, yet they are all quite unlike each other in appearance.
   II. Contrary to the way they look, these boats are amazingly stable.
   III. The small windows and the sturdy materials are inexpensive and durable.
(A) I and III only
(B) II only
(C) III only
(D) I, II, and III
(E) II and III only

33. Proof of the fact that the Great Lakes gill net fish tug was a successful design can be found in
(A) the fact that it can be repaired with tar paper
(B) the statement that nothing beats them for ugliness, but their owners love them for their looks
(C) the fact that the few steel tugs now being built still use the same old design
(D) the author's statement that these tough little boats incorporate a full range of practical virtues
(E) the author's words: sleet and snow cannot ice the nets stored inside

34. The word "bounty" as used in the second sentence of the first paragraph most nearly means
    (A) treasure
    (B) cash reward
    (C) small amount
    (D) mishmash
    (E) paucity

35. In the passage, the author uses all of the following *except*
    (A) simile
    (B) metaphor
    (C) contrast
    (D) generalization
    (E) documentation

"We are all in the gutter, but some of us are looking at the stars," wrote Oscar Wilde about life. The same applies to language: We all make mistakes (somebody just wrote in to point out a badly constructed sentence in one of my columns), but some of us at least try to maintain standards. It is not easy, and the best may stumble. Thus the worthy Irving Howe writes, in the first page of *The New York Times Book Review* (April 19), about "main protagonists." Now, the protagonist is *the* main actor in something and has, since Greek times, always been in the singular. "Protagonists" is incorrect (unless you refer to the protagonists of two or more dramas), and "main protagonists" (main main actors) is redundant to boot. A double-barreled error, but even the ablest among us, harried by the exigencies of rapid-fire journalism, are not immune to lapses.

What worries me more is rock-bottom illiteracy: in the gutter and looking at the sewers. David Sheff of *New West* sent me a good-sized National Airlines poster the other day, depicting a charming flight attendant (formerly stewardess) and bearing this caption: "Watch us shine with more flight's to Houston." Be honest: did your jaw drop when you read that "flight's"? I showed the poster to some civilized friends, and it took them quite a bit of prodding to notice the howler. So there you have it: Half the population (I guess) thinks that any plural ending in *s* requires an apostrophe, and the other half stands idly by without squirming, if, in fact, it even notices.

Where does all this come from? Who is the chief culprit? Surely, the schools, both lower and higher,

and the distemper of the times that influences them. Let me give you examples. Jim Deutsch of Greenville, Mississippi, has just sent me a copy of a letter published in *American Studies International* (Winter 1977), in which Toby Fulwiler protests what seems to be a fairly obvious plagiarism of a paper he wrote. But he twice misspells plagiarize as *plagerize*, which the editors duly note with a *sic*. If Mr. Fulwiler is that concerned with plagiarism, he might at least ascertain how it is spelled, especially since he is the Director of Freshman English at Michigan Technological University. It is clear, furthermore, that he knows neither Latin (*Plagiarius*: a kidnapper) nor any major modern language in which the spelling of the word is made manifest by the pronunciation, e.g., French (plagiat) or German (Plagiat). But it may be asking too much of a contemporary director of freshman English that he know other languages; English, though, should still be part of his competency.

36. The author's primary purpose in this passage is to
    (A) draw attention to the errors made by critics and professors
    (B) draw attention to the fact that he himself makes errors in sentence construction
    (C) make his readers conscious of the need to maintain standards
    (D) protest the use of redundancies
    (E) impress us with his knowledge of Greek

37. In his last sentence, the author, to make a point about Mr. Fulwiler's error, uses
    (A) broad generalization
    (B) irony
    (C) analogy
    (D) repetition
    (E) ellipsis

38. Which person does the author criticize most harshly?
    (A) Irving Howe
    (B) David Sheff
    (C) Jim Deutsch
    (D) The editors of *American Studies International*
    (E) Toby Fulwiler

39. Of the following, the error not mentioned in the passage is
(A) improper use of the apostrophe for possessives
(B) incorrect spelling
(C) sentence structure
(D) use of an apostrophe to indicate a plural ending
(E) incorrect diction

40. The word "exigencies" as used [in the] sentence of the first paragraph means
(A) enemies
(B) poverty
(C) persistence
(D) urgencies
(E) philosophies

STOP
WORK ONLY ON THIS SECTION UNTIL THE TIME ALLOTTED IS OVER.

Time—30 minutes

35 Questions

In the mathematical sections, use any available space on the page for scratchwork in solving problems. Then indicate the *one* correct answer by darkening the appropriate oval on the answer sheet.

You may wish to refer to the following formulas and relationships in solving some of the problems.

Triangle:
The sum of the angles of any triangle is one straight angle, or 180 degrees.

The area of a triangle $= \frac{1}{2}$ (base $\times$ altitude).

In a right triangle, the square of the hypotenuse $=$ the sum of the squares of the legs.

Circle of radius r:
Area $= \pi r^2$
Circumference $= 2\pi r$
There are 360 degrees of arc in a circle.

Definitions of Symbols
$=$ is equal to $\leq$ is less than or equal to
$\neq$ is unequal to $\geq$ is greater than or equal to
$<$ is less than $\parallel$ is parallel to
$>$ is greater than $\perp$ is perpendicular to

Note: Figures are drawn as accurately as possible *except* when it is stated in a specific problem that its figure is not drawn to scale. All figures lie in a plane unless otherwise indicated. All numbers used in this test are real numbers.

1. If $36 < K^2 < 64$ and K is a positive integer, then $K =$
   (A) 6
   (B) 7
   (C) 8
   (D) 36
   (E) 49

2. How much money can be saved by buying 60 ball-point pens at $2 per dozen than by buying them for 20¢ each.
   (A) $4.50
   (B) $3.40
   (C) $3.00
   (D) $2.40
   (E) $2.00

3.

In the figure, $PR = 30$, $PQ = 6$ and M is the midpoint of QR. What is the length of MR?
   (A) 12
   (B) 15
   (C) 17
   (D) 18
   (E) $18\frac{1}{2}$

4. If $4p + 7q + 2p = 20p$, find p in terms of q.
   (A) $2q$
   (B) $7q - 14$
   (C) $14 - 7q$
   (D) $\frac{1}{2}q$
   (E) Cannot be determined from the information given

5. How many meters of fencing are needed to enclose a circular flower bed the radius of which is 7 meters?
   (A) 11
   (B) 22
   (C) 44
   (D) 66
   (E) 124

6. Two nations produce $\frac{1}{5}$ and $\frac{3}{10}$, respectively, of the world production of aluminum. What fraction of world production do the two nations produce together?
   (A) $\frac{2}{5}$
   (B) $\frac{1}{2}$
   (C) $\frac{1}{4}$
   (D) $\frac{3}{5}$
   (E) $\frac{2}{3}$

7. If a particular magazine costs m cents, how many magazines can you buy for d dollars?
   (A) $\frac{100m}{d}$
   (B) $\frac{d}{m}$
   (C) $\frac{100d}{m}$
   (D) $\frac{m}{d}$
   (E) $\frac{d}{100m}$

8. If 5 is 25% of $n + 5$, what does n equal?
   (A) 4
   (B) 15
   (C) 16
   (D) 20
   (E) 25

9. An equilateral triangle has a perimeter of p. If $\frac{2p}{3} = \frac{6}{7}$, then one side of the triangle is
   (A) $\frac{7}{2}$
   (B) $\frac{6}{7}$
   (C) $\frac{3}{2}$
   (D) $\frac{7}{6}$
   (E) $\frac{3}{7}$

10. If $x^2 = 36$ and $y^2 = 49$, what is the *least* possible value of $y - x$?
    (A) 1
    (B) -1
    (C) 13
    (D) -13
    (E) 6

11. A cube has an edge of 4. If the cube is split into cubes with edges of 2, what is the total surface area of the smaller cubes?
    (A) 32
    (B) 64
    (C) 96
    (D) 120
    (E) 192

12.

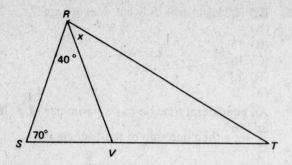

In triangle *RST* above, *RV* = *VT*. Find the number of degrees in angle *x*.
(A) 25
(B) 30
(C) 35
(D) 40
(E) 45

13. What percent of 15 pounds is 6 ounces?

(A) $2\frac{1}{2}$

(B) $12\frac{1}{2}$

(C) 25

(D) $37\frac{1}{2}$

(E) $62\frac{1}{2}$

14.

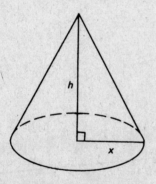

The formula for the volume, *V*, of a cone is *V* $= \frac{1}{3}Bh$ where *B* is the area of the circular base and *h* is the height of the cone. If the volume of the cone above is 32π and its height is 6, find the radius, *r*, of the circular base.

(A) 4π
(B) 7π

(C) $5\frac{1}{2}$

(D) 4
(E) 3

15. In triangle *PQR*, base *PQ* and altitude *RS* to this base have lengths equal to the same integer. Which of the following could *not* be the area of the triangle *PQR*?
(A) 1
(B) 2
(C) 8
(D) 18

(E) $24\frac{1}{2}$

16. A circle of radius *r* has a circumference equal to *c*. A square of side *r* has a perimeter equal to *p*. Which one of the following inequalities is correct?
(A) $O < C < p$
(B) $p < C < 2p$
(C) $2p < C < 3p$
(D) $2p < 2C < 3p$
(E) $3p < 3C < 4p$

17. If the ratio of *r* to *s* is 2 to 5 and the ratio of *s* to *t* is 3 to 4, then the ratio of *r* to *t* is

(A) $\frac{1}{2}$

(B) $\frac{2}{3}$

(C) $\frac{3}{10}$

(D) $\frac{8}{15}$

(E) $\frac{15}{8}$

Questions 18–35 each consist of two quantities, one in Column A and one in Column B. Compare the two quantities and on the answer sheet blacken oval

A if the quantity in Column A is greater;
B if the quantity in Column B is greater;
C if the two quantities are equal;
D if the relationship cannot be determined from the information given.

All letters such as x, y and n represent real numbers. A symbol appearing in both columns represents the same quantity in Column A as it does in Column B.

In some questions, information concerning one or both of the quantities to be compared is centered above the two columns.

Column A	Column B

18. 30% of 40   40% of 30

19. $(3n^2)$ $n < 0$ $3n^2$

20.

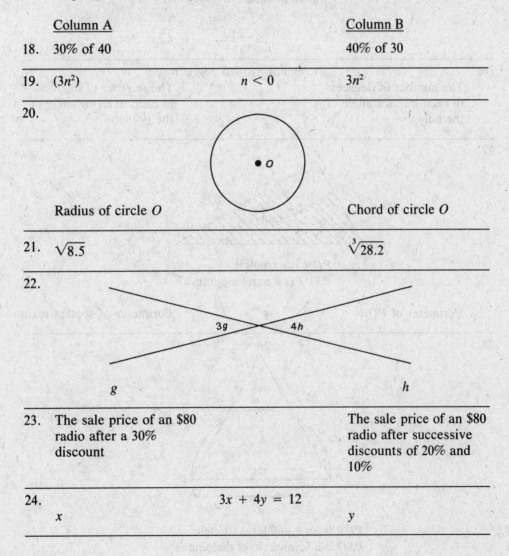

Radius of circle O Chord of circle O

21. $\sqrt{8.5}$ $\sqrt[3]{28.2}$

22.

$3g$ $4h$

      g h

23. The sale price of an $80 radio after a 30% discount   The sale price of an $80 radio after successive discounts of 20% and 10%

24. $3x + 4y = 12$

   x y

25.

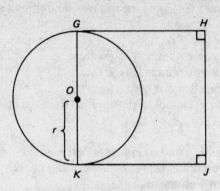

$$t = \frac{\text{area of circle } O}{\text{area of square } GHJK}$$

Column A	Column B
t	$\dfrac{3}{4}$

---

26. A regular n-sided polygon

Column A	Column B
The number of degrees in each interior angle of the polygon	The number of degrees in each exterior angle of the polygon

---

27.

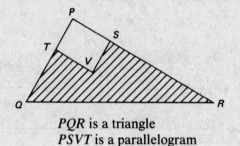

PQR is a triangle
PSVT is a parallelogram

Column A	Column B
Perimeter of PQR	Perimeter of shaded region

28.

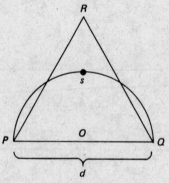

PQR is an equilateral triangle
PSQ is a semicircle of diameter d

Column A	Column B
Area of triangle	Area of semicircle

Column A	Column B

29. The number of prime factors of 330 — The number of prime factors of 210

30.
$$\frac{p}{7} = \frac{7}{p}$$

$$p < 0$$

$\dfrac{p}{14}$ — $-\dfrac{1}{7}$

31.
$$rst = 0,\ r > s$$

rt — st

---

32. y^2 — $y(y + 2)$

Questions 33–35 refer to the figure below.

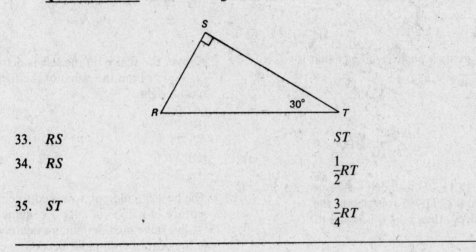

33. RS — ST

34. RS — $\dfrac{1}{2}RT$

35. ST — $\dfrac{3}{4}RT$

STOP
WORK ONLY ON THIS SECTION UNTIL THE TIME ALLOTTED IS OVER.

1. If $y + \dfrac{2}{7} = \dfrac{5}{7}$, then $y + \dfrac{1}{7} =$

    (A) $\dfrac{3}{7}$

    (B) $\dfrac{4}{7}$

    (C) $\dfrac{5}{7}$

    (D) 1

    (E) $\dfrac{8}{7}$

2. What is the greatest positive integer that is less than $\sqrt{340}$?
    (A) 15
    (B) 16
    (C) 17
    (D) 18
    (E) 19

3. If p is equal to 11,793 rounded to the nearest thousand and q is 11,793 rounded to the nearest hundred, then $p - q$ is equal to
    (A) 0
    (B) 100
    (C) 200
    (D) 300
    (E) 2000

4. Point R is on one side of a square and point S is on the opposite side. If the perimeter of the square is 36, what is the longest possible length of RS?
    (A) 8
    (B) 9

    (C) $9\sqrt{3}$

    (D) $5\sqrt{2}$

    (E) $9\sqrt{2}$

5. A produce salesman sells apples for 20¢ each and oranges for 25¢ each. If he sells $4.00 worth of apples and oranges what is the *least* number of apples he could have sold (not zero)?
    (A) 2
    (B) 3
    (C) 4
    (D) 5
    (E) 6

6.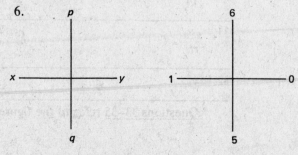

    Above, the figure on the left is defined as $(x + y)^{pq}$. Find the value of the figure above on the right.
    (A) 0
    (B) 1
    (C) 11
    (D) 30
    (E) 31

7. The cost of gold paint needed to cover the surface of a cube of edge 3 centimeters is $24. At the same cost per square centimeter, what is the cost of gold paint needed to cover the surface of a cube of edge 6 centimeters?
    (A) $6
    (B) $12
    (C) $24
    (D) $48
    (E) $96

8. If 9 short notes can be typed in 12 minutes, what is the number of such notes that can be typed in 8 hours at the same rate?
    (A) 40
    (B) 180
    (C) 360
    (D) 540
    (E) 600

9. A woman bowls 134, 145, and 150 in her first 3 games. What score must she make on her next game so that her average for the 4 games will be 149?
(A) 156
(B) 163
(C) 165
(D) 167
(E) 170

10. If the circumference of a circle is *numerically* equal to the area of the circle, the *circumference* of the circle is
(A) 4
(B) 2π
(C) $\pi\sqrt{2}$
(D) π
(E) 4π

11. In which of the following expressions can the 5's be cancelled out without changing the value of the expression?

(A) $\dfrac{p^5}{q^5}$

(B) $\dfrac{5p - q}{5}$

(C) $\dfrac{\dfrac{p}{5}}{\dfrac{5}{q}}$

(D) $\dfrac{5p^2 + 5q^2}{5}$

(E) $5p + 5q$

12. Peter lives 3 miles south of the school. Bill, who lives west of the school, finds that the direct distance from his house to Peter's is 1 mile shorter than the distance by way of the school. How many miles west of the school does Bill live?

(A) $\dfrac{3}{4}$ (D) $2\dfrac{1}{4}$

(B) $1\dfrac{1}{4}$ (E) $\sqrt{11}$

(C) $1\dfrac{3}{4}$

13. If $r > s$ and $s > t$, which of the following represents the *least* number?
(A) $t - r$
(B) $r - t$
(C) $s - t$
(D) $s - r$
(E) $t - s$

14.

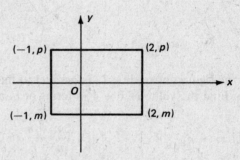

The area of the rectangle in the above figure is
(A) $p - m$
(B) $3(p - m)$
(C) $3(p + m)$
(D) $p + m$
(E) $3(m - p)$

15.

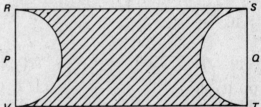

Given rectangle *RSTV* with semicircles *P* and *Q* with diameters of 10, as shown above. If *TV* = 25, what is the area of the shaded region?
(A) $250 - 20\pi$
(B) $250 - 50\pi$
(C) 225π
(D) $250 - 25\pi$

(E) $250 - \dfrac{25\pi}{2}$

16. If $p + q = 3n$ and $q + n = 4$, then, in terms of n, $p =$
(A) $4n + 4$
(B) $2n + 4$
(C) $2n - 4$
(D) $2n - 1$
(E) $4n - 4$

17.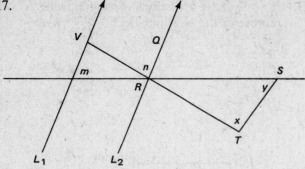

In the figure above, line L_1 is parallel to line L_2. Find the value of $x + y$ in terms of m and n.

(A) $m + n$

(B) $2m + 2n$

(C) $m - n$

(D) $\dfrac{2m + n}{m + n}$

(E) $\dfrac{2m + n}{2}$

18. If p is an integer, which of the following must also be integer(s)?

    I. $\dfrac{p + 3}{3}$

    II. $\dfrac{3p + 6}{3}$

    III. $\sqrt{p^2 - 2p + 1}$

(A) II only

(B) III only

(C) II and III only

(D) I and II only

(E) I, II, and III

19. An iron rod 85 centimeters long is cut into two pieces such that the length of the shorter is $\dfrac{2}{3}$ the length of the longer. How many centimeters in length is the shorter piece?

(A) 17

(B) 27

(C) 34

(D) 51

(E) 57

20. The degree measures of the three angles of a triangle are x, y, and z. If z is the average of x and y, find the value of z.

(A) 20°

(B) 40°

(C) 60°

(D) 90°

(E) It cannot be determined from the information given

21. A boy starts mowing a lawn at 10 a.m. and by 11:20 a.m. has finished $\dfrac{4}{5}$ of it. If he continues working at the same rate, at what time will he finish mowing the lawn?

(A) 11:36 a.m.

(B) 11:40 a.m.

(C) 11:52 a.m.

(D) 12:00 noon

(E) 12:40 p.m.

Questions 22 and 23 refer to the following graph.

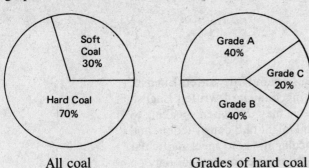

All coal   Grades of hard coal

22. The graphs above show the distribution of coal production in a certain state. The graph on the left shows the percentages of hard and soft coal and that on the right shows the distribution of grades of hard coal. What percent of the total production was grade B hard coal?
   (A) 14
   (B) 21
   (C) 28
   (D) 34
   (E) 40

23. In the circle graph on the left, how many degrees are there in the central angle of the sector for soft coal?
   (A) 108
   (B) 120
   (C) 144
   (D) 160
   (E) 252

24. If a theater ticket, including a 15% tax, costs $11.50, then the amount of the tax is
   (A) $.77
   (B) $1.00
   (C) $1.15
   (D) $1.50
   (E) $1.72

25. A cubic centimeter of a certain metal weighs 10 grams. What is the weight in grams of a cube of this metal that is 2 centimeters on each edge?
   (A) 20
   (B) 40
   (C) 50
   (D) 60
   (E) 80

STOP
WORK ONLY ON THIS SECTION UNTIL THE TIME ALLOTTED IS OVER.

Time—30 minutes

50 Questions

This section tests your ability to use standard written English, the kind used in more formal writing. Standard written English is quite different from the English we may use when speaking to friends. In the sentences below, you might find constructions and forms that you would use at particular times to meet particular needs, but you are being asked to determine correctness only on the basis of what would be acceptable in standard written English.

<u>Directions</u>: Some of the following sentences contain errors in grammar, usage, diction (choice of words), and idiom. Some of the sentences are correct. No sentence, however, contains more than one error. If a sentence has an error, it will be in one of the lettered and underlined words or phrases. Assume there are no errors in the parts of the sentence that are not underlined. *If there is an error in any underlined part, note the letter under it, and blacken the corresponding space on the answer sheet. If the sentence is free of errors, blacken answer space (E). Follow the guidelines for standard written English when determining the answer.*

1. The advertisement stated that the personnel office <u>was looking</u> for
                                                        A
   candidates who <u>were willing</u> to work long hours, <u>travel extensively</u>, and
                        B   C
   <u>have clerical skills</u>. <u>No error</u>
        D   E

2. <u>Despite</u> the many days of rehearsals, <u>not one</u> of the cast members had
      A   B
   <u>their</u> lines memorized <u>as the director had requested</u>. <u>No error</u>
      C   D   E

3. "<u>Any</u> messages for my sister <u>and I</u>?" asked Joanne when <u>she</u> stopped at
        A   B   C
   the desk after the <u>day's</u> outing. <u>No error</u>
                          D   E

4. Do you know <u>who</u> Mr. Johnson meant when <u>he referred</u> to the student
                    A   B
   <u>whose</u> work <u>was</u> incomplete. <u>No error</u>
      C   D   E

5. My <u>brother John</u> weighs more <u>than me</u>, although <u>we are</u> approximately
          A   B   C
   the <u>same</u> height. <u>No error</u>
          D   E

6. To be a superb cook, it is necessary to measure carefully, use only clean
   A   B

   utensils, and choosing all the ingredients with great discrimination.
                 C   D

   No error
   E

7. When a person is learning to drive, you must first study the rules of
                   A   B

   traffic and safety before getting behind the wheel. No error
   C   D   E

8. Graphologists believe that it is possible to determine from a single
                       A   B

   handwriting sample an individual's personality, character, and
                         C

   how he thinks. No error
   D   E

9. Next year's car buyers will have to pay almost ten times as much for a
        A

   compact model than they paid a decade ago for a car of similar size.
                B   C   D

   No error
   E

10. Mrs. Nolan is reputed to be the best of all the other cooks in the
                 A   B   C   D

    neighborhood. No error
                  E

11. Although Wendell had divided the day's catch evenly among the two
                                   A   B

    boys, Phil continued to complain that he had been given the smaller
                                             C   D

    share. No error
           E

12. Before last month's misadventure when the fishing boat capsized, no boat
                   A   B   C

    had ever sank in these waters. No error
    D   E

13. In his treatise on Shakespeare, Professor Brown made several illusions to
       A   B

    the historians from whose works Shakespeare had drawn material for his
                    C   D

    plays. No error
           E

14. The doctor objected to him going, maintaining that the stress and strain of
                        A   B

    a long journey could impede the progress of his recovery. No error
                     C   D   E

15. It has <u>long been</u> known that the earth, which seems so solid and
            A
    permanent, <u>is</u>, <u>in fact</u>, constantly changing, with earthquakes, volcanic
            B   C
    eruptions, and the rise of mountains giving evidence of <u>its</u> unsettled
                                                        D
    interior. <u>No error</u>
              E

16. Only one of the <u>crew members</u> in the <u>airline's</u> employ <u>lack</u> the credentials
                        A   B   C
    necessary <u>for overseas</u> flight. <u>No error</u>
                    D   E

17. Contrary to the <u>economists'</u> prediction that the <u>coming</u> inflation would be
                        A   B
    signaled by <u>a round</u> of wage increases, the salary index <u>has fell</u> slightly.
                    C   D
    <u>No error</u>
        E

18. <u>Being that</u> we were among the first to arrive, we had the opportunity to
        A
    examine <u>the offerings</u> and to estimate <u>their</u> value before the sale <u>began</u>.
                B   C   D
    <u>No error</u>
        E

19. The new maid opened the door timidly, stood uncertainly in the doorway
    <u>until</u>, as if <u>propelled</u>, she dashed into the room, <u>set</u> the plate down, and
        A   B   C
    <u>fled</u>. <u>No error</u>
        D   E

20. <u>Whose</u> to blame if current <u>taxation policies</u> of the federal government <u>are</u>
        A   B   C
    not <u>uniformly</u> applied at all economic levels of society? <u>No error</u>
            D   E

21. The people <u>who</u> remain my closest friends are those <u>which</u> share my
                A   B
    social values <u>and my</u> political <u>leanings</u>. <u>No error</u>
                        C   D   E

22. The <u>President's</u> impassioned plea for individual cooperation and corporate
            A
    <u>compliance with</u> his plan to halt inflation has had the <u>resultant effect</u> on
            B   C
    the stock market which <u>had been predicted</u>. <u>No error</u>
                                D   E

23. The first lesson that new recruits must learn <u>is</u> <u>obedience and respect for</u>
                                                   A   B

the rules <u>which govern</u> each and every aspect of life in the Marine <u>Corps</u>.
           C   D

<u>No error</u>
E

24. Although we <u>had had</u> time for farewells earlier, <u>I</u> objected to <u>them</u>
                 A   B   C

rushing <u>off</u> without a last embrace. <u>No error</u>
         D   E

25. <u>During</u> his many years <u>on the bench</u>, Judge Jones voted with the liberals
     A   B

<u>in the majority of</u> cases, and <u>being conservative</u> in only a small number of
         C   D

cases. <u>No error</u>
        E

Directions: In each of the sentences below, a part or the whole of the sentence is underlined. Following each sentence will be five different ways of writing the underlined segment—the first an exact repeat of the underlined original, the other four different. *If you think the underlined segment is correct as it stands, you will select choice (A) as your answer. If you think the underlined segment is incorrect as it stands, select the one of the remaining lettered choices that you think makes the sentence correct.* For whichever of the five lettered choices you select as correct, blacken the corresponding space on your answer sheet.

This portion of the examination tests your ability to determine correctness and effectiveness of expression according to the requirements of standard written English. You are to take into account grammar, diction (choice of words), sentence construction, and punctuation. *Do not select a version that changes the original sense of the sentence as given.* Choose the version that offers the clearest, most precise sentence according to the guidelines imposed.

26. Some teachers <u>try to not only teach subject matter but to also inculcate</u> ethical and spiritual values as well.
   (A) try to not only teach subject matter but to also inculcate
   (B) try not only to teach subject matter but also to inculcate
   (C) try, not only teaching subject matter, but inculcating also
   (D) try to teach subject matter and
   (E) try not to only teach subject matter but also to inculcate

27. Delores was not permitted to enter the school <u>because she had brung her dog with her</u>.
   (A) because she had brung her dog with her
   (B) since she had brung her dog with her
   (C) because she had brung her dog along with her
   (D) because her dog was with her
   (E) because she had brought her dog with her

28. The Mayor was, as usual, <u>late to the meeting, the people</u> showed their displeasure with him by booing.
    (A) late to the meeting, the people
    (B) late, to the meeting, the people
    (C) late to the meeting, and the people
    (D) late to the meeting the people
    (E) late to the meeting of the people who

29. <u>Charlotte inferred, with a sly wink</u>, that Viola was not to be trusted.
    (A) Charlotte inferred, with a sly wink,
    (B) Charlotte inferred with a sly wink,
    (C) Charlotte inferred with a sly wink
    (D) Charlotte implied, with a sly wink,
    (E) Charlotte implied with a sly wink,

30. <u>Brad asked incredulously, "Did he say, 'I'm not going to attend.'?"</u>
    (A) Brad asked incredulously, "Did he say, 'I'm not going to attend.'?"
    (B) Brad asked incredulously "Did he say, 'I'm not going to attend.'?"
    (C) Brad asked incredulously, "Did he say, 'I'm not going to attend?' "
    (D) Brad asked incredulously, "Did he say he wasn't going to attend?"
    (E) Brad, incredulous, asked if he said he wasn't going to attend.

31. We all knew <u>him to be skillful, perseverant, and he liked to have fun</u>.
    (A) him to be skillful, perseverant, and he liked to have fun
    (B) him to be skillful, persevering, and he liked to have fun
    (C) him to be skillful, perseverant, and fun-loving
    (D) he was skillful, perseverant, and he liked to have fun
    (E) he was skillful, perseverant and like to have fun

32. <u>Because he knew that the country home was not their's</u>, he refused the invitation to spend the Christmas holidays there.
    (A) Because he knew that the country home was not their's,
    (B) Knowing that the country home was not their's,
    (C) He, knowing that the country home was not their's,
    (D) Because he knew that the country home was not theirs,
    (E) Knowing that the country home was not theirs

33. The average consumer does not get
    <u>his money's worth all the time, but you soon get used to that</u>.
    (A) his money's worth all the time, but you soon get used to that
    (B) his money's worth all the time, but he soon gets used to that
    (C) his moneys worth all the time, but you soon get used to that
    (D) his money's worth all the time but you soon get used to that
    (E) their money's worth all the time, but you soon get used to that

34. <u>Its the only chance the team will have to play its rescheduled game</u>.
    (A) Its the only chance the team will have to play its rescheduled game.
    (B) Its the only chance the team will have, to play its rescheduled game.
    (C) Its the only chance the team will have to play it's rescheduled game.
    (D) It's the only chance the team will have to play its rescheduled game.
    (E) It's the only chance the team will have to play their rescheduled game.

35. The responsibility rests <u>on whoever approved the building plans</u>.
    (A) on whoever approved the building plans
    (B) on whosoever approved the building plans
    (C) on him who approved the building plans
    (D) on whomever approved the building plans
    (E) on whomever it was who approved the building plans

36. André Watts <u>has scarcely no equals</u> as a concert pianist.
    (A) has scarcely no equals
    (B) has scarcely an equal
    (C) has scarcely some equals
    (D) has few equals
    (E) has hardly no equals

37. It is easy <u>for we teachers to instruct students</u> in the use of the slide rule.
    (A) for we teachers to instruct students
    (B) for we, teachers, to instruct students
    (C) for us to instruct students
    (D) for us teachers how to instruct students
    (E) for us teachers to instruct students

38. <u>I have held this view five years ago, and I still hold it today</u>.
    (A) I have held this view five years ago, and I still hold it today.
    (B) I held this view five years ago, and I still hold it today.
    (C) Holding this view for five years, and I still hold it today.
    (D) I still hold this view of five years ago today.
    (E) I held this view for five years that I hold today.

39. <u>Practicing for the big game, Rod saw them at the stadium</u>.
    (A) Practicing for the big game, Rod saw them at the stadium.
    (B) Practicing for the big game Rod saw them at the stadium.
    (C) Practicing, Rod saw them at the stadium for the big game.
    (D) Practicing at the stadium, for the big game, they were seen by Rod.
    (E) Rod saw them practicing at the stadium for the big game.

40. He has <u>always been active and concerned about programs</u> for the handicapped.
    (A) always been active and concerned about programs
    (B) always been active in and concerned about programs
    (C) always been active in and concerned about programming
    (D) always been active, and concerned about programs
    (E) always been both active and concerned regarding programs

GO ON TO THE NEXT PAGE

The directions that follow are the same as those given at the beginning of this section. They are repeated for your convenience, for easy reference, as you work on the questions below.

<u>Directions</u>: Some of the following sentences contain errors in grammar, usage, diction (choice of words), and idiom. Some of the sentences are correct. No sentence, however, contains more than one error. If a sentence has an error, it will be in one of the lettered and underlined words or phrases. Assume there are no errors in the parts of the sentence that are not underlined. *If there is an error in any underlined part, note the letter under it, and blacken the corresponding space on the answer sheet. If the sentence is free of errors, blacken answer space (E).* Follow the guidelines for standard written English when determining the answer.

41. Eric's family <u>had immigrated</u> from Norway in the first decade of the new
                 A

    century, joining the eager throngs <u>who</u> sought the streets paved with gold
                                          B

    <u>about which</u> they <u>had been told</u>. <u>No error</u>
       C   D   E

42. <u>After looking over</u> the preparation materials, Matthew said, "It seems to
        A

    me that the examinations contain <u>hardly nothing</u> which we have not
                                   B

    studied; in fact, the unit <u>tests which</u> we took during the semester appear
                          C

    <u>to have been</u> equally difficult. <u>No error</u>
        D   E

43. <u>Feeling odd</u> in his civilian attire, he walked through the village looking for
       A

    familiar landmarks, aware <u>already</u> that the place he <u>had retained</u> in his
                        B   C

    mind's eye was very much <u>different than</u> this reality. <u>No error</u>
                       D   E

44. She <u>raced breathlessly</u> back to Ricardo, shouting, "I <u>can't bear</u> the beauty
          A   B

    of it all, the sun turning the <u>meadows gold</u>, the birds singing, and the
                              C

    flowers smelling <u>so sweetly</u>. <u>No error</u>
                 D   E

45. "I <u>couldn't of</u> done it," he explained, "<u>because</u> at the time this occurred,
        A   B

    I was <u>occupied</u> with my laboratory experiment, <u>and I</u> have my log to
         C   D

    prove it. <u>No error</u>
           E

46. Unable to decide <u>between</u> the tweed jacket and the <u>camel's hair</u>, he took
                   A   B

    <u>the both</u> of them, only to find, when he reached the cashier, that he
    C

    <u>had left</u> his checkbook at home. <u>No error</u>
    D   E

47. It isn't <u>like</u> she was <u>new to</u> the school; she had been a student <u>there</u> for
          A   B   C

    two years <u>prior to</u> the incident. <u>No error</u>
              D   E

48. It is important to take <u>one's</u> rings <u>off</u> before washing dishes, since
                            A   B

    <u>continuous</u> immersion in water may damage the stone or <u>weaken</u> the
    C   D

    setting. <u>No error</u>
            E

49. By the time the ambulance arrived, the old woman was <u>besides</u> herself
                                                     A

    with anxiety, unable to move from her husband's side, <u>yet fearing</u> that if
                                                B

    she did not personally conduct the attendants <u>to the site</u>, they might
                                                C

    somehow <u>fail to</u> find it. <u>No error</u>
            D   E

50. Although <u>the rise</u> in cattle production is <u>being felt</u> in the wholesale
            A   B

    markets, there are <u>less</u> varieties of prime cuts of beef to be found at the
                    C

    retail level <u>than before</u>. <u>No error</u>
              D   E

STOP
WORK ONLY ON THIS SECTION UNTIL THE TIME ALLOTTED IS OVER.

Answer Key
Practice Test 2

Section I

1.	C	13.	B	24.	B	35.	E
2.	B	14.	D	25.	A	36.	E
3.	B	15.	D	26.	D	37.	B
4.	C	16.	B	27.	C	38.	D
5.	D	17.	D	28.	B	39.	B
6.	C	18.	D	29.	E	40.	E
7.	A	19.	C	30.	D	41.	C
8.	A	20.	B	31.	E	42.	B
9.	B	21.	C	32.	D	43.	D
10.	C	22.	D	33.	B	44.	B
11.	A	23.	D	34.	D	45.	D
12	C						

Section II

1.	E	11.	B	21.	C	31.	B
2.	D	12.	B	22.	A	32.	D
3.	B	13.	B	23.	D	33.	A
4.	A	14.	E	24.	E	34.	C
5.	E	15.	D	25.	C	35.	C
6.	C	16.	C	26.	D	36.	A
7.	C	17.	C	27.	E	37.	E
8.	D	18.	E	28.	D	38.	A
9.	C	19.	D	29.	C	39.	D
10.	A	20.	D	30.	A	40.	B

Section III

1.	A	11.	B	21.	B	31.	C
2.	E	12.	D	22.	A	32.	E
3.	C	13.	A	23.	D	33.	C
4.	B	14.	E	24.	D	34.	A
5.	A	15.	B	25.	A	35.	E
6.	B	16.	C	26.	C	36.	C
7.	D	17.	D	27.	E	37.	B
8.	D	18.	A	28.	C	38.	E
9.	E	19.	C	29.	E	39.	A
10.	B	20.	D	30.	A	40.	D

How to Prepare for the Scholastic Aptitude Test (SAT)

Section IV

1.	B	10.	D	19.	A	28.	A
2.	E	11.	E	20.	D	29.	C
3.	A	12.	C	21.	B	30.	B
4.	D	13.	A	22.	A	31.	D
5.	C	14.	D	23.	B	32.	D
6.	B	15.	A	24.	D	33.	B
7.	C	16.	B	25.	A	34.	C
8.	B	17.	C	26.	D	35.	A
9.	E	18.	C	27.	C		

Section V

1.	B	8.	C	14.	B	20.	C
2.	D	9.	D	15.	D	21.	B
3.	C	10.	E	16.	E	22.	C
4.	E	11.	D	17.	A	23.	A
5.	D	12.	B	18.	C	24.	D
6.	B	13.	A	19.	C	25.	E
7.	E						

Section VI

1.	D	14.	A	27.	E	39.	E
2.	C	15.	E	28.	C	40.	B
3.	B	16.	C	29.	D	41.	A
4.	A	17.	D	30.	D	42.	B
5.	B	18.	A	31.	C	43.	D
6.	C	19.	E	32.	D	44.	D
7.	B	20.	A	33.	B	45.	A
8.	D	21.	B	34.	D	46.	C
9.	B	22.	C	35.	A	47.	A
10.	C	23.	B	36.	B	48.	C
11.	B	24.	C	37.	E	49.	A
12.	D	25.	D	38.	B	50.	C
13.	B	26.	B				

Explanatory Answers Practice Test 2

SECTION I

1. **C.** *Grave*: serious, solemn.
   Opposite: *frivolous*.

2. **B.** *Meager*: scanty.
   Opposite: *profuse*.

3. **B.** *Precede*: go before, preface.
   Opposite: *ensue*.

4. **C.** *Martial*: warlike.
   Opposite: *pacific*.

5. **D.** *Extol*: eulogize, praise highly.
   Opposite: *castigate*.

6. **C.** *Implicate*: involve as being concerned in a matter (as in a crime).
   Opposite: *absolve*, free from consequences, etc.

7. **A.** *Abhorrence*: detestation, loathing.
   Opposite: *adoration*.

8. **A.** *Munificent*: characterized by great generosity.
   Opposite: *penurious*.

9. **B.** *Obdurate*: unyielding.
   Opposite: *relenting*.

10. **C.** *Heinous*: abominable.
    Opposite: *admirable*.

11. **A.** *Credulous*: gullible.
    Opposite: *skeptical*, having doubt.

12. **C.** *Vindictive*: vengeful.
    Opposite: *forgiving*.

13. **B.** *Rigorous*: rigidly severe.
    Opposite: casual, *relaxed*.

14. **D.** *Bizarre*: markedly unusual, whimsically odd.
    Opposite: *normal*.

15. **D.** *Partial*: prejudiced in favor of a person, side, etc.
    Opposite: *disinterested*, absence of prejudice. "Uninterested" means having no interest, being indifferent.

16. **B.** A *virulent* disease, one that is highly infective or malignant (not malevolent) would certainly force someone to *curtail*, or cut short, his participation. No one can contract a congenital disease, since "congenital" means "existing at birth."

17. **D.** The word "other" tells us that the blank is like meat in makeup. The word of choice is *proteins*. In an exothermic process, we would expect that *heat* would be given off.

18. **D.** Logic tells us that propaganda is designed to increase the energy and arouse the will of the citizens to win. "Harness," "stimulate," and "nurture" are possible choices, but among second words, only *imbue* fits in from the point of view of meaning and linguistics. Usage forbids the constructions "arouse them with" or "include them with" to complete this sentence. *Imbue* means "to inspire."

19. **C.** The construction "while many . . . were . . . , many others were mere . . ." suggests that the blank will be in contrast to what is expressed at the outset. Many difficulties were "substantial," or of a material or tangible nature, while others were mere *apprehensions* or suspicions or fears of future troubles.

20. **B.** *Gills* are the respiratory organs for obtaining oxygen from water. The second word of choice is *breathe*.

21. **C.** The construction starting "While . . . " implies that her "natural" movements resulted from something quite different. (A) and (C) are both possibilities in terms of

being composed of opposites, but "logic" could hardly result in movement, natural or otherwise. The answer is *spontaneously . . discipline.*

22. **D.** *Claiming . . denying* is the only possible pair.

23. **D.** While all the choices indicate that Caldwell's feelings have suffered, only *lacerated*, which means "to tear roughly," is specific enough.

24. **B.** Logic tells us that the first blank must be filled by a verb that means "went," and that the adverb after the "but" must indicate that those who went, returned. The choice, therefore, is *fared . . always.*

25. **A.** The construction, "Even . . . when we do not seem to perspire . . . ," seems to call for the conclusion that we have insensible *perspiration.* The word *evaporation* fulfills the meaning of the sentence.

26. **D.** *Saturday* is followed by *Sunday*; the *eve* of a holiday is followed by the *holiday* itself.

27. **C.** A *spy* can be characterized as *secretive* in his behavior; similarly, a *fan* can be characterized as *partisan* in his behavior. While an elephant can be characterized as heavy, that characterization relates to physical appearance, not behavior.

28. **B.** A *glutton* has an excessive or obsessive desire for *food*, just as a *miser* has an excessive or obsessive desire for *money.*

29. **E.** A person is officially declared a *saint* at the ceremony of *canonization.* In the same manner, a person is officially declared a *king* at the ceremony of *coronation.*

30. **D.** *Prudery* is an excessive display of *modesty*; *Pedantry* is an excessive display of *scholarship.*

31. **E.** The *braggart* is not characterized by *humility* (the modest sense of one's importance); similarly, the *rebel* is not characterized by *conventionality* (accepted standards of behavior).

32. **D.** A *saw* can be used to cut a *log*, just as *scissors* can be used to cut *cloth.* A *jackknife*

can be used for whittling, but the *whittlings* would be analogous to sawdust, not a log.

33. **B.** A *storm* must *subside* eventually. *Energy* must *flag* (diminish or droop) eventually. We cannot say that a *rebellion* must *quell.* Rather, someone can quell a rebellion, but not all rebellions can be quelled eventually.

34. **D.** *Roosevelt*, upon his death, was succeeded in office by his vice-president, *Truman*, just as *Lincoln*, upon his death, was succeeded by his vice-president, *Johnson.*

35. **E.** We seek a *port* to find safety from a *storm*; similarly, we seek a *haven* to find safety from *oppression.*

36. **E.** The last sentence of paragraph 1 tells us that the noise was made by a calving glacier. The first sentence of the last paragraph makes clear that "calving" means breaking off of sections.

37. **B.** The food chain is given in the next-to-the-last sentence of the second paragraph.

38. **D.** In the last paragraph, the author says that the sound gave some perspective of the glacier's dimension. To the eye, the ice that broke away was insignificant, but to the ear, the sound was stentorian. We can infer that "stentorian" means very loud.

39. **B.** The third paragraph tells us what the voices of the glacier are. Sentence 3 refers to item IV, and sentences 4 and 5 refer to item III.

40. **E.** The first sentence of the last paragraph makes clear that "calving" means breaking up or splintering.

41. **C.** Sentence 5 states that "Dispute is possible as to the lasting artistic value and the ultimate perfection of his music . . . "

42. **B.** Sentence 7 gives the chain of transmission of musical ideas.

43. **D.** Fourth sentence from the end tells us Liszt used this principle in various symphonic poems and his concertos, rebutting item I. In the next sentence, the author states that this principle was used in the music of the seventeenth century, so Liszt could not have been the first to use it. Item III is affirmed by the paragraph's last sentence.

44. **B.** In the sentence that begins, "In the matter of musical form . . . ," the author points out why the term "cyclic" construction was applied to Liszt's work.

45. **D.** The answer cannot be (A), because the author says that he is concerned only with Liszt's use of the romantic ideas of his age, after referring to Liszt's biography in passing. Nor can the answer be (B), because the author is writing from the perspective of one familiar with the modern French and Russian schools. The content is too discursive and, perhaps, too limited in appeal to have been written by a feature writer. A musicologist, one concerned with musical analysis and history, would be a far more likely choice than a conductor, unless, of course, that conductor was, to some extent, a musicologist.

SECTION II

1. **E.** *Rapture*: ecstatic joy.
   Opposite: *depression*.

2. **D.** *Apathy*: lack of interest or concern.
   Opposite: *enthusiasm*.

3. **B.** *Secrete*: conceal, place out of sight.
   Opposite: *flaunt*, display ostentatiously.

4. **A.** *Sagacious*: wise.
   Opposite: *foolish*.

5. **E.** *Questionable*: open to dispute.
   Opposite: *authoritative*.

6. **C.** *Hone*: make sharp.
   Opposite: *dull*.

7. **C.** *Expunge*: blot out, erase.
   Opposite: *restore*.

8. **D.** *Garrulous*: wordy, talkative.
   Opposite: *taciturn*.

9. **C.** *Tendentious*: showing a definite bias.
   Opposite: *unbiased*.

10. **A.** *Effulgent*: shining forth brightly.
    Opposite: *murky*, obscure, thick with mist.

11. **B.** Paragraph 3 confirms (A) and (C) as having been stated. (D) is implied by the fact that car manufacturers have had to recall millions of cars. Item (E) is implied in the last sentence.

12. **B.** In the fourth paragraph, figures are given for both U.S. and foreign cars. Be sure to add the two totals to get approximately 49 million.

13. **B.** The pound referred to in the saying is the unit of money in England. A paraphrase of the adage would be: When a person tries to save pennies by a foolish economy, he may find that instead of saving pennies he has created a situation in which he must spend pounds to correct his error.

14. **E.** In the last paragraph, the author says that a minor recall can cost $5 to $10 million, while a major recall can cost up to $50 million. Combining the two figures, we get $5 to $50 million.

15. **D.** The author is using irony when he suggests that the carmakers would even consider celebrating the tenth anniversary of NHTSA. The passage makes clear that the carmakers are opposed to the Act because it has cost them millions in recalls.

16. **C.** Paragraph 4 states the point in item (A); paragraph 1 makes the point in item B; the last clause of paragraph 3 confirms item (D), and the second sentence of that paragraph implies, when it says that terror is not always the effect of the application of force, that force does not always succeed as a deterrent.

17. **C.** The author does not mention treaties (item A), nor suggest anyone's surrender (item B). He never discusses economic sanctions (item D), and it is the argument in favor of force that he treats with some disdain. In paragraph 3, sentence 3, the author says that if conciliation fails, the opportunity for the use of force is still left. We can infer that his purpose is to persuade his reader to try conciliation, the act of gaining goodwill through pleasing acts.

18. **E.** We must infer that the author would be consistent in advocating conciliation rather than force in any situation.

19. **D.** Paraphrased, this sentence would read: Above are my reasons for not approving (*entertaining that high opinion*) of the use of force as many do—whose opinions I respect in other matters (*for whose sentiments in other particulars I have great respect*).

20. **D.** The author's judgments are made pragmatically; that is, only on the basis of whether or not force works, not on moral or ethical grounds.

21. **C.** In paragraph 2, the author concludes that paleolithic man's power of generalization was extremely feeble because he was only beginning to use abstractions (or conceptual language). We can conclude, therefore, that the statement in item (C) represents the author's view.

22. **A.** The author cites paleolithic man's realistic art to make the point that he was unable to generalize and that, therefore, his language must have been nonconceptual, and, finally, in some respects he was not much ahead of the apes.

23. **D.** From sentence 3 on, in the first paragraph, the author makes the point that neolithic man's art used "hieroglyphical symbols, each representing an intellectual abstraction." In paragraph 2, he develops the idea that neolithic man must have had conceptual language and, by extension, the power of generalization as explained in the explanation for question 21.

24. **E.** The author clearly states that paleolithic man thought in particular images. He could not, therefore, have felt that such ability marks man's highest level of development. Furthermore, the phrase "Nature and the eternities," has no meaning and is not used or implied by the author.

25. **C.** The last sentence says that while nature does not change, the way man sees the world ("the outlines . . . are continuously changing") does. We can conclude that

since paleolithic man's art and neolithic man's art, though differing markedly, are valid expressions of man's view of nature, any other view, realistic or abstract, would also be valid.

26. **D.** The construction, "even for a trip . . . ," requires the use of *seldom* or "never" in the first blank. Obviously, however, the valley could not have been mountain "cluttered," since, then, the valley would not have been a valley. It had to be a mountain *girded* valley.

27. **E.** The word "euphemistically" tells us that "inventory losses" is a cover-up phrase used to mask a more offensive truth: theft, or *pilferage*, which is *plaguing* retailers.

28. **D.** If a man's reputation for probity (uprightness and honesty) was great enough, even if his testimony was *refuted* (shown to be erroneous), people might think his testimony *incontrovertible*, or not disputable.

29. **C.** If the law were the belated ratification of a coup, it would not represent the result of our full bicameral procedure. But, if it were *by no means* the belated ratification of a coup, it would *rather* (on the contrary) represent those procedures.

30. **A.** The "but" tells us that though some hold this belief, it does not jibe (agree) with the findings of research. The first words of choices (A), (B), and (D) are agreement words, but "supported" cannot be used before "with," and *ever* makes no sense as the second word. The answer is *consonant . . . the well-to-do*.

31. **B.** A *hat* is an article of apparel and a *brim* is a part of the hat; similarly, a *coat* is an article of apparel and a *lapel* is a part of a coat. A *crown*, while it is worn on the head, is not an article of clothing, and the *jewel* is an adornment rather than an integral part. A *pocket* is, itself, only a part.

32. **D.** To *crumple* is to fold in a random manner, just as to *tear* is to cut in a random manner.

33. **A.** *Whither* is the opposite of *whence*. The former means to what *destination*, and the latter means from what *origin*.

34. **C.** *Pillar* supports *ceiling*, just as *corroboration*, the act of confirming previous testimony, would support an *alibi*.

35. **C.** *Rubber* is characterized by *elasticity*; similarly, *steel* is characterized by *rigidity*.

36. **A.** A *raisin* is a dried *grape*, just as a *prune* is a dried *plum*.

37. **E.** A *score* is produced by a composer such as *Mozart*; similarly, a *painting* is produced by an artist such as *Picasso*.

38. **A.** The *safety valve* is an automatic device that prevents the *boiler* from blowing up. In the same way, the *fuse* automatically prevents the *motor* from burning itself out.

39. **D.** The *lord* is the key figure in *feudalism*; the *entrepreneur*, the person who takes the risk in business, is the key figure under *capitalism*.

40. **B.** The *gourmet* is the expert in the matter of *fine food*, and the *lepidopterist* is the expert on the *butterfly*.

SECTION III

1. **A.** *Slander*: defame, malign.
   Opposite: *glorify*, magnify in worship.

2. **E.** *Fidelity*: faithfulness.
   Opposite: *perfidy*, treachery.

3. **C.** *Negligible*: so trifling that it may safely be neglected.
   Opposite: *significant*, important, momentous.

4. **B.** *Boorish*: rudeness of manner.
   Opposite: *urbane*, polished.

5. **A.** *Fortify*: strengthen.
   Opposite: *enfeeble*.

6. **B.** *Equitable*: just, fair.
   Opposite: *unfair*.

7. **D.** *Nebulous*: vague, hazy.
   Opposite: *distinct*.

8. **D.** *Clandestine*: conducted with secrecy, usually for an illicit purpose.
   Opposite: *overt*, open to view.

9. **E.** *Laconic*: terse, sparing of words.
   Opposite: *verbose*.

10. **B.** *Immiscible*: not capable of being mixed.
    Opposite: *mixable*.

11. **B.** The phrase, "made up for his . . . ," indicates that something is missing or wanting. The answer must be *lack . . originality*, because the second word of choice (E), "vacuity," meaning inanity, could not make up for want of education.

12. **D.** It would be logical that people who are biologically dependent on one another could not exist without *cooperation*, and that, therefore, the *violent* resolution of disputes would be suicidal, in a manner of speaking, like a Siamese twin stabbing his twin brother.

13. **A.** The construction starting, "While adolescents . . . " implies that the following clause will have a contrasting meaning that would suggest "on the other hand." While choice (C) supplies a pair of opposites, the meaning does not sound as sensible as when *independence . . security* are inserted.

14. **E.** The phrase, "wasteful and extravagant practices," guides us to the selection of *squandered . . patrimony* (heritage).

15. **B.** A summary would be "short" or *concise*. We select the latter because it means condensed as well as brief. Besides, the second word, *omitted*, makes sense when inserted in the sentence, whereas "precluded," in choice (A), does not.

16. **C.** The only pair which makes sense is *power . . civilized*. From the point of view of correct usage, "threats" cannot be exercised over anyone, nor can "a writ" or "forbearance." "Authorization" is an incorrect choice of word; the correct word would be "authority."

17. **D.** The phrase, "and the means of showing

pecuniary strength," indicates that the blank preceding it should be filled with the word *pecuniary*, which means monetary. The second word of choice (D), *conspicuous*, completes the meaning of the sentence: You show that you are rich by working as little as possible, and by spending money on very noticeable things.

18. **A.** We see that the blank before "belied" is obviously an adverb, but we do not concern ourselves with which one, as yet. "Simplicity," however, is "belied"—proven false—by the blank, into which we insert *complexity*, which completes the logic of the sentence and provides us with the first word, *perversely*, which suggests contrariness.

19. **C.** "That" is a demonstrative pronoun which refers to the preceding clause, "we presume . . . guilty," and therefore it is indicating that *presumption*.

20. **D.** The colon after the opening clause indicates that what is to follow will illustrate Milton's complexity of character. The colon also may indicate, as it does here, that what is to follow will be a series of phrases. From the point of view of style, we can expect that the series of phrases will have similar construction. Milton's complexity is described in a series of paired opposites: "dogmatic" and "flexible," "diffident" (unduly timid) yet *arrogant, provincial* (narrow in outlook) but "catholic" (comprehensive and universal in outlook).

21. **B.** *Cotton* is a particular *fabric*; similarly, *chestnut* is a particular *wood*.

22. **A.** A diseased or damaged *tooth* is treated by putting in a *filling*; a diseased or damaged *bone* may be similarly treated by a bone *graft*.

23. **D.** When the *pitcher* misses the strike zone, the throw is called a *ball*. Similarly, when the *batter* misses the pitch, his swing is called a *strike*.

24. **D.** A *nemesis* is one who inflicts *retribution*; a *benefactor* is one who gives *assistance* or benefits.

25. **A.** *Amusement*, which suggests quiet mirth or laughter is like *hilarity* except that the latter is more boisterous and, therefore, stronger. *Indignation* is deep, righteous anger, but *fury* implies an overmastering passion verging on madness and is, therefore, stronger.

26. **C.** An *incorrigible* person cannot be corrected or *reformed*, just as an *untenable* position cannot, by definition, be *defended*.

27. **E.** *Constantinople* is the old name for *Istanbul*, just as *Petrograd* is the old name for *Leningrad*.

28. **C.** *Ptarmigan* and *gnat* are alike in that each is spelled with an unpronounced initial letter; similarly, *column* and *aplomb* are alike in that each is spelled with an unpronounced final letter.

29. **E.** This analogy is a function analogy. A *general commands*, and a *senator legislates*.

30. **A.** *Ambiguous* and *equivocal* are synonymous, both meaning having two or more significations (meanings). *Sanctimonious* and *hypocritical*, too, are synonymous, both meaning putting on a show of virtue or religiosity. *Doubtful* and *indubitable* are opposites: "indubitable" means doubtless. *Inflammable* and *incombustible* are opposites: "inflammable" means capable of being set on fire; "incombustible" means not capable of being set on fire. *Animated* and *enervated* are almost opposites: "animated" means lively; "enervated" means lacking force or strength.

31. **C.** Choice (C) is confirmed by sentence 4 of paragraph 1.

32. **E.** In paragraph 2, sentence 2, the author says that the boats are much alike in appearance, so item I is false. Sentence 3 of paragraph 3 affirms the statement in item II, while sentence 6 of the same paragraph affirms the statement in item III.

33. **C.** The last sentence points out that it is a tribute, etc., that the old design is still used for the few boats now being built.

34. **A.** Substitute the other meanings to see that only *treasure* fits the sentence. If he had

only a "small amount," "paucity," or "mishmash," the next sentence, which says that anyone without this background would be at a disadvantage, would not make sense. "Cash reward" makes no sense at all.

35. **E.** The figure of speech in sentence 4, paragraph 2 is a simile. "Beady-eyed windows" is a metaphor. The author employs contrast throughout: sentence 3, paragraph 1 gives one instance of this. He uses generalization when he says that an outsider could starve before he is well started; when he says that as a class these boats have gathered more scales, etc.; and in his description of these boats in paragraph 3.

36. **C.** Throughout the passage, the author writes of errors in the use of language, but his purpose, expressed in his topic sentence, is to have us look to the stars, i.e., "at least try to maintain standards."

37. **B.** The author obviously does expect someone in Mr. Fulwiler's position to know other languages. Saying that it may be too much to ask is putting it ironically.

38. **E.** Mr. Howe's error is excused by the author's "... even the ablest among us ... are not immune to lapses." Sheff and Deutsch are mentioned only for having sent material, and the editors of *American Studies International* are not mentioned at all. For a single spelling error (repeated, it's true), Mr. Fulwiler is subjected to criticism for failure to check the dictionary and is sneered at as lacking what the author obviously feels is appropriate scholarly background.

39. **A.** The author cites the misspelling of "plagiarize," his own error in sentence structure in a previous column, the use of the apostrophe in pluralizing "flights," and Mr. Howe's incorrect choice of the plural "protagonists," but he does not mention use of the apostrophe in the formation of possessives.

40. **D.** The word "harried" followed by the phrase "rapid-fire journalism" provide the clues that lead us to the idea of "pressures," or *urgencies.*

SECTION IV

1. **B.** If $36 < K^2 < 64$, then
$$6 < K < 8.$$
Since K is an integer, it must be equal to 7.

2. **E.** The cost of 60 ball-point pens at $2 per dozen is $\frac{60}{12} \times 2 = 5 \times 2 = \$10.00$. The cost of buying them for 20¢ each is $60 \times .20 = \$12.00$. Thus, the saving is $2.00.

3. **A.** $QR = PR - PQ = 30 - 6 = 24$

$$QM = \frac{1}{2}QR = \frac{1}{2}(24) = 12.$$

4. **D.** $6p + 7q = 20p$
$$7q = 20p - 6p$$
$$7q = 14p$$

$$p = \frac{1}{2}q.$$

5. **C.** $C = 2\pi r$
$$= 2 \cdot \frac{22}{7} \cdot 7$$
$$C = 44.$$

6. **B.** $\frac{1}{5} + \frac{3}{10} = \frac{2}{10} + \frac{3}{10}$

$$= \frac{5}{10} = \frac{1}{2}.$$

7. **C.** Change d dollars to $100d$ cents.
Then the number of magazines to be bought is
$$\frac{100d}{m}.$$

8. **B.** $5 = \frac{1}{4}(n + 5)$. Multiply both sides by 4.

$20 = n + 5$

$n = 15$.

9. **E.** Each side of the triangle is $\frac{p}{3}$.

$\frac{2p}{3} = \frac{6}{7}$. Divide both sides by 2.

$\frac{p}{3} = \frac{3}{7}$.

10. **D.** If $x^2 = 36$, then $x = \pm 6$.
If $y^2 = 49$, then $y = \pm 7$.
The least value of $y - x$ is obtained by taking the least value of y and the greatest value of x.
Thus, $y - x = -7 - (+6)$
or $y - x = -7 - 6 = -13$.

11. **E.** A cube of edge 4 has a volume of $4^3 = 64$. A cube of edge 2 has a volume of $2^3 = 8$. Thus the larger cube can be split into 8 smaller cubes. The surface area of a cube of edge 2 is $6(2)^2 = 24$. The total surface area of all 8 smaller cubes is $8(24) = 192$.

12. **C.** Since $RV = VT$, angle $T = x$ degrees. Angle $RVS = 180 - 110 = 70$ degrees. Angle $RVS = x + x = 2x = 70$. Thus, $x = 35°$.

13. **A.** Change 15 pounds to $15(16) = 240$ ounces.

Then, $\frac{6}{240} = \frac{1}{40} = .025 = 2\frac{1}{2}\%$.

14. **D.** $V = \frac{1}{3}Bh = \frac{1}{3}\pi r^2 h$

$32\pi = \frac{1}{3}\pi r^2(6)$

$32 = 2r^2$

$r^2 = 16$

$r = 4$.

15. **A.** Let $PQ = RS = n$ (an integer).

$A = $ Area of $\triangle PQR = \frac{1}{2} \cdot PQ \cdot RS$

$= \frac{1}{2} - n^2$

Thus, $n^2 = 2A$

or $n = \sqrt{2A}$.

n would be an integer for all the given values of A except $A = 1$.

16. **B.** $c = 2\pi r$ and $p = 4r$.
Since $\pi = 3.14$, $C = 6.28r$.
Thus, the value of C is between p and $2p$, or $p < C < 2p$.

17. **C.** $\frac{r}{s} = \frac{2}{5}$ and $\frac{s}{t} = \frac{3}{4}$.

To obtain the ratio $\frac{r}{t}$, multiply the left members of the above equations and their right members. Thus,

$\frac{r}{s} \cdot \frac{s}{t} = \frac{2}{5} \cdot \frac{3}{4}$

$\frac{r}{t} = \frac{3}{10}$.

18. **C.** $40(.3) = 12$ and $30(.4) = 12$, so that the two quantities are equal.

19. **A.** $(3n)^2 = 9n^2$ and n^2 is positive, so that $9n^2 > 3n^2$.

20. **D.** The length of the chord may vary from 0 to the length of the diameter, so that we cannot determine its relationship to the radius.

21. **B.** Since $8.5 < 9$, then $\sqrt{8.5} < 3$.
Since $28.2 > 27$, then $\sqrt[3]{28.2} > 3$.
Thus, $\sqrt[3]{28.2} > 8.5$.

22. **A.** Since the indicated angles are vertical angles, then $3g = 4h$, or

$g = \frac{4}{3}h$ so that $g > h$.

23. **B.** $\$80(.70) = \$56.00$ (A)
$\$80(.80) = \$64.00$ First discount price
$\$64(.90) = \$57.60$ Sale price (B)
Thus, (B) is greater than (A).

24. **D.** $3x + 4y = 12$,
when $x = 0$, $y = 3$ and $y > x$.
when $y = 0$, $x = 4$ and $x > y$.
Thus, relationship cannot be determined.

25. **A.** Area of circle $= \pi r^2$.
Area of square $= (2r)^2 = 4r^2$.

$$t = \frac{\pi r^2}{4r^2} = \frac{\pi}{4}$$

$$= \frac{3.14}{4} > \frac{3}{4}.$$

26. **D.** Each interior angle $= \dfrac{180°(n-2)}{n}$.

Each exterior angle $= \dfrac{360°}{n}$.

We cannot determine which is greater unless we know the value of n.

27. **C.** In parallelogram $PSVT$, $TV = PS$ and $PT = SV$. Perimeter of $\triangle PQR = QR + RS + SP + PT + TQ$. Perimeter of shaded region $= QR + RS + SV + VT + TQ$. In view of the above equalities, the two perimeters are equal.

28. **A.** Area of $\triangle PQR = \dfrac{d^2}{4}\sqrt{3} = \dfrac{1.73}{4}d^2 = .43d^2$.

Area of semicircle $= \dfrac{1}{2}\pi\dfrac{d^2}{4} = \pi\dfrac{d^2}{8} = \dfrac{3.14d^2}{8} = .39d^2$. Thus, the triangle is greater in area.

29. **C.** $330 = 33 \times 10 = 11 \times 3 \times 5 \times 2$ (4 prime factors). $210 = 21 \times 10 = 7 \times 3 \times 5 \times 2$ (4 prime factors). The number of prime factors is the same in both cases.

30. **B.** $\dfrac{p}{7} = \dfrac{7}{p}$

$p^2 = 49$

$p = -7$ since $p < 0$

$\dfrac{p}{14} = \dfrac{-7}{14} = -\dfrac{1}{2} < -\dfrac{1}{7}.$

31. **D.** If $rst = 0$, then at least one of the three factors is equal to zero. If $t = 0$, then $rt = st = 0$. Since we do not know the signs of r or s, we cannot compare rt and st in magnitude.

32. **D.** If $y = 0$, the two expressions are equal. If $y > 0$, $y(y + 2) = y^2 + 2y > y^2$. We cannot compare the two quantities.

33. **B.** Since $\angle S = 90°$ and $\angle T = 30°$, then $\angle R = 60°$. Thus, $ST > RS$.

34. **C.** In the 30°–60°–90° triangle, $RS = \dfrac{1}{2}RT$.

35. **A.** Let $RT = x$, then $RS = \dfrac{x}{2}$ and

$$ST = \frac{x}{2}\sqrt{3} = \frac{1.73}{2}x = .86x > .75x.$$

Thus $ST > \dfrac{3}{4}RT$.

SECTION V

1. **B** $y + \dfrac{2}{7} = \dfrac{5}{7}.$

Subtract $\dfrac{2}{7}$ from both sides.

$$y = \frac{5}{7} - \frac{2}{7} = \frac{3}{7}$$

$$y + \frac{1}{7} = \frac{3}{7} + \frac{1}{7} = \frac{4}{7}.$$

2. **D.** $17^2 = 289$.

$18^2 = 324$, or $\sqrt{324} = 18$.

Thus, $\sqrt{340} > 18$, so that 18 is the greatest positive integer less than $\sqrt{340}$.

3. **C.** $p = 12{,}000$
$q = 11{,}800$
$p - q = 200.$

4. **E.**

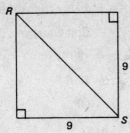

The side of the square is $\frac{36}{4} = 9$. The longest possible length of RS is obtained by making RS a diagonal of the square. In this case $RS = 9\sqrt{2}$.

5. **D.** If he sold 2 apples, they would sell for 40¢, leaving $3.60 for the oranges. But $3.60 is not divisible by 25¢, so this is not possible. Try the other possible answers in this way.

   If he sells 5 apples, he gets $1.00, leaving $3.00 for the oranges. This number is divisible by 25¢, so that 5 is the least number of apples he could have sold.

6. **B.** $(x + y)^{pq} = (1 + 0)^{6(5)} = 1^{30}$
   $= 1.$

7. **E.** The surface area of a cube of edge e is given by $S = 6e^2$. Doubling e would multiply S by 4, since the e is squared in the formula. Thus, the cost of gold paint would also be multiplied by 4; so that the cost would be $24 \times 4 = 96.$

8. **C.** 12 minutes $= \frac{12}{60} = \frac{1}{5}$ hr.

   $$\frac{9}{\frac{1}{5}} = \frac{x}{8}$$

   $$\frac{1}{5}x = 72$$

   $$x = 360.$$

9. **D.** Let n = her score on the next game.

   $$\frac{134 + 145 + 150 + n}{4} = 149$$

   $$\frac{429 + n}{4} = 149$$

   $$429 + n = 596$$

   $$n = 167.$$

10. **E.** Let r = radius of circle.
    $$2\pi r = \pi r^2$$
    $$r^2 = 2r. \text{ Divide by } r.$$
    $$r = 2$$
    $$C = 2\pi r = 4\pi.$$

11. **D.** $\frac{5p^2 + 5q^2}{5} = \frac{5(p^2 + q^2)}{5} = p^2 + q^2.$

    Thus, the 5's may be cancelled out. This is not true in any of the other expressions.

12. **B.**

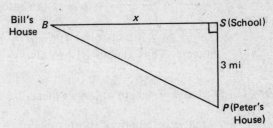

    $PB = \sqrt{x^2 + 9} = (x + 3) - 1$
    $\qquad\qquad = x + 2.$
    $\qquad\qquad$ Square both sides.
    $$x^2 + 9 = (x + 2)^2$$
    $$\cancel{x^2} + 9 = \cancel{x^2} + 4x + 4$$
    $$4x = 5$$
    $$x = 1\frac{1}{4}.$$

13. **A.** The least number is obtained by subtracting the largest of the three numbers from the smallest of them. Since r is the greatest number and t is the least quantity, then $(t - r)$ is the least number of the five choices.

14. **B.** The area of the rectangle in the figure is given by the formula
    $$A = bh$$
    $$b = 2 - (-1) = 2 + 1 = 3$$
    $$h = p - m,$$
    so that $A = 3(p - m).$

15. **D.** Area of $RSTV = 25(10) = 250.$
    Area of two semicircles
    $\qquad = $ Area of one circle
    $\qquad = \pi r^2 = \pi(5)^2 = 25\pi$
    Area of shaded region $= 250 - 25\pi.$

16. **E.** $p + q = 3n$ and $q + n = 4$,
    $\qquad$ or $q = 4 - n$.
    $\qquad$ Then, $p + (4 - n) = 3n$
    $\qquad\qquad\quad p + 4 - n = 3n$
    $\qquad\qquad\qquad\quad p = 4n - 4$.

17. **A.** $\angle m = \angle QRS$ since they are corresponding angles of parallel lines. $\angle VRS = \angle n + \angle m$. Since $\angle VRS$ is an exterior angle of triangle RST, $\angle VRS = \angle S + \angle T$, or $m + n = x + y$.

18. **C.** $\dfrac{p + 3}{3}$ is not always an integer (Let $p = 1$).

    $\dfrac{3p + 6}{3} = \dfrac{3(p + 2)}{3} = p + 2$ (an integer).

    $\sqrt{p^2 - 2p + 1} = \sqrt{(p - 1)^2} = p - 1$ (an integer). Thus II and III are always integers.

19. **C.** $\quad$ Let x = length of longer piece,

    then $\dfrac{2}{3}x$ = length of shorter piece

    $x + \dfrac{2}{3}x = 85$. Multiply both sides by 3.

    $3x + 2x = 255$

    $\qquad 5x = 255$

    $\qquad\quad x = 51, \dfrac{2}{3}x = \dfrac{2}{3}(51) = 34$.

20. **C.** $x + y + z = 180°$

    $z = \dfrac{x + y}{z}$,

or $2z = x + y$. Substitute in

first equation

$\qquad 2z + z = 180°$

$\qquad\quad 3z = 180°$

$\qquad\quad\ z = 60°$.

21. **B.** $\quad$ He mows $\dfrac{4}{5}$ of the lawn in $1\dfrac{1}{3}$ hours $\left(\dfrac{4}{3}\right)$.

    To do another $\dfrac{1}{5}$ of the lawn will take $\dfrac{1}{4} \times$

    $\dfrac{4}{3} = \dfrac{1}{3}$ hour = 20 minutes. Thus, he will

    finish at 11:20 plus 20 minutes or 11:40 a.m.

22. **C.** $\quad$ Grade B hard coal = $.70 \times .40 = .28$
    $\qquad\qquad\qquad\qquad\qquad\qquad = 28\%$.

23. **A.** $\quad$ Central angle = $.30 \times 360°$
    $\qquad\qquad\qquad\qquad = 108°$.

24. **D.** $\quad$ Let x = cost of ticket before tax,
    $\qquad$ then $.15x$ = tax
    $\qquad\quad x + .15x = 11.50$
    $\qquad\qquad 1.15x = 11.50$
    $\qquad\qquad\ 115x = 1150$
    $\qquad\qquad\qquad x = \$10$
    $\qquad$ Tax = $\$11.50 - 10.00$
    $\qquad$ Tax = $\$1.50$.

25. **E.** $\quad$ The volume of the 2 cm. cube is given by

    $V = e^3$

    $\qquad = 2^3 = 8$ cc

    Weight = $8 \times 10 = 80$ grams.

SECTION VI

1. **D.** Lack of parallel construction. All the things the candidate was required to do should have been expressed as similar actions. The sentence would have to be rewritten to say, "The advertisement stated . . . for candidates with clerical skills who were willing to work long hours and travel extensively."

2. **C.** Lack of agreement between pronoun and antecedent. "Their" should read "his" or "her."

3. **B.** Incorrect case. The preposition, "for," takes the objective case. The phrase should read, " . . . my sister and me."

4. **A.** Incorrect case. The sentence should read, "whom," since the pronoun is the object of the verb "meant."

5. **B.** Incorrect case. After the conjunction "than," use the same case for the second member of an unequal comparison as you use for the first.

6. **C.** Lack of parallel construction. " . . . it is necessary to measure . . . , to use . . . , and to choose" (not *choosing*). . . .

7. **B.** Incorrect shift in person. "When a person . . . he" (not *you*) . . .

8. **D.** Lack of parallel construction. " . . . an individual's personality, character, and thinking" (not *how he thinks*).

9. **B.** The correct construction to use for comparison is, " . . . as much . . . as . . . "

10. **C.** Mrs. Nolan is reputed to be the best of *all* the cooks etc., not the best of all the *other* cooks.

11. **B.** Error in diction. "Among" is used for three or more, while "between" is used for two.

12. **D.** Error in grammar. The past participle of "sink" is "sunk."

13. **B.** Error in diction. The word intended was "allusions."

14. **A.** Error in case. The preferred form in standard written English would be "his going."

15. **E.** No error.

16. **C.** Error in agreement of subject and verb. The subject, "one," is singular, and the verb should be "lacks."

17. **D.** Error in grammar. The past participle of "fall" is "fallen."

18. **A.** Illiterate substitute. Substitute "since" or "because" for "being that."

19. **E.** No error. Sentence correct as given.

20. **A.** Error in diction. Substitute "who is" or "who's" for "whose."

21. **B.** The pronoun "which" is usually used only for things or for people in an impersonal sense. Use "who" instead of "which."

22. **C.** Redundant expression. "Resultant" implies "effect."

23. **B.** "Obedience" takes the preposition "to," while "respect" takes the preposition "for." When two words taking different prepositions are used together, both prepositions must be used, each following its respective word: "obedience to and respect for . . . "

24. **C.** Be wary of this construction. The possessive case, "their," is preferred in more formal writing.

25. **D.** Lack of parallelism. Substitute "with the conservatives" for the underlined portion.

26. **B.** The correlative conjunctions "not only . . . but also . . . " connect elements in parallel form. Further, do not split the conjunctions by inserting words between "not" and "only" or between "but" and "also."

27. **E.** The past participle of "bring" is "brought."

28. **C.** As written, the question contains two sentences in one. The error is called a comma splice. Instead of a comma, there could be a period after the word "meeting," or the run-on sentences could be correctly connected through the use of the coordinating conjunction "and," as in choice (C).

29. **D.** Error in diction. "Infer" means "draw a conclusion." The correct word, "imply," means "hint or suggest."

30. **D.** Choice (D) is properly punctuated.

31. **C.** Lack of parallel construction. "We . . . knew him to be," should be followed by a series that uses the same kind of construction for each trait. Having used the adjectives "skillful" and "perseverant," the writer should have used another adjective or descriptive, as in choice (C).

32. **D.** Error in spelling of possessive form. "Theirs," "yours," "ours," and "hers" do not use the apostrophe.

33. **B.** Error in construction: shift from third person to second person. The sentence should have read, "The average consumer . . . , his money's worth . . . , but he (not *you*). . . . "

34. **D.** The first word of the sentence, "Its," should be "It's" because it represents a contraction of "it" and "is."

35. **A.** The sentence is correct as given. "Whoever" is in the nominative because it is the subject of the clause.

36. **B.** "Scarcely" is a negative and cannot be used with another negative as in the construction given.

37. **E.** The preposition "for" takes the objective pronoun "us."

38. **B.** The limiting phrase, "five years ago," indicates that the view was held in the past, but not extending to the present. The verb in the main clause must, therefore, be in the past tense.

39. **E.** Squinting modifier. We cannot tell which Rod was doing: practicing for the big game when he saw them at the stadium, or seeing them practicing at the stadium for the big game.

40. **B.** When two words take different prepositions, both must be used, each following its respective word.

41. **A.** Error in diction. "Immigrated" means came to a country to take up permanent residence. The correct word would be "emigrated."

42. **B.** Error in logic. "Hardly" is a negative which means "probably not" and its use with "nothing" is not acceptable in standard written English.

43. **D.** Error in diction. Usage dictates the use of "different from."

44. **D.** Error in grammar. The construction calls for the use of the predicate adjective, "sweet," rather than the adverb, "sweetly."

45. **A.** Illiterate substitution. The correct verb is "couldn't have."

46. **C.** The use of the definite article, "the," is only colloquial or local.

47. **A.** The use of "like" for "as if" is not acceptable in standard written English.

48. **C.** Error in diction. "Continuous" means "without cessation." The writer intended to indicate that frequent and prolonged immersion in water could damage the stone or weaken the setting of a ring.

49. **A.** Error in diction. "Besides" means "in addition." The term intended, "beside herself," is an idiomatic expression meaning "almost out of one's senses from a strong emotion."

50. **C.** "Less" refers to quantity rather than number in standard written English. The word of choice would be "fewer."

SAT Practice Test 3

ANSWER SHEET

When you have chosen your answer to any question, blacken the corresponding space on the answer sheet below. Make sure your marking completely fills the answer space. If you change an answer, erase the previous marking completely.

Section I—Verbal

1 Ⓐ Ⓑ Ⓒ Ⓓ Ⓔ	13 Ⓐ Ⓑ Ⓒ Ⓓ Ⓔ	24 Ⓐ Ⓑ Ⓒ Ⓓ Ⓔ	35 Ⓐ Ⓑ Ⓒ Ⓓ Ⓔ
2 Ⓐ Ⓑ Ⓒ Ⓓ Ⓔ	14 Ⓐ Ⓑ Ⓒ Ⓓ Ⓔ	25 Ⓐ Ⓑ Ⓒ Ⓓ Ⓔ	36 Ⓐ Ⓑ Ⓒ Ⓓ Ⓔ
3 Ⓐ Ⓑ Ⓒ Ⓓ Ⓔ	15 Ⓐ Ⓑ Ⓒ Ⓓ Ⓔ	26 Ⓐ Ⓑ Ⓒ Ⓓ Ⓔ	37 Ⓐ Ⓑ Ⓒ Ⓓ Ⓔ
4 Ⓐ Ⓑ Ⓒ Ⓓ Ⓔ	16 Ⓐ Ⓑ Ⓒ Ⓓ Ⓔ	27 Ⓐ Ⓑ Ⓒ Ⓓ Ⓔ	38 Ⓐ Ⓑ Ⓒ Ⓓ Ⓔ
5 Ⓐ Ⓑ Ⓒ Ⓓ Ⓔ	17 Ⓐ Ⓑ Ⓒ Ⓓ Ⓔ	28 Ⓐ Ⓑ Ⓒ Ⓓ Ⓔ	39 Ⓐ Ⓑ Ⓒ Ⓓ Ⓔ
6 Ⓐ Ⓑ Ⓒ Ⓓ Ⓔ	18 Ⓐ Ⓑ Ⓒ Ⓓ Ⓔ	29 Ⓐ Ⓑ Ⓒ Ⓓ Ⓔ	40 Ⓐ Ⓑ Ⓒ Ⓓ Ⓔ
7 Ⓐ Ⓑ Ⓒ Ⓓ Ⓔ	19 Ⓐ Ⓑ Ⓒ Ⓓ Ⓔ	30 Ⓐ Ⓑ Ⓒ Ⓓ Ⓔ	41 Ⓐ Ⓑ Ⓒ Ⓓ Ⓔ
8 Ⓐ Ⓑ Ⓒ Ⓓ Ⓔ	20 Ⓐ Ⓑ Ⓒ Ⓓ Ⓔ	31 Ⓐ Ⓑ Ⓒ Ⓓ Ⓔ	42 Ⓐ Ⓑ Ⓒ Ⓓ Ⓔ
9 Ⓐ Ⓑ Ⓒ Ⓓ Ⓔ	21 Ⓐ Ⓑ Ⓒ Ⓓ Ⓔ	32 Ⓐ Ⓑ Ⓒ Ⓓ Ⓔ	43 Ⓐ Ⓑ Ⓒ Ⓓ Ⓔ
10 Ⓐ Ⓑ Ⓒ Ⓓ Ⓔ	22 Ⓐ Ⓑ Ⓒ Ⓓ Ⓔ	33 Ⓐ Ⓑ Ⓒ Ⓓ Ⓔ	44 Ⓐ Ⓑ Ⓒ Ⓓ Ⓔ
11 Ⓐ Ⓑ Ⓒ Ⓓ Ⓔ	23 Ⓐ Ⓑ Ⓒ Ⓓ Ⓔ	34 Ⓐ Ⓑ Ⓒ Ⓓ Ⓔ	45 Ⓐ Ⓑ Ⓒ Ⓓ Ⓔ
12 Ⓐ Ⓑ Ⓒ Ⓓ Ⓔ			

Section II—Verbal

1 Ⓐ Ⓑ Ⓒ Ⓓ Ⓔ	11 Ⓐ Ⓑ Ⓒ Ⓓ Ⓔ	21 Ⓐ Ⓑ Ⓒ Ⓓ Ⓔ	31 Ⓐ Ⓑ Ⓒ Ⓓ Ⓔ
2 Ⓐ Ⓑ Ⓒ Ⓓ Ⓔ	12 Ⓐ Ⓑ Ⓒ Ⓓ Ⓔ	22 Ⓐ Ⓑ Ⓒ Ⓓ Ⓔ	32 Ⓐ Ⓑ Ⓒ Ⓓ Ⓔ
3 Ⓐ Ⓑ Ⓒ Ⓓ Ⓔ	13 Ⓐ Ⓑ Ⓒ Ⓓ Ⓔ	23 Ⓐ Ⓑ Ⓒ Ⓓ Ⓔ	33 Ⓐ Ⓑ Ⓒ Ⓓ Ⓔ
4 Ⓐ Ⓑ Ⓒ Ⓓ Ⓔ	14 Ⓐ Ⓑ Ⓒ Ⓓ Ⓔ	24 Ⓐ Ⓑ Ⓒ Ⓓ Ⓔ	34 Ⓐ Ⓑ Ⓒ Ⓓ Ⓔ
5 Ⓐ Ⓑ Ⓒ Ⓓ Ⓔ	15 Ⓐ Ⓑ Ⓒ Ⓓ Ⓔ	25 Ⓐ Ⓑ Ⓒ Ⓓ Ⓔ	35 Ⓐ Ⓑ Ⓒ Ⓓ Ⓔ
6 Ⓐ Ⓑ Ⓒ Ⓓ Ⓔ	16 Ⓐ Ⓑ Ⓒ Ⓓ Ⓔ	26 Ⓐ Ⓑ Ⓒ Ⓓ Ⓔ	36 Ⓐ Ⓑ Ⓒ Ⓓ Ⓔ
7 Ⓐ Ⓑ Ⓒ Ⓓ Ⓔ	17 Ⓐ Ⓑ Ⓒ Ⓓ Ⓔ	27 Ⓐ Ⓑ Ⓒ Ⓓ Ⓔ	37 Ⓐ Ⓑ Ⓒ Ⓓ Ⓔ
8 Ⓐ Ⓑ Ⓒ Ⓓ Ⓔ	18 Ⓐ Ⓑ Ⓒ Ⓓ Ⓔ	28 Ⓐ Ⓑ Ⓒ Ⓓ Ⓔ	38 Ⓐ Ⓑ Ⓒ Ⓓ Ⓔ
9 Ⓐ Ⓑ Ⓒ Ⓓ Ⓔ	19 Ⓐ Ⓑ Ⓒ Ⓓ Ⓔ	29 Ⓐ Ⓑ Ⓒ Ⓓ Ⓔ	39 Ⓐ Ⓑ Ⓒ Ⓓ Ⓔ
10 Ⓐ Ⓑ Ⓒ Ⓓ Ⓔ	20 Ⓐ Ⓑ Ⓒ Ⓓ Ⓔ	30 Ⓐ Ⓑ Ⓒ Ⓓ Ⓔ	40 Ⓐ Ⓑ Ⓒ Ⓓ Ⓔ

Section III—Mathematical

1 Ⓐ Ⓑ Ⓒ Ⓓ Ⓔ	8 Ⓐ Ⓑ Ⓒ Ⓓ Ⓔ	14 Ⓐ Ⓑ Ⓒ Ⓓ Ⓔ	20 Ⓐ Ⓑ Ⓒ Ⓓ Ⓔ
2 Ⓐ Ⓑ Ⓒ Ⓓ Ⓔ	9 Ⓐ Ⓑ Ⓒ Ⓓ Ⓔ	15 Ⓐ Ⓑ Ⓒ Ⓓ Ⓔ	21 Ⓐ Ⓑ Ⓒ Ⓓ Ⓔ
3 Ⓐ Ⓑ Ⓒ Ⓓ Ⓔ	10 Ⓐ Ⓑ Ⓒ Ⓓ Ⓔ	16 Ⓐ Ⓑ Ⓒ Ⓓ Ⓔ	22 Ⓐ Ⓑ Ⓒ Ⓓ Ⓔ
4 Ⓐ Ⓑ Ⓒ Ⓓ Ⓔ	11 Ⓐ Ⓑ Ⓒ Ⓓ Ⓔ	17 Ⓐ Ⓑ Ⓒ Ⓓ Ⓔ	23 Ⓐ Ⓑ Ⓒ Ⓓ Ⓔ
5 Ⓐ Ⓑ Ⓒ Ⓓ Ⓔ	12 Ⓐ Ⓑ Ⓒ Ⓓ Ⓔ	18 Ⓐ Ⓑ Ⓒ Ⓓ Ⓔ	24 Ⓐ Ⓑ Ⓒ Ⓓ Ⓔ
6 Ⓐ Ⓑ Ⓒ Ⓓ Ⓔ	13 Ⓐ Ⓑ Ⓒ Ⓓ Ⓔ	19 Ⓐ Ⓑ Ⓒ Ⓓ Ⓔ	25 Ⓐ Ⓑ Ⓒ Ⓓ Ⓔ
7 Ⓐ Ⓑ Ⓒ Ⓓ Ⓔ			

Section IV—Mathematical

1 Ⓐ Ⓑ Ⓒ Ⓓ Ⓔ	10 Ⓐ Ⓑ Ⓒ Ⓓ Ⓔ	19 Ⓐ Ⓑ Ⓒ Ⓓ	28 Ⓐ Ⓑ Ⓒ Ⓓ
2 Ⓐ Ⓑ Ⓒ Ⓓ Ⓔ	11 Ⓐ Ⓑ Ⓒ Ⓓ Ⓔ	20 Ⓐ Ⓑ Ⓒ Ⓓ	29 Ⓐ Ⓑ Ⓒ Ⓓ
3 Ⓐ Ⓑ Ⓒ Ⓓ Ⓔ	12 Ⓐ Ⓑ Ⓒ Ⓓ Ⓔ	21 Ⓐ Ⓑ Ⓒ Ⓓ	30 Ⓐ Ⓑ Ⓒ Ⓓ
4 Ⓐ Ⓑ Ⓒ Ⓓ Ⓔ	13 Ⓐ Ⓑ Ⓒ Ⓓ Ⓔ	22 Ⓐ Ⓑ Ⓒ Ⓓ	31 Ⓐ Ⓑ Ⓒ Ⓓ
5 Ⓐ Ⓑ Ⓒ Ⓓ Ⓔ	14 Ⓐ Ⓑ Ⓒ Ⓓ Ⓔ	23 Ⓐ Ⓑ Ⓒ Ⓓ	32 Ⓐ Ⓑ Ⓒ Ⓓ
6 Ⓐ Ⓑ Ⓒ Ⓓ Ⓔ	15 Ⓐ Ⓑ Ⓒ Ⓓ Ⓔ	24 Ⓐ Ⓑ Ⓒ Ⓓ	33 Ⓐ Ⓑ Ⓒ Ⓓ
7 Ⓐ Ⓑ Ⓒ Ⓓ Ⓔ	16 Ⓐ Ⓑ Ⓒ Ⓓ Ⓔ	25 Ⓐ Ⓑ Ⓒ Ⓓ	34 Ⓐ Ⓑ Ⓒ Ⓓ
8 Ⓐ Ⓑ Ⓒ Ⓓ Ⓔ	17 Ⓐ Ⓑ Ⓒ Ⓓ Ⓔ	26 Ⓐ Ⓑ Ⓒ Ⓓ	35 Ⓐ Ⓑ Ⓒ Ⓓ
9 Ⓐ Ⓑ Ⓒ Ⓓ Ⓔ	18 Ⓐ Ⓑ Ⓒ Ⓓ	27 Ⓐ Ⓑ Ⓒ Ⓓ	

Section V—Mathematical

1 Ⓐ Ⓑ Ⓒ Ⓓ Ⓔ	8 Ⓐ Ⓑ Ⓒ Ⓓ Ⓔ	14 Ⓐ Ⓑ Ⓒ Ⓓ Ⓔ	20 Ⓐ Ⓑ Ⓒ Ⓓ Ⓔ
2 Ⓐ Ⓑ Ⓒ Ⓓ Ⓔ	9 Ⓐ Ⓑ Ⓒ Ⓓ Ⓔ	15 Ⓐ Ⓑ Ⓒ Ⓓ Ⓔ	21 Ⓐ Ⓑ Ⓒ Ⓓ Ⓔ
3 Ⓐ Ⓑ Ⓒ Ⓓ Ⓔ	10 Ⓐ Ⓑ Ⓒ Ⓓ Ⓔ	16 Ⓐ Ⓑ Ⓒ Ⓓ Ⓔ	22 Ⓐ Ⓑ Ⓒ Ⓓ Ⓔ
4 Ⓐ Ⓑ Ⓒ Ⓓ Ⓔ	11 Ⓐ Ⓑ Ⓒ Ⓓ Ⓔ	17 Ⓐ Ⓑ Ⓒ Ⓓ Ⓔ	23 Ⓐ Ⓑ Ⓒ Ⓓ Ⓔ
5 Ⓐ Ⓑ Ⓒ Ⓓ Ⓔ	12 Ⓐ Ⓑ Ⓒ Ⓓ Ⓔ	18 Ⓐ Ⓑ Ⓒ Ⓓ Ⓔ	24 Ⓐ Ⓑ Ⓒ Ⓓ Ⓔ
6 Ⓐ Ⓑ Ⓒ Ⓓ Ⓔ	13 Ⓐ Ⓑ Ⓒ Ⓓ Ⓔ	19 Ⓐ Ⓑ Ⓒ Ⓓ Ⓔ	25 Ⓐ Ⓑ Ⓒ Ⓓ Ⓔ
7 Ⓐ Ⓑ Ⓒ Ⓓ Ⓔ			

Section VI—Written English

1 Ⓐ Ⓑ Ⓒ Ⓓ Ⓔ	14 Ⓐ Ⓑ Ⓒ Ⓓ Ⓔ	27 Ⓐ Ⓑ Ⓒ Ⓓ Ⓔ	39 Ⓐ Ⓑ Ⓒ Ⓓ Ⓔ
2 Ⓐ Ⓑ Ⓒ Ⓓ Ⓔ	15 Ⓐ Ⓑ Ⓒ Ⓓ Ⓔ	28 Ⓐ Ⓑ Ⓒ Ⓓ Ⓔ	40 Ⓐ Ⓑ Ⓒ Ⓓ Ⓔ
3 Ⓐ Ⓑ Ⓒ Ⓓ Ⓔ	16 Ⓐ Ⓑ Ⓒ Ⓓ Ⓔ	29 Ⓐ Ⓑ Ⓒ Ⓓ Ⓔ	41 Ⓐ Ⓑ Ⓒ Ⓓ Ⓔ
4 Ⓐ Ⓑ Ⓒ Ⓓ Ⓔ	17 Ⓐ Ⓑ Ⓒ Ⓓ Ⓔ	30 Ⓐ Ⓑ Ⓒ Ⓓ Ⓔ	42 Ⓐ Ⓑ Ⓒ Ⓓ Ⓔ
5 Ⓐ Ⓑ Ⓒ Ⓓ Ⓔ	18 Ⓐ Ⓑ Ⓒ Ⓓ Ⓔ	31 Ⓐ Ⓑ Ⓒ Ⓓ Ⓔ	43 Ⓐ Ⓑ Ⓒ Ⓓ Ⓔ
6 Ⓐ Ⓑ Ⓒ Ⓓ Ⓔ	19 Ⓐ Ⓑ Ⓒ Ⓓ Ⓔ	32 Ⓐ Ⓑ Ⓒ Ⓓ Ⓔ	44 Ⓐ Ⓑ Ⓒ Ⓓ Ⓔ
7 Ⓐ Ⓑ Ⓒ Ⓓ Ⓔ	20 Ⓐ Ⓑ Ⓒ Ⓓ Ⓔ	33 Ⓐ Ⓑ Ⓒ Ⓓ Ⓔ	45 Ⓐ Ⓑ Ⓒ Ⓓ Ⓔ
8 Ⓐ Ⓑ Ⓒ Ⓓ Ⓔ	21 Ⓐ Ⓑ Ⓒ Ⓓ Ⓔ	34 Ⓐ Ⓑ Ⓒ Ⓓ Ⓔ	46 Ⓐ Ⓑ Ⓒ Ⓓ Ⓔ
9 Ⓐ Ⓑ Ⓒ Ⓓ Ⓔ	22 Ⓐ Ⓑ Ⓒ Ⓓ Ⓔ	35 Ⓐ Ⓑ Ⓒ Ⓓ Ⓔ	47 Ⓐ Ⓑ Ⓒ Ⓓ Ⓔ
10 Ⓐ Ⓑ Ⓒ Ⓓ Ⓔ	23 Ⓐ Ⓑ Ⓒ Ⓓ Ⓔ	36 Ⓐ Ⓑ Ⓒ Ⓓ Ⓔ	48 Ⓐ Ⓑ Ⓒ Ⓓ Ⓔ
11 Ⓐ Ⓑ Ⓒ Ⓓ Ⓔ	24 Ⓐ Ⓑ Ⓒ Ⓓ Ⓔ	37 Ⓐ Ⓑ Ⓒ Ⓓ Ⓔ	49 Ⓐ Ⓑ Ⓒ Ⓓ Ⓔ
12 Ⓐ Ⓑ Ⓒ Ⓓ Ⓔ	25 Ⓐ Ⓑ Ⓒ Ⓓ Ⓔ	38 Ⓐ Ⓑ Ⓒ Ⓓ Ⓔ	50 Ⓐ Ⓑ Ⓒ Ⓓ Ⓔ
13 Ⓐ Ⓑ Ⓒ Ⓓ Ⓔ	26 Ⓐ Ⓑ Ⓒ Ⓓ Ⓔ		

SAT Practice Test 3

SECTION I

Time—30 minutes

45 Questions

For each of the numbered questions in this section, choose the best answer according to the instructions, and blacken the corresponding blank space on the answer sheet.

In each of the questions below, a capitalized word is followed by five words or phrases lettered (A) through (E). Select the word or phrase most nearly *opposite* in meaning to the capitalized word.

Since some of the questions require that you distinguish fine shades of meaning, consider all choices carefully before you select your answer.

1. EARTHY:
   (A) terrestrial
   (B) glowing
   (C) caustic
   (D) refined
   (E) defined

2. INDUCEMENT:
   (A) sweetener
   (B) dismissal
   (C) deterrent
   (D) bonus
   (E) duress

3. EXUBERANT:
   (A) dissuaded
   (B) urban
   (C) vexed
   (D) incensed
   (E) dispirited

4. ORNATE:
   (A) agreeable
   (B) rococo
   (C) bothersome
   (D) averse
   (E) austere

5. TIRADE:
   (A) waterfall
   (B) panegyric

6. LITHE:
   (A) inflexible
   (B) dislike
   (C) despise
   (D) limber
   (E) adore

7. FECUND:
   (A) erudite
   (B) recondite
   (C) assigned
   (D) volatile
   (E) barren

8. INDIGENOUS:
   (A) veracious
   (B) serene
   (C) foreign
   (D) inchoate
   (E) coincidental

9. PERUSE:
   (A) skim
   (B) circle
   (C) scrutinize
   (D) hoodwink
   (E) convince

(C) placebo
(D) leap
(E) silence

10. PURBLIND:
    (A) imaginative
    (B) farsighted
    (C) dazed
    (D) receptive
    (E) bigoted

11. JOCOSE:
    (A) saltatory
    (B) sentimental
    (C) rueful
    (D) solemn
    (E) conciliatory

12. HARMONIOUS:
    (A) consonant
    (B) symphonic
    (C) discordant
    (D) tonic
    (E) phonemic

13. LOYALTY:
    (A) calmness
    (B) perfidy
    (C) fervor
    (D) tension
    (E) perfection

14. DUPLICITY:
    (A) candor
    (B) pairing
    (C) conceit
    (D) deceit
    (E) simplicity

15. OVERT:
    (A) below
    (B) unseemly
    (C) cowardly
    (D) surreptitious
    (E) surrogate

Each of the sentences below has one or more blank spaces indicating where a word (or words) has been omitted. Each sentence is followed by five words or sets of words lettered from (A) through (E). Select the lettered word or set of words which, inserted to replace the blanks, *best* fits in with and completes the meaning of the sentence as a whole.

16. The most extraordinary thing about the marriage is that it happened at all, for on the surface the two could not have been more _____.
    (A) furtive
    (B) contemporary
    (C) rational
    (D) incompatible
    (E) gracious

17. To the wealthy plantation owners who _____ them, they are merely a pack of serfs, indistinguishable bundles of brown rags; among themselves, however, they are as passionate, as vengeful, as _____ of their honor as medieval knights.
    (A) regard . . respectful
    (B) employ . . concerned
    (C) despise . . timorous
    (D) ignore . . devoted
    (E) exploit . . jealous

18. Books are the _____ that a great genius leaves to mankind, which are delivered down from generation to generation, as presents to the _____ of those who are yet unborn.
    (A) present . . ancestors
    (B) products . . parents
    (C) legacy . . posterity
    (D) gifts . . desires
    (E) message . . history

19. Youth is the only season for enjoyment, and the first twenty-five years of one's life are worth all the rest of the longest life of man, even though those five-and-twenty be spent in _____ and contempt, and the rest in the possession of wealth, honors, and _____.
    (A) penury . . respectability
    (B) jail . . parsimony
    (C) sin . . one's senses
    (D) Russia . . esteem
    (E) meditation . . gluttony

20. They worked well together because they were perfectly complementary: Beatrice was good at gathering material, Sidney could digest and organize it; Beatrice was the _____ one, Sidney had the historical and political sense; Beatrice was emotional and moody, Sidney was cheerful and _____.
(A) flighty . . tender
(B) literary . . optimistic
(C) strong . . dependent
(D) gullible . . pretentious
(E) artistic . . flighty

21. O'Hara's seriousness as a writer is revealed in his willingness to _____ such unfashionable writers as Tarkington, Lewis, and Galsworthy as the main influences on his work, even while recognizing that they were _____ by gentlemanly qualms.
(A) assess . . stimulated
(B) disown . . guilty
(C) praise . . cursed
(D) credit . . inhibited
(E) criticize . . characterized

22. However flimsy and politically contrived his charges against the Administration, they created _____ and brought _____ to the man who introduced them.
(A) contempt . . dismay
(B) gossip . . censure
(C) hostility . . a halt
(D) excitement . . attention
(E) dissension . . contumely

23. Not until the middle of the last century, with the development of valved instruments that could _____ in every key, and with the prodding of such composers as Berlioz and Wagner, did the symphony orchestra _____ the form it still substantially has today.
(A) play . . assume
(B) participate . . invent
(C) improvise . . circumvent
(D) harmonize . . avoid
(E) accompany . . resume

24. Like Hudson, he has a sharp and sympathetic eye for natural history, and his book _____ in vivid pictorial glimpses of the landscape, but it is in his accounts of _____ history of Patagonia that he is most absorbing.
(A) reveals . . early
(B) resounds . . oral
(C) falls short . . modern
(D) teems . . the unwritten
(E) abounds . . human

25. Frederick Law Olmsted's and Calvert Vaux's great scheme for those 840 acres has long been _____ to be the nation's model urban park—a remarkable mix of landscaping and engineering, designed with significant _____ goals as well as esthetic ones.
(A) hoping . . intellectual
(B) thought . . artistic
(C) overestimated . . political
(D) overlooked . . philanthropic
(E) understood . . social

In each of the questions below, a related pair of words or phrases, in capital letters, is followed by five pairs of words or phrases lettered from (A) to (E). Select that lettered pair which expresses a relationship that is *most* similar to that of the capitalized pair.

26. PATTERN : DRESSMAKER ::
(A) script : writer
(B) folkways : patriarch
(C) script : director
(D) houseplan : architect
(E) baseball : umpire

27. DUKE : ARISTOCRACY ::
(A) governor : government
(B) Brahmin : caste
(C) beggar : sufferance
(D) priest : clergy
(E) bourgeoisie : middle class

28. REALTOR : LAND ::
  (A) notary : deed
  (B) banker : loan
  (C) scientist : atom
  (D) broker : bonds
  (E) physicist : relativity

29. RETICENT : RESERVED ::
  (A) fleeting : transient
  (B) scarce : abundant
  (C) order : chaos
  (D) discharged : retained
  (E) cow : bovine

30. ENTHUSIASM : INDIFFERENCE ::
  (A) ardor : fervor
  (B) zeal : apathy
  (C) concern : acerbity
  (D) health : nurture
  (E) remorse : coarseness

31. BUSHEL : GRAIN ::
  (A) karat : gold
  (B) ounce : prevention
  (C) carat : gemstone
  (D) pound : sterling
  (E) troy : avoirdupois

32. CROWDING : CONGESTION ::
  (A) indefatigable : untiring
  (B) compression : repression
  (C) concise : precise
  (D) short : sweet
  (E) brightness : brilliance

33. COKE : COAL ::
  (A) bread : cake
  (B) cola : heat
  (C) dough : yeast
  (D) bread : dough
  (E) chicle : gum

34. DRAGON : DINOSAUR ::
  (A) amphibian : marine
  (B) fabulous : real
  (C) primeval : medieval
  (D) minute : enormous
  (E) progenitor : progeny

35. BORE : PROLIX ::
  (A) senator : elected
  (B) excitement : stimulus
  (C) tedium : monotony
  (D) boor : oafish
  (E) ruffian : civil

Each of the reading passages below is followed by several questions about the contents of the passage. In answering the questions, base your responses on what is *stated* or *implied* in the passage.

Of Schubert himself we have a vivid image— short (five feet exactly) and a bit on the pudgy side, a potato nose, curly brown hair, gold-rimmed spectacles that he didn't take off even when he went to bed; consuming whatever wine or coffee he could afford or charge; the center of a circle of adoring friends who looked after him, provided him with places to live, joined him on hiking-tours (how much "walking" we find in his music), and with whom he played cards and charades; an unassuming little man whose Viennese accent was as dense as the knödel in his soup, and who somehow, blithely, without laborious sketching or erasing, composed masterpieces on tablecloths and on the backs of menus.

While it is true that correspondence between the young musician and his friends substantiates much of these impressions, Schubert's works were not all of the same spirit, nor all accomplished in a single burst of creative energy. We have, furthermore, the wrong idea if we imagine his works as going unnoticed and Schubert himself hopelessly neglected except within the circle of his friends. True, his fame was local, and the E-flat Piano Trio was the only work of his to be published abroad in his lifetime. But in fact, something like an eighth of his music was in print when he died. Not bad for a prolific musician with no connections, without an important career as a performer, and lacking all talent for self-promotion. Vienna, moreover, was a considerable musical center, and it meant something to be known there. On 7 March 1821, Johann Michael Vogl, a star of the Court Opera, sang the *Erlkönig* at an important charity concert, and that was the end of Schubert's obscurity in the capital.

Schubert never attained the success in the theater for which he so ardently longed, neither did he ever hear a professional performance of any of his symphonies, but for the rest, his music was sung and played, admired, and talked about.

36. Of the following statements, which is (are) true of Schubert's work?
    I. His work was unacclaimed except within his own coterie.
    II. His works were not performed professionally during his lifetime.
    III. All his works were written in friendless isolation.
    IV. Only one work was published abroad during his lifetime.
    V. More than a tenth of his work was in print when he died.
    (A) I and IV only
    (B) I and II only
    (C) IV only
    (D) IV and V only
    (E) II, III, and IV only

37. Schubert's personality is least characterized by
    I. self-aggrandizement
    II. pretension
    III. asceticism
    IV. gregariousness
    (A) I, II, and III only
    (B) I, II, and IV only
    (C) III only
    (D) IV only
    (E) I, II, III, and IV

38. The author's purpose in this passage seems to be
    (A) to demean the composer
    (B) to clear up common misconceptions about the composer's life
    (C) to reappraise Schubert's works
    (D) to analyze Schubert's compositions
    (E) to examine the influences on his composing

39. The author implies that certain traits, skills, or attributes were necessary or useful to a person seeking recognition in Schubert's time. Which of those listed below is not among them?

(A) An important performing career
(B) Important friends
(C) A talent for self-promotion
(D) Public performance of one's work
(E) A circle of adoring friends

40. The author's conclusion about Schubert's artistic life seems to be that
    (A) by and large Schubert was not to be pitied as having been a neglected genius
    (B) Schubert never achieved success in his field
    (C) Schubert suffered obscurity in the capital until after his death and the performance of the *Erlkönig*
    (D) Schubert blithely composed masterpieces on tablecloths and on the backs of menus, without laborious sketching or erasing
    (E) Schubert's works were all in the same spirit, accomplished in a single burst of creative energy

There are historians still at work who were high school students during the First World War, and for all the senior members of the historical profession the events of the 1920s and 1930s were among the great experiences that determined their lives and conditioned their outlooks. Until the 1950s it was fashionable for historians to look upon the most modern and contemporary era of history as beyond the limits of their subject. It used to be thought that the history of an era could be written only when it lay half a century or so in the past, when, so to speak, the historical dust has settled and the historian could take an "objective" view of what had happened, free from the passions and concerns of the present. The study of the contemporary era was something to be left to political scientists, sociologists, and journalists, all of whom were supposedly lacking in the austere dignity of the historian.

In the past two decades academic historians have abandoned this attitude, and the history of the contemporary world of the past half century has received careful and critical analysis. The line between the past and present had grown less distinct. Historians have come more and more to agree with Benedetto Croce's view that in a sense they are studying "an eternal present" and that the world of the past is largely understood in terms of current experience. The feudal world of the twelfth century is illuminated by our knowledge of changes in underdeveloped societies today; the pattern of the Industrial Revolution of the eighteenth century had been repeated in many twentieth-century societies; the experience of contemporary revolutions enables us to understand more clearly the course of the French Revolution and the attitudes of its leaders. There is a growing consensus that historians, sociologists, political scientists, and cultural anthropologists are all studying the same subject, the nature of social change, and the examination of this problem with reference to the recent and contemporary era is as valid an undertaking for the historian as the study of any period before 1914.

41. According to this passage,
    (A) historians have gone beyond the limits of their professions
    (B) senior members of the historical profession should write only about the 1920s and 1930s
    (C) only after the passing of at least half a century can the history of an era be properly written
    (D) it is now considered academically acceptable for historians to write histories of the contemporary era
    (E) high school students have much to learn from a study of the First World War, especially if they intend to become historians

42. Benedetto Croce's view that historians are studying ''an eternal present'' most nearly means
    (A) times may change, but history does not
    (B) the past and the present are one and the same
    (C) the study of the present is so time-consuming as to appear to take forever
    (D) understanding the present will keep us from repeating the mistakes of the past
    (E) our knowledge of today's world permits us a clearer understanding of the world of the past

43. The word *objective* as used in the first paragraph of the passage most nearly means
    (A) goal
    (B) dispassionate
    (C) concerned
    (D) personalized
    (E) protesting

44. The last sentence of the passage most nearly indicates that
    (A) scientists and historians are really in competition with one another
    (B) historians ought to leave the study of the present to the political scientists and cultural anthropologists, or stop pretending that their profession's goals are really different
    (C) what historians are really studying is the nature of social change
    (D) there is no real difference between historians and sociologists
    (E) only the study of the period before 1914 would be a valid undertaking for the historian

45. Which of the following statements is neither expressed nor implied in the reading passage?
    (A) The feudal world is illuminated by our knowledge of underdeveloped societies today.
    (B) Before 1950 historians tended to look upon the modern era as beyond the scope of their profession.
    (C) In the 1940s study of the contemporary era was left to the journalist.
    (D) The French Revolution, studies of the present show, revealed the attitudes of its leaders.
    (E) Historians now undertake studies they formerly shunned.

STOP
WORK ONLY ON THIS SECTION UNTIL THE TIME ALLOTTED IS OVER.

For each of the numbered questions in this section, choose the best answer according to the instructions, and blacken the corresponding blank space on the answer sheet.

In each of the questions below, a capitalized word is followed by five words or phrases lettered (A) through (E). Select the word or phrase most nearly *opposite* in meaning to the capitalized word.

Since some of the questions require that you distinguish fine shades of meaning, consider all choices carefully before you select your answer.

1. COURTEOUS:
   (A) civil
   (B) uncouth
   (C) arrogate
   (D) disregard
   (E) impolitic

2. INVARIABLE:
   (A) immutable
   (B) contentious
   (C) mixable
   (D) uncorruptible
   (E) changing

3. ABSTAIN:
   (A) prevent
   (B) prevail
   (C) cleanse
   (D) indulge
   (E) depart

4. EXONERATE:
   (A) disgrace
   (B) award posthumously
   (C) complain
   (D) implicate
   (E) write in

5. FATUOUS:
   (A) corporeal
   (B) inconsiderable
   (C) sensible
   (D) variegated
   (E) insincere

6. PROLIFIC:
   (A) barren
   (B) repetitive
   (C) unique
   (D) farfetched
   (E) irresolute

7. EBULLIENT:
   (A) boiling
   (B) downcast
   (C) swollen
   (D) formidable
   (E) flowering

8. GERMANE:
   (A) significant
   (B) flimsy
   (C) conflicting
   (D) flexible
   (E) irrelevant

9. SCRUPULOUS:
   (A) unprincipled
   (B) cancerous
   (C) uncaring
   (D) weighty
   (E) conscientious

10. EGREGIOUS:
    (A) unnecessary
    (B) vital
    (C) carefree
    (D) excusable
    (E) glaring

Each of the reading passages below is followed by several questions about the contents of the passage. In answering the questions, base your responses on what is *stated* or *implied* in the passage.

When President Carter vowed that "the U.S. will not be the first supplier to introduce into a region newly developed, advanced weapons systems which could create a new or significantly higher combat capability," most observers took the president to mean he would not let the U.S. take the first step in changing the balance of power in any region of the world. On Valentine's Day, 1978, in an arms deal that included aircraft for Israel and Egypt, Mr. Carter announced his intent to sell sixty F-15 Eagle aircraft to Saudi Arabia.

The F-15 Eagle is the most sophisticated combat aircraft flying. Newly developed, having entered service with our Air Force only in January 1976, it perfectly fits the president's definition of the kind of weapon this country would not be the first to introduce. It is highly advanced, though not so much for its advertised combat range of 2,800 miles which, because of extravagant consumption of fuel, it often fails to achieve. It is advanced because it is fast and maneuverable. It has frequently registered speeds in excess of Mach 2.54 (1,676 mph), and at combat weight, with half its internal fuel, it can climb faster and turn more sharply than any other aircraft. Indeed, the F-15 can make a turn of more than 14 degrees per second, and during that turn it can sustain more than five times its own weight without losing airspeed. That, as any pilot can tell you, is nothing short of miraculous. Finally, the Eagle is advanced because it carries the Hughes AN/APG-63 fire control radar, which has a target detection range of more than 100 miles, a system Air Force General Vogt describes as "a decade ahead of anything else."

It appeared that Carter has gone against his word, and intended to introduce an advanced weapons system into the Middle East, changing the balance of power there. Drew Middleton wrote then that "until now, Israel had been the sole recipient in the Middle East of advanced American weaponry." The following day, in an editorial that generally supported the Carter proposal, the *New York Times* conceded that the sale of sixty F-15s to the Saudis would "alter the balance of forces in the Middle East."

11. The primary purpose of this passage is
(A) to describe the capabilities of the F-15 Eagle
(B) to praise the president for vowing not to alter the balance of power in any region of the world
(C) to indicate that Mr. Carter intended to go against his avowed policy of not acting to affect the balance of power, anywhere
(D) to accuse the *New York Times* of contradicting itself
(E) to suggest that Drew Middleton had leaked the president's plan to send sixty F-15s to the Saudis

12. The author maintains that the F-15 Eagle is highly advanced for the following reason (reasons):
   I. It has an extravagant rate of fuel consumption.
  II. It is faster than any other aircraft.
 III. It can climb faster and turn more sharply than any other aircraft.
 IV. It carries the Hughes fire control radar.
(A) I and II only
(B) II and III only
(C) I and IV only
(D) III and IV only
(E) I, II, III, and IV

13. To advance his argument, the author uses
(A) emotional appeals
(B) contrast and comparison
(C) dramatic irony
(D) figurative language
(E) a logical, factual approach

14. The author quotes Drew Middleton in order to show that
    (A) the president was switching some support from Israel to Saudi Arabia and was, therefore, altering the balance of power in the Middle East
    (B) Israel would continue to receive favored treatment
    (C) Middleton and the *New York Times* were impartial
    (D) the Saudis merited the support of the U.S.
    (E) the president had been misquoted

15. The author, to strengthen and support his view that Carter intended to introduce an advanced weapons system into the Middle East,
    (A) dwells on the advantages of the F-15
    (B) quotes General Vogt on the Hughes fire control radar
    (C) points out that the arms deal includes aircraft for Israel and Egypt as well as for Saudi Arabia
    (D) states that the *New York Times* editorial generally supported the Carter proposal, but it also admitted that the deal would alter the status quo in the Middle East
    (E) suggests that Carter had gone against his word

Common terns have one nesting peculiarity in their favor. They avoid unvegetated outer beaches (the areas most frequented by sunbathers and swimmers) in favor of patches of beach grass and goldenrod. The least tern (*Sterna albifrons*), a smaller species that prefers open, sandy beaches, is now considered threatened in the east, and the Pacific coast race is endangered—its numbers diminished by human recreational activities within its colonies and, perhaps, by pesticides as well.

Human beachgoers also have strong preferences. They crowd together close to restaurants, restrooms, and other facilities. Seen from the air, the dispersion of humans near the parking lot on West End Beach produces a bell-shaped curve characteristic of a "normally distributed" population. Only a few people frequent the dunes and beaches away from the parking lot and facilities, thus leaving the bird colony relatively free of human intruders. The main contact between birds and people is the almost constant stream of automobile traffic on the road through the colony. On any summer day, however, instances of human intrusion into the colony do occur, and it is important to examine how birds and intruders react to each other.

Common terns usually produce a clutch of three well-camouflaged brown and speckled eggs. The nest itself is a simple indentation in the ground, embellished during the incubation period with straw or bits of shell. An uninitiated human intruder or natural predator cannot easily see the eggs. Once one knows what to look for, however, hundreds of nests can be found in a short time.

On rare occasion, people come to such colonies to collect eggs for food in the tradition of some European and South American cultures. Although such activities are strictly illegal, they do take place and can entirely eliminate a breeding population of birds. Fortunately, the West End Beach colony, despite its accessibility, has not been subject to egging. Vandalism, however, does occur. Footsteps are often seen leading into the colony and ending at a nest containing a broken egg. Perhaps this is due to a misplaced foot or to simple curiosity—a desire to see what is inside an egg. But sometimes the footsteps lead to a pile of wantonly broken eggs.

Much rarer is the vandal who deliberately kills the chicks. In one case a person drove a beach buggy through a colony in an apparent attempt to demolish nests. The colony at Breezy Point in Queens was destroyed by vandals in 1972 when it contained 2,000 pairs of common terns. A bird bander who periodically checked on the fortunes of that colony arrived one day to find the beach grass ablaze. Two adolescents told him that they had set the fire to see what the birds would do. As might be expected, the birds left.

16. It is fortunate that common terns avoid unvegetated outer beaches because
    (A) this leaves the beaches free for sunbathers and swimmers
    (B) the least tern would have to compete with them for nesting space, otherwise
    (C) their colony is thus relatively free of human intrusion
    (D) their nest and eggs can thus be well camouflaged
    (E) their presence there would interfere with egg gathering

17. The main contact between the terns and the beachgoers is
    (A) the area near the restrooms and restaurants
    (B) the steady flow of traffic along the road through the colony
    (C) the steady flow of vandals who wantonly destroy eggs
    (D) at the surf during periods of heavy recreational use
    (E) at beaches on the Pacific coast

18. While the author states that human intrusions into the colony do occur, he differentiates among intruders. Which of the following statements does not make a point made by the author?
    (A) Egg gathering for food is comparatively rare in tern colonies.
    (B) Occasionally people break an egg out of curiosity.
    (C) Sometimes evidence indicates the deliberate destruction of eggs for no known reason.
    (D) A tern colony was completely destroyed by vandals in 1972.
    (E) Vandals frequently attempt to kill chicks.

19. The word *wantonly* as used in the last sentence of the next to the last paragraph most nearly means
    (A) extravagantly
    (B) headstrong
    (C) without regard for what is right or humane
    (D) unrestrained
    (E) dissolute

20. The least tern is a threatened species in the east because
    (A) it is so much smaller than the common tern
    (B) human recreational activities intrude upon its nesting areas
    (C) it is not ''normally distributed''
    (D) its colonies are polluted by automobiles
    (E) its eggshells are broken by vandals

It was in 1839 that William Henry Fox Talbot read a paper to the Royal Society which had as its title: ''Some account of the Art of Photogenic Drawing, or the process by which Natural Objects may be made to delineate themselves without the aid of the artist's pencil.'' He was quite aware of photography as a kind of automation that eliminated the syntactical procedures of pen and pencil. He was probably less aware that he had brought the pictorial world into line with the new industrial procedures. For photography mirrored the external world automatically, yielding an exactly repeatable visual image. It was this all-important quality of uniformity and repeatability that had made the Gutenberg break between the Middle Ages and the Renaissance. Photography was almost as decisive in making the break between mere mechanical industrialism and the graphic age of electronic man. The step from the age of Typographic Man to the age of Graphic Man was taken with the invention of photography. Both daguerreotypes and photographs introduced light and chemistry into the making process. Natural objects delineated themselves by an exposure intensified by lens and fixed by chemicals. In the daguerreotype process there was the same stippling or pitting with minute dots that was echoed later by Seurat's *pointillisme*, and is still continued in the newspaper mesh of dots that is called ''wire-photo.'' Within a year of Daguerre's discovery, Samuel F. B. Morse was taking photographs of his wife and daughter in New York City. Dots for the eye (photograph) and dots for the ear (telegraph) thus met on top of a skyscraper.

A further cross-fertilization occurred in Talbot's invention of the photo, which he imagined as an extension of the *camera obscura*, or pictures in ''the little dark room,'' as the Italians had named the picture play-box of the sixteenth century. Just at the time when mechanical writing had been achieved by movable types, there grew up the pastime of looking at moving images on the wall of a dark room. If there is sunshine outside and a pinhole in one wall, then the images of the outer world will appear on the wall opposite. The new discovery was very exciting to painters, since it intensified the new illusion of perspective and of the third dimension that is so closely related to the printed word. But the early spectators of the moving image in the sixteenth century saw those images upside down. For this reason the lens was introduced—in order to turn the picture right side up. Psychically, we learn to turn our visual worlds right side up by translating the retinal impression from visual into tactile and kinetic terms. Right side up is apparently something we feel but cannot see directly.

21. The author refers to photography as a kind of automation. He means by this that
    (A) photography yields exact reproductions of images
    (B) a mechanical object produces an image, eliminating the human who used to do it
    (C) photography is an industrial process like printing
    (D) photography produced more pleasing images than painting or drawing
    (E) photography provides a more faithful image than does the artist

22. Photography was thought to be little more than an outgrowth of the *camera obscura* which was
    (A) a room in which slide shows were given
    (B) a dark room where film was developed and printed
    (C) a modified little theater where pantomimes were enacted
    (D) a dark room with a pinhole in one wall; images from the sunny outside world appeared on the wall opposite the pinhole
    (E) a little-known camera invented by Talbot

23. We can infer that the Royal Society referred to in the first sentence was
    (A) an organization of monarchists who supported Queen Victoria
    (B) an institution for the perpetuation of academic studies
    (C) a society, supported by the government of England, which concerns itself with scientific developments
    (D) founded to foster the art of photography and keep it competitive with other graphic arts
    (E) used as a clearinghouse for typographic, graphic, and communication industries

24. The invention of photography is compared with the invention of the Gutenberg printing press in this passage because they have in common that
    (A) they arrived at critical phases of history
    (B) they both provide for uniform and repeatable reproduction
    (C) their products are both used in the communication of information
    (D) they were eventually combined to be used in both books and periodicals
    (E) they were data processing systems

25. The title that best expresses the ideas of this passage is
    (A) The automated eye
    (B) The image is the message
    (C) Photography: a communications breakthrough
    (D) Daguerreotypes, tintypes, and prototypes
    (E) The *camera obscura*

GO ON TO THE NEXT PAGE

Each of the sentences below has one or more blank spaces indicating where a word (or words) has been omitted. Each sentence is followed by five words or sets of words lettered (A) through (E). Select the lettered word or set of words which, inserted to replace the blanks, *best* fits in with and completes the meaning of the sentence as a whole.

26. Lorenzo and Matthew were _____ by Landford's waspish criticism, but without exchanging so much as a word, they _____ chose to ignore him.
    (A) angered . . overt
    (B) inflamed . . solemnly
    (C) pleased . . politely
    (D) stung . . tacitly
    (E) hurt . . emphatically

27. The most _____ evidence against him was an eyewitness account that attested to his _____ at the scene of the crime.
    (A) recriminating . . footprints
    (B) sweeping . . resentment
    (C) heinous . . involvement
    (D) cogent . . disappearance
    (E) incriminating . . presence

28. In the seventeenth century, doctors listened carefully to their patients and looked at them carefully, too; diagnosis was an intellectual problem, carried on entirely without the technical _____ so visible and apparently _____ in any modern practitioner's office.
    (A) know-how . . lacking
    (B) conditions . . gratuitous
    (C) apparatus . . indispensable
    (D) refinements . . counterproductive
    (E) library . . unread

29. The speaker began his address by saying that what he valued most was _____, what he most abhorred was _____.
    (A) brevity . . verbosity
    (B) prolixity . . redundancy
    (C) wealth . . procrastination
    (D) inevitable . . irrefutable
    (E) originality . . copiousness

30. Had the voters known of Clarke's _____, they would never have _____ his candidacy.
    (A) frugality . . repealed
    (B) fecklessness . . opposed
    (C) venality . . countenanced
    (D) stamina . . encumbered
    (E) mendacity . . defeated

In each of the questions below, a related pair of words or phrases, in capital letters, is followed by five pairs of words or phrases lettered from (A) through (E). Select that lettered pair which expresses a relationship that is *most* similar to that of the capitalized pair.

31. SCEPTER : MONARCH ::
    (A) purple : grape
    (B) lion : serenity
    (C) gavel : chairperson
    (D) moss : vagabond
    (E) rose : thorn

32. QUACK : CHARLATAN ::
    (A) panacea : cure-all
    (B) remedy : dosage
    (C) tonic : snake oil
    (D) injection : intravenous
    (E) hypodermic : hypochondriac

33. PLUMP : CORPULENT ::
    (A) investment : speculation
    (B) flattered : adulated
    (C) turkey : elephant
    (D) slim : skinny
    (E) snake : crocodile

34. CARAPACE : ARMADILLO ::
    (A) cartilage : marrow
    (B) shell : turtle
    (C) quills : porcupine
    (D) tongue : anteater
    (E) transistor : radio

35. EXCULPATE : IMPLICATE ::
   (A) hint : suggest
   (B) conclude : deduce
   (C) honor : obey
   (D) exonerate : incriminate
   (E) debate : berate

36. SALESMAN : VOLUBLE ::
   (A) leader : supine
   (B) host : prudent
   (C) leader : decisive
   (D) artist : successful
   (E) ruler : autocratic

37. STABLE : IMMUTABLE ::
   (A) stallion : mare
   (B) valid : invalid
   (C) cipher : code
   (D) sometimes : always
   (E) unusual : unique

38. CURMUDGEON : CANTANKEROUS ::
   (A) trout : piscine
   (B) termagant : shrewish
   (C) terrapin : aqueous
   (D) frog : amphibious
   (E) pine : coniferous

39. INSULT : HUMILIATION ::
   (A) anger : arousal
   (B) amusement : entertainment
   (C) tears : crying
   (D) commendation : pride
   (E) jeering : disappointment

40. OSLO : NORWAY ::
   (A) Riga : Latvia
   (B) Milan : Italy
   (C) Rio de Janeiro : Brazil
   (D) Bombay : Calcutta
   (E) Toronto : Canada

STOP
WORK ONLY ON THIS SECTION UNTIL THE TIME ALLOTTED IS OVER.

Time—30 minutes

25 Questions

In the mathematical sections, use any available space on the page for scratchwork in solving problems. Then indicate the *one* correct answer by darkening the appropriate oval on the answer sheet.

You may wish to refer to the following formulas and relationships in solving some of the problems.

Triangle:
The sum of the angles of any triangle is one straight angle, or 180 degrees.

The area of a triangle $= \frac{1}{2}$ (base $\times$ altitude).

In a right triangle, the square of the hypotenuse = the sum of the squares of the legs.

Circle of radius r:
Area $= \pi r^2$
Circumference $= 2\pi r$
There are 360 degrees of arc in a circle.

Definition of Symbols

$=$ is equal to	$\leqq$ is less than or equal to
$\neq$ is unequal to	$\geqq$ is greater than or equal to
$<$ is less than	$\parallel$ is parallel to
$>$ is greater than	$\perp$ is perpendicular to
$\approx$ nearly equal to	$\cong$ congruent to

Note: Figures are drawn as accurately as possible *except* when it is stated in a specific problem that its figure is not drawn to scale. All figures lie in a plane unless otherwise indicated. All numbers used in this test are real numbers.

1. If $6 \times 6 \times t = 18 \times 18 \times 18$, then $t =$
   (A) 3
   (B) 9
   (C) 54
   (D) 108
   (E) 162

2. The temperature at the bottom of a ski lift is $12°$ and at the top is $-18°$. How many degrees higher is the temperature at the bottom than at the top?
   (A) $6°$
   (B) $-6°$
   (C) $30°$
   (D) $-30°$
   (E) $40°$

3. How many 9-inch pieces of molding can be cut from a 6-foot piece?

(A) $\frac{2}{3}$ (D) 8

(B) $1\frac{1}{2}$ (E) 12

(C) $4\frac{1}{2}$

4.

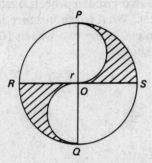

In the figure above, the circle with center at O has a radius of 2. Diameters PQ and RS are perpendicular. Semicircles are drawn with diameters PO and OQ as shown. Find the shaded area.

(A) π

(B) $\frac{\pi}{2}$

(C) 2π

(D) $\frac{3\pi}{2}$

(E) 4π

5. A boy runs $\frac{4}{5}$ of the distance around a circular track in m minutes. How many minutes does it take him to run around the entire track at the same rate?

(A) $\frac{m}{4}$ (D) $\frac{5}{4m}$

(B) $\frac{5m}{4}$ (E) $\frac{4}{m}$

(C) $\frac{4m}{5}$

6. An aircraft flies 3 miles in 15 seconds. What is its speed in miles per hour?
(A) 440
(B) 520
(C) 600
(D) 720
(E) 800

7. In a class of 30 students, the average on a certain test is p. The teacher decides to raise each mark 10 points. What is the new average?
(A) $p + 10$
(B) $p + 30$
(C) $p + 300$
(D) $10p$
(E) $p + 3$

8.

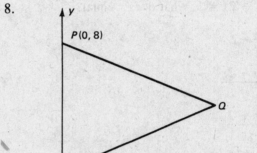

Figure not drawn to scale.

In the graph above, the area of triangle OPQ is 64. Find the length of the altitude from Q to OP.
(A) 8
(B) 10
(C) 12
(D) 14
(E) 16

9. How many degrees between the hands of a clock at 6:30 p.m.?
(A) 0
(B) 10
(C) 15
(D) 20
(E) 30

10. Find the value of t in the equation:
$$5t - .5t = 9.$$
(A) 0
(B) 2
(C) 4
(D) 6
(E) 9

11. A rectangular flower bed 16 yards long by 12 yards wide is surrounded by a walk 3 yards wide. The number of square yards in the area of the walk is
(A) 93
(B) 168
(C) 177
(D) 186
(E) 204

12. If $r(y - 2) = b$, what does y equal?

(A) $\dfrac{b}{r} - 2$

(B) $\dfrac{b + 2r}{r}$

(C) $\dfrac{b + 2}{r}$

(D) $\dfrac{b + 2r}{2}$

(E) $\dfrac{r}{b + 2}$

13. Which number is the best estimate of $\sqrt{61}$?
(A) 2.5
(B) 7.3
(C) 7.8
(D) 8.1
(E) 9.2

14. In the tally system, the number 7 is represented by ⦀⦀ ||. In writing the number 39 in the tally system, how many tallies are uncrossed?
(A) 0
(B) 1
(C) 2
(D) 3
(E) 4

15.

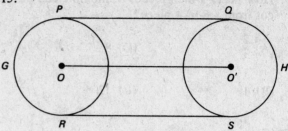

A conveyor belt 6 feet long is drawn tightly around two circular wheels each 1 foot in diameter. What is the distance in feet between the centers of the two wheels (OO' in the figure above)?
(A) π

(B) $6 - \pi$

(C) $\dfrac{\pi - 6}{2}$

(D) $\dfrac{3\pi}{2}$

(E) $\dfrac{6 - \pi}{2}$

16. Which of the following has no finite value that can be determined?

(A) $\dfrac{0}{3}$

(B) 3×0

(C) $0 - 3$

(D) $\dfrac{3}{0}$

(E) None of these

17. John has half as much money as Bob. If Bob gives John $5.00, John will have $4.00 less than Bob has then. How much money did John and Bob have together originally?
(A) $23
(B) $27
(C) $42
(D) $48
(E) $51

18.

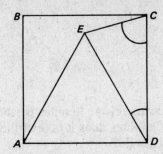

In the figure above, *ABCD* is a square and *ADE* is an equilateral triangle. How many degrees in ∠*ECD*?

(A) 75   (D) 60
(B) 70   (E) 55
(C) 65

19.

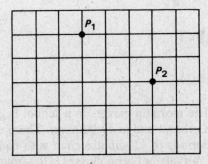

In the figure above, the coordinates of P_1 are (2,4). What are the coordinates of P_2?

(A) (2,5)
(B) (5,2)
(C) (2,2)
(D) (5,1)
(E) (5,5)

20. If $r + s = 100$ and $\frac{r}{s} = \frac{1}{4}$, then $s - r =$

(A) −100
(B) 30
(C) 50
(D) 60
(E) 75

21. What is the surface area of a cube with a volume of $64k^3$?

(A) $16k^2$ (D) $16k^3$
(B) $96k^2$ (E) $256k^3$
(C) $64k^2$

22. If the tax on a radio priced at $125 is $20, at the same rate how much should the tax be on a radio priced at $175?

(A) $16
(B) $24
(C) $28
(D) $32
(E) $35

23. If p is an integer, which of the following cannot equal zero?

   I. $p - 1$
   II. $p + 1$
   III. $p^2 - 1$
   IV. $p^2 + 1$

(A) only II and IV
(B) only III
(C) only IV
(D) only I and III
(E) only II, III, and IV

24. If the radius of circle P is 60% of the radius of circle Q, the area of circle P is what percent of the area of circle Q?

(A) 36
(B) 40
(C) 64
(D) 80
(E) 120

25.

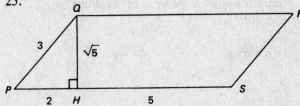

In the figure above, *PQRS* is a parallelogram with measurements as shown. The length of diagonal *PR* is

(A) $\sqrt{5}$
(B) 3
(C) 7
(D) $\sqrt{58}$
(E) $\sqrt{86}$

STOP
WORK ONLY ON THIS SECTION UNTIL THE TIME ALLOTTED IS OVER.

1. The number of inches in k yards is

   (A) $\dfrac{k}{36}$

   (B) $\dfrac{k}{12}$

   (C) $3k$

   (D) $12k$

   (E) $36k$

2. If $n - x = n$, then x equals

   (A) 0

   (B) n

   (C) $\dfrac{n}{2}$

   (D) $2n$

   (E) $\dfrac{2}{n}$

3. Six pints is what percent of 2 gallons?

   (A) 30

   (B) $33\dfrac{1}{3}$

   (C) $37\dfrac{1}{2}$

   (D) $137\dfrac{1}{2}$

   (E) 300

4. If a car travels at 50 miles per hour, how many minutes does it take at this rate to travel 1 mile?

   (A) $\dfrac{5}{6}$

   (B) $1\dfrac{1}{6}$

   (C) $1\dfrac{1}{4}$

   (D) $1\dfrac{1}{5}$

   (E) $1\dfrac{1}{3}$

5. The morning classes in a school begin at 9:00 a.m. and end at 12:00 noon. There are 4 class periods of 42 minutes each with equal intervals between classes. How many minutes are there in each interval?

   (A) 3

   (B) 4

   (C) $3\dfrac{1}{2}$

   (D) $4\dfrac{1}{2}$

   (E) $4\dfrac{1}{4}$

6. Every seat in a bus was taken and 5 people were standing. At the next stop 12 people got off and 6 got on. How many seats were empty after this stop if everyone was seated?

   (A) 1
   (B) 2
   (C) 4
   (D) 5
   (E) 7

7. A rectangular fish tank is 4 feet long, 3 feet wide and 2 feet high. If the water in the tank rises to a level 4 inches from the top of the tank, how many cubic feet of water are there in the tank?
(A) 8
(B) 12
(C) 16
(D) 20
(E) 24

8. Which of the following number triples *cannot* be the sides of a *right* triangle?
(A) 9, 12, 15
(B) 10, 24, 26
(C) 8, 11, 15
(D) 8, 15, 17
(E) 7, 7, 7√2

9.

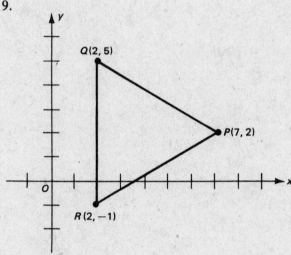

In the figure above, what is the area of triangle *PQR*?
(A) 10
(B) 12
(C) 15
(D) 21
(E) 30

10. A dealer bought *n* articles for *x* dollars one year and for *y* dollars ($y > x$) the following year. What was his increase in cost, in dollars per article?

(A) $\dfrac{y - x}{n}$

(B) $\dfrac{x - y}{n}$

(C) $\dfrac{y}{n}$

(D) $\dfrac{y}{x}$

(E) $\dfrac{n}{y - x}$

11. The diagonals of a parallelogram divide the figure into four triangles which are
(A) isosceles
(B) equal in area
(C) congruent
(D) similar
(E) equilateral

12. If *p* and *q* are positive numbers, which of the following is (are) always true?

I. $\sqrt{p^2 - q^2} = p - q$

II. $\sqrt{p^2 q^2} = pq$

III. $\sqrt{\dfrac{p^2}{q^2}} = \dfrac{p}{q}$

(A) I and II only
(B) II and III only
(C) III only
(D) I, II, and III
(E) II only

13. Line segment *PQ* is 24 inches long; point *R* is located on *PQ* so that *PR* is to *RQ* as 5 is to 3. What is the length in inches of *RQ*?
(A) 3
(B) 6
(C) 8
(D) 9
(E) 15

14. A student has taken n tests and has an 80% average. What must he get on his next test to raise his average to 82%?
    (A) $2n - 82$
    (B) $n + 82$
    (C) $2n + 82$
    (D) $2n + 80$
    (E) $2n - 80$

15. If $5p + 8 = 3 + 5q$, find the value of $p - q$.
    (A) 1

    (B) $2\frac{1}{5}$

    (C) -1

    (D) $-2\frac{1}{5}$

    (E) It cannot be determined from the information given

16. Which of the following is the best

    approximation for $\sqrt{\dfrac{2.698}{.031} - 9.03}$?

    (A) 3
    (B) 5
    (C) 7
    (D) 9
    (E) 11

17.

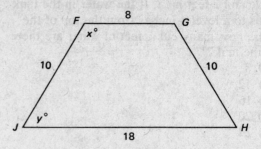

In the isosceles trapezoid above, the lengths of the sides are as shown. Then $x - y =$
(A) 90
(B) 60
(C) 45
(D) 30
(E) 20

Questions 18–35 each consist of two quantities, one in Column A and one in Column B. Compare the two quantities and on the answer sheet blacken oval

A if the quantity in Column A is greater;
B if the quantity in Column B is greater;
C if the two quantities are equal;
D if the relationship cannot be determined from the information given.

All letters such as x, y and n represent real numbers. A symbol appearing in both columns represents the same quantity in Column A as it does in Column B.

In some questions, information concerning one or both of the quantities to be compared is centered above the two columns.

Column A	Column B
18. 30% of 70	70% of 30

19.
$$2 < p < 7$$
$$7 < q < 10$$

p	q

20.
r, s, and t are positive integers
$$r > 1$$

$r(s + t)$	$rs + t$

21. $\dfrac{1}{3} \times \dfrac{1}{4}$ $\dfrac{1}{3} \div \dfrac{1}{4}$

22.
$$r = 2s$$

$6s + 3$	$2r + 3$

23. $11 \times 180 \times 7$ $9 \times 180 \times 12$

24.

n	q

25. Area of circle with diameter d Area of square with side $\dfrac{3}{4}d$

Column A	Column B

Questions 26 and 27 refer to figure below.

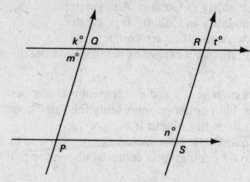

Figure not drawn to scale.
PQRS is a parallelogram

26.	k	n

27.	m + k	n + t

28. $r > s, r, s \neq 0$

$\dfrac{1}{r}$	$\dfrac{1}{s}$

Questions 29 and 30 refer to diagram below.

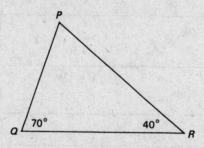

Figure not drawn to scale.

29.	PQ	QR

30.	PR	QR

31. $x \geqq 0, y - 2x = 5$

x	y

32.	$\sqrt[3]{28.2}$	$\sqrt{8.92}$

33. $0 < k < 1$

k^2	k

34.

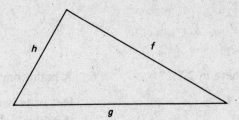

Figure not drawn to scale.

f $g - h$

35.

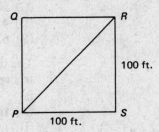

$PQRS$ is a square

| The number of seconds it takes a man to walk from P to R directly at 5 feet per second | The number of seconds it takes a man to run from P to Q and Q to R at 8 feet per second |

STOP
WORK ONLY ON THIS SECTION UNTIL THE TIME ALLOTTED IS OVER.

Time—30 minutes

25 Questions

1. How many thousandths are there in 2.7%?
   (A) .27
   (B) 2.7
   (C) 27
   (D) 270
   (E) 20.7

2. $.04 \div \dfrac{4}{.5} =$

   (A) .005
   (B) .05
   (C) .5
   (D) 5
   (E) .32

3. A book club charges 10¢ for the first 3 days and 6¢ for each additional day the book is borrowed. If a borrower pays $1.18 for the loan of a book, for how many days was the book borrowed?
   (A) 15
   (B) 18
   (C) 20
   (D) 21
   (E) 24

4. An equilateral triangle 3 inches on each side is divided up into equilateral triangles 1 inch on each side. What is the maximum number of the smaller triangles that can be formed?
   (A) 3
   (B) 6
   (C) 9
   (D) 12
   (E) 15

5. The length of a rectangular court is 6 feet shorter than twice its width, w. The perimeter of the court is
   (A) $3w - 6$
   (B) $6w - 6$
   (C) $4w - 12$
   (D) $3w - 12$
   (E) $6w - 12$

6. A bathroom floor that is $7\dfrac{2}{3}$ feet long and 6 feet wide is covered with tiles, each of which is a square 4 inches on a side. How many tiles cover the floor?
   (A) 45
   (B) 75
   (C) 207
   (D) 414
   (E) 620

7. The degree measures of the three angles of a triangle are in the ratio of 2:3:5. The triangle is
   (A) right
   (B) isosceles
   (C) equilateral
   (D) acute with no equal angles
   (E) obtuse with no equal angles

8. If $\dfrac{r + 40}{s + 20} = 1$, s is what percent of r?

   (A) 75
   (B) 150
   (C) 200
   (D) 50
   (E) It is impossible to tell from the given information

9. If an isosceles triangle has sides of x and $2x + 1$, what is its perimeter?
   (A) $5x + 1$
   (B) $4x + 1$
   (C) $5x + 2$
   (D) $3x$
   (E) It is impossible to tell from the given information

10. If the area of one circle is twice that of another, what is the ratio of the radius of the larger circle to that of the smaller?

(A) $\dfrac{\sqrt{2}}{2}$

(B) $\dfrac{1}{2}$

(C) $\dfrac{1}{4}$

(D) $\sqrt{2}$

(E) 2

11.

3 teaspoons	=	1 tablespoon
16 tablespoons	=	1 cup
8 ounces	=	1 cup

Using the table above, 2 ounces equals how many teaspoons?

(A) 6

(B) 12

(C) $42\dfrac{2}{3}$

(D) 10

(E) $1\dfrac{1}{2}$

12. A gong sounds every 35 minutes starting at midnight. On the same night, exactly how many minutes will pass after 4:12 a.m. until the gong sounds again?

(A) 7
(B) 9
(C) 14
(D) 19
(E) 28

13. A wheel of diameter 30 inches revolves 120 times in going a certain distance. What is the total number of times a wheel of 15-inch diameter would revolve to go the same distance?

(A) 240
(B) 160

(C) 100
(D) 80
(E) 60

14. $\dfrac{1}{1 + \dfrac{x}{1 + \dfrac{x}{1 + x}}} = 1$; then $x =$

(A) -1

(B) 0

(C) 1

(D) 2

(E) $\dfrac{1}{2}$

15.

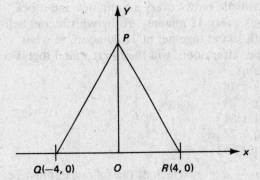

In the figure above, triangle PQR is equilateral. The coordinates of point P are

(A) $(0,4)$

(B) $(4\sqrt{3},0)$

(C) $(8\sqrt{3},0)$

(D) $(0,8\sqrt{3})$

(E) $(0,4\sqrt{3})$

16. The time in city A is 3 hours later than in city B. A plane leaves city A at 5 p.m. for city B and arrives there 4 hours later. What time is it in city B upon arrival?

(A) 6 a.m.
(B) 6 p.m.
(C) 2 p.m.
(D) 3 p.m.
(E) 4 p.m.

17.

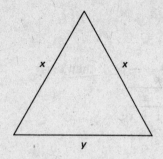

In the figure above, $10 < x < 20$. Which of the following gives all possible values of y?
(A) $0 < y < 20$
(B) $0 < y < 40$
(C) $5 < y < 20$
(D) $10 < y < 40$
(E) $20 < y < 80$

18. A whistle blows every 14 minutes and a bell rings every 12 minutes. If the whistle and bell both sound together at 12:00 noon, at what time, after noon, will they first sound together again?
(A) 2:48
(B) 2:24
(C) 1:54
(D) 1:24
(E) 12:42

19. If $p - q = r$, which of the following must be true?

  I. $3p - 3q = 3r$

  II. $p^2 - q^2 = r^2$

  III. $\dfrac{p}{r} = \dfrac{q}{r}$

(A) I and II only
(B) II and III only
(C) I only
(D) II only
(E) I and III only

20. A milk can contains g gallons of milk. If the milk is withdrawn at the rate of w quarts a minute for 20 minutes, how many gallons of milk will remain in the can?
(A) $g - 20w$
(B) $g - 5w$
(C) $5w - g$
(D) $20w - g$
(E) $g - 80w$

21. A block of wood $9'' \times 3'' \times 12''$ is to be cut into cubes that are the largest that can be cut from this block. How many of them will there be?
(A) 6
(B) 8
(C) 10
(D) 12
(E) 14

22. In right triangle RST, the ratio of the legs is 2:3. If the area of the triangle is 75, what is the length of the hypotenuse ST?
(A) 4
(B) $4\sqrt{5}$
(C) $13\sqrt{5}$
(D) $5\sqrt{3}$
(E) $5\sqrt{13}$

23. What is the surface area in square feet of a cube with a volume of 125 cubic feet?
(A) 25
(B) 27
(C) 64
(D) 100
(E) 150

24.

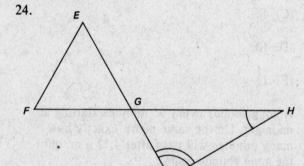

In the diagram above, EFG is an equilateral triangle. Sides FG and EG are extended through G to H and K and another triangle is formed. The sum of the measures in degrees of angles K and H is
(A) 60
(B) 120
(C) 135
(D) 140
(E) 150

25. If $p = 4q$ and $q = 2r$, find r in terms of p.

(A) $\dfrac{p}{2}$

(B) $\dfrac{p}{4}$

(C) $\dfrac{p}{8}$

(D) $4p$

(E) $8p$

STOP
WORK ONLY ON THIS SECTION UNTIL THE TIME ALLOTTED IS OVER.

Time—30 minutes

50 Questions

This section tests your ability to use standard written English, the kind used in more formal writing. Standard written English is quite different from the English we may use when speaking to friends. In the sentences below, you might find constructions and forms that you would use at particular times to meet particular needs, but you are being asked to determine correctness only on the basis of what would be acceptable in standard written English. <u>Directions</u>: Some of the following sentences contain errors in grammar, usage, diction (choice of words), and idiom. Some of the sentences are correct. No sentence, however, contains more than one error. If a sentence has an error, it will be in one of the lettered and underlined words or phrases. Assume there are no errors in the parts of the sentence that are not underlined. *If there is an error in any underlined part, note the letter under it, and blacken the corresponding space on the answer sheet. If the sentence is free of errors, blacken answer space (E). Follow the guidelines for standard written English when determining the answer.*

1. If <u>anyone</u> has <u>any</u> doubts about the value of this tour, refer <u>them</u> to <u>me</u>.
      A   B   C   D
   <u>No error</u>
    E

2. <u>Any</u> student <u>who's</u> locker is not cleaned out <u>by</u> next Wednesday <u>will have</u>
    A   B   C   D
   to report to the Dean. <u>No error</u>
                    E

3. The young woman <u>who</u> was <u>just named</u> as the winner in the prestigious
                  A   B
   Naumberg Competition has <u>scarcely no</u> equal as a <u>violist</u>. <u>No error</u>
                      C   D   E

4. Despite the fact that you and <u>she</u> went to the same schools, <u>Ellen's</u>
                         A   B
   experiences <u>were</u> quite different from <u>your's</u>. <u>No error</u>
           C   D   E

5. In a departure <u>from</u> our previous <u>concentration</u> on cognitive <u>skills</u>, we are
                  A   B   C
   going to focus on the <u>affective</u> behavior in the early years. <u>No error</u>
                      D   E

6. Between <u>you and I</u>, the reason he <u>gave</u> for leaving school in the middle of
            A   B
   the semester was just <u>to conceal</u> the fact that he <u>was failing</u>. <u>No error</u>
                     C   D   E

7. <u>Neither</u> the chairperson <u>nor</u> the members of the committee <u>are</u> available
    A   B   C
<u>for</u> public comment at this time. <u>No error</u>
 D   E

8. It is difficult <u>to detect</u> errors in <u>these kinds</u> of statistics, <u>since</u> the raw
                  A   B   C
data <u>is</u> unavailable. <u>No error</u>
     D   E

9. "There is <u>no such</u> animal!" the man said <u>as he</u> watched the giraffe
           A   B
<u>gallop across</u> the fields, <u>having made his escape</u>. <u>No error</u>
   C   D   E

10. We still <u>have not had</u> a definitive statement <u>as to</u> the <u>exact affects</u> on us
            A   B   C
of a nuclear accident <u>at the proposed</u> power plant. <u>No error</u>
                   D   E

11. The man <u>who</u> I pointed out <u>to</u> you <u>just moved</u> into the house <u>next to ours</u>.
          A   B   C   D
<u>No error</u>
  E

12. <u>After putting</u> the engine through exhaustive tests, the engineers finally
     A
discovered <u>that the load</u> was too great for the <u>compressor, causing</u> the
           B   C
casing <u>to burst</u>. <u>No error</u>
       D   E

13. <u>When</u> I reached <u>class</u>, <u>I realized</u> I <u>took</u> the wrong book. <u>No error</u>
    A   B   C   D   E

14. <u>After much discussion</u>, the librarian <u>and myself</u> agreed that the students in
          A   B
the sophomore class, <u>since they were</u> on the late session, would be
                      C
permitted to use the reference <u>room in the mornings</u>. <u>No error</u>
                              D   E

15. When we <u>arose</u> the next <u>morning, we</u> discovered that the river <u>rose</u>
          A   B   C
another foot during the night, <u>making the crossing</u> impossible. <u>No error</u>
                             D   E

16. <u>Being that</u> Miss Brunswick was <u>new to the job</u>, the other computer
     A   B
analysts <u>were as</u> helpful to her <u>as they could be</u> without neglecting their
         C   D
own work. <u>No error</u>
         E

17. <u>All of the</u> students except <u>Terry and us</u> will be expected to turn in <u>his</u>
       A   B   C

    assignments before <u>the end of the following week</u>. <u>No error</u>
                        D   E

18. When the opening day of the convention <u>arrived</u>, I <u>uttered</u> a silent prayer
                                         A   B

    <u>that each</u> member of the huge staff <u>knows</u> his assignment. <u>No error</u>
     C   D   E

19. <u>Although</u> I would never admit it publicly, I secretly believe that very
       A

    <u>few people</u> are better at grammar and writing <u>than</u> <u>me</u>. <u>No error</u>
       B   C   D   E

20. Large schools make new entrants feel as if they <u>were mere ciphers</u>, small
                                                 A

    cogs in <u>a giant machine</u>, but <u>you</u> very soon <u>feel at home</u>. <u>No error</u>
            B   C   D   E

21. Listening to the performances of the <u>two</u> finalists, we <u>were soon</u>
                                   A   B

    convinced that <u>the first</u> was <u>the better</u> of the two. <u>No error</u>
              C   D   E

22. He walked slowly through the woods, <u>under the great trees</u>, the golden
                                      A

    autumn leaves <u>clinging to</u> his clothes <u>as they</u> softly <u>had fallen</u> on him.
             B   C   D

    <u>No error</u>
     E

23. <u>When I look</u> back on the many family dinners Mother <u>had prepared</u> over
       A   B

    the years, I wonder <u>why</u> she never expected Dad <u>and I</u> to help. <u>No error</u>
                   C   D   E

24. <u>Did you</u> notice how <u>beautifully</u> the sky looked that day <u>just after</u> the rain
       A   B   C

    <u>had stopped</u>? <u>No error</u>
       D   E

25. We thought we <u>had made</u> adequate arrangements <u>for seating</u>, but a larger
              A   B

    <u>amount</u> of people <u>showed up</u> than we had expected. <u>No error</u>
      C   D   E

Directions: In each of the sentences below, a part or the whole of the sentence is underlined. Following each sentence will be five different ways of writing the underlined segment—the first an exact repeat of the underlined original, the other four different. *If you think the underlined segment is correct as it stands, you will select choice (A) as your answer. If you think the underlined segment is incorrect as it stands, select the one of the remaining lettered choices that you think makes the sentence correct.* For whichever of the five lettered choices you select as correct, blacken the corresponding space on your answer sheet.

This portion of the examination tests your ability to determine correctness and effectiveness of expression according to the requirements of standard written English. You are to take into account grammar, diction (choice of words), sentence construction, and punctuation. *Do not select a version that changes the original sense of the sentence as given.* Choose the version that offers the clearest, most precise sentence according to the guidelines imposed.

26. When the ship reached the naval base,
    a full compliment of officers and men was waiting to board it.
    (A) a full compliment of officers and men was waiting
    (B) a full compliment of officers and men were waiting
    (C) a full compliment of officer's and men were waiting
    (D) a full complement of officers and men was waiting
    (E) a full complement of officers and men were waiting

27. The temperature had risen into the nineties, every man, woman, and child looked ready to pass out.
    (A) risen into the nineties, every man, woman, and child
    (B) risen into the nineties. Every man, woman, and child
    (C) risen into the nineties every man, woman, and child
    (D) risen into the nineties, every man woman and child
    (E) risen into the nineties, because every man, woman, and child

28. Ellison and the others searched everywhere for him,
    in vain; when the sun rose, they found him, at last, lifeless beneath the tree.
    (A) in vain; when the sun rose, they found him,
    (B) in vain; when the sun rose they found him
    (C) in vain, when the sun rose, they found him,
    (D) in vain. When the sun rose, they found him,
    (E) in vain—they found him when the sun rose

29. When Hawkins saw what Thompson was doing, he broke his hatchet and threw it into the deepest part of the lake.
    (A) was doing, he broke his hatchet
    (B) was doing he broke his hatchet
    (C) was doing, he broke his own hatchet
    (D) was doing; he broke his hatchet
    (E) had done, he had broken his hatchet

30. Although I was sure he would never do so, he said
he would try and raise the money to liquidate his debt to me.
(A) he would try and raise the money to liquidate his debt
(B) he would try to raise the money to liquidate his debt
(C) he would try and raise enough money to liquidate his debt
(D) he would, "try and raise the money to liquidate his debt
(E) he would try to liquidate his debts

31. West Germany and Japan are as strong if not stronger than they were
before World War II, economically, if not militarily.
(A) are as strong if not stronger than they were
(B) are as strong as if not stronger than they were
(C) are as strong if not stronger then they were
(D) are as strong and stronger than they were
(E) are as strong as if not stronger than they had been

32. Egyptian architecture had reached the highest peak of any other nation up
to that time.
(A) had reached the highest peak of any other nation
(B) had reached the highest peak, of any other nation
(C) has reached the highest peak of any other nation
(D) had reached the highest peak of any nation
(E) had attained the highest peak of any other nation

33. Not only would I vote for him again, but I would also campaign for him.
(A) again, but I would also campaign for him
(B) again, but also I would campaign for him
(C) again but also campaign for him
(D) again, but also campaign for him
(E) again, but I would campaign for him as well

34. Driving toward the desert,
badly weathered but still visible, a sign proclaimed, "You are entering Mt.
Pleasant, the Eden of the West."
(A) badly weathered but still visible, a sign proclaimed,
(B) badly weathered but still visible, a sign proclaimed
(C) badly weathered but still visible, we saw a sign that proclaimed,
(D) badly weathered and still visible, a sign proclaimed,
(E) we saw a sign, badly weathered but still visible, that proclaimed,

35. I think back with fondness upon all the things I loved to do when I
was young: swimming, riding, rock climbing, and jigsaw puzzles.
(A) was young: swimming, riding, rock climbing, and jigsaw puzzles
(B) was young: swimming, riding, rock climbing, and doing jigsaw
    puzzles
(C) had been young: swimming, riding, rock climbing, and jigsaw puzzles
(D) had been young: swimming, riding, rock climbing, doing jigsaw
    puzzles
(E) was young. Swimming, riding, rock climbing, and doing jigsaw
    puzzles

36. He looked at those early paintings with wonder and
asked himself, "Are those really mine or are they someone elses?"
(A) asked himself, "Are those really mine or are they someone elses?"
(B) asked himself "Are those really mine or are they someone elses?"
(C) asked himself, "Are those really mine or are they someone else's?"
(D) asked himself if those were really his or someone elses.
(E) asked himself, "Are those really mine or someone elses?"

37. Every member of the candidate's staff did his best to get out the vote.
(A) did his best to get out the vote
(B) did their best to get out the vote
(C) did their best to get the vote out
(D) did his best to get the voters out
(E) had done his best to get out the vote

38. The research is done first, and then you write the report.
(A) The research is done first,
(B) First you do the research,
(C) First the research is done,
(D) First having done the research
(E) First the research

39. Jud quickly became aware that the aim of their innocent-sounding
plans to organize a militia were really a plot to seize control of the
settlement.
(A) plans to organize a militia were really a plot
(B) plans to organize militia were really a plot
(C) plans, to organize a militia was really a plot
(D) plans to have an organized militia were really a plot
(E) plans to organize a militia was really a plot

40. Take stock of your assets and then you should try to decide what course of
action to take.
(A) Take stock of your assets and then you should try to decide
(B) Take stock of your assets and then try to decide
(C) Take stock of your assets; then you should try to decide
(D) Take stock of your assets! Decide
(E) First take stock of your assets, and then you can try to decide

GO ON TO THE NEXT PAGE

The directions that follow are the same as those given at the beginning of this section. They are repeated for your convenience, for easy reference, as you work on the questions below.

<u>Directions</u>: Some of the following sentences contain errors in grammar, usage, diction (choice of words), and idiom. Some of the sentences are correct. No sentence, however, contains more than one error. If a sentence has an error, it will be in one of the lettered and underlined words or phrases. Assume there are no errors in the parts of the sentence that are not underlined. *If there is an error in any underlined part, note the letter under it, and blacken the corresponding space on the answer sheet. If the sentence is free of errors, blacken answer space (E).* Follow the guidelines for standard written English when determining the answer.

41. Bob <u>set</u> the vase down carefully while Joan and <u>I</u> made sure that <u>neither</u>
       A   B   C
    the baby nor the dog would <u>get</u> in his way. <u>No error</u>
                              D   E

42. Bill began to despair when he <u>learned</u> that everyone except <u>he</u> had
                                  A   B
    already heard from the graduate schools <u>to which</u> they <u>had applied</u>.
                                      C   D
    <u>No error</u>
      E

43. If I <u>was</u> in your place, I <u>would be</u> very much concerned about the future
        A   B
    and <u>would</u> certainly be taking steps <u>to improve</u> my situation. <u>No error</u>
        C   D   E

44. After Erskine had <u>ran</u> the mile, he <u>jogged slowly</u> <u>around the track</u> for
                     A   B   C
    <u>ten more</u> laps. <u>No error</u>
      D   E

45. Knowing all that we did about his <u>past</u>, we <u>couldn't</u> hardly believe <u>that</u> he
                               A   B   C
    would <u>desert</u> the cause. <u>No error</u>
         D   E

46. <u>Its</u> <u>altogether</u> irresponsible <u>of him</u> to think that he can substitute guile <u>for</u>
    A   B   C   D
    cooperation, and charm for study. <u>No error</u>
                              E

47. Uncle Dan always allowed <u>we</u> boys to visit his shop during the holidays
                           A
    <u>and, when</u> we left, <u>each of us had</u> a special gift he <u>had made for</u> us.
      B   C   D
    <u>No error</u>
      E

48. <u>Even</u> after repeated <u>questioning, May</u> steadfastly denied <u>having known</u>
      A   B   C

    <u>either of the accused.</u> <u>No error</u>
          D   E

49. As I entered the dusty room, I saw the <u>child's</u> drawings still tacked to the
                                                A

    walls and the toys <u>laying</u> on the rug, almost <u>as if</u> young David had
                            B   C

    <u>stepped out</u> for a moment. <u>No error</u>
        D   E

50. My friend and <u>myself</u> made our way <u>through</u> the darkened auditorium and
                     A   B

    slipped quietly <u>into</u> our seats just as the curtain <u>rose</u>. <u>No error</u>
               C   D   E

STOP
WORK ONLY ON THIS SECTION UNTIL THE TIME ALLOTTED IS OVER.

Answer Key
Practice Test 3

Section I

1.	D	13.	B	24.	E	35.	D
2.	C	14.	A	25.	E	36.	D
3.	E	15.	D	26.	C	37.	A
4.	E	16.	D	27.	D	38.	B
5.	B	17.	E	28.	D	39.	E
6.	A	18.	C	29.	A	40.	A
7.	E	19.	A	30.	B	41.	D
8.	C	20.	B	31.	C	42.	E
9.	A	21.	D	32.	E	43.	B
10.	A	22.	D	33.	D	44.	C
11.	D	23.	A	34.	B	45.	D
12.	C						

Section II

1.	B	11.	C	21.	B	31.	C
2.	E	12.	D	22.	D	32.	A
3.	D	13.	E	23.	C	33.	D
4.	D	14.	A	24.	B	34.	B
5.	C	15.	D	25.	C	35.	D
6.	A	16.	C	26.	D	36.	C
7.	B	17.	B	27.	E	37.	E
8.	E	18.	E	28.	C	38.	B
9.	A	19.	C	29.	A	39.	D
10.	D	20.	B	30.	C	40.	A

Section III

1.	E	8.	E	14.	E	20.	D
2.	C	9.	C	15.	E	21.	B
3.	D	10.	B	16.	D	22.	C
4.	A	11.	E	17.	C	23.	C
5.	B	12.	B	18.	A	24.	A
6.	D	13.	C	19.	B	25.	E
7.	A						

Section IV

1.	E	10.	A	19.	B	28.	D
2.	A	11.	B	20.	A	29.	B
3.	C	12.	B	21.	B	30.	C
4.	D	13.	D	22.	D	31.	B
5.	B	14.	C	23.	B	32.	A
6.	A	15.	C	24.	A	33.	B
7.	D	16.	D	25.	A	34.	A
8.	C	17.	B	26.	C	35.	A
9.	C	18.	C	27.	C		

Section V

1.	C	8.	E	14.	B	20.	B
2.	A	9.	C	15.	E	21.	D
3.	D	10.	D	16.	B	22.	E
4.	C	11.	B	17.	B	23.	E
5.	E	12.	E	18.	D	24.	B
6.	D	13.	A	19.	C	25.	C
7.	A						

Section VI

1.	C	14.	B	27.	B	39.	E
2.	B	15.	C	28.	A	40.	B
3.	C	16.	A	29.	C	41.	E
4.	D	17.	C	30.	B	42.	B
5.	E	18.	D	31.	B	43.	A
6.	A	19.	D	32.	D	44.	A
7.	E	20.	C	33.	B	45.	B
8.	D	21.	E	34.	E	46.	A
9.	D	22.	D	35.	B	47.	A
10.	C	23.	D	36.	C	48.	E
11.	A	24.	B	37.	A	49.	B
12.	E	25.	C	38.	B	50.	A
13.	D	26.	D				

Explanatory Answers
Practice Test 3

SECTION I

1. **D.** *Earthy*: gross, low.
   Opposite: *refined*.

2. **C.** *Inducement*: that which brings about or persuades.
   Opposite: *deterrent*, that which discourages.

3. **E.** *Exuberant*: extremely joyful.
   Opposite: *dispirited*.

4. **E.** *Ornate*: elaborately adorned.
   Opposite: *austere*.

5. **B.** *Tirade*: prolonged outburst of bitter denunciation.
   Opposite: *panegyric*, eulogy, oration in praise.

6. **A.** *Lithe*: limber, supple, flexible.
   Opposite: *inflexible*.

7. **E.** *Fecund*: fruitful, productive.
   Opposite: *barren*, unproductive.

8. **C.** *Indigenous*: native to (some place).
   Opposite: *foreign* (to).

9. **A.** *Peruse*: read with thoroughness.
   Opposite: *skim*.

10. **A.** *Purblind*: deficient in imagination.
    Opposite: *imaginative*.

11. **D.** *Jocose*: humorous, playful.
    Opposite: *solemn*.

12. **C.** *Harmonious*: forming a pleasantly consistent whole.
    Opposite: *discordant*.

13. **B.** *Loyalty*: faithfulness.
    Opposite: *perfidy*, faithlessness.

14. **A.** *Duplicity*: deceitfulness.
    Opposite: *candor*, sincerity.

15. **D.** *Overt*: open to public view.

Opposite: *surreptitious*, underhanded, stealthy.

16. **D.** What could make it surprising that the two should have gotten married? Only that they didn't get along or were, in other words, *incompatible*.

17. **E.** Only two choices could possibly be used with the prepositional phrase "of their honor," and only choice (E) makes the sentence meaningful.

18. **C.** That which one leaves to mankind is probably a *legacy*, and it is left to the unborn children or *posterity* of those yet unborn.

19. **A.** The sentence structure leads us to expect that the life of the first twenty-five years is being pictured as providing the opposite of the rest of life. The sense, then, is that youth, even when spent in poverty, is worth the rest of life even if it is spent with the fruits of achievement. The answer: *penury . . respectability*.

20. **B.** The first clause says that the two complement one another. The colon tells us that the rest of the sentence will illustrate that clause. *Literary* complements "historical and political," for it suggests that one had the ideas and the other wrote them up. Certainly, *optimistic* complements "emotional and moody."

21. **D.** We assume that the action that shows seriousness in relation to unfashionable writers is the willingness to either *praise* or *credit* them. The second blank can take only *inhibited* and still make sense.

22. **D.** The implication of the first clause is that no matter how weak, no matter the motivation, the charges helped the man who

made them by creating *excitement* and *attracting* attention.

23. **A.** The implication is clear that the orchestra was then able to *assume* the form it still has today, since none of the other choices make any sense. The orchestra could not "invent" the form or "circumvent" the form it has today. It could not "avoid" the form it has today, and it certainly could not "resume" a form it had not yet had.

24. **E.** Since the sense of the sentence seems to be that the book has much in the way of vivid pictorial glimpses, etc., the choice lies between (D) and (E). However, "teems" would take the preposition "with" instead of "in." The answer is *abounds . . human*.

25. **E.** The choices are really limited to "thought" and *understood* for the first blank. However, "artistic" is redundant when followed by "esthetic." *Social* completes the sentence best.

26. **C.** The *pattern* serves as a guide for the *dressmaker*, just as the *script* serves as a guide for the *director*.

27. **D.** The *duke* is a part of and a member of the nobility, which is a hereditary *aristocracy*, and the *priest* is a part of and a member of the *clergy*.

28. **D.** The *realtor* is an agent in the sale of other people's *land*, just as the *broker* is an agent in the sale of other people's *bonds*.

29. **A.** *Reticent* and *reserved* are synonymous, both meaning shy and somewhat withdrawn. *Fleeting* and *transient* are synonymous, both meaning short-lived.

30. **B.** *Enthusiasm* and *indifference* are opposed in meaning, as are *zeal* and *apathy*. *Zeal* and *apathy* are, respectively, synonyms of *enthusiasm* and *indifference*, thus making a perfect analogous pair.

31. **C.** The *bushel* is a unit of measure for *grain*; the *carat* is a unit of measure for a *gemstone*. The *karat* does not measure *gold* in the same way, since it is really an expression of the ratio of pure gold to base metal. In a sense, the karat is an expression of quality.

32. **E.** *Crowding* is like *congestion* except that the latter represents the same quality to a greater degree. Likewise, *brightness* is like *brilliance*, except that the latter represents the quality of brightness at a greater intensity.

33. **D.** *Coke* is produced by baking *coal* in an oven, just as *bread* is produced by baking *dough* in an oven.

34. **B.** (Note that this is a vertical analogy; the first term of the given pair forms a relationship with the first term of one of the choices, and the second word of the given term forms an analogous relationship with the second word of the same choice item.) A *dragon* is a large, *fabulous* reptile, just as a *dinosaur* is a large *real* reptile.

35. **D.** A *bore* can be characterized as *prolix*, or long-winded; similarly, a *boor*, or dull, insensitive peasant, can be characterized as *oafish*, or stupid.

36. **D.** Sentence 3, paragraph 2 tells us that item I is not true. The last sentence of the same paragraph contradicts item II. In paragraph 1, the author pictures him at "the center of a circle of adoring friends," and in paragraph 2 he again refers to the circle of Schubert's friends in the second sentence. Item IV, however, is affirmed in the next sentence, and item V is stated as true in the sentence after that.

37. **A.** In the third from last sentence in paragraph 2, the passage mentions Schubert as lacking a talent for self-promotion, another way of saying that he lacked a talent for self-aggrandizement. In the last sentence of paragraph 1 he is characterized as unassuming, so he is not pretentious. He is not characterized by asceticism as we can see by reading the first sentence, which says he consumed whatever coffee or wine he could afford or charge. However, he is described as being at the center of a circle of friends, so item IV does characterize him best. Therefore, the answer is (A).

38. **B.** The author points out that, contrary to common belief, Schubert's music was sung and played, admired, and talked about (see

the last sentence). He also points out that an eighth of Schubert's music was in print, so he could not really be termed neglected, contrary to the popular notion of Schubert's lack of recognition during his lifetime.

39. **E.** In pointing out what Schubert accomplished, and noting, in sentence 5, paragraph 2, that he had no connections, not much of a career as a performer, and no talent for self-promotion, the author clearly implies that these were usually important for achieving recognition. A couple of sentences further on, he says that Schubert's obscurity ended when the *Erlkönig* was performed in Vienna, and, just prior to that he indicated that to be known in Vienna meant something. The author does not suggest that Schubert's circle of adoring friends was an important factor in his achieving recognition.

40. **A.** The answer is summed up in the last paragraph: While Schubert did not attain the success in the theater he had hoped for, he was not unknown or unadmired during his own time.

SECTION II

1. **B.** *Courteous*: polite.
   Opposite: *uncouth*, unmannerly, rude.

2. **E.** *Invariable*: static, unchanging.
   Opposite: *changing*.

3. **D.** *Abstain*: refrain from.
   Opposite: *indulge*, gratify one's desires.

4. **D.** *Exonerate*: free of blame.
   Opposite: *implicate*, involve, as being concerned in a matter (crime, etc.).

5. **C.** *Fatuous*: foolish.
   Opposite: *sensible*.

6. **A.** *Prolific*: productive, fruitful, abundant.
   Opposite: *barren*.

7. **B.** *Ebullient*: overflowing with enthusiasm.
   Opposite: *downcast*.

8. **E.** *Germane*: relevant, pertinent.
   Opposite: *irrelevant*.

41. **D.** In sentence 1, paragraph 2, the author says that historians have abandoned the attitude of the past that contemporary history was not the concern of historians, and have given the past half century of contemporary history careful and critical analysis.

42. **E.** Sentence 3, paragraph 2, clearly supports choice *E* when it says " . . . that the world of the past is largely understood in terms of current experience."

43. **B.** The passage refers to "an 'objective' view of what had happened, free from the passions . . . "

44. **C.** The passage is saying, here, that all social scientists are dealing with the same problem, the nature of social change, and that this is a valid undertaking for the historian.

45. **D.** Choice (A) is expressed in sentence 4, paragraph 2. Choice (B) is expressed in sentence 2, paragraph 1. Choice (C) is expressed in the last sentence of paragraph 1. Choice (E) is expressed or implied in sentence 1, paragraph 2. Choice (D) is neither expressed or implied.

9. **A.** *Scrupulous*: having strict regard for what one considers right.
   Opposite: *unprincipled*.

10. **D.** *Egregious*: flagrant, glaring, conspicuously bad.
    Opposite: *excusable*.

11. **C.** In the first paragraph, sentence 1, Mr. Carter is quoted as saying that he would not act to affect the balance of power anywhere. The second paragraph indicates that the F-15 is a weapon of great potential, armed with a system that is "a decade ahead. . . . " The last paragraph says that even the president's supporters admit that the sale of the F-15 would "alter the balance. . . . " Item (A) is only evidence of item (C). The other items are not even remote possibilities as answers.

12. **D.** Item I is a disadvantage. Item II is not

stated. The passage says that the F-15 is fast, but it does not say it is the fastest. Item III is affirmed by sentence 5, paragraph 2, and item IV is supported by the last sentence in the same paragraph.

13. **E.** The passage is written without the use of figurative language or rhetorical devices. The author simply makes calm, factual-sounding statements which seem to support each other and lead the reader to accept the author's conclusion.

14. **A.** In sentence 2, the last paragraph, Middleton is quoted as saying, "until now . . ." which implies that now things are different. He is showing that the statement in item (A) is correct. His quote presents a view opposite to item (B). The other items are not possibilities.

15. **D.** He mentions the *New York Times* editorial to show that even Mr. Carter's supporters admit that the president is doing what he said he would not do.

16. **C.** Sentences 1 and 2 of paragraph 1 show item (C) to be correct.

17. **B.** Item (B) is affirmed by the next-to-the-last sentence in paragraph 2.

18. **E.** Sentence 1, paragraph 4 makes the point in item (A). The last sentence of that paragraph makes the point in item (C) (the word "wantonly" means without motive or provocation). The next-to-the-last sentence of paragraph 4 supports item (B). Item (D) offers a point made by the author in sentence 3 of the last paragraph. Item (E) is directly contradicted by the first sentence of the last paragraph and is, therefore, a point not made by the author.

19. **C.** "Wantonly" not only means without motive or provocation, but also without regard for what is right or humane. The paragraph clearly implies that the eggs have been broken without motive or provocation and, therefore, without regard for what is right or humane.

20. **B.** Sentence 3, paragraph 1 tells us that the least tern is threatened in the east because

of human recreational activities within its colonies.

21. **B.** Sentence 2, paragraph 1 gives the answer. " . . . pen and pencil" stand for the person who wields them.

22. **D.** The description of the *camera obscura* in paragraph 2 matches the statement in item (D).

23. **C.** The Royal Society, we may infer, is a society concerned with new discoveries or inventions. Choices (A) and (B) are obviously out. (D) and (E) are not acceptable because a society would not have been founded to foster photography before photography was invented, and there was no communication industry, as we know it, in 1839.

24. **B.** Sentence 4 of the first paragraph says that photography was characterized by the qualities of uniformity and repeatability. The next sentence says that these qualities also characterized the Gutenberg break (meaning the printing press).

25. **C.** Since the "title" question actually asks for the choice that best sums up the passage as a whole, the answer must be choice (C). "The automated eye" is too vague. Choice (E) does not in any way sum up the passage as a whole. Only choice (C) can be correct. The passage is about the invention of photography, and the author clearly makes the point that the invention is a decisive new development, or breakthrough.

26. **D.** We would expect someone to be *stung* by waspish criticism, and *tacitly* means unvoiced or unspoken.

27. **E.** *Incriminating* evidence would involve a person in a crime, and an eyewitness account of someone's *presence* at the scene of the crime would indeed be incriminating.

28. **C.** Something seventeenth-century doctors diagnosed without would be *apparatus*, "know-how," "refinements," or a *library*. Of second-word choices, however, only *indispensable* is suitable.

29. **A.** We can infer that what he valued was the

opposite of what he abhorred: *brevity* and *verbosity* are the only antonyms among the options offered.

30. **C.** If the voters had known of something good about Clarke, they would have supported him; if they had known of something bad, they would have opposed him. The only pair that fits is *venality* (corruptibility) and *countenanced*. "Fecklessness" means feebleness or incompetence. The voters would have "opposed" a feckless candidate. "Mendacity" means untruthfulness. The voters would have "defeated" an untruthful candidate.

31. **C.** A *scepter* is a rod or wand that is the symbol of power of a *monarch* or ruler. A *gavel* is a symbol of the power of a *chairperson*, one who presides over a meeting.

32. **A.** *Quack* and *charlatan* are synonymous words meaning fake or fraud. *Panacea* means *cure-all* or universal remedy.

33. **D.** *Plump* is similar in meaning to *corpulent*, but *corpulent* describes a greater degree of stoutness or plumpness. Similarly, *slim* is similar in meaning to *skinny*, but *skinny* signifies a greater degree of thinness than *slim*.

34. **B.** The *carapace* is a part of an *armadillo*. It is a shell covering the dorsal part of that animal. Similarly, the *shell* is a part of a *turtle*; it covers the dorsal part of that animal. While the *quills* are a part of a *porcupine*, the quills do not form a shell-like covering of the dorsal part of that animal. The *tongue* of the *anteater* does not relate to that animal in the same manner as the carapace does to the armadillo.

35. **D.** *Exculpate* and *implicate* are opposite in meaning, as are *exonerate* and *incriminate*. Furthermore, *exculpate* means "to exonerate," or "to free of blame," and *implicate* and *incriminate* both mean "to involve in" (a crime).

36. **C.** It is a good for a *salesman* to be characterized as *voluble* (fluent, having an easy flow of language). Similarly, it is good for a *leader* to be characterized as *decisive*. While it is good for an *artist* to be described as *successful*, this characterization is not analogous to the one given, since *decisive* and *voluble* describe behavior, while *successful* describes an outcome.

37. **E.** *Stable* and *immutable* are close in meaning. *Stable* means not changing, while *immutable*, a somewhat stronger word, means unchangeable. *Immutable* is an absolute. Of the choices, only the second words of choices (D) and (E) contain absolutes. However, *sometimes* is not as close in meaning to *always* as *unusual* is to *unique*. If choice (D) offered "usually" instead of *sometimes*, (D) would be an acceptable choice.

38. **B.** A *curmudgeon* (irascible, churlish person) can be characterized as *cantankerous* (quarrelsome, irritable, contentious). A *termagant* (brawling, turbulent woman) can be characterized as *shrewish* (violent-tempered or nagging).

39. **D.** Just as *insult* may cause a feeling of *humiliation*, so too, *commendation* can cause a feeling of *pride*.

40. **A.** *Oslo* is the capital of *Norway*, and *Riga* is the capital of *Latvia*.

SECTION III

1. **E.** $6 \times 6 \times t = 18 \times 18 \times 18$.
   Divide both sides of the equation by 6×6.
   $t = 3 \times 3 \times 18$
   $t = 162$.

2. **C.** $12 - (-18) = 12 + 18$
   $\qquad\qquad\quad = 30°$.

3. **D.** 9 inches $= \dfrac{9}{12}$ feet $= \dfrac{3}{4}$ foot.

   $6 \div \dfrac{3}{4} = \dfrac{\cancel{6}^{2}}{1} \times \dfrac{4}{\cancel{3}_{1}} = \dfrac{8}{1} = 8.$

4. **A.** Area of circle $O = \pi r^2 = \pi(2)^2 = 4\pi$.
Area of quadrant POS + quadrant ROQ
$= \frac{1}{2}(4\pi) = 2\pi$.

Since the radius of the smaller semicircle is 1, then the area of each smaller semicircle is $\frac{\pi}{2}$ and the area of the two small semicircles is $2\left(\frac{\pi}{2}\right) = \pi$. The shaded area $= 2\pi - \pi = \pi$.

5. **B.** If he goes around $\frac{4}{5}$ of the track in m minutes, then he runs $\frac{1}{5}$ of the track in $\frac{m}{4}$ minutes, since $\frac{1}{5} = \frac{1}{4}$ of $\frac{4}{5}$. Thus, to run the entire track would take $m + \frac{m}{4} = \frac{4m}{4} + \frac{m}{4}$
$= \frac{5m}{4}$ minutes.

6. **D.** If it flies 3 miles in 15 seconds, then it flies 12 miles in 60 seconds (1 minute). If it flies 12 miles in 1 minute, then it flies $12 \times 60 = 720$ miles in 60 minutes, or 720 miles per hour.

7. **A.** The sum total of the 30 scores is $30p$. If each mark is raised 10 points, the sum total becomes $30p + 30(10) = 30p + 300$. The average is then $\frac{30p + 300}{30} = p + 10$.

8. **E.** Area of triangle
$OPQ = \frac{1}{2}(OP \times \text{altitude})$.

$64 = \frac{1}{2}(8h)$

$64 = 4h$

$h = 16$.

9. **C.** At 6:30 p.m., the large hand points to the six and the small hand is half-way between the six and the seven. Since the number of degrees of arc between the six and the seven is $\frac{360°}{12} = 30°$, the angle between the

hands at 6:30 is $\frac{1}{2}(30°) = 15°$.

10. **B.** $5t - .5t = 9$.
Multiply both sides by 10.
$50t - 5t = 90$
$45t = 90$
$t = 2$.

11. **E.**

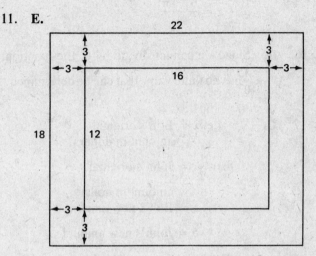

$22 = 16 + 3 + 3$
$18 = 12 + 3 + 3$

The area of the flower bed is $16 \times 12 = 192$ sq. yd. The area of the large rectangle in the figure above is $22 \times 18 = 396$ sq. yd. The area of the walk is $396 - 192 = 204$ sq. yd.

12. **B.** $r(y - 2) = b$

$ry - 2r = b$

$ry = b + 2r$

$y = \frac{b + 2r}{r}$.

13. **C.** Since $\sqrt{64} = 8$ and $\sqrt{49} = 7$; then $\sqrt{61}$ must be slightly less than 8. The only possible choice is 7.8.

14. **E.** Since every crossed group is made up of 5 tallies, there are $\frac{39}{5} = 7$ such groups with 4 tallies uncrossed.

15. **E.** Let $OO' = x$, then
$PQ = RS = x$ (external tangents).
Then PGR and QHS are semicircles and

their sum is equal to the circumference C of one of the circles. $C = \pi D = \pi$ feet.

$$6 = x + x + \pi$$
$$6 = 2x + \pi$$
$$6 - \pi = 2x$$
$$x = \frac{6 - \pi}{2}.$$

16. **D.** Since we cannot divide by 0, the function $\frac{3}{0}$ has no finite value that can be determined.

17. **C.** Let x = Bob's original amount in dollars,

then $\frac{1}{2}x$ = John's original amount in dollars.

$x - 5$ = Bob's new amount

$\frac{1}{2}x + 5$ = John's new amount

$$\frac{1}{2}x + 5 = (x - 5) - 4$$
$$\frac{1}{2}x + 5 = x - 9.$$

Multiply both sides by 2.

$$x + 10 = 2x - 18$$

$x = 28$ (Bob's original amount)

$\frac{1}{2}x = 14$ (John's original amount)

$\$28 + \$14 = \$42$ (amount together).

18. **A.** Since $\angle ADE = 60°$ and $\angle ADC = 90°$, then $\angle EDC = 90 - 60 = 30°$. Since $ED = DC$, the base angles of triangle EDC are each

$$\frac{180 - 30}{2} = \frac{150}{2} = 75°.$$

19. **B.** To locate the origin from P_1, go left 2 units

and down 4 units. It can then be seen that P_2 is 5 units to the right of the origin and 2 units up. So that the coordinates of P_2 are (5,2).

20. **D.** If $\frac{r}{s} = \frac{1}{4}$, then $4r = s$.

Substitute $s = 4r$ in the equation
$$r + s = 100$$
$$r + 4r = 100$$
$$5r = 100$$
$$r = 20$$
$$s = 4r = 80,$$
so that $s - r = 80 - 20 = 60$.

21. **B.** The volume V and surface area S of a cube are given by the formulas $V = e^3$ and $S = 6e^2$, where e is the edge of the cube.

$$V = 64k^3$$
$$e^3 = 64k^3$$
$$e = 4k$$
$$S = 6e^2 = 6(4k)^2 = 96k^2.$$

22. **C.** Let t = tax on a radio priced at \$175,

then $\frac{125}{20} = \frac{175}{t}$

$$125t = 3500$$
$$t = \$28.$$

23. **C.** Regardless of the value of p, p^2 must be greater than or equal to 0. Therefore, $p^2 + 1$ must be greater than or equal to 1.

24. **A.** Let the radius of circle $Q = 1$, then the radius of circle $P = .6$. Area of circle $Q = \pi(1)^2 = \pi$. Area of circle $P = \pi(.6)^2 = .36\pi$. Thus, the area of circle P is 36% of the area of circle Q.

25. **E.** Drop a perpendicular RT from R to PS extended. Then triangle $PQH \cong$ triangle RTS, so that $RT = QH = \sqrt{5}$ and $ST = PH = 2$. In right triangle PRT, $\overline{PR}^2 = \overline{PT}^2 + \overline{RT}^2 = 9^2 + (\sqrt{5})^2 = 81 + 5 = 86$. $PR = \sqrt{86}$.

SECTION IV

1. **E.** There are 36 inches in 1 yard.
   In k yards, there are $36k$ inches.

2. **A.** $n - x = n$.
   Subtract n from both sides.
   $-x = 0$
   or $x = 0$.

3. **C.** 1 gallon = 4 quarts = 8 pints.
   2 gallons = 16 pints.

   $$\frac{6}{16} = \frac{3}{8} = 37\frac{1}{2}\%.$$

4. **D.** 50 miles per hour = 50 miles in 60 minutes.
   1 mile will take $\frac{60}{50} = \frac{6}{5} = 1\frac{1}{5}$ minutes.

5. **B.** The morning classes run 3 hours, or 180 minutes. There are 3 passing intervals. Four periods of 42 minutes each take 168 minutes, leaving $180 - 168 = 12$ minutes for 3 intervals, or 4 minutes per interval.

6. **A.** When 12 people got off, that left 7 empty seats. When 6 got on, there was only 1 empty seat left.

7. **D.** The fish tank is 2 feet high. The water level is 4 in. $= \frac{4}{12} = \frac{1}{3}$ ft. from the top of the tank. The height of the water is $2 - \frac{1}{3} = 1\frac{2}{3}$ ft.

   $V = LWH$

   $V = 4(3)\left(1\frac{2}{3}\right)$

   $= 4(5)$

   $V = 20$ cu. ft.

8. **C.** The 9-12-15 is a 3-4-5 combination multiplied by 3. The 10-24-26 is a 5-12-13 combination multiplied by 2. The 8-15-17 satisfies the relationship $8^2 + 15^2 = 17^2$. The 7-7-7$\sqrt{2}$ is a right, isosceles triangle. However, $8^2 + 11^2$ does not equal 15^2 since $64 + 121 \neq 225$; thus these numbers cannot be the sides of a right triangle.

9. **C.** Consider QR as the base of the triangle. $QR = 5 - (-1) = 5 + 1 = 6$. The altitude from P to QR is $7 - 2 = 5$. Then

   $$A = \frac{1}{2}bh$$

   $$= \frac{1}{2}(6)(5) = 15.$$

10. **A.** The increase for n articles was $(y - x)$ dollars. Thus, the increase per article was $\frac{y - x}{n}$ dollars.

11. **B.** One diagonal of the parallelogram divides the figure into two congruent triangles. The other diagonal bisects the first diagonal, thus providing a median in each of the two congruent triangles. Since a median bisects the area of a triangle, the resulting four triangles are equal in area.

12. **B.** Let $p = 5$ and $q = 2$. Substitution in I, II, and III will show that only II and III are true.

13. **D.**

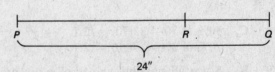

   Let $PR = 5x$ and $RQ = 3x$. Then
   $$5x + 3x = 24$$
   $$8x = 24$$
   $$x = 3$$
   $$RQ = 3x = 3(3) = 9.$$

14. **C.** His total of scores on n tests is $80n$. Let x = his score on the next test;

    then $\frac{80n + x}{n + 1} = 82$

    $$80n + x = 82n + 82$$

    $$x = 2n + 82.$$

15. **C.** $\quad 5p + 8 = 3 + 5q$
    $$5p - 5q = 3 - 8$$
    $$5(p - q) = -5$$
    $$p - q = -1.$$

16. D. $\sqrt{\dfrac{2.698}{.031} - 9.03} \approx \sqrt{\dfrac{2.70}{.03} - 9}$

$$\approx \sqrt{90 - 9}$$

$$\approx \sqrt{81} = 9.$$

17. B.

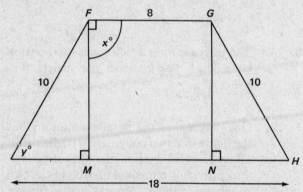

Drop perpendiculars *FM* and *GN* to base *JH*. Then $MN = FG = 8$ and $JM = NH = 5$. Since $JM = \dfrac{1}{2}FJ$, angle $JFM = 30°$ and angle $y = 60°$. Since angle $MFG = 90°$, it follows that $x - y = 90 + 30 - 60 = 60°$.

18. C. 30% of 70 = .3(70) = 2.1.
70% of 30 = .7(30) = 2.1.

19. B. Since all possible values of q are greater than all possible values of p, it follows that $q > p$.

20. A. $r(s + t) = rs + rt$.
Since $r > 1$ and s and t are positive, $rs + rt > rs + t$.

21. B. $\dfrac{1}{3} \times \dfrac{1}{4} = \dfrac{1}{12}$.

$\dfrac{1}{3} \div \dfrac{1}{4} = \dfrac{1}{3} \times \dfrac{4}{1} = \dfrac{4}{3} = 1\dfrac{1}{3} > \dfrac{1}{12}$.

22. D. Substitute $r = 2s$ in $2r + 3$, giving $2(2s) + 3 = 4s + 3$. If s were zero, $6s + 3 = 4s + 3 = 3$. Hence, we cannot compare these two values without knowing more about the values of r and s.

23. B. Since 180 is common to both products, let

us compare $11 \times 7 = 77$ with $9 \times 12 = 96$. Apparently $96 > 77$.

24. A. Since n is an exterior angle of the triangle containing angles p and q, it follows that $n > q$.

25. A. Area of circle $= \pi r^2 = \pi \left(\dfrac{d}{2}\right)^2$

$$= \dfrac{\pi d^2}{4} = \dfrac{3.14}{4} d^2.$$

Area of square $= \left(\dfrac{3}{4} d\right)^2$

$$= \dfrac{9}{16} d^2.$$

$\dfrac{3.14}{4} = .78; \qquad \dfrac{9}{16} = .56.$

Therefore the area of the circle is greater.

26. C. Angle k = angle PQR (vertical angles). Angle n = angle PQR, since they are opposite angles of a parallelogram. Therefore $k = n$.

27. C. $\qquad m + k = 180°$ (supplementary)
$\qquad\qquad n = \measuredangle QRV$ (corresponding angles of parallel lines)
$\measuredangle QRV + t = 180°$ (supplementary)
or $n + t = 180°$,

so that $m + k = n + t$.

28. D. If $r > s$, $\dfrac{1}{r} < \dfrac{1}{s}$ if r and s are positive.

However, this relationship will not be true if one or both of these variables are negative.

29. B. Angle $P = 180° - (70 + 40) = 180 - 110 = 70°$.
Therefore, $QR > PQ$ since the longer side lies opposite the larger angle.

30. C. Since $\angle P = \angle Q = 70°$, it follows that the sides opposite are equal; that is, $PR = QR$.

31. B. $y - 2x = 5$, $x \geqq 0$
$y = 2x + 5$.
Since y is 5 more than twice x and $x \geqq 0$, it follows that $y > x$.

32. A. $\sqrt[3]{28.2} > \sqrt[3]{27} = 3$

$\sqrt{8.92} < \sqrt{9} = 3.$

Since the item in Column A > 3 and that in Column B < 3, (A) must be the answer.

33. B. If $0 < k < 1$, then $k^2 < k$, since the squaring of a positive fraction less than 1 produces a still smaller positive fraction.

34. A. Since the sum of the two sides of a triangle is greater than the third side,

$f + h > g.$
Subtracting h from both sides, we get
$f > g - h.$

35. A. $PR = 100\sqrt{2} \approx 100(1.41) \approx 141$ ft. Walking PR at 5 feet per second takes about $\frac{141}{5}$ = 28.2 seconds. $PQ + QR = 200$ ft., so that running from P to Q and Q to R takes $\frac{200}{8}$ = 25 seconds. So that Column A > Column B.

SECTION V

1. C. $2.7\% = .027 = 27$ thousandths.

2. A. $.04 \div \frac{4}{.5} = .04 \times \frac{.5}{4}$

$= .04 \times \frac{5}{40}$

$= .04 \times \frac{1}{8} = \frac{.040}{8} = .005.$

3. D. Let $n =$ the number of *additional* days.
$10 + 6n = 118$
$6n = 108$
$n = 18$
$n + 3 = 21.$

4. C.

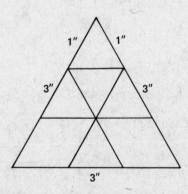

The figure above shows the division of the larger triangle into 9 smaller ones.

5. E. Let $w =$ width,
then $l = 2w - 6$ (length).
perimeter $= 2l + 2w$

$= 2(2w - 6) + 2w$
$= 4w - 12 + 2w$
$= 6w - 12.$

6. D. Each tile is $\frac{4}{12} = \frac{1}{3}$ ft. on a side. The number of tiles lengthwise is

$7\frac{2}{3} \div \frac{1}{3} = 7\frac{2}{3} \times 3 = 23.$

The number of tiles along the width is

$6 \div \frac{1}{3} = 6 \times 3 = 18.$

The total number of tiles is $23 \times 18 = 414.$

7. A. Let the three angles be $2x$, $3x$ and $5x$.
Then $2x + 3x + 5x = 180$
$10x = 180$
$x = 18.$
$5x = 5(18) = 90.$
Therefore, the triangle is a right triangle.

8. E. $r + 40 = s + 20$
$r = s - 20.$
From this information above, it is impossible to determine what percent s is of r.

9. C. It is not possible for two sides to be equal to x because the sum of two sides would be less than the third side ($x + x < 2x + 1$). Therefore, two sides must be equal to $2x + 1$ and the perimeter $= (2x + 1) + (2x + 1) + x = 5x + 2.$

10. **D.** Let A equal the area of the larger circle and let $r = $ its radius. Let B equal the area of the smaller circle and let $s = $ its radius.

Then $A = \pi r^2$ and $B = \pi s^2$

$$\frac{A}{B} = \frac{\pi r^2}{\pi s^2} = \frac{2}{1}.$$

Taking the square root of both ratios on the right, we get

$$\frac{r}{s} = \frac{\sqrt{2}}{1} = \sqrt{2}.$$

11. **B.** Since

8 ounces = 1 cup,

$$2 \text{ ounces} = \frac{1}{4} \text{ cup} = 4 \text{ tablespoons}$$

$$= 12 \text{ teaspoons}.$$

12. **E.** $4:12 = 4(60) + 12 = 252$ minutes after midnight. Since midnight, the gong sounds $\frac{252}{35} = 7$ times and 7 minutes left over. Therefore, it sounds again 28 minutes later $(35 - 7)$.

13. **A.** The smaller wheel has a circumference that is half as large as the larger. Hence, it must revolve twice as many times, or 240 revolutions.

14. **B.** For the complex fraction on the left side of the equation to equal 1, the denominator must also equal 1. This is only possible if $x = 0$.

15. **E.** Triangle OPR is a 30°-60°-90° triangle. Since $OR = 4$, $PR = 8$ and $OP = 4\sqrt{3}$. The coordinates of P are $(0, 4\sqrt{3})$.

16. **B.**

A ⊢———————— (3 hr. later) ————————⊣ B

Leaves 5 p.m.

When the plane leaves city A at 5 p.m., it is 3 hours earlier in city B, or 2 p.m. Four hours later it is 6 p.m. upon arrival.

17. **B.** $y < 2x$ so that $y < 40$. But y can have a minimum value as close to zero as we wish to make it. So that $0 < y < 40$.

18. **D.** The number of minutes after twelve noon is the least common multiple (LCM) of 14 and 12. The LCM is the product of all distinct factors of 14 and 12, each taken the greatest number of times it occurs in either of the two quantities. Since $14 = 7 \cdot 2$ and $12 = 3 \cdot 2^2$, the LCM $= 7 \cdot 3 \cdot 2^2 = 84$. Thus, the bell and whistle will sound together again at 1:24.

19. **C.** If we multiply both sides of $p - q = r$, we obtain I, so that this is true. By substituting $p = 5$, $q = 3$ and $r = 2$, we see that II and III are not, in general, true statements.

20. **B.** g gallons = $4g$ quarts. $20w$ quarts are withdrawn so that $4g - 20w$ quarts remain.

$$\frac{4g - 20w}{4} = g - 5w \text{ gallons}.$$

21. **D.** The largest cubes that can be cut from the given block are $3''$ on an edge. Dividing the volume of the block by the volume of each cube, we find the number of cubes.

$$\frac{\overset{3}{\cancel{9}} \times \cancel{3} \times \overset{4}{\cancel{12}}}{\cancel{3} \times \cancel{3} \times \cancel{3}} = 12.$$

22. **E.** Let the legs be $2x$ and $3x$.

$$\text{Area} = \frac{1}{2}(2x)(3x) = 75$$

$$3x^2 = 75$$
$$x^2 = 25$$
$$x = 5.$$

The legs are 10 and 15.

Then $(ST)^2 = 10^2 + 15^2$

$$= 100 + 225 = 325$$

$$ST = \sqrt{325} = \sqrt{25 \cdot 13} = 5\sqrt{13}.$$

23. **E.** If e is the edge of the cube, then
$$V = e^3 = 125$$
$$e = 5$$
$$S = 6e^2 = 6(5)^2$$
$$= 6(25) = 150.$$

24. B. Angle HGK = angle EGF = 60°, so that $\angle H + \angle K = 120°$.

25. C. $p = 4q$ and $q = 2r$, so that $p = 4(2r) = 8r$. Therefore, $r = \dfrac{p}{8}$.

SECTION VI

1. C. Error in agreement. The antecedent of the pronoun "them" is "anyone," a singular subject. Substitute "him" for "them."

2. B. Error in spelling. The intended word is "whose."

3. C. Error in logic or grammar. "Scarcely" like "hardly" is a negative which means "probably not." Its use with "no" forms a double negative that is not acceptable in standard written English.

4. D. Error in spelling or in formation of possessive. "Yours" is a possessive that does not need an apostrophe.

5. E. Sentence is correct as given.

6. A. Error in case. "Between" is a preposition and it takes an object. Substitute "me" for "I."

7. E. The verb "are" agrees with the second of the correlative subjects, "members," which is plural.

8. D. Error in agreement. "Data" is a plural noun.

9. D. Squinting modifier. Who has made his escape, man or giraffe?

10. C. Error in diction. The correct word here would be "effects."

11. A. Error in grammar. Substitute "whom" for "who" since the pronoun is the object of "pointed out."

12. E. The sentence is correct as given.

13. D. Error in tense. Substitute "had taken" to indicate the past of some time in the past.

14. B. Error in diction. "Myself" is not used instead of "I" in standard written English.

15. C. Error in tense. Substitute "had risen."

16. A. Substandard, colloquial substitution. "Being that" is an unacceptable substitute for "because."

17. C. Error in agreement. The antecedent, "All of the students," calls for the use of the pronoun "their."

18. D. Error in tense. The verb should be either "knew" or "know." The former would be acceptable for ordinary usage since it is the orthodox use of the past tense; the latter would be acceptable as a subjunctive, since it expresses a wish of the speaker.

19. D. The coordinating conjunction "than" takes the pronoun "I" here because the other element of the comparison, "few people" is in the nominative case.

20. C. Incorrect shift from third person to second person. Should read as follows: "Large schools make new entrants feel as if they . . . , but they (not *you*) very soon . . . at home."

21. E. Sentence is correct as given.

22. D. Error in tense. Use the past tense—a time in the past not extending into the present.

23. D. Error in case. The verb "expected" takes an object. Substitute "me" for "I."

24. B. Error in grammar. "How _____ the sky looked" calls for a predicate adjective, not an adverb. Substitute "beautiful" for "beautifully."

25. C. Error in diction. The correct word is "number." "Amount" is used for things in bulk, like "a large amount of money" as against "a large number of dollars."

26. D. Error in diction. "Compliment" means expression of praise, whereas "complement" means full number or full allowance.

It is used as a singular noun, and it takes the verb "was," in this case.

27. **B.** Comma splice. Two sentences have been joined into one. They should be set apart by the use of a period after the word "nineties."

28. **A.** Sentence is correct as given.

29. **C.** Faulty reference. The pronoun "his" does not clearly indicate which person the writer means, Hawkins or Thompson.

30. **B.** Substandard colloquial substitution. Change "and" to "to."

31. **B.** Error in structure. Complete statement "as strong *as*," before going on to second comparison, "if not stronger."

32. **D.** Comparatives, but not superlatives, may be completed by use of "other."

33. **B.** Error in parallelism. When using correlative conjunctions, keep conjunctions together, i.e., "Not only . . . but also." In this case, "but" and "also" have been separated by "I would."

34. **E.** Dangling or squinting modifier. As given, the sense seems to be that the sign was driving toward the desert.

35. **B.** Lack of parallel construction. The list of things enjoyed shifts from gerunds to artifacts. The correction is another gerund.

36. **C.** Error in case or in spelling. The last word should be a possessive; there should be an apostrophe before the final "s."

37. **A.** Sentence is correct as given.

38 **B.** Shifted voice. The writer moves from the passive in the first clause to the active in the second clause. If the research *is done*,

the paper *is written*. If *you do* the research, *you write* the paper.

39. **E.** Error in agreement. " . . . the aim of their . . . plans . . . was . . . a plot. . . ." "Aim" is a singular noun which should agree with the verb "was."

40. **B.** Shift in mood. The writer shifts from the imperative to the indicative.

41. **E.** Sentence is correct as given.

42. **B.** Error in case. The pronoun "except" takes the objective "him."

43. **A.** Error in mood. A condition contrary to fact calls for the subjunctive "were."

44. **A.** Error in diction. Past participle of "run" is "run."

45. **B.** Error in logical construction. "Hardly" is a negative. Substitute "should" for "shouldn't" to avoid an unacceptable double negative.

46. **A.** Error in spelling. "Its" should read "It's" or "It is." Remember that "its" is the possessive form of "it," and that "it's" is the spelling for the contraction of "it" and "is."

47. **A.** Error in case. "Allowed" takes an object, "us."

48. **E.** Sentence is correct as given.

49. **B.** Error in diction. Use "lying" instead of "laying." The former is intransitive, and the latter is transitive.

50. **A.** Error in diction. "Myself" is a reflexive pronoun used as an object or as an intensive. It is not used as subject in standard written English.

SAT Practice Test 4

ANSWER SHEET

When you have chosen your answer to any question, blacken the corresponding space on the answer sheet below. Make sure your marking completely fills the answer space. If you change an answer, erase the previous marking completely.

Section I—Verbal

1 Ⓐ Ⓑ Ⓒ Ⓓ Ⓔ	13 Ⓐ Ⓑ Ⓒ Ⓓ Ⓔ	24 Ⓐ Ⓑ Ⓒ Ⓓ Ⓔ	35 Ⓐ Ⓑ Ⓒ Ⓓ Ⓔ
2 Ⓐ Ⓑ Ⓒ Ⓓ Ⓔ	14 Ⓐ Ⓑ Ⓒ Ⓓ Ⓔ	25 Ⓐ Ⓑ Ⓒ Ⓓ Ⓔ	36 Ⓐ Ⓑ Ⓒ Ⓓ Ⓔ
3 Ⓐ Ⓑ Ⓒ Ⓓ Ⓔ	15 Ⓐ Ⓑ Ⓒ Ⓓ Ⓔ	26 Ⓐ Ⓑ Ⓒ Ⓓ Ⓔ	37 Ⓐ Ⓑ Ⓒ Ⓓ Ⓔ
4 Ⓐ Ⓑ Ⓒ Ⓓ Ⓔ	16 Ⓐ Ⓑ Ⓒ Ⓓ Ⓔ	27 Ⓐ Ⓑ Ⓒ Ⓓ Ⓔ	38 Ⓐ Ⓑ Ⓒ Ⓓ Ⓔ
5 Ⓐ Ⓑ Ⓒ Ⓓ Ⓔ	17 Ⓐ Ⓑ Ⓒ Ⓓ Ⓔ	28 Ⓐ Ⓑ Ⓒ Ⓓ Ⓔ	39 Ⓐ Ⓑ Ⓒ Ⓓ Ⓔ
6 Ⓐ Ⓑ Ⓒ Ⓓ Ⓔ	18 Ⓐ Ⓑ Ⓒ Ⓓ Ⓔ	29 Ⓐ Ⓑ Ⓒ Ⓓ Ⓔ	40 Ⓐ Ⓑ Ⓒ Ⓓ Ⓔ
7 Ⓐ Ⓑ Ⓒ Ⓓ Ⓔ	19 Ⓐ Ⓑ Ⓒ Ⓓ Ⓔ	30 Ⓐ Ⓑ Ⓒ Ⓓ Ⓔ	41 Ⓐ Ⓑ Ⓒ Ⓓ Ⓔ
8 Ⓐ Ⓑ Ⓒ Ⓓ Ⓔ	20 Ⓐ Ⓑ Ⓒ Ⓓ Ⓔ	31 Ⓐ Ⓑ Ⓒ Ⓓ Ⓔ	42 Ⓐ Ⓑ Ⓒ Ⓓ Ⓔ
9 Ⓐ Ⓑ Ⓒ Ⓓ Ⓔ	21 Ⓐ Ⓑ Ⓒ Ⓓ Ⓔ	32 Ⓐ Ⓑ Ⓒ Ⓓ Ⓔ	43 Ⓐ Ⓑ Ⓒ Ⓓ Ⓔ
10 Ⓐ Ⓑ Ⓒ Ⓓ Ⓔ	22 Ⓐ Ⓑ Ⓒ Ⓓ Ⓔ	33 Ⓐ Ⓑ Ⓒ Ⓓ Ⓔ	44 Ⓐ Ⓑ Ⓒ Ⓓ Ⓔ
11 Ⓐ Ⓑ Ⓒ Ⓓ Ⓔ	23 Ⓐ Ⓑ Ⓒ Ⓓ Ⓔ	34 Ⓐ Ⓑ Ⓒ Ⓓ Ⓔ	45 Ⓐ Ⓑ Ⓒ Ⓓ Ⓔ
12 Ⓐ Ⓑ Ⓒ Ⓓ Ⓔ			

Section II—Verbal

1 Ⓐ Ⓑ Ⓒ Ⓓ Ⓔ	11 Ⓐ Ⓑ Ⓒ Ⓓ Ⓔ	21 Ⓐ Ⓑ Ⓒ Ⓓ Ⓔ	31 Ⓐ Ⓑ Ⓒ Ⓓ Ⓔ
2 Ⓐ Ⓑ Ⓒ Ⓓ Ⓔ	12 Ⓐ Ⓑ Ⓒ Ⓓ Ⓔ	22 Ⓐ Ⓑ Ⓒ Ⓓ Ⓔ	32 Ⓐ Ⓑ Ⓒ Ⓓ Ⓔ
3 Ⓐ Ⓑ Ⓒ Ⓓ Ⓔ	13 Ⓐ Ⓑ Ⓒ Ⓓ Ⓔ	23 Ⓐ Ⓑ Ⓒ Ⓓ Ⓔ	33 Ⓐ Ⓑ Ⓒ Ⓓ Ⓔ
4 Ⓐ Ⓑ Ⓒ Ⓓ Ⓔ	14 Ⓐ Ⓑ Ⓒ Ⓓ Ⓔ	24 Ⓐ Ⓑ Ⓒ Ⓓ Ⓔ	34 Ⓐ Ⓑ Ⓒ Ⓓ Ⓔ
5 Ⓐ Ⓑ Ⓒ Ⓓ Ⓔ	15 Ⓐ Ⓑ Ⓒ Ⓓ Ⓔ	25 Ⓐ Ⓑ Ⓒ Ⓓ Ⓔ	35 Ⓐ Ⓑ Ⓒ Ⓓ Ⓔ
6 Ⓐ Ⓑ Ⓒ Ⓓ Ⓔ	16 Ⓐ Ⓑ Ⓒ Ⓓ Ⓔ	26 Ⓐ Ⓑ Ⓒ Ⓓ Ⓔ	36 Ⓐ Ⓑ Ⓒ Ⓓ Ⓔ
7 Ⓐ Ⓑ Ⓒ Ⓓ Ⓔ	17 Ⓐ Ⓑ Ⓒ Ⓓ Ⓔ	27 Ⓐ Ⓑ Ⓒ Ⓓ Ⓔ	37 Ⓐ Ⓑ Ⓒ Ⓓ Ⓔ
8 Ⓐ Ⓑ Ⓒ Ⓓ Ⓔ	18 Ⓐ Ⓑ Ⓒ Ⓓ Ⓔ	28 Ⓐ Ⓑ Ⓒ Ⓓ Ⓔ	38 Ⓐ Ⓑ Ⓒ Ⓓ Ⓔ
9 Ⓐ Ⓑ Ⓒ Ⓓ Ⓔ	19 Ⓐ Ⓑ Ⓒ Ⓓ Ⓔ	29 Ⓐ Ⓑ Ⓒ Ⓓ Ⓔ	39 Ⓐ Ⓑ Ⓒ Ⓓ Ⓔ
10 Ⓐ Ⓑ Ⓒ Ⓓ Ⓔ	20 Ⓐ Ⓑ Ⓒ Ⓓ Ⓔ	30 Ⓐ Ⓑ Ⓒ Ⓓ Ⓔ	40 Ⓐ Ⓑ Ⓒ Ⓓ Ⓔ

Section III—Verbal

1 Ⓐ Ⓑ Ⓒ Ⓓ Ⓔ	11 Ⓐ Ⓑ Ⓒ Ⓓ Ⓔ	21 Ⓐ Ⓑ Ⓒ Ⓓ Ⓔ	31 Ⓐ Ⓑ Ⓒ Ⓓ Ⓔ
2 Ⓐ Ⓑ Ⓒ Ⓓ Ⓔ	12 Ⓐ Ⓑ Ⓒ Ⓓ Ⓔ	22 Ⓐ Ⓑ Ⓒ Ⓓ Ⓔ	32 Ⓐ Ⓑ Ⓒ Ⓓ Ⓔ
3 Ⓐ Ⓑ Ⓒ Ⓓ Ⓔ	13 Ⓐ Ⓑ Ⓒ Ⓓ Ⓔ	23 Ⓐ Ⓑ Ⓒ Ⓓ Ⓔ	33 Ⓐ Ⓑ Ⓒ Ⓓ Ⓔ
4 Ⓐ Ⓑ Ⓒ Ⓓ Ⓔ	14 Ⓐ Ⓑ Ⓒ Ⓓ Ⓔ	24 Ⓐ Ⓑ Ⓒ Ⓓ Ⓔ	34 Ⓐ Ⓑ Ⓒ Ⓓ Ⓔ
5 Ⓐ Ⓑ Ⓒ Ⓓ Ⓔ	15 Ⓐ Ⓑ Ⓒ Ⓓ Ⓔ	25 Ⓐ Ⓑ Ⓒ Ⓓ Ⓔ	35 Ⓐ Ⓑ Ⓒ Ⓓ Ⓔ
6 Ⓐ Ⓑ Ⓒ Ⓓ Ⓔ	16 Ⓐ Ⓑ Ⓒ Ⓓ Ⓔ	26 Ⓐ Ⓑ Ⓒ Ⓓ Ⓔ	36 Ⓐ Ⓑ Ⓒ Ⓓ Ⓔ
7 Ⓐ Ⓑ Ⓒ Ⓓ Ⓔ	17 Ⓐ Ⓑ Ⓒ Ⓓ Ⓔ	27 Ⓐ Ⓑ Ⓒ Ⓓ Ⓔ	37 Ⓐ Ⓑ Ⓒ Ⓓ Ⓔ
8 Ⓐ Ⓑ Ⓒ Ⓓ Ⓔ	18 Ⓐ Ⓑ Ⓒ Ⓓ Ⓔ	28 Ⓐ Ⓑ Ⓒ Ⓓ Ⓔ	38 Ⓐ Ⓑ Ⓒ Ⓓ Ⓔ
9 Ⓐ Ⓑ Ⓒ Ⓓ Ⓔ	19 Ⓐ Ⓑ Ⓒ Ⓓ Ⓔ	29 Ⓐ Ⓑ Ⓒ Ⓓ Ⓔ	39 Ⓐ Ⓑ Ⓒ Ⓓ Ⓔ
10 Ⓐ Ⓑ Ⓒ Ⓓ Ⓔ	20 Ⓐ Ⓑ Ⓒ Ⓓ Ⓔ	30 Ⓐ Ⓑ Ⓒ Ⓓ Ⓔ	40 Ⓐ Ⓑ Ⓒ Ⓓ Ⓔ

Section IV—Mathematical

1 Ⓐ Ⓑ Ⓒ Ⓓ Ⓔ	10 Ⓐ Ⓑ Ⓒ Ⓓ Ⓔ	19 Ⓐ Ⓑ Ⓒ Ⓓ	28 Ⓐ Ⓑ Ⓒ Ⓓ
2 Ⓐ Ⓑ Ⓒ Ⓓ Ⓔ	11 Ⓐ Ⓑ Ⓒ Ⓓ Ⓔ	20 Ⓐ Ⓑ Ⓒ Ⓓ	29 Ⓐ Ⓑ Ⓒ Ⓓ
3 Ⓐ Ⓑ Ⓒ Ⓓ Ⓔ	12 Ⓐ Ⓑ Ⓒ Ⓓ Ⓔ	21 Ⓐ Ⓑ Ⓒ Ⓓ	30 Ⓐ Ⓑ Ⓒ Ⓓ
4 Ⓐ Ⓑ Ⓒ Ⓓ Ⓔ	13 Ⓐ Ⓑ Ⓒ Ⓓ Ⓔ	22 Ⓐ Ⓑ Ⓒ Ⓓ	31 Ⓐ Ⓑ Ⓒ Ⓓ
5 Ⓐ Ⓑ Ⓒ Ⓓ Ⓔ	14 Ⓐ Ⓑ Ⓒ Ⓓ Ⓔ	23 Ⓐ Ⓑ Ⓒ Ⓓ	32 Ⓐ Ⓑ Ⓒ Ⓓ
6 Ⓐ Ⓑ Ⓒ Ⓓ Ⓔ	15 Ⓐ Ⓑ Ⓒ Ⓓ Ⓔ	24 Ⓐ Ⓑ Ⓒ Ⓓ	33 Ⓐ Ⓑ Ⓒ Ⓓ
7 Ⓐ Ⓑ Ⓒ Ⓓ Ⓔ	16 Ⓐ Ⓑ Ⓒ Ⓓ Ⓔ	25 Ⓐ Ⓑ Ⓒ Ⓓ	34 Ⓐ Ⓑ Ⓒ Ⓓ
8 Ⓐ Ⓑ Ⓒ Ⓓ Ⓔ	17 Ⓐ Ⓑ Ⓒ Ⓓ Ⓔ	26 Ⓐ Ⓑ Ⓒ Ⓓ	35 Ⓐ Ⓑ Ⓒ Ⓓ
9 Ⓐ Ⓑ Ⓒ Ⓓ Ⓔ	18 Ⓐ Ⓑ Ⓒ Ⓓ Ⓔ	27 Ⓐ Ⓑ Ⓒ Ⓓ	

Section V—Mathematical

1 Ⓐ Ⓑ Ⓒ Ⓓ Ⓔ	8 Ⓐ Ⓑ Ⓒ Ⓓ Ⓔ	14 Ⓐ Ⓑ Ⓒ Ⓓ Ⓔ	20 Ⓐ Ⓑ Ⓒ Ⓓ Ⓔ
2 Ⓐ Ⓑ Ⓒ Ⓓ Ⓔ	9 Ⓐ Ⓑ Ⓒ Ⓓ Ⓔ	15 Ⓐ Ⓑ Ⓒ Ⓓ Ⓔ	21 Ⓐ Ⓑ Ⓒ Ⓓ Ⓔ
3 Ⓐ Ⓑ Ⓒ Ⓓ Ⓔ	10 Ⓐ Ⓑ Ⓒ Ⓓ Ⓔ	16 Ⓐ Ⓑ Ⓒ Ⓓ Ⓔ	22 Ⓐ Ⓑ Ⓒ Ⓓ Ⓔ
4 Ⓐ Ⓑ Ⓒ Ⓓ Ⓔ	11 Ⓐ Ⓑ Ⓒ Ⓓ Ⓔ	17 Ⓐ Ⓑ Ⓒ Ⓓ Ⓔ	23 Ⓐ Ⓑ Ⓒ Ⓓ Ⓔ
5 Ⓐ Ⓑ Ⓒ Ⓓ Ⓔ	12 Ⓐ Ⓑ Ⓒ Ⓓ Ⓔ	18 Ⓐ Ⓑ Ⓒ Ⓓ Ⓔ	24 Ⓐ Ⓑ Ⓒ Ⓓ Ⓔ
6 Ⓐ Ⓑ Ⓒ Ⓓ Ⓔ	13 Ⓐ Ⓑ Ⓒ Ⓓ Ⓔ	19 Ⓐ Ⓑ Ⓒ Ⓓ Ⓔ	25 Ⓐ Ⓑ Ⓒ Ⓓ Ⓔ
7 Ⓐ Ⓑ Ⓒ Ⓓ Ⓔ			

Section VI—Written English

1 Ⓐ Ⓑ Ⓒ Ⓓ Ⓔ	14 Ⓐ Ⓑ Ⓒ Ⓓ Ⓔ	27 Ⓐ Ⓑ Ⓒ Ⓓ Ⓔ	39 Ⓐ Ⓑ Ⓒ Ⓓ Ⓔ
2 Ⓐ Ⓑ Ⓒ Ⓓ Ⓔ	15 Ⓐ Ⓑ Ⓒ Ⓓ Ⓔ	28 Ⓐ Ⓑ Ⓒ Ⓓ Ⓔ	40 Ⓐ Ⓑ Ⓒ Ⓓ Ⓔ
3 Ⓐ Ⓑ Ⓒ Ⓓ Ⓔ	16 Ⓐ Ⓑ Ⓒ Ⓓ Ⓔ	29 Ⓐ Ⓑ Ⓒ Ⓓ Ⓔ	41 Ⓐ Ⓑ Ⓒ Ⓓ Ⓔ
4 Ⓐ Ⓑ Ⓒ Ⓓ Ⓔ	17 Ⓐ Ⓑ Ⓒ Ⓓ Ⓔ	30 Ⓐ Ⓑ Ⓒ Ⓓ Ⓔ	42 Ⓐ Ⓑ Ⓒ Ⓓ Ⓔ
5 Ⓐ Ⓑ Ⓒ Ⓓ Ⓔ	18 Ⓐ Ⓑ Ⓒ Ⓓ Ⓔ	31 Ⓐ Ⓑ Ⓒ Ⓓ Ⓔ	43 Ⓐ Ⓑ Ⓒ Ⓓ Ⓔ
6 Ⓐ Ⓑ Ⓒ Ⓓ Ⓔ	19 Ⓐ Ⓑ Ⓒ Ⓓ Ⓔ	32 Ⓐ Ⓑ Ⓒ Ⓓ Ⓔ	44 Ⓐ Ⓑ Ⓒ Ⓓ Ⓔ
7 Ⓐ Ⓑ Ⓒ Ⓓ Ⓔ	20 Ⓐ Ⓑ Ⓒ Ⓓ Ⓔ	33 Ⓐ Ⓑ Ⓒ Ⓓ Ⓔ	45 Ⓐ Ⓑ Ⓒ Ⓓ Ⓔ
8 Ⓐ Ⓑ Ⓒ Ⓓ Ⓔ	21 Ⓐ Ⓑ Ⓒ Ⓓ Ⓔ	34 Ⓐ Ⓑ Ⓒ Ⓓ Ⓔ	46 Ⓐ Ⓑ Ⓒ Ⓓ Ⓔ
9 Ⓐ Ⓑ Ⓒ Ⓓ Ⓔ	22 Ⓐ Ⓑ Ⓒ Ⓓ Ⓔ	35 Ⓐ Ⓑ Ⓒ Ⓓ Ⓔ	47 Ⓐ Ⓑ Ⓒ Ⓓ Ⓔ
10 Ⓐ Ⓑ Ⓒ Ⓓ Ⓔ	23 Ⓐ Ⓑ Ⓒ Ⓓ Ⓔ	36 Ⓐ Ⓑ Ⓒ Ⓓ Ⓔ	48 Ⓐ Ⓑ Ⓒ Ⓓ Ⓔ
11 Ⓐ Ⓑ Ⓒ Ⓓ Ⓔ	24 Ⓐ Ⓑ Ⓒ Ⓓ Ⓔ	37 Ⓐ Ⓑ Ⓒ Ⓓ Ⓔ	49 Ⓐ Ⓑ Ⓒ Ⓓ Ⓔ
12 Ⓐ Ⓑ Ⓒ Ⓓ Ⓔ	25 Ⓐ Ⓑ Ⓒ Ⓓ Ⓔ	38 Ⓐ Ⓑ Ⓒ Ⓓ Ⓔ	50 Ⓐ Ⓑ Ⓒ Ⓓ Ⓔ
13 Ⓐ Ⓑ Ⓒ Ⓓ Ⓔ	26 Ⓐ Ⓑ Ⓒ Ⓓ Ⓔ		

SAT Practice Test 4

Time—30 minutes

45 Questions

For each of the numbered questions in this section, choose the best answer according to the instructions, and blacken the corresponding blank space on the answer sheet.

In each of the questions below, a capitalized word is followed by five words or phrases lettered (A) through (E). Select the word or phrase *most nearly opposite* in meaning to the capitalized word.

Since some of the questions require that you distinguish fine shades of meaning, consider all choices carefully before you select your answer.

1. DELETE:
   (A) submit
   (B) conserve
   (C) edit
   (D) insert
   (E) correct

2. INEPT:
   (A) competent
   (B) facile
   (C) useful
   (D) fitting
   (E) artful

3. FRENZY:
   (A) delirium
   (B) chaos
   (C) untoward
   (D) salient
   (E) calm

4. POMPOUS:
   (A) excelling
   (B) portable
   (C) portentous
   (D) sedate
   (E) unassuming

5. URBANE:
   (A) unsophisticated
   (B) unspoiled
   (C) untutored
   (D) uncultivated
   (E) antisocial

6. PIQUANT:
   (A) peaceful
   (B) tasty
   (C) jejune
   (D) teasing
   (E) resentful

7. RECALCITRANT:
   (A) demonstrative
   (B) hardened
   (C) amenable
   (D) refined
   (E) benevolent

8. AUSPICIOUS:
   (A) unprotected
   (B) unsponsored
   (C) opportune
   (D) ill-omened
   (E) circumstantial

9. CASTIGATE:
   (A) reprove
   (B) acclaim
   (C) ventilate
   (D) retaliate
   (E) construe

10. DESULTORY:
(A) retentive
(B) unopposed
(C) orotund
(D) methodical
(E) perverse

11. ARTLESS:
(A) cunning
(B) talented
(C) trendy
(D) primitive
(E) smart

12. VIGILANT:
(A) watchman
(B) alert
(C) sleepless
(D) arsonist
(E) negligent

13. CONCRETE:
(A) soft
(B) discrete
(C) asphalt
(D) wispy
(E) abstract

14. SUSCEPTIBLE:
(A) disabled
(B) immune
(C) averse
(D) enraptured
(E) open

15. INIMICAL:
(A) unique
(B) corrupt
(C) friendly
(D) curious
(E) raucous

Each of the sentences below has one or more blank spaces indicating where a word (or words) has been omitted. Each sentence is followed by five words or sets of words lettered from (A) through (E). Select the lettered word or set of words which, inserted to replace the blanks, *best* fits in with and completes the meaning of the sentence as a whole.

16. In a rational world, we will need leaders who can look beyond unfettered national _____ to a condition of effective law applied to the states themselves.
(A) debts
(B) ambitions
(C) alliances
(D) sovereignty
(E) boundaries

17. Although no such action was required because the pact had been the result of compulsory _____, the union submitted the new contract with the Postal Service to the membership for _____.
(A) negotiation . . abeyance
(B) legislation . . recommendations
(C) regulation . . amendment
(D) arbitration . . ratification
(E) attendance . . compliance

18. The lobbyists for the railroads advocate a _____ of ICC regulated freight rates, and an easing of the regulation of other rail activities in order to allow the railroad industry to be _____ with the other carriers.
(A) rollback . . competitive
(B) tightening . . conversant
(C) boycott . . aggressive
(D) kickback . . equitable
(E) rebate . . compared

19. Despite continuing growth and financial success, the company's _____ in the business community and with the general public has been _____ by scandals that reflect a get-it-done-I-don't-care-how philosophy of management.
(A) popularity . . reversed
(B) influence . . heightened
(C) sapience . . stultified
(D) refutation . . shattered
(E) image . . tarnished

20. While his predecessor was considered aloof and _____, communicating only with a small, inner circle, the new chairman is seen by associates as warm and _____.
    (A) assiduous . . sedulous
    (B) reclusive . . introverted
    (C) self-contained . . surreptitious
    (D) dictatorial . . egalitarian
    (E) presumptuous . . contemptible

21. Potential women congressional candidates still face _____ obstacles, particularly a lack of primary campaign contributions and a lack of _____ to the "old-boy" network that donates it.
    (A) formidable . . access
    (B) temporal . . allegiance
    (C) psychological . . attention
    (D) pitfall . . excess
    (E) rigid . . connection

22. The crop failure, the third in as many years resulting from natural _____, could severely _____ Vietnam's plans for economic recovery.
    (A) sources . . intensify
    (B) turmoil . . obstruct
    (C) calamities . . hamper
    (D) enemies . . deflect
    (E) floods . . inundate

23. A recent study found that part-time employees generally provide higher productivity, greater loyalty, and _____ absenteeism than full-time employees, while putting less strain on company _____.
    (A) more . . policies
    (B) fewer . . budgets
    (C) less . . payrolls
    (D) increased . . programs
    (E) decreased . . personnel

24. Personnel practices in some large companies include character analysis from handwriting, and it is not unusual for the personnel office to retain a consulting _____.
    (A) psychologist
    (B) analyst
    (C) chiropodist
    (D) engineer
    (E) graphologist

25. The German High Command underestimated the _____ of radar to the British, although they themselves had radar at the time and knew its _____.
    (A) cost . . value
    (B) value . . potential
    (C) potential . . defects
    (D) effectiveness . . cost
    (E) benefit . . fecklessness

In each of the questions below, a related pair of words or phrases, in capital letters, is followed by five pairs of words or phrases lettered from (A) through (E). Select that lettered pair which expresses a relationship that is *most* similar to that of the capitalized pair.

26. AVERSION : ABHORRENCE ::
    (A) revenge : recriminations
    (B) respect : reverence
    (C) scorn : disdain
    (D) duress : suppress
    (E) detestation : dislike

27. NECESSITY : INVENTION ::
    (A) procrastination : time
    (B) honor : thieves
    (C) honey : bees
    (D) stitch : time
    (E) angels : tread

28. CRESTFALLEN : ELATED ::
    (A) happy : sad
    (B) forlorn : woebegone
    (C) careful : wary
    (D) dejected : jubilant
    (E) depressed : repressed

29. QUENCH : THIRST ::
    (A) absolve : innocent
    (B) quell : fears
    (C) allay : alloy
    (D) reject : accept
    (E) requite : repay

30. NIBBLE : DEVOUR ::
    (A) sip : quaff
    (B) encompass : encircle
    (C) slurp : swallow
    (D) hinder : hurt
    (E) crush : crunch

31. LAUD : EULOGIZE ::
    (A) deplore : deny
    (B) criticize : complain
    (C) aid : abut
    (D) pine : enjoy
    (E) repine : grumble

32. GAS GAUGE : AMMETER ::
    (A) gallons : volts
    (B) empty : negative
    (C) fuel : current
    (D) low : high
    (E) full : overheating

33. PYROMANIAC : FIRE ::
    (A) kleptomaniac : theft
    (B) bibliophile : religion
    (C) claustrophobe : heights
    (D) ailurophobe : cat lover
    (E) megalomaniac : Hitler

34. FRIDAY : THURSDAY ::
    (A) spring : summer
    (B) hit : hurt
    (C) August : July
    (D) Roosevelt : Cleveland
    (E) seven : eight

35. ASCETIC : DENIAL ::
    (A) aesthete : retention
    (B) philosopher : anger
    (C) diplomat : revenge
    (D) epicure : indulgence
    (E) conspirator : acquisition

Each of the reading passages below is followed by several questions about the contents of the passage. In answering the questions, base your responses on what is *stated* or *implied* in the passage.

A quarter of a century ago, most psychologists thought that a child's development followed two fairly discrete paths. He mastered new motor skills as his organism matured, but his intellectual growth was primarily governed by experience. Modern research suggests that the physiological maturing process also plays a major role in cognitive growth, which unfolds in the same well-ordered sequences in most environments.

To illustrate this point, let us look at a special set of new reactions that seems to emerge quite suddenly at eight to twelve months of age. Certain events that bored a child a couple of months earlier appear to take on new interest; others that he responded to with equanimity then make him inhibited or even fearful now. He becomes wary if presented with a jack-in-the-box or a moving mechanical toy and hesitates before reaching for an unfamiliar object that he would once have grabbed gleefully. At four months he probably smiled at strange adults; now he may cry if one approaches. Soon after his first birthday, he will also stop what he is doing if a strange child comes near. Most important, his behavior now suggests that he can

remember events that happened moments before and can make use of that information.

A classic experiment devised by Swiss psychologist Jean Piaget demonstrates this improvement in memory. An adult hides an attractive toy under a small cloth while the infant watches. A child under seven months typically does not reach for the cloth, as though he has forgotten about the toy once it is removed from view. After eight months, most children confidently reach for the hidden toy. With each succeeding month, the child becomes capable of tolerating a longer delay between the hiding of the toy and the moment when he is allowed to reach for it. What he has achieved is the ability to hold past knowledge on the memory stage and juxtapose it with information currently being absorbed. This process of evaluation and comparison is one of the fundamental components of thought.

The enhanced ability to remember and evaluate is one reason the eight-month-old appears more purposeful in his activity. It may also explain why he soon begins to show a fear of separation. The probability that a child will protest, cry, or stop his playing when he sees his mother or principal caretaker leave emerges at about the same time in all cultures.

36. Twenty-five years ago, psychologists believed that motor skills developed as the organism matured, but that mental skills
    (A) evolved as a result of the infant's direct experiences
    (B) were directly related to genetic structure
    (C) were slower to manifest themselves
    (D) were a function of the total child
    (E) had no relation to physical maturity

37. Which of the following, according to the passage, characterize (characterizes) the changes that take place as a child reaches eight to twelve months?
    I. Responds with equanimity to all things.
    II. Reaches warily or hesitantly for an unfamiliar object that he previously would have grabbed gleefully.
    III. Remembers events that have just happened, and can use the information.
    IV. Smiles at strange adults.
    (A) I and IV only
    (B) II and III only
    (C) III only
    (D) I, II, III, and IV
    (E) II only

38. The term "cognitive growth" as used in paragraph 1 most nearly means
    (A) motor skills
    (B) intellectual growth
    (C) emotional control
    (D) purposeful behavior
    (E) reflex actions

39. The author's main purpose is to indicate that current research believes
    (A) that the psychologists of twenty-five years ago were correct in their belief that intellectual growth was primarily governed by experience
    (B) that children, regardless of their physiological development, fear separation from their mothers
    (C) the ability of children to learn and think follows a fairly specific sequence of development in which physiological maturation plays a major role

(D) children show very little change in their thought processes and reactions during the first year of life
(E) that new reactions only seem to emerge suddenly in children, but that they have been present all along

40. Which of the following statements would, if demonstrated to be true, prove the author's belief about intellectual growth?
    I. Cognitive growth unfolds in the same well-ordered sequences in most environments.
    II. The same new reactions set in for most children quite suddenly between eight and twelve months of age.
    III. In all cultures, children show fear of separation from their mothers or principal caretakers at about the same stages of physiological development.
    (A) III only
    (B) I, II, and III
    (C) II only
    (D) I and III only
    (E) I only

The night, like clean water and the wolf, is getting away from us. Our cities are filled with children who have never seen the Milky Way. It is against the law to drive slowly down an empty country road under a full moon with your headlights off. Observations of the night sky from California's Mount Palomar are washed out by the blaze of illumination from Los Angeles to the north and San Diego to the south. Mercury vapor lamps in San Jose slash the film record of celestial observations at Lick Observatory with dark spectral lines.

The comfort and mystery of a night full of stars and nocturnal creatures are eroding before us. The stars have become the victims of artificial lights; the dark woods at midnight are victims of neglect.

For those of us who live in urban and suburban areas, the loss of darkness is entirely the fault of too many headlights, streetlights, parking lot lights, burglar lights, searchlights, swimming pool lights, midway lights. Indeed, outdoor lighting is growing at a rate of twenty-three percent a year versus a population growth of one percent a year. So passes the starry night.

But we are losing the night in a much more subtle way. We have come to think of it as a nuisance, an inconvenience, like sagebrush and mosquitoes. As an essentially urban people, our senses blunted by noise and bad air, we find little to interest us in an environment that renders our primary sense—sight—all but useless and calls on our little-used senses of smell, balance, hearing, and direction.

Yet the gifts of night, while more obscure, more abstract than those of the daylight hours, are no less valuable. In an age when it is all but impossible to find refuge from machinery, the night is as important to the human psyche as is pure water to the body. When the human eye can no longer see Arcturus, we will have lost a perspective. When the deep night of the forest, like the Arctic night of winter or the night of the Mariana Trench becomes only a metaphor for the absence of life, then we will shrink as a civilization. The stuff of our mysteries will collapse around us.

We cannot afford to lose the night any more than we can afford to lose poetry.

41. The primary purpose of this passage is to
(A) promote a cause
(B) raise a question
(C) describe a happening
(D) arouse our awareness
(E) analyze an argument

42. Of the following statements, which is (are) in agreement with the passage?
    I. Outdoor lighting is making the sky so bright that many people in urban areas have never seen more than a few of the stars of our own galaxy.
    II. Excessive artificial lighting has caused us to lose our night vision.
    III. Illumination from the large urban areas on the Pacific coast is interfering with astronomical observations.
(A) I, II, and III
(B) I and III only
(C) I only
(D) II and III only
(E) II only

43. It can be inferred from the first two sentences of paragraph 5 that the author of this passage
(A) is in favor of spectator sports being presented at night
(B) finds the daylight hours less valuable than the nighttime
(C) bemoans the diminishing acuteness of his senses
(D) feels that the gifts of night can be spiritually restorative to people caught up in the hustle and bustle of their daily lives
(E) is opposed to all forms of outdoor lighting

44. The author expresses his alarm about the impact of outdoor lighting. Which of the following is (are) cause for alarm according to the passage?
    I. Mercury vapor lamps in San Jose
    II. Headlights, burglar lights, and traffic signals
    III. The outdoor illumination of large urban areas
(A) I only
(B) II only
(C) III only
(D) I and III only
(E) I and II only

45. The last line of the passage most nearly means:
(A) The same people who like poetry are probably night persons as well.
(B) The stars and the moon have inspired much poetry, and the loss of the latter would probably cause the loss of the former, and vice versa.
(C) Poetry arouses deep emotions in people and, even though it may not have commercial value, it is rewarding for us in ways that are obscure and abstract. Similarly, night arouses emotional feelings in us, and we cannot afford to give up the comfort of night for the comfort of light.
(D) Night is a mystery we cannot comprehend, but perhaps the time will come someday when we will understand it.
(E) Both night and poetry are important aspects of romance.

STOP
WORK ONLY ON THIS SECTION UNTIL THE TIME ALLOTTED IS OVER.

SECTION II

Time—30 minutes

40 Questions

For each of the numbered questions in this section, choose the best answer according to the instructions, and blacken the corresponding blank space on the answer sheet.

In each of the questions below, a capitalized word is followed by five words or phrases lettered (A) through (E). Select the word or phrase most nearly *opposite* in meaning to the capitalized word.

Since some of the questions require that you distinguish fine shades of meaning, consider all choices carefully before you select your answer.

1. BENEVOLENT:
   (A) cruel
   (B) despotic
   (C) involuntary
   (D) accursed
   (E) good-natured

2. MATURE:
   (A) ripe
   (B) aged
   (C) capable
   (D) puerile
   (E) powerless

3. COPIOUS:
   (A) unwieldy
   (B) meager
   (C) plentiful
   (D) in stock
   (E) resourceful

4. DEPLETE:
   (A) augment
   (B) omit
   (C) revise
   (D) envy
   (E) desire

5. OMINOUS:
   (A) sweltering
   (B) suspicious
   (C) all-powerful
   (D) undetermined
   (E) propitious

6. VEHEMENT:
   (A) undercoat
   (B) imperious
   (C) timid
   (D) dispassionate
   (E) uncontrolled

7. GELID:
   (A) firm
   (B) quaking
   (C) quiescent
   (D) burning
   (E) latent

8. PRODIGAL:
   (A) gifted
   (B) untalented
   (C) frugal
   (D) hard-pressed
   (E) qualified

9. DIAPHANOUS:
   (A) sweeping
   (B) flowing
   (C) heavy
   (D) putrescent
   (E) absorbent

10. INCIPIENT:
    (A) dormant
    (B) exciting
    (C) tasteless
    (D) foregone
    (E) concluding

Each of the reading passages below is followed by several questions about the contents of the passage. In answering the questions, base your responses on what is *stated* or *implied* in the passage.

Around Seward they still tell of the hunter who was on the beach at Humpy Cove that day, skinning a hair seal when the first wave came.

He and his partner were hunting the rough coast of Resurrection Bay for seals back in 1964, when such hunting was still lawful. A tough way to turn a dollar, and they were working their way back up Resurrection toward Seward through the snow squalls and wet gray winds of March.

The hunter had shot a seal on the narrow beach at Humpy and gone ashore to skin it when the ground began bucking beneath his feet like a deck in a tide rip. There was a deep rushing noise like a high wind just overhead, but there was no wind, and the spruces above the beach swayed and whipped in the windless air. He looked up at the boat offshore, hearing his partner's yell, and far out on the gray-green surface of Resurrection Bay he could see something wrong with the water, something that grew swiftly as it came on. Knife still in hand, he turned and ran for the trees.

Up through the branch of a big spruce, climbing as high and as fast as he could, suddenly finding that he still held the knife and driving the blade into the tree and embracing the trunk just as the first tsunami engulfed the beach.

The great wave brought the boat with it, over the beach and into the trees, then receding and taking the boat out to sea again. The next wave was even higher than the first, a vast swell of water that rose up over the shore and into the forest, sweeping the boat even farther inland and bringing it to the spruce tree where the seal hunter clung. Unbelieving, he saw the boat just beneath him— and stepped down onto the deck as the sea began to run back. A fantastic stroke of luck on one of southern Alaska's most unlucky days—Good Friday, 1964. A few miles north at the head of Resurrection Bay, docks gone, wharves and railroads gone, great ships aground and oil tanks smashed, its waterfront a mass of splintered and twisted wreckage, Seward was burning.

But, for the seal hunter and his partner, Resurrection Bay had lived up to its name. Two weeks later he went back to Humpy Cove and climbed the tree and got his skinning knife.

11. We can infer from this passage that in the article from which it is taken, the author will, in the next few paragraphs, be writing about
    (A) changes in the conservation laws dealing with seal hunting
    (B) other close calls that the seal hunter and his friend experienced
    (C) emergency procedures to follow when a tidal wave strikes
    (D) the earthquake, the tidal wave it caused, and the other effects they had on the area around Seward
    (E) the need for new regulations to prevent further damage to the Alaskan ecosystem

12. A tsunami is, we can infer, a
    (A) riptide
    (B) huge manta ray
    (C) tidal wave
    (D) wind of tornadolike force
    (E) violent earth tremor

13. The only one of the following that the author did not employ to achieve literary effects in the passage is
    (A) figurative language
    (B) contrast
    (C) anticlimax
    (D) delineation of character
    (E) punning

14. The city of Seward is located
    (A) on the beach at Humpy Cove
    (B) sixty-four miles south of Resurrection Bay
    (C) two weeks journey by boat from Alaska
    (D) at the foot of tsunami
    (E) at the head of Resurrection Bay

15. The seal hunter's life was saved when
    (A) he drove the knife into the trunk of the tree and held onto the haft
    (B) he caught the first tidal wave and surfed on to safety farther inland
    (C) the great wave receded, taking the boat back to Seward
    (D) he shot the seal and skinned it, covering the spruce tree to which he clung

(E) the second wave swept farther inland than the first one, so that the boat floated up to the tree that he had climbed, and remained there just long enough for him to drop into it before the water receded, carrying the boat back to the bay

Let me confess to a bias in favor of the authentic traveler, as opposed to the tourist, whose most intense experience usually has to do with the shortcomings of his accommodations. The equipment of the authentic traveler comprises not credit cards, but a certain number of human qualities, such as stamina, patience, indifference to personal comfort, a gift for being at the same time detached and absorbed, a knack for ferreting out odd information, and the ability to make the most of chance encounters.

Bruce Chatwin falls into that commendable category. There are few parts of the globe I am less curious about than Patagonia, yet he coaxed me into joining him for the 205 pages it took to cross that semiarid landscape. He has written a book that deserves to stand on a small shelf containing the work of far better-known writers, such as Graham Greene's *Journey Without Maps*, W. Somerset Maugham's *The Gentleman in the Parlour* and Paul Theroux's *The Great Railway Bazaar*.

The authentic traveler sets out alone, with the modest aim of roaming around a place and letting things happen to him. He is available for experiences, not always pleasant: Riding in the Andes, Mr. Chatwin's saddle girth snapped and his horse threw him into sharp rocks, and he cut his hand to the bone. Walking through the bogs of Tierra del Fuego, he fell into a river, "head first into black mud, and I had a hard time getting out."

But these were minor interruptions. Inspired by a piece of skin, on display in his grandmother's living room, that had been taken from a brontosaur found in Patagonia, Mr. Chatwin crossed the part of South America that includes the lower thirds of Argentina and Chile. Although it is sparsely populated, he found a seemingly inexhaustible supply of English sheep ranchers there. The British presence in Patagonia, apparently so extensive that the area deserves admittance to the

Commonwealth, forms the spine of the book. We are told of the mining concern that posted its orders in English and Gaelic, of the homes where cucumber sandwiches and bound sets of *Country Life* are in evidence. We are introduced to the Scottish rancher who wears kilts and plays the pipes, and to the Englishwoman growing strawberries in Tierra del Fuego.

If the book were nothing more than a study of how the English maintain quaint customs in remote environments, its appeal would be limited. Fortunately, Mr. Chatwin has an inquiring mind, and part of the pleasure lies in his digressions. Mr. Chatwin's mind, like a crowded attic without cobwebs, produces curios and discontinued models, presented in a manner that is laconic without being listless, literate without being pedantic, and intent without being breathless.

16. Which of the following characterize the tourist, according to the author?
    I. A desire to encounter the unexpected
    II. Deep concern about the comfort of his accommodations
    III. His equipment comprises credit cards and a travel guidebook
    (A) I only
    (B) I and III only
    (C) I and II only
    (D) II and III only
    (E) II only

17. The "small shelf" referred to in paragraph 2 implies that
    (A) there are few books written about travel
    (B) the author of the passage has a small collection of travel books
    (C) better-known writers have written far better books on travel than this one
    (D) the author prefers to read about tourism rather than travel
    (E) only a handful of writers have written praiseworthy books on travel

18. The main thread of Mr. Chatwin's book, we can infer, is
    (A) the unusual presence of the British in Patagonia and the quaint customs and habits they maintain
    (B) the material describing scenic highlights
    (C) the discovery of a brontosaur in Patagonia
    (D) the series of mishaps experienced by Mr. Chatwin
    (E) the presentation of curios and discontinued models from Mr. Chatwin's attic

19. The author of this passage, in his writing, makes use of
    (A) humor and satire
    (B) contrast and figurative language
    (C) hyperbole and alliteration
    (D) cause and effect
    (E) dramatic irony

20. By which of the following statements can the author's reaction to Mr. Chatwin's book be summed up?
    (A) He feels that the book has only a limited appeal.
    (B) He is not particularly interested in Patagonia and he would have preferred a book about some other part of the globe.
    (C) He likes the book, but not as much as others that he has read by better-known authors.
    (D) He is delighted with both the style and content of the book and feels that it ranks with the great travel books of all time.
    (E) He feels the book is nothing more than a study of how the English maintain quaint customs in remote environments.

The study of the twentieth century does offer special problems for the historian. The closer to the present the events that are being considered, the harder it is for the historian to get a firm perspective and to distinguish the important from the peripheral. There are, furthermore, some peculiar problems for the contemporary historian. Although the scholar who investigates the last fifty years of European history has a wealth of data, he encounters frustrating obstacles when he wants to examine the papers of important leaders. If the leader himself is not still alive and reluctant to be subjected to the scrutiny of academic scholarship, then his family and disciples are frequently determined to protect his reputation. Thus the papers of David Lloyd George, British prime minister during the First World War, are still not open to the public and many diplomatic records of the 1930s are still closed to general inquiry. A peculiar problem that the political historian of the contemporary era encounters is the fugitive nature of a great deal of twentieth-century communications as a result of telephone conversations and face-to-face conferences greatly facilitated by airplane travel. It may turn out that historians will know more about the motivations of nineteenth-century statesmen who left behind vast personal and official correspondence than of many comparably important twentieth-century leaders.

The shape of twentieth-century European history as it now appears in historical literature is an ambiguous and paradoxical combination of the themes of progress and achievement on the one hand, and disappointment and retrogression on the other. The last half century has seen the resolution, by and large, of the social problems caused by the industrial revolution in the Western world and the achievement of a generally high standard of living by the working classes as a result of the coming of the welfare state. The two decades since the Second World War have also witnessed the emancipation of the non-European peoples from direct Western imperialist exploitation and control. The last half century has been an era of unprecedented advance in theoretical and applied science and the understanding and control of nature by mankind to a degree scarcely dreamed of in 1914. On the other hand, the dangerous boom in world population, the colossal devastation and degradation of human life by authoritarian regimes, and the threat to the survival of the human race imposed by nuclear and biological weapons have made the twentieth-century not only an era of progress and prosperity, but also one of hitherto unimaginable desperation, terror, and violence.

21. Which of the following is *not* a problem faced by the contemporary historian?
    (A) There is an abundance of data on the last fifty years of European history.
    (B) The papers of some of the European leaders of the past seventy years are still not available for general inquiry.
    (C) An important leader's family and disciples may try to protect that leader's reputation.
    (D) It is hard to get a firm perspective on the events of the relatively recent past.
    (E) A good deal of twentieth-century communication is verbal rather than written.

22. Which of the following most strongly supports the author's contention that historians may turn out to know more about the motivations of nineteenth-century statesmen than those of comparable twentieth-century leaders?
    (A) The papers of some of the great leaders are missing.
    (B) Nineteenth-century statesmen left behind vast personal and official correspondence.
    (C) Most twentieth-century leaders wish to protect their personal reputations.
    (D) David Lloyd George's papers are still not available to the general public.
    (E) Copyright laws protect the inner thoughts of current leaders.

23. The word *fugitive* as used in the next-to-the-last sentence of the first paragraph most nearly means
    (A) runaway
    (B) escapee
    (C) vagabond
    (D) fleeting
    (E) underhanded

24. According to this passage, which statement or statements represent the view of twentieth-century European history as it now appears in historical literature?
    I. By and large the social problems caused by the Industrial Revolution have been resolved in the last fifty years.
    II. Many non-European peoples still have not been emancipated from direct imperialist exploitation.
    III. Nuclear and biological weaponry pose a threat to the survival of the human race.
    (A) I and III only
    (B) I only
    (C) II and III only
    (D) I, II, and III
    (E) III only

25. Which pairing below best illustrates the paradoxical combination referred to in the second paragraph?
    (A) biological warfare and the H-bomb
    (B) moon landings and the Hindenburg
    (C) the American standard of living and the Russian standard of living
    (D) polio vaccines and cerebral palsy
    (E) decreased birth mortality and concentration camps

GO ON TO THE NEXT PAGE

Each of the sentences below has one or more blank spaces indicating where a word (or words) has been omitted. Each sentence is followed by five words or sets of words lettered from (A) through (E). Select the lettered word or set of words which, inserted to replace the blanks, *best* fits in with and completes the meaning of the sentence as a whole.

26. Domestic hens lay eggs at any time of the year, although egg production is highest during the spring months; the _____ of domestic hens, however, normally laid during the _____ only.
    (A) fossils . . winter
    (B) ancestors . . spring
    (C) descendants . . other
    (D) enemies . . off
    (E) rooster . . odd

27. The quality of tap water, although nominally under the control of federal legislation, is still largely _____ on the enforcement of a jumble of often-conflicting regulations by _____ officials who vary in their enthusiasm for maintaining water quality.
    (A) reliant . . appointed
    (B) dependent . . state and local
    (C) based . . elected
    (D) centered . . corrupt and venal
    (E) reported . . unconcerned

28. Women _____ to higher management levels need more than the advice and guidance that a mentor gives; they need the knowledge and skills learned when theory and principles are _____ to concrete situations.
    (A) applying . . inappropriate
    (B) urged . . responsive
    (C) advanced . . inconsistent
    (D) aspiring . . applied
    (E) passed over . . common

29. Some observers believe that many police and fire strikes could be _____ if disputes were _____ to binding arbitration or a public referendum.
    (A) shortened . . averse
    (B) averted . . submitted
    (C) defeated . . closed
    (D) broken . . subordinated
    (E) lengthened . . taken

30. The movie is not only a supreme expression of mechanism, but _____ it offers as product the most magical of consumer commodities, namely _____.
    (A) incidentally . . paintings
    (B) unintentionally . . romance
    (C) paradoxically . . dreams
    (D) parenthetically . . vicarious thrills
    (E) quixotically . . escape

In each of the questions below, a related pair of words or phrases, in capital letters, is followed by five pairs of words or phrases lettered from (A) through (E). Select that lettered pair which expresses a relationship that is *most* similar to that of the capitalized pair.

31. HOMESTEADER : SETTLER ::
    (A) rancher : cowpoke
    (B) wetback : traveler
    (C) greenhorn : trapper
    (D) Okie : migrant farmer
    (E) voyageur : teamster

32. MOLECULE : ATOM ::
    (A) tree : leaf
    (B) hydrogen : oxygen
    (C) book : plot
    (D) bouquet : flower
    (E) flower : stamen

33. ADVENTURER : TIMOROUS ::
    (A) poltroon : savage
    (B) buffoon : suave
    (C) baboon : coarse
    (D) lampoon : satire
    (E) patroon : landowner

34. PORPOISE : AQUATIC ::
    (A) blowfish : terrestrial
    (B) sloth : aerial
    (C) zebra : arboreal
    (D) whale : mammal
    (E) eel : aquatic

35. ATTACK : DEFEND ::
    (A) divulge : reveal
    (B) indulge : gratify
    (C) wither : bloom
    (D) welter : swelter
    (E) swoon : faint

36. EXPUNGE : OBLITERATE ::
    (A) annihilate : eradicate
    (B) proliferate : perforate
    (C) garret : garrote
    (D) condemn : condone
    (E) extrude : obtrude

37. BOGUS : SPURIOUS ::
    (A) felonious : feline
    (B) fitting : inappropriate
    (C) spontaneous : premeditated
    (D) authentic : bona fide
    (E) incombustible : inflammable

38. CASHMERE : FABRIC ::
    (A) glove : horsehide
    (B) ceramic : pot
    (C) pine : forest
    (D) vinyl : plastic
    (E) ceramic : clay

39. TOADY : OBSEQUIOUS ::
    (A) martinet : easygoing
    (B) snob : egalitarian
    (C) dandy : foppish
    (D) skinflint : generous
    (E) harridan : genteel

40. EPHEMERAL : EVERLASTING ::
    (A) timeless : eternal
    (B) fixed : permanent
    (C) transitory : perpetual
    (D) fantastic : real
    (E) intransigent : impermeable

STOP
WORK ONLY ON THIS SECTION UNTIL THE TIME ALLOTTED IS OVER.

For each of the numbered questions in this section, choose the best answer according to the instructions, and blacken the corresponding blank space on the answer sheet.

In each of the questions below, a capitalized word is followed by five words or phrases lettered (A) through (E). Select the word or phrase *most nearly opposite* in meaning to the capitalized word.

Since some of the questions require that you distinguish fine shades of meaning, consider all choices carefully before you select your answer.

1. FALLIBLE:
   (A) risible
   (B) misshapen
   (C) unforgiving
   (D) unerring
   (E) imperfect

2. VIVACIOUS:
   (A) experimental
   (B) tormented
   (C) blithe
   (D) languid
   (E) forsworn

3. RELINQUISH:
   (A) forget
   (B) retain
   (C) remember
   (D) quell
   (E) encumber

4. SPONTANEITY:
   (A) impromptu
   (B) promptness
   (C) premeditation
   (D) procrastination
   (E) rectitude

5. BRUSQUE:
   (A) suave
   (B) harsh
   (C) standoffish
   (D) advanced
   (E) retarded

6. ARDOR:
   (A) indifference
   (B) contumely
   (C) conserving
   (D) élan
   (E) misfortune

7. PERIPHERAL:
   (A) wandering
   (B) central
   (C) stationary
   (D) containing
   (E) obstinate

8. PERFUNCTORY:
   (A) restricted
   (B) painstaking
   (C) matter-of-fact
   (D) offhand
   (E) intentional

9. ENTHRALLING:
   (A) tedious
   (B) impious
   (C) captivating
   (D) persuasive
   (E) rebutting

10. VACILLATING:
    (A) obtuse
    (B) humble
    (C) lubricating
    (D) somnolent
    (E) decisive

Each of the sentences below has one or more blank spaces indicating where a word (or words) has been omitted. Each sentence is followed by five words or sets of words lettered from (A) through (E). Select the lettered word or set of words which, inserted to replace the blanks, *best* fits in with and completes the meaning of the sentence as a whole.

11. On the Bay of Fundy, because of the great range of tide, vessels can come to the docks for only a few hours on each _____ to take on or discharge cargo, taking care to leave promptly to avoid being _____ in mud at low water.
    (A) shift . . buried
    (B) tide . . stranded
    (C) current . . anchored
    (C) day . . overnight
    (E) trip . . shallow

12. The evolutionary _____ of the praying mantis rests on the eagerness of the female to eat anything, including the _____.
    (A) development . . twig
    (B) demise . . progeny
    (C) role . . nest
    (D) chain . . links
    (E) dilemma . . male

13. Although archaeologists have long been convinced that the Near East is the region where man first made the _____ from a wandering to a settled life, the early stages of this transition have been _____ in the mists of time.
    (A) transition . . shrouded
    (B) transcription . . clouded
    (C) transposition . . curtained
    (D) exodus . . trapped
    (E) adaptation . . swallowed

14. Because urban surface transportation often comes almost to a complete _____, the cost of delivering anything to anyone is rising steeply and the _____ of owning a car for any purpose but fleeing the city over the weekend is becoming clearer and clearer.
    (A) circle . . pleasure
    (B) reversal . . prospect
    (C) letdown . . confusion
    (D) overkill . . refusal
    (E) standstill . . futility

15. When the Declaration of Independence was finally approved, only the president and the secretary of the Continental Congress _____ their signatures; the delegates added theirs as their individual states _____ the action of Congress.
    (A) underlined . . defied
    (B) indited . . repealed
    (C) endorsed . . reviewed
    (D) affixed . . confirmed
    (E) removed . . disclaimed

16. Farmers are interested in science, in modern methods, and in theory, but they maintain a healthy _____ of book learning.
    (A) suspicion
    (B) respect
    (C) fondness
    (D) attitude
    (E) contempt

17. The supervisor of construction was charged with gross _____ when the crane, which had been inadequately chocked, _____ into the excavation.
    (A) laxity . . totalled
    (B) malfeasance . . floated
    (C) negligence . . rolled
    (D) liability . . fell
    (E) sabotage . . retreated

18. We expect great _____ in modern construction, but we are astonished to see the close _____ employed by the builders of the Egyptian pyramids: "Neither needle nor hair" can be inserted at the joints between the great stone blocks.
    (A) innovations . . reliance
    (B) improvements . . supervision
    (C) size . . relationships
    (D) precision . . tolerances
    (E) strength . . patterns

19. The complainant agreed to drop charges against young Fortesque, whose parents pleaded for _____ for him on the grounds of his youth, but only on condition that the lad make complete _____.
   (A) relentment . . obloquies
   (B) clemency . . restitution
   (C) regard . . confession
   (D) exoneration . . remission
   (E) internment . . obeisance

20. Despite the extreme _____ in its population, the alewife continues to be the most _____ fish in Lake Michigan.
   (A) diversity . . desirable
   (B) range . . superfluous
   (C) profusion . . commercial
   (D) instability . . neglected
   (E) fluctuations . . abundant

In each of the questions below, a related pair of words or phrases, in capital letters, is followed by five pairs of words or phrases lettered from (A) through (E). Select that lettered pair which expresses a relationship that is *most* similar to that of the capitalized pair.

21. ORATOR : ORATION ::
   (A) judge : decision
   (B) sprinter : prize
   (C) cabinet : craftsman
   (D) jury : trial
   (E) president : inauguration

22. OAK : DECIDUOUS ::
   (A) tree : mahogany
   (B) cow : herbivorous
   (C) acorn : leaf
   (D) trunk : branch
   (E) horse : equestrian

23. RUPTURE : BREAK ::
   (A) placate : disturb
   (B) exude : discharge
   (C) release : upset
   (D) envy : greed
   (E) horse : saddle

24. FLAME : SCORCH ::
   (A) fire : whisky
   (B) sympathy : injury
   (C) brick : building
   (D) avid : eager
   (E) acid : corrode

25. ESOTERIC : MANIFEST ::
   (A) invaluable : inevitable
   (B) priceless : worthless
   (C) feckless : faithful
   (D) exotic : exegesis
   (E) common : ordinary

26. STAVE : BARREL ::
   (A) slat : blind
   (B) corset : stay
   (C) waterline : hull
   (D) staff : cane
   (E) trigger : clip

27. PICTURE : FRAME ::
   (A) package : paper
   (B) egg : shell
   (C) diamond : setting
   (D) photograph : mat
   (E) package : string

28. SQUALL : DRIZZLE ::
   (A) tiff : brawl
   (B) squabble : scuffle
   (C) brawl : spat
   (D) tempest : teapot
   (E) quibble : quake

29. DEMUR : CONCUR ::
   (A) erroneous : felonious
   (B) inflation : sensation
   (C) normal : formal
   (D) object : agree
   (E) concrete : discrete

30. GARAGE : CAR ::
   (A) shed : lawnmower
   (B) boathouse : bayfront
   (C) gondola : blimp
   (D) plane : hogan
   (E) hangar : dirigible

Like many other people, Lee Peterson's interest in eating wild plants was sparked by the late Euell Gibbons. In 1968, a friend showed Lee one of Gibbons' books, and he set out to discover and sample the edible wild plants on the Maine coast, where he worked at a boys' camp.

Adventurous and more than ordinarily knowledgeable as a botanist, Lee Peterson quickly found his way around in the bewildering profusion of leafy things. There were books in print that extolled the delights of wild foraging, and others, described exactly how to prepare what Italians call *verdura trovata* (found vegetables) for the table, but few people had the skills to sort out the characteristics distinguishing an edible species from its toxic relatives.

If a budding naturalist confuses, let's say, a chickadee with a blackpoll warbler, no harm is done except perhaps to the viewer's ego. But if that same neophyte mixes up the wild carrot with the somewhat similar fool's parsley or poison hemlock, the results can be a great deal more unfortunate.

Adult Americans, despite the surge of interest in stuffing wild leaves and roots into their mouths, so far have brought surprisingly little harm down on themselves. In 1976, the most recent year for which the Division of Poison Control in the Food and Drug Administration has records, only forty-seven adults and a dozen or so children were hospitalized after accidentally eating poisonous wild plants. Perhaps one or two deaths a year are attributed to this cause.

But the need for detailed field identification remained. At first, Lee Peterson merely put together a pamphlet on the edible wild plants of Connecticut and distributed it in health food stores. Impressed by his thoroughness, his father urged him to expand his work to cover all of the eastern half of North America.

The present book is the result. It will certainly become the standard guide for anyone who ventures to provide the family table with wild fare more exotic than dandelion greens.

For easy reference, there are separate sections where the reader finds the habitats and season in which the plants are at their best, the uses for each plant, and species to avoid. (Among those marked with skull and crossbones are bouncing Bet, star-of-Bethlehem, and wild indigo.)

31. Lee Peterson's book is different from previous books on edible wild plants in that
(A) it extols the delights of wild foraging
(B) it provides information on how to prepare vegetables for the table
(C) it gives field information on edible wild plants of North America
(D) it provides detailed field information that helps people to distinguish edible species from toxic ones
(E) it is more knowledgeable than other botanical books

32. Peterson's interest in edible wild plants can be traced back to
(A) the work he did at a boys' camp in Maine
(B) the report by the Division of Poison Control on deaths from eating wild plants
(C) the influence of Euell Gibbons
(D) his study of botany in college
(E) his interest in health foods

33. The word "neophyte," as used in paragraph 3, most nearly means
(A) beginner
(B) convert
(C) nonbeliever
(D) veteran
(E) ignoramus

34. Which of the following is nontoxic?
(A) bouncing Bet
(B) fool's parsley
(C) wild indigo
(D) star-of-Bethlehem
(E) wild carrot

35. According to the author of the passage,
(A) adult Americans show little interest in edible wild plants
(B) dandelion greens rank among the most exotic of wild plants
(C) Lee Peterson's book will become the standard guide in the field
(D) a surprising number of people have poisoned themselves by eating toxic plants
(E) few people need the skills to sort out the characteristics distinguishing an edible species from its toxic relatives

In darkness softened by spring, sands touched silver by the moon await a visitation from the sea. Offshore, just beyond the point where the surf rears up booming from the inky water, masses of small, slim fish course back and forth just below the surface. From above, the flashing forms are fleetingly visible, like meteors streaking through the night sky.

The only motion along the ribbon of beach, however, is that of the waves. One by one, crested with foam, they surge into the shallows. The waves swirl up toward the night's high-tide mark, reached only a few minutes before, then slide back, smoothing the sand on their return to the sea.

Three days have passed since the two-week tidal cycle peaked along the Pacific rim of southern California. The time has come for the beach to serve as a moonlit stage for a haunting natural drama. It will demonstrate how infinitely complex are the adaptations that allow living things to perpetuate their kind. And it will show that in ways beyond understanding, small beings ruled by instinct can sense forces generated by the cosmos.

A wave sweeps up the beach in a boil of foam. Out of the dissolving froth, a small shape materializes. It is a fish, silvery as the moonshine that highlights it, with a back the blue-green color of the deep tropical sea. Momentarily, the fish lies still on the smooth, wet sand. Then, as a wave engulfs it, the fish slips over and catches the wash back out to sea. Seconds later, some yards away, parting waves reveal another little fish, and it stays but a moment, too.

As the minutes pass, more fish are stranded individually, here and there along the beach, but they do not remain long. They herald the main event of the night, a spawning run of their species, the grunion, a member of the silversides family.

From the far side of the breakers, thousands of grunion are riding the waves toward the shore. Wave upon wave will hurl knots and clumps of shimmering fish upon the sand just below the high-tide mark. Amidst the spume, the heaps of fish will disperse into thousands of wriggling bodies intent upon procreation. There on the night-veiled beach, the grunion will mate. Their fertilized eggs will be left buried in the sand, proclaiming that the grunion is the only fish in the sea to spawn on land.

The eggs are buried high enough on the beach so that they stay dry until the tidal cycle has progressed for several more days. Meanwhile, out of reach of marine predators, the embryonic grunion in the eggs develop quickly. By the time the tidal cycle has ebbed and nears its zenith again, the grunion are ready to hatch. But they will not do so unless churned by the waves, the touch of which will free them from their egg prisons.

36. The title that best expresses the main idea of this passage is
(A) the mating call of the tides
(B) the grunion on land and in the sea
(C) the fish that spawns on land
(D) an amazing biological happening
(E) time, tide, and the grunion

37. The most unusual aspect of the grunion's life cycle is that
(A) it lays its eggs above the high-water mark
(B) it waits until the tidal cycle has peaked before it looks for a mate
(C) it demonstrates the complexity of living creatures
(D) it spawns just below the high-tide mark
(E) after it spawns, it lies still on the sand for ten minutes

38. A very useful aspect of the grunion's spawning method is that
(A) the embryonic grunion is safe from harm from marine predators
(B) the grunion's eggs stay dry until hatched
(C) the males know where they are supposed to fertilize the eggs
(D) other predators are unable to anticipate the tidal changes
(E) the tides will have ebbed by the time the grunion is ready to hatch

39. We can infer from the passage that the grunion lays its eggs
(A) at the high-tide mark of the two-week cycle so as to assure that the young mature properly
(B) in such a fashion as to assure safety from all predators
(C) beyond the reach of the waves in order to avoid marine life
(D) on a low enough tide to be able to get back safely from spawning
(E) just below the high-tide mark on the third day after the peak of the tidal cycle so as to assure that the sea will come up high enough on the cycle to touch and free the young from their egg prisons

40. At the end of the third paragraph, the author refers to ''forces generated by the cosmos.'' Which statement below relates to that reference?

(A) The grunion course back and forth beyond the booming surf.

(B) By the time the tidal cycle has ebbed and nears its zenith again, the grunion are ready to hatch.

(C) Their fertilized eggs will be left buried in the sand, proclaiming that the grunion is the only fish in the sea to spawn on land.

(D) One by one, crested with foam, they surge into the shallows.

(E) The time has come for the beach to serve as a moonlit stage for a haunting natural drama.

STOP
WORK ONLY ON THIS SECTION UNTIL THE TIME ALLOTTED IS OVER.

SECTION IV

Time—30 minutes

35 Questions

In the mathematical sections, use any available space on the page for scratchwork in solving problems. Then indicate the *one* correct answer by darkening the appropriate oval on the answer sheet.

You may wish to refer to the following formulas and relationships in solving some of the problems.

Triangle:
The sum of the angles of any triangle is one straight angle, or 180 degrees.

The area of a triangle $= \frac{1}{2}$ (base $\times$ altitude).

In a right triangle, the square of the hypotenuse = the sum of the squares of the legs.

Circle of radius r:
Area $= \pi r^2$
Circumference $= 2\pi r$
There are 360 degrees of arc in a circle.

Definition of Symbols
$=$ is equal to	$\cong$ congruent to
$\neq$ is unequal to	$\leq$ is less than or equal to
$<$ is less than	$\geq$ is greater than or equal to
$>$ is greater than	$\parallel$ is parallel to
$\approx$ nearly equal to	$\perp$ is perpendicular to

Note: Figures are drawn as accurately as possible *except* when it is stated in a specific problem that its figure is not drawn to scale. All figures lie in a plane unless otherwise indicated. All numbers used in this test are real numbers.

1. One half of a certain number equals $\frac{1}{3}$. What does $\frac{1}{4}$ of this number equal?

    (A) $\frac{2}{3}$

    (B) $\frac{1}{6}$

    (C) $\frac{1}{3}$

    (D) $\frac{1}{4}$

    (E) $\frac{4}{3}$

2. If $p - 3 = q + 3$, what does $q - p$ equal?
    (A) 6
    (B) 1
    (C) 0
    (D) -1
    (E) -6

3. If rain is falling at the rate of 3 centimeters per hour, how many centimeters of rain will fall in m minutes?

(A) $\dfrac{1}{20m}$

(B) $\dfrac{20}{m}$

(C) $\dfrac{m}{20}$

(D) $\dfrac{40}{m}$

(E) $20m$

4. What is the cost of sending a telegram of 32 words if the first 15 words cost x cents and each additional word costs y cents?
(A) $x + 17y$
(B) $y + 17x$
(C) $15x + 17y$
(D) $17x + 15y$
(E) $x + 32y$

5. A car that averages 18 miles to the gallon requires how many gallons of gasoline, to the nearest gallon, for a 2,175 mile trip?
(A) 12
(B) 38
(C) 86
(D) 121
(E) 356

6.

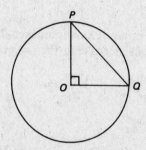

In the figure above, two legs of the right triangle are radii of circle O, whose area is 64π. The area of the triangle is
(A) 16π
(B) 32π
(C) 64
(D) 48
(E) 32

7. A circle is inscribed in a square of side 12. The length of the longest chord in the circle is
(A) 12
(B) $12\sqrt{2}$
(C) $6\sqrt{2}$
(D) 6
(E) $6\sqrt{3}$

8. Eight blocks on one side of a scale balance three blocks and a 2-pound weight on the other side. What is the weight, in pounds, of all eleven blocks?

(A) $\dfrac{2}{5}$

(B) $1\dfrac{1}{5}$

(C) $3\dfrac{1}{5}$

(D) $4\dfrac{2}{5}$

(E) $5\dfrac{1}{4}$

9. Which of the following is *not* the product of two consecutive *odd* integers?
(A) 15
(B) 35
(C) 99
(D) 143
(E) 183

10. If x and y are integers, both divisible by 7, which of the following is (are) *always* true?

I. $x - y$ is divisible by 7.
II. $x + y$ is divisible by 14.
III. xy is divisible by 49.

(A) I and II only
(B) II and III only
(C) I and III only
(D) I, II, and III
(E) I only

11.

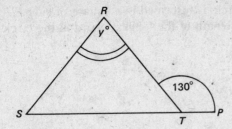

In the figure above, triangle *RST* is an isosceles triangle with *RS* = *RT*. Find the value of *y*.
(A) 80°
(B) 75°
(C) 70°
(D) 65°
(E) 60°

12. It takes one-half pint of paint to cover the 6 faces of a given cube. How many pints of this paint are needed to cover the faces of a cube each of whose edges is twice as long as those of the given cube?
(A) 1
(B) 2
(C) $2\frac{1}{2}$
(D) 3
(E) 6

13. If $\frac{17}{10}y = 0.68$, $y =$
(A) .04
(B) .4
(C) 1.6
(D) 1.9
(E) 4

14. If the ratio of *p* to *q* is 2 to 5 and the ratio of *q* to *r* is 6 to 7, then the ratio of *p* to *r* is
(A) $\frac{2}{7}$
(B) $\frac{1}{2}$
(C) $\frac{12}{35}$
(D) $\frac{7}{15}$
(E) $\frac{15}{7}$

15. Of the following, which *cannot* be the ratio of the lengths of the sides of a triangle?
(A) 7:9:11
(B) 9:12:15
(C) 4:5:6
(D) 1:1:1
(E) 2:4:6

16. If the sum, *S*, of 6 numbers is 5 more than the average of the 6 numbers, then *S* =
(A) 6
(B) 8
(C) 10
(D) $4\frac{1}{5}$
(E) $7\frac{2}{5}$

17. The radius of a circle is increased 20%. What is the percent increase in the area of the circle?
(A) 20
(B) 32
(C) 40
(D) 44
(E) 144

Questions 18–35 each consist of two quantities, one in Column A and one in Column B. Compare the two quantities and on the answer sheet blacken oval

A if the quantity in Column A is greater;
B is the quantity in Column B is greater:
C if the two quantities are equal;
D if the relationship cannot be determined from the information given.

All such letters such as x, y and n represent real numbers. A symbol appearing in both columns represents the same quantity in Column A as it does in Column B.

In some questions, information concerning one or both of the quantities to be compared is centered above the two columns.

	Column A	Column B
18.	$\dfrac{10}{21}$	$\dfrac{8}{15}$
19.	$2\sqrt{6}$	6

20. p and q are positive numbers

	Column A	Column B
	$\dfrac{4p + q}{pq}$	$\dfrac{4 + \dfrac{q}{p}}{q}$

21. $\dfrac{r}{3} = \dfrac{s}{4}$

	Column A	Column B
	$4r$	$3s$

	Column A	Column B
22.	$\left(\dfrac{7}{15} + \dfrac{16}{33}\right) \times 423$	423

23. $\dfrac{x}{y} = \dfrac{4}{7}$

	Column A	Column B
	x	y

24. k is an integer

	Column A	Column B
	The remainder when $k^2 + k$ is divided by 2	0

25. $t > 0$

	Column A	Column B
	t^3	t

Column A		Column B

Questions 26–30 refer to the figure below.

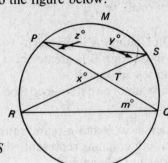

26. Length of arc *PMS*   Length of chord *PS*

27. y $\frac{1}{2}$ the number of degrees in minor arc *PR*

28. x $\frac{1}{2}$ the number of degrees in minor arc *PR*

29. z x

30. z m

31. x $6x = 5k,\ 4y = 3k,\ k > 0$ y

32. $\sqrt{.09}$ $\frac{\pi}{7}$

33. The average of $5n$, $3n$ and 7 $n > 0$ The average of $2n$, $6n$ and 9

34.

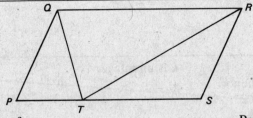

Perimeter of parallelogram *PQRS*   Perimeter of triangle *QRT*

35. $2x$ $\dfrac{x^3}{y^6} = \dfrac{1}{8}$ y^2

STOP

WORK ONLY ON THIS SECTION UNTIL THE TIME ALLOTTED IS OVER.

SECTION V

Time—30 minutes

25 Questions

1. A metal rod 8 feet long weighs 44 pounds. What is the weight in pounds of a rod 10 feet long composed of the same metal?
   (A) 48
   (B) 51
   (C) 55
   (D) 58
   (E) 62

2. If $\dfrac{3p}{q} = 5$, find the value of $\dfrac{3p - q}{q}$.

   (A) 3

   (B) 4

   (C) 5

   (D) $4\dfrac{3}{5}$

   (E) It is impossible to find with the information given

3. If t is the average of 2, 3, 5, 8 and t, find the value of t.

   (A) $2\dfrac{1}{2}$

   (B) 3

   (C) $3\dfrac{1}{2}$

   (D) 4

   (E) $4\dfrac{1}{2}$

4. A stick 40 inches long is cut into two pieces so that the length of one piece is $\dfrac{2}{3}$ the length of the other piece. How many inches are there in the shorter piece?
   (A) 16
   (B) 18
   (C) 22
   (D) 24
   (E) 28

5. The diagonal of a rectangle is 15 centimeters and its height is 9 centimeters. Find the area of the rectangle in square centimeters.
   (A) 54
   (B) 86
   (C) 98
   (D) 108
   (E) 125

6. There are five times as many nurses in a hospital as doctors. Which of the following *cannot* be the number of nurses in the hospital?
   (A) 30
   (B) 35
   (C) 40
   (D) 45
   (E) 52

7. In a class of 20 students, the average grade on a test is 78. They do not all have the same grade. Which of the following must then be true?
   I. Half the students have grades below 78.
   II. At least one student has a grade of 78.
   III. At least one student has a grade above 78.

   (A) I only
   (B) II only
   (C) III only
   (D) I and II only
   (E) II and III only

8.

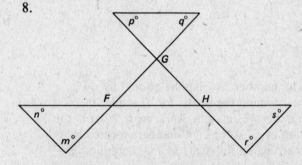

In the figure above, the value of $m + n + p + q + r + s =$
(A) 250
(B) 280
(C) 320
(D) 360
(E) 400

9. Town X has a population of 40,000 which is increasing 2,000 per year. Town Y has a population of 125,000 which is decreasing 3,000 per year. In how many years will the populations of the two towns be equal?
(A) 13
(B) 14
(C) 15
(D) 16
(E) 17

10. The point $P(3,4)$ is one corner of a square of area 25 lying in the coordinate plane with its sides parallel to the coordinate axes. Which one of the following choices *cannot* be the coordinates of a point Q diagonally opposite P?
(A) $(8,9)$
(B) $(-2,9)$
(C) $(-2,-1)$
(D) $(8,-1)$
(E) $(-1,-2)$

11. All of the following have the same value *except*

(A) $\dfrac{5}{8}$

(B) .625

(C) $\dfrac{15}{24}$

(D) $\dfrac{45}{70}$

(E) $\sqrt{\dfrac{25}{64}}$

12. The number 234 may be altered by rearranging the digits; for example, the number 423 may be so formed. What is the sum of all three-digit numbers formed by rearranging the digits of 234, including 234 itself?
(A) 1998
(B) 1664
(C) 999
(D) 1566
(E) 1656

13. Which of the following integers *cannot* be written as the sum of two *prime* numbers?
(A) 16
(B) 23
(C) 24
(D) 28
(E) 30

14. In a given sequence of numbers, the first term is 2 and each successive term is formed by taking $\dfrac{1}{4}$ of the cube of the preceding term. What is the eleventh term of the sequence?
(A) 1

(B) $\dfrac{3}{2}$

(C) 2
(D) 18
(E) 180

15. If p is 50% more than q, then q is what percent less than p?

(A) $66\dfrac{2}{3}$

(B) 50
(C) 40

(D) $33\dfrac{1}{3}$

(E) 25

16. A gallon of oil is poured into a cubical container 7 inches on an edge. About how high, in inches, does the oil rise in the container? (1 gallon = 231 cu. in.)
(A) 3.8
(B) 4.2
(C) 4.7
(D) 5.2
(E) 5.6

17.

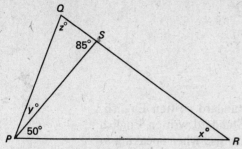

In the figure above, $y + z - x =$

(A) 55
(B) 60
(C) 65
(D) 70
(E) 75

18. If the ratio of r to s is 9 times the ratio of s to r, then $\dfrac{r}{s}$ could be

(A) $\dfrac{1}{9}$ (C) 3

(D) 6

(E) 9

(B) $\dfrac{1}{3}$

19. The diagonal of a rectangular door is $6\dfrac{1}{2}$ feet long. The longer side of the door is 6 feet. What is the area of the door in square feet?
(A) 156
(B) 60
(C) 39
(D) 17
(E) 15

20. If a vehicle goes 300 miles on 15 gallons of gas, how many more miles per gallon must it get to go the same 300 miles on 12 gallons?
(A) 1   (D) 7
(B) 3   (E) 9
(C) 5

21. How much must a man deposit in a bank so that he has $400 in his account one year later,

if the simple interest rate is 4%?
(A) $365.76
(B) $384.62
(C) $416.00
(D) $392.64
(E) $388.65

22. If p dishes cost d dollars, n dishes at the same rate will cost, in dollars,

(A) $\dfrac{pd}{n}$ (D) $\dfrac{np}{d}$

(B) $\dfrac{nd}{p}$ (E) $\dfrac{p}{nd}$

(C) npd

23. Six tractors working together can plow a field in 12 hours. How many hours will it take 8 tractors to plow the field?
(A) 9
(B) 10
(C) 12
(D) 15
(E) 18

24. Three men, X, Y, and Z, invest respectively $1400, $1800 and $2200 in a business. How much of the first year's profit of $1500 should Y get if each man shares the profits in proportion to his investment?
(A) $800.
(B) $750.
(C) $700.
(D) $620.
(E) $500.

25. A teacher drives 40 miles to her school every morning in 55 minutes. If she leaves 7 minutes late one morning, how many miles per hour must she drive to arrive at the time she normally does?
(A) 42   (D) 50
(B) 45   (E) 54
(C) 48

STOP
WORK ONLY ON THIS SECTION UNTIL THE TIME ALLOTTED IS OVER.

This section tests your ability to use standard written English, the kind used in more formal writing. Standard written English is quite different from the English we may use when speaking to friends. In the sentences below, you might find constructions and forms that you would use at particular times to meet particular needs, but you are being asked to determine correctness only on the basis of what would be acceptable in standard written English.

Directions: Some of the following sentences contain errors in grammar, usage, diction (choice of words), and idiom. Some of the sentences are correct. No sentence, however, contains more than one error. If a sentence has an error, it will be in one of the lettered and underlined words or phrases. Assume there are no errors in the parts of the sentence that are not underlined. *If there is an error in any underlined part, note the letter under it, and blacken the corresponding space on the answer sheet. If the sentence is free of errors, blacken answer space (E).* Follow the guidelines for standard written English when determining the answer.

1. Being as we were new to the academy, we girls had to register, pick up
   A   B   C
   our uniform issue, and then proceed to orientation. No error
                          D   E

2. Due to the uncertainty of the president's position on price controls, an
   A   B   C
   unanticipated raise in interest rates has occurred. No error
                 D   E

3. Bob told me that Mr. Epworth, his employer, discussed future
            A
   possibilities with him and says that he has some challenging ideas in mind
                   B   C   D
   for Bob. No error
            E

4. While it is only one week since his surgery, Jim feels confidently that he
   A   B   C
   will be able to resume his duties shortly. No error
                   D   E

5. His cynicism could not hold out, however, in the face of the
       A   B   C
   overwhelming evidence of this candidate's sincerity. No error
                                D   E

6. School <u>won't</u> be the same for <u>Jim and I</u> now that his course of study
        A   B

   requires <u>his working</u> two quarters <u>out of</u> four. <u>No error</u>
          C   D   E

7. An enormous <u>amount of time</u> and money is <u>being spent</u> on programs to
               A   B

   increase participation in government, but <u>less and less</u> people are voting
                                       C

   in local and federal elections <u>with each passing year</u>. <u>No error</u>
                           D   E

8. <u>The thinking</u> of the new economic theorists <u>has effected</u> changes in
     A   B

   several <u>critical government</u> regulations, particularly in those dealing
             C

   <u>with social legislation</u>. <u>No error</u>
      D   E

9. <u>Stopping</u> at ports of call on the <u>cruise ship's itinerary</u> becomes a
     A   B

   <u>race against time</u> as everyone dashes into and out of shops comparing,
      C

   bargaining, buying, and then, laden with their trophies, <u>rushes</u> back to the
                                            D

   dock. <u>No error</u>
       E

10. The cattlemen <u>feared</u> that the new organization of sheep raisers had
              A

    staked <u>it's</u> claim to the only watering hole on the range, a move
        B

    <u>which could increase</u> the vulnerability of the <u>cattlemen's</u> position in the
         C   D

    territory. <u>No error</u>
           E

11. The interviewer at the employment office <u>said, "I will</u> speak first
                                     A

    <u>to the one among</u> the applicants <u>who arrived earliest</u> and filled out <u>their</u>
         B   C   D

    papers first. <u>No error</u>
             E

12. The young recruit <u>was directed</u> by the <u>sergeant-major</u> to take <u>his</u> rifle to
                  A   B   C

    the quartermaster and <u>have it exchanged</u> for the new model. <u>No error</u>
                        D   E

13. Simms <u>had learned</u> too late that his health <u>had already been</u> <u>affected</u> by
         A   B   C

    his almost <u>continuous</u> exposure to radiation from the damaged pile.
            D

    <u>No error</u>
     E

14. If he <u>didn't cheat</u> at <u>every opportunity</u>, I <u>would have beaten</u> him <u>handily</u>.
        A   B   C   D

<u>No error</u>
E

15. <u>I've</u> been told that the accommodations at the Plaza Hotel <u>where</u> <u>your</u>
  A   B   C

planning to stay are <u>the most</u> luxurious in town. <u>No error</u>
             D   E

16. <u>Only after</u> I had reached the library <u>did I</u> realize <u>that</u> I <u>forgot</u> my library
    A   B   C   D

card. <u>No error</u>
      E

17. The news article <u>inferred</u> that our school has <u>more severe</u> problems with
               A   B

truancy <u>and</u> cutting <u>than</u> <u>any of the other</u> schools. <u>No error</u>
        C   D   E

18. When the <u>Water Department</u> crew <u>arrived</u> at the scene, they <u>discovered</u>
              A   B   C

that the sudden frost <u>had busted</u> the pipe. <u>No error</u>
                 D   E

19. At first you have <u>to move</u> slowly until <u>you</u> have built up <u>one's</u> skills, but
              A   B   C

then you move ahead <u>with rapidity</u>. <u>No error</u>
             D   E

20. <u>They surrounded the building</u>, set up barricades, <u>evacuated the people</u> in
              A   B

the neighboring houses, <u>brought in sharpshooters</u>, fired bright flares to
                            C

illuminate the area, and <u>helicopters hovered overhead</u>. <u>No error</u>
                        D   E

21. <u>It's</u> always difficult to determine <u>whether or not</u> to pursue a particular
  A   B

vocation, <u>but</u> <u>particularly so</u> when economic conditions are uncertain.
         C   D

<u>No error</u>
E

22. Many of us <u>prefer</u> pro football games <u>to watching the programs</u> on the
           A   B

educational <u>TV station</u>, even though we know <u>that public</u> television
          C   D

deserves our support. <u>No error</u>
              E

23. After Kelly <u>had nosed out</u> Berriman in the first heat of the 100-meter
                        A

    <u>sprint, breaking</u> the meet record <u>by almost</u> a second, the officials decided
            B   C

    that he had been fouled, and <u>he</u> was disqualified. <u>No error</u>
                                    D   E

24. <u>As the last chords</u> of the dramatic finale <u>fade</u> away, the enthusiastic
            A   B

    audience arose <u>as one man</u> and <u>applauded</u> vigorously. <u>No error</u>
                        C   D   E

25. The child was almost in tears <u>as</u> he told his mother that everyone <u>but</u>
                                    A   B

    Everest and <u>he</u> had <u>been</u> permitted to go on the picnic. <u>No error</u>
                    C   D   E

> Directions: In each of the sentences below, a part or the whole
> of the sentence is underlined. Following each sentence will be
> five different ways of writing the underlined segment—the first
> an exact repeat of the underlined original, the other four different.
> *If you think the underlined segment is correct as it stands, you
> will select choice (A) as your answer. If you think the underlined
> segment is incorrect as it stands, select the one of the remaining
> lettered choices that you think makes the sentence correct.* For
> whichever of the five lettered choices you select as correct,
> blacken the corresponding space on your answer sheet.
>
> This portion of the examination tests your ability to determine
> correctness and effectiveness of expression according to the re-
> quirements of standard written English. You are to take into ac-
> count grammar, diction (choice of words), sentence construction,
> and punctuation. *Do not select a version that changes the original
> sense of the sentence as given.* Choose the version that offers the
> clearest, most precise sentence according to the guidelines im-
> posed.

26. When the last of the guests had long since departed, and after
    <u>he had lain down for a brief rest, a violent knocking</u> at the door awakened
    him.
    (A) he had lain down for a brief rest, a violent knocking
    (B) he had laid down for a brief rest, a violent knocking
    (C) lying down for a brief rest, a violent knocking
    (D) having lain down for a brief rest, a violent knocking
    (E) he had layed down for a brief rest, a violent knocking

27. The first thing Jessica did upon receiving Morgan's demands,
    <u>aside from becoming furious, was tearing</u> his letter to shreds.
    (A) aside from becoming furious, was tearing
    (B) aside from becoming furious was, tearing
    (C) aside from becoming furious was tearing,
    (D) aside from becoming furious, was tear
    (E) besides becoming furious, was tearing

28. Mr. Swift thought that
his daughter was mistaken, she should have accepted the oil company's
offer of indemnities for the damages to her car.
(A) his daughter was mistaken, she should have accepted the oil
company's
(B) his daughter was mistaken, she should have accepted the oil
companies
(C) his daughter was mistaken. She should have accepted the oil
company's
(D) his daughter had made a mistake in not accepting the oil company's
(E) his daughter mistaken for not accepting the oil company's

29. The last two innings of the
fifth World Series game was tremendously exciting, I thought.
(A) fifth World Series game was tremendously exciting,
(B) fifth World Series game were tremendously exciting,
(C) fifth World Series game, was tremendously exciting
(D) Fifth World Series game was tremendously exciting
(E) fifth world series game was tremendously exciting

30. When just a young recruit, the commanding general gave him an important
assignment that permitted him to establish his reputation for exceptional
valor and ingenuity.
(A) When just a young recruit, the commanding general gave him
(B) When just a young recruit the commanding general gave him
(C) When just a young recruit, the Commanding General gave him
(D) When he was just a young recruit, the commanding general gave him
(E) When he was young and just a recruit, the commanding general gave
him

31. Of all the designs submitted for this competition,
Marie's and your's were considered the most professional by far.
(A) Marie's and your's were considered the most professional by far
(B) Marie's and your's was considered the most professional by far
(C) Marie's and yours were considered the most professional by far
(D) Marie's and your's were considered the most professional, by far
(E) Maries and yours were considered the most professional by far

32. Astonished, Neville
asked, "Did he really say, 'You can't fire me; I quit!'?"
(A) asked, "Did he really say, 'You can't fire me; I quit!'?"
(B) asked "Did he really say, 'You can't fire me; I quit!'?"
(C) asked, "Did he really say 'You can't fire me; I quit!'?"
(D) asked, "Did he really say, 'You can't fire me; I quit?' "
(E) asked, "Did he really say that you can't fire me, "I quit!'?"

33. They did not object so much to his being late as they did to his
carelessness.
(A) They did not object so much to his being late as
(B) They did not object so much to him being late, as
(C) They did not object to his being late so much, as
(D) They did not object so much to him being late as
(E) They did not object so much to his lateness as

34. Crocker, despite his service on many fronts to our community, has and most likely always will be remembered for that one terrible blunder.
    (A) has and most likely always will be remembered for
    (B) has been and most likely always will be remembered for
    (C) had and most likely always will be remembered for
    (D) has always been and most likely will also be
    (E) most likely will always be remembered, as he has been, for

35. I was angry when I saw that one of my wrenches were missing.
    (A) one of my wrenches were missing
    (B) one of my wrenches was gone
    (C) one of my wrenches was missing
    (D) one of my wrenches had been missing
    (E) one wrench was missing

36. Most people soon learn that experience is the best, even if sometimes the most demanding, teacher, if you survive to apply the lessons.
    (A) demanding, teacher, if you survive to apply the lessons
    (B) demanding, teacher, if they survive to apply the lessons
    (C) demanding teacher, if you survive to apply the lessons
    (D) demanding, teacher if you survive to apply the lessons
    (E) demanding, teacher, if you can survive the lessons

37. Having agreed to return home the following week, Marcus, the prize money concealed in the lining of his vest, boarded the early morning plane for Rome.
    (A) week, Marcus, the prize money concealed in the lining of his vest,
    (B) week Marcus, the prize money concealed in the lining of his vest,
    (C) week, the prize money concealed in the lining of his vest, Marcus
    (D) week, Marcus, the prize money was concealed in the lining of his vest,
    (E) week, Marcus, the prize money being concealed in the lining of his vest,

38. The Shah was to have been warned of the imminent coup, but by the time the intelligence agency were in touch with the palace, it was too late.
    (A) by the time the intelligence agency were in touch with the palace,
    (B) by the time the intelligence agency was in touch with the palace,
    (C) by the time the intelligence agency had gotten in touch with the palace,
    (D) by the time the intelligence agency was to be in touch with the palace,
    (E) by the time the intelligence agency would have called the palace,

39. Armstrong decided to hold a clearance sale on all the ladies' and childrens' bicycles, regardless of year of make, that were in stock.
    (A) all the ladies' and childrens' bicycles, regardless of year of make,
    (B) all the ladies' and children's bicycles, regardless of year of make,
    (C) all the lady's and children's bicycles, regardless of year of make,
    (D) all the ladies' and childrens' bicycles regardless of year of make
    (E) all, regardless of year of make, the ladies and childrens bicycles

40. The District Attorney's office will take no
action, until its investigators issue a report on their findings.
   (A) action, until its investigators issue a report
   (B) action, until it's investigators issue a report
   (C) action, until after its investigators have issued a report
   (C) action until its investigators, issue a report
   (E) action until its investigators issue a report

The directions that follow are the same as those given at the beginning of this section. They are repeated for your convenience, for easy reference, as you work on the questions below.

Directions: Some of the following sentences contain errors in grammar, usage, diction (choice of words), and idiom. Some of the sentences are correct. No sentence, however, contains more than one error. If a sentence has an error, it will be in one of the lettered and underlined words or phrases. Assume there are no errors in the parts of the sentence that are not underlined. *If there is an error in any underlined part, note the letter under it, and blacken the corresponding space on the answer sheet. If the sentence is free of errors, blacken answer space (E).* Follow the guidelines for standard written English when determining the answer.

41. Although we hated admitting it, it was obvious to all of us alumni that the
                    A   B   C
   victory was their's. No error
                   D   E

42. The trouble with the inexpensive underwear was that after a couple of
       A   B
   washings it had shrank so badly that I could not wear it. No error
                  C   D   E

43. Ellen had always felt that her brother was a superior student, and it took
            A   B
   her many years to realize that she was as capable as him. No error
                                  C   D   E

44. I wonder whose car has been left in the "No Parking" zone? No error
              A   B   C   D   E

45. The driver of the station wagon was at fault since the other car was
                 A   B
   stationery when he collided with it. No error
        C   D   E

46. There are a pair of heavy woolen socks in your knapsack, left over from
    A   B   C
   your backpacking trip. No error
            D   E

47. If you would have done your assignments regularly, you would not
       A   B

now be facing the possibility of a failing grade in this course. No error
  C   D   E

48. Strangely enough, we finally realized, it had all began innocently enough,
                A   B   C

set off by that one foolish remark of Joan's. No error
                              D   E

49. Von Faulkenstein clicked his heels, bowed stiffly and, turning away
                                                      A

with a sneer of disdain, stomping off down the long, dimly-lit corridor.
     B   C   D

No error
   E

50. Could it have been they who were responsible for the damage to the
                 A   B   C

store's window displays? No error
   D   E

Answer Key
Practice Test 4

Section I

1.	D	13.	E	24.	E	35.	D
2.	A	14.	B	25.	B	36.	A
3.	E	15.	C	26.	B	37.	B
4.	E	16.	D	27.	A	38.	B
5.	A	17.	D	28.	D	39.	C
6.	C	18.	A	29.	B	40.	B
7.	C	19.	E	30.	A	41.	D
8.	D	20.	D	31.	E	42.	B
9.	B	21.	A	32.	C	43.	D
10.	D	22.	C	33.	A	44.	D
11.	A	23.	C	34.	C	45.	C
12.	E						

Section II

1.	A	11.	D	21.	A	31.	D
2.	D	12.	C	22.	B	32.	D
3.	B	13.	D	23.	D	33.	B
4.	A	14.	E	24.	A	34.	E
5.	E	15.	E	25.	E	35.	C
6.	D	16.	E	26.	B	36.	A
7.	D	17.	E	27.	B	37.	D
8.	C	18.	A	28.	D	38.	D
9.	C	19.	B	29.	B	39.	C
10.	E	20.	D	30.	C	40.	C

Section III

1.	D	11.	B	21.	A	31.	D
2.	D	12.	E	22.	B	32.	C
3.	B	13.	A	23.	B	33.	A
4.	C	14.	E	24.	E	34.	E
5.	A	15.	D	25.	B	35.	C
6.	A	16.	A	26.	A	36.	C
7.	B	17.	C	27.	C	37.	D
8.	B	18.	D	28.	C	38.	A
9.	A	19.	B	29.	D	39.	E
10.	E	20.	E	30.	E	40.	B

Section IV

1.	B	10.	C	19.	B	28.	A
2.	E	11.	A	20.	C	29.	B
3.	C	12.	B	21.	C	30.	D
4.	A	13.	B	22.	B	31.	A
5.	D	14.	C	23.	D	32.	B
6.	E	15.	E	24.	C	33.	B
7.	A	16.	A	25.	D	34.	A
8.	D	17.	D	26.	A	35.	C
9.	E	18.	B	27.	C		

Section V

1.	C	8.	D	14.	C	20.	C
2.	B	9.	E	15.	D	21.	B
3.	E	10.	E	16.	C	22.	B
4.	A	11.	D	17.	B	23.	A
5.	D	12.	A	18.	C	24.	E
6.	E	13.	B	19.	E	25.	D
7.	C						

Section VI

1.	A	14.	A	27.	D	39.	B
2.	D	15.	C	28.	C	40.	E
3.	C	16.	D	29.	B	41.	D
4.	C	17.	A	30.	D	42.	C
5.	E	18.	D	31.	C	43.	D
6.	B	19.	C	32.	A	44.	D
7.	C	20.	D	33.	E	45.	C
8.	E	21.	E	34.	B	46.	A
9.	E	22.	B	35.	C	47.	B
10.	B	23.	D	36.	B	48.	C
11.	D	24.	B	37.	A	49.	C
12.	C	25.	C	38.	C	50.	E
13.	E	26.	A				

Explanatory Answers
Practice Test 4

SECTION I

1. **D.** *Delete*: strike out, remove.
   Opposite: *insert*.

2. **A.** *Inept*: without skill.
   Opposite: *competent*, having skill.

3. **E.** *Frenzy*: violent mental or emotional agitation.
   Opposite: *calm*.

4. **E.** *Pompous*: ostentatiously lofty, pretentious, full of pretense.
   Opposite: *unassuming*.

5. **A.** *Urbane*: polished, sophisticated, worldly.
   Opposite: *unsophisticated*.

6. **C.** *Piquant*: interesting, provocative.
   Opposite: *jejune*, dull, insipid.

7. **C.** *Recalcitrant*: hard to deal with, manage, or operate.
   Opposite: *amenable* (ageeable, tractable).

8. **D.** *Auspicious*: favorable, promising success.
   Opposite: *ill-omened*.

9. **B.** *Castigate*: criticize severely.
   Opposite: *acclaim*.

10. **D.** *Desultory*: lacking in consistency, fitful.
    Opposite: *methodical*.

11. **A.** *Artless*: free of deceit or craftiness.
    Opposite: *cunning*.

12. **E.** *Vigilant*: ever awake and alert.
    Opposite: *negligent*.

13. **E.** *Concrete*: constituting an actual thing or instance.
    Opposite: conceived apart from any concrete realities, *abstract*.

14. **B.** *Susceptible*: liable to (some mood, influence, agency).
    Opposite: *immune* (exempt, not liable to).

15. **C.** *Inimical*: hostile.
    Opposite: *friendly*.

16. **D.** *Sovereignty* fits the blank as opposed to a condition where the laws apply to the states themselves, since sovereignty would imply independent power.

17. **D.** Compulsory *arbitration* would imply that the decision was binding upon the parties involved, yet the union asked the membership for approval, or *ratification*.

18. **A.** What would the lobbyists for the railroads want? A *rollback*, naturally! If the rates were rolled back and the regulations were eased, the railroad industry would be *competitive* with other carriers.

19. **E.** We wouldn't expect to see the word "popularity" applied in this sentence. Companies are not concerned about popularity, as a person might be, but rather with *image*. The image would certainly be *tarnished* by scandals of the sort mentioned.

20. **D.** The sentence's structure would imply that the first set of characterizations would be the opposite of the second set. The words *dictatorial* and *egalitarian* provide the appropriate antonyms and complete the sentence meaningfully.

21. **A.** The obstacles are *formidable* (discouraging as to size, difficulty, etc.): lack of campaign contributions and lack of *access* (admittance, or the ability to approach) to those who donate funds is a formidable obstacle.

22. **C.** The only item that could cause crop failure would be natural *calamities*. A writer would not be likely to speak of "natural floods" or "turmoil." Floods, for the most part, are not artificial, and turmoil is not natural.

Hamper is the only remaining second word that works logically. Crop failures could only hamper or "obstruct" plans for recovery, but choice (B) has been ruled out.

23. **C.** Since the third of a series of findings of the study was not introduced by a disclaimer such as "but," the assumption is that the third finding was also an advantage: either *less* or decreased absenteeism. While decreased could be a correct choice for the first blank, personnel, the second paired word has no logical relationship to the context of the sentence. Whereas *payrolls* has, since part-time employees would undoubtedly be paid less than full-time employees.

24. **E.** Since the sentence refers to handwriting analysis, we may infer that the sentence is talking about someone who is retained as a handwriting analyst, or *graphologist*.

25. **B.** Choice (A) would make no sense. It would not matter to the German High Command whether the British spent a little or a great deal on radar. What would matter is that radar proved of great *value* to the British, and that they, the German High Command, underestimated that value even though they should have realized how valuable it would be since they already had radar and knew its *potential* (possibility for development).

26. **B.** *Aversion* and *abhorrence* are similar in meaning, but the former is not as intense. *Aversion* means repugnance, and *abhorrence* means extreme repugnance. *Respect* and *reverence*, too, are similar in meaning, but with a degree of difference: *respect* means admiration for someone's worth as a person, and *reverence* means extreme respect.

27. **A.** According to the adage, *necessity* is, metaphorically, the mother of *invention*; similarly, *procrastination* is, metaphorically, the thief of *time*. To further strengthen the analogy, the first word in each pair is the subject of the sentence, and the second word is the object of the preposition in the predicate nominative construction.

28. **D.** *Crestfallen*, which means dejected, is the opposite of *elated*; *dejected* is the opposite of *jubilant*, which means elated.

29. **B.** When we *quench* our *thirst*, we allay (relieve or mitigate) it. When we *quell* our *fears*, we allay them.

30. **A.** To *nibble* is to bite gently or slightly, while to *devour* is to swallow or eat voraciously. Similarly, to *sip* is to take small tastes, while to *quaff* is to drink copiously and heartily.

31. **E.** *Laud* means praise, or *eulogize*, and *repine* means complain, fret, or *grumble*.

32. **C.** In this vertical relationship, *gas gauge* indicates the amount of *fuel*, just as an *ammeter* measures the amount of *current*. (A) is incorrect because the gas gauge does not necessarily measure in *gallons*, and the ammeter does not measure *volts* but amperes. While, in choice (B), there is a relationship between gas gauge and *empty*, and ammeter and *negative* that seems analogous, closer examination will show that *empty* is an absolute measurement indicated by a gas gauge, but *negative* is only a relative measurement.

33. **A.** A *pyromaniac* is a person with a compulsive need to set a *fire*. Similarly, a *kleptomaniac* is, by definition, a person with a compulsive need to commit a *theft*. A *claustrophobe* does not commit an act against *heights* but, rather, fears heights, and therefore choice (C) is not analogous to the given pair.

34. **C.** *Friday* and *Thursday* express a sequential relationship: Friday follows Thursday. Similarly, *August* follows *July*. *Spring* precedes *summer*, so choice (A) is in the wrong order. *Hurt* and *hit* are in the wrong order, too, but even if they were not, they would express a cause-and-effect relationship rather than a sequential one. The other two choices have their terms in the wrong order, too.

35. **D.** An *ascetic* practices self-*denial*, and an *epicure* engages in self-*indulgence* in pursuit of pleasure.

36. **A.** Sentence 2, paragraph 1 confirms choice (A).

37. **B.** Sentence 2, paragraph 2 contradicts item I. Sentence 4 of the same paragraph contradicts item IV. Sentence 3 of paragraph 2 confirms item II, and the last sentence of that paragraph affirms item III.

38. **B.** Since the previous sentence referred to the position of psychologists of a quarter of a century ago in regard to "intellectual growth," we may infer that this sentence is juxtaposing the views of modern research in regard to the same matter, but terming it "cognitive growth."

39. **C.** In the first paragraph, the author presents the thesis of modern psychology and in the subsequent paragraphs presents supporting material for that thesis, which is paraphrased in choice (C).

40. **B.** Item I is set forth as a belief of modern psychologists in regard to cognitive growth. Item II is an amplification of item I. Item III is a specific example of items I and II.

41. **D.** Since the author does not propose changes or advocate any particular action to stop what is happening, we may infer that he is calling our attention to what is happening in order to arouse our awareness of it, leaving advocacy to some future time, perhaps.

42. **B.** Item I is supported by the author's statements in sentence 2, paragraph 2, and sentence 1, paragraph 3. Item III is underlined by the last two sentences in paragraph 1.

The reader might, perhaps, not know that Mount Palomar is an observatory, but Lick Observatory is clearly called to our attention.

43. **D.** The author never mentions spectator sports (choice A); he talks about outdoor lighting in other paragraphs, not paragraph 5 (choice E); he writes of the blunting of other senses, and of an environment that makes our sense of sight almost useless, in paragraph 4 (choice C); and says, in paragraph 5, that the daylight hours are no more valuable than the night hours (choice B). His first two sentences in paragraph 5, quite clearly indicate that he values the night, and that he values it for its importance to the psyche, permitting us to infer that he feels the night to be spiritually restorative.

44. **D.** Item II is incorrect because the author never mentions traffic signals. The other two items are clearly confirmed in paragraphs 1 and 3.

45. **C.** The conclusion in choice (A) is not supported by the statement. The author says nothing about what kind of people like either night or poetry. Choice (B) is a meaningless statement. Choice (D) has no relationship to the question of the similarity of poetry and night. Choice (E) brings in "romance," something the author does not mention or imply. Choice (C) makes a sensible comparison of the value to us of night and poetry, and makes a case for the importance of each of them.

SECTION II

1. **A.** *Benevolent*: desiring to do good.
Opposite: *cruel*, willfully causing pain or distress to others.

2. **D.** *Mature*: fully developed in mind and body.
Opposite: *puerile*, childishly foolish, immature.

3. **B.** *Copious*: plentiful.
Opposite: *meager*.

4. **A.** *Deplete*: decrease or exhaust the supply.
Opposite: *augment*, add to, increase.

5. **E.** *Ominous*: threatening evil.
Opposite: *propitious*, presenting favorable conditions.

6. **D.** *Vehement*: impassioned, intense, ardent.
Opposite: *dispassionate*.

7. **D.** *Gelid*: freezing.
Opposite: *burning*.

8. **C.** *Prodigal*: extravagant, wasteful.
Opposite: *frugal*.

9. **C.** *Diaphanous*: very sheer and light.
Opposite: *heavy*.

10. **E.** *Incipient*: beginning to appear, initial.
Opposite: *concluding*.

11. **D.** The author builds up suspense about what is going to happen, and when we understand that he is leading up to the earthquake and tidal wave, which is an important matter, we expect to learn more about that matter.

12. **C.** The first words of paragraph 5 obviously refer to *tsunami*.

13. **D.** "... bucking ... like a deck in a tide rip" is an example of figurative language that eliminates choice (A). The author contrasts when comparing the hunters' good luck with Alaska's bad luck, eliminating choice (B). The author uses anticlimax in the final paragraph when he mentions the hunter's returning to pick up his knife. This unimportant act is certainly anticlimactic when compared with the seriousness of the tidal wave. Choice (C) is, therefore, eliminated. Choice (E) is eliminated by the author's use of a pun on the name of the bay. The seal hunter and his partner had almost been killed by the tidal wave, but they had been brought back to life, or resurrected. The only literary effect the author had not used was choice (D). He tells us nothing about the hunter except that he was almost killed but managed to escape.

14. **E.** The last sentence of paragraph 5 tells us that Seward is located "... at the head of Resurrection Bay."

15. **E.** Paragraph 5, sentences 2 and 3, tells us that choice (E) is the correct one.

16. **E.** Sentence 1, paragraph 1, tells us that the tourist's "most intense experience usually has to do with the shortcomings of his accommodations." From this we can infer that the tourist is deeply concerned about the comfort of his accommodations. However, items I and III do not characterize the tourist. The former characterizes the authentic traveler, according to the author, and the latter is only half correct, for though the author indirectly indicates that credit cards comprise the equipment of the tourist, he makes no reference to travel guidebooks as being part of the tourist's equipment.

17. **E.** The verb "deserves" indicates that the author thinks highly of Mr. Chatwin's book, and he implies that there would be only a few books of similar quality, requiring only a small shelf to accommodate them.

18. **A.** In sentence 4, paragraph 4, the author says that the British presence in Patagonia forms the spine of the book. The word "spine" is used figuratively to mean the framework, or the main theme—in other words, the main thread of the book. This statement supports choice (A).

19. **B.** The author uses contrast freely: paragraph 1, when he compares the tourist and the traveler; paragraph 5, when he characterizes Mr. Chatwin's writing as "laconic without being listless, literate without being pedantic, and intent without being breathless." He uses figurative language in paragraph 2 when he speaks of this book as deserving "to stand on a small shelf," instead of merely saying that it was one of a very few good books; when he writes that the British presence "forms the spine of the book;" and when he refers to Mr. Chatwin's mind as being like a crowded attic without cobwebs.

20. **D.** The author says the book's appeal would be limited if it "were nothing more than a study ...," but he goes on to say that it is more than that, so choice (A) is incorrect. Choice (B) is correct as far as it goes, but the author goes on to say that Mr. Chatwin "coaxed me into joining him ...," so choice (B) is incorrect. In paragraph 2 he says quite the opposite of choice (C). Sentence 2 of the last paragraph contradicts sentence 1 which is the only basis for

choice (E), and eliminates that choice. Paragraphs 2 and 5 affirm the statement in choice (D).

21. **A.** Sentence 1 of the opening paragraph indicates that a series of problems will be listed. Sentence 2 affirms the statement in choice (D). Sentence 5 corroborates choice (C). Sentence 6 supports choice (B), and sentence 7 supports the statement in choice (E). The one that is not a problem is the statement in choice (A).

22. **B.** Choice (B) is affirmed by the last sentence in the first paragraph.

23. **D.** Telephone conversations and face-to-face conferences provide data of a fleeting, transient, or fugitive nature.

24. **A.** Sentence 2, paragraph 2 makes the point in item I, and the last sentence of that paragraph supports item III. Item II is contradicted by sentence 3 of the same paragraph.

25. **E.** The paradoxical combination referred to is progress and achievement on the one hand, and disappointment and retrogression, on the other. The decrease of birth mortality is an achievement; the existence of concentration camps was, and is, disappointment and retrogression. In choice (A), both terms are disappointments; in choice (B), both can be considered achievements; in choice (C), labeling either term would be a subjective matter; and in choice (D), while polio vaccines can be termed achievements, cerebral palsy, as a natural phenomenon, falls into neither category.

26. **B.** The indicator word "however" leads us to expect that if domestic hens lay eggs at any time, their *ancestors* would lay eggs only some of the time, such as in the *spring*.

27. **B.** The statement that the quality of water is nominally (ostensibly, or in name only) under the control of federal legislation leads us to expect to learn that it is actually under the control of something opposed to federal, or *state and local*. The word *dependent* is compatible with the meaning of the rest of the sentence. While the first word of choice (A) could fit, the second

word, "appointed," does not oppose the idea of federal.

28. **D.** The only words that could fit into the first blank before the preposition "to" are "advanced" and *aspiring*. Only *applied*, of the two second words, completes the meaning of the sentence successfully.

29. **B.** The only pair that works is *averted . . submitted*. "Averse" makes no sense in choice (A), nor does "closed" in choice (C). The strikes would not be *broken* if they were submitted to binding arbitration, but choice (D) doesn't even offer that option. It offers the word "subordinated," which makes no sense at all. As to choice (E), that would be a possibility if "would" were substituted for "could," because observers would then be expressing a belief, whereas in the sentence as it stands, using choice (E) implies that observers are advocating the lengthening of such strikes.

30. **C.** The word "but" implies that contradiction is in the offing, something opposed to "supreme expression of mechanism." *Paradoxically* suggests the simultaneous existence of mechanism and *dreams* in the same medium.

31. **D.** Just as a *homesteader* is a *settler*, so, too, an *Okie* is a *migrant farmer*.

32. **D.** A *molecule* is usually composed of more than one *atom*. Similarly, a *bouquet* is usually composed of more than one *flower*.

33. **B.** An *adventurer* cannot be characterized as *timorous* (fearful). A *buffoon* (a person given to coarse jesting) cannot be characterized as *suave* (smooth, elegant, polished).

34. **E.** A *porpoise* is an *aquatic* animal, i.e., a porpoise lives in water. An *eel* is an *aquatic* animal, i.e., an eel lives in water.

35. **C.** *Attack* is the opposite of *defend*. *Wither* is the opposite of *bloom*.

36. **A.** *Expunge* and *obliterate* are synonymous, as are *annihilate* and *eradicate*.

37. **D.** *Bogus* and *spurious*, which both mean fake,

are synonyms. *Authentic* and *bona fide*, which both mean genuine, are synonyms, too. *Incombustible* means cannot be burned, but *inflammable* means can be burned.

38. **D.** *Cashmere* is a type of *fabric*. Similarly, *vinyl* is a type of *plastic*.

39. **C.** Just as a *toady* can be characterized as *obsequious* (servilely compliant or deferential), so, too, a *dandy* (a man excessively concerned about clothes) can be characterized as *foppish* (excessively refined and fastidious in taste and manners).

40. **C.** *Ephemeral* is the opposite of *everlasting*, since *ephemeral* means fleeting or transient. *Transitory* (fleeting, or transient) is the opposite of *perpetual* (lasting forever).

SECTION III

1. **D.** *Fallible*: liable to err.
   Opposite: *unerring*.

2. **D.** *Vivacious*: lively, sprightly.
   Opposite: *languid*, lacking in vigor.

3. **B.** *Relinquish*: cede, yield.
   Opposite: *retain*.

4. **C.** *Spontaneity*: the quality of being unrehearsed.
   Opposite: *premeditated*, planned beforehand.

5. **A.** *Brusque*: blunt, rough.
   Opposite: *suave*, smooth, polished.

6. **A.** *Ardor*: passion, enthusiasm.
   Opposite: *indifference*.

7. **B.** *Peripheral*: pertaining to the boundary.
   Opposite: *central*.

8. **B.** *Perfunctory*: superficial, without interest.
   Opposite: *painstaking*, careful, taking pains.

9. **A.** *Enthralling*: captivating, charming.
   Opposite: *tedious*, tiresome.

10. **E.** *Vacillating*: wavering, indecisive.
    Opposite: *decisive*.

11. **B.** Trial and error will indicate that only choice (B) works, and that the answer is *tide . . stranded*.

12. **E.** The *dilemma* of the *male* praying mantis is that to approach the female he must risk being eaten.

13. **A.** The gap between a wandering and a settled life would be closed by some sort of *transition*. Since this happened a long time ago, the transition would have been hidden or *shrouded* by the mists of time. Note that "this transition" clearly refers to the antecedent blank.

14. **E.** The word that suggests itself as following "complete" is *standstill*, "reversal," or "circle," but the only second word of any of those options that works is *futility*.

15. **D.** What could people have done with their signatures? The answer that suggests itself first is *affixed*. The word *confirmed* completes the sense of the sentence. The delegates would only have added theirs when their individual states confirmed the action of Congress.

16. **A.** The "but" indicates that what farmers maintain is somewhat opposed to the idea of being interested. The only possible choices are *contempt* and *suspicion*. "Contempt" would be too strongly opposed to "interest." Besides, "contempt" would not take the preposition "of," but rather "for."

17. **C.** The supervisor could not have been charged with "liability." He might have been held liable, or accused of liability, but what he was charged with was *negligence*. In other words, he was accused of carelessness. Furthermore, if the crane was improperly chocked, it would have *rolled* into the excavation, and that would have constituted negligence.

18. **D.** The clause after the colon clearly suggests that the *tolerances* between the great stone blocks must have been very close. The

word *precision* accurately completes the meaning of the sentence.

19. **B.** What could the parents have pleaded for? Among the choices offered, only *clemency* (leniency, mercy) or "exoneration" (freedom from blame) are possibilities, and the latter is not something that can be pleaded for. Only the evidence or some explicit testimony can exonerate. It would be reasonable for the complainant to drop the charges if complete *restitution* (repayment) were made.

20. **E.** A single fish could not have diversity in its population, so choice (A) is wrong. The word *range* would take the preposition "of" not "in," so choice (B) is out. If the word *profusion* were used, it would substitute for the entire phrase, as follows: "Despite its profusion, the alewife . . . ," so choice (C) is wrong. Choice (D) makes no sense. Even though its population shows wide *fluctuations*, the alewife remains the most *abundant* fish. In other words, even at their lowest population levels, the alewife outnumbers all other fish in Lake Michigan.

21. **A.** An *orator* delivers an *oration*. Similarly, a *judge* delivers a *decision*.

22. **B.** Just as an *oak* can be characterized as *deciduous* (losing its leaves annually), so, too, a *cow* can be characterized as *herbivorous*, or grass-eating.

23. **B.** *Rupture* and *break* are synonymous, as are *exude* and *discharge*.

24. **E.** *Flame* can *scorch*, and *acid* can *corrode*.

25. **B.** *Esoteric*, which means known to a few, is the opposite of *manifest*, which means clearly apparent and obvious. Similarly, *priceless* is the opposite of *worthless*.

26. **A.** A *stave* is a thin, shaped piece of wood that helps make up the sides of a *barrel*. Similarly, a *slat* is a thin piece of wood or metal that helps make up a window *blind*.

27. **C.** A *picture* is bordered by, displayed by, and held in place by a *frame*. A *diamond* is bordered by, displayed by, and held in place by a *setting*. A *photograph* is not held in place by a *mat*.

28. **C.** A *squall* is a violent rainstorm; a *drizzle* is a very gentle rain. A *brawl* is a violent fight; a *spat* is a petty quarrel. In both instances the words describe similar things with a degree of difference.

29. **D.** *Demur* and *concur* are antonymous, as are *object* and *agree*. This is a "perfect" analogy because the first words of the two pairs are synonymous, and so are the second words.

30. **E.** A *garage* is a place for storing a *car*. A *hangar* is a place for storing a *dirigible*. While a *shed* is a place where one can store a *lawnmower*, that relationship is not as analogous as choice (E) because the car and the dirigible are both large means of transportation.

31. **D.** Sentence 2, paragraph 2, eliminates choices (A) and (B). Choice (C) is incorrect; the book covers only the eastern half of North America. The passage makes no such claim as is indicated in choice (E). Choice (D) is indicated in sentence 1, paragraph 5, in the last paragraph, and is implied in paragraph 2, where the author says that there were books on the delights of foraging and books on preparation of edible wild plants, but few people could distinguish the edible plants from the toxic ones.

32. **C.** Choice (C) is supported by the statement in the opening sentence.

33. **A.** Paragraph 3 first refers to a budding naturalist, and then says, "But if that same neophyte . . . ." A "neophyte" must, therefore, be a beginner.

34. **E.** The second sentence of paragraph 3 clearly implies that wild carrot is nonpoisonous and fool's parsley and hemlock are poisonous. Since bouncing Bet, star-of-Bethlehem, and wild indigo are all marked with the skull and crossbones, the poison symbol, they must be toxic.

35. **C.** Sentence 1, paragraph 4 says quite the opposite of choice (A). The next-to-the-last

paragraph clearly indicates that the author of the passage considers wild dandelion to be far less than exotic, which rules out choice (B). The author, contrary to the statement in choice (D), says that adult Americans have done themselves surprisingly little harm while eating wild plants. As for choice (E), the author actually says that few people *have* the skills needed to sort out toxic species from the others. Choice (C) is the answer, according to sentence 2 of the next-to-the-last paragraph.

36. **C.** Choice (A) is completely nonspecific. Choice (B) is close, but the main point of the passage is the unusual fact that the grunion spawns on land.

37. **D.** If the grunion did not spawn just below the high-tide mark, one of two equally fatal things would happen: the eggs would be washed away too soon, or the matured hatchling would never be set free by the churning waves.

38. **A.** Sentence 2 of the last paragraph substantiates the selection of choice (A).

39. **E.** This answer is substantiated by sentence 1, paragraph 3, sentence 1, last paragraph, and the last two sentences of the passage.

40. **B.** The forces generated by the cosmos are the tides, which result from the gravitational pull of the moon and the sun.

SECTION IV

1. **B.** Let x = the certain number.

    $\frac{1}{2}x = \frac{1}{3}$. Multiply both sides by 6.

    $3x = 2$

    $x = \frac{2}{3}$

    $\frac{1}{4} \cdot \frac{2}{3} = \frac{1}{6}$

2. **E.** $p - 3 = q + 3$. Add -3 and $-p$ to both sides.

    $-6 = q - p$

    or $q - p = -6$.

3. **C.** 3 cm. per hour $= \frac{3}{60}$

    $= \frac{1}{20}$ cm. per minute

    In m minutes,

    $m\left(\frac{1}{20}\right) = \frac{m}{20}$ cm. will fall.

4. **A.** After x cents for the first 15 words, another 17 words must be paid for at y cents per word. Cost $= x + 17y$.

5. **D.** $\frac{2,175}{18} = 120\frac{5}{6}$ gallons

    $= 121$ gallons

    (to nearest gallon).

6. **E.** Let $r = OP = OQ$ = radius of circle, then $\pi r^2 = 64\pi$

    $r^2 = 64$

    $r = 8$.

    Area of triangle $= \frac{1}{2}(OQ)(OP)$

    $= \frac{1}{2} \cdot r \cdot r = \frac{1}{2} \cdot 8 \cdot 8$

    $= 32$.

7. **A.**

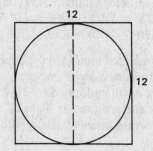

The longest chord in the circle is the diameter of the circle, which is equal to the side of the square, or 12.

8. **D.**   Let w = weight in pounds

of one block,

then $8w = 3w + 2$

$5w = 2$

$w = \dfrac{2}{5}$ lb. (wt. of one block)

$11w = 11\left(\dfrac{2}{5}\right) = \dfrac{22}{5} = 4\dfrac{2}{5}$ lb.

9. **E.** Examine each choice of answer.

$15 = 5 \cdot 3$
$35 = 7 \cdot 5$
$99 = 11 \cdot 9$
$143 = 11 \cdot 13$
$183 = 3 \cdot 61$ which cannot be factored further into consecutive odd integers.

10. **C.** Let $x = 7p$ and $y = 7q$ where p and q are integers.

I. $x - y = 7p - 7q$
      $= 7(p - q)$ which is always divisible by 7.

II. $x + y = 7p + 7q$
      $= 7(p + q)$—not *always* divisible by 14.

III. $xy = (7p)(7q)$
      $= 49 pq$—*always* divisible by 49.

Thus, I and III are always true. Another method is to substitute integers for x and y, but try various combinations of odd and even integers.

11. **A.** In isosceles triangle RST, angle $RST = \angle RTS = 180° - 130° = 50°$. Therefore, $y = 180 - 2(50) = 180 - 100 = 80°$.

12. **B.** The surface area (S) of a cube is given by the formula $S = 6e^2$, where e = edge. Doubling e will multiply S by $2^2 = 4$. Thus, the new surface area is 4 times as great and requires 4 times as much paint.

$4\left(\dfrac{1}{2}\right) = 2$ pints.

13. **B.** $\dfrac{17}{10}y = 0.68$. Multiply both sides by 10.

$17y = 6.8$. Divide by 17.

$y = \dfrac{6.8}{17} = .4.$

14. **C.** $\dfrac{p}{q} = \dfrac{2}{5}, \dfrac{q}{r} = \dfrac{6}{7}$. Multiply the left members by each other and the right members by each other.

$\dfrac{p}{q} \cdot \dfrac{q}{r} = \dfrac{2}{5} \cdot \dfrac{6}{7}; \dfrac{p}{r} = \dfrac{12}{35}.$

15. **E.** The sum of two sides of a triangle must be greater than the third side. This is true in all choices except (E), where $2 + 4$ is not greater than 6.

16. **A.** The average of the numbers is $\dfrac{S}{6}$. Then,

$S = 5 + \dfrac{S}{6}$. Multiply by 6.

$6S = 30 + S$

$5S = 30$

$S = 6.$

17. **D.** Let the radius, $r = 10$. A = Area = $\pi r^2 = 100\pi$. The increased radius = $10 + .2(10) = 12$. B = Increased area = $\pi(12)^2 = 144\pi$.

$B - A = 144\pi - 100\pi = 44\pi$

$\dfrac{B - A}{A} = \dfrac{44\pi}{100\pi} = 44\%.$

18. **B.** Since $\dfrac{10}{20} = \dfrac{1}{2}, \dfrac{10}{21} < \dfrac{1}{2}.$

Since $\dfrac{8}{16} = \dfrac{1}{2}, \dfrac{8}{15} > \dfrac{1}{2},$

so that $\dfrac{8}{15} > \dfrac{10}{21}.$

19. **B.** $6 = \sqrt{6}\sqrt{6}$. Since $\sqrt{6} > 2$, then $\sqrt{6}\sqrt{6} > 2\sqrt{6}.$

20. **C.** $\dfrac{4 + \dfrac{q}{p}}{q} = \dfrac{4p + q}{pq}$. (Multiply numerator

and denominator by p.)

21. **C.** $\dfrac{r}{3} = \dfrac{s}{4}$ (Cross-multiply.)

$4r = 3s$.

22. **B.** $\dfrac{7}{15}$ and $\dfrac{16}{33}$ are each less than $\dfrac{1}{2}$. Thus,

$\left(\dfrac{7}{15} + \dfrac{16}{33}\right)$ must be less than 1. So that,

$\left(\dfrac{7}{15} + \dfrac{16}{33}\right)$ 423 < 423.

23. **D.** $\dfrac{x}{y} = \dfrac{4}{7}$

$7x = 4y$

$y = \dfrac{7}{4}x$.

However, we do not know if x and y are each zero, positive or negative numbers. Thus we cannot compare their magnitudes.

24. **C.** $\dfrac{k^2 + k}{2} = \dfrac{k(k + 1)}{2}$.

k and $(k + 1)$ are consecutive integers and one of them must be even (divisible by 2). Thus the remainder is equal to zero.

25. **D.** If $t > 1$, then $t^3 > t$. If $t = 1$, then $t^3 = t$. If $0 < t < 1$, then $t^3 < t$. Thus, comparison cannot be made.

26. **A.** The arc PMS is greater than the chord PS, since a straight line is the shortest distance between two points.

27. **C.** $y = \dfrac{1}{2}$ arc PR, since an angle inscribed in a circle is measured by one-half its intercepted arc.

28. **A.** x is greater than y because an exterior angle of a triangle (PST) is greater than either

remote interior angle and $y = \dfrac{1}{2}$ arc PR.

29. **B.** x is greater than z, since the exterior angle of a triangle is greater than either remote interior angle.

30. **D.** We have no information that will help in comparing z and m.

31. **A.** $6x = 5k, 4y = 3k$

$x = \dfrac{5}{6}k, \quad y = \dfrac{3}{4}k$.

Since $k > 0, \dfrac{5}{6}k = \dfrac{10}{12}k > \dfrac{9}{12}k = \dfrac{3}{4}k$. So that $x > y$.

32. **B.** $\sqrt{.09} = .3$

$\dfrac{\pi}{7} = \dfrac{3.14}{7} \approx .45.$

So that $\dfrac{\pi}{7} > \sqrt{.09}$.

33. **B.** Av. of $5n, 3n$ and $7 = \dfrac{8n + 7}{3}$.

Av. of $2n, 6n$ and $9 = \dfrac{8n + 9}{3}$.

Since $n > 0, 8n + 9 > 8n + 7$. So that the average in Column B > average in Column A.

34. **A.** In triangle $PQT, PQ + PT > QT$. In triangle $RST, SR + ST > RT$. Thus, the perimeter of parallelogram is greater than the perimeter of triangle QRT.

35. **C.** Take the cube root of both sides of

$\dfrac{x^3}{y^6} = \dfrac{1}{8}$ yielding $\dfrac{x}{y^2} = \dfrac{1}{2}$,

or $2x = y^2$.

Note that $x^3 = \dfrac{1}{8}y^6$; since y^6 is positive, x^3,

and therefore x, is positive. So that no problem of signs is in question here.

SECTION V

1. **C.** Let x = weight in pounds of 10-foot rod, then $\frac{8}{44} = \frac{10}{x}$. Cross-multiply.

   $8x = 440$

   $x = 55$.

2. **B.** $\frac{3p - q}{q} = \frac{3p}{q} - \frac{q}{q} = 5 - 1 = 4.$

3. **E.** $\frac{2 + 3 + 5 + 8 + t}{5} = t$

   $18 + t = 5t$

   $18 = 4t$

   $t = 4\frac{1}{2}.$

4. **A.** Let y = length of longer piece in inches, then $\frac{2}{3}y$ = length of shorter piece in

   inches.

   $y + \frac{2}{3}y = 40$. Multiply both sides by 3.

   $3y + 2y = 120$

   $5y = 120$

   $y = 24$ (longer piece)

   $\frac{2}{3}y = \frac{2}{3}(24) = 16$(shorter piece).

5. **D.**

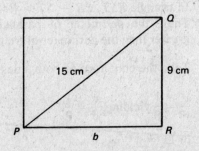

   $PQ = 15 = 3(5)$, $QR = 9 = 3(3)$.
   Thus, triangle PQR is a 3-4-5 right triangle multiplied by 3, or a 9-12-15 triangle. Therefore, $b = 12$, and area of the triangle is $12 \times 9 = 108$ sq. cm.

6. **E.** The number of doctors is $\frac{1}{5}$ the number of nurses and must be a whole number. Since $\frac{1}{5}$ of 52 is not a whole number, 52 cannot be the number of nurses. The other choices are all divisible by 5.

7. **C.**   I. Half the students need not have grades below 78.
   II. No student need have a grade of 78.
   III. Some students must have grades above 78 in order to average 78, since they did have a variation of grades. Therefore, III only is true.

8. **D.** Note the vertical angles at F, G and H. Then
   $m + n + \angle GFH = 180°$
   $p + q + \angle FGH = 180°$
   $r + s + \angle GHF = 180°$. Add these up.
   $m + n + p + q + r + s +$ sum of angles of $\triangle FGH = 540°$. Subtract 180 from both sides.
   $m + n + p + q + r + s = 360°$.

9. **E.** Let n = no. of years for population to be equal.
   $40,000 + 2,000n = 125,000 - 3000n$
   $5,000n = 85,000$
   $n = 17$.

10. **E.** Since the area is 25, the side of the square is 5. Possible coordinates of Q are $(3 + 5, 4 + 5)$ or $(8,9)$, $(3 - 5, 4 - 5)$, or $(-2,-1)$; $(3 + 5, 4 - 5)$, or $(8,-1)$; and $(3 - 5, 4 + 5)$, or $(-2,9)$. Choice (E) is not one of these possibilities.

11. **D.** $\frac{5}{8} = .625$

   $\frac{15}{24} = \frac{5}{8}$

   $\sqrt{\frac{25}{64}} = \frac{5}{8}$

   $\frac{45}{70} = \frac{9}{14} \neq \frac{5}{8}.$

12. **A.**
$$\begin{array}{r} 423 \\ 432 \\ 234 \\ 243 \\ 342 \\ \underline{324} \\ 1998 \end{array}$$
Note: Each vertical column of digits is made up of two 3's, two 2's and two 4's, so that each column adds up to 18. This helps to speed up the addition.

13. **B.** $16 = 13 + 3$; $24 = 17 + 7$; $28 = 23 + 5$; $30 = 17 + 13$. However, 23 is an odd number and must be the sum of an odd and an even number. It cannot be $21 + 2$, since 21 is not *prime*. All other even numbers but 2 are not *prime*. Hence, 23 cannot be written as the sum of two prime numbers.

14. **C.** First term = 2.

Second term $= \dfrac{1}{4}(2^3) = \dfrac{1}{4}(8) = 2$.

Third term $= \dfrac{1}{4}(2^3) = 2$.

All terms of the sequence are 2.

15. **D.** Let $q = 100$,
then $p = q + .50q$
$p = 100 + .50(100) = 150$
q is now 50 less than p.

$\dfrac{50}{150} = \dfrac{1}{3} = 33\dfrac{1}{3}\%$.

So that q is $33\dfrac{1}{3}\%$ less than p.

16. **C** Let the oil rise to a height of h inches.
Then $7 \times 7 \times h = 231$. Divide by 7.
$$7h = 33$$
$$h = 4.7 \text{ inches.}$$

17. **B.** The 85° angle is an exterior angle of triangle *PSR*, so that $85 = 50 + x$, or $x = 35$. In triangle *PQS*, $y + z + 85 = 180$, so that $y + z = 95$. Thus, $y + z - x = 95 - 35 = 60°$.

18. **C.** $\dfrac{r}{s} = 9\left(\dfrac{s}{r}\right) = \dfrac{9s}{r}$. Cross-multiply.

$r^2 = 9s^2$

$\dfrac{r^2}{s^2} = 9$ Take square root of both sides.

$\dfrac{r}{s} = 3$.

19. **E.**

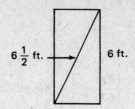

$6\dfrac{1}{2} = \dfrac{13}{2}$, $6 = \dfrac{12}{2}$.

So that $x = \dfrac{5}{2}$. (5-12-13 triangle where each side is divided by 2.) Area $= 6\left(\dfrac{5}{2}\right) = 15$ sq. ft.

20. **C.** $\dfrac{300}{15} = 20$ miles per gallon.

$\dfrac{300}{12} = 25$ miles per gallon.

Thus, 5 miles more per gallon.

21. **B.** Let $P = $ amount deposited,
then $P + .04P = 400$
$$1.04P = 400$$
$$P = \dfrac{400}{1.04} = \$384.62.$$

22. **B.** $\dfrac{p}{d} = \dfrac{n}{x}$

$px = nd$

$x = \dfrac{nd}{p}$.

23. **A.** Let $h = $ no. of hours for 8 tractors to plow field. The number of tractors is inversely proportional to the number of hours.

$\dfrac{6}{8} = \dfrac{h}{12}$

$8h = 72$

$h = 9$.

24. **E.** X—$1400.

Y—$1800.

Z—$\dfrac{$2200}{$5400}$.

Y receives $\dfrac{1800}{5400} = \dfrac{1}{3}$ of the profit

$\dfrac{1}{3}$ of $1500 = $500.

25. **D.** She must now drive 40 miles in $55 - 7$ $= 48$ minutes $= \dfrac{48}{60} = \dfrac{4}{5}$ hour.

$$R = \dfrac{D}{T} = 40 \div \dfrac{4}{5}$$

$$= \dfrac{\overset{10}{\cancel{40}}}{1} \times \dfrac{5}{\cancel{4}_1} = 50 \text{ mph.}$$

SECTION VI

1. **A.** Illiterate substitution. "Being that" is incorrectly substituted for "since."

2. **D.** Error in diction. The correct word is "rise."

3. **C.** Error in tense. Mr. Epworth spoke to Bob in the past, and he "said," not "says."

4. **C.** Error in grammar. Verbs pertaining to the five senses often complete their meanings with a predicate adjective that modifies the subject. In this case, the word is "confident" not "confidently."

5. **E.** Sentence is correct as given.

6. **B.** Error in grammar. The object of the preposition "for" should be "Jim and me."

7. **C.** Error in diction. In standard written English, "less" is used to refer to amount rather than number. Substitute "fewer and fewer."

8. **E.** Sentence is correct as given.

9. **E.** Correct as given.

10. **B.** Error in spelling. The possessive of the impersonal third person pronoun is "its," without the apostrophe.

11. **D.** Error in agreement. The antecedent is "the one," and the pronoun should be "his."

12. **C.** Faulty reference. To whom does the pronoun "his" refer?

13. **E.** No error. Tenses are correct as given.

14. **A.** Error in tense. Substitute past tense "hadn't cheated" for "didn't cheat."

15. **C.** Error in diction. The correct word is "you're," the contraction for "you are."

16. **D.** Error in tense. Substitute "had forgotten" for "forgot."

17. **A.** Error in diction. The correct word here would be "implied" or "hinted" or "suggested."

18. **D.** Error in grammar or diction. "Burst" is the correct past participle of "burst." "Bust" and "busted" are colloquial expressions.

19. **C.** Shift in person. The sentence starts in the second person. It should not shift to the third person, "one's."

20. **D.** Shift in structure. Substitute "had helicopters hovering overhead," or some similar construction that continues having the "they" party doing something.

21. **E.** No error. Sentence is correct as given.

22. **B.** Lack of parallel construction. We may prefer "football games" to "programs on the educational TV station," but we can't prefer "games," a noun, to "watching," a participle.

23. **D.** Faulty reference. To whom does "he" refer? Who was fouled? Who was disqualified?

24. **B.** Error in tense. Substitute "faded" for "fade."

25. **C.** Error in grammar. "Everyone but him" is the correct construction. "But" is a preposition and takes the objective case.

26. **A.** No error. The sentence is correct as given.

27. **D.** Error in construction. In this case, the use of the infinitive is indicated. The "to" before "tear" is understood.

28. **C.** Comma splice. Two main clauses have been joined by a comma. They should be separated by a period.

29. **B.** Error in agreement. The subject "last two innings" is plural. The verb should be changed to "were," to bring it into agreement with the subject.

30. **D.** Misplaced modifier. The clause "When just a young recruit," modifies "the commanding general," but that does not fit the meaning of this sentence. Note how the correction removes all ambiguity.

31. **C.** Error in construction of the possessive. "Yours" is a possessive pronoun. It does not take an apostrophe.

32. **A.** No error. Sentence is correct as given.

33. **E.** Lack of parallelism. "Lateness" is a noun that parallels "carelessness." "His being late" is a participial phrase and is not parallel to "carelessness."

34. **B.** Error of omission. While acceptable in conversation and in informal writing, the omission of part of the auxiliary verb is not acceptable here.

35. **C.** Error in agreement. The subject of the clause is "one" and the verb must be in the imperfect tense and singular in order to agree.

36. **B.** Shift in person. The sentence starts in the third person; it should not shift to the second person.

37. **A.** No error. Sentence is correct as given.

38. **C.** Error in tense.

39. **B.** Error in formation of possessive. The possessive of "children" is "children's."

40. **E.** Error in punctuation. No comma is needed in this sentence.

41. **D.** Error in formation of possessive. "Theirs" is a possessive pronoun that does not require the use of the apostrophe.

42. **C.** Error in diction. The past participle of "shrink" is "shrunk."

43. **D.** Error in case. Use the nominative case for the subject of the understood verb: "capable as he (is)."

44. **D.** Error in punctuation. This sentence is not a question; it is a declarative sentence.

45. **C.** Error in diction. The correct word would be "stationary."

46. **A.** Error in agreement. A "pair" is a singular noun. The sentence should read, "There *is* a pair . . . ."

47. **B.** Error in tense. Substitute "had" for "would have."

48. **C.** Error in diction. The past participle of "begin" is "begun."

49. **C.** Error in tense. The sentence should read " . . . bowed stiffly and, . . . stomped off. . . ."

50. **E.** No error. Sentence is correct as given.

NOTES

NOTES

NOTES